THE ART & SCIENCE
OF TRIAL ADVOCACY

THE ART & SCIENCE OF TRIAL ADVOCACY

SECOND EDITION

L. TIMOTHY PERRIN
Professor of Law
Pepperdine University School of Law

H. MITCHELL CALDWELL
Professor of Law
Pepperdine University School of Law

CAROL A. CHASE
Professor of Law
Pepperdine University School of Law

 LexisNexis

Library of Congress Cataloging-in-Publication Data

Perrin, L. Timothy.
  The art and science of trial advocacy / L. Timothy Perrin, H. Mitchell Caldwell,
  Carol A. Chase. — 2nd ed.
    p. cm.
  ISBN 978-1-4224-8223-0 (perfect bound)
1. Trial practice—United States. I. Caldwell, Harry M. II. Chase, Carol A. III. Title.
  KF8915.P474 2011
  347.73'7—dc22

                                                                    2011002403

NOTE TO USERS
To ensure that you are using the latest materials available in this area, please be sure to periodically check the LexisNexis Law School web site for downloadable updates and supplements at www.lexisnexis.com/lawschool.

Editorial Offices
121 Chanlon Rd, New Providence, NJ 07974 (908) 464-6800
201 Mission St., San Francisco, CA 94105-1831 (415) 908-3200
www.lexisnexis.com

MATTHEW BENDER   (2011-Pub.3607)

DEDICATIONS

For Lucy, Hannah, Sam, and Will with thanks for their love and laughter.

–L. Timothy Perrin

For Joyce, Eric, Jack and Kay for their unflagging enthusiasm and support.

–H. Mitchell Caldwell

For John, Warren, Meredith, Harrison, Bonnie and Bob, with gratitude for their love and support.

–Carol A. Chase

ACKNOWLEDGMENTS

The authors gratefully acknowledge the generous support they have received from Pepperdine University School of Law in the preparation of this book; and in addition they express heartfelt gratitude to their trial practice students who planted the seeds of inspiration for this book. The authors are deeply indebted to the faculty support staff and, in particular, to Candace Warren, Roberta Nebgen, Sheila McDonald, and Courtenay Stallings for their tireless assistance (and patience) in preparing this manuscript. They gratefully acknowledge the invaluable contributions of Richard Gabriel and Sharon Gross to Chapter Six and Christopher Frost to Chapter Eleven. Finally, they would like to thank the following law students for their research and editorial assistance: Nathan Newman, Brett Fenoglio, Ryan McNamara, Bryan Rotella, Joshua Pakstis, and Brittany Kelley.

PREFACE

More than seven years have passed since the publication of *The Art & Science of Trial Advocacy* and during that time we have been gratified by the positive response to our book from students, professors, and practitioners. While much has changed in the world since publication of the book, the fundamentals of trial advocacy remain very much the same. Successful trial advocates understand that their credibility—their ethos—is central to trial success. You can not control the facts in the case, but you can control what you do with the facts. Effective advocates do not sacrifice their credibility with the factfinder by stretching, distorting, or otherwise misusing the evidence in the case.

If the fundamentals are unchanged, then why publish a second edition of the book? The answer is that while effective trial advocacy is still rooted in the same values as before, the tools of advocacy continue to evolve. In particular, the rapid development of technology and its use in the courtroom is changing the way that trials are conducted and the way that lawyers present evidence and argue to the jury. Some of these changes are for the better and some for the worse. In this edition, we have sought to pay particular attention to the use of technology. We have added "Tech Tips" throughout the book, providing specific suggestions regarding how technology might be used to enhance advocacy at various points of the trial. In addition, we have emphasized the technologies available to trial lawyers as they prepare and present evidence.

Technology is merely a tool, of course. It will not magically turn poor advocacy into effective advocacy, or transform the boring and uninteresting into something that is compelling and persuasive. Yet, most jurors live in a world that is high-tech and are conditioned to enjoy plenty of visual and aural stimulation, preferably at the same time. Effective advocates are aware of and responsive to the expectations of jurors; thus, we must master the available technologies and become adept at their use.

In addition to this updated edition of the book, we have also put together additional tools to assist the aspiring or less experienced trial advocate. As part of the on-line resources that are available for readers of this book, we have developed two videotaped trials—one civil and one criminal—to provide an application of the principles of trial advocacy contained herein. The advocates and witnesses in the trials are Pepperdine law students and we hope that the addition of this visual simulation of advocacy in practice will prove helpful and instructive. The student efforts are not perfect and indeed are not intended to represent the perfect example of good advocacy, to the extent there is such a thing, but provide another means of thinking deeply about the art and science of trial advocacy.

Our best wishes to you in your pursuit of success and meaning in this honorable profession.

Tim Perrin
Harry Caldwell
Carol Chase
October 2010
Malibu, California

TABLE OF CONTENTS

TABLE OF AUTHORITIES

UNITED STATES SUPREME COURT CASES

UNITED STATES CIRCUIT COURT CASES

Chapter One

INTRODUCTION TO TRIAL ADVOCACY

I. ART & SCIENCE

Trial advocacy is both an art and a science. And, by the same token, trial advocates must be both artists and scientists.

The science of trial advocacy consists in part of the rules, procedures, and protocols of trial. There are right ways to ask questions and wrong ways, legitimate objections and frivolous ones. Empirical research in the fields of communication and learning theory establishes that there are certain principles of effective advocacy which transcend the nature of the case or the identity of the party. Trial advocacy is a craft that can be learned; however, perfecting it involves dedication to the rules and strategies that must be studied. Make no mistake about it: There *is* a science of trial advocacy, and trial advocates must become steeped in it.

At the same time, however, trial advocacy is also an art. A trial lawyer faced with fashioning an argument out of a set of facts or trying a case before a jury is akin to Picasso with a blank canvas, Rodin with a shapeless mound of clay, or Michelangelo before the empty expanse of the ceiling of the Sistine Chapel. Just as every aspiring Picasso must be adept at using the tools of his trade and understanding the properties of paint and the changeability of color, so must trial advocates appreciate the tools at their disposal, the "properties" of persuasion, and the unpredictability of jurors. They must become skilled at the use of language and the art of rhetoric; they must develop their imaginations and listen to their creative instincts. But advocates develop their themes and craft their arguments for jurors, not blank canvasses, and those jurors come with built-in biases and prejudices and with pre-formed notions of how the world works. Accordingly, while creativity and imagination are essential tools for the successful advocate, an understanding of the science of juror psychology is equally important.

Thus, this book will explore both the art *and* science of trial advocacy. We address the rules and procedures that govern trials and the tools utilized by trial advocates—objections, offers of proof, rules of evidence, and the like. We explain the "how to" aspects of each part of the trial and include a multitude of examples. We also explore the artistry of trial advocacy, from the development of appealing themes and theories to the significance of making an emotional connection with the jury.

Trial advocacy is about much more than a mastery of questioning techniques, the rules of evidence, or the handling of exhibits. Although each of those tasks must be mastered, they are no more than a beginning. Successful trial advocacy requires an understanding of human psychology, principles of communication, and learning theory. It requires the ability to think ahead and to plan strategically, a willingness to work hard, and a commitment to find the truth. Trial practice can be rewarding and exhilarating, satisfying and meaningful. If we did not know that to be true, we would not have written this book. Yet, the competent trial of a case before a jury is a complex endeavor and, when viewed as a whole, mastery of this sophisticated undertaking may understandably seem daunting. Accordingly, it is important to first take a wide view of advocacy and persuasion, to examine the advocate's role in an adversary system, the procedural context in which that advocacy takes place, and the various tools of persuasion at the advocate's disposal.

II. THE ADVERSARY SYSTEM

Lawyers live and work in a system steeped in conflict. For trial lawyers, every case involves conflict, a dispute about what happened, or a contest over who is to blame. Cases with no disagreement rarely make it into the hands of a trial lawyer or before a jury. And the adversary system, as its name suggests, assumes the existence of conflict and the presence of adversaries. The task of trial lawyers is to take their client's version of reality—the client's truth—and persuade the jury to adopt it as the "Truth." The system's foundational premise is that, if both sides are competently represented and if both sides present their competing versions of reality to an impartial decision maker, the outcome will reflect what actually happened—the truth will be discovered and justice will be dispensed.

A. Fallible Participants

It would undoubtedly overstate the case to say that the adversary system always produces justice or that juries always discover the truth. The system depends on frail and fallible human beings. Judges may make bad rulings or unfairly favor one side over another. Jurors on occasion are governed by their emotions or motivated by an agenda that may cause them to render incorrect verdicts. Overworked or incompetent lawyers may fail to recognize the strongest evidence or make the best arguments. As several high profile jury verdicts in the 1990s and 2000s demonstrated, sometimes the adversary system breaks down and fails in its fundamental task. Such cases, however, are aberrations, not the norm. Most lawyers competently represent their clients. Most judges fairly and impartially preside over trials. Most jurors admirably perform their fact-finding function. Indeed, the adversary system has rightly been called the highest form of dispute resolution because of its ability to bring about the peaceful resolution of so many disputes.

Nonetheless, the genius of the adversary system can also be its downfall. The conflict that ensures the presence of competing adversaries can devolve into contentiousness and hostility. Parties motivated to persuade the decision maker of the rightness of their claims or defenses can turn into parties who are motivated to win at all costs. The structures and procedures of the trial process designed to ensure fairness and efficiency can be used as weapons to curtail the claims of meritorious litigants. The search for truth can be prostituted, leaving behind the attainment of justice as a casualty.

The larger point is that lawyers play the central role in the adversary system. They are the insiders, the ones with knowledge of the secret handshakes and ceremonial rituals, and they dictate to a large degree whether the system functions properly. Judges, jurors, law enforcement officers, and others have an important role to play as well, of course, but it is the lawyers who decide which claims or defenses to assert, which witnesses to present at trial, which objections to raise, and which questions to ask. In fact, one of the distinctive marks of the adversary system is the amount of autonomy given to the parties and thus to their lawyers. The system relies on the advocates to represent their clients with care and competence; to marshal all of the facts that support their clients' claims; to construct a coherent case theory out of those facts; and to persuasively present those claims to a jury. And it relies on the advocates to maintain balance and perspective in their work and to take seriously their role as officers of the court.

B.   Gladiators & Gunslingers?

Popular culture is seemingly obsessed with the law, and more specifically, with trials and trial lawyers. Television has produced one show after another featuring trial lawyers: for example, "Law and Order," "Boston Legal," "The Practice," and "Ally McBeal," to name only a few. There seems to be a never-ending supply of simulated court programs, from "The People's Court" to "Judge Judy," "Texas Justice," and a host of others. An entire television network, Court TV, devotes itself to televising trials. Movie producers have done more than their share with movies such as "The Verdict," "My Cousin Vinny," "The Devil's Advocate," and scores of others. In literature, one can choose from *To Kill a Mockingbird*, *A Civil Action*, or the latest novel from John Grisham, Scott Turow or many others. The news media contributes gavel-to-gavel coverage of the latest trial of the century, whether it is Michael Jackson's or Phil Spector's criminal trials, or some other high profile crime.

The images portrayed by the entertainment industry and presented by the news media suggest almost without fail that trials are sporting events or duels and that lawyers are athletes or gunslingers. They paint lawyers as modern day gladiators, going to battle in a courtroom instead of a colosseum. The prevailing notion seems to be that lawyers use every available advantage to win, whether ethical or not. That may make good entertainment or interesting news reporting, but trials are not games that can be scored at the end of the day, and lawyers are not gunslingers or gladiators—or at least they should not be. The image of the trial as a mere game trivializes the pursuit of justice, making a trial simply another form of entertainment with no lasting consequences. The image of the trial as war turns trial lawyers into mercenaries and diminishes their important role as officers of the court charged with pursuing what is right and just.

C. Officers of the Court

The reality is that trials are about real flesh-and-blood individuals; individuals who have been hurt and those who are alleged to have caused the injury, individuals who have been victimized and individuals who are alleged to have done the victimizing. Hence, trials are solemn events that directly affect people's lives. Justice is at stake. In the face of such high stakes, trial lawyers have a difficult task. On the one hand, as advocates, trial lawyers must diligently, faithfully, and skillfully represent their clients. But, on the other hand, as officers of the court, lawyers must pursue justice and refuse to allow anything to interfere with the system's search for the truth.

The role of lawyers as advocates is captured in part by the familiar refrain that lawyers must "zealously" represent their clients. And throughout this book we will demonstrate what zealous advocacy looks like—how advocates can exploit their opponents' weaknesses while maximizing their clients' advantages. But the call to zealous representation is only part of what effective advocacy is about. An unyielding commitment to the system and to the principles the system exists to protect— truth and justice—is also part and parcel of the lawyer's calling. "Telling the truth" and "playing fair" are not antiquated notions of a bygone era. They are the cornerstones of an adversary system and the guarantors of justice.

The adversary system, by its very "adversary-ness," tempts advocates to emphasize their loyalty to their clients at the expense of their duties to the court and to opposing counsel. The conflict imbedded in every lawsuit and the financial incentive inherent in litigation create a climate in which some advocates deem it permissible, or even necessary, to compromise their values and to cut corners when it comes to ethical principles. The laundry list of such tactics is long and disturbing: withholding a damaging document from the other side; coaching a witness to shade the truth to avoid a harmful admission or to gain an advantage; retaining an expert solely because of his willingness to render a favorable opinion; suggesting in the opening statement the existence of evidence that does not exist; disrupting the opponent's examination with groundless objections; haranguing an opposing witness with questions during cross-examination that do not have a good faith basis; and seeking a verdict not supported by the facts and the law. We will address the ethical obligations of trial lawyers at every stage of the pretrial and trial processes and we will espouse a vision of trial advocacy wherein the lawyers take those ethical principles seriously.

That is not to suggest that there is one correct result in every case or that the lawyers in a case are obliged to ensure a particular outcome regardless of their client's interests. In most cases that are tried before a jury, the known facts are incomplete or they point to more than one possible interpretation. Undoubtedly, the notion of "truth," in any absolute sense, is hard to identify in any definitive way in real-life trials. Most cases tried before juries are closely contested, involving at least two quite different views of what happened. It is in those cases that trial advocacy matters most. In cases with one-sided facts, jurors will likely reach the obvious verdict regardless of the advocacy skill of the lawyers. In cases with closely divided facts, the outcome will turn on which witnesses the jury believes and on which advocate the jury trusts.

Successful trial advocacy depends not on which lawyer can argue the longest or the loudest. Nor does it depend on which lawyer knows the most tricks of the trade. Tricks and gimmicks do not win lawsuits. Successful trial lawyers are not performers on a stage or shysters working con games. Successful advocacy is not the result of some calculated manipulation of the jury. To the contrary, cases are won by:

- preparation that is intense, careful, thorough, and leaves no-stone-left-unturned

- effective presentation of the party's case such that the jurors appreciate the larger significance of the dispute

- trustworthy and likeable advocates who shoot straight with the jury and display respect and courtesy to everyone in the courtroom

Trial lawyers' successes come from hard work and attention to the details; from the advocate's sincerity and authenticity; from facts marshaled and presented in such a way that they appeal to both logic and emotion; and from a cause or a principle that the jurors will claim as their own.

III. COURTROOM ETIQUETTE

Before diving headfirst into the trial process, there is basic courtroom etiquette that every aspiring trial lawyer should be aware of. It is important to note that each court has its own distinct rules and procedures. Because these rules and procedures can vary greatly from jurisdiction to jurisdiction—and even courtroom to courtroom—you should familiarize yourself with a particular court's procedures before making an appearance. There are, however, a few general rules that should be followed no matter what court you are in:

- **Lawyer Punctuality:** First and foremost, it is important to always be on time when making an appearance in court. The court's time is generally very limited and expensive. Making a judge wait may cost money, and gives him or her reason to dislike you. In extreme cases of tardiness or absence, sanctions or bench warrants could be issued. Unfortunately, just because you are on time, does not mean your case will be called at that time.

- **Attire:** If you are addressing the court, you should be wearing formal business attire. If you are just observing or taking care of procedural matters, business casual attire is appropriate.

- **Decorum While Waiting:** As stated above, there are often long waits associated with spending a day in court. While in the courtroom, do not read, listen to music, sleep, or talk. All electronic devices such as PDAs, cell phones, and pagers should be turned off immediately upon entering the courtroom.

- **Addressing the Court:**

  ○ When your matter is first called: proceed to the front of the court and stand behind your assigned seat, or the podium.

  ○ When the Judge or Jury enters or leaves the courtroom, you should rise unless otherwise instructed. You should also stand anytime you address the judge, or the judge addresses you. This includes when you respond to questions, make statements, or make objections. You should also stand when you are addressing a witness (unless the jurisdiction's practice is to sit during examination of witnesses).

  ○ Address the Judge as "Your Honor" and ONLY "Your Honor." Although "Sir" or "Ma'am" seems respectful, some judges are very particular about only being called "Your Honor" and you do not want to be in his or her disfavor over something so trivial.

  ○ Speak in full words. Do not reply by murmuring "mmhmm" or shaking your head. It is important that you say yes or no, so that the court reporter can accurately and clearly document the events of the courtroom.

  ○ The area between the lawyer's tables and the Judge's bench is called the "well." In most jurisdictions, if you are going to enter or cross the well to show an exhibit, approach the bench, or hand something to a witness, you must first ask permission. For example, "Your Honor, may I traverse the well to show exhibit 2?" or "Your Honor, may I approach the witness to present People's Exhibit 5 and refresh her memory?"

  ○ Never directly address opposing counsel in open court. All communication must go through the court. Communication with opposing counsel should be triangulated through the judge. For example:

- Correct: "Your Honor, can you please ask Opposing Counsel to provide me with a copy of Exhibit 2?"

- Incorrect: "John, you forgot to give me a copy of Exhibit 2."

IV. TRIALS

A. The Pretrial Process and Trial Preparation

Preparation for trial begins the first moment the lawyer is retained to represent a client. It is the preparation phase on which most trial lawyers, particularly those trying civil cases, will spend the majority of their time. In civil cases, the pretrial process includes drafting pleadings, making and responding to motions, discovering what the other side knows and disclosing what the advocate's client knows, deposing fact and expert witnesses, and meeting pre-trial deadlines for designating witnesses and identifying exhibits.

Preparation is, undoubtedly, the most important factor in successful advocacy at trial. Effective trial advocates are those who are totally and completely prepared. They have mastered the facts and the law; they are prepared for every contingency. In the days and weeks immediately preceding a trial, trial preparation becomes all-consuming for trial advocates. Other work must be put aside and all attention must be focused on the trial of the case. This kind of intense, indefatigable preparation is exhausting, but also exhilarating.

An exhaustive treatment of the pretrial process is beyond the scope of this book, but one should note that there is a logical pattern that cases follow before trial. Civil cases are, of course, initiated by a complaint. The complaint is followed by appropriate responsive pleadings from the defendants. Federal courts and some state jurisdictions require an early meeting between counsel and with the presiding judge to establish a schedule for the case and to set various deadlines. The pleadings are followed by discovery, which may include mandatory disclosures of certain basic information as well as formal requests for information, in the form of interrogatories, requests for production of documents, requests for admission, and depositions. After the initial discovery phase, the parties designate their expert witnesses, if any, and produce written reports from each testifying expert. One or more of the parties may file motions for summary judgment or other motions that seek whole or partial disposition of the case in the party's favor. In federal court, the parties will be required to prepare a Joint Pretrial Order setting forth each party's contentions, a summary of disputed and undisputed facts, a witness list, exhibit lists, expected deposition testimony to be offered at trial, motions *in limine*, and perhaps the questions the parties would like the court to ask the jury during *voir dire*. At the final pretrial conference, the court rules on any objections to the proposed exhibits, motions *in limine*, and any other contested matters.

Criminal cases, on the other hand, typically follow one of two paths. In those state jurisdictions that utilize preliminary hearings, the process is initiated with a complaint charging the defendant with a crime. After the defendant enters a not guilty plea at the arraignment, the case is set for a preliminary hearing. That hearing usually occurs within days of the arraignment. At the preliminary hearing, the state's threshold for holding the defendant to answer on the charge is proof that there is probable cause to believe the defendant committed the offense. This hearing typically consists of the state putting on a bare bones case, frequently involving testimony from only the victim and/or the arresting officer. The defense then has the opportunity to cross examine the state's witnesses. It is unusual for the defense to call its own witnesses at these hearings. In the likely event the magistrate finds that the state has met its burden, the defendant is held to answer and an arraignment date is set. The state, in light of the preliminary hearing, again reviews the case and the supporting evidence. In the event the government elects to continue the prosecution, an information is filed. The defendant is then arraigned in the court of general jurisdiction on the information and a trial date is set.

The other path leading to a criminal trial, favored in federal court, is the issuance of an indictment by a grand jury. The grand jury, with the assistance of representatives from the prosecutorial authority, questions pertinent witnesses and decides whether the evidence supports the issuance of an indictment, which must be based upon probable cause to believe the defendant committed the offense. After an indictment is issued, the defendant is arraigned and a trial date is set.

Under both procedures, the parties attend a pre-trial conference at which they attempt to negotiate a disposition of the case with the judge's assistance. It is at this time, failing a disposition, that motions are scheduled and pretrial deadlines are established. Suppression, dismissal, and continuing discovery motions earmark this phase of the pretrial proceedings. Prior to trial, each side will be required to provide a witness list, exhibits list, motions *in limine*, and proposed jury instructions, and each side must comply with discovery requirements concerning exculpatory or witness background material.

B. Settlement or Trial?

In every filed case there comes a time when the parties and advocates must decide whether to settle with the adversary through negotiation or some alternative form of resolution, such as mediation, or to go to trial. In many jurisdictions, perhaps most, some effort to settle civil cases before trial is mandatory, either in the form of judicial settlement conferences, mediation, or nonbinding arbitration. As many as 96 percent of all civil cases that are filed settle before trial, and a substantial majority of criminal cases result in a guilty plea before trial.

The reasons for the high rates of settlement before trial are not difficult to deduce. Trials are particularly high-risk events. No one can predict with any degree of confidence the precise outcome of a particular case tried before a judge or jury. A familiar axiom among trial lawyers is that a jury trial is a crap shoot. Understandably, instead of "rolling the dice" and going to trial, most trial lawyers decide most of the time that a known outcome, some kind of a compromise, is better than an unknown outcome. Cases that actually do go to trial tend to be cases that involve (1) close factual determinations that are particularly difficult to predict, (2) opposing lawyers with vastly differing perspectives on the validity or value of the claims or in a criminal case the relative merits of the state's evidence, or (3) litigants who are more interested in advocating a principle or vindicating a perceived wrong than in necessarily making an otherwise prudent decision.

Once parties decide to proceed to trial, they must make a second decision: whether to try the case before a jury or a judge. In a limited number of cases, such as civil cases involving claims at equity, there may be no choice inasmuch as a jury trial may not be available. In other cases, the parties may not want to demand a jury for strategic reasons. Nevertheless, in cases in which there is a right to a jury, either party can demand to have the case tried before a jury. Typically, plaintiffs in civil cases and defendants in criminal cases prefer juries whenever possible, though there are exceptions to these generalizations, of course. Parties might elect to try a case before a judge because of particularly complex facts or issues or a perceived ability to accurately predict how the judge will rule in the case. Yet, most contested cases are tried to juries, and accordingly, this book will devote most of its attention to jury trials. At the same time, however, principles of good advocacy are the same whether the trier of fact is a judge or a jury. The lessons in this book apply to advocacy before judges, arbitrators, and juries or any other forum in which lawyers are called upon to be persuasive.

C. Jury Selection

The final prelude to a jury trial is, of course, actual selection of the jury. As suggested above, in civil cases in which the advocate chooses to invoke a party's right to jury trial, the advocate must demand a jury trial before the trial begins. The election for a jury must be in writing, and a jury fee must be paid as well. In the absence of a timely election, the party risks being precluded from having a jury seated. In contrast, the assumption in criminal cases is that a jury will be impaneled, although criminal defendants can waive their right to a jury trial.

From a panel of prospective jurors, the *venire*, the court empanels the jurors and alternates. Although termed "jury selection," that is, in fact, a misnomer. The "selection" of jurors is beyond the control of the lawyers; the most a trial advocate can hope to accomplish is to "de-select" the individuals on the *venire* who appear to be most unsympathetic to the advocate's client. To facilitate this objective, potential jurors are questioned by the judge, and in most instances by the lawyers, in an effort to uncover any biases or views which might negatively affect the person's ability to impartially decide the case. Additionally, this is an opportunity for the lawyers to begin shaping and developing their cases and to begin building a rapport with the jurors.

The process of questioning potential jurors is called *voir dire*. At the conclusion of *voir dire*, all parties may exercise challenges (either challenges for cause or peremptory challenges) to remove prospective jurors from the panel. Challenges for cause are unlimited and are directed toward some disability that would prevent the juror from satisfying the statutory requirements for jury service, such as a previous or existing relationship with any of the parties, a felony conviction, or an inability to understand English. Peremptory challenges, on the other hand, are challenges for any reason at all (with a few exceptions, such as for race or gender) and are limited in number depending on the jurisdiction and nature of the case. The parties exercise their peremptory challenges based on their predictions about a particular prospective juror's sympathy with or hostility against the party's case. When all parties have exhausted their challenges, or when all parties have agreed that they will not exercise any additional challenges, the jurors are impaneled and sworn.

D.   Opening Statements

Each party has an opportunity to present an opening statement prior to the presentation of evidence. The opening statement is the first opportunity for advocates to fully and completely speak to the jurors about their cases. Thus, an opening statement should not merely summarize the anticipated testimony, but rather should present the advocate's case in a compelling and powerful way. Advocates should personalize their clients, shape the factual overview of the case, minimize weaknesses, and set forth the theory of the case. In short, the opening is the advocate's opportunity to tell his side of the story and to make a positive first impression with the jury.

The primary limit on what advocates can say during the opening statement is the rule against argument, which precludes advocates from drawing conclusions or making inferences for the jury or otherwise going beyond the evidence that will be introduced during the trial. The defendant has the right to reserve his or her opening statement until the conclusion of the plaintiff's or prosecution's case-in-chief, or to waive the opening altogether, though it rarely, if ever, makes sense to do so.

E.   The Cases-in-Chief

The party bearing the burden of proof (typically the plaintiff or prosecutor) presents his case first. The party must offer evidence sufficient to prove the existence of each element necessary under the applicable substantive law to establish a *prima facie* case. Should the party fail, the defendant is entitled to judgment as a matter of law or judgment of acquittal.

Evidence is primarily presented through witness testimony, which plays a crucial role in ultimate success or failure at trial. During direct examination, each witness is questioned by the party who called him. The form and content of the questions and answers are regulated by the rules of evidence. In most jurisdictions, questions on direct examination must not lead the witness to the desired answer, and the answers must be relevant to the disputed issues and must be based on the witness' personal knowledge. The goal of direct examination is for the witness to relate to the jury any pertinent information known by the witness, not by the advocate. Accordingly, the witness must testify in his or her own words.

Following direct examination, witnesses are subjected to cross examination by opposing counsel. In federal courts and in many states, cross-examination is limited to those events or issues raised during direct examination and any matters that affect the witness' credibility. Cross-examination is the hallmark of the adversary system, ensuring that all parties in the trial have the opportunity to confront and question their accusers. It is a hostile act in which the primary goal is to discredit the witness or otherwise undermine the witness' testimony. In contrast to direct examination, most questions on cross should be leading, and the jury's attention should be on the examiner, not the witness.

At the conclusion of the cross-examination, the direct examiner may conduct a redirect examination limited to the areas addressed during cross-examination. Likewise, re-cross-examination is limited to those areas covered during redirect. The process continues until both sides have exhausted their questions for the witness or until the judge halts the examination.

The plaintiff or prosecutor presents all of his witnesses during his case-in-chief. In addition, during the case-in-chief the parties may introduce into evidence stipulations, exhibits, and demonstrative evidence. After presenting all of their evidence in the case, the plaintiff or prosecutor then "rests." At that point, the defendant can move for judgment if the plaintiff or prosecutor has failed to present sufficient evidence to prove a *prima facie* case. In federal civil cases, the motion is called a motion for judgment as a matter of law; in most state courts, it is called a motion for directed verdict; and in criminal cases it is a motion for an acquittal.

After the plaintiff or prosecutor rests, the defendant has the opportunity to present his case-in-chief. The defendant's case follows the same structure and format as the plaintiff/prosecutor's case. At the conclusion of the defendant's case, either party, plaintiff or defendant, can move for judgment against the opposing party. The question for the judge in deciding the motion is whether there is sufficient evidence to support the non-movant's case that a reasonable jury could find in the party's favor. Not surprisingly perhaps, motions seeking summary disposition of the case are rarely granted.

F. The Rebuttal Cases

Following the defendant's case-in-chief, the plaintiff/prosecution may present a rebuttal case. Like the case-in-chief, the plaintiff/prosecution has an opportunity to present evidence to the fact-finder through witness testimony and trial exhibits. Unlike the case-in-chief, however, the scope of the rebuttal is limited to evidence that rebuts the claims or defenses presented in the defendant's case-in-chief.

At the conclusion of the plaintiff/prosecution rebuttal case, the defendant also has an opportunity to present rebuttal evidence that refutes the plaintiff's/prosecution's rebuttal case. Again, the evidence offered must tend to rebut evidence offered in the immediately preceding plaintiff/prosecution rebuttal case.

After the defendant's rebuttal case, the plaintiff/prosecution may offer evidence that rebuts the immediately preceding defendant's rebuttal case in what is known as a surrebuttal case. This process continues until all of the parties have exhausted their store of evidence or have exhausted the judge's patience. When the last party to present evidence rests, it signals the end of the presentation of evidence in the trial.

G. Closing Arguments

Closing arguments follow the presentation of evidence and provide advocates their last opportunity to persuade the jurors of the correctness of their claims or defenses. During closing argument, lawyers should integrate the evidence into the law and attempt to convince the triers of fact that the advocate's view of the facts should prevail. Unlike the opening statement, when argument is specifically precluded, the closing argument, as its name suggests, is the appropriate time for argument by counsel. Advocates are not limited to reviewing the evidence introduced during the trial, and, in fact, should try to avoid merely rehashing the evidence. Rather, they can and should explain to the jury what the evidence means and why it logically leads to a particular verdict. In doing so, advocates may use analogies, anecdotes, rhetorical questions, and literary references or other tools of argument to make their points. The closing argument is a time for creativity on the part of advocates as they use every available means to persuade the fact finder.

The party with the burden of proof (typically the plaintiff or prosecutor) presents the first argument, then the defense presents his closing argument, followed by the plaintiff/prosecutor's rebuttal argument. The rebuttal is limited to those areas discussed during the defense argument, and only the plaintiff or prosecutor may make a rebuttal argument.

H. Jury Instructions

The last step before the jury begins its deliberations, at least in most jurisdictions, is for the judge to read the jury instructions. Jury instructions inform the jurors of the law that they are to apply in determining the outcome of the case. Every jurisdiction has a set of jury instructions designed to cover essentially all claims and defenses as well as other issues that may arise in a case. Before trial, the advocates submit their list of proposed instructions to the court and after the close of the evidence the court hears arguments from counsel (outside the presence of the jury) about which instructions should be given to the jury. Occasionally a situation may arise when the "form instructions" are inadequate. In that case, the court will construct its own instruction with the aid of counsel. The jury instructions also include a verdict form that asks the jury to determine which party should prevail or to answer a series of questions, which will enable the judge to make that determination.

I.   Verdicts and Post-Trial Motions

After the jury receives the judge's instructions, it begins its deliberations. The jury selects a foreperson and then discusses the trial evidence and attempts to reach a decision. In most jurisdictions, the jury's verdict in criminal cases must be unanimous, but in civil cases unanimity is not required. In civil cases with twelve-person juries, agreement of nine or ten (depending on the jurisdiction) is typically sufficient. The verdict represents the decision of the jury or judge (in a non-jury trial). If the jury is unable to reach a verdict, the judge will declare a mistrial and the case will have to be tried again. If the jury does reach a verdict, the party that did not prevail may request that the verdict be set aside and that judgment be entered in that party's favor and/or may move for a new trial. These are steps made in preparation for an appeal.

V.   PERSUASION

Beyond the particular rules and objectives of trial, advocates must persuade the trier of fact. More than 2300 years ago, the great philosopher Aristotle identified three components of persuasive rhetoric: ethos, logos, and pathos. Ethos represented the moral character of the speaker; logos, the logical force and power of the argument; and pathos, the emotional appeal of the argument.[1] More than two millennia later, Aristotle's words still ring true. In the new millennium, trial advocates must demonstrate their trustworthiness, make arguments supported by the force of logic, and tap into the emotional reserves of jurors.

The ability to communicate effectively depends heavily on context—the particular needs of the speaker, the make-up of the audience, and the specific circumstances present. The injured person describing pain sensations to a doctor will communicate very differently than the stand-up comedian doing her act at a comedy club or a lawyer addressing a jury. The injured person seeks to inform the doctor about her injuries in hopes of receiving treatment and, ultimately, healing; the comedian seeks to humor the audience in hopes of getting a laugh and, ultimately, acceptance, respect, and another gig; the advocate seeks to persuade the jury in hopes of obtaining a favorable verdict and, ultimately, justice.

---

[1] *See* 3 THE GREAT IDEAS 645 (Mortimer J. Adler, ed. 1985).

Advocates must respect the cumbersome rules of court and still present the facts in a memorable and compelling way. That is, the advocate's message must be accurate, factual, and legally adequate, but also absorbing, captivating, and emotionally forceful. Similarly, the advocate, as messenger, must not only be lawyerly, making sure that all the "i's" are dotted and "t's" are crossed, but also credible and likeable. Thus, before we can begin to consider the particulars of trying a case—from avoiding argument at opening statement to deciding how to ask non-leading questions on direct—we must understand certain basic principles of communication.

The science of trial advocacy includes a rich body of social science data about communication and learning, much of it in the specific context of trials. In addition to the ancient principles of communication identified by Aristotle, the available empirical data supports a number of additional principles of effective communication at trial, relating to the optimum organization of trial presentations, the best means of presentation, and the specific content of the presentation. We identify three principles that apply to the messenger, trial advocates, and seven more that apply to the message. These keys constitute overarching principles of effective communication for trial lawyers, applying to every part of the trial and to every attempt by advocates to persuade.

A. Keys for Messengers

1. *Credibility*

The first and most important component of persuasive communication is the credibility of the advocate, or what Aristotle called "ethos."[2] Aristotle framed ethos as consisting of three parts: good sense, good moral character, and good will. Thus, the concept of ethos extends beyond the connotation of the English word "credibility," to the judgment displayed by advocates (their "good sense"), the respectfulness and courtesy shown by advocates (their "good will"), and even their personal rectitude or "moral character." Advocates go about the task of building their ethos from the very beginning of trial. It is the most important task of the trial lawyer.

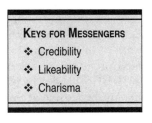

KEYS FOR MESSENGERS
❖ Credibility
❖ Likeability
❖ Charisma

Credible advocates are those who keep their promises to the jury; show respect to the judge, witnesses, opposing counsel, and opposing parties; and assert only credible arguments supported by the facts and the law. They avoid tricks or gimmicks, freely reveal problems in their cases or weaknesses with their witnesses, and play fair no matter the costs to their cases or clients. Cultivation of the jury's trust requires that

---

[2] RICHARD D. RIEKE AND RANDALL K. STUTMAN, COMMUNICATION IN LEGAL ADVOCACY 109 (1990).

advocates demonstrate their mastery over the facts, thus confirming the jury's perception of the advocate's superior knowledge, while simultaneously demonstrating a commitment to fairness and justice, thus rebutting the jury's skepticism that advocates are paid partisans.

a. Look and Act Like an Expert

The first and foremost means of garnering the jury's trust and respect is for advocates to demonstrate that they are experts both in regard to the subject matter of the lawsuit and the procedural aspects of the trial. Advocates who know what they are doing receive greater deference from the jury than advocates who appear befuddled or incompetent. Advocates who are completely and thoroughly prepared earn the jury's trust whereas unprepared lawyers fritter away the jury's reservoir of good will.

This principle applies to every area of life. When you have a plumbing problem, you are likely to call a plumber. After all, he is the expert. And when the plumber arrives, the homeowner will begin with a presumption that the plumber knows about plumbing. However, the plumber can quickly lose the benefit of the doubt by what he says or how he acts. If he expresses ignorance or confusion about how to repair the problem or actually worsens the problem by his attempted repair, the homeowner's presumption of competence will quickly give way to doubt and perhaps even despair. In the same way, jurors begin a trial assuming that the advocates know what they are doing and know what happened in the case, but that assessment is subject to constant revision. Moreover, just as the homeowner knows that the plumber has a financial incentive to exaggerate the nature of the plumbing problem, so do jurors believe that most lawyers have a financial incentive to mislead jurors at trial. So jurors go about evaluating the advocates before them just like we evaluate the plumbers in our homes, watching and listening as they decide whether the advocates know what they are doing and what happened between the parties, whether the advocates are, in fact, experts.

The extent to which the jury perceives that the advocate is knowledgeable about the case turns in large part upon the advocate's display of mastery over the facts—mastery over every fact, every claim or defense, and every demonstrative aid or exhibit. That kind of expertise comes only after careful, painstaking preparation. From the first words spoken during *voir dire* and continuing through the final rebuttal closing argument, advocates demonstrate, for better or for worse, the extent of their pretrial preparation.

In the same way, advocates build their credibility by demonstrating their mastery over the procedural rules and regulations of the trial. Lawyers inspire confidence in jurors when they display the confidence and quiet assurance that they know what is going to happen because they have done this many times before. The more comfortable and in control the advocate appears in the courtroom, the more the jurors will feel comfortable and at ease in the jury box.

b. Demonstrate Fairness and Objectivity

Advocates also build and maintain their credibility by demonstrating that they are not motivated by partisan loyalty to their clients, financial interests, or any other corrupting influence. The renowned trial lawyer and legal commentator Gerry Spence says: "The first trick of the winning argument is the trick of abandoning trickery."[3] Instead of being deceptive or manipulative, the trial advocate should be genuine, sincere, straightforward, and authentic. That kind of trustworthiness supplants the preconceptions held by many jurors that lawyers are greedy scoundrels who will say and do anything to prevail. Overcoming such stereotypes requires that advocates:

- keep their promises,

- disclose weaknesses in their case,

- make concessions and agree to stipulations,

- avoid weak or inconsistent arguments,

- resist the use of legalese or technical jargon,

- reject gimmicks or tricks, and

- dress and behave conservatively.

i. Keep Your Promises

It should be obvious from these tips that maintaining credibility is not rocket science. After all, most of these tips arise out of principles we learned in grade school. The key is for advocates to gain an appreciation of how significant their credibility is to the client's ultimate success and how much the advocate can do to shape and influence the jury's perceptions. For example, the first principle on the list—keep your promises—is a simple truth of profound importance. The jury trusts advocates who show themselves to be trustworthy. If an advocate represents that certain evidence will be admitted, a certain witness called, or a certain argument refuted, the advocate must ensure that the promise is kept. Broken promises are a serious betrayal of the jury's trust and may overshadow favorable facts or meritorious claims.

ii. Disclose Weaknesses

A second means of showing the advocate's objectivity is to disclose the weaknesses in one's own case, whether the weakness is a witness' prior conviction, inconsistencies in the eyewitness' identification of the defendant, or a pre-existing injury of the plaintiff. Disclosing such information directly rebuts the jury's notion that the advocate is merely out to win (*justice be damned!*). Some lawyers refer to such disclosures as "drawing

---

[3] GERRY SPENCE, HOW TO ARGUE AND WIN EVERY TIME 47 (1995).

the sting," or by the more graphic label "pricking the boil." This step may be painful, but it is necessary for the long-term health and success of the case. When advocates preemptively prick the boils in their cases, the jurors gain respect for them and are more willing to believe them when advocates identify their case strengths. The advocate's willingness to voluntarily disclose hurtful information shows a commitment to truth even when that commitment conflicts with the party's own self-interest. Most importantly, the advocate gains a measure of control over the method and timing of the disclosure of damaging material.

iii.   Make Appropriate Concessions

Advocates enhance their credibility when they concede points they have failed to establish or which the opposing party has proven. Stipulate the facts or issues that are collateral or undisputed. Concessions on subsidiary issues or other points not fatal to the advocate's case demonstrate the advocate's fairness and objectivity. Stipulations show that the advocate is agreeable and considerate of the jury's time. And when the advocate then refuses to compromise on a point, drawing a figurative line in the sand, the jury will take notice and will understand that the issue must be important and the facts must favor the advocate's side of the argument.

iv.   Avoid Weak Arguments

Advocates earn the jury's trust based on the merit of their arguments. The jury will respond to the advocate who offers only strong arguments and not weak ones. Thus, advocates should resist the urge to argue every point or every contention no matter how trivial or insignificant yet valid. Instead, they should be selective, arguing only the points supported by competent, credible evidence. An argument—whether inside a courtroom or not—is only as strong as its weakest link and an advocate's credibility is only as strong as the plausibility of his weakest argument. The words "but even if" are words of weakness, words that mean "ignore everything I said before."[4] They are words that have no place in any argument.

v.   Use Plain Language

The words chosen by advocates make them more or less credible. The advocate should be plain-spoken and easily understood. The more the lawyer tries to impress the jury with his vocabulary, the more distance he will put between himself and the jurors and the less they will relate to him. The trial is the time for plain English and lots of pictures. Think USA Today, not New York Times. Or better yet, think internet, not newspaper. The jurors are used to less text, more graphics, less word power, more visual stimulation. The advocate who communicates with the jury in clear and descriptive terms will be better received, and thus more trusted, than one who does not.

---

[4] *See* HERBERT J. STERN, TRYING CASES TO WIN 71-75 (1991).

vi.   Avoid Gimmicks or Tricks

Advocates destroy their credibility when the jury perceives that they are using gimmicks or tricks to manipulate the outcome in their favor. The motivation to win often causes advocates to develop ways of evading the rules to gain an advantage. For example, advocates ask questions on cross-examination or make assertions during opening or closing that they know are improper, and then immediately "withdraw" the question or the assertion, hoping that the jury's exposure to the information will have the desired effect. Advocates interpose frivolous objections solely to disrupt the opponent's rhythm. Advocates feign an inability to hear the witness' answer so that they can ask the witness to repeat verbatim an important answer. Tricks such as these will surely backfire as the jurors realize that they are being manipulated and that the advocate deems it necessary to resort to gimmicks to prevail.

Other tricks that should be avoided are:

- Rhetorical manipulations – arguing intensely for one thing, as though it proves something it does not, often confuses the jury, and is intellectually dishonest.

- Evasion – by evading specific, albeit hurtful issues, the jury is allowed to come to its own conclusions without hearing "your take" on problematic issues. Furthermore, as previously discussed, evading hurtful information or facts compromises an advocate's credibility.

- Ambiguity – do not use equivocal language to avoid committing to one version of the facts. There is only one truth, and you want the jury to believe that your story is the one that represents that truth. By not committing to one interpretation of the events, it seems as though you do not even believe in your client's case.

vii.   Avoid Ostentatious Dress

Finally, the lawyer gains credibility by dressing and acting like someone worthy of trust. Trials are not the time for ostentatious attire or expensive jewelry. The goal is to blend in, not stand out. Trials are also not the time for making social or political statements or for being provocative. The advocate should not wear pins or ribbons that have political or social significance. All aspects of the appearance of advocates, from the car they drive to the clothes and the jewelry they wear, to the way they act, should cause the jurors to take them seriously and to view them as professionals. Advocates communicate something by how they dress, and they should use even that as an opportunity to build their credibility with the jury.

During the trial, the jurors constantly ask themselves: Can I trust the lawyers? Can I trust the evidence? Are the advocates simply paid partisans trying to win at all costs? Or are they professionals concerned with trying to find the truth? At every turn advocates must demonstrate their even-handedness, their respect for the process and all the trial participants, as well as their fair, but firm, belief in their case. A lawyer who has the jury's trust has a powerful weapon; he will get the benefit of the doubt from the jury, which is an advantage of inestimable value.

2.   *Likeability*

The second essential component of persuasive communication—the advocate's likeability—is just as important as the first. If advocates are unable to develop a rapport with their audience (the jurors), then no technique in the world can bring about comprehension or retention of their message. The principle is simple enough: People tend to trust and like people who are like them. To the extent that advocates appear to have the same values and experiences as the jurors, the jurors perceive the advocate as credible and likeable.[5]

In the Western television shows at the advent of the television era, the viewer could always identify the good guys because they wore the white hats. In the same way advocates should strive to wear the white hat and be identified as one of the good guys. Such "likeability" leads to a strong, positive rapport between the jury and the advocate, and ultimately will cause the jury to give the advocate the benefit of the doubt on contested issues.

How does the advocate foster such a relationship? It all starts with the way the advocate treats the other participants in the trial and the court personnel in the courtroom. The trial lawyer must genuinely and sincerely show respect to each and every person. Every single one. When advocates act with some degree of humility and strive to live by the golden rule when in the courtroom, jurors will take notice. Respect and courtesy must extend to the court clerk, the bailiff, the court reporter, and to every witness—even hostile ones. This courtesy should extend outside the courtroom because advocates never know when a juror is watching or eavesdropping. Strive to be the one lawyer in the courtroom who gets along with everyone, the one who makes it impossible for the jury not to like him or her. Respect requires avoidance of the following;

- haranguing

- harassing or insulting remarks

- yelling or screaming

- interrupting or cutting off

- *ad hominem* attacks

- sarcasm

Having said that, there will come a time in many trials when a witness or an opposing lawyer will forfeit any right to the advocate's respect

---

[5]   *See* MICHAEL T. NIETZEL & RONALD C. DILLEHAY, PYSCHOLOGICAL CONSULTATION IN THE COURTROOM, 143 (1986).

or deference. They will lie or evade or cheat. The jury will want the advocate to hold them accountable for their misconduct. Then, and only then, the gloves can come off and the proverbial fur can fly. But until that moment, courtesy and respect should be the advocate's watchwords.

Likeability also comes from taking advantage of opportunities to demonstrate to the juror that the advocate is no different from them. One means of doing that is through personal disclosures to the jury, when appropriate. For example, in the beginning moments of *voir dire* counsel should tell the jury a bit about himself and perhaps use a personal anecdote to help the jury understand how experiences and backgrounds give us certain biases and prejudices. The closing argument provides another opportunity to share personal experiences that reveal important truths about the case. These disclosures help break down the barrier between juror and lawyer and make the lawyer seem more accessible and approachable.

In the same way, advocates enhance their likeability by not taking themselves too seriously. The ability to laugh during the lighter moments of trial or to admit misstatements or mangled questions demonstrates a certain human quality that jurors will appreciate. The lawyer who can show some self-deprecation when appropriate in front of the jury will gain the jurors' respect and even affection. For example:

- After a particularly poorly phrased question: "I'm sorry, that question was so unintelligible I don't even know what the point was. Let me try that again."

- After an objection for improper argument has been sustained during the advocate's opening statement: "I apologize, Your Honor, that was argumentative. I'll try to avoid that from here on."

The old adage is that you get more flies with honey than vinegar. Jurors are not flies, but they most certainly are attracted to advocates they like and with whom they have a rapport. Genuine kindness, courtesy, and respect will go a long way toward success for trial advocates.

3. *Charisma*

The final trait possessed by many persuasive advocates—charisma—is undoubtedly the most difficult to teach. Charisma is the sheer "star power" of the advocate. Charisma is the ability of the speaker to grab the audience's attention, keep the audience interested, and move the audience according to the speaker's will.

Some trial lawyers, just as some people, are blessed with powerful personalities that attract people like magnets. They seem to have been born with larger than life personas—they have authoritative voices, magnetic personalities, contagious smiles, and a sixth sense about how to get people to do what they want them to do. It is imprinted in their DNA. A winning personality cannot be taught. Charm does not come in a bottle. Charisma cannot be packaged and sold.

Yet, you do not have to be a Svengali to be successful at trial. Advocates with squeaky voices, dour faces, and introverted personalities can persuade juries and be successful at trial. The keys to success for those who are not blessed with natural charisma are the same ones discussed above: thorough preparation, transparent sincerity, mastering the tools of advocacy, understanding the psychology of jurors, and, perhaps most importantly, settling cases with bad facts! On the other hand, the keys for success for those blessed with an abundance of charisma are two-fold: (1) avoid relying on your ability to charm as a substitute for the hard work and attention to detail required for success; and (2) resist appearing so slick or smooth that the jury begins to question the sincerity and trustworthiness of the advocate.

B.   Keys for the Message

The persuasive power of advocates who are credible, likable, and charismatic is substantial, but not absolute. The most likable and charming advocates will fail to persuade if their messages are incoherent, inconsistent, or unintelligible. In fact, the organization, presentation, and content of the message matters as much as the stature of the advocate and his rapport with the jury. Which messages are most persuasive to jurors? What devices help jurors retain the most information? What tools keep jurors interested in a party's claim or defense? In this section we will identify principles that will maximize retention, increase interest, and ultimately lead to greater persuasiveness. These principles of communication include primacy, recency, pathos, simplicity, imagery, frequency, and logical coherence.

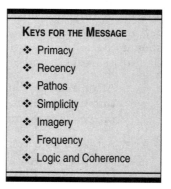

KEYS FOR THE MESSAGE
- ❖ Primacy
- ❖ Recency
- ❖ Pathos
- ❖ Simplicity
- ❖ Imagery
- ❖ Frequency
- ❖ Logic and Coherence

1. *Primacy*

The first principle of communication—*primacy*—comes first in the list of principles of effective communication for obvious reasons. Primacy is a critical tool for the organization and presentation of material at trial. Primacy teaches that information presented first is more effectively recalled by the listener and heavily influences the listener's impression of everything that follows.[6] At least two aspects of human nature are at work. First, during the first moments of a speech or a presentation the interest of the audience is greatest. The audience will likely never be so attentive again. That attentiveness translates into better retention of the information later. Second is the matter of first impressions. Once formed, first impressions are nearly impossible to change. Truth be told, it is instinctive

---

[6] MARGARET ROBERTS, TRIAL PSYCHOLOGY 23 (1987).

for most people to take sides on issues and people as quickly as possible. Neutrality is an unnatural and uncomfortable state of being. In fact, based upon nothing more than a cursory exchange of pleasantries, people form an opinion about another's character and then they filter everything they subsequently learn about him through that filter. Thus, once people form a favorable impression of a person or company, they will explain away negative information acquired later, rationalizing its meaning or importance so that they avoid having to change their view of that person or company.

The principle of primacy means that the beginning of the trial is critically important. The very first moments of *voir dire* and the opening statement provide invaluable opportunities for counsel to create memorable and favorable impressions of their clients and cases with the jury. It means that defendants should never waive their opening statement. It also means that advocates should almost never save a critical piece of evidence—a smoking gun—for later in the case. Later may be too late, because the jurors may have already made up their minds about the case.

The impact of primacy is not limited to the beginning of trial. It applies to the beginning of every examination, after every recess, and even with the introduction of each new topic during a direct examination. Every time there is a new start in the trial, there is a chance for counsel to take advantage of the benefits of primacy. Each examination must begin with something that matters, most often with the personal background of the witness. The opening statement and closing argument must begin with powerful and memorable introductions that immediately focus the jury's attention on why the party should win and on the issues that really matter in the case. After each recess, counsel should look for chances to begin a new topic or introduce important testimony. During direct examinations counsel should periodically introduce new topics to the jury (through the use of "headlines") or use a visual aid as a means of restarting the benefits of primacy yet again.

2. *Recency*

In contrast to primacy, the principle of recency holds that the last thing a person hears about a topic will be best remembered. The principle is rooted in the commonsense notion that the attention of jurors improves as they perceive that the end of the presentation is near. The brain marks an end point and more easily encodes, stores, and recalls the last portions of the presentation.[7] Accordingly, just as advocates must develop memorable beginnings and work to exploit the benefits of primacy, so must they ensure that they end each speech or examination just as powerfully.

The principle of recency means that the rebuttal closing argument, the literal last word from the lawyers in the case, is a critically important opportunity for the advocate to leave the jury with memorable words or images. It means that lawyers should take great pains to avoid ending an

---

[7] Robert S. Wyer, Jr. & Thomas K. Srull, *The Processing of Social Stimulus Information: A Conceptual Integration, in* PERSON MEMORY: THE COGNITIVE BASIS OF SOCIAL PERCEPTION 227, 254-55 (Reid Hastie, et al. eds. 1980).

examination on a sustained objection. That is not the memorable impression any advocate wants to leave the jury with. It means that the moments at the end of each day of trial or just before a recess are opportunities to take advantage of the principle of recency and the jurors' heightened attention. Many advocates instinctively create a dramatic conclusion by highlighting a key fact at the end of testimony or at the end of an opening statement or closing argument because of the theatrical effect it has on the jurors. That instinct, it turns out, is good trial strategy.

3. *Pathos*

On the face of things, the task of jurors is to find the facts through the use of their logic, reason, and common sense. That is what judges instruct jurors to do in their final instructions to the jury and that is what the system expects of jurors. However, reason is rarely the lone basis for any decision, much less the jury's decision reflected by its verdict. After all, jurors are no more or less human in the jury deliberation room than they are outside of it, and they are no more or less able to ignore the influence of their emotions during deliberations than in their everyday lives. For jurors, as for everyone else, emotions often impel them to make a decision not supported by reason or to feel more strongly about something than a purely rational analysis would justify. Emotions create a powerful and sometimes irresistible impetus to decide an issue a particular way.

Pathos, of course, is a term coined by the ancient Greeks to identify those emotions we all have—feelings of pity, sorrow, or sympathy on the one hand, and feelings of anger, hostility, and rage on the other. And pathos, undoubtedly, is an essential and powerful element of all persuasive discourse. Parties and witnesses who gain the sympathy of the jurors have a significant advantage over their opponent. Parties who evoke the jurors' hostility or outrage operate at a substantial disadvantage compared to parties who do not. It is essential that by the end of the trial jurors feel some degree of sympathy, or better yet, empathy for the client.

The challenge for trial lawyers is to introduce pathos into the case, to make compelling emotional appeals to the jury, without running afoul of the rules of evidence and procedure that preclude any such explicit appeals. Advocates are specifically precluded from appealing to passion or prejudice, such as by suggesting that the jury should find for the plaintiff because he is severely injured or impoverished or against the defendant because of its wealth and power. In a few cases, however, the law cooperates and actually facilitates arguments steeped in pathos. For instance, when punitive damages are in issue, plaintiff's counsel may seek punishment of the defendant wrongdoer for the purpose of deterring similar misconduct in the future. Righteous indignation is not only appropriate, but necessary in those situations. When damages are being sought for personal injuries or death, issues of loss and pain give rise in a natural way to evidence of the plaintiff's feelings and those of his family. In criminal cases, prosecutors may have a similar opportunity in the sentencing phase of a trial when they can argue the fair and just punishment for the defendant as well as the grief and suffering of the victim.

In most cases, however, the emotional appeal will present more of a challenge, but it is no less important. The infusion of pathos must simply be more subtle and less explicit. The techniques for doing so could fill a volume or more themselves and will be discussed at some length throughout this work. The use of pathos starts with the development of the case theme. The central theme of every case should do more than simply tell the jury why the party should win, it should also connect the jury to some reason why they should care about the party winning. Logic *and* emotion must be tapped. Advocates must pay attention to the human element in their case, regardless of the particular facts involved. Every case is about people and their failures and successes, their victories and defeats. A breach of contract case is not simply about whether one party failed to perform a set of obligations. It is about the most sacred of all human acts, the making of a promise; it is about betrayal of that trust or perhaps about greed or pride. Advocates must look for the larger themes in the case, the universal truths the case stands for, and then show the jury how and why the case is larger than its facts.

Another means of introducing pathos into a case is through personalizing parties and witnesses, moving beyond their professional personas in the case and exploring the ways in which they are like the jurors sitting in the jury box. By revealing certain biographical information about parties (or witnesses), an advocate increases the likelihood that jurors will identify with them. The credibility and persuasiveness of advocates and their witnesses is often directly proportional to the perceived similarity between those witnesses and the jurors. This similarity can be reflected by overall appearance (*e.g.*, dress, grooming, body type, or mannerisms), demographics (*e.g.*, age, education, gender, or race), background (*e.g.*, where they were born and raised, where they were educated, or where they reside), lifestyle characteristics (*e.g.*, hobbies, organization membership, or past experiences related to the case), or perceived values (*e.g.*, right to life or personal responsibility).

The important role of pathos in juror decision-making requires that lawyers do more than coldly and efficiently elicit the facts from their witnesses. They must also draw out the emotional dimension of the experiences of their witnesses—the rape victim's feeling at the time she was raped, the employee's feelings when he received word that he was being fired, or the criminal defendant's reaction to being wrongfully accused.

When we speak of pathos, we are not espousing a cheap, calculated manipulation of the juror's emotions as some gimmick to obtain large damage awards. We are not advising the exploitation of a party's emotional despair to gain a tactical advantage at trial. Efforts to manipulate or exploit parties or jurors have no place at trial and, in any event, they usually backfire. The jury will see through the tactic and the advocate's credibility will be destroyed. Instead of a tool for crass manipulation, we see the use of pathos at trial as necessary to help jurors understand the full story of what happened and to gain an accurate perspective of the conflict.

In short, jurors may think with their heads, but they often decide with their hearts.

4. *Simplicity*

Trials can quite easily become complex affairs. The stilted language of the law, the arcane vocabulary of trial lawyers, convoluted claims or defenses, and highly technical or specialized witness testimony conspire to make the task of jurors very challenging, and quite frankly beyond the ability of many people. The sheer volume of material produced during a typical trial—the witnesses, exhibits, and arguments—may cause jurors to suffer from information overload and leave them unable to remember all or even most of the information presented. Complexity is the enemy of effective communication; confusion is one of the trial lawyer's greatest foes.

Accordingly, trial lawyers must work to keep their messages clear, straightforward, and understandable. The principle of simplicity is not an excuse for avoiding difficult issues in the case or oversimplifying complicated or ambiguous facts. To the contrary, it means that advocates should avoid making cases more complicated than they already are or obscuring the message of the case by their organization, vocabulary, or presentation. Simplicity manifests itself at trial in at least three ways:

* word choices

* content choices

* presentation choices

Start with the importance of words. A lawyer's vocabulary should never interfere with a juror's understanding of the evidence. Trials are not the time or place for lawyers to show off their intelligence or their Ivy League vocabularies. Instead, lawyers should use plain language when they address the jury and should prepare their witnesses to do the same. Words with four and five syllables should be used sparingly. Terms of art should be avoided. Legalese should be eliminated.

In addition, advocates should avoid the lawyerly temptation to ask every possible question or make every conceivable argument. Simplicity includes separating the wheat from the chaff and eliminating the clutter from your case. Jurors appreciate brevity. They respect the advocate who does not waste their time with frivolous questioning or meritless arguments. One strong argument is preferable to multiple weak arguments. "Everything, including the kitchen sink," advocacy simply does not work. To the contrary, effective advocacy requires ruthless editing. Limit distractions. Minimize digressions. Spend as much time as it takes to make your case or to discredit your opponent's, but not one second longer!

Finally, simplicity requires that lawyers present their cases in ways designed to make the facts easy for the jury to understand and remember. For example, the advocate's use of "headlining" and "blocking" during direct examination will simplify the task of jurors. This technique, which is discussed in detail in Chapter Six, breaks down the direct into discreet parts and then introduces each new part with a statement that announces the subject matter. Such a simple tool serves to increase juror retention, interest, and comprehension. Another means of keeping things simple is through the use of demonstrative and visual aids. Show and tell is not just a children's game, it is an essential part of effective advocacy.

5. *Imagery*

People are essentially "visual learners." Jurors will likely forget what they are merely told, whereas information they are told *and* shown is likely to be remembered. It is that simple. The ability to store and recall visual images is remarkable. Researchers have found that "jurors remember 85 percent of what they see as opposed to only 15 percent of what they hear."[8] They are accustomed to electronic stimulation from televisions and computers and are more likely to read the graphic-rich *USA Today* than the text-heavy *New York Times*, if, in fact, they read any newspaper at all. They expect to get their news in pithy sound bites with accompanying pictures and colorful explanatory graphics. This growing visual dependency on the part of jurors means that demonstrative and other visual aids are necessary to:

Tech Tip
Visual Aids

✓ Visual aids speak louder than words.

✓ Choose simplicity over complexity.

✓ Engage your audience with common-knowledge terminology.

✓ Continuously use a visual for a particular theme.

✓ Be sensitive to visual details; make it visually pleasing.

- maintain juror interest,

- enhance juror retention, and

- satisfy juror expectations.

a. The Importance of Technology

Demonstrative and visual aids are essential to clear and effective communication at every phase of the trial—during the opening statement and closing argument and during the witness examinations. The pictures or images do not have to be dramatic or costly to be effective. They might range from the rudimentary—photographs, overhead transparencies, time lines, charts, diagrams, or lists—to the more complicated—PowerPoint slides, video re-creations or demonstrations, and computer animations or simulations. The evidence may be something as obvious as the murder weapon in a criminal case or the contract in a civil case, something as surprising as a plaster mold of the defendant's shoe print or the actual engine from the plaintiff's allegedly defective car.

The liberal use of exhibits and demonstrative aids maintains (and heightens) juror interest in at least three ways: (1) it creates a change in the courtroom environment, varying from the norm of so many talking heads; (2) it gives the jurors something on which to focus their attention other than

---

[8] *See* Lionel Standing, et al., *Perception and Memory for Pictures: Single-Trial Learning of 2500 Visual Stimuli*, 19 PSYCHONOMIC SCI. 73 (1970).

the witness, the advocates, or the ceiling; and (3) it stimulates another of the jurors' senses—their sense of sight. And the jurors will remember the point better because it appeals to both their sense of hearing and seeing.

Consider a case presented two ways, one with a demonstrative aid and one without. Take any case and almost any issue. In a simple car accident case, the plaintiffs could present their case solely through the testimony of eyewitnesses without the use of any demonstrative evidence whatsoever. They could do it that way, but why? How difficult would it be for the jury, based on nothing but oral descriptions, to understand the layout of the intersection where the accident took place or the nature of the damage to the cars or the sequence of events leading to the accident? The preferable alternative is to show the jury a diagram of the intersection, along with full color photographs of it or videotape, so that the jurors can have the sense of having been to the intersection (perhaps counsel could even arrange a jury view of the accident site, if it would be helpful). In addition, counsel would want to have pictures of the cars as they appeared after the collision and of the plaintiffs and their injuries from the accident.

> **Tech Tip**
> *Strategy*
>
> ✓ Before agreeing to the admission of an adverse party's digital images, demand a copy of the original digital image.

If the case is substantial enough, counsel might have a computer animation developed showing the jury exactly how the accident happened. If there were any issues of chronology, counsel might create a timeline showing when critical events happened and in what sequence. The police report, if helpful, might be enlarged and shown to the jury. During closing argument, counsel might create a chart listing all of plaintiff's medical expenses and other damages in discussing damages.

The contrast could not be clearer. One approach is sure to leave the jury bored and confused (and maybe disappointed, or even angry). The other approach at least gives counsel the hope of keeping the jury tuned in and interested during the trial with some sense of what happened and when.

b. The Use of Technology in the Courtroom

The tentacles of technology currently touch every branch of our lives, including the law. In today's high tech world, it is not only logical that technology would be a part of the courtroom, but also that its use is essential to provide the best and most persuasive presentation of the evidence. Understandably, it behooves every advocate to be educated and knowledgeable about the best uses of technology for various circumstances. Therefore, before trial, an advocate should methodically

> **Tech Tip**
> *Basic Tools*
>
> ✓ Laptop notebook (MAC or PC), which includes USB printing capabilities and a CD/DVD burner
> ✓ USB 2.0
> ✓ Microsoft Word and/or WordPerfect
> ✓ Multifunction flatbed inkjet printer-scanner-copier
> ✓ Access to Adobe Acrobat Pro or Reader for .PDF files

think through how best to use equipment and software in order to maximize her case.

i. Forms of Technology

a. Presentation Software

Among the most common presentation software is *Microsoft's PowerPoint* and *Apple's 'Keynote'*. In a document-intensive case laden with information, other programs may be more effective and efficient, such as, *Sanction, Trial Director, Acrobat,* and *Trial Pro*. Specifically, these versatile presentation programs offer immediate document recall via barcode and modification of displayed images.

Pros of Presentation Software	*Cons*
- Appeals to various senses - If used properly, can aid in persuading audience - Focus audience to key points of case - User friendly - Common program - Ability to create lists, timelines, charts, and diagrams; to label photographs and to project documents in color and with motion and sound	- Too much text in the slides can drown audience with information - If not comfortable with and knowledgeable in program's application, it can hinder the advancement of your case - Can become a cumbersome tool that conflicts with the natural flow of communication

Technology Presentation Packages are Excellent For
- Displaying maps (aerial, street maps, etc.) - Recreating an accident - Using flow charts to explain complicated issues - Timelines - Storyboards - Establishing timelines (with pictures) - Displaying autopsy/injury photos - Putting your "hook" phrase on a slide during opening and closing argument - Humanizing the deceased in a criminal and civil case - Highlighting the confession of the defendant with a callout box containing admissions - Calling attention to the contract the defendant signed showing his responsibility to the homeowner - Playing the videotaped will of the decedent

In addition, other presentation software focuses on enhancing, editing, and manipulating images. A popular example of this software is *Adobe Photoshop 7*. This type of software can highlight key components of a case.

b. Document Cameras

Document cameras are an advanced type of projector. They have the ability to project any document and picture onto a large screen without requiring computer hook-ups. ELMO is a widely used document camera operated in many courtrooms. Witnesses have the opportunity to interpret, explain, and comment on the document being observed by the jurors.

Pros of Document Cameras	Cons
- Simple program – If you can use an over-head projector, you can use a document camera! - Allows a witness to engage with an exhibit to better explain their testimony - Many courtrooms are equipped with document cameras - Allows the use of hardcopies: documents, photos, etc. - Can electronically rotate image - Some document cameras can record and electronically store images	- A large number of people are still not familiar with its operating process - Added time-consuming steps are needed if digital cameras are not available for use

c. Video Recording

Another technology option for advocates is video presentations produced by a camera or computer. Counsel should address three significant issues when using video technology: (1) authentication, (2) personal knowledge, and (3) potential unfair prejudice. Video presentations may be admissible if the video presents opinions by experts or testimony by witnesses, and if a foundational connection exists between the presentation and the witness. Also, counsel should not wait to provide opposing counsel and the court with video footage on the day of trial or mediation; instead, the potential video presentation should be made available in accordance with the court's direction or in response to discovery requests.

A video presentation allows an advocate to build an emotional bridge between the client and the jurors by a common means of communication, a film. Some examples of the effective use of video evidence might include:

- The life of the client before the harm

- The interviewee's response after becoming aware of the harm

- The observations made by the interviewer of the injured client

- The client's effort to recover

- The present state of the client

- The wishes and desires of the client

A video presentation can be a very effective tool if used properly. The response to the video presentation can become a turning point towards persuading an audience in a very profound way.

ii. Choosing the Best Equipment

As you are preparing your case, you may find that different forms of technology may be necessary for different types of exhibits. In order to help you keep your presentation as effective as possible, the preferred types of input and output devices are listed below according to each specific type of exhibit.

> **Tech Tip**
> *Preparation*
>
> Before committing to technology in a new courtroom, be sure to notice:
>
> ✓ Available equipment provided by the court
> ✓ Jury perception and visibility of presentation
> ✓ Acoustics
> ✓ Position and number of outlets
> ✓ Possible compatibility issues between Mac and PC – for example, Macs need a video adapter (VGA) for use with the majority of projectors.

Exhibit Types	Best Input	Easiest Output
Photographs	ELMO Document Camera	Projector and screen
Charts and graphs	Laptop computer	Individual juror monitors
Text documents	Laptop computer	Projector and screen
Maps, drawings, diagrams	ELMO Document Camera	Projector and screen
Small objects	ELMO Document Camera	Projector and screen
X-Rays and CAT scans	ELMO Document Camera	Large high-resolution monitor
Timelines	Laptop computer	Projector and screen
Tables, printouts	ELMO Document Camera	Projector and screen
Videotape excerpts	Laptop computer/DVD or VHS	Large high-resolution monitor
Sound recordings	Laptop computer	High-resolution audio speakers
Animations, simulations	Laptop computer	Projector and screen

6. *Frequency*

The sixth fundamental principle of communication is frequency. It rests on a common sense proposition: the more times people hear something, the more likely they are to remember it and believe that it is true.[9] Frequency enhances recall. Frequency enhances recall. Frequency enhances recall. Got it?

One might naturally ask at this point whether the principle of frequency directly and unavoidably conflicts with the principle of simplicity. This is simply a way of saying that the need for repetition at trial creates a difficult and challenging task for advocates. They must repeat the key points of the case enough times for the jurors to understand them, remember them, and accept them as true, but not so often that the jurors feel patronized, bored, or, worst of all, alienated. The principle of repetition, carried too far, can leave jurors feeling that counsel has nothing to say (because he keeps saying the same thing over and over) or that counsel believes the jurors are idiots (because he feels the need to say the same thing over and over). A common complaint of jurors after trials is that the lawyers spent too much time saying the same thing, repeating the same points.

Yet, despite these potential downsides, frequency is an important tool of persuasion and it most certainly does not conflict with the notion of simplicity. The need for repetition simply recognizes the inability of jurors to separate the important from the unimportant without some help, and the reality that it is easy for jurors to drown in the sea of information that comprises a typical trial.

Some words, phrases, and ideas must be repeated throughout the trial because of their centrality to a party's argument. A party's central theme certainly fits into that category. If the party's theme of the case is that the defendant corporation chose profits over people, sales over safety, then the jury should hear those words during *voir dire*, opening statement (at the beginning and the end), and closing argument. Moreover, the witness examinations should explore the defendant's decision-making process and how the defendant made an economic decision to not make the change. During cross-examination of the defendant's executives, counsel can directly ask: "Isn't it true that you put profits over the welfare of your customers?" and "Isn't it true that you cared more about sales than about safety?" The repetition of the key words "profits," "sales," and "safety" again invoke the plaintiff's theme for the jurors.

Repeating points without inducing boredom or suffering an objection requires some imagination on counsel's part. One tool that can help is the use of demonstrative or visual aids. Often counsel can have a witness narrate certain events or points and then gain a measure of repetition by having the witness go through the events again, this time with the aid of a diagram or chart. Similarly, repetition can be attained during the direct examination on key points or critical action sequences through the use of close-ended questions. For instance, after the witness has given a

---

[9]   John T. Cacioppo & Richard E. Petty, *Effects of Message Repetition and Position on Cognitive Response, Recall, and Persuasion*, 37 J. PERSONALITY & SOC. PSYCH. 97, 105-07 (1979).

narrative answer about the events, counsel can go back and ask questions about aspects of the events not covered by the witness' answer and in doing so, work through the critical events an additional time.

7. *Logic and Coherence*

The final principle of effective communication harkens to Aristotle's notion of logos and his emphasis of the importance of logic and reason in persuasive rhetoric. Advocates must develop and advance logical and coherent arguments at trial because otherwise the argument fails the test of reason and the advocate's credibility suffers a fatal blow. This principle dictates that advocates:

- identify the facts that the jury will likely find to be true,

- develop one central theme for the case that incorporates those facts,

- resist reliance on any facts that are inconsistent with the central theme, and

- make only strong, credible arguments.

Few trial techniques can compare to the power of an argument supported by the credible evidence in the case and bolstered by the force of logic and common sense.

The task of ignoring some of the claims or defenses available to a party and resisting the urge to argue alternative or inconsistent claims, requires that lawyers forget the lessons they learned in law school, which encourage students to identify every argument (on both sides) and to consider alternative and even inconsistent positions in analyzing problems. The words "but even if" are part and parcel of the law student's language, a phrase introducing an alternative argument ("But even if D killed the victim, it was in self-defense"). For trial lawyers, the words "but even if" are the death knell to persuasiveness at trial. They suggest that the advocate is unsure what happened or, more sinister yet, is espousing a number of arguments in hopes that one will stick. Advocates must overcome their fears and their training and identify their strongest argument in light of the facts the jury will likely find to be true. Then they must make that argument without hedging their bet. In reality, the attempts at hedging, rather than making things safer and more comfortable for the party and advocate, do much more harm than good. The jury is left to question the credibility and expertise of the advocates without clear answers as to what it should believe about the party's arguments.

Effective communication is challenging even under the best of circumstances. It is downright treacherous for trial lawyers who have to navigate a thicket of procedural and evidentiary rules and still find a way to persuade the total strangers who sit in the jury box that their arguments are the truth. Challenging, but not impossible. Treacherous, but not unattainable. The road to success begins with the techniques described above. They apply to trial preparation and to every aspect of the trial itself. Review the principles regularly. Consider their applications. Think through their uses. Become an effective trial advocate.

Chapter Two

CASE DEVELOPMENT

I. OVERVIEW & OBJECTIVES

Most trial lawyers spend only a relatively small percentage of their professional lives in the courtroom actually trying cases. From the busiest public defender to the most senior prosecutor, from the insurance defense lawyer to the litigator who has yet to find a case that cannot be settled, lawyers spend most of their time preparing for trial, not in trial. Further, every trial lawyer who has ever tried a case knows that cases are won or lost based largely on the adequacy of the lawyer's preparation. But preparation involves more than a thorough investigation of the facts or comprehensive discovery of what the other side knows. Preparation involves more than doing, it also involves thinking—analyzing the issues in the case, sifting the important facts from the unimportant, and developing the themes and theories.

This book is not about the pretrial process. We do not discuss the drafting of pleadings, techniques of investigation, tactics for discovery, strategy at depositions or preliminary hearings, timing or strategy of making or responding to motions for summary judgment, intricacies of independent medical examinations, requirements for expert witness reports, or the other myriad aspects of pretrial preparation. That does not mean that those aspects of the process are unimportant or irrelevant to whether an advocate obtains a favorable settlement or verdict. They may well be determinative in a case, but that is beyond the scope of this chapter and this book.

We will discuss, however, the ultimate purpose of pretrial activity. Pleadings, discovery, and motions uncover the facts and narrow the issues. And at the end of that process, whether it takes months or years, advocates should know the disputed issues in the case and should possess the pertinent facts. Then, the advocate's task is to develop those facts and make them into a winning case, one that is coherent and cogent, powerful and persuasive.

II. DEVELOPING THE CASE FOR TRIAL

Case development is the process of sifting through all the facts and data collected through the discovery process–both formal and informal— to ultimately identify those facts that are important and useful and distinguish them from those facts that are not, to build a case that is both legally sufficient and factually compelling. The first step in the process is the assessment of the legal requirements for the party's charge, claim, or defense. Thus, an advocate should follow these four steps in developing their cases:

- assess the legal requirements of proof for the party

- sift the important evidence from the unimportant

- construct a legal and factual theory

- develop a case theme

A. Assess Legal Requirements

Regardless of how interesting or riveting a party's case may be, it is of no value if the evidence presented by the party fails to satisfy the legal requirements. Thus, the process of thinking about a case begins with the jury instructions, which are surely the best source for quickly determining the elements of a charge, claim, or defense. Most jurisdictions have pattern jury instructions for common criminal or civil claims or defenses. Jury instructions provide advocates with an early insight into the necessary proof requirements and the precise information the jurors will likely be told about the law of the case at the end of the trial. The legal requirements provide the bare minimum standard of proof that the party must satisfy.

There must be competent evidence of every element of the party's claim or defense or evidence sufficient to defeat the opponent's claim or defense.

The advocate must know the basic legal requirements early in the representation because that information colors everything that comes later. The claims that are pleaded, the information that is sought, and the witnesses that are questioned, all follow from the party's understanding of the law that applies to the case. For example, in a personal injury case in which plaintiff was injured while not wearing a seatbelt, it makes a significant difference if the law allows defendant to use plaintiff's failure as evidence of contributory negligence on plaintiff's part. If that evidence is excluded in the jurisdiction (as it is in some jurisdictions), the defendant must pursue other claims or defenses, not the seatbelt defense. From the outset of undertaking a representation, advocates must know the precise elements of their claims and defenses and must use the pretrial process to collect sufficient evidence to prove each element.

Jury instructions can influence how the advocate organizes and prepares his or her case from start to finish. In the beginning stages of preparation, jury instructions can help the advocate understand the basic applicable law and are crucial tools in shaping the preparation for the entire trial.

Most jurisdictions have pattern jury instructions that cover almost all issues that may arise during trial. The benefit of pattern instructions is that they are already pre-accepted by the judge and they are almost always accurate statements of law. However, lawyers have the option of using the pattern instructions, or drafting their own. The instructions are always subject to discussion by both sides, and the judge will make the ultimate determination as to which instructions will be used. In reality, pattern instructions are routinely used, unless one of the following applies:

- There is no current jury instruction on the issue.

- The law has changed since the pattern instructions were written.

- A well thought out argument compels the advocate to share a particular reason as to why the pattern instructions could be improved in a legally accurate, more relevant fashion.

B. Sift Important Evidence from Unimportant

The second step is evaluation of all the evidence collected by the party, including witnesses, documents, physical evidence, or demonstrative evidence. Some of the evidence will be critically important to the party's case, while other evidence will not be helpful in establishing the party's claims or defenses. Every witness does not have to be presented. Every document does not have to be introduced. Every fact does not have to be revealed. Successful advocates prune their cases of unhelpful evidence, trimming the unproductive portions of the case and sifting out facts that do not advance the party's contentions.

There are no hard and fast rules for this process of pruning and sifting. It is very much a matter of intuition and instinct as the advocate considers what evidence the jury is likely to believe and what evidence the judge will likely admit. As advocates gain experience in the courtroom and increase their exposure to the fact-finding of judges and juries, they refine and sharpen their ability to discern what evidence should be used and what evidence should be eliminated. However, as a general rule, advocates, in evaluating the evidence in their cases, should look for evidence that satisfies four criteria: relevance, reliability, resilience, and resonance.

- *Relevance*: All evidence must, at the very least, satisfy the legal requirement of relevance. It must advance a party's claim or defense or rebut an opponent's claim or defense. Evidence that is not relevant should not be part of the advocate's case.

- *Reliability*: Evidence must also be reliable and trustworthy. The integrity of the advocate is at stake when she offers a witness or introduces an exhibit before the jury in that she implicitly vouches for her witnesses and for the evidence she introduces. Thus, the evidence must be worthy of the juror's trust, or the advocate must explain to the jurors in advance the reasons for offering suspect evidence or witnesses.

- *Resilience*: Evidence should be resilient and durable. It must stand the test of time and survive adversarial testing. Evidence that is easily rebutted or attacked by the opponent or is contrary to common sense should be rejected when possible.

- *Resonance*: Evidence should also resonate with the jurors; it should appeal to their sense of fairness and justice and touch their emotions. Undoubtedly, not every piece of evidence will have that effect, but advocates should be alert for evidence that will connect with the jurors and will help make the case seem bigger than the individual facts themselves.

C. Construct Legal and Factual Theories

The third part of the advocate's mental preparation for trial is to take the facts—the testimonial evidence as well as the real, documentary, and demonstrative evidence—and to construct from those facts legal and factual theories. The factual theory of the case is the advocate's synthesis of what happened and why; the legal theory is the advocate's view of why those facts are legally sufficient to state a claim or defense or to disprove the opponent's claim or defense. Depending on the complexity of the case, the trial lawyer should be able to state his theory in no more than a few sentences. The theory of the case is the answer an advocate would give if asked in a social setting, "So what is the Jones case all about?" When advocates hem and haw in response to that question, it means that they have not yet developed a clear and concise theory of the case.

1. *Legal Theories*

The legal theory of the case must take into account the legal requirements for the claim or defense, and identify the evidence that establishes each element. For parties bearing the burden of proof, it is particularly important that they develop a legal theory of the case. In a criminal prosecution for rape, for example, the prosecutor must know the statutory elements of rape in the jurisdiction. If the elements require the government to prove that the victim resisted the attacker, the prosecutor will have to include, as part of his legal theory of the case, how he will prove that element. From the defense perspective, the defendant may be acquitted either if he did not commit the act or he committed the act but reasonably believed that the "victim" had consented. The defense cannot pursue both possibilities in the same case (or at least should not pursue them both simultaneously) and the particular theory chosen will, of course, depend upon the particular facts surrounding the rape.

Similarly, in a defamation case in which defendant claims that plaintiff was a public figure, thus requiring a show of malice by the plaintiff, plaintiff will have to determine his preferred battleground. Should plaintiff argue that he is not a public figure, but that even if he was, the defendant acted maliciously? Or should plaintiff argue malice from the outset, knowing that if the jury finds malice, the public figure issue will become a moot point. Later in this section, we will discuss in more detail the dangers of arguing alternative theories. For now, however, recognize that a legal theory is a necessity in every case for the practical reason that parties must have a clear sense of the legal requirements for their claims and defenses and a clear roadmap of how they will meet those requirements.

2. *Factual Theories*

The advocate's factual theory should explain what happened and why. In developing factual theories, advocates must:

- take into account each established fact in the case,

- avoid contradicting any disputed fact that the jurors will likely find to be true,

- select a theory that maximizes the party's chance to prevail, and

- reject any claims or defenses that are inconsistent with other claims or defenses.

a. **Consistent with the Facts**

In almost every case that goes to trial, there are facts that favor each side, facts that are often directly in conflict. The jury's job is to resolve those conflicts. However, before the case ever gets to the jurors the advocate must anticipate what they will do, which facts they will believe and which facts they will not believe. Sometimes that is easy enough because the fact is undisputed or so one-sided that it is hard to imagine the jurors will not accept it as true. At other times, on closely contested issues, predicting the jurors' fact finding can be extraordinarily difficult. But it must be done, to the extent possible, because advocates must ensure that their theories take into account all the facts that will be clearly established at trial and do not contradict those facts that the jurors will most likely find to be true.

Return now to the hypothetical rape prosecution. Assume that it is undisputed through the evidence (including perhaps DNA test results, eye-witness testimony, or the defendant's own statements) that the defendant had sexual intercourse with the victim. Thus, the defendant could not have a theory that he was not there and did not commit the crime. Instead, one defense theory might center on the reasonableness of the defendant's belief that the "victim" had consented. Assuming that the victim claims that she did not consent to the defendant's advances, the advocate must develop a theory that will explain the "he said/she said" contradiction. There may be several options. Perhaps the defendant was mistaken, but the mistake was reasonable in view of his existing relationship with the "victim" and her conduct at the time of the incident. Alternatively, perhaps the victim consented but later regretted her consent, and now seeks to "undo" the act by disputing the consent. Or, perhaps she consented, but is now attempting to avoid the consequences (say an unpleasant or violent response from her boyfriend or spouse) by accusing the defendant of rape. Many other possible theories exist, but one thing is clear: The theory relied upon by the advocate must comport with the facts known to the advocate, must incorporate the established facts, and must not contradict any fact the jurors are likely to believe. If the defendant had no previous relationship with the victim or if the victim had no significant other at the time, the theory must reflect that.

Assume that the defense theory is that the intercourse was consensual and that the victim has chosen to falsely accuse the defendant of rape to calm her abusive boyfriend. That theory is consistent with the defendant's testimony, including comments the defendant claims the victim made to him while they were together, and it supplies the motive the jurors need to discredit her testimony. The theory, if proven, could logically lead to an acquittal.

b. On a Favorable Battle Site

The theory of the case must maximize the advocate's opportunity to win. That is obvious. Advocates should select the high ground from which they can win. They should fight on their turf, not their opponent's. The case theory identifies the battleground. An advocate works from a position of power when his theory establishes the turf on which the case will be tried. For example, in a trial about a truck driver's negligence in colliding with plaintiff's car, in which the evidence of negligence is overwhelming, defendant may be wise to concede liability and fight the case over the severity of plaintiff's injuries. Depending on the facts, that is a battle that may be winnable, while contesting liability would be futile.

The other possibility is to try to turn the difficult facts to the advocate's advantage. A notable example of a trial lawyer who did just that is Donald Re in his defense of John Delorean. Consider the backdrop for Re's representation. In 1982, ten years after leaving General Motors, Delorean had founded and was running Delorean Motor Company. He lived the good life. He was married to a former fashion model and shuttled between three multi-million dollar homes in Manhattan, New Jersey, and California. But the reality was that the "Delorean" was not selling well and his company was close to bankruptcy. Delorean needed $20 million. He learned of an opportunity in the illicit drug business. Unknown to Delorean, however, the source of this "opportunity" was a government informant. The consummation of the eventual "drug deal" was videotaped and depicted a triumphant Delorean accepting a suitcase filled with cocaine and then offering a champagne toast for "a lot of success for everyone."

Difficult facts indeed. Donald Re had the daunting task of designing a blueprint for Delorean's defense. To allow the prosecution to set the agenda would be fatal. His case theory had to shift the battleground away from Delorean's actions. Indeed, should the jury dwell on the damning conduct of Delorean, a conviction would surely be the outcome. Re had to shape the overall view of the jurors, pick the vantage point or the perspective from which the jurors would view the facts in the light most favorable to his client. And that meant focusing on the misdeeds of the government. Re recognized that he must demonize the government agents, turning the trial into a scathing condemnation of the actions and motivations of the investigators, in their blind quest to topple a newsworthy figure, at the expense of the real victim: John Delorean. Re's theory was basic: "The agents weren't concerned with the facts. They weren't concerned with intent. They were on a headlong rush to glory because they could nail this guy."[1] The result? An acquittal of Delorean.

Re's strategy was by no means novel. In 1912, when Clarence Darrow was on trial for bribing a juror, the evidence of Darrow's guilt was similarly overwhelming. Darrow, recognizing his dilemma, successfully shifted the focus of the trial away from his actions by questioning the government's motivation in bringing the prosecution.

 ## Illustration of Theory Development

Darrow: What am I on trial for, gentlemen of the jury? You have been listening here for three months. What is it all about? If you don't know then you are not as intelligent as I believe. I am not on trial for having sought to bribe a man named Lockwood. There may be and doubtless are many people who think I did seek to bribe him, but I am not on trial for that, and I will prove it to you. No man is

---

[1] MICHAEL S. LIEF, ET AL., LADIES AND GENTLEMEN OF THE JURY 303 (1998).

> being tried on that charge. I am on trial because I have been a lover of the poor, a friend of the oppressed, because I have stood by labor for all these years, and have brought down upon my head the wrath of the criminal interests in this country. Whether guilty or innocent of the crime charged in the indictment, that is the reason I am here, and that is the reason that I have been pursued by as cruel a gang as ever followed a man.

The defense's efforts on behalf of O.J. Simpson followed in that same tradition. The right theory allows the advocate to capture the high ground by moving the trial to the most advantageous battlefield.

c.   Consistent with Other Claims or Defenses[2]

A party's claims or defenses should be consistent with each other and that consistency should be reflected by the party's theories of the case. This notion works against law school training wherein prospective lawyers are encouraged (and even required) to make every argument and to advance every contention. Even the procedural rules that govern lawsuits and trials encourage such tactics, allowing parties to plead alternative and even inconsistent theories. (Fed R. Civ. Pro. 8(e).) And when developing a case, an attorney might choose, for a variety of legitimate reasons, to plead theories that are actually inconsistent with each other. For instance, an advocate might choose to allege that the defendant did not engage in tortious conduct, and also plead that the plaintiff was not damaged by the defendant's conduct. Indeed, an attorney may be remiss not to do so early in the case, when facts and theories have not been completely discovered or developed, particularly since a party may later be precluded from arguing a theory it has not included in its pleadings. And since a jury will likely never see the pleadings themselves, there is little or no risk in doing so.

However, when those instincts are brought into a courtroom before a jury the result may be disastrous. For instance, in a personal injury trial the defense theory might be that the plaintiff was not injured, and even if he was, the defendant was not the cause of the injury. Or in a homicide case, the defense might argue that defendant was not at the scene, and in any event, the victim's death was accidental. Or in a trial involving a contractual dispute, the defense argument may be that the contract is unenforceable, and furthermore, even if it is enforceable, the defendant is excused from performance by the contract's terms.

The primary danger of asserting such "multiple choice" theories is that it imperils the advocate's credibility before the jury. Inconsistent arguments

---

[2]   *See* Caldwell, Perrin & Christopher L. Frost, *The Art and Architecture of Closing Argument,* 72 TULANE L. REV. 961 (2002) (earlier version). Used with permission.

raise in the minds of jurors the very real possibility that the advocate is not concerned about the truth, but only with winning. The tactic also suggests a lack of confidence in one's own case and perhaps even a certain degree of desperation. The advancement of multiple theories in a case is the equivalent of throwing in "everything but the kitchen sink" in the hope that something will prove persuasive.

The classic example of the lawyer who advanced every possible argument is described by Irving Younger who recalls that at common law, advocates were entitled to reply to a plaintiff who claimed that his cabbages had been eaten by the defendant's goat as follows:

You had no cabbages.

If you did, they were not eaten.

If they were eaten, it was not by a goat.

If they were eaten by a goat, it was not my goat.

And if it was my goat, he was insane.[3]

An attorney is most effective when he conveys a commitment to the truth. And an attorney who makes inconsistent arguments fails that most basic test. Moreover, an attorney who appears unsure or hesitant about the correct outcome will have a difficult time persuading others of its correctness. Jurors will likely ask themselves why they should believe a particular theory when the attorney presenting that theory does not even seem to believe it. Multiple choice theories are likely to elicit just such a response. "If the attorney feels so passionate about the primary theory, why does he give me another option?" In other words, while the lawyer may view this type of presentation as thorough and meticulous, the jury will likely perceive this approach as game-playing or even worse, manipulative and dishonest.

Take a murder trial. Assume that an individual is accused of murder in the first degree. The defense attorney discovers evidence to support the position that his client did not commit the crime. At the same time, the lawyer finds evidence that the crime was committed without premeditation (a central element to first degree murder), such that a lesser included offense would be more appropriate. The advocate may be tempted to argue both theories. And the attorney might even justify this logic by rationalizing his decision as being in the best interest of the client, who faces life in prison if convicted of first-degree murder. Unfortunately, the jury will not engage in the same mental gymnastics as the attorney, but instead will expect an attorney whose client is truly innocent to argue for nothing less than an acquittal.

---

[3] *See* James W. McElhaney, McElhaney's Trial Notebook 49 (2nd ed. 1987). Copyright 1987 American Bar Association and James W. McElhaney. Reprinted with permission.

Indeed, there is something to be said for standing for nothing less. An adamant attorney may even appear righteously indignant at the thought of his client suffering at the hands of an overzealous prosecutor. Compare this image before the jury, and that of an attorney arguing multiple choice theories, striving to convince a jury that his client is not guilty of any crime, and yet seemingly resigned or even relieved at the possibility that his client may serve time for manslaughter instead of murder. The contrast is shocking.

There is one situation that often requires the advocate to present juries with a choice of theories, and that is the situation confronting civil defense lawyers in cases involving claims for damages. Should the defense lawyer challenge both liability and damages, or only liability? The risk, of course, is that by presenting evidence and making arguments about the extent of plaintiff's damages, the advocate seems to implicitly concede the liability issues. However, by focusing solely on liability the lawyer risks unreasonably high damages in the event of a plaintiff's verdict. One dramatic example of that risk comes from *Pennzoil v. Texaco*. The lead lawyer for the defendant made the tactical choice to ignore damages because of his belief that the plaintiff's case on liability was weak. The jury found for the plaintiff and awarded astronomical damages because it had only plaintiff's theory of damages to consider.[4] The jurors returned what was then the largest civil verdict in American history just as the plaintiff's attorneys had asked them to do.

The *Pennzoil* case serves as a reminder of the risk of not arguing both liability and damages. The process of educating the jury about the need for the advocate to argue and present evidence on both liability and damages must begin during *voir dire* and continue through closing argument. The lawyer might explain that necessity as follows:

 ## Illustration of Arguing Liability *and* Damages

Lawyer: Ladies and Gentlemen, let me make one thing perfectly clear: Jones Industries is not liable to the plaintiff in this case. Jones did nothing wrong and, in fact, did everything possible to make the safest and best product possible. I wish I could stop right there, because that should be the end of the case. But plaintiff did not stop there, he also told you about the injuries he claims he has and he asked you for a large amount as damages in this case, and so I can't stop where I should be able to. I have to address plaintiff's injuries and his damage claims, not because plaintiff is entitled to any damages—he is not—but because my obligation to Jones Industries requires that I respond to each and every claim and allegation raised by plaintiff regardless of its merit.

---

[4] Stephan Landsman, *The Civil Jury in America*, 62 Law & Contemp. Prob. 285, 287, 295 (1999).

At the very least, the jury will appreciate the advocate's candor and her sense of duty in addressing each issue in the case. At the most, the jury will not hold the damage arguments against the advocate during deliberation as some kind of concession to liability.

D. Develop a Case Theme

1. *Meaning and Resonance*

The final step in the preparation of a case for trial is development of a case theme. Development of a theme requires the advocate to synthesize the facts into the core truth that the case represents—the essence of the case, its soul. An artistic creation, whether a painting, musical composition, or closing argument, that fails to strike a universal message may be momentarily acknowledged, perhaps even appreciated in passing, but it will not transcend the moment or inspire the audience. Those who master their craft understand the need for a theme—a central idea that harnesses the power of the work and focuses its message.

To return to a concept discussed earlier, the advocate is searching for an idea or image that will resonate with the jurors, that will cause them to fully and deeply understand what the case is about. The extremely successful and popular writer and storyteller, Stephen King, says that as he reflects on his stories before they are published he asks himself "the Big Questions," including:

- "Is this story coherent?"

- "What are the recurring elements?"

- "Do they entwine and make a theme?"

Then King reveals the most important part of his storytelling: "What I want most of all is resonance, something that will linger for a while in [the] [r]eader's mind (and heart) after he or she has closed the book and put it on the shelf."[5] Advocates must ask the same questions in pursuit of the same goal.

2. *Finding the Right Theme*

Where do case themes come from? Common life experiences make for the most powerful and effective themes, but the universe of potential sources for thematic statements is limited only by the advocate's creativity. Themes might be drawn from literary sources—books, folk lore, or the Bible—or from popular culture references such as current events, movies, plays, or advertising slogans, or from a simple play on words, such as figures of speech, a catchy rhyme, or an alliteration.

Consider some examples of themes created by master trial advocates, together with a brief explanation of the facts in each case.

---

[5] STEPHEN KING, ON WRITING 214 (2000).

Illustrations of Themes

- "If the lion gets away, Kerr McGee has to pay.[6] This theme was used by Gerry Spence in his closing argument for the family of Karen Silkwood in their lawsuit against Kerr-McGee. Plaintiffs claimed that the defendant had failed to protect its employees from the risks of exposure to plutonium. Spence's theme, which evoked the image of a lion escaping despite the best efforts of its owner, was simple and rhythmic, but it was also memorable, powerful, and pointed. It encapsulated the reason his client should win. Spence obtained a multimillion-dollar verdict from the jury.

- "Terry Nichols was building a life, not a bomb."[7] In the defense of Terry Nichols, prosecuted for conspiring with Timothy McVeigh to bomb the federal building in Oklahoma City, Michael Tigar's simple, alliterative theme not only attempted to refute the underlying charges, but also communicated the positive message that Nichols was trying to make a life for his family and would not have risked it all to help McVeigh commit his heinous crime. Tigar successfully convinced the jury to spare Nichols from the death penalty.

- "Three starkly descriptive words, deceit, exploitation, and greed have been and are indeed today the guiding beacons which have directed the cigarette industry."[8] John Ciresi's theme, on behalf of the State of Minnesota and Blue Cross and Blue Shield of Minnesota, used powerful terms to describe the conduct of the tobacco industry, foreshadowing the evidence of the defendants' many lies and half truths about the health effects of smoking. Plaintiffs settled before closing arguments for more than six billion dollars.

Each of these themes uses simple words to create a powerful and memorable image of the case, an image that reveals to the jury the essence of the case. Consider these potential themes in hypothetical cases:

- In the hypothetical rape case described above, in which the defendant claims that the victim consented and now claims rape to avoid conflict with her angry boyfriend: "She said yes, she must face her mess."

---

[6] *See Estate of Silkwood v. Kerr-McGee Corp.*, Cause No. 76-0888 (D. Ct. Okla. 1979) (closing argument of Gerry Spence), *reprinted in* COVER ET AL., *supra* at note 2, at 994–95.

[7] *See United States v. Nichols*, No. 96-CR-68, 1997 WL 677907, at *25, *41, *54 (D. Colo. Nov. 3, 1997) (Michael Tigar's opening statement for Terry Nichols).

[8] *See State v. Phillip Morris, Inc.*, No. C1-94-8565, 1998 WL 36940, at *4 (Minn. Dist. Ct. Jan. 26, 1988) (John Ciresi's opening statement for the State of Minnesota).

- In a breach of contract case for the plaintiff, in which defendant allegedly reneged on a commitment to fund production of plaintiff's invention: "Broken promises, shattered dreams."

- The defendant in a product liability case in which plaintiff claims that she was injured when the airbags in her car (made by defendant) inflated with excessive force: "Saving lives first, everything else second."

Once a prospective theme is found, it must be screened for its appropriateness to the facts of the case. Naturally, the theme must fit the facts, not the other way around. The theme should be consistent with the advocate's factual and legal theories and, of course, must not conflict with undisputed facts or even disputed facts that the jury is likely to believe. Such a theme will be rejected by the jury as nonsensical, thus undermining the advocate's arguments, impairing his credibility, and creating an easy point of attack for opposing counsel.

The theme must not only be factually appropriate but also must be screened for its appeal to the jury. The theme must connect with the jury's life experiences and its values. For instance, the usefulness of a biblical theme may depend on the location of the trial and the composition of the jury. In certain areas, a biblical theme might isolate or offend a member of a different religious background or an atheist. Similarly, an obscure or abstract literary reference may be lost on less-sophisticated jurors.

As demonstrated above, good themes are typically short, one to two sentences at most, and should be easily remembered. They should contain "impact" or "buzz" words that refer to the key issues the advocate seeks to emphasize. The theme should be intriguing and powerful, a message that the jury will not grow weary of hearing over and over again. And the theme should be repeated often, beginning in *voir dire* and continuing throughout the trial. Repetition of the theme is essential for it to take hold.

III. MAINTAINING CONTROL OVER THE CASE AT TRIAL

There is one additional aspect to case preparation, beyond doing the work of gathering the facts and the evidence, and beyond thinking about the case and developing themes and theories. The final step is preparing to manage the nuts and bolts of the trial, the logistical part of trying a case. And even though the exercise of effective case management may not be as stimulating as developing case themes or as familiar as assessing legal requirements, it will play a significant role in ensuring that jurors form favorable impressions of trial counsel.

Advocates who appear to be in control of the courtroom environment, who have mastery of the facts and ready access to the information they need in the courtroom, are perceived by jurors as being more credible. Such advocates inspire confidence; they put the jurors at ease. And yet, trial

Tech Tip

If you feel that computer-based organizational systems are more your style than traditional paper files, try *CaseMap* by LexisNexis. *CaseMap* is a case analysis tool that allows you to gather, import and label all the facts, pleadings, documents, emails, and discovery relevant to your case by putting all the information into categorized and indexed spreadsheets. It also has a jump-start wizard to help new users get started, and a search engine that suggests pertinent sources based on keywords. *CaseMap* also includes a one-step citation checker, which makes sure all case law searched is still relevant law each time you pull up your case file.

lawyers face a difficult task. Even the simplest of trials is a complicated endeavor involving the organization of documents, the planning and presentation of arguments, the scheduling and examination of witnesses, and the possibility of unforeseeable events. In large, complex cases, there may be hundreds of witnesses and millions of pages of documents, creating tremendous organizational challenges. In simple, single party cases, the organizational challenges are fewer to be sure. Counsel, however, still must have ready access to each exhibit in the case, organization of the materials needed for the examinations, arguments, past statements or testimony by the witnesses, and so on.

Good case management requires effective organization. Regardless of the method preferred, whether computer based organizational systems or more traditional paper files, the materials needed must be well organized and easily accessible. The aim of this section is to help the advocate recognize what needs to be done from the beginning in order to effectively manage the case at trial.

The starting point for effective organization at trial is for the advocate to have someone assist him during the trial. Trials are difficult solo acts. Another set of ears and eyes, a person to take notes, someone to provide a different perspective and to serve as a sounding board can make an important difference. This person may be a legal assistant or junior lawyer. He should be familiar with the case and the case materials and able to assist the advocate in maintaining organization and control during the trial. Sometimes lawyers must try cases alone, because of economics perhaps or because no one is available to help, and those advocates may find it useful to use the client as an assistant, a note taker, and observer.

The second step toward effective organization is a trial notebook. The trial notebook should contain all the important information to which the lawyer will need quick access at the trial, with tabs or dividers to make it easy to find and retrieve the information. It should be put together as the trial date draws near. Depending on the size and complexity of a case, the precise contents of the trial notebook may vary, but generally it should include:

- An address reference page (with contact information for the client, witnesses, opposing counsel, and others the advocate may need to connect during the trial)

- A "things to do" list (to ensure that nothing is missed in the final frantic days before trial)

- Separate tabs for the advocate's case themes, legal theories, and factual theories (for the purpose of making a quick note when a word or phrase comes to the advocate's mind)

- The index of pleadings filed in the case

- A copy of the current complaint in a civil case or, in a criminal case, the indictment, information, or complaint

- A copy of the current answer filed by defendant(s)

- Copies of any motions *in limine* filed by the parties

- A list of potential witnesses and the order in which they will be called, with any special notes regarding availability

- A chart listing each exhibit the party expects to offer into evidence, with columns to indicate when the exhibit is offered into evidence and whether it is admitted by the court

- Notes for *voir dire*, including lines of questions and lists of favorable and unfavorable characteristics, attitudes, or experiences for jurors

- A chart for jury selection (to facilitate keeping track of the jurors and their responses to questions)

- Jury instructions requested by plaintiff or prosecutor

- Jury instructions requested by defendant[s]

- The jury charge that is ultimately approved by the court

- Notes for opening statement

- Notes for closing argument

- Separate tabs for each witness the advocate will take on direct or cross-examination

In large cases one notebook may not handle all the information needed and the advocate may need multiple trial notebooks. In addition to the trial notebook, advocates may prepare a separate file folder for each witness examination. The folder should include everything the advocate will need to examine or cross-examine the witness at trial, including, (1) copies of all documentary exhibits that will be used during the witness' testimony, (2) any writings made by the witness, (3) any witness statements or testimony in the case and/or summaries of that testimony, (4) notes to assist the attorney in the examination, and (5) the executed proof of service of the subpoena if one was served on the witness.

Regardless of the size or complexity of the case, the advocate must be able to find any document she might need during the trial, whether it is a prior inconsistent statement of a witness or an internal memorandum of a corporate defendant. If the attorney appears disorganized in trying to find the document, fumbling for it or asking for the court's indulgence as she scrambles to find it, she will pay a price while standing before the jury (and the judge). Careful and logical organization will prevent most such lapses, eliminating any distractions that might interfere with the party's presentation of its case.

Chapter Three
MOTIONS

I. OVERVIEW AND PURPOSE OF MOTIONS

Rulings on pretrial motions can shape entire trials by determining what comes into evidence and what does not. Motions deal with the provocative and contentious—Will the damning internal memo be admitted? Was the defendant in custody for *Miranda* purposes?—as well as the mundane—Which witnesses will be excluded from the courtroom? Advocates who prevail on these critical issues will have a strategic advantage throughout the trial. The focus in this chapter will be on motions that directly impact the trial because they:

- seek a ruling on the admissibility of a particular piece of evidence,

- seek to exclude witnesses from the trial,

- seek a ruling directing entry of a verdict during the trial, or

- seek a mistrial, a new trial, or to set aside the verdict reached by the jury.

A motion is simply a request to the court for a ruling. Motions may be made in writing or orally and may or may not include the filing of briefs. The making of any motion, however, requires consideration of the strategic advantages to be gained from the motion, the procedural requirements for the motion, and the oral and written presentation of the motion.

II. EVIDENTIARY MOTIONS

Evidentiary motions, when made pretrial, are usually referred to as motions *in limine*. Every seasoned trial lawyer has encountered situations in which a ruling on the admissibility of evidence can affect not just the outcome of a trial, but also the strategy that a lawyer may wish or need to pursue during trial. For instance, assume that the prosecutor's primary witness in an armed robbery case has made an unwavering identification of the defendant as the robber. However, a year before trial, that same witness spent two months in a mental hospital following a nervous breakdown. The prosecutor, concerned that defense counsel will attempt to elicit this information during cross-examination of the witness, believes that evidence should be excluded as irrelevant or, at a minimum, excluded because any minimal relevance is substantially outweighed by the danger of unfair prejudice. Moreover, the witness has told the prosecutor that he does not want to testify if it means that he will be forced to discuss his mental illness. Although the prosecutor knows that the witness can be compelled to testify by subpoena and court order, the prospect of having her case rest upon a witness who is uncooperative, embarrassed, or flustered is, to say the least, unappealing.

The prosecutor has a clear-cut choice. She could raise her objection to the impeaching evidence at the time the witness actually testifies and do her best to calm and reassure the witness. Or, she could make a motion *in limine* seeking a pretrial ruling on the admissibility of the evidence. If the judge rules in her favor and excludes the impeaching evidence, both the lawyer and the witness can approach the witness' testimony with confidence. Even if the judge denies the motion, the attorney is in a better position, because she has some time to repair or avoid the potential damage to her case. The prosecutor can now better advise her witness on how to handle cross-examination questions concerning her hospitalization and, perhaps more importantly, can raise the concern on direct examination and thus mitigate the harmful impact.

A.   Motions *in Limine*

The decision of whether to assert a motion *in limine* requires careful consideration of a number of factors. It is not necessarily a foregone conclusion that all issues that could be raised should be raised. Advocates must weigh the advantages and disadvantages of making the motion. Should the advocate decide to make the motion, he must comply with any court requirements or rules that govern the filing of pretrial motions. Next, the lawyer must prepare to argue the motion before the judge. And finally, the lawyer must anticipate the effect of an adverse ruling.

1.   *Considerations in Deciding Whether to Make Motions* in Limine

The majority of motions *in limine* seek the exclusion of evidence from trial. However, motions *in limine* are not limited to exclusion. The term "motion *in limine*" refers only to the timing of the motion, not the content. Any evidentiary ruling—either admission or exclusion—might be sought through a motion *in limine*.

The first step in deciding whether to move *in limine* to exclude evidence is to identify harmful evidence for which there is a basis for exclusion.

In criminal cases this might include evidence obtained in violation of a defendant's constitutional rights, such as evidence seized in an unlawful search in violation of the Fourth Amendment, but most evidentiary motions will be based upon the rules of evidence. Accordingly, grounds for exclusion must be based upon those rules. Likewise, in seeking admission of evidence there must be a rule of evidence that authorizes admission of the evidence. The advocate's ability to identify harmful evidence for which there is a basis for exclusion or helpful evidence that should be admitted depends upon two things: (1) thorough case preparation, which will enable the advocate to anticipate the opponent's evidence, and (2) thorough understanding of the applicable rules of evidence.

a.   Reasons Not to File Motions *in Limine*

Even after the advocate has identified a piece of evidence that could be the subject of a motion *in limine,* it does not necessarily mean that the motion should be made pretrial. The lawyer may prefer to raise the matter during trial at the time the evidence is actually offered. Any evidence vulnerable to exclusion can be excluded following a timely objection at trial. It requires less time and effort for the advocate to merely rise and state, "Objection, impermissible character evidence," than it does to plan, draft, file, and argue a motion *in limine*. Also, the basis for the objection may be more readily apparent to the judge who by that time knows the case and better understands the context of the motion. Indeed, judges may actually prefer not to rule on the motion *in limine*, because they do not know enough about the facts and theories of the case and they do not want to be wrong. Of course, during trial, when the evidence is offered and the objection is made, the judge must rule; there is nowhere to hide. In addition, a party might choose not to bring a motion *in limine* because of the chance that the objectionable evidence will not be offered at trial—perhaps because opposing counsel does not appreciate its potential effect or is unaware of its existence.

There is an additional reason advocates may choose not to file motions seeking *admission of evidence* and it follows the old saying that one should "let sleeping dogs lie." That is, the counsel, by filing the motion, virtually guarantees that the opponent will oppose the motion, whereas if no motion was filed and the evidence was simply introduced during the course of the trial, no objection may be forthcoming. Some evidence is so obviously prejudicial or harmful to the opponent—such as prior convictions of a witness—that the opponent will object at trial even if the proponent does not seek an *in limine* ruling on its admission. With other evidence, however, counsel will be wise to avoid stirring up an objection when one might not be made.

b.   Reasons to File Motions *in Limine*

Despite the reasons to forego making a motion *in limine*, there are typically stronger reasons to do so. First and foremost, prevailing on the motion may protect against any mention of the excluded matter. Opposing counsel cannot *voir dire* on the excluded matter, nor refer to it during opening statement, or during witness examinations. Additionally, when the matter is left for objection at trial, the advocate risks missing the objection or making the objection late, such that an answer or partial answer may be blurted out. In that event, even if the objection is sustained and the answer stricken, the "bell has been rung" and the jury will be unlikely to disregard the answer.

A second reason for obtaining a ruling on the admissibility of potentially harmful evidence is that if the motion is unsuccessful, the advocate has time to develop a strategy to minimize the harm from losing the objection. In the hypothetical given at the outset of this chapter, if the prosecutor failed to convince the court to exclude evidence of the eyewitness' mental illness, she could minimize the impact of the evidence by working with the eyewitness to present the information to the jury on direct examination, rather than waiting for the defense attorney to "spring" it during cross-examination. Preemptive disclosure of harmful information minimizes both the negative impact on the case and embarrassment to the witness, who now can control both the timing of the disclosure of her illness and the way in which the information is presented. Compare the effect of the following:

Illustration of Cross-Examination with No Disclosure

On cross-examination:

Lawyer: Isn't it true that you were confined to a mental hospital about a year ago?

Witness: Well, yes, but....

Lawyer: And wasn't that because you suffered a complete mental breakdown?

Witness: Yes, but...

Lawyer: So you don't do well in stressful situations, do you?

Illustration of Direct Examination with Disclosure

On direct examination:

Lawyer: Now, have you been hospitalized at all during the past few years?

Witness: Yes. I was hospitalized a year ago.

Lawyer: What led you to hospitalization?

Witness:	After my father was killed in an automobile accident and my wife left me, things sort of spiraled out of control. At the urging of my sister, I sought medical assistance and agreed that I needed to be hospitalized for treatment of what was diagnosed as essentially a nervous breakdown.
Lawyer:	When were you released from the hospital?
Witness:	Ten months ago.
Lawyer:	Are you still under a doctor's care for your illness?
Witness:	Well, I periodically see my doctor to, you know, just follow up. But I am not taking any kind of medication or doing anything differently.
Lawyer:	Are you now affected by any of the symptoms that led to your hospitalization?
Witness:	No.
Lawyer:	Were you affected by any of the symptoms of your illness on the date of the robbery.
Witness:	No. I have been fine since my release from the hospital.

Information elicited for the first time during cross-examination might cause jurors to doubt the veracity or reliability of the witness who, after all, has suffered from a mental illness, which he did not disclose during his direct examination. Whereas, if the information is elicited in a sympathetic way on direct, it may not only engender the jurors' sympathy and admiration for what the witness has overcome, but it may also give the jurors another reason to credit the testimony of the witness—the witness' willingness to testify truthfully, even about potentially embarrassing information.

Not all judges are comfortable ruling on the admissibility of evidence without the benefit of the factual context the judge would have if she reserved her ruling until trial. In other words, the ruling on a motion *in limine* may be deferred by the judge until it arises during trial. Even in this event, there are distinct advantages to be gained from having made the motion. At a minimum, the advocates will have been able to "preview" their opponents' arguments about why the disputed evidence should be excluded or admitted. They may also gain insight about how the judge is inclined to rule on the issue or whether there are particular concerns that have caused the judge to hesitate to rule in their favor. Advocates can use this information to bolster their renewed arguments for or against admissibility with an eye toward addressing any concerns voiced by the judge. And perhaps most importantly, the judge, at the urging of counsel bringing the motion, may preclude mention of the challenged evidence during jury selection and opening statement even if he does not definitively rule in the party's favor. Therefore, even if the motion should ultimately fail, the opponent's opportunity to exploit the evidence may be limited.

While the strategic benefits of obtaining a pretrial ruling comprise the strongest arguments for seeking a ruling *in limine*, there are other considerations that should influence a lawyer's decision as well. One such consideration is that motions *in limine* provide an opportunity to obtain a more carefully considered and, hopefully more favorable and accurate ruling. Trial objections must be ruled upon "on the spot." Except for a hurried, whispered argument at sidebar—which itself is rarely permitted—trial attorneys have relatively little opportunity to influence or inform the judge's ruling on objections. Judges are very mindful that the jury's time and attention are limited and are reluctant to interrupt the trial for an extended hearing on an evidentiary objection. Thus, the objection itself is generally limited to merely stating the legal ground for the objection. For example, "Objection, impermissible character evidence." The response, if any, is similarly limited, such as, "Proper impeachment under Rule 609." Even a more extended response may not be more than two or three sentences. The judge then issues a ruling, based upon nothing more than what she has heard or seen during the trial and her understanding of the rules of evidence. These "on the spot" rulings may be much less reliable—and are almost certainly less considered—than a ruling made in the more leisurely setting of pretrial motions, replete with points and authorities and oral argument. In other words, if advocates anticipate that their opponents will offer harmful but most likely excludable evidence, moving *in limine* provides the opportunity to thoroughly present the grounds for exclusion to the judge and the opportunity for the judge to carefully consider those grounds.

A final consideration is that motions *in limine* provide the advocate an opportunity to educate the judge about the facts of the case and the advocate's case theories. The impact of this judicial education can extend far beyond the motion *in limine* itself. The judge will make each trial ruling influenced by what she has learned in the pretrial motions. In particular, in the event that the judge reserves her ruling on the motion *in limine*, when the advocate renews the motion at trial the judge will have the benefit of having learned more about the case, and about the advocate's reasons for objecting to the evidence. Thus, she will be better able to make a considered ruling during the trial.

There are at least two other benefits that may flow from making pretrial motions, even though by themselves these additional considerations would not ordinarily cause an advocate to make the motion. First, the oral argument provides an opportunity to test the opponent's mettle and to learn more about the opponent's case theory while the advocate still has an opportunity to adjust her trial strategy. Second, the pretrial hearing provides an opportunity for the advocate to gain information about the trial judge's style, temperament, and any inclinations or biases that might affect the case. This information can be particularly useful if the advocate has not previously appeared before the judge.

2. *Bringing Motions* in Limine

Court rules governing motions *in limine* are far from uniform. They vary both in terms of when and how the motions are considered and in terms of what form they should take. Thus, it is essential for advocates to consult their local rules of court and any pretrial orders issued by the presiding judge to determine the specific procedural steps that must be undertaken to bring a motion *in limine*. Some courts require full briefing. Others require written notice. Some may not require written notice or briefing. Almost all judges maintain pretrial schedules that require motions *in limine* to be made a specified number of court days before the date set for trial. Others may permit oral motions to be made on the date set for trial immediately before the jury is empanelled.

If the court permits written briefing, there is seldom any good reason to forego briefing the motion, even if a written brief is not required. Briefing permits judges to familiarize themselves with the issues before the argument, and further, gives the judges something they can refer to during the argument and rely on in making a ruling. Additionally, in the event that the judge reserves ruling, the written briefs become part of the case record and can be referred to by the judge at trial when the objection is renewed. Finally, if the court's ruling is contested as erroneous on appeal, the briefs in the record will be useful in preparing the appeal.

3.   *Typical Motions* in Limine

There is a vast array of evidence that might prompt a party to make a motion *in limine*, extending to the very limits of the rules of evidence. An examination of each potential motion exceeds the scope of this book. However, advocates do tend to make certain boilerplate motions in every case and make other case-specific motions with sufficient frequency to merit brief discussion.

a.   Boilerplate Motions *in Limine*

Many advocates make certain motions *in limine* as a matter of course in most every case and make others that depend on the specific facts and issues at hand. Below we set forth examples of several "boilerplate" motions to exclude evidence and limit attorney comments.

 ## Illustrations of Boilerplate Motions *in Limine*

(i)   *Representations about testimony from witnesses who are absent, unavailable, or will not be called to testify either live or by deposition.* Although this motion simply restates the obvious, that counsel must not tell the jury during voir dire or the opening statement about testimony counsel does not have a good faith belief will be offered during the trial, it is often asserted to remind opposing counsel of its obligations and to create a record in the event that counsel does attempt to discuss testimony from a witness who does not take the stand.

(ii)   *Reference to a party's failure to call a witness equally available to both sides.* In civil cases, there is no limit on a party's ability to argue that the jury should draw adverse inferences from an opponent's failure to call a witness under their control, an employee or expert, for instance. In criminal cases, there is no limit on drawing such inferences against the prosecution. Fifth Amendment concerns, of course, place some limits on the prosecutor from commenting on why certain witnesses were not called by the defense. Sometimes, advocates will go one step further and argue that the jury should infer from the opponent's failure to call a bystander or other individual equally available to all parties that the witness' testimony would have been adverse to the opponent's position. This motion in limine makes the point that no inference can properly be drawn from one's failure to call an unattached witness, especially since the party seeking to get the benefit of the inference also had the ability to subpoena and examine the witness.

(iii) *The personal beliefs of counsel about the justice of his client's case, the credibility of witnesses, or the amount of damages.* Again, this is a well-accepted principle of trial advocacy, yet it is frequently violated by overzealous advocates. This common motion seeks to remind opponents (and the judges) of the rule.

(iv) *Questions to the venire about damages, including attempts to commit the prospective jurors to specific dollar amounts.* In civil cases defendants must be concerned about attempts by plaintiff's lawyers to question prospective jurors about damages. The injection of specific dollar amounts in a case involving largely non-economic damages can contaminate the jury pool and seriously prejudice the defendant. This motion seeks to preclude plaintiff's counsel from requesting jurors to commit to specific dollar amounts as damages before any evidence is presented.

(v) *Any mention of damages.* In a civil case where the question of damages has been bifurcated from the issue of liability, plaintiff's counsel should be precluded from even broaching the extent or the amount of damages during *voir dire* or opening statement, from eliciting damages testimony during witness examinations, or from arguing damages at closing argument.

b. Case-Specific Motions *in Limine* in Civil Cases

The examples above are simply illustrative, not exhaustive, of the types of matters that trial lawyers may include in their motions *in limine* in many cases. There are also specific evidentiary issues that arise in civil and criminal cases, which necessitate motions *in limine*. Examples of case-specific motions in civil cases might include the following:

Illustrations of Case-Specific Motions *in Limine* in Civil Cases

(i) *Evidence of any settlement or compromise of claims entered into by any party*. In a case in which the plaintiff has settled with some but not all defendants or in which a defendant has settled, but because of the terms of the agreement remains a party in the case, counsel for the settling party may want to move for a ruling prohibiting any reference to the fact of settlement or the discussions that led to it. Under the Federal Rules, settlements are not admissible to prove liability or the lack of liabilty (Fed. R. Evid. 408), and parties should use motions *in limine* to prevent opposing counsel from disclosing the existence of a settlement or the existence of settlement negotiations during *voir dire*, opening statement, or the examination of witness.

(ii) *Evidence of the wealth or resources of the defendant corporation, until and unless the jury finds that a basis exists for the award of punitive damages*. In any case in which damages are being sought from the defendant, defense counsel must be concerned about plaintiff's attempts to get evidence about the defendant's wealth or resources before the jury. Those references may come in a variety of forms from a casual mention during *voir dire* about the size of the corporation to testimony about the revenue of the defendant in recent years. The evidence is entirely irrelevant except on the issue of the appropriate amount of punitive damages, and a motion *in limine* can help preclude such evidence from making its way before the jury during the liability or compensatory damage phases of the trial.

(iii) *References to the existence or maintenance of liability insurance by the defendant*. Defendants in personal injury cases do not want jurors to consider the possibility that the damages, if any, may not be coming out of the defendant's pocket, but instead from an insurance company's pockets. Rule 411 of the Federal Rules of Evidence specifically excludes such references at trial. Nonetheless, plaintiffs will try to find a way to get such references before the jury, such as by asking the prospective jurors during *voir dire* if they have anything to do with the insurance industry or with claims adjusting. Defendants typically attempt to prevent such questioning, instead insisting that plaintiff's counsel ask each prospective juror specific questions about their employment without asking general questions about any experience in the insurance industry.

(iv) *Expert testimony by someone who is unqualified to testify, an expert testifying to unreliable theories or techniques, or an expert testifying to opinions that have an inadequate basis*. Pre-trial challenges to experts in civil cases are relatively common because of the significant role played by experts in modern litigation. A favorable ruling on a motion to exclude the opponent's primary expert on liability may well mean summary disposition of the case because of the party's inability to prove its *prima facie* case. As discussed in the next section and in Chapter 10, recently heightened reliability requirements for experts have contributed to an increase in challenges to expert witnesses.

c. Case-Specific Motions *in Limine* in Criminal Cases

In criminal cases, depending on the facts, one might file motions *in limine* to address the following matters:

Illustrations of Case-Specific Motions *in Limine* in Criminal Cases

(i) *Reference to improperly obtained evidence of the defendant's past statements to the police.* Few pieces of evidence are more difficult for defendants to overcome than their own prior incriminating statements to the police. It is not the kind of matter that defense counsel should wait and object to when the evidence is offered during trial. Mention of the prior statements during *voir dire* and/or the opening statement will be difficult, if not impossible, to erase from jurors' minds even if the judge later excludes the evidence. The most common grounds for exclusion are that the statements were obtained in violation of *Miranda* or were part of plea bargaining, and thus are protected under the rules of evidence (Fed. R. Evid. 410).

(ii) *Crimes, wrongs, or acts of the defendant offered by the prosecution to prove the defendant's motive, intent, knowledge, preparation, plan, identity, modus operandi, or other non-propensity purpose or conduct of a third party offered by the defendant to prove the third party's motive, identity, or modus operandi.* Prosecutors love to offer evidence of the defendant's past conduct pursuant to Rule 404(b) of the Federal Rules of Evidence because of its powerful effect on jurors, and defendants routinely move *in limine* to seek exclusion of such evidence as not relevant or as unfairly prejudicial. Less frequently, defendants offer what is called "reverse 404(b)" evidence as proof that someone other than the defendant had the motive to commit the crime or had a similar *modus operandi*. The admission or exclusion of the evidence typically turns on the court's balancing of the probative value of the evidence with its potential for causing unfair prejudice to the adversely affected party or the risk of confusion of the issues for the jury. (Fed. R. Evid. 403.) The balancing standard is weighted toward admission.

(iii) *Prior convictions of the defendant or other witness offered for impeachment purposes*. For defendants, the court's decision whether to admit or exclude a prior conviction may dictate whether they will testify in their own defense. The adverse impact to the defendant from the admission of a prior conviction can hardly be overstated. Jurors tend to view the defendant in a distinctly negative light once they learn that he is a convicted felon. Thus, defense counsel typically make every effort to get a pretrial ruling on the admission of such evidence as part of the basic planning of the defense case. Under the federal rules, the burden is on the prosecution to show that the probative value of the conviction on the issue of the defendant's credibility outweighs the danger of unfair prejudice. (Fed. R. Evid. 609(a)(1).)

(iv) *Expert testimony by someone who is unqualified to testify, an expert testifying to unreliable theories or techniques, or an expert testifying to opinions that have an inadequate basis*. Expert testimony is also a frequent subject of motions *in limine* by parties on both sides of the docket in criminal cases. The requirement that expert opinions must be based on reliable theories and techniques has opened the door to challenges of the forensic and social sciences in particular. Thus, by way of example, the prosecution may want to challenge the admission of defendant's expert evidence on battered women's syndrome or the results from a polygraph examination and the defendant may want to challenge the prosecution's testimony from a forensic document examiner or a voiceprint expert. Recent Supreme Court decisions and amendments to Rule 702 of the Federal Rules of Evidence have heightened the requirements for expert witness testimony and it is not uncommon for advocates to challenge the reliability of an expert's underlying theory or technique. The discussion of the standards for the admission of expert witness testimony is discussed in greater detail in Chapter Ten.

These areas are ripe for motions *in limine* because in each instance the evidence would permanently impair the ability of the jurors to decide the case, at least from the perspective of the moving party. And the evidence in each example is substantial and potentially disastrous if admitted.

4. *Arguing Motions* **in Limine**

When arguing a motion *in limine*, the advocate's audience is the presiding judge, not the jury: a circumstance that dictates the manner and content of the advocate's presentation. First of all, the advocate arguing the motion can assume that the judge is familiar with the governing legal principles, at least in a general sense, though she may need assistance in understanding how those principles justify a ruling in the advocate's favor. Second, it may be less important for the advocate to worry about holding the attention of the judge than when he is arguing to the jury. The judge will be keen to understand the arguments so that she can rule correctly and avoid reversal. Third, the judge should be able to quickly grasp the impact and meaning of the argument because of the judge's experience— perhaps as a trial lawyer and certainly as a trial judge. Thus, it is often the case that the advocate's preparation for argument can focus on how to tie governing legal rules to the particular facts of the case.

At the same time, however, advocates who successfully and effectively argue motions before judges must be persuasive and that effort begins with the principles of persuasion discussed in Chapter One. That does not mean that each advocate's *style* will be the same, or even remotely similar; but, it does mean that trial lawyers who want to be successful oral advocates, regardless of their particular idiosyncrasies, must work to gain the judge's trust and respect and must make arguments that are well-grounded in the law and persuasive on the facts. When engaging in oral advocacy before the court, advocates must:

- Express their arguments clearly and concisely

- Structure their arguments persuasively

- Connect their arguments to the central issues in the case

- Preemptively rebut the opponent's arguments

- Distinguish adverse authority

- Listen and watch for cues from the judge

a. Clear and Concise Arguments

Advocates enhance their standing before the court by making clear and concise arguments. Judges have busy calendars and they appreciate lawyers who do not waste the court's time. That especially applies to motions *in limine*, which are often argued immediately before the beginning of jury selection. The court may well feel the need to get the prospective jurors into the courtroom as soon as possible to begin the *voir dire* process. At the outset of the argument, counsel should briefly describe the evidence that is the subject of the motion and the legal grounds for exclusion (or admission). Counsel should then discuss the reasons that require admission or exclusion of the evidence.

 Illustration of Introduction of Motion *in Limine*

Lawyer:	Your Honor, we have three motions *in limine* on behalf of Mr. Wilkinson. The first motion seeks to exclude any mention or discussion during the trial of a conviction suffered by Mr. Wilkinson more than six years ago for larceny, because the conviction is inadmissible under Rule 609 of the Federal Rules of Evidence. The second motion...

b. Persuasive Organization

Any good argument begins with good organization. And good organization requires careful planning and forethought. Too many advocates fail to think through the oral argument of their motions *in limine*, believing that they will be able to successfully argue the motion extemporaneously. Many such efforts are pedestrian at best, consisting of nothing more than restatements of the rule, platitudes, and generalities.

Effective organization begins with identification of all of the party's potential arguments for admission or exclusion of the evidence, followed by consideration of which arguments are likely to be most persuasive to the court. The advocate's best argument should be placed first, while weak arguments should be eliminated altogether. Inconsistent arguments should be avoided as well. Advocates should anticipate the arguments of opposing counsel and structure their argument to demonstrate the fallacy or weakness in the opponent's argument.

Consider one example of a potentially weak argument for exclusion of evidence regularly offered by trial advocates—that the probative value of the offered evidence is substantially outweighed by the danger of unfair prejudice. Every jurisdiction has a provision for the exclusion of such evidence (in the Federal Rules it is Rule 403), and judges hear such arguments all the time. And they usually reject the argument because the standard under Rule 403 is tilted toward admission and because they tend to view such arguments as desperate, last-ditch pleas. When planning the structure and organization of their presentations, counsel should accordingly recognize that arguments based in whole or part on Rule 403 or its equivalent, may be quickly dismissed by the court. The consequence of Rule 403's overuse is that (1) advocates, if possible, must avoid joining Rule 403 arguments with arguments under other more favorable substantive rules of evidence, such as hearsay or character evidence, because the effect is to weaken the entire argument, and (2) when attempting to exclude evidence under Rule 403, advocates should be specific about the exact nature of the potential prejudice and the precise unfair prejudice to the party.

One device that will substantially improve the structure and clarity of the advocate's argument is the use of a list. Enumerating the five reasons that support the exclusion of a piece of evidence advances one's case much more than a rambling argument that may encompass five points but does so in a disjointed fashion that is impossible for the court to follow.

c. Connect Arguments to Central Issues

The argument itself should be specific both as to the law that applies to the evidentiary issue and the pertinent facts in the case, but at the same time, it should be thematic so that the court's attention is focused on the significance of the disputed evidence in the case. Almost all evidentiary decisions are contextual; admission or exclusion depends on the particular evidence being offered and the purpose for which it is being offered. Moreover, most judges are not well-informed about the specific facts and allegations in the cases before them. That is particularly true in jurisdictions that use master calendars, in which cases are not assigned to particular judges, but rather each newly filed motion in the case is assigned to a judge for consideration of only that matter. Yet, even in direct calendar courts, wherein each case is assigned to a single judge who presides over all proceedings in the case, judges rarely have the time to become steeped in the facts or allegations of one case. Thus, counsel must provide the court with the necessary factual context so that the judge can appreciate the potential implications of her ruling for admission or exclusion of the evidence and can make an informed ruling on the motion.

It is one thing to tell the judge that the murder victim's line of work as a scam artist is relevant under Rule 401 of the Federal Rules of Evidence and should be admitted because it shows that others had a motive to kill her. It is quite another to argue that the central issue—the only issue—in the case is identity. In the illustration below, the defense responds to the prosecution's motion to exclude evidence of the victim's direct mail order business and the existence or identity of alleged victims of her scams without specific evidence from the defense that the alleged victims could have committed the murder.

 Illustration of Argument in Opposition to Motion *in Limine*

Defense Lawyer: The central issue in this case, Your Honor, is who killed Mary Bonaparte. Who committed the murder? And the prosecution's evidence is entirely circumstantial, no one will testify that they saw Mr. Shrake [the defendant] commit the crime. There will be no eyewitnesses to the murder. The details of Ms. Bonaparte's unsavory work are essential for the jury to appreciate the number of people she had ripped off, the number of people who hated her with a passion, the number of people who wished her ill. The evidence of the victim's dark life of fraud goes to the heart of the defense case, right to the core of the defense claim that someone other than Mr. Shrake committed the murder. Under Rule 404(b) [of the Federal Rules of Evidence] the evidence is admissible to show the motive of many others to do Ms. Bonaparte harm. In fact, it would be unfair to Mr. Shrake to exclude the evidence. It would create a false impression with jurors that the only person who had any hostility toward Ms. Bonaparte was Mr. Shrake, and that's simply not true. The jurors need to know, they must know, of the Ms. Bonaparte who was a scam artist, a con woman, a hustler. If they don't know about that Mary Bonaparte, they simply will not be able to fairly and accurately determine who killed her.

d.   Rebuttal of Opponent's Arguments; Distinguishing Adverse Authority

The argument should not merely advance the advocate's own contentions, but should also anticipate and refute the opponent's arguments. Particularly, those advocates who speak first are in a powerful position to characterize their opponents' arguments, explain their inapplicability, and/or discount their validity. At the same time, if there is authority adverse to the advocate's position, counsel must disclose it to the court, whether or not the opponent does so. Disclosure is required by the Model Rules of Professional Conduct, of course, but it is also required by basic principles of effective advocacy and common sense. Counsel has at least three options in the face of adverse authority. She can argue that (1) the cited case or authority does not apply to the facts in the case; (2) the case is distinguishable from the current case; or (3) the holding of the case should be overturned and a different rule adopted.

e.   Watching and Listening for Cues from the Judge

Unlike the jurors, judges are active decision-makers. They can and will interrupt the advocates to ask questions, to interject their perceptions of the issue, or to indicate which way they are inclined to rule. Advocates must pay attention to those musings because they can help focus the advocate's argument and direct the advocate's energies. Yet, these verbal cues are often missed by advocates because they are too busy delivering their argument, making sure they deliver it all, right down to the last word. Sometimes the advocate's entire argument is not necessary for him to prevail and other times the specific argument being advanced by the lawyer is simply not persuasive to the judge. Listen, watch, and react accordingly.

5.   *Effect of an Adverse Ruling on a Motion in Limine*

An adverse ruling on a motion *in limine* can create difficult choices for trial advocates. For example, in the hypothetical at the outset of the chapter, if the judge rules the eyewitness' history of mental illness is admissible, the advocate must decide whether to

- attempt to soften the impact of the evidence by raising it during the direct examination of her witness; or

- conceal the history of mental illness and then object to the opponent's attempt to introduce it during the cross-examination.

The first option—pricking the boil—is sound trial strategy, but, at least in federal court, likely constitutes waiver of any error from the trial court's ruling, meaning that the advocate will be unable to contest the correctness of the ruling on appeal.[1] Parties cannot complain on appeal

---

[1]   *See Ohler v. United States*, 529 U.S. 753, 754–55 (2000).

about the admission of evidence they introduce. If, on the other hand, the advocate chooses to preserve the court's pretrial ruling for later review by an appellate court, she must avoid referring to it during direct examination. Traditionally, the court's pretrial ruling has not preserved the claim of error for purposes of appeal. Instead, parties were required to renew their objections at the time that the evidence was introduced during the trial. However, Rule 103 of the Federal Rules of Evidence provides that "definitive" pretrial rulings do in fact preserve the claim of error and that advocates need not renew their objections (which are certain to be overruled) during trial. However, if the court's pretrial ruling is tentative or conditional, the objection must be renewed to preserve error. State court practices vary on the effect of pretrial rulings, and the advocate must ascertain whether a renewed objection at trial is required in order to preserve the appealability of the unfavorable pretrial ruling.

If a renewal of the objection is required, the advocate is forced to choose between a strategy that preserves the issue on appeal—*i.e.*, not trying to soften the blow, but rather objecting when the evidence is offered with the knowledge that the objection is certainly doomed to be overruled—or a strategy that waives the error on appeal but lessens the impact of the harmful evidence by presenting it on direct examination. In other words, the dilemma confronted by the advocate is between pricking the boil, at the expense of forgoing on appeal on the issue, and allowing the evidence to be presented by the advocate's opponent, which will almost always be more harmful to the advocate's case. Criminal defendants face an even starker choice, because they must take the stand *and* suffer impeachment on cross-examination (without any attempt to defuse the attack) to preserve the claim of error for appeal.

If a motion *in limine* made by the opposing party is successful, meaning that evidence the advocate wanted to offer at trial has been ruled inadmissible, then to preserve the appealability of that ruling it may be necessary for the advocate to attempt to offer the evidence at trial. In federal court, Rule 103 provides that such efforts would be unnecessary if the court's pretrial ruling was definitive. Preferably, counsel should try to avoid having to offer evidence that the judge will exclude in front of the jury. If possible, counsel should seek a ruling from the trial judge that her pretrial ruling will be preserved without having to offer the evidence at trial or should make the necessary record outside the jury's presence.

B. Evidentiary Motions at Trial

Most evidentiary objections at trial are made orally as the evidence is about to be introduced. Making and responding to trial objections is covered in Chapter Nine. Occasionally, however, an advocate will become aware of the existence of potentially damaging evidence only after the trial has begun, but before her opponent offers it into evidence. The same concerns that would motivate the advocate to make a motion *in limine* may cause the advocate to attempt to seek an advance ruling on the admissibility of the evidence. Whether the court is willing to consider such a motion after the trial has begun is within the discretion of the judge, but the advocate is wise to raise the issue as soon as it becomes evident. The time to bring the issue to the court's attention is the first opportunity after the issue arises when the jury is not present in the courtroom. Because the jury has been impaneled, and has already begun considering the evidence being presented, the judge will not want to have an extended period of briefing the issue or lengthy arguments. To do so delays the trial and wastes juror time. Nevertheless, counsel should offer to file a brief statement of the grounds for exclusion prior to oral argument. The advocate should be prepared for an immediate hearing on the issue, which would preclude such a filing.

III. Motion for Exclusion of Witnesses

Both in criminal and in civil cases, the advocate can request that witnesses be excluded so they cannot hear the testimony of other witnesses. The purpose of this motion is to prevent collusion by witnesses who shape their testimony according to the prior testimony of other witnesses. Exclusion of witnesses is specifically permitted under the Federal Rules of Evidence and similar provisions in nearly every non-federal jurisdiction. (Fed. R. Evid. 615.) There are some limitations. For example, parties have a right to be present during the trial, including representatives of corporations or other business entities. Their participation in the trial assists their attorneys and serves to make the verdict more acceptable to them. Other exceptions to the general rule may include:

- expert witnesses who need to be present in order to hear witness testimony based upon which the expert will be asked to render an opinion;

- detectives or investigators in criminal cases who are essential for the prosecution to present its case; and

- victims of the crime who may be excepted from the order of exclusion in some jurisdictions.

For most other witnesses, there is no good reason to permit them to hear the testimony of other witnesses, and the advocate can move to exclude them from the courtroom. Once requested by a party, the court *must* exclude the witnesses who are subject to the motion. Counsel may desire to raise the matter before the opening statement to ensure that the opponent's witnesses do not get the benefit of hearing the opening presentations, though the request can be made at any time during the trial.

IV. Motions for Directed Verdict, Judgment as a Matter of Law, or For a New Trial

In addition to the evidentiary motions, there are other trial and post-trial motions that an advocate can make that can have a direct impact on the case. They fall into two categories: The first is a motion for a verdict or entry of judgment based upon an opponent's failure to offer sufficient evidence to support a verdict or judgment in his favor. The second is a motion for a mistrial (and a new trial) based upon the occurrence of an event that has irreparably prejudiced one party.

A. Motions for Directed Verdict or Judgment as a Matter of Law

The legal ground for a motion directing a particular verdict or entry of judgment is that the record reveals a failure of proof as a matter of law. In other words, such motions are proper when, construing the evidence presented by the opponent in the light most favorable to his case, the evidence fails to create a fact issue as to one or more elements of the claim or defense being advanced by the opponent. In some jurisdictions, including federal court, these motions are referred to as motions for judgment as a matter of law. The more traditional nomenclature, still employed by some jurisdictions, is motion for a directed verdict (if the jury has not yet deliberated) or motion for judgment notwithstanding the verdict (when the evidence does not support the verdict actually reached). Whatever the name, the motions share a common theme: The opposing party has had his opportunity to present evidence and the evidence presented, even if fully believed, does not justify a verdict for the opponent because the party's evidence fails to support some essential element of the claim or defense.

These motions are typically oral motions made during or immediately after trial. Motions that are made prior to jury deliberation are properly made at two stages of the trial. The defendant may move for a directed verdict/judgment as a matter of law at the conclusion of the plaintiff/prosecutor's presentation of evidence if the plaintiff's evidence, even if believed, fails to prove each essential element needed for the cause of action or crime. The defendant's motion must attack a claim on which the plaintiff or prosecutor bears the ultimate burden of persuasion. In other words, when the plaintiff/prosecutor has rested, the motion may be made. The defendant should take care to make the motion outside the presence of the jury. Either the defendant or the plaintiff may move for a directed verdict/judgment as a matter of law at the close of the presentation of all evidence in the case. Finally, after the jury verdict is announced, the party against whom the verdict is entered may move for entry of judgment as a matter of law if the evidence fails to support the verdict.

B. Motions for Mistrial or for a New Trial

A motion for a mistrial or for a new trial differs from the motions for a judgment as a matter of law or for directed verdict both with respect to the result sought and with respect to the supporting grounds for the motion.

1. *Motion for a New Trial*

A motion for a new trial is typically made after an unfavorable verdict has been reached. It is often made in conjunction with a motion for judgment notwithstanding the verdict. Whereas the latter motion is properly granted only when the record indicates that the party against whom a jury verdict was entered is entitled to judgment as a matter of law, the motion for a new trial may be based upon the inadequacy of the evidence or the existence of an error or errors during the trial that likely caused an improper verdict to be reached. Essentially, the errors upon which the motion is based must be the type of error that would require reversal, and an order for a new trial, if raised on appeal. Grounds for a new trial might include, for example, juror misconduct, the erroneous admission of evidence, or opposing counsel's misconduct by referring to excluded evidence or engaging in improper argument. In many jurisdictions, a motion for a new trial is a necessary prerequisite to filing an appeal. If granted, the verdict is set aside and the case is set for retrial.

2.   *Motion for a Mistrial*

A motion for a mistrial may be made at any time after the jury is empanelled, but before the verdict is entered. A mistrial leads to the retrial of the case. Motions for mistrial are often made after a jury has reached a deadlock in its deliberations and is unable to reach a verdict. Other than the jury deadlock situation, a motion for a mistrial may be made whenever the jury has been so infected by exposure to inadmissible evidence that the court is unable to cure the error by issuing a limiting instruction, or because of the misconduct of counsel, one of the parties, or jurors. Curative limiting instructions are generally considered to have remarkable powers, curing most of the most troubling errors, and thus, courts only rarely grant mistrials. In criminal cases, however, there are certain additional circumstances likely to give rise to a mistrial, namely the prosecutor's violation of the defendant's Fifth Amendment privilege against self-incrimination. If the prosecutor comments to the jury on the defendant's failure to testify, and thus commits the so-called *Griffin* error, a motion for mistrial may well be granted by the court.

Chapter Four

JURY SELECTION

I.   OVERVIEW & OBJECTIVES

A.   Preconceptions and First Impressions

Many jurors arrive at tentative verdicts in the case by the conclusion of jury selection.[1] Empirical research confirms the astonishing reality that many jurors identify their "side" of the case during *voir dire* and hold to those perceptions throughout the trial.[2] As a result, it is beyond dispute that the preconceptions jurors bring to the courthouse and their first impressions of the trial and its participants are monumentally significant factors in the decision process of every trial and need to identified and taken into account by trial advocates.

---

[1] *See* MARGARET C. ROBERTS, TRIAL PSYCHOLOGY 41 (1987).

[2] *See id.*

Juror preconceptions are formed from each individual's vast body of beliefs. They are the product of a lifetime of experiences. Many preconceptions are held in common (*i.e.*, drunk driving is dangerous) while others are not so universal (*i.e.*, the death penalty is a deterrent of crime). A wide variety of events and issues can trigger juror preconceptions. The juror's view of the cause of action being claimed or the crime being charged is likely to be affected by those factors that create preconceptions in all of us.

Just as significant as the preconceptions the jurors bring to the trial are the first impressions jurors form of the parties and their lawyers. A positive initial impression of the attorney or party can predispose a juror to favor the view of events sought by that lawyer or his client. Conversely, an unfavorable view can have the opposite effect. These early impressions should not be left to mere chance, but rather should be created as the result of a carefully planned effort from the very beginning of the trial. Because the jurors have heard little of the merits of the case during the initial juror questioning, their first impressions result from the demeanor and appearance of the parties and lawyers and from the questions asked. At no point in the entire trial process is the concept of primacy more significant than during that first contact between the jurors, the advocate, and his client. Those critical first impressions will have a lasting, if not decisive, impact on the jurors' ultimate determination of the case.

B.   Who You Want and What You Want Them to Do

The objectives of *voir dire* can be broken into three basic areas:

- getting the "best" group of individuals on the jury for the advocate's case

- predisposing those individuals to the advocate's view of the case

- developing a positive rapport with the jurors

Getting the "right" or "best" group of individuals to serve as jurors is, of course, basic and critical. And yet, jury selection is not so much identifying "ideal" people to serve as jurors, but rather deselecting individuals that the advocate perceives as unfavorable to his case. It is somewhat counterintuitive to view events from the perspective of excluding the unfavorables rather than seeking out the favorables. However, advocates cannot choose those jurors who are favorable because they ultimately have little control over who actually serves on the jury. The most the advocate can do is to exclude those who appear to be the most unfavorable. Consequently, getting the "right" jurors actually means eliminating those jurors who are most likely to hurt the advocate's chances of success.

The process of ferreting out unfavorable jurors is frequently undertaken without adequate information. Given the limits on questioning, both in terms of time and content, most advocates readily admit that exercising their challenges to prospective jurors is little more than guesswork or hunches or, worse yet, succumbing to stereotypes. Consequently, it is vital to maximize *voir dire* questioning to obtain meaningful and helpful information about each prospective juror.

Interrelated with the question of who will (or will not) sit on the jury is the task of how to educate the prospective jurors about the parties and facts. It is a curious procedure that dictates that the persuasion process begins even before the final composition of the jury is determined. Advocates must begin persuading even though many of the prospective jurors will ultimately not even be seated on the case. Nonetheless, the tasks of selection and persuasion are inexorably intertwined.

The third objective of *voir dire*, rapport building, is at least as important as the first two. First impressions die hard. And because *voir dire* is the first opportunity for advocates to interact with the prospective jurors, it is important to begin the attorney-juror relationship on a positive note. Persuasion begins with trust and respect. Advocates must strive from the beginning to alleviate the anxiety of the potential jurors while developing relationships with them, and focusing on creating positive first impressions of their clients, cases, and themselves.

II.   THE MECHANICS OF *VOIR DIRE*

The actual process of how courts empanel a jury varies dramatically from jurisdiction to jurisdiction, from court to court within a particular jurisdiction, and even from judge to judge within a particular courthouse. No other aspect of trial has the variance of procedure that is encountered during jury selection. If time and circumstances permit, advocates should watch the judge who will preside over their trial conduct a jury selection before the trial begins. In any event, it is essential that the advocate learn what jury selection procedures are followed by the particular judge before beginning *voir dire*. Some courts prefer that the lawyers conduct all of the questioning. In others, the judge undertakes the entire questioning while the lawyers are allowed to submit written questions that they would like the judge to ask. Yet, in other courts, a hybrid approach is used in which both the judge and the advocates question the prospective jurors. However, even under this approach the limits on questioning undertaken by the advocates may vary dramatically from courtroom to courtroom. Occasionally, part of the juror screening process is done by means of a written questionnaire. Trial judges have wide discretion in deciding how *voir dire* will be conducted in their courtrooms. Nevertheless, every *voir dire* includes roughly the same components and ends the same way. Those various components are discussed below.

A.   Jury Questionnaires

One option available to assist in the *voir dire* process is a written questionnaire. An advantage of having the prospective jurors answer the questions set forth in the questionnaire is that it saves time, eliminating much of the oral questioning. The questionnaires can elicit background information, such as employment history, spouse's employment history, prior jury service, any undue hardship in serving on the jury, and information about the jurors' attitudes on matters relevant to the trial. For instance, in a criminal trial, some questions may seek jurors' attitudes about the crime problem plaguing our country, or whether the criminal justice system is too harsh or too lenient. In civil trials, the questions might ask for the jurors' opinions about the number of lawsuits filed in America or whether the prospective jurors believe that corporate America is more interested in profit than in safety.

Historically, questionnaires have been reserved for complex or high profile trials, such as death penalty cases or cases involving controversial individuals or issues. However, the benefits of questionnaires are anything but a foregone conclusion. Supporters cite the greater breadth of questioning that can be undertaken and the greater sense of candor on the part of prospective jurors in disclosing sensitive information through a questionnaire instead of through oral questioning in open court. However, in refusing to allow the use of questionnaires, many courts cite two primary concerns. First, even if both sides join in requesting questionnaires, the court does not want to be in a position to arbitrate which specific questions will be included or how those questions will be worded. Second, administering questionnaires consumes valuable court time.

Generally, courts will not permit the use of questionnaires unless both parties agree to use them and reach agreement on the questions to be included. Courts are understandably reluctant to be placed in the position where they must resolve disputes over which questions should be included and how they should be phrased. An advocate who wants to use questionnaires is well served in getting agreement and cooperation from opposing counsel for the use of the questionnaire and the specific questions that will be included before the questionnaire is presented for approval by the court.

The second concern focuses on the amount of time consumed by questionnaires. Because questionnaires are generally handed out at the beginning of jury selection, there will be a delay while the prospective jurors fill out the questionnaires. Proponents can counter the undue delay concern by suggesting that the jurors complete the questionnaires while court and counsel are clearing up any pre-trial matters. Another time-saving concession is to agree that neither side will repeat questions asked in the questionnaires—but only ask follow-up questions, case-specific questions, and questions that deal with possible challenges for cause. If used properly, the questionnaires could actually reduce the time that the court expends on the jury selection process. Yet, the reality is that even when these concerns are met, most courts remain reluctant to permit the use of questionnaires in ordinary, run-of-the-mill cases.

B. Beginning the Process

In most jurisdictions, jury selection begins when a large group of prospective jurors (the *venire*) is ushered into the courtroom. The number summoned will depend on the size of the jury to be empanelled, the number of peremptory challenges allocated to the parties, and the nature and complexity of the case. The judge will make general remarks to the group as a whole, including an introduction of the parties and their lawyers. Some courts will read the charge if it is a criminal case or summarize the contentions of the parties in a civil case. Judges may allow the advocates to introduce themselves and their clients and permit the advocates to make a brief statement as to the nature of the case. This "mini-opening statement" facilitates *voir dire* questioning by giving the prospective jurors a generalized understanding of the case.

C. Hardship Questioning

Following the introductions, some courts will solicit "hardship" claims from the prospective jurors. The claimed hardships may range from medical problems to employment concerns or family care situations. The judge will question each juror about the specifics of the claimed hardship. If the judge determines that a hardship exists, that prospective juror will be excused from service. Even though the advocates are not typically involved in "hardship" questioning, the lawyers should note those jurors whose hardship claims were denied, for they may be reluctant to serve and that may affect their ultimate view of the case.

D. Questioning by the Judge

At the conclusion of any "hardship" questioning, if she has not already done so, the judge will usually read or have read the complaint (misdemeanor), information, indictment (felony) in a criminal case, or summarize the contentions of the parties in a civil case. The questioning of the jurors may proceed in any number of formats. In a death penalty case, the prospective jurors may be questioned individually, whereas in other cases the prospective jurors may be questioned as a group (the entire *venire* all at once); or in some courts, only those jurors randomly seated in the jury box may be questioned. The jurors will be questioned concerning their general biographical background, including occupation, spouse's occupation, occupation of adult children, and prior jury service. After the judge elicits basic biographical information, he focuses the questioning on discovering each juror's suitability to decide the particular case before them. The extent of the judge's questioning, and the extent to which the judge allows the advocates to ask questions, varies widely.

E. Questioning by the Advocates

Since some time elapses between the initial introductions and the questioning, advocates should re-introduce themselves and introduce and personalize their client before beginning their questioning.

 ## Illustration of the Advocate Introducing Himself and His Client

Lawyer:	Thank you, Your Honor. It has been a while since Judge Thomas introduced everyone and I would like to take this opportunity to re-introduce myself and Jack Smith, sitting here beside me.

> My name is Ed Malone. I've been a lawyer for four years. Most of my work is in cases like this in which a person has been accused of a crime. But before I struck out on my own, I was a deputy prosecutor in this very county for two years.
>
> I have the privilege of representing Jack Smith. [*Lawyer walks to client and, standing behind him, continues.*] Mr. Smith is a local man with a devoted wife and two children. Mr. Smith works as a roofer for a local contracting company. He has been steadily employed for over ten years . . . .

Following the introduction, the advocate should provide an overview of the case and then begin questioning the prospective jurors about their experiences and attitudes. The type and extent of that questioning is discussed in Part IV of this Chapter.

F.   Challenges to Prospective Jurors

At some point during the juror questioning, the advocates will have the opportunity to challenge any of the seated prospective jurors for cause. The timing of those challenges varies. It may be done following the conclusion of all questioning, or at the conclusion of the advocate's own questioning, or at the time that such a challenge arises, depending on the particular practice of the judge. As discussed below, there are several options available to the court once a challenge for cause is made.

At the conclusion of all challenges for cause, jury selection moves to the peremptory challenge phase. And once again there are multiple methods used in courts for the exercise of peremptory challenges. Broadly speaking, there are two approaches. Some courts use a "blind challenge" system in which the parties exercise their challenges outside the presence of the opposing party, such that both parties might strike the same members of the venire; and some courts use an "open challenge" system, in which the parties exercise their challenges in open court in the presence of the venire and the opposing party. In the open challenge approach, plaintiff's counsel or the prosecutor makes the first peremptory challenge. Because the challenge is exercised in front of other potential jurors, advocates must be respectful and courteous to the person who is being dismissed. Not only is that the right thing to do, but it is also the wise thing to do. Counsel's rude or impolite treatment of the dismissed panelist may cause the remaining *venire* members to harbor ill will toward counsel, and that is especially true for those members who had befriended the dismissed individual.

 Illustration of Thanking and Excusing a Prospective Juror

Lawyer: Your Honor, at this time the defense would like to thank and excuse Mr. Luckman. [*turning to Mr. Luckman*] Mr. Luckman, thank you for your time and service.

Courtesy and respect should be the norm. Use the person's name, sincerely thank him for his willingness to serve, and make eye contact with him to reinforce the point. A lawyer who extends such courtesies will be viewed more favorably than one who does not.

1. *Challenges for Cause*

Challenges for cause require a showing by counsel that a juror does not satisfy the statutory requirements for jury service or cannot render an impartial verdict. (Fed. R. Civ. Pro. 47; Fed. R. Crim. Pro. 24.) This may be because of a stated bias, a relationship the person has with a party, the person's inability to understand English, a felony conviction in the person's past, or any other statutory ground for disqualification provided in the jurisdiction. There is no limit to the number of each party's challenges for cause. Challenges for cause are usually made out of the presence of the prospective jurors.

In the event an advocate has identified a prospective juror who appears to be not only unfavorable but also perhaps a candidate for a cause challenge, counsel should ask questions to firm up the basis for a cause challenge. For instance, assume that during a prosecutor's *voir dire*, it developed that a prospective juror had previously experienced some confrontations with the police. The *voir dire* questioning may proceed along these lines:

 Illustration of *Voir Dire* Questioning to Firm Up a Challenge for Cause

Prosecutor: Mr. Evans, you indicated that you have had more than one confrontation between yourself and the police, is that correct?

Prospective Juror: Over the past several years I've had some dealings with them.

Prosecutor: And would it be fair to say that those dealings would have been adversarial—kind of "you against them"?

Prospective Juror: Not always, but a couple of times.

Prosecutor: I take it then that you were arrested?

Prospective Juror: That's a fact.

Prosecutor: On any of those occasions did you disagree with the officer's account of the events that led to your arrest?

Prospective Juror: Well, let's just say that sometimes they saw events different from me.

Prosecutor: Mr. Evans, there is going to be police officer testimony in this case. And the judge is going to instruct you that you are to evaluate their testimony fairly and objectively. Do you think because of your past contacts that may be difficult for you to do?

Prospective Juror: I don't know. I would try to do my best.

Prosecutor: Mr. Evans, I appreciate your candor.

The prosecutor will challenge this prospective juror for cause. The court then has several options. First, the court could rule on the challenge immediately without further questioning. This option is appropriate if the apparent bias is material and does not appear to be the result of some miscommunication or misunderstanding by the prospective juror. Second, the court could initiate its own questioning to determine if the apparent bias justifies dismissal. Generally, questioning by the court to determine bias is ineffective, because most prospective jurors will represent that they can be fair despite the preconceptions they appear to harbor. Third, the court could allow the opposing lawyer (the defense lawyer in this example) to attempt to rehabilitate the challenged juror. If defense counsel has already undertaken his *voir dire* questioning, the court may allow him to question only the challenged juror and only about the basis of the challenge. If opposing counsel has not yet had an opportunity to *voir dire* the venire, the court may defer its ruling on the challenge until after that *voir dire*. Naturally, defense counsel will want to "rehabilitate" this challenged member of the venire, not because the person ultimately will be "selected" to serve, but because if the challenge for cause is eventually denied, the prosecutor will have to exercise a peremptory challenge on the prospective juror, thus causing the prosecutor to expend one of his limited peremptory challenges.

 ## Illustration of Rehabilitating a Challenged Juror

Defense lawyer: Mr. Evans, you indicated that because of your past problems with law enforcement you may tend to view police testimony skeptically, is that correct?

Prospective Juror: It's not so easy to forget the past.

Defense Lawyer: I understand that, Mr. Evans. However, if you are selected in this case you will take an oath to follow the law, and accordingly you will be instructed to evaluate the testimony of a police officer as you would anyone else's testimony. Would you be able to follow the law?

Juror: I would try my best.

Defense Lawyer: Do you believe you could put aside your personal feelings and follow the law and decide this case on the evidence?

Juror: I think I could.

Defense Lawyer: If you are ultimately selected to sit on this case, would you be able to be fair and impartial to both sides?

Juror: Yes, I would.

---

2. *Peremptory Challenges*

Peremptory challenges allow counsel to simply challenge or strike a member from the prospective jury panel without a showing of cause. Because peremptory challenges are within the discretion of the advocates, no reason for the challenge need be given. The only limitations are that the attorneys may not use peremptory challenges to exclude persons based upon their race or gender.

Unlike challenges for cause, which are not limited, each party has a finite number of peremptory challenges. This number varies by jurisdiction and by the nature of the case. For instance, in federal court, each side receives three peremptory challenges in a civil case and in a criminal misdemeanor case. (28 USC §1870; Fed. R. Crim. Pro. 24(b).) In a non-capital federal felony criminal trial, the prosecutor has six peremptory challenges and the defense has ten, and in a capital federal case each side has twenty peremptory challenges. (Fed. R. Crim. Pro. 24(b).) In state courts there is substantial variance in the allocation of peremptory challenges. In California, for example, peremptory challenges are issued according to the type of case before the court, with twenty challenges given to each side in a criminal case where the potential sentence is death or life without the possibility of parole, ten in all other criminal cases, and six in civil cases. (CAL. CODE CIV. PRO. § 231.)

G. Swearing in the Jury

In the "blind challenge" system, jury selection ends when both parties submit their lists of peremptory challenges. In an "open challenge" system, jury selection is complete when counsel have either exhausted their peremptory challenges, or when there are consecutive passes on peremptory challenges, or when both sides have stated that they accept the panel as constituted. There may be some advantage gained by being the first party to announce that she accepts the jury panel as presently constituted, because it conveys to the jury that the party is satisfied that the jurors will act fairly and impartially. However, this should not outweigh the use of a peremptory challenge if an unsatisfactory juror remains in the panel. With the completion of jury selection, the jurors are sworn in. It is at this point in a criminal trial that jeopardy attaches.

H. Selecting Alternate Jurors

In some cases, courts will also seat alternate jurors. The alternate jurors sit in the jury box with the "regular" jurors so that they perceive the testimony and arguments from the same perspective as the other jurors. However, alternate jurors do not participate in deliberations unless a seated juror becomes unable to fulfill his duty. In that event, the deliberations will begin anew with the newly seated, formerly alternate, juror. The number of alternate jurors will vary according to the court's discretion. In a shorter trial, the court may opt for one or two alternates, and in a longer trial, the court may have four, five, or more alternate jurors. The guiding concern is to ensure the availability of the requisite number of jurors to complete deliberations so that the court is not forced to declare a mistrial.

III. PRELIMINARY CONSIDERATIONS

While the foregoing description of the mechanics of jury selection was necessarily general in nature, because of the absence of uniformity of the process, the next two sections provide more specific guidance about the preparation for and actual questioning during *voir dire*. The advocate's opportunity to speak directly with the jurors during *voir dire* is an invaluable opportunity that must not be wasted or misused.

A. Evaluate the Case for Emotional or Prejudicial Undercurrents

No case is tried in a vacuum, and prior to the start of jury selection, advocates should be aware of issues in the case or events in the community that may impact the viewpoints of prospective jurors on those issues or otherwise color their view of the case. Likewise, the subject matter of some trials, such as cases involving murder, rape, child abuse, domestic violence, asbestos contamination, breast implants, and medical malpractice, to name a few, may evoke strong emotions. In cases that have such emotionally charged facts, the advocates must be prepared to ask the questions that will deal effectively with juror preconceptions about those facts. A trial lawyer cannot ignore the events and circumstances that form the contemporary societal backdrop for her trial.

The backdrop of the trial may be affected by local events, such as a high school principal expelling several students for passing out birth control information, or by events of national interest, such as the tragic events of September 11, 2001. In the case of the high school principal expelling students, juror attitudes concerning the propriety of the principal's actions would be significant if, for example, that principal was a witness in an unlawful termination case involving a former teacher. Even though one event is unrelated to the other, the jurors' perception of the principal's credibility will be affected by their views of his earlier actions. In the wake of 9/11, criminal defense attorneys must be concerned about juror attitudes toward individuals of Arab descent or individuals accused of terrorist-type activities. These attitudes must be probed and explored and commitments to fairness and impartiality must be obtained from the prospective jurors. Prospective jurors are likely to have formed firm opinions based on such local and national events, which, in turn, may affect their ability to impartially judge issues in the trial.

By way of illustration, assume that a defendant charged with rape goes to trial in a community that had recently endured a wrenching and publicly reported criminal trial involving day care workers who allegedly sexually abused children in their care. In the *voir dire* for the rape case, it would be necessary for a lawyer defending the rape suspect to acknowledge the background against which the trial is taking place and to get assurances from the jurors that they would not allow any preconceptions formed during that previous trial to color their view of the current case. Such questions might proceed as follows:

Illustration of Probing Juror Attitudes Concerning Local Events or Sentiments

Defense Lawyer: I am sure most, if not all, of you are familiar with the trial in which the people who ran a day care center were found guilty of molesting some of the children in their school. That was an awful case with awful facts and most of us can't help feeling anger when we hear about such things. One way we might be tempted to vent our anger and our frustration would be to strike out at anyone who is even accused of a sex related offense. Now, I know you folks wouldn't knowingly let that happen, but sometimes we might not even be fully aware of our feelings. I think it is important to be open and talk about such matters so that we can enter this trial unencumbered by hidden feelings that might make it hard to judge this case fairly and impartially.

How about you, Mrs. Harris? Did you follow the day care case?

Advocates need to be aware of these undercurrents and prepare appropriate questions designed to uncover juror attitudes.

B.   Consider Common Attitudes and Experiences Desired in Prospective Jurors

As noted, jury selection is not so much a *selection* process as a *deselection* process. Advocates cannot "choose" jurors, they can only excuse them. Deselection, intelligently undertaken, requires that advocates identify the traits, attitudes, and experiences in potential jurors that will not be favorable to their clients. Conversely, advocates should also have in mind a profile of their "ideal" juror, or at least the kinds of experiences or attitudes they would like to have in their ideal jurors. This exercise of identifying both undesirable and desirable characteristics is not only vital to the intelligent "selection" of a jury, but has the additional benefit of requiring a pre-trial analysis of the case from a number of perspectives. The advocate can begin the jury selection process only after achieving a thorough understanding of how she, her client, and her case are likely to be perceived by all prospective jurors.

Historically, lawyers have exercised peremptory challenges based on nothing more than gut instincts and hunches, or on racial or ethnic stereotypes. It was perhaps the clearest example of advocacy as art because the process was anything but scientific. Even some of the reputed masters of trial advocacy, including giants of the profession like Francis Wellman and Clarence Darrow, advocated such a jury selection strategy. First, consider Wellman's advice:

> Irish are sometimes prejudiced against the Hebrews and vice versa. Germans are apt to be stubborn but inclined to be generous as well. Hebrews as a rule make fine jurors except where they harbor prejudices. Young men as a rule are much safer than old men, unless the lawyer is representing a defendant; then he wants older men.[3]

Next, read Darrow's counsel:

> An Irishman is called into the box for examination. There is no reason for asking about his religion; he is Irish; that is enough. We may not agree with his religion, but it matters not; his feelings go deeper than any religion. You should be aware that he is emotional, kindly and sympathetic. If he is chosen as a juror, his imagination will place him in the dock; really, he is trying himself. You would be guilty of malpractice if you got rid of him, except for the strongest reasons.
>
> An Englishman is not so good as an Irishman, but still, he has come through a long tradition of individual rights, and is not afraid to stand alone; in fact, he is never sure that he is right unless the great majority is against him. The German is not so keen about individual rights except where they concern his own way of life; liberty is not a theory, it is a way of living. Still, he wants to do what is right, and he is not afraid. He has not been among us long, his ways are fixed by his race, his habits are still in the making. We need inquire no further. If he is a Catholic, then he loves music and art; he must be emotional, and will want to help you; give him a chance.[4]

Darrow loves the Irish as jurors and Wellman prizes the "Hebrew." But they both view jurors as nothing apart from their ethnicity or age. The reality is that those ethnicities tell us nothing about any juror's particular experiences, about what each juror believes, or how a specific juror views the world. In today's diverse and increasingly pluralistic world, it would be foolish to rely on stereotypes based on a prospective juror's race or zip code. That may have worked in the courtrooms frequented by Wellman and Darrow, but it would surely fail if adopted as a modern jury selection strategy.

Instead, advocates must go beyond ethnicity or place of residence and consider the attitudes and experiences of the prospective jurors. We are

---

[3] *See* Francis L. Wellman, Day in Court 125 (1914).

[4] Clarence Darrow, *Attorney for the Defense*, Esquire, May 1936, at 3, 211.

all the product of our experiences, a complex compilation of sometimes strikingly inconsistent viewpoints. Advocates must ask: What experiences would best position jurors to appreciate and understand, and perhaps to even connect at some deep level with the party's story? What attitudes and predilections would cause them to view the facts favorably to the party?

For example, in a case involving claims of racial discrimination by an employer against African-American employees, it is unwise and far too simplistic to think that the defendant should simply strike all of the African-American members of the venire, just as it is wrong to conclude that the plaintiff should try to keep every African-American on the panel. From the plaintiff's viewpoint, prospective jurors who have overcome great adversity in their own lives or who have a particularly finely tuned sense of responsibility might view the plaintiffs' claims with some disdain, despite the fact that they have black skin by birth. Such jurors might be desirable for the defendant.

Similarly, in a domestic violence case, the prosecution should not immediately assume that its ideal jurors will be women, nor should the defense reflexively seek to exclude all women from the panel. Not only is such a strategy illegal, inasmuch as it violates the Equal Protection Clause under *JEB v. Alabama*,[5] but also it defies common sense. The better approach, once again, is to explore the attitudes and experiences of the prospective jurors, by asking, "Who has a low tolerance for conflict, or, in contrast, is not bothered by the presence of conflict? Who has been exposed to domestic violence or has seen its impact on others and who has not? Who feels like a victim, from either real or imagined slights, and who believes that each person has control and responsibility over what happens to them?" These questions and many more will begin to illuminate which panelist may pose the greatest risk for one side or the other.

None of this is to say, however, that more mundane matters, such as occupation and familial relationships, are not important pieces of infor- mation. Such information can be immensely helpful and important to an advocate in exercising peremptory challenges. For instance, in a medical malpractice case, the plaintiff's lawyer most likely would want to exclude a prospective juror who is married to a medical doctor. Without knowing anything more about this prospective juror, that fact alone may well put her at odds with plaintiff's case. Though, of course, it remains possible that the prospective juror may in fact believe that most doctors are incompetent or motivated by greed and would be sympathetic to plaintiff's claim. Of course, that same prospective juror might be ideal for the defense.

Identifying the attitudes and experiences on the part of prospective jurors that will best serve a party's interests in a case is substantially more difficult than simply identifying the person's ethnicity or occupation. For that reason, lawyers in larger cases that can handle the expense, regularly rely on jury consultants to assist in the jury selection process. One of the tasks frequently undertaken by the consultant is to research prevailing

---

[5]   511 U.S. 127 (1994).

attitudes in the community and to compile the profiles of individuals who respond favorably to the client's claims or defenses. Through the use of surveys, mock juries, and demographic research, jury consultants can provide invaluable insight into the kind of people the party wants as jurors, and more importantly, those it does not want.

In the large majority of cases that cannot afford the luxury of hiring outside jury consultants, lawyers must use all available resources and develop a profile of the experiences and attitudes they would like for their jurors to have. This should go beyond the practice of labeling and stereotyping. The advocate's available resources include many of the sources already discussed, including mastery over the case facts themselves and the issues raised by those facts, familiarity with current events or issues in the larger community, research into the demographics of the jury pool—where the jurors are drawn from and any significant differences in the make-up of the neighborhoods included in the pool—and counsel and advice from colleagues with long term roots in the community. The advocate must then ask good questions, listen to the answers, and follow-up when appropriate.

The advocate should also attempt to ascertain whether prospective jurors are leaders or followers. A potential juror's background or occupation may make him particularly suitable to lead jury deliberations. Lawyers, medical doctors, college professors and high-ranking corporate executives are likely candidates to be forepersons. Additionally, prospective jurors with strong personalities may exercise "control" during deliberations even if they are not selected as forepersons. An advocate who is concerned about how a potential foreperson or jury leader might view the case will be well advised to strike that potential juror or run the risk of ceding jury leadership to the opponent.

Occasionally during questioning an advocate will encounter a hostile juror. The hostility may be the product of a personality clash between the advocate and the prospective juror, or it could be a reaction to the subject matter of the trial. An advocate should avoid questioning that juror once the hostility becomes evident because he will almost certainly excuse that prospective juror and so should curtail the opportunity for that juror to affect the other potential jurors by letting them hear responses hostile to the advocate's position. Additionally, continued questioning could cause the attorney to appear antagonistic or unnecessarily confrontational to the remaining prospective jurors.

IV. THE THREE PHASES OF THE QUESTIONING PROCESS

Attorney questioning during *voir dire* consists of three distinct phases:

- **Information:** The first phase elicits basic biographical information about the jurors;

- **Insight:** The second phase includes specific inquiries into jurors' backgrounds, experiences, and attitudes that shed light on how the jurors will likely view the particular issues in the case; and

- **Indoctrination:** The third phase indoctrinates prospective jurors about the parties' contentions and concerns in the case.

Information. Insight. Indoctrination.

Advocates should approach *voir dire* by recognizing that most prospective jurors are anxious. Most people fear speaking in a public setting. That fear is compounded when the setting is a trial courtroom replete with judge, lawyers, and all the solemn and formal trappings of the legal system. Further exacerbating juror anxiety is the fear of the unknown. Most prospective jurors do not fully understand what their role will be or what will be expected of them. Juror anxiety, though understandable, creates a challenge for advocates because it impedes the free flow of information that is essential to an effective *voir dire*.

And so the questioner's first task is to overcome that juror anxiety, to ensure that she is able to elicit sufficient information for her to intelligently identify the least favorable prospective jurors. The three-step approach to *voir dire* recognizes the reality of juror anxiety and the foolishness of beginning *voir dire* with questions on difficult or sensitive topics. There will be time for those later. *Voir dire* should begin instead with questioning that requires short answers on non-threatening matters and gradually escalates to more penetrating and invasive inquiries. Proceeding in this way allows advocates to put the jurors at ease and build a relationship with them before moving into the deeper waters of *voir dire*.

A.   First Phase—Preliminary Matters

1.   *Methodology and Purpose*

At the start of the questioning, the attorney should reintroduce himself and his client. This opportunity should be fully exploited—advocates should have their clients stand and then introduce and personalize them for the jury. Additionally, anybody else at counsel table should be introduced. For instance, if the prosecutor has an investigator at the counsel table or defense counsel has a second chair, they should be introduced as well. Counsel should also introduce the facts of the case in a brief and non-argumentative manner. Although most jurisdictions do not allow extended remarks by counsel at the outset of *voir dire*, it is typically permissible to apprise the jurors of the basic contentions of the advocate's client. Some kind of brief overview is necessary to provide the jurors context for the questions that follow.

After advocates introduce their claims in the case, they should spend a few moments helping the prospective jurors understand the nature and purpose of *voir dire*. The jurors need to appreciate that the advocate's questions are not gratuitous efforts to pry into the panelist's affairs, but instead, part of a critically important attempt to identify the most fair and impartial jurors to decide the case. A personal story or example can serve as a valuable tool to explain that one's experiences can permanently shape a person's outlook and even impair a person's objectivity.

Illustration of Overview of Case and Explanation of *Voir Dire*[6]

Lawyer: [*After introducing herself and her client*] Ladies and Gentlemen, Fred Thornton and his wife of 13 years, Sarah, set out to buy a house right here in South Hills after Fred received a job transfer to here. And you will hear that they were excited about buying their first home. But that excitement didn't last long. They got a real estate broker, Ms. Sandoval, and she showed them a house in the Highland subdivision, a house owned by the defendant, Mr. Riley. Mr. Thornton liked the house and Sarah did too and so they made an offer. An offer the defendant rejected. And we contend, Fred and Sarah Thornton contend, that the reason Mr. Riley rejected that offer and a subsequent one was not because the offers were too low, or were somehow inadequate, but because the Thorntons are African-American. You will learn a lot more about the evidence that supports this claim of racial discrimination through the witnesses who testify, but it is important at the outset that you understand why the Thorntons are here. The Thorntons have suffered a great deal because of the defendant's refusal to treat them like everyone else, physically, emotionally, economically, and so they have brought their claims to this forum—to you—for a hearing.

This is my chance to ask you questions and to discuss with you some of the issues in the case to try to determine who can best serve as a juror in this case. And I want you to understand that the questions I'm asking are not intended to embarrass you or put you on the spot. Not at all. I simply want to find out about your background and experiences so that we can know whether you are in the best position to evaluate the facts in this case. We are all the product of our experiences and we are all effected by what we have done, where we were raised, what we do for a living and so on. It all shapes our view of the world. My wife is a chair-side assistant for an orthodontist. She helps straighten people's teeth! And she loves her job, loves the people she works with, loves working with teeth. That experience alone might make it hard for her to be a fair juror in a lawsuit against an orthodontist. She might have a hard time not quietly rooting for the orthodontist or giving him the benefit of the doubt, just because of her experience in the field with her orthodontist.

The other thing to remember as I ask you my questions is that I need for you to all be completely forthcoming and honest about your experiences and attitudes. And I know you all will do that. If you need to discuss something that's embarrassing or difficult, just let me know and we can take it up with the judge in private.

Okay, now let me start with you, Mrs. Fifer . . . .

---

[6] This illustration is based on the hypothetical case *Green v. Hall and Rose*, Kenneth S. Broun (Rev. 4th ed. 1992, National Institute of Trial Advocacy).

After the introductory remarks, counsel should proceed to the initial phase of questioning. It has the dual purposes of putting the prospective jurors at ease and gathering information that provides a biographical portrait of each juror. Prospective jurors appreciate an advocate who recognizes "speaker anxiety" and helps ease them into the process. And, a juror who is nurtured, not rushed, is more likely to be forthcoming during the difficult and more intrusive areas of inquiry in the second and third phases of the questioning process.

The easiest way to induce jurors to open up is to get them to talk about themselves, their jobs, their children, and their accomplishments. In doing so, both goals of the first phase are served; the jurors become acclimated to the process and the advocate gathers essential information. First phase questioning should inquire about each prospective juror's employment. And in the event a juror is unemployed or retired, ask about their past employment. If a juror is married or otherwise involved in a significant relationship, that information should be elicited, as well as the occupation of the significant other. Additionally, if a juror has adult children, ask about what they do for a living. If the oldest son is a lawyer, or a doctor or a chemical engineer, it may bear on the trial. The use of open-ended questions facilitates the flow of this valuable biographical information. Encourage jurors to talk freely and to volunteer information that they feel is relevant. It is particularly important during this first phase to ask some questions of each prospective juror. Give everyone an opportunity to "break the ice" and to overcome their anxiety.

A good technique to "get the ball rolling" is to ask the entire panel a nonthreatening, simple question that anyone would have an answer to. For example, "How many of you have been annoyed by telemarketers calling during dinnertime?" The advocate should ask the question while raising her hand and smiling; this encourages the jurors to interact without feeling as though they will be the only one with their hand raised. If several people raise their hands, note who they are, and then single out each of those jurors for individual follow up questions.

2. *Specific Background Inquiries*

Once a juror reveals general information there is frequently the need to ask follow-up questions seeking greater detail or clarity. For instance, if a juror states that he is a doctor, the advocate should ask whether he is a Ph.D. or a physician and inquire into his area of practice or specialty. If a juror indicates that her daughter is a lawyer, she should be asked about the type of law her daughter practices.

3. *Familiarity with the Case or the Parties*

It is essential to ask if the prospective jurors know anything about the case or know any of the people involved in the case. This is a particular concern if the case has generated some notoriety, which can easily happen in smaller communities. Of particular concern, of course, is whether a juror's familiarity with the facts or the people involved may have caused the juror to form opinions concerning either.

4. *Prior Jury Experience*

Each prospective juror should be asked about prior jury service, including whether the prior jury service involved a civil or criminal trial and what cause of action or crime had been alleged. It is permissible and advisable to ask the person if the jury reached a verdict, but it is not appropriate to inquire about the actual verdict that was reached in that prior case.

 Illustration of Questioning as to Prior Jury Experience

Lawyer: Mr. Smith, without telling us about the verdict or any other outcome, we need to know if you have ever served as a juror before?

Prospective Juror: Yes, about two years ago.

Lawyer: Was that here in this county?

Prospective Juror: As a matter of fact, it was right here in this courthouse.

Lawyer: I see. Was that a civil or criminal case?

Prospective Juror: It was for auto theft. So I guess it was criminal.

Lawyer: Again Mr. Smith, without telling us what the verdict was, was the jury able to reach a verdict?

Prospective Juror: Yes, we were.

Lawyer: Thank you, Mr. Smith.

Jurors with previous jury service may have had experiences during that prior trial, or trials, which they found troubling and which may have some spillover effect on the present case. Thus, it is wise to ask each juror how she felt about her prior experience as a juror. Advocates may be able to point out significant differences between the prior trial and the current trial and correct any misperceptions, thus beginning the juror education process. For instance, in a civil case, if the prior trial was a criminal case, the difference in burden of proof must be explained.

 Illustration of Questioning on Burden of Proof

Plaintiff's Lawyer: Mr. Smith, since that previous case involved a criminal trial, the burden on the prosecution was to prove the defendant's guilt beyond a reasonable doubt. Do you recall that?

Prospective Juror: Yes, I do.

Lawyer: Since this case is a civil trial, my burden as the lawyer for Mrs. Brown, the plaintiff, is simply to prove her case by a

	preponderance of the evidence. Do you recall the distinction between the two burdens of proof?
Prospective Juror:	Well, I think I do. The burden in a criminal case is much greater than in a civil case.
Lawyer:	That's right. In a criminal case the state's burden is to prove guilt beyond any reasonable doubt, whereas in this case the plaintiff's burden is simply more likely than not.
Prospective Juror:	Just a little more than the defendant?
Lawyer:	That's right. Do you think you would be able to apply that standard in this case?
Prospective Juror:	Yes, I think I could.

5. *Law Enforcement Contacts*

Advocates in criminal cases should ask about each prospective juror's contacts or relationships with law enforcement personnel, including security guards, firemen, probation officers, social service workers, or anyone even peripherally involved in law enforcement. If a defense attorney must attack police testimony, he should not permit prospective jurors who have strong relationships with law enforcement personnel to remain on the panel. For instance, the mother of a police officer is unlikely to be receptive to an argument that another police officer acted improperly or lied on the witness stand.

6. *Prior Contacts with Professionals*

Most civil trials and many criminal trials involve expert witnesses, ranging from medical doctors to engineers to psychologists. In such cases it is important to ask about prospective jurors' contact or relationship with the type of professionals involved in the trial. In a medical malpractice case, for example, a juror whose daughter is undergoing treatment for cancer may bring an entirely different prospective to the trial than the other prospective jurors.

B. Second Phase—Insights into Case-Specific Attitudes

Once basic biographical information has been elicited and every juror has had an opportunity to speak, the advocate should move the questioning into more case-specific areas. During this second phase, the focus should turn to the specific aspects of the prospective juror's experience and attitudes that may bear on this trial. For example, in a criminal case involving rape, with a victim who is a female college student living in an on-campus dorm, the lawyer might ask whether any of the prospective jurors or their children attend college (or did so in the past) and whether they live on-campus (or did so when they attended). Likewise, in the prosecution of a member of a motorcycle gang, the defense attorney should elicit each prospective juror's feelings about motorcycles and groups of motorcycle riders who associate together. The aim of the questioning is to uncover biases that will affect the juror's view of the evidence so that the lawyer can intelligently exercise challenges. The attorney should attempt to uncover any relevant juror biases concerning race, cultural differences, or alternative life-styles. Questions in these sensitive areas may prove awkward to ask. It may even be necessary to write out sensitive questions in advance and to avoid trying to "wing it." Questions about reading materials and movies may shed light on juror inclinations, as will questions concerning groups, clubs, or organizations. Be tactful, but do not avoid tough questions.

As with phase one questioning, information elicited in phase two questioning may provide an opportunity to educate the jurors. For instance, a prospective juror who is a gun enthusiast may consider himself an "expert" in a murder trial involving a gun. This could lead to an outcome based improperly on facts and experiences obtained outside the courtroom rather than upon evidence presented in the courtroom. Instructing the "expert" about his duty and responsibility to consider only the evidence admitted at trial also instructs the remainder of the panel as to their duties should the "expert" attempt to dominate deliberations.

1. *Prior Brushes with the Law*

It is especially important in criminal cases to inquire whether a prospective juror has had any prior negative experience with law enforcement personnel. It follows that individuals with past criminal problems may harbor some ill will toward the prosecution and police officers, and this may be their opportunity to "get even." Whether true or not, a prior arrest or criminal prosecution is a significant event that may well color that individual's ability to be fair and impartial to both sides. Additionally, counsel must ask if any family members or close friends have suffered arrest or prosecution. Again, such a negative contact could well influence the prospective juror's attitude concerning events crucial to the trial.

Jurors may be understandably reluctant to divulge this kind of information. Many judges advise prospective jurors that they may disclose sensitive information outside the presence of the rest of the panel.

In attempting to elicit sensitive information consider the following approach. Sometimes disclosure begets disclosure.

 Illustration of Questioning to Elicit Negative Contacts with Law Enforcement

Lawyer: Several years ago, my brother was arrested for possession of cocaine. Now I've got to tell you that was a real shock to me and my whole extended family. We were puzzled, concerned, and even ashamed. As the lawyer in the family, it was up to me to help my brother as his case worked its way through the courts. To some extent it colored how I looked at police officers, my fellow prosecutors, as well as how I looked at narcotics, jail and a family's anxiety. I guess the point of my story is this—my brother's experience had a real effect on me. It made me view a number of things from an entirely new perspective. I was different because of the experience. It was important for me to realize that.

Now, I suspect that some of you have had an experience where either you or someone you know has had some problem with the law. And, as I experienced, that probably gave you a new perspective. We need to know about and talk a little about whether your experience might effect how you would view events that happened in the trial.

Has anyone experienced the kind of situation I went through with my brother?

2. *Attitudes Toward Professions Involved in the Case*

In a medical malpractice action, both plaintiffs and defendants must be concerned about how the prospective jurors view doctors and other health care professionals. Plaintiffs who are suing doctors for their alleged mistakes do not want jurors who believe that doctors are perfect and never make mistakes, and defendants do not want jurors who have had bad experiences with doctors or the medical profession as a whole. And so, both plaintiffs and defendants must explore the prospective jurors' experiences with doctors and attitudes toward them.

Imagine that the plaintiff in a medical malpractice case accuses the doctor of negligently performing a heart transplant operation on plaintiff's husband, resulting in the patient's death. Obviously, heart transplant surgeons are highly skilled and the procedure itself is quite complex, and the risk of jurors refusing to entertain the possibility of doctor negligence is great. Consequently, the need to address the jurors' attitudes toward doctors is particularly pronounced.

 ## Illustration of Questions About Attitudes Toward Doctors[7]

Plaintiff's Lawyer: As I've told you, the allegations in this case focus mainly on Doctors Attenboro and Wiley. We claim that they made certain critical mistakes in performing the surgery on Mr. Jackson, leading

---

[7] Illustration based on hypothetical case *Farrel et al. v. Strong Line, Inc. et al.*, Thomas F. Geraghty (1994, National Institute for Trial Advocacy).

	to his death. If you serve as a juror in this case you will be called on to evaluate the conduct of these two heart transplant surgeons. And I'd like to know about your experiences with doctors. Mr. Gonzales, how about you? What has been your experience with doctors?
Prospective Juror:	Well, I guess its been okay. I've never been really sick or anything.
Plaintiff's Lawyer:	I remember that when I was growing up people considered doctors to be like God, just a little below God-status, almost incapable of making a mistake. How would you characterize your view of doctors in that regard? Do you see them as kind of like that—as almost perfect?
Prospective Juror:	I wouldn't say that. I mean they're human just like the rest of us and I know they make mistakes sometimes. I've read about doctors leaving their instruments in people after they're all sewn up and stuff like that, so I know it happens.
Plaintiff's Lawyer:	Based on what you know, how do you think mistakes like that might happen?
Prospective Juror:	I don't know. I suppose just being careless or not paying attention. I know there's a lot to think about and worry about in a surgery.
Plaintiff's Lawyer:	Thank you, Mr. Gonzales, I really appreciate your thought on that. Ms. Rhodes, what is your view of doctors?

There is, of course much more ground still to cover with regard to the jurors and their views of doctors. The advocate would want to know about any specific experiences the jurors have had with doctors, either positive or negative, with the doctor as a hero or life-saver or with the doctor as mistake prone and arrogant. The advocate will want to know more than is sought in the example above about the perceived healing power of doctors and about their perceived vulnerabilities. And the advocate will want to leak out facts from the case as appropriate to plant a seed about the culpability of the defendant doctors.

3.   *Attitudes About Race, Gender, or Ethnicity*

In a case that involves questions of race, gender, or ethnicity, either directly or indirectly, counsel must explore the jurors' attitudes about those delicate issues. In a case involving claims of discrimination in the workplace based on race or gender, the need for the questions is patently clear. However, in other cases, in which the central contentions of the parties do not include race or gender related claims the need may be equally great because of any number of factors. It may be that the defendant is African-American in a largely Anglo community; it may be that the defense claims the defendant has been framed by a racist cop; it may be that the defendant is a person of middle-eastern descent accused of conspiring against the United States; it may be that the plaintiff is an undocumented immigrant from Mexico who alleges he was wrongly beaten by the police; it may be that the victim in a domestic violence prosecution has now recanted her accusations against the defendant and claims she lied; and the list goes on. The attitudes of the prospective jurors about people of different races and genders and nationalities may reveal much about that jurors' ability to view the claims of a party in a favorable or unfavorable light.

Broaching the matter of race can be awkward at best and downright unpleasant at worst. Advocates must avoid being confrontational—the question "Mr. Blake, do you hold to any racial biases?" is most definitely not the way to go. Instead, advocates are better served by approaching the issue from the perspective of some current event, something that will give the jurors a relatively safe topic to discuss but will reveal their attitudes and perspectives. When the O.J. Simpson criminal case was being tried, it would have provided an excellent barometer of juror attitudes concerning race. Perhaps a more current example would be attitudes toward racial profiling (especially after the events of September 11) or the jurors' perspectives on the value of and continuing need for affirmative action.

Assume that in the example below plaintiffs have brought an employment discrimination claim, alleging that they were the victims of reverse discrimination—that the defendant employer (a historically black college) refused to promote them or give them pay raises because they were white. The defendant's counsel is questioning the jurors.

 ## Illustration of *Voir Dire* on Attitudes About Race

Defense Lawyer: This case, as you've already heard, involves claims that the plaintiffs were treated differently and unfairly simply because they were white. Now, Eastern College vigorously denies they were treated differently or unfairly because of the color of their skin. Nonetheless, you will hear a lot during the course of this case about affirmative action and issues relating to race and color. It's unavoidable. So I want to ask you some questions about your feeling about race relations in America today. Some of you may remember a little while back when then President Clinton announced his Race Initiative and he appointed a commission to study a number of race related issues and he said that he wanted to begin a new conversation in America about race. Do you think that was something that we needed in this country? Mr. Sackheim, let's start with you. Do you remember reading about that?

Prospective Juror: I remember. It seems like we spend a lot of time talking about this stuff, but nothing ever really changes. I think we focus too much on the color of a person's skin. It doesn't matter to me what race someone is, the question is whether they do the job, what kind of person are they.

Defense Lawyer: Thank you for that, Mr. Sackheim. Your response leads me to ask about your views of affirmative action for minorities. In California, for example, they passed a proposition eliminating affirmative

	action in its universities and its government hiring and contracting. How do you feel about that development?
Prospective Juror:	I think it's probably a good thing. It's time to get past all that stuff it seems to me. I don't know exactly how that works out there in California, but it sounds like something I would probably support.
Defense Lawyer:	Thank you, Mr. Sackheim, for your candor. Ms. Villanueva, what do you think about the President's conversation on race in America. Do we need that?
Prospective Juror:	I think so. There are still too many people left behind without a chance to succeed. Everybody should get a fair chance and right now ... I don't know, it doesn't seem like it's working so good.
Defense Lawyer:	Why is it do you think that some people don't have a fair chance to succeed?
Prospective Juror:	No jobs. No chance to go to college, to get ahead. It's tough.
Defense Lawyer:	Thank you, Ms. Villanueva. Ms. Dowdy, do you agree with Ms. Villanueva? How do her comments strike you?

The advocate has now "primed the pump." A wide-ranging discussion on the topics of race and affirmative action will allow the advocates on both sides to better understand juror attitudes on the critical issue in the trial.

C.   Third Phase—Indoctrination & Commitment

By beginning slowly and only gradually moving the *voir dire* into the deeper waters of phase two and then phase three, the advocate should have developed a relationship and some measure of trust with the prospective jurors. The focus in phase three shifts from inquiry into the jurors' backgrounds and personal experiences that might have a bearing on the trial to the legal concepts involved in the trial.

One challenge in this third phase of questioning is to educate the prospective jurors concerning important legal concepts without improperly instructing them on the law. For instance, the advocate must discuss, when appropriate, such concepts as reasonable doubt, preponderance of the evidence, presumption of innocence, negligence, and comparative negligence.

The second objective of this phase of questioning is to disclose potential weaknesses or vulnerabilities in the advocate's case and to obtain commitments from the jury that they will not decide the issue or case against the party based on that one solitary fact. Common examples of such potential vulnerabilities might include:

- the defendant's failure to testify

- the criminal defendant's past criminal conviction or so-called "prior bad acts"

- the alleged bias of the prosecution's main witness who is testifying in exchange for reduced jail time or other leniency

- the defendant's status as a corporation

- backlash against the defendant's business—insurance (including HMOs), tobacco, guns, pharmaceutical drug manufacturers, and so on

- the plaintiff's pursuit of a large amount of monetary damages for her injuries

By way of example, corporate defendants must address their status during *voir dire* and must deal with the preconceptions of prospective jurors that the defendant is entitled to less protection or consideration simply because it is a corporation. This "David/Goliath" perception is always a concern to the Goliaths. Consequently, the corporate defendant's lawyer should seek a commitment from each juror that they will accord the corporation the same care and concern as the plaintiff. Just as defendants must be concerned about potential backlash against them simply because of the nature of their business, so must civil plaintiffs, at least in personal injury cases, be concerned about backlash against them for greedily seeking money for their injuries. This concern may be more pronounced now than ever before, in light of ongoing tort reform efforts and some sentiment that personal injury litigation is akin to the lottery. Those perceptions must be addressed.

In criminal cases, concerns about the jury's commitment to the presumption of innocence (particularly if the defendant does not testify) or its willingness to seriously consider the defendant's case once it learns he is a convicted felon, also require time and attention during *voir dire*. Each prospective juror should be asked for a commitment to reserve judgment until they hear the defendant's case, to resist the urge to convict him for his prior mistakes or for not testifying in his defense in this case.

A commitment from each prospective juror on these issues is critical because it creates a bond between the advocate and the prospective jurors, one that the advocate can fully exploit during his closing argument by reminding the jurors that they made it and by demonstrating to the jurors why the commitment should be kept in light of the facts of the case. The following examples illustrate phase three questioning.

1. *Why Discuss Damages if There is No Liability?*

Defense counsel in civil cases face a dilemma concerning whether they should address damages when they believe there is no liability. Should counsel address plaintiff's damages claim even though he fears that in so doing he is at least implicitly conceding liability? If counsel ignores damages in the hope that the jury will find no liability on the part of his client and he is wrong, the plaintiff's damages claim will go unanswered and the results could be catastrophic. Thus, counsel must address damages and the time to begin is in *voir dire*.

 ## Illustration of Preemptive Strike as to Damages

Defense Lawyer:	Mr. Davis (prospective juror), let me address this next concern to you since you have previous experience as a juror in a civil case. As you will recall in that trial, the party bringing the law-suit had to establish two things, first, that the defendant was liable, that he did something wrong, and second, that the plaintiff was injured or damaged. Now, Mr. Davis, let's suppose, just for the sake of argument, that the jurors found that the defendant did nothing wrong, that he was not liable. In that case, there would not be any reason for the jurors to even discuss damages, would there?
Prospective Juror:	I guess that's right. Since he didn't do anything wrong he wouldn't have to pay anything.
Defense Lawyer:	Exactly. Now in this trial we are starting today, the woman I represent, Joan Spano, doesn't believe she was in any way at fault during the car accident and she and I are confident the facts will show that. But we expect opposing counsel to put on evidence showing how badly injured the plaintiff was. Now I expect that we are going to take issue with the extent of his injuries. Mr. Davis, do you believe that if we do put on evidence that the plaintiff wasn't hurt as badly as he claims we are somehow admitting that we were at fault?
Prospective Juror:	I see where you are going. If you did nothing wrong, why worry about damages?
Defense Lawyer:	Well put, Mr. Davis. What do you think?
Prospective Juror:	Based on that other trial in which I was a juror, I would put on whatever evidence you had. I was amazed with how differently people understood the evidence.
Defense Lawyer:	Would you hold it against Mrs. Spano as far as liability goes if I put on evidence showing the plaintiff was not badly hurt?
Prospective Juror:	No, I would just think it's a lawyer doing a thorough job for his client.

---

2. *Where There's Smoke, There's Fire*

Most jurors in criminal cases, whether they are willing to admit it or not, are prone to believe that just because the accused has been arrested and charged, he must be guilty of *something*. The defense attorney should confront the jurors with this prevalent belief and attempt to dispel its validity.

 ## Illustration of Eliciting Juror's Attitude Concerning Bias Based on the Fact of Defendant's Arrest

Defense Lawyer: Mrs. Klein (prospective juror), do you think that because a person has been arrested and charged with a crime he most likely did that crime?

Prospective Juror: I know I'm not supposed to think that, but I guess being perfectly honest, I do think there must be something to it.

Defense Lawyer: I appreciate your candor, Mrs. Klein. I think deep down most people would agree with your feelings. But what we have to recognize this morning is that if you are selected as a juror in this case you will take an oath to follow the law. And one of the most fundamental laws you will be given is that the defendant is presumed innocent. That means regardless of the fact that he has been charged with a crime, you are to begin the trial believing that he is innocent. The notion that a person is presumed innocent until proven guilty is not just high-sounding language, but rather a real and viable concept that we need to confront here and now. Will you be able to follow the law?

Prospective Juror: Yes, I believe that I will be able to do so.

Defense Lawyer: Just to take things a step further. If you had to render a verdict now with no evidence being presented either way, would you agree that your verdict must be "not guilty"?

Prospective Juror: I understand your point. I would have to find "not guilty" because he is presumed innocent.

---

3. *"If He Didn't Do It, Why Won't He Take the Witness Stand and Tell Us?"*

Another difficult concept for jurors to understand is the criminal defendant's right not to testify. If the defense attorney does not intend to put the defendant on the stand, or is undecided whether he will do so, he must make the choice of whether to discuss this with the jury during *voir dire*. He can decide not to mention it at all and hope that the jury does not draw a negative conclusion, or he can confront the issue and explain the principle behind a defendant's Fifth Amendment right, hoping that this explanation will somewhat mitigate the negative impact.

These, of course, are strategy decisions that must be viewed in light of the whole case.

 ## Illustration of Dealing with Presumption of Guilt if Criminal Defendant Does Not Testify

Defense Lawyer: When our forefathers drafted the American Bill of Rights they held that a person accused of a crime had a fundamental right not to testify. It is one hundred percent the duty and responsibility of the state to come forward and independently establish whether a crime has been committed by the accused. Mr. Peterson (the defendant) has that fundamental right just as you and I do. And should he claim the same privilege that is available to all of us, the judge is going to tell you that that's okay. That's his right. Mrs. Wright (prospective juror), do you understand that Mr. Peterson has the right to not testify?

Prospective Juror: I do.

Defense Lawyer: If for whatever reason he exercises that right and does not testify will you hold that against him?

Prospective Juror: Well, I guess I would like to hear what he has to say about things.

Defense Lawyer: I appreciate your candor and your curiosity. However, there are bigger concerns, such as his constitutional right not to testify. Will you be able to respect that?

Prospective Juror: Yes, I will.

---

4. *Reasonable Doubt is Not Proof Beyond All Doubt*

Jurors struggle to understand the burden of proof in criminal cases. The concept of reasonable doubt is understood by many jurors to be "beyond a shadow of a doubt" or simply "beyond all doubt." Failing to distinguish these preconceptions from the true legal standard could prove fatal to the prosecution's case.

There are several techniques the prosecutor may employ to dispel such misconceptions. One technique is to tell the jury that they will probably hear two different versions of how the alleged crime took place—the prosecution's side and then the defense's side. It must be stressed that the mere existence of two sides does not create reasonable doubt. The jurors must evaluate each version. Another technique is to simply discuss in straightforward terms what the "reasonable" in reasonable doubt means.

Illustration of Dealing with Reasonable Doubt from the Prosecutor's Perspective

Prosecutor: Ladies and gentlemen, the People have the burden of proving the defendant's guilt beyond a reasonable doubt and to an abiding conviction. That is the level of proof that I carry. The key word in that definition is reasonable. I do not need to prove my case beyond a doubt, or beyond all doubt, or beyond a shadow of a doubt. The defendant is guilty if the case is proven beyond a reasonable doubt. Mr. Marks (prospective juror), do you have any quarrel with that? Would you be able to follow the law concerning that level of proof?

Prospective Juror: I never really understood that before. I always thought it was beyond a shadow of doubt.

Prosecutor: That's a common misunderstanding. So you now appreciate that simply because the defense offers some other explanation for what happened, the defendant's explanation must be reasonable to you.

Prospective Juror: I understand what you are saying.

Prosecutor: So now that you have a clearer understanding of my burden, will you be able to follow that law?

Prospective Juror: Of course I will.

V.   PRINCIPLES OF *VOIR DIRE* QUESTIONING

❖ Principle Number One: Reduce Barriers

A common complaint among former jurors is that the lawyers seemed more interested in recording the jurors' responses than in listening to those responses. The attorney who stands at a podium buried behind a legal pad, writing down detailed responses to questions, is missing a significant opportunity to establish a positive relationship with the jury and to see the all-important non-verbal answers from the prospective jurors. Recalling specific answers is important, however, it should not supplant the development of a positive relationship with the jury.

> **PRINCIPLES OF *VOIR DIRE* QUESTIONING**
> ❖ Reduce Barriers
> ❖ Ask Open-Ended Questions
> ❖ Facilitate a Group Discussion
> ❖ Focus First on One; Then the Group
> ❖ Avoid "Blue Sky" Questions
> ❖ Disclosure Begets Disclosure
> ❖ Raise Material Weaknesses
> ❖ Avoid Excluding or Embarrassing Anyone
> ❖ Ask the Global, Catch-all Question Last

Podiums, legal pads, and note cards stand as barriers between the advocate and the prospective jurors. Unless the judge demands the use of the podium, advocates should move to the front of jury box, and stand before the prospective jurors as they engage them at *voir dire*.

Some courts refer to jurors by number, while others refer to each juror by name. If the court uses names, commit the names of the prospective jurors to memory. If the *voir dire* questioning includes thirty or more prospective jurors at once, it may be impossible to do so, of course. However, if only six or twelve jurors are questioned at a time, advocates should be capable of memorizing the names on a short-term basis. In addition, counsel should limit, to the extent possible, reliance on notes during *voir dire*. One means of doing so is to ensure that a colleague or legal assistant sits through *voir dire* with the examining lawyers. *Voir dire* requires at least two people such that one person can make notes of the specific responses of the prospective jurors while the other actually asks the questions and focuses on developing a positive rapport with jurors. Without the hindrance of notes and with the jurors names in mind, the questioning will be more natural and the prospective jurors will be more comfortable and more likely to open up and provide complete and candid responses. Additionally, referring to jurors by names without benefit of notes helps personalize the process and lays the foundation for a positive juror-advocate relationship.

❖ Principle Number Two: Ask Open-Ended Questions

An indicator of the success or lack of success at *voir dire* is the amount of time the lawyer talks compared to the amount of time the prospective jurors talk. Long questions that draw monosyllabic responses are not helpful in getting a sense of who the prospective jurors are and how they might react to the advocate's client, her side of events, or to specific testimony. Rather, it is vital that the prospective jurors provide explanatory answers. Questions that permit, or encourage, explanation and questions directed to juror attitudes, will produce responses that enable the advocate to intelligently exercise challenges. Questions asking "why?" or "how do you feel about that?" or "could you please explain what you mean?," encourage the prospective jurors to provide in depth answers.

 ### Illustration of Open-Ended Questioning

Lawyer: As you have no doubt figured out, the defendant is the medical doctor who treated Mr. Carroll. And since a doctor is involved it is necessary that we ask you some questions about relationships you have or have had with doctors. Mrs. Conners (prospective juror), are you currently under treatment by a doctor?

Prospective Juror: Yes, I am.

Lawyer: Without prying into your personal affairs, Mrs. Connors, how would you describe the relationship you have with your doctor?

Prospective Juror: I think he's doing a good job. I'm satisfied with him.

Lawyer: Mrs. Connors, what is it about him that leads to your conclusion?

This last question probes the details of the relationship. It provides an opportunity for the prospective juror to fully discuss her relationship with her doctor. If the advocate had left off with the prospective jurors initial response ("I'm satisfied with him."), she would not have gotten a true sense of this prospective juror's feelings about her doctor and doctors in general. Create an opportunity for the prospective jurors to be expansive.

❖ Principle Number Three: Facilitate a Group Discussion

Encourage an atmosphere in which everyone feels free to contribute. Masters of the art of *voir dire* are able to prime the pump; once they get a response from one juror they are able to build on it and bring others into the discussion. Such a free-wheeling exchange of views on issues relevant to the trial is more apt to produce fruitful information.

Illustration of Questioning that Facilitates a Group Discussion

Lawyer: Mrs. Rich (prospective juror), we are going to hear testimony that Mr. Roberts received extensive medical treatment from a number of doctors. In fact, we are going to hear from several doctors during this trial, and I think it is important to get a sense from you as to how you view doctors. For instance, would you be more likely to trust a person simply because he or she is a doctor?

Juror Rich: I have a lot of respect for doctors. I probably would tend to trust them more than other people.

Lawyer: Why is that?

Juror Rich: Doctors are special, they know what is good for us. I trust them with my health so I guess I would trust what they would say while testifying.

Lawyer: Thank you Mrs. Rich. Mr. King (prospective juror), do you agree with Mrs. Rich? Would you tend to trust doctors more?

Juror King: Of course not. They are just like everyone else only looking out for themselves.

Lawyer: Why do you say that?

Once the lawyer has initiated the discussion with one prospective juror he can bring others into the discussion in a more spontaneous way that truly facilitates a free flow of information.

❖ Principle Number Four: Focus First on One, Then the Group

Most people in a group setting would prefer to maintain a low profile. The old army adage that you should never volunteer for anything represents the feelings of most prospective jurors. If a question is asked generally of the entire group, there very well may be an uncomfortable silence. The advocate must either move on to another question or single out one of the reluctant jurors. The "selected" juror by her initial silence has already indicated her diffidence to the question, yet now she is forced to give a response against her will. It is usually preferable to direct a question to a particular juror first and then, following her response, expand the inquiry to the group as a whole. Again, once the "pump is primed" people are more inclined to join in.

❖ Principle Number Five: Avoid "Blue Sky" Questions

The relevance of every question during *voir dire* should be immediately apparent to the prospective jurors. A question eliciting information that is unrelated to the facts, at least as the jurors understand them, will be viewed with confusion at the least, or suspicion and distrust at the worst. This is especially true for questions that probe into personal or sensitive areas. The jurors first must be told of the need to make the inquiry. Advocates should selectively leak out sufficient facts so that the prospective jurors understand the reason for the questions. No question should just come out of the "blue."

For instance, in the trial of a woman accused of murdering her husband, defense counsel may broach the subject of domestic violence. From the lawyer's prospective, because she is aware of instances of domestic violence by the decedent, the subject demands discussion. But if the prospective jurors are unaware of those facts, inquiry into this subject will come as a complete surprise. Prospective jurors may well become suspicious of the questioner, or concerned that they are being manipulated. The defense counsel in that instance would be better served by first explaining the reason for inquiring into the subject of domestic violence.

 Illustration for Giving Context to the Line of Questioning

Lawyer: Ladies and Gentlemen, now that we have gotten a sense of your backgrounds I want to inquire into some of your life experiences as they relate to issues in this case. One of those issues will be domestic violence. Mrs. Whitaker is going to take the stand and testify that she was a victim of domestic violence at the hands of her husband. So you can see that we need to discuss this issue and how any experiences you or your family members or friends might have had would affect how you view such testimony. Now Mrs. Seaver, just to get the discussion started, do you have any family members or close friends who have been affected by domestic violence?

❖ Principle Number Six: Disclosure Begets Disclosure

Every trial involves sensitive issues and areas that require inquiry, whether it involves probing for prior criminal contacts in a criminal case, or sensitive financial matters in a civil case. And, typically, prospective jurors are reluctant to discuss such matters. Nonetheless this is information trial lawyers need. Prior to probing into difficult areas it is helpful for the advocate to make some kind of disclosure so that prospective jurors will feel less vulnerable when they are asked to do so. First the advocate "opens up" and discloses something personal about himself and how his experience effected his subsequent views on the topic under discussion, and then the jurors are more willing to reciprocate and "open up" about matters they ordinarily would be unwilling to discuss. For instance, it is important that a prosecutor know if any prospective jurors have criminal backgrounds. That information is not typically forthcoming. And an advocate bold enough to come right out and ask, "have any of you been arrested or convicted?" is most likely to be met with stony silence. A preferable approach is set forth in Section IV, B, 1 of this chapter.

In seeking such sensitive information it may be best to lay the question out to the entire panel instead of directing it to a particular juror. This may be the exception to the rule of focusing first on one juror and then expanding the discussion to the whole (see Principle Four). The concern is that by focusing the inquiry on a particular juror, that juror may feel that the advocate is somehow singling her out or even accusing her. It is certainly preferable to have a "volunteer" step up. Once that first juror does so, be certain to thank her and acknowledge how difficult and important the disclosure was.

❖ Principle Number Seven: Raise Material Weaknesses

Every trial lawyer in every trial will be confronted with problem areas or weaknesses. Perfect cases do not go to trial. The true measure of effective advocacy is the ability to overcome the problems and present a compelling and winnable case despite the problems. The greater the problem, the greater the need for effective advocacy.

Problems may surface in many areas. Some are obvious, such as a criminal defense attorney confronted with her client's previous conviction, or a plaintiff's counsel whose client made damaging admissions at the scene of the accident. Some problems are more subtle, such as a loss of memory by a significant witness or use of an expert witness who always testifies on behalf of corporate defendants. While the problems will vary from case to case, the need to disclose them to the jury will be a constant.

Mitigating or integrating weaknesses is a task that runs the length and breadth of the trial. It is not relegated to closing argument or even direct examination, but must be raised during jury selection and then shaped throughout the balance of the trial. There are significant credibility enhancing advantages to be gained by disclosing weakness early. It enables the advocate to control how the problem will be initially perceived and, more importantly, to gain credibility for making the disclosure.

Throughout this chapter we have emphasized the power of first impressions and how those first impressions will largely dictate the client-juror relationships and advocate-juror relationships throughout the trial. An advocate who takes the opportunity to be candid with the jurors and to disclose problems to them will most likely be viewed as someone who can be trusted throughout the trial. An advocate who fails to disclose runs the risk that the jurors will feel misled as to the particular problem and, more significantly, will view the advocate's efforts throughout the trial with suspicion and distrust.

Another significant advantage of first disclosure is that the disclosing advocate has the opportunity to place the weakness in the context of the entire trial, thus mitigating some of its harmful impact. If the advocate does not take the initiative and disclose a weakness before the other party has the opportunity to do so, the advocate is ceding control of the "problem area" to opposing counsel, allowing her to characterize and exploit the weaknesses to her full advantage.

Not every weakness merits disclosure during jury selection. Rather, *voir dire* disclosure should be limited to weaknesses significant enough to draw attention during opposing counsel's cross-examination or closing argument.

 ## Illustration of "Pricking the Boil"

Plaintiff's Lawyer: Mr. Fenwick (prospective juror), you are going to hear testimony from Mr. Cochran (the plaintiff) that he apologized to the defendant at the scene of the accident. Many of us would view an apology as an admission of fault, but you are going to also hear from Mr. Cochran that he wasn't admitting any fault on his part but rather that he just felt bad about the accident. Would you be able to listen carefully to Mr. Cochran's whole testimony, including his reasons for saying what he did?

Prospective Juror: I would listen to his testimony carefully. But it does sound odd if he wasn't in the wrong that he would apologize.

Plaintiff's Lawyer: I appreciate your concern. Would you agree with me that during stressful events, sometimes people do and say things without reflection and sometimes may not even be fully aware of the significance of their words?

Prospective Juror: I would have to hear what he has to say.

Plaintiff's Lawyer: Fair enough, sir. I appreciate your candor.

❖ Principle Number Eight: Avoid Excluding or Embarrassing Anyone

As the advocate questions the prospective jurors during *voir dire*, she should be careful to involve all of the prospective jurors. Some advocates will systematically work through the jurors in the order in which they are seated. Using this approach ensures that no one will be forgotten. Other advocates prefer to question jurors based on considerations such as commonality of backgrounds or interests, or even based on previous answers. Regardless of the approach, recognize that a juror who has been overlooked will feel excluded and very probably will resent the exclusion. No one likes to be left out and the lawyer who is responsible for the exclusion may pay for the omission.

Additionally, advocates must be careful not to inadvertently antagonize or embarrass anyone. This can happen innocently enough. For instance, the questioner may ask, "What college did you attend?" Someone who did not attend college may be embarrassed or even offended by such an inquiry. Or, on ascertaining that a woman does not have job outside the house, the questioner may comment, "So, you don't work?" Such a comment may well draw ire not only from that juror but also from others as well. Additionally, be careful of creating an intellectual gap between you and any of the prospective jurors. Occasionally jurors will have trouble understanding an important concept. It is important to be patient and courteous in further explaining that concept. Advocates must strive to talk to the jurors, as equals, without speaking either above them and creating an intellectual gap or below them and thus being condescending. Be courteous and thoughtful throughout the questioning. If you have inadvertently embarrassed someone, sincerely and promptly apologize.

❖ Principle Number Nine: Ask the Global, Catch-all Question Last

The worst nightmare for any advocate is to fail to elicit a critical piece of information about a prospective juror; information that affects the juror's fitness to serve. There is no way to make certain that every possible area is covered by specific questions and even if there was, there is not sufficient time allotted to ask them all. Accordingly, advocates should end their *voir dire* with a broadly phrased, open-ended question that invites the jurors to share anything about themselves that they believe may be of importance in their ability to serve as a juror.

Illustration of Closing Question

Lawyer: Before I sit down, I have just one final question: As you have lis-
                        tened today and answered the questions that have been asked,
                        has anything come to mind to cause you to doubt in any way that
                        you could serve as a fair and impartial juror in this trial? Anyone?
                        Seeing no acknowledgments, I thank you for your kind attention
                        and your thoughtful responses to my questions.

VI.   OBJECTIONS AND OBJECTION STRATEGY AT *VOIR DIRE*

As long as advocates are permitted to inquire of the prospective jurors they will attempt to indoctrinate the jurors to their view of events. There is often a fine line between proper questioning and improperly attempting to predispose the jurors to a favorable view of the case. Most of the objections that can be lodged during *voir dire* focus on this point.

A.   Asking the Jury to Prejudge the Evidence

Counsel cannot ask the jury to prejudge the evidence. For example, it is improper to ask a member of the venire in a murder case what weight they would give to the fact that the murder weapon was registered to the defendant. This is not the same as asking jurors whether certain evidence will make them unable to provide an impartial verdict, which could possibly lead to a peremptory challenge or challenge for cause. Obtaining commitments from the jury that they will give credence to a certain piece of evidence or testimony is also improper. Note that this differs from obtaining a commitment from the jury that they will not hold something against a party or will not find against a party solely based on one fact or event. An example of improperly asking the jury to prejudge the evidence would arise if a plaintiff's attorney asked: "If it turns out that the plaintiff had been speeding when he was hit by the defendant would you find that to be unsafe or negligent behavior that would prevent you from allowing the plaintiff to recover any damages?"

B.   Arguing the Law or Facts; Attempting to Indoctrinate the Jurors on the Law

Arguing the law or facts during *voir dire* is a second potential objection. While it is necessary and appropriate for counsel to impart some case facts to the jury, giving specific facts meant to precondition jurors to vote a certain way is improper. It is always improper to use *voir dire* to argue the facts of the case. For instance, it would be improper for defense counsel in a negligence suit to ask, "Since the plaintiff clearly placed himself in peril by running the red light, could you in good faith find against Mrs. Smith when it was the plaintiff who acted so unreasonably?" It is also impermissible to instruct the jury on matters of the law, such as the elements of a claim or defense. The judge will do this at trial. It *is* proper to ask whether jurors will follow the jury instructions even if they do not agree with the law. Thus, it is proper to ask if a juror would have difficulty imposing the death penalty in a murder case.

C. Asking a Question That is Not Related to an Intelligent Exercise of a Peremptory Challenge or Challenge for Cause

Attorneys must ensure that their questioning during *voir dire* is relevant to the case and helpful in the exercise of challenges. A question such as "Did you know the defendant owns forty Italian suits?" is inappropriate if the case has nothing to do with those suits. One way to make sure the questioning is relevant is to ask whether the question is related to an intelligent exercise of a challenge for cause or peremptory challenge. The question above is meant only to spark jealousy against the defendant. A positive or negative answer to that question would not be sufficient to sustain a challenge for cause.

D. Introducing Prejudicial or Inflammatory Material

It is impermissible to introduce inadmissible evidence or inflammatory material about a party or counsel during *voir dire*. This follows the general rule that the purpose of *voir dire* is not to prejudice the jury in favor of or against a particular party. For example, evidence that the civil defendant has liability insurance or evidence that a party entered into a settlement is usually not admissible in evidence, and thus, is not permissible during *voir dire*.

E. Excluding Prospective Jurors Based on Race or Gender

By definition, a peremptory challenge is a challenge made for any reason or no reason at all, and historically, advocates have had almost unfettered discretion in exercising peremptory challenges. However, in *Batson v. Kentucky*[8] and *J.E.B. v. Alabama*,[9] the United States Supreme Court held that advocates violate the Equal Protection Clause when advocates base their challenges on the prospective jurors' race or gender. For example, in a criminal case, the prosecutor, perhaps concerned that jurors of the same ethnicity may be particularly sensitive to the defendant and thus view his defense more favorably than others, may attempt to exclude

---

[8] 476 U.S. 79 (1986).

[9] 511 U.S. 127 (1994).

such persons. Any such attempt may constitute the so-called *"Batson* error" and should draw immediate objection.

 Illustration of a *Batson* Objection

Prosecutor:	Your Honor, at this time the People would like to ask the court to thank and excuse Mr. Adbul, juror Number Five. [*turning to Mr. Abdul*] Mr. Adbul, thank you for your time and service, sir.
Defense Lawyer:	Your Honor, may we approach?
Court:	Come forward.

[Discussion at sidebar.]

Defense Lawyer:	Your Honor, Mr. Adbul is the second Arab-American the prosecutor has excluded. I fear there is no reason for excluding Mr. Adbul other than that he is of the same ethnicity as the defendant.
Prosecutor:	Mr. Adbul was excluded only because during questioning it was brought out that he was convicted of assault four years ago. And as he said when questioned about that incident, he felt unjustly accused and continues to harbor ill will toward the police. As a result, I do not believe he will be able to fairly evaluate the police officer testimony that will constitute a significant portion of my case.
Defense Lawyer:	I would not characterize Mr. Adbul's answers as indicating any ill will toward the police. He did say that he felt he was not treated fairly, but at no point did he indicate any hostility to the police. Your Honor, I believe the prosecutor is attempting to exclude Arab-Americans from this jury and is attempting to conjure up some thin facade to cover his actions.

Once a prima facie showing of systematic exclusion based on race or gender has been made, it is incumbent on the advocate whose actions are being challenged to provide a race or gender-neutral reason for his peremptory strike. The judge then must decide the legitimacy of the reasons given for the challenge. *Batson* challenges in federal courts focus on race and gender; however, a number of state courts have expanded the classes of individuals subject to these challenges.

F.   Challenging the Systematic Exclusion of Identifiable Groups from Jury Service

The final possible objection during jury selection is actually a challenge to the method by which prospective jurors are initially identified and selected for jury service by the applicable governmental body. Federal law, for example, provides that "litigants ... entitled to trial by jury shall have the right to ... juries selected at random from a fair cross section of the community." (28 U.S.C. §1861.) If the process denies a party to the suit his right to a fairly representative pool of jurors, the party can object to the entire pool, and, if successful, obtain the dismissal of the prospective jurors in favor of a more representative one. The challenge must be supported by evidence of the under inclusion of a particular, identifiable group.

Chapter Five

OPENING STATEMENT

I. OVERVIEW AND PURPOSE

The opening statement is critically important because it is the advocate's first opportunity to tell the full and complete story of the case—to humanize the client, to detail the evidence, to convey the party's theme. This irreplaceable first opportunity to persuade the jury merits careful preparation and confident execution.

Consider for a moment the scene in the courtroom when the advocate rises to begin the opening statement: After some period of questioning of the prospective jurors about their likes and dislikes, their experiences and attitudes, the jurors have been empanelled. They have been given some generalities about the case, briefly introduced to the parties and lawyers, told by the judge about the seriousness of their task, and have taken an oath to decide the case impartially. They are ready, more ready than they will ever be again, to hear from the parties about the case and to begin their service as jurors.

From the first moment that the jurors see the parties and their lawyers they begin forming all kinds of impressions about them based on their appearance, body language, demeanor, and many other visual clues. Through the *voir dire* process, the jurors develop impressions about the lawyers' personalities and their presentation styles. However, the opening statement is the first chance for the jurors to begin forming opinions about the merits of the dispute. Human nature dictates that jurors will not stay neutral about the disputed issues any longer than they must. From the beginning of the trial, the jurors are deciding whom they can trust and whom they cannot, who is in the right and who is in the wrong.

Those initial impressions quickly harden into fixed judgments, judgments that are extremely difficult to soften and nearly impossible to change. The axiom that a juror's first impressions "harden like cement" is the reality for trial lawyers. Conventional wisdom among lawyers is that as many as eighty percent of jurors align themselves with one side or the other after the opening statement, and do not shift their loyalty thereafter.[1] Although the validity of the eighty percent statistic is somewhat doubtful, the larger point is undisputed. The psychological principle of primacy makes the opening statement's position at the beginning of the trial of first importance. The opening statement colors each juror's impression of the facts and heavily influences how the jurors view the information they learn later in the trial. Such an opportunity comes only once during the trial and must be seized and exploited to its full potential.

Accordingly, the advocate's primary objective during the opening is to gain the allegiance of the jurors. To accomplish that objective, advocates must pursue a number of specific goals during the opening statement. They must:

- introduce the central theme

- humanize their client

- tell a coherent and compelling story about why their client should prevail

- disclose and defuse case weaknesses

- anticipate and deflect the opponent's arguments

- develop a rapport with the jury

---

[1] *See* Michael F. Colley, *The Opening Statement: Structure, Issues, Techniques,* TRIAL, Nov. 1982, at 54 (citing H. KALVEN & H. ZEISEL, THE AMERICAN JURY (1966).

A.   Of Roadmaps and Jigsaw Puzzles

The classic description of the opening statement by lawyers is that it is a "roadmap." In fact, many lawyers begin their opening statements with just such an analogy: "The opening statement is like a roadmap. It provides you with an overview of the evidence in the case so that you will better appreciate 'where you are' when the various witnesses testify." The roadmap analogy has given way to myriad others, including: the opening statement is like a movie preview that is shown before a feature film, the picture on a jigsaw puzzle box, or a birds-eye view of the evidence. These analogies are accurate, and they may be helpful to lawyers in reminding them of the role of the opening statement. However, they work against effective advocacy because they suggest that the opening statement is merely preliminary, a prelude to the important stuff that is yet to come. Good advocacy dictates that advocates never minimize their own words and the shopworn "roadmap" analogy does just that.

Thus, the lawyer who seeks to use the opening statement as a tool of persuasion should avoid such tiresome descriptions of the opening. After all, why describe what the advocate is doing at all? Better to just do it. Tell the story. Humanize the client. Connect with the jury. Announce the theme. If you are successful, the jury will decide that above anything else the opening statement is a helpful tool in putting the evidence and parties into proper context and providing a means of understanding how the evidence fits into one coherent story.

B.   The Prohibition on Argument

There remains, however, one substantial obstacle to the use of the opening statement as a tool of persuasion. That obstacle is the rule against argument, which constitutes the primary limit on what the advocate can say during the opening statement. The rule purports to preclude the lawyer from "arguing" during the opening statement. Yet, this "rule," though often cited by lawyers and judges, is ill-defined and poorly understood. To complicate things further, actual application of the rule against argument varies from jurisdiction to jurisdiction, and even from judge to judge. The only thing that is truly uniform is the fact that all lawyers argue to some degree in their opening statements. It is almost unavoidable.

The reason for mentioning the rule against argument at this point is contextual. Later in this chapter we discuss in depth the prohibition against argument in the opening statement. The rule lurks around the dark corners of every opening statement, threatening to interrupt the opening with an objection from opposing counsel or an admonition from the judge. The rule and the uncertainty of its application cause lawyers untold moments of anxiety and, at least in theory, limit the extent to which the opening statement can be converted into simply another chance to argue the case. The rule against argument creates an intractable tension for advocates in making their opening statements. On the one hand, advocates know that they must make an indelible impression on the fact finder by telling their story fully and persuasively, but on the other hand, they must also adhere to the rules of procedure by avoiding "argument." Successfully navigating that tension is the challenge confronting every advocate at opening statement.

II. PREPARING THE OPENING STATEMENT

The tendency to lose interest is strongest when jurors do not understand the relevancy of what the advocate is saying. The advocate can make the relevance of their statements clear, and keep the interest of the jurors, by constructing a solid framework for her opening statement. The preparation of the opening statement should begin long before the trial itself begins. In fact, the preparation of the opening statement is an ongoing process during the discovery phase of a case. As the facts become known, as the witnesses are interviewed and deposed, as the contentions of the opposing side are revealed and specified, and as the case theme is developed, the content and structure of the opening statement should be constantly and carefully drafted and redrafted by the advocate. The content of the opening should be prudently thought through well in advance of trial, not haphazardly tossed together the night before it is to be made. Advocates must review the entire case file—every witness statement, all of the deposition testimony, each expert report, the entire universe of produced documents, and so on—to ensure that they have a complete grasp of all the facts of the case. And they must focus on their goals and objectives for the opening statement. That important part of the preparation process requires some consideration of several dangerous misconceptions of the opening statement that advocates must avoid.

A. The Opening Statement Is Not ...

The opening statement is not the time to provide jurors a procedural overview of the trial. One of the authors of this book once observed a lawyer deliver an extraordinarily short opening statement, less than two minutes, which consisted of nothing more than the following: "Ladies and gentlemen, this is the opening statement. It is my chance to tell you about the case, to give you a roadmap of the trial. After I sit down, Mr. Smith will get up and have a chance to talk to you. Then I will call several witnesses, starting with Ms. Jones. She will tell you about what she saw at the intersection on May 1, 1998. Then I will call ..." What a wasted opportunity! The lawyer forfeited an irreplaceable opportunity to connect with the jury.

The opening statement is also not the time to give the jury a mere recounting of the facts in the case. Because of the rule against argument, some advocates maintain this kind of minimalist notion of the opening, believing that it serves as nothing more than a time to acquaint the jurors with the key facts, but not the time to give those facts context or to persuade the jury of the correctness of the party's view of those facts. The result is a mind-numbing recitation of facts, certain to leave the jurors scratching their heads. The pay-off with the jury from this approach is equal to the effort invested; it does nothing to cause the jurors to align themselves with the advocate's client.

Finally, the opening statement is not the time to transform into a professor of political science or to quote from Cicero about the importance of truth or to tell a story involving Abraham Lincoln about the critical role of juries in a democracy. There may well be a time for such civic-mindedness during the trial (although it is doubtful), but the opening statement is surely not the place for such efforts. The jurors are poised to hear about the people they see before them, to learn who did what to whom, and to decide who is in the right and who is not. The sooner advocates satisfy each juror's longing to know and to understand, the better off they will be.

B.   Development of a Theme

Of course, the right way to plan an opening statement is the same as the right way to plan a direct examination or a cross-examination or a closing argument. The first step is to have a clear and understandable central theme. The theme must connect with the jurors' common experiences and synthesize the advocate's case into one or two statements.

An effective theme connects the facts with the "human" element of the case. Without fail, every case, regardless of how dry the facts may appear, has a human element to it—broken promises, a life cut short, a party motivated by greed, a corporation putting profits ahead of people, a defendant attempting to avoid responsibility for a wrong, a plaintiff searching for someone to blame (in all the wrong places). Invocation of the human element causes the story to resonate with the all-too-human fact finders and makes the case seem larger than the facts themselves.

C.   Preparing to Tell the Story

The opening statement is an exercise in storytelling, and constructing the story of the case is, in essence, an exercise in constructing an argument. The advocate must mentally envision the evidence as it will come before the trier of fact—the direct and cross-examination of each witness, exhibits that will be introduced, and arguments that will be made. Who will the jury believe? What evidence will the jury trust? The answers to those questions will dictate the contours of the story the lawyer will tell; the lawyer must not rely on facts or exhibits that the jury will likely mistrust and must explain those weaknesses in the case that might cause the jury to question the party's claims or defenses.

Once advocates sift through the evidence and analyze the legal requirements, they must actually construct their client's stories. Every client has a story to tell no matter their status in the case, whether plaintiff or defendant, the state or the accused, the individual or the corporation, the wronged or the alleged wrongdoer. Telling the client's story during the opening makes sense for a number of reasons. Perhaps most significantly,

> **Tech Tip**
>
> ✓ Use *Powerpoint Storyboard* to sequence visual slides that depict a story in a film-like fashion.
>
> ✓ Add text, audio, pictures and video
>
> ✓ Use common story components
>
> ✓ Utilize the electronic tabbing feature to adjust the flow of the story

social scientists have discovered that jurors construct a story from the case facts with or without the advocate's help.[2] Jurors process the competing facts presented to them during the trial as a story and make every effort to fit both side's versions of the facts into their "story." The fact that juries tend to learn and understand the case in story form anyway mandates that the advocate take on the role of storyteller.

Perhaps the more obvious reason for turning the opening statement into a narrative is that everyone loves a good story. The "story" will arouse the jury's interest, and in doing so, will enhance the jury's retention of the material. The jury's familiarity with stories provides a basic framework for revealing the facts in the case. For example, good stories always have conflict between the characters or between characters and nature or circumstances, and some resolution of the conflict. You can count on heroes and villains, suspense and tragedy, good overcoming evil. Effective advocates recognize this reality and tell the stories in their cases using the same themes: courageous heroes, greedy, cowardly, or uncaring villains, the triumph of good over evil, the abuse of power, the fall of the mighty, and so on.

Good stories share not only certain themes, but also a similar structure. They introduce listeners to the important characters, show them the development and consequence of the conflict, and then point them toward the resolution. The advocate's story should do the same. The question at the end of the preparation process is whether the opening statement conveys the party's case in powerful and compelling terms and gives the jury clear and understandable reasons why the jury should align itself with that party. If the opening statement successfully accomplishes those goals, then the advocate has an excellent start toward ultimate success.

III. CONTENT OF THE OPENING STATEMENT

The content of the opening statement depends upon a multitude of variables, including the nature of the case, the contentions of the parties, the disputed issues, and whether the advocate is going first or second. There is no secret formula or a one-size-fits-all approach for successful opening statements. However, there are certain common elements found in good opening statements and a general structure that good opening statements often share. For example, consistent with the principles of primacy and recency, the opening statement should begin strong and end strong and weaknesses should be disclosed somewhere in the middle. Of course, that frequently delivered piece of advice does not really help much. What

---

[2] *See* Nancy Pennington & Reid Hastie, *The Story Model for Juror Decision Making*, in INSIDE THE JUROR: THE PSYCHOLOGY OF JUROR DECISION MAKING 192, 194 & 217 (R. Hastie, ed., 1993).

does it mean to start strong? How does one disclose a weakness? This section explores the structure and content of an effective opening statement, followed by seven principles that are essential for delivery of a persuasive opening statement.

A.   The Importance of Language

The first challenge of the opening statement, and the most important one, consists of choosing the words the advocate will speak; for those words are the advocate's primary tool of persuasion. And, of course, it is quite possible to describe the same event in starkly contrasting ways—with words that are interesting and active or with words that are dull and passive. The difference between "hit" and "smash" or between "fired" and "let go" are obvious. Even something as simple as introducing the advocate's role in the case can vary dramatically depending on the advocate's word choice. Compare these two radically divergent approaches:

Passive, dull:	I have been retained to represent the defendant in this case.
Active, interesting:	I have the privilege and responsibility of representing Dr. Mary Smith here today.

Words matter. The advocate's choice of words can dramatically impact the jury's level of retention and the extent to which the jury is persuaded by the opening. Choose the active voice whenever possible. Choose words that have a visceral impact on the listener.

Passive, weak:	Ms. Jones was hit by the defendant's car.
Active, strong:	The defendant's car smashed into Ms. Jones.
Passive, weak:	Ms. Jones was let go by the defendant for reporting what she saw.
Active strong:	The defendant fired Ms. Jones for being a whistleblower and reporting the criminal wrongdoing she witnessed.

The opening should also consist of short, simple words that everyone on the jury will easily understand. The trial is not the time or place for advocates to display their linguistic brilliance. Four and five syllable words should be used sparingly, only when no shorter alternative is available. Terms of art should be avoided. Words known to confuse should be eliminated. For example, instead of "willful and wanton," the advocate might speak of the party's "callous lack of concern about the lives of its customers"; instead of "negligent," the advocate might use "careless" or "unreasonable."

The language of the opening statement must also reflect the fact that the opening is a predictive exercise. That is, during the opening the advocate must predict what evidence the jurors will actually hear during the trial and which witnesses will actually testify. As a result, the opening statement must include some predictive words and phrases: "The evidence will show," "You will hear," or something similar. This predictive language is necessary in the opening as a reminder to the jurors that they are not hearing the actual evidence, but only the prediction of counsel about the evidence. But, of course, that is also the potential problem. Those very reminders can serve to soften the impact of the advocate's words and limit their persuasiveness. Thus, predictive phrases should be used sparingly during the opening. For instance, when beginning to tell the story, the prosecutor might say: "The people will prove these facts ..." and then proceed with the story. It is unnecessary and unwise to preface each statement or even each topic with another predictive phrase.

There may be times, however, when the advocate intentionally chooses to use predictive words for the purpose of gaining an advantage with the jury. The words, "I will prove to you," for example, are bold and active words. They provide the advocate a means of creating a bond with the jury by putting the advocate's own credibility on the line, while not violating the rule against personally vouching for witnesses or evidence.[3] The use of "I" or "we" can be particularly effective when put together with the central contention the party must prove in the case. Thus, the advocate might say: "Ladies and gentlemen, I will prove to you that the defendant murdered both Ms. Brown and Mr. Goldman and that he did so in cold blood and after careful planning." This example also demonstrates another beneficial use of predictive terminology. A well placed, "the evidence will show" may cause particularly argumentative statements to sound less argumentative, thus avoiding an objection or, at the least, avoiding an adverse ruling from the court. Upon suffering a sustained objection for being argumentative, the advocate may well fall back at that point to using some predictive phrase.

Finally, the advocate should avoid lapsing into present tense during the opening statement. The facts in the case happened in the past or the case would not be at trial, and they should be discussed in the past tense. The use of present tense, while perhaps appearing to heighten interest by creating the appearance that the events are unfolding even now, gives the opening statement the feel of a sports broadcast, not a formal legal proceeding. And it creates a false impression. The facts are not happening even now. The advocate's ethos demands that she not use the present tense for events that happened in the past.

B.   Hook the Jury

The primacy principle dictates that the first words out of an advocate's mouth should be meaningful and attention getting. As noted above, conventional introductions are a waste of the precious moments at the beginning of the opening. This is no time to remind the jury of the advocate's name; there will be time for that later. It is also no time to explain to the jury what the advocate is doing and why. The judge will likely do that anyway, and if he does not the advocate should not either. The jury will figure it out. The first moments of the opening should grab the attention

---

[3]   *See* 1 HERBERT J. STERN, TRYING CASES TO WIN 22–23, 142–44 (1991).

of the jurors and give them a preview of why they should conclude that the advocate and his client are in the right.

The "grab" may come in many forms: a staccato recitation of the key facts in the case, an announcement of a party's theme, the use of a well known quote, or the emphasis of a key statement by a witness. The advocate might use repetition, dramatic pauses, or voice inflection (or all three) to communicate to the jury the significance of what is being said. For example:

Illustration of Grab by Prosecution in Rape Case[4]

Prosecutor: Ruthless force ... Raw power ... Rape ... About midnight on June 1, 2001, the defendant, [*pointing*] that man(!), broke into the home of Marilyn Miller, stormed into her bedroom, thrust a knife against her neck, ruthlessly held her down, and brutally raped her as she screamed and struggled. The defendant's brutal act, perpetrated against a complete stranger, haunts Ms. Miller every day, every hour, every minute. Today you will see her bravely confront her attacker, the defendant, and through her testimony we will prove beyond a reasonable doubt that the defendant is guilty of the rape of Ms. Miller.

Illustration of Grab by Plaintiff in Defamation Case[5]

Plaintiff's Lawyer: Words are powerful weapons, capable of great destruction. They can maim and destroy and kill. A tongue full of venom and wrath has the power to take away another's honor and good name in a heartbeat. Words like "Adulterous affair!" "Adulterer!" "Immoral activity!" These are the weapons wielded by the defendant against George Bellig, false and baseless allegations of misconduct that have already inflicted great harm and threaten much more. And sadly, as we will prove to you, the defendant made these false allegations not for some noble cause, but out of jealousy and anger.

As illustrated in each example, the "grab" should conclude with the advocate's thesis statement about the case, which tells the jury who should win and why. In a medical malpractice case, the doctor might conclude the grab as follows:

---

[4]   This illustration is based on the hypothetical case *State v. Stone*, James H. Seckinger (4th ed. 1990, National Institute of Trial Advocacy).

[5]   This illustration is based on the hypothetical case *Reiter v. McKyton*, Judge Jerry R. Parker (1995, Texas Young Lawyers Association).

 Illustration of Thesis Statement at Conclusion of Grab[6]

Defense Lawyer: Ladies and gentlemen, I will prove to you that Dr. Madden performed the heart surgery with great care and competence and that the cause of the suture break was a defect in the manufacture of the suture by the defendant corporation and not anything that Dr. Madden did.

At that point, only after the advocate has grabbed the jury's attention, advocates should introduce themselves and their clients. Of course, even in this seemingly mundane matter advocates should prepare what they will say. The introduction of the client should be more than a *pro forma* ritual. The lawyer's words and his actions will tell the jury much about whether the lawyer truly believes in the client's case. Avoid stock phrases or impersonal references. Instead, advocates must communicate to the jury that they are more than mere guns for hire. The advocate stands before the jurors with a great responsibility, yes, but even more so with the privilege of representing another person or entity and with the honor of speaking on their behalf.

C. Personalize the Client

The introduction of the advocate and client should segue seamlessly into the next part of the opening: the personalization of the client. Personalization is critically important in every case, regardless of whether it concerns collection of a debt, recovery of damages for personal injuries, or defense of a criminal charge, and regardless of whether the client is a sympathetic plaintiff, a sinister-looking criminal defendant, or a corporation.

The importance of personalization follows from the nature of juror decision-making. During the course of a trial, jurors must make numerous decisions about who to trust and who not to trust and about who is in the right and who is not in the right. These decisions are based as much on intuition as on cold logic, as much on which party the jury likes as on which party has the better argument. That is not to say that jurors are poor decision-makers or that they are easily manipulated. Rather, it means that they are normal, every day folks, and they tend to believe and trust people with whom they are most familiar. The more we know about a person and his situation, the more we can sympathize with that person and relate to him. These truths, established through years of empirical research,[7] demand that advocates take the time to personalize their clients.

---

[6]   This illustration is based on the hypothetical case *Farrel et al. v. Strong Line, Inc. et al*, Thomas F. Geraghy (1994, National Institute of Trial Advocacy).

[7]   *See, e.g.,* MICHAEL T. NIETZEL & RONALD C. DILLEHAY, PSYCHOLOGICAL CONSULTATION IN THE COURTROOM 136 (1986).

The personalization process should include basic biographical information about the party, such as where the person lives, what the person does for a living, who makes up the person's family, and the like. It should also include case specific information, such as how the person has been affected by the events at issue. Obviously, the nature of the personalization will vary depending on the nature of the case and the status of the party. In a civil case involving an injured plaintiff suing to recover for injuries, the plaintiff presents an inherently sympathetic image, perhaps suggesting that counsel should avoid creating the impression that she is cynically using the injuries to garner sympathy.

 ## Illustration of Personalization of Plaintiff[8]

Plaintiff's Lawyer: The one person who could tell you exactly what happened at that street crossing isn't here in this courtroom and cannot be here because, tragically, she is dead. Kathryn Potter died as a result of that collision and so you will not hear her voice or see her smile or feel her presence. And sadly, that is the void that Jeffrey Potter lives with every day. His wife and best friend, Kathryn, is gone. Just like that. Jeff and others will do their best to tell you about Kathryn. Her electric smile and friendly eyes. Kathryn and Jeff had been married nearly four years when she was taken away. Their life together was something out of a fairy tale. They often joked that their lives seemed charmed. They adored each other and spent every available moment together. They looked forward to having children, to raising a family, to growing old together. Kathryn Potter had just completed her graduate studies and received a hard-earned and much-anticipated Ph.D. in chemistry. She had just started her professional life, obtaining an exciting position with an international pharmaceutical company. She was full of life, full of hope, full of excitement for the future. Jeff Potter's days seem longer now than before, and much sadder. He plows ahead, goes to work, sleeps, eats, worships, and relies on his friends and family. But the void remains, the emptiness is ever-present. Jeff's life will never be the same and that is why Jeff Potter comes before you today.

The corporate defendant, on the other hand, may present an impersonal and unsympathetic image. And yet, the careful selection of a corporate representative can provide wonderful personalization opportunities. Corporate defendants should select a representative who is knowledgeable about the facts, personable, and someone with whom jurors can identify, as opposed to a distant-seeming senior administrator. The advocate should

---

[8] This illustration is based on the hypothetical case *Potter v. Shrackle*, James H. Seckinger and Kenneth S. Broun (4th ed. 1990, National Institute of Trial Advocacy).

personalize the representative first, making the representative embody what is good and noble about his corporate employer. If successful, the jury will see that the company is a community of hard-working people striving for a common purpose. Take, for example, a personal injury case brought against a national petro-chemical refining company for injury to a sub-contractor at one of its refineries. The representative should be someone from the local refinery, not the national risk manager, and should have some knowledge of the events in dispute. Assume that the defendant refining company chose a shift foreman as its representative in the described case, the very foreman who was on duty at the time of the accident. Counsel might personalize the corporation as follows:

 ## Illustration of Personalization of Corporate Defendant

Defense Lawyer: The defendant in this case is not some nameless, faceless conglomerate concerned only with making money at the expense of the safety of its workers. That image, suggested by plaintiff, may feed into people's stereotypes, but it does not match the evidence or the reality in this case. PC Refining is people like Hank Durston, right here. Hard working, productive, reliable, loyal. Hank started working for PC back when it only had one refinery, 35 years ago. He came to work for PC straight out of high school. He started at the bottom of the ladder and through persistence and hard work and commitment he advanced through the ranks until three years ago he became a shift foreman. Hank often says that he's done every job there is to do at a PC refinery, from cleaning bathrooms to hiring and firing workers. Since he started at PC, Hank has married his high school sweetheart, become a father four times over and recently, a grandfather. He's never lived anywhere other than right here; he's never worked anywhere other than at PC. He will tell you about the culture at PC Refining, that it is more like a family than a corporation and that it is a place that puts the safety of its workers first, far above profits or productivity. If it was any other way, Hank Durston wouldn't have stayed for so long.

The prosecution in criminal cases may appear to present unique challenges when it comes to personalization. At first blush it may appear that prosecutors have no client and thus have no one to personalize. But closer examination shows otherwise. In the first place, prosecutors represent the people and should proudly wrap themselves in the glory of being the people's representative in the courtroom. In the second place, prosecutors speak for the victim or victims of the crime and may want to spend the early moments of the opening introducing the jury to the victim.

Illustration of Personalization by Prosecutor

Prosecutor: Ladies and gentlemen, I have the high honor and great privilege to represent the people of the state of Texas. That means that I am here not on behalf of a single person or even a group of people, but on behalf of every citizen of this state. I speak for the people, a great responsibility to be sure. And one of those citizens for whom I am particularly honored to speak today is Kathy Jones, the victim of the defendant's crime. At the time of the rape, Ms. Jones had lived in Texas for only a month or so. She had moved here in search of a new beginning, a fresh start. You may hear about some of her less-than-spotless past, about some brushes with the law she had as a teen and about some bad choices she made in the past. But don't let that distract you from seeing Kathy Jones for who she is and who she was before the rape. She was vibrant, carefree, full of life, ready to move ahead. Twenty-five years old with a future full of possibilities. She was planning to return to school and prepare to become a teacher, a kindergarten teacher. Kathy has put those plans on hold since the rape. The future is much less certain.

Before beginning this process of personalization, counsel should signal the transition to the jury by walking over to the client and standing next to him or her. Counsel's movement will help shift the jury's attention to the client. Counsel may even place his hand on the client's arm or shoulder as he talks about the client. The advocate's personal touch sends important messages to the jury about the client and the relationship between the lawyer and the client. Such a touch may be particularly important for criminal defense lawyers whose clients stand charged with committing a violent crime or violating some social norm, but it is appropriate in every case. It tells the jury that the client is flesh-and-blood, accessible, non-threatening and that the lawyer believes in the client's case and, perhaps more importantly, believes in the client.

The language that advocates use to refer to their clients is just as critical as where they stand or whom they touch. Most importantly, advocates should always use clients' names when referring to them, as an additional means of personalization. Yet, advocates should only rarely refer to their clients by just first name during the opening statement, for several reasons. First, some judges require that lawyers use only last names when referring to witnesses or others in the courtroom, without exception. Next even in courtrooms that do not impose that requirement, early use of the first name may suggest too much familiarity between the advocate and the client. A more formal relationship makes it easier for the lawyer to maintain an appearance of dispassionate impartiality. At the same time, advocates should avoid impersonal references to their clients, such as "plaintiff," "defendant," or "my client." The latter reference can be particularly damaging as it reminds the jury that this is just another job for the lawyer, another client in another courtroom, and nothing more.

The converse of personalization is depersonalization, which is what advocates want to do with the opposing party and the opposition's witnesses. Depersonalization begins with substituting the opposing party's status for the party's name. Thus, instead of "James White," the plaintiff should always be referred to by defense counsel as "plaintiff," or some other impersonal label. If the defendant is a corporation, it might even be called "the defendant corporation" to maximize the effect. There is much in a name and repeatedly labeling the opposing party and its witnesses with impersonal and less-than-attractive labels will undoubtedly impact the jury. Depersonalizing the other side does not mean the advocate should treat poorly the opposing lawyer or client. That may antagonize or alienate the jury. It is much safer to treat everyone in the courtroom, including the opposition, with respect and courtesy at all times.

D. Tell the Story

Storytelling is one of those naturally acquired skills that is too often dulled by three years of legal education. In law school students learn a new language, a new way of thinking, and a frustratingly compartmentalized way of viewing human tragedy and triumph. If they are not careful, lawyers can come to see events as product liability claims or breached contracts and can come to see people as tortfeasors, victims or murderers instead of appreciating the people affected by the events. When telling the story during the opening statement, advocates must avoid their lawyerly tendencies and instead must think about the events involved in the case as a story. And indeed, the trial is about the story of an individual or individuals. The advocate's task then is to tell a story that engages the imagination of the jurors and captures their loyalty. Success is achieved if the story moves jurors beyond understanding to empathy with the client and his situation. To do so, four keys must be observed:

- structure the story logically

- keep the story interesting

- tell the complete story, but omit needless detail and clutter

- make the story persuasive, not just informative, while avoiding argument

Needless to say, stating these keys is much easier than executing them, but none of them is impossible. Each of the keys is discussed separately below.

1. *A Logical Structure*

a. Chronology

The organization of the opening statement is not a simple matter. Just as there are many ways to structure a story, there are many ways to structure the body of an opening statement. The most common approach adopted by lawyers is chronological for obvious reasons. Jurors generally think in a linear fashion and are quite comfortable with stories that unfold from the earliest event to the latest. A chronology keeps the opening statement simple, straightforward, and understandable. For advocates, chronology reduces preparation time. However, blind allegiance to chronological order must be avoided. Chronology, for all of its simplicity, also limits the flexibility of the storyteller. The first event in the sequence may not be a particularly interesting one or it may put the advocate's client in a negative light. At the same time, the last event may be anticlimactic or unhelpful to proving the case theory. A slavish adherence to chronology yields control of the opening to the events, regardless of their persuasiveness or pertinence.

b. Witness-by-Witness

The second most popular approach to the opening is to summarize the expected testimony of the witnesses in the case, one witness after another. Again this approach has the advantage of simplicity. In fact, any capable ten year old could summarize the expected testimony of a group of witnesses. However, the disadvantages far outweigh that lone benefit. The witness-by-witness summary does not satisfy the jurors' desire to process the case information as a story. To the contrary, the story is told in a disjointed and fragmented way as the limited knowledge of each witness is described. Moreover, this approach limits the advocate's ability to emphasize key pieces of evidence or to present a cogent and compelling account of the key events. The witness-by-witness approach is the lazy lawyer's means of presenting an opening statement, one that largely forfeits the potential impact of the opening.

c. Logical Structure

There is an alternative to the extremes presented above. A logical structure is neither chronological nor witness-by-witness, but rather is tailored to the facts of the case. It requires thoughtful preparation, careful attention to the needs and desires of the jury, a logical analysis of the evidence in the case, and a dose of imagination. The right organization for an opening statement, of course, depends on the facts that will be established, the issues that will be contested, and the law that will be applied.

Nevertheless, chronology is often the best starting place simply because most stories proceed chronologically. But the advocate must be prepared to deviate from the chronology when necessary to emphasize a point or to demonstrate the relationship between two seemingly unrelated events. Juxtaposing events that happened at different times but are inextricably linked in the case can serve as a powerful tool before the jury. For example, telling the jury about the defendant manufacturer's decision to design their car with exposed gas tanks, knowing that some people would die from explosions upon impact, and then jumping ahead to the collision that killed the plaintiff's husband can demonstrate the consequence of the defendant's decision in a powerful way, despite the fact that it omits many events about which the jury will hear. Similarly, in a personal injury case, it may make sense to start with damages, to describe the plaintiff's injuries and their impact, and then to move back to the events leading up to the accident. And in a wrongful termination case, the story might begin with the moment the plaintiff was fired or the moment that the plaintiff was led off the premises, and then move back to the events that led up to the firing. The point is that the facts should be revealed in a way that emphasizes the key pieces of evidence, demonstrates the critical relationships between important events and people, and keeps the story interesting for the jury. In short, the advocate should organize the facts in a logical manner that will persuade the jury of the correctness of the client's cause.

2.   *An Interesting Story*

Once an effective organization is in place, the advocate must turn to the content of the story itself and examine the facts with an eye toward the specific aspects that will most interest the jury. What points should the advocate emphasize? Five basic principles should guide the preparation process:

- Focus on the human interest aspects of the conflict and look for themes that go beyond the particular dispute, such as the triumph of good over evil or the destructive power of greed.

- Emphasize details to increase the story's sense of reality.

- Use literary devices to create suspense or trauma and to provide insights into the case.

- Use visual aids—exhibits, charts, timelines, lists, and the like—to enhance understanding and retention of key points.

- Keep language active and understandable.

The larger point, of course, is that good storytelling has much to do with not only stimulating the jurors' minds, but also with appealing to their hearts and connecting with their emotions. A coldly efficient recitation of facts, one fact after another, will not get a warm reception from most jurors and will not motivate those jurors to align themselves with that party. The techniques identified above each involve going beyond the cold, bare legal necessities and into the kinds of things that keep people going back to read each new John Grisham novel. This is not an appeal to "sappiness" or an explicit appeal to the jurors' sympathies. Either of those approaches is doomed to failure with the jury and is subject to objection by the other side. Instead, the advocate, in the course of describing the tort or the breach of contract or the act of discrimination, should look for the details that lend an air of authenticity to the events. The fact that the baby has just said "Da-da" for the first time when the plaintiff went off to work on the day he was summarily (and wrongfully) discharged, or the fact that the plant safety director had just talked to her husband on the phone about the plant's industry recognition for safety when she received word that an employee of a sub-contractor had mistakenly hooked up to a hydrogen hose. The insights into the lives of the participants, the small snapshots of their families and their hopes and dreams, their successes and failures, help connect the jury to their experiences in the case at hand.

In the same way, advocates should make use of literary devices in their opening statements, when appropriate. Foreshadowing future events in the opening grab or at the beginning of the body of the opening can help to maintain the jury's interest. Using irony, compare and contrast, and other such devices can also spice up the opening. For example, assume that plaintiff is seeking damages for the death of her firefighter husband. The defendant claims the rescuer was negligent in attempting the rescue. In the example below, defendant's counsel uses compare and contrast to make the point.

Illustration of Defendant's Opening Using Compare and Contrast[9]

Defense Lawyer: Even rescuers must do it right. Even rescuers must be careful. Working under emergency circumstances demands discipline. We are here today because a firefighter, for all his heroism, didn't do it right. He wasn't careful. He did not exercise the necessary discipline. And when Ty McGuire [the defendant] found himself at the base of a cliff unable to move because of a shattered leg, his rescuer, instead of illuminating the path, plunged into darkness; and instead of walking over the uneven terrain, stumbled and slipped on the wet rocks; and instead of recognizing and avoiding danger, he ran off that very cliff.

The use of visual images during the opening will undoubtedly enhance the jurors' interest in what they are hearing. Many lawyers are reluctant to use visual aids during the opening out of fear that it is somehow improper or simply from force of habit. The truth, of course, is that the lawyer is not precluded in any way from using visual aids during the opening provided that the visual fairly depicts expected evidence and is not argumentative. The possibilities, which are discussed in more detail

---

[9] This illustration is based on the hypothetical case *Wrigley v. McGuire*, (2002, Association of Trial Lawyers of America).

in section IV below, are limited only by the expected evidence at trial. It is remarkable how something as simple as holding up the murder weapon, playing the defendant's taped confession, showing the photographs taken soon after the accident, or preparing a timeline of the key events in the case can help the story come to life and increase the jury's retention of the facts.

Finally, interest is also heightened by the advocate's effective use of language. As noted earlier, the language of the opening statement should be active and energetic, not passive and lifeless, and should avoid legalisms and long, multi-syllabic words or terms meant to impress others of the advocate's brilliance. Abraham Lincoln, the author of the Gettysburg Address and master of the English language, spoke the language of the rural juries he tried cases before, when riding the circuit in Illinois, telling them that he "reckoned" such and such was true. If Lincoln could adopt the language of his juries in rural Illinois, advocates can and must do no less. The advocate's motto during the trial should be: "simple words, interesting stories."

3. *A Full and Complete Story*

One of the myths perpetuated by the notion that the opening statement is just a roadmap or the picture on the jigsaw puzzle box is that it is nothing more than a brief overview of the case, a brief summary of the evidence in the case. The truth is that the critical role that the opening statement has in forming impressions about the merits of the case demands that advocates fully and completely describe their cases during the opening. Advocates should not withhold critical pieces of evidence for the purpose of unveiling them later (it may be too late!) or strategically avoid committing themselves to a particular strategy until after some of the critical witnesses have testified (again, it may be too late when the advocate decides on a strategy) or, worst of all, delay making an opening statement until the conclusion of the plaintiff's or prosecution's case.

The opening statement is the time to give the jurors a comprehensive description of the case, not an executive summary, to tell the jurors each and every reason your client should win, not just the most easily understood one. The tactic of withholding some perceived "smoking gun" during the opening so that the other side does not get a full preview of the advocate's case and so the advocate can maximize the surprise when the evidence is disclosed is a commonly advanced strategy. Presumably, advocates are concerned that early disclosure will inform the opponent that the advocate has the evidence and will reveal how the advocate plans to use the evidence, thus giving the opponent an opportunity to develop an explanation or to find some counter proof. These concerns are overblown, because if the "smoking gun" is truly powerful, then after-developed explanations will not be persuasive and the advocate will be able to destroy any such explanations during closing argument. On the other hand, choosing to withhold the explosive evidence from the jury at a time when the jury is still deciding who is right and who is wrong could be fatal to the outcome. If the advocate waits to make disclosure, when the evidence is finally unveiled the jury may be aligned with the opponent and thus willing to explain away the "smoking gun," as people often do when confronted with weaknesses in their own positions.

The one exception to this principle might be when the advocate has a piece of impeachment evidence and advance disclosure would allow the witness on direct examination to avoid or at least blunt the impeachment attack. Even in this situation, however, the default position should be disclosure.

The same principle applies when the criminal defense attorney is representing a defendant facing damning evidence and has no alibi or recognized defense. The lawyer is left with nothing to argue other than the prosecution's failure to meet its burden of proof. Admittedly, defense lawyers in that predicament face a tough choice when they rise to deliver their opening statements. They cannot rightly dispute the prosecution's facts. They have little more than the burden of proof to argue to the jury and yet they may not fully know the prosecution's weaknesses until after cross-examination of the prosecution's witnesses. Should the defense lawyer deliver an opening statement dedicated to the great strength of our criminal justice system and its insistence on giving the state the burden to prove guilt rather than giving defendants the obligation to prove innocence? Or even more dramatically, should such lawyers simply reserve their opening statements until after the prosecution's case-in-chief. To each question the answer is an emphatic "no!" The defense lawyer with little or no defense should use the opening statement to condition the jury for those areas where doubt may arise—the uncertain eyewitness identification or the absence of a motive. The advocate's best chance to create doubt is during the opening statement before any evidence has been presented, not later after the jury has heard the prosecution's witnesses and already concluded that the defendant is guilty.

4.   *A Persuasive Story Without Argument*

The final key to maximizing the opportunity presented by the opening statement is to tell a persuasive story. Notwithstanding misconceptions to the contrary, the opening is a time for advocacy of the party's position, not for a mere summary of the expected evidence. The goal of persuasion dictates everything the advocate does during the opening: from creating and announcing a theme, to personalizing the client, to structuring the opening in a logical manner, to telling the jury an interesting and complete account of what happened.

There remains, of course, one imposing obstacle to persuasion in the opening, and that is the rule against argument. And yet, the notion that persuasion is improper in the opening is a myth, because the rule against argument only purports to preclude one of *the means* used to persuade during the opening, not *the act* of persuasion itself. The traditional rule of thumb used by lawyers to decide what is argumentative is the "witness test," which asks whether the party has a witness who can competently testify to the point being expressed during the opening statement. If the answer is "yes," then the statement is not argumentative, but if the answer is "no," the statement may be argumentative and not appropriate for the opening statement.

As is discussed in greater detail below, the witness test is not a perfect tool for enforcing the rule against argument and is not strictly enforced by most judges. Nevertheless, it provides a kind of barometer for understanding the nature and extent of persuasion that is possible during the opening. In some cases, the rule against argument may preclude the advocate from explicitly drawing inferences from the evidence. That is, under the witness test the advocate might be precluded from telling the jury, "The defendant was driving 85 miles an hour in a 50 mile per hour zone, and thus, he was speeding." He could, however, use these words:

 ## 1st Illustration of Avoiding Argument

Plaintiff's Lawyer: The speed limit was 50 miles an hour. Signs were posted to that effect on the highway and the defendant was familiar with this stretch of highway. But we will prove to you that the defendant was traveling at a speed greater than 50 miles per hour, and not just 10 miles an hour or 20 miles an hour greater. No. He was traveling at 85 miles an hour, 35 miles an hour over the posted speed limit.

Despite the conservative witness test, however, advocates are still able to draw explicit inferences for the jury provided the inferences are supported by the testimony of an expert witness. The rules of evidence of every jurisdiction empower experts to testify in the form of an opinion and to draw inferences from the evidence for a jury.[10] A design engineer might testify that the automobile made by the defendant was designed in an unsafe manner, a human factors engineer might testify that the defendant's warnings were inadequate to apprise potential users of the risks created by the product, or a medical doctor might testify that the defendant's conduct during surgery was entirely consistent with the standard of care for surgeons. In each instance, the experts' opinions draw inferences for the jury, telling them how they should view the evidence in the case. And in each instance, it would be entirely appropriate for the advocate to tell the jury during the opening statement of the unsafe design, or the inadequate warnings, or the satisfaction of the standard of care. Thus, it is fair to say that the outer limit of what is permissible under the rule against argument is staked by the expert opinion rules.

For instance, in her opening statement in a criminal trial, defense counsel might say as follows:

---

[10] *See, e.g.,* Fed. R. Evid. 702; CAL. EVID. CODE § 801; *see also* Samuel P. Gross, *Expert Evidence,* 1991 WIS. L. REV. 1113, 1140.

2nd Illustration of Avoiding Argument

Defense Counsel: The evidence will establish that Bruce Davis [the defendant] had no idea of right or wrong at the time he stabbed his wife. You will learn that for most of his adult life he has been in and out of psychiatric hospitals and has been administered a vast array of powerful anti-psychotic drugs. In the weeks leading up to his wife's death, he suffered from severe depressive episodes during which he had no idea of where he was or even who he was. When his treating psychiatrist testifies, he will tell you that when Mr. Davis took his wife's life, he was insane. That is, he had no idea of what was right or wrong, nor any ability to appreciate the nature of his act.

Even when the rule against argument would seem to preclude the advocate from drawing the explicit inference for the jury, the advocate can present the material in a persuasive manner. For example, assume that a critical issue in the case is the credibility of the plaintiff, who has given several conflicting accounts of her handling of the firearm before it discharged and injured her. The rule against argument would preclude the advocate from explicitly telling the jury in the opening that the evidence would show that the plaintiff was a liar. However, the defense lawyer can in the opening tell the jury about the various accounts of the events given by the plaintiff, point out the specific inconsistencies, and identify what the evidence will show about her motivation when she made the statements. Simply by putting the inconsistent statements side-by-side for the jury, the advocate makes the point without ever specifically telling the jury what it means.

Advocates argue through the facts of the case by how they arrange those facts and by which facts they choose to emphasize. The advocate must carefully organize the story so that the key points are made even when the advocate is unable to make the point explicitly.

E.   Disclose Weaknesses

The body of the opening statement is not only the time to tell the story of the case in compelling and interesting ways, but it is also the time to make full disclosure to the jury about any skeletons the advocate's client or witnesses have in their closets. Every litigated case has weaknesses. It is not so much a matter of if the case has weaknesses, but what the weaknesses are, and it is not so much a matter of *whether* advocates should disclose those weaknesses, but *how* advocates should do so.

The opening statement is a particularly critical time to make disclosures because the advocate can shape the jurors' impressions of the evidence. The client's prior criminal conviction might be fairly described as "a youthful indiscretion" and his prior inconsistent statements as simply the earnest efforts of one falsely accused to remember everything that happened.

By shaping the juror's images of the key people and events in the case, the advocate substantially complicates the opponent's efforts to exploit the weaknesses, and in some cases causes the opponent to look petty and unfair.

The objective is for the disclosure to not look like a disclosure, so as to not unduly emphasize the point. The optimum means of accomplishing that task is by integrating any weaknesses into the party's overall case theme. For example, assume that several eyewitnesses gave inconsistent accounts of an accident with regard to certain details, such as the location of the plaintiff/pedestrian at various times and the point of impact, but each witness' testimony was consistent with the accident happening outside of the crosswalk, thus suggesting that the car had the right of way at the time of the accident. The defendant, rather than treating the witness' inconsistencies as weaknesses to be disclosed, should integrate them into his theory of the case. The lack of perfect precision, he might point out, results from the diverse perspective of the witnesses, not the untrustworthiness of any of them. In fact, it would be suspicious if the stories lined up perfectly, perhaps an indication that the witnesses had concocted a false account of what happened. Human memory is not photographic, and the inconsistencies give the testimony the "ring of truth." Although this point could not be made explicitly in the opening because that would be argumentative, counsel could prepare the jury for it by discussing the inconsistencies of the witnesses, pointing out their different perspectives, and emphasizing their key areas of agreement.

Some weaknesses defy integration. The advocate must ask three questions:

- Is disclosure necessary?

- When should the disclosure be made?

- What should the advocate actually disclose?

1. *Whether to Disclose*

The decision of whether to make the disclosure in the first place should turn on two factors: the materiality of the weakness and the likelihood that the other side knows about the weakness. Obviously, there is no need to disclose information that the other side does not have or could not know. That is not an invitation to conceal evidence or to otherwise abuse the discovery process, but a simple recognition that parties do not always ask all the questions they should or prepare a case as thoroughly as they should. Some weaknesses will go undiscovered. But most will not and advocates should only cautiously rely on the hope that the other side is in the dark. If the probabilities point toward the opposing counsel knowing the weakness, then the weakness must be disclosed.

The other factor—materiality—requires a contextual analysis of the weakness. Does the information have any bearing on an issue in the case that makes a difference in the outcome? If the weakness is not material, the advocate, by the act of "disclosing" it, actually suggests to the jury that the evidence does matter in the case, that it is, in fact, material. And the disclosing party opens the door for the opponent to emphasize the immaterial weakness as well. Thus, the disclosure of a defendant's petty theft conviction when the defendant is charged with a violent crime such as rape or murder would be foolish. The conviction is not material to the case, but its preemptive disclosure to the jury suggests to the contrary.

Before making a disclosure, counsel should consider filing a motion *in limine* challenging the admission of the evidence. For some types of weaknesses there may be no colorable claim that the evidence should be excluded. Typically, however, there will be such a claim. As discussed in Chapter Three, the motion *in limine* is an indispensable tool because it provides advocates with the chance to learn the opponent's view of the evidence, to gauge the court's attitude toward the evidence, and potentially to gain exclusion of the weakness, in which case disclosure is unnecessary.

2.   *When to Disclose*

The timing of the disclosure depends on the nature of the material to be disclosed. The conventional wisdom is that weaknesses should be disclosed in the middle of the opening statement, not at the beginning or the end. The principle of primacy dictates that advocates do not want jurors to first learn their clients' flaws before they have formed a favorable impression of them. The principle of recency mandates that the jurors not be left with a weakness as the last thing they hear. At the same time, however, the disclosure should flow naturally from the structure of the opening. The worst possible approach is to abruptly change topics when making the disclosure, effectively emphasizing the weakness. In short, the disclosure should not look like a disclosure. If the weakness involves past indiscretions by a party, the disclosure might best come at the end of the personalization section. If the weakness is an inconsistency in the client's testimony, it might be explained at the appropriate point in the story. If the weakness is a pre-existing injury for a civil plaintiff, it might be disclosed during the personalization section during the discussion of damages.

3.   *What to Disclose*

The actual making of the disclosure proves surprisingly difficult for most lawyers. The act itself is counterintuitive. Lawyers are trained to advocate for their clients by advancing their best case, while disclosing weaknesses requires the advocate to freely and willingly reveal negative and harmful information about the client or a witness. The result is that most lawyers make half-hearted disclosures, if they do so at all. The disclosures are sometimes so general that they raise more questions than they answer. In modern parlance, this might be called the Clintonian approach: "I had an inappropriate relationship ..." Such disclosures likely do more harm than good.

Instead, the disclosure should be full and complete. It should include necessary details both to inform the jury about the events and to deprive the opponent of any chance to demonstrate later in the trial that the disclosing advocate failed to tell the whole story. A comprehensive disclosure effectively steals the other side's thunder. The disclosure not only gives the advocate the appearance of being more interested in truth than in winning, but it also gives the advocate some measure of control over the weakness, allowing the advocate to explain the events and give them much-needed context.

Assume, for instance, in a criminal prosecution, the critical eyewitness initially identified another as the shooter. The prosecutor must disclose and mitigate this weakness during her opening statement.

 ## Illustration of Disclosure of Weakness in Opening Statement

Prosecutor: You are going to hear from a man who actually witnessed the murder. Paul Evans lived in the apartment complex where Christy White was murdered. And on that early morning something woke him, and when he looked out his window he saw the defendant, a large unkempt bearded man, running after Christy. He saw the defendant knock Christy to the ground and shoot her in the head.

Later that afternoon, the police picked up a large, unkempt bearded man who lived in a nearby apartment building. They brought a very nervous and even reluctant Paul Evans to the station to look at this man. Mr. Evans took one quick sideways glance and as he rushed from the room, said something like, "Get me out of here. That's him."

The lieutenant in charge of the investigation will come before you and testify that Evans was nervous and distraught about being in the same room as the man. The lieutenant will tell you he erred in bringing Evans into that room, and that Evans' identification under those circumstances was meaningless.

Two weeks later, when the defendant was arrested, Mr. Evans, this time from behind one-way glass, unhesitatingly picked the defendant from an eight-man line-up that also included that original man.

Mr. Evans will come before you during this trial and again will identify the defendant as the man who shot Christy Wells. Other evidence will also point toward the defendant and we will prove that Mr. Evans' initial identification of another was an all-too-human error, but an error nonetheless, and that his later identification of defendant is correct and reliable.

F.   Create a List

Two essential goals of any opening statement are to synthesize the evidence for the jury and to help the jurors understand what is important and what is not, what matters and what does not. At every point in the opening, from the personalization of the client to the disclosure of weaknesses, the advocate strives to help the jury make those critical judgments. Yet, the risk remains that the jurors may get lost in the advocate's narrative and may not appreciate or understand the difference between the wheat and the chaff in the case. One way for advocates to clarify their message and simplify the jury's task is to use a list during the opening statement. The list serves as a useful tool for the advocate because it forces the advocate to identify the key pieces of evidence in the case, and thus reduce the case to its most basic essentials. It also serves as a useful tool for jurors because it enhances their retention of the material presented.

The list should come rather late in the opening, after the story has been told and the expected evidence discussed. At that point, a list, either pre-prepared or written as each point is disclosed, should be revealed to the jury. The list should identify the key reasons that the party should win the case. It may include, among other things, critical pieces of evidence, central people or events, unexplained holes in the opponent's case, or important legal standards or principles. For example, the prosecution's list in the criminal prosecution of O.J. Simpson, had all of the evidence been introduced, might have looked something like this:

Illustration of a List

1.   Past Abuse

2.   Blood—Nicole's House

3.   Blood—O.J.'s Bronco

4.   The Second Glove

5.   The Chase

The points should be short, two or three words at most. They should be memorable, the pithier the better. In a sound bite era, jurors expect, well, sound bites. The points should not be argumentative or too conclusory. The points above are largely factual, though one might quibble with the term "abuse" and the term "chase." Caution is wise in selecting the words for the list; the last thing an advocate wants is to be forced to erase or cross out points that have already been written because they are ruled argumentative.

```
┌─────────────────────────────────────┐
│              Tech Tip               │
│           Create a Visual           │
│                                     │
│  ✓  Use 2 or 3 words at the most     │
│  ✓  Be memorable                     │
│  ✓  Do not be too argumentative or   │
│     conclusory                      │
│  ✓  Briefly discuss each listed point│
│  ✓  Just use key points              │
│  ✓  Reveal one point after another – not all │
│     at once                         │
│  ✓  Remember never to turn your back to │
│     the jury when diagramming, outlining, or │
│     using a PowerPoint list.        │
└─────────────────────────────────────┘
```

The advocate likely will have discussed the information set forth in the points on the list earlier in the opening. Thus, the discussion of each point should be brief. The objective is for the jury to see the picture painted by the evidence without the advocate having to explicitly make the point for the jury.

Some may view the list itself as argumentative simply because it singles out certain evidence. However, that fact alone does not render it argumentative. If a witness will competently testify to the facts included on the list, it is not argumentative. However, counsel may improperly argue by introducing the list as constituting the important evidence in the case. For example, "And as we hear from the various witnesses there are four critical things to keep in mind." Instead the segue to the list should be subtle and understated, referring to the evidentiary support of the items in the list ("We will prove to you five things, . . .").

Another objection that may be offered is that the items on the list are cumulative to what has already been said. However, counsel's statements in the opening are not "evidence" and should not fall prey to such an objection. Moreover, the list is not cumulative of counsel's oral remarks because it appeals to the jurors' visual senses, not their aural ones, and it organizes the evidence in a different and helpful manner.

G.   Anticipate the Opponent's Arguments

The value of the opening statement in helping the jury form initial impressions about the case is a double-edged sword. The jury forms initial impressions not only about the advocate's case, but also about the claims of the opponent. Thus, it is not enough for advocates to focus on their cases or the correctness of their contentions, advocates must also rebut the contentions of their opponents. This is particularly true for the advocate who speaks first, because he can preemptively characterize the contentions of the opponent.

Under the rules of modern litigation, which include broad discovery in civil and criminal cases, an advocate has little excuse for not knowing the other side's claims and contentions before the trial begins. Advocates should know not only the oppositions' contentions by the time of trial, but also the identity of its witnesses, the expected testimony of its experts, and so forth. The best time to start attacking the other side's case is before the other side has even made their case. For example, if a case involves an alleged product defect and the defendant claims the plaintiff was injured because she misused the product, the plaintiff can use the opening statement to point out that the evidence will not support the defense and urge that the defendant, rather than accepting responsibility for the defect, is blaming the victim for the injury. By the time the defendant rises to lay out its contributory negligence defense, it will face a difficult uphill battle.

The presiding judge may limit discussion of the opponent's case during opening statement. Indeed, some trial judges strictly limit opening statements, providing the jury with only an overview of the party's own evidence. According to this view, any discussion of the opponent's case constitutes improper argument. This approach, which harkens back to a different era of trial advocacy, makes little sense in light of the pretrial discovery available today, and is unsupported by either case authority or common sense. Yet, some judges continue to impose this limitation on opening statement, and advocates must be prepared to adjust accordingly.

In criminal trials an additional caveat is necessary. Unlike other advocates, the prosecutor is constrained by the Fifth Amendment in discussing expected testimony by the criminal defendant or defense evidence generally. The defendant's privilege against self-incrimination protects him from giving compelled testimony and it precludes the government from attempting to imply guilt based on the defendant's exercise of that right. The prosecutor should refrain from discussing any expected testimony by the defendant; the defendant does not have to testify and it is improper for the government to explicitly or implicitly make an issue out of whether the defendant testifies. Infringement of these rights of a criminal defendant can lead to a mistrial and perhaps even dismissal of charges on double jeopardy grounds.

While the prosecutor must refrain from commenting upon the defendant's anticipated testimony, she can discuss what the defendant has already said to the police or the grand jury (which is admissible hearsay evidence even if the defendant does not testify) and can anticipate defenses such as self-defense or lack of premeditation. Thus, if the defendant told the police in an interview that he does not have a witness who can support his alibi for the crime because he was chipping golf balls after dark on his front lawn alone, the prosecution can discuss that admission in the opening.

 ## Illustration of Discussion of Defendant's Past Statements

---

Prosecutor: The defendant claims that he was elsewhere at the time of the murders, but he can point to no one who was with him or who saw him when these murders were being committed. He claims he was chipping golf balls in the dark on his front lawn all by himself. That's his story. That's what he told the police after the murders.

When the defendant has already made statements or defense witnesses have previously testified before the grand jury or in a preliminary hearing, the prosecution can freely discuss the evidence without running afoul of the defendant's rights because that evidence is admissible at trial. Only *criminal* defendants receive this protection from the Fifth Amendment. In civil cases, for example, there is no Fifth Amendment constraint that would prevent counsel from freely commenting on the opponent's expected testimony or evidence or on the opponent's anticipated failure to present evidence.

H.   Respond to the Opponent's Assertions

The advocate who goes second suffers from several disadvantages and at least one additional responsibility. Unlike the lawyer for the plaintiff or prosecution, the defense lawyer faces a jury "corrupted" by the partisan presentation of the opponent and saturated with the opponent's view of the facts in the case. In a very real sense, the seal has been broken and the minds of the jurors have been invaded. Thus, it is impossible for the advocate to exert the kind of control over the case facts that is available to the plaintiff simply because the advocate is going second. Moreover, the advocate must overcome any favorable impression created by the first advocate, which may well be a difficult task.

The second advocate also must respond to the claims and characterizations of her opponent, which requires a greater degree of flexibility and preparation on her part. The opening statement is not the time for a canned speech in disregard of everything that went before. Rather the advocate must recognize what has already been said, avoid needless repetition, and acknowledge the facts and theories with which the advocate agrees. Most importantly, however, the advocate must identify the assertions of the plaintiff's counsel or the prosecutor that will not be supported by the evidence and must demonstrate the weaknesses of the opponent's theories.

Responding to the opponent's statements requires that advocates actively listen to the opening. Although advocates should anticipate much of what the other side will say in the opening, they should not assume that they know everything. There may be a surprise claim or an unknown piece of evidence or even a misstatement that the advocate can exploit. Opportunities to demonstrate the exaggerations or misstatements of the opposing counsel must not be missed, as every point counts in the battle for the jury's trust.

I. End Strong

The final part of the opening is, of course, the conclusion. The principle of recency dictates that the advocate must go out with a bang, not a whimper. Some advocates find it impossible to quit talking. Either they keep talking and talking because they have not planned any means of ending or they end abruptly and without warning, leaving the jury surprised and unnerved. The ending should be just as carefully planned as the beginning. The ending should be interesting and memorable, without being trite. The classic ending for the opening, "We are confident that after you have heard the evidence you will find in favor of _____" is not particularly imaginative. With a little effort and some creativity, thoughtful and prepared advocates can do better.

One helpful approach is for the ending to return to the beginning, and grab and repeat the same key words or phrases. The symmetry of beginning and ending with the same words can be quite effective. Similarly, as set forth in the following illustration, the advocate might state the case theme again and reinforce the key facts of the case.

 Illustration of Conclusion of Defense Opening Statement[11]

Defense Lawyer: No one is ever going to deny that that firefighter was a true hero. He put his life on the line for another. But as we will hear throughout this trial, even heroes have to do it right. Even heroes cannot plunge into darkness, slip and stumble on slippery rocks and run into the unknown. At the conclusion of this trial I am confident you will find that this tragic death was caused by the rescuer's own negligence, his own lack of discipline.

IV.   PRINCIPLES FOR EFFECTIVE OPENING STATEMENTS

❖   Principle Number One: No Wind-Up, No Throat Clearing

The temptation at the beginning of any speech or presentation is for the speaker to spend some time warming up before getting to the substance of what he has to say. The speaker might start with a humorous story, a brief bio, comments about the weather, references to current events, or perhaps all of the above. This kind of "wind up" calms the speaker's nerves and serves as an attempt to establish a rapport with the audience.

Lawyers often follow the same approach for the same reasons. They begin by essentially clearing their throats, relating to the jury any number of inane introductory remarks. What follows is a

> **PRINCIPLES FOR EFFECTIVE OPENING STATEMENTS**
> - ❖ No Wind-up, No Throat Clearing
> - ❖ Use Pictures, Lists, Timelines, and Exhibits
> - ❖ Avoid Unnecessary Clutter and Detail
> - ❖ Avoid Promising Too Much
> - ❖ Never Waive or Reserve the Opening
> - ❖ No Scripts, No Podium, No Reading
> - ❖ Keep the Opening Short

---

[11] This illustration is based on the hypothetical case *Wrigley v. McGuire*, (2002, Association of Trial Lawyers of America).

list of the top ten "throat clearing" statements that advocates often include in their opening statements, but which are entirely unhelpful and should be avoided. For example, "This is what we lawyers call 'the opening statement.'" The problem, of course, is that everyone calls this part of the trial "the opening statement," not just lawyers, and the insider reference is offensive, condescending, and self-defeating. On top of that, it is totally unnecessary, as the judge will have already imparted that information. Other examples to be avoided include,

- "The opening statement is like a roadmap."

- "The opening statement is like the picture on the cover of the jigsaw puzzle box."

- "The opening statement is like a movie preview."

- "The opening statement is like _____ [fill in the blank]."

This is perhaps the most common and least effective way to begin an opening statement. The jury does not need instruction from the advocate about the purpose of the opening statement—the judge will give them whatever instruction they need. The opening statement analogy is nothing but a waste of the precious first moments of the opening. The goal is to grab the jurors' interest, and not one of these analogies is interesting in a meaningful way. It is tempting to spend the first part of the opening thanking the jurors or giving a civics lesson or both.

- "I want to start by thanking you for fulfilling your civic duty by being here today."

- "The jury is the foundation of our democracy. As [Alexis de Tocqueville] [Abraham Lincoln] [fill in the blank] once said: _____."

There is a time for thanking the jurors for their service, but it comes at the end of the trial, not the beginning. The civics lesson does nothing to advance the advocate's position.

Of all the egregious mistakes advocates can make during their opening, surely nothing is worse than uttering these words:

- "What the lawyers say during the opening statement is not evidence. That means that nothing I say and nothing the defendant's lawyer, Mr. Smith, says is evidence for you to consider in deciding this case."

They essentially instruct the jury to disregard what the advocate is saying, negating the advocate's carefully prepared remarks. It is like wearing a large sign during the opening that says, "Ignore me."

While advocates should be sensitive to the need to avoid wasting the jury's time, there is nothing gained, and much lost, by starting your opening statement by minimizing its importance.

- "I know that you would prefer to be somewhere else right now, so I'll try to make this as brief and painless as possible."

Advocates should have genuine gratitude for the service of jurors and even heartfelt sympathy for the sacrifices that some jurors make, they should not suggest that the case is unimportant or subject to some kind of shortcut. To the contrary, the advocate's attitude should be that the case has extreme importance for the litigants, and thus will last as long as it needs to last, but no longer. No apologies necessary.

Characterizations of the case are unhelpful at best and confusing at worst.

- "This is a [simple] or [complicated] or [interesting] or [distasteful] case."

The better approach is for the advocate to tell the jury about the case without describing it in such general terms.

The point is that advocates should begin with something that matters, something that gets the jurors into the facts of the case. Advocates can ask themselves, "what is this case about?" and start with the answer they uncover. Even then, however, they may be tempted to start the opening by saying to the jury, "Ladies and gentlemen, this case is about the destructive power of greed." That's well and good, but the words "this case is about" are needless clutter. Why not start with something more powerful and persuasive?

Illustration of Grab by Prosecution

Prosecutor: Greed destroys. . . . It destroys relationships, careers, even lives. And today you will hear about the destructive power of greed, the greed of the defendant, [pointing] sitting right over there. You will see the incredible destructive force of the defendant's greed and the things it led him to do. We will prove to you that the defendant, motivated by greed, stole more than 1 million dollars from Acme Office Products, and in the course of doing so, destroyed everything that was important to him.

The leaner and tighter the advocate's message is, the greater the impact. The fewer the words needed to communicate the message, the better. Every word counts during those first few minutes of the opening when the jurors are most attentive and least attached to one side or the other. Time must not be wasted with trite expressions or overused clichés.

❖ Principle Number Two: Use Pictures, Lists, Timelines, and Exhibits

Regardless of the eloquence of the speaker and the logic of his presentation, the opening statement is a failure if the jury is unable to remember what the advocate said or why the advocate's points were important. Retention reigns supreme for every advocate. And the one proven way to ensure that the jury retains the advocate's opening statement is through the use of sensory aids. People fall into three different camps when it comes to learning: visual, auditory, and kinesthetic. Auditory learners are easy to please; as long as the advocate can properly organize the information and make it easy to follow, the aural jurors will grasp the information simply by hearing it. Visual learners will do best when they can see the evidence before them. Using a variety of visual aids—such as charts, maps, lists, models, or demonstrations—will help to hold the attention of visual learners. Kinesthetic learners need to touch objects in order to best process information. To connect to these jurors, the advocate may allow them to hold records, feel physical models, or use language that evokes physical sensations. Generally, most people remember best what they hear *and* see, not what they only hear. Thus, if the advocate cannot employ techniques that will reach all three types of learners, she should at least provide the jury with helpful visual cues during the opening to greatly enhance retention by the jury.

As noted above, lawyers are occasionally reluctant to use demonstrative aids during the opening out of concern for the rule against argument and in recognition of the fact that exhibits have not yet been authenticated or admitted into evidence. Neither concern is insurmountable, and neither concern should cause advocates to rely solely on their words in the opening statement. The concern about argument simply means that advocates must ensure that any demonstrative aid they use is not unfairly argumentative and that it is based on evidence the party expects to elicit during the trial. Similarly, the unadmitted status of exhibits simply requires that the advocate have a good faith belief that the exhibit will be authenticated and admitted during the trial and allow the opponent to examine the exhibit before it is used in the opening. Some judges require advocates to obtain judicial approval before using demonstrative aids or exhibits during opening statement.

The potential range of exhibits that might be used during the opening statement is broad. Start with some obvious ones. In a murder case, the prosecution ought to show the jury the murder weapon during the opening; she should hold up the gun and describe the damage it has wrought. The visceral impact of the weapon makes the advocate's message more memorable and more powerful. In a breach of contract case, the plaintiff can enlarge the contract and display it for the jury in all its glory, emphasizing the portions that were breached by the defendant. In a patent infringement case, the plaintiff can show the jury the two competing products or devices to let them see the heart of the dispute right from the outset.

In addition to exhibits that arise out of the core of the dispute, advocates can look to demonstrative aids to serve an explanatory role for the jury. For example, in a case arising out of a car accident, a diagram or photograph of the scene of the accident is essential. It is difficult for jurors (or anyone for that matter) to understand how a car accident happened based solely on an oral description. A picture, however, greatly simplifies the process. In a case of some complexity, in which the timing or sequence

of events is important, a timeline for the jury may prove beneficial. Again, jurors will struggle
to keep straight the relationship
between a series of events based
on only one telling of the events.
The timeline will assist the jury
in understanding the context of
the issues in the case and the
relationship of events to each
other. One caveat about timelines: avoid putting too much
information before the jury at
one time. Too much detail will create confusion and will distract the jury
from the most important events or dates. Keep the timeline simple and
easily readable.

> **Tech Tip**
> *Use PowerPoint Slides or a Document
> Camera for Demonstrative Aids*
>
> - Bullet point lists
> - Labeled photos
> - Timelines
> - Text documents with emphasis added by
>   using boxes, circles, lines, or highlighting.
> - Organizational charts

Another helpful demonstrative aid is videotape. More and more,
bystanders or news organizations capture important events on videotape.
A video of the critical events can give the jurors important context and
understanding while also appealing to their desire to be entertained by
electronic means. Similarly, use audio recordings if they exist and will
likely be admissible at trial. For example, a tape recording of the defendants conspiring to distribute illegal drugs would almost certainly be
much more memorable and interesting to the jury than the advocate's
description of the conversation. As the tape is playing, display photographs of the individuals speaking on the tapes to help familiarize the
jury with them.

Before the advocates use demonstrative evidence during the opening they should apprise the judge of their intent to do so, and show the
opposing counsel exactly what they intend to show the jury. Just as counsel
always has the right to examine every exhibit shown to a witness or the
jury, so counsel should be given the chance to inspect such items before
they are used in the opening. Counsel might say, "Your Honor, we intend
to use this timeline during our opening remarks to the jury. It simply lists
certain events and the dates on which they happened. We have shown it to
opposing counsel. We believe that it would assist the jury in understanding
the evidence that we will produce during the trial." Most judges will readily
allow the evidence to be used, assuming it is not argumentative or based
upon inadmissible evidence.

Sometimes the simplest visual aid is the best. In this age of increasing
sophistication and technological innovation, advocates are tempted to use
as much technological gadgetry simply because its there. Resist the temptation! Nothing is so exquisitely painful as an advocate availing herself of
some presentation software (such as PowerPoint) and then becoming so
reliant on it that it becomes a substitute for effective advocacy. Advocates
who have a slide for everything that comes out of their mouths have
misused the technology and wasted an excellent opportunity. If every point
is represented visually, then the benefits are lost and the jury is sure to

suffer from visual overload. Balance is the key. Sometimes the best thing the advocate can do is go to the chalk board (or dry erase board) and handwrite a list of the three or four key pieces of evidence in the case.

❖ Principle Number Three: Avoid Unnecessary Clutter and Detail

One of the most difficult tasks at opening statement is to give the jurors a comprehensive understanding of the case without confusing them with unnecessary clutter and detail. Needless details are distractions; they are not necessary to an understanding of the story, and only tend to confuse. There is a fine line between giving the jurors enough to understand the case, but not so much that they become confused. One prime example of such detail is the names of marginal or peripheral people involved in the case. Instead of names, use characterizations. They are easier for the jurors to remember and distract less attention away from the few names in the case that are important. Thus, instead of "Fred Jones," use "the car mechanic," and instead of "Dr. Sue Smith," use "the treating physician."

Similarly, do not clutter the opening statement with a series of dates or a set of compass directions or a street address. Dates are difficult to remember and are meaningless except as they relate to the critical events in the case. It is much more helpful to tell the jury that "two weeks before the accident, Ms. Green [the plaintiff] took her car into Mr. Jones' car repair shop," than to tell them that she did so on "On August 1, 2009." The date by itself is meaningless. The same is true of compass directions. The fact that the car was traveling "westbound" will probably only confuse most jurors, not help them. The jurors will spend the next several moments trying to figure out which way is west, and will not hear the next sentence or two. Directions must be *shown* to the jurors visually to have any real value. For instance, "The defendant was driving on Kirby Street and as he approached Mathis he prepared to make a left turn." Use a chart to illustrate. Always look for opportunities to simplify by eliminating details that create clutter rather than enhance the credibility of the message.

❖ Principle Number Four: Avoid Promising Too Much

The importance of the opening statement creates a strong temptation to exaggerate the evidence and promise more than the advocate can deliver. And yet, the central importance of the advocate's ethos—his credibility with the jury—emphasizes the need for him not to yield to this temptation. Of course, that is easier said than done. Dangers lurk around every representation, and every claim. Will that witness actually testify at trial? Will those witnesses, when they testify, say the things represented by counsel? Will the judge admit the exhibits? Will the proof actually establish the party's claims? Thorough and comprehensive preparation will inoculate the advocate against most of the dangers of promising too much. The rest is managed by a dose of caution in making grandiose claims about uncertain matters.

Conversely, when the other side makes promises, the advocate should take note, and if they are not kept by the evidence, such unkept promises are fertile fodder for closing argument.

❖ Principle Number Five: Never Waive or Reserve the Opening

A couple peculiarities of the opening statement are that the parties can waive their right to make an opening statement altogether, and defendants have the right to delay their opening statements until after the opponent (the plaintiff or prosecutor) has presented its case-in-chief. Criminal defendants occasionally choose to reserve their opening statements so that they will know precisely the prosecution's evidence and can effectively identify the holes in the prosecution's proof. Alternatively, the defendant's decision to testify may not be made until after the prosecution's case, so defense counsel may prefer to defer the opening statement to a time when the defendant's anticipated testimony may be safely referenced. Or, a defense attorney may be concerned that an opening statement given prior to the plaintiff's or prosecutor's case will be forgotten before the defense case and, therefore, will not guide the jury through the defense case. Typically, reservation is for those cases in which the defense hinges on the argument that the prosecution failed to satisfy the burden of proof.

Waiver is never a good idea, and reservation of the opening is usually equally misguided. Such a strategy allows plaintiffs or prosecutors to tell their side of the story without interruption and to present their witnesses without giving the jury any sense or appreciation of how the defense views those witnesses. It will mean that the jurors will be less critical of plaintiff's or prosecution's evidence. The limited and fragmented nature of cross-examination is insufficient to overcome the absence of an opening. By the time the defense presents its view of the case and tells its side of the story it may be too late to unveil the defense theory. The jurors will have already aligned themselves with the plaintiff or prosecutor and accordingly will not be nearly as receptive to the defense arguments as they were at the beginning. Advocates should always make a full and complete opening statement at the beginning of the case.

❖ Principle Number Six: No Scripts, No Podium, No Reading

Effective communication requires the removal of any barriers between the speaker and the audience. Some barriers are intangible, such as the barriers of language or culture, while others are physical, such as the barrier of the podium or the script. Without regard to the precise nature of the barrier, they each have the potential to rob a speech of its desired rhythm and blunt its potential impact.

Advocates must appreciate the extent to which these barriers can interfere with their efforts and must diligently strive to eliminate them. It is not enough to have the facts or the law in a party's favor, though that is preferable to the alternative. One's style of presentation matters. Jury perceptions count. Advocates who adopt a persuasive style improve their chances of success.

The litany of "to do's" is familiar to anyone who has had a basic speech class.

First the negatives:

- Do not use the podium (unless the judge requires it)

- Do not read or otherwise rely on notes

- Do not memorize

- Do not pace

- Do not stand still

Now the positives:

- Do stand directly in front of the jury box (unless the judge prohibits it)

- Do maintain eye contact with the jurors

- Do learn the opening statement so that the delivery is natural

- Do move around during the opening, but purposefully

- Do use gestures and voice modulation and inflection to emphasize points

The points fit into four basic categories: (1) where to stand; (2) where to look; (3) where to go; and (4) what to do with your hands.

1.   *Where to Stand*

The obvious place to start is with the best position for delivery of the opening statement. Consider several alternatives: One possibility is to give the opening statement from behind the podium, located between the counsel tables, perpendicular to the jury box; a second possibility is to deliver the opening from directly in front of the jury box, but behind a podium; and a third possibility is to deliver the opening from directly in front of the jury box, without a podium or anything else between the advocate and the jury. Which position is conducive to better communication, to a greater connection between advocate and jurors? The latter position, of course, because the advocate has removed all physical barriers. The podium hides the advocate, suggesting a lack of openness on the advocate's part. It also anchors advocates to one spot, limiting their mobility. And finally, it provides an attractive place to put notes and ensures that counsel will frequently look down at those notes and perhaps even start reading. Avoid the podium like the plague. Move it to a corner. Refuse to use it even if—especially if—the other side succumbs to the temptation to use it.

In some courtrooms, particularly some federal courtrooms, judges require the lawyers to stay at the podium for every part of the trial, including the opening statements. Advocates who find themselves in such a situation must make the best of it. Instead of standing behind the podium, stand to the side of it (most judges give the lawyer some leeway as long as the lawyer can always touch the podium). Avoid the temptation to hide behind the podium or to be unduly anchored to it. Move to one side then the other. Do not use the podium as a repository for notes. Find ways to leave the podium as often as possible, such as through the use of demonstrative aids. In the opening that might mean that the advocate creates a chart, draws a diagram, or puts a list on the board. Look for ways to limit the podium's impact.

2. *Where to Look*

Novice lawyers face one overwhelming emotion when they stand to deliver the opening statement: paralyzing fear. The fear reveals itself in any number of ways: the fear of facing the jurors, the fear of failing miserably, the fear of looking foolish, the fear of having nothing to say. Fear intimidates lawyers into writing out a script of their opening statement and then reading to the jury from the script. The advocate's notes provide an antidote for the fear. They ensure that the advocate will have something to say and that it will make sense. However, reading the opening statement is the death knell for the persuasiveness of the advocate and the interest of the jurors.

The use of notes during the opening exacts a high price. It precludes the advocate from maintaining eye contact with the jury. Eye contact is critical because the advocate who looks at the jurors while talking to them will be perceived as credible and trustworthy. We immediately trust those who look into our eyes when they talk to us, for they seem to have nothing to hide. Moreover, once advocates free themselves from the slavery of their notes, they are free to have a dialogue with the jurors, to observe their body language and to notice their nonverbal responses.

There really is no excuse for using notes during the opening. The opening can be prepared and learned before the trial and it comes before the presentation of evidence. An advocate who is adequately prepared to try a case should be able to deliver the opening without notes. Doing so maximizes the opportunity presented by the opening. Inexperienced trial attorneys who believe they need the "security" of notes may want to use a list, prepared as a visual aid for jurors, as a substitute. If this device is used, however, the advocate must be careful not to overuse it by staring at it rather than making eye contact with jurors.

On the other hand, advocates should not memorize their opening statements. It is easy to discern when someone is giving a canned speech. The word choice seems artificial, the delivery too smooth. The message that advocates send to jurors when they memorize their openings is that the opening is just a performance. The advocate is merely playing a part; he is just a mouthpiece for the client.

Instead of memorization at one extreme or reading at the other, advocates should be familiar with their openings inside and out, without memorizing each word or phrase. A bit of stumbling, searching for the right word is a good thing. It reveals the advocate's authenticity and genuineness. A pause by the advocate to collect her thoughts often provides jurors with a welcome opportunity to reflect upon what has been said.

3.   *Where to Go*

Purposeful movement by the advocate during the opening statement helps the jurors maintain their interest in what the advocate is saying. Too much movement, such as pacing back and forth in front of the jury box, distracts the jury from listening to the advocate's words. Too little movement—standing in the same place for the entire presentation—bores the jurors and reduces their retention of the opening. But some movement helps the advocate transition from one topic to another or serves to emphasize a point. The key is to ensure that the movement is purposeful and not the result of nervousness or mindless habit. For example, as the advocate begins to personalize the client, she might move back to the client at counsel table. After the personalization, the advocate might move to the front of the jury box to tell the story of the case. At the critical moment in the story, the advocate might move in closer to the jury, while lowering his voice. As he moves from one topic to another, the advocate might purposefully move from one side of the jury box to the other. At the appropriate time, the advocate should walk to the flip board to prepare a timeline, go to the blackboard to put up a list, or use the easel to display an important document. The possibilities are unlimited, but the key is that when movement has a purpose it enhances the message and increases the jurors' interest.

4.   *What to Do with Your Hands*

The final dilemma faced by most advocates is what they should do with their hands. There is no consensus on advocates' use of their hands. Is it okay to put your hands in your pockets? One hand? Both hands? Should you use hand gestures? Never? Rarely? Frequently?

Despite the myriad questions and the conflicting answers, the best approach to the use of the advocates' hands is surprisingly easy: Do what comes naturally. The worst possible approach is to use artificial gestures or to stiffly refuse to allow a hand to find a way into a pocket. Few things are more painful than watching an advocate deliver an entire opening statement with her hands held behind her back. This pose is so unnatural it becomes a distraction. Once again, of course, authenticity and sincerity should serve as the advocate's guides. There is no harm in putting a hand in a pocket; such a pose evokes a certain informality and familiarity. Gestures can enhance the words being spoken, providing emphasis and meaning.

The list of what should be avoided includes anything that will distract the jury from hearing the words being spoken. For example, playing with keys or change in pockets so that they jingle, fiddling with a pen or marker while speaking, or making the same gesture over and over again. Advocates can identify distracting nervous habits and idiosyncrasies by watching themselves on videotape. The tape will reveal the gestures, movements, and habits that help and those that do not.

❖ Principle Number Seven: Keep the Opening as Short as Reasonable Under the Circumstances

There is no magical length for opening statements. It is impossible to say whether the right length for the opening in a particular case is 10 minutes, 20 minutes, 2 hours or more without knowing the case and understanding the contested issues. However, the advocate should be sensitive to the limited attention span of the jury and should not needlessly use up his good will with the jurors by testing their patience at the outset of the trial. A key barometer that an advocate has gone too long is when some jurors begin looking off or fidgeting. Advocates should spend as much time as they need to give their opening, but not a second longer. As discussed at some length above, the opening should contain no civics lessons, no needless ingratiating, and no excessive repetition. Instead, it should be efficient, using as few words as possible.

V. THE LAW OF OPENING STATEMENT

A. The Rule Against Argument[12]

The prohibition on argument is the fundamental characteristic that distinguishes the opening statement from the closing argument. But what constitutes argument? Surprisingly, this most fundamental question is one of the least analyzed or understood principles of trial practice. Appellate courts rarely have occasion to discuss the meaning of "argument," because of the infrequency with which trial court rulings on the propriety of opening statement remarks are the subject of appeal. Because of this lack of guidance, trial judges have appropriated Justice Potter Stewart's obscenity test and applied it to "argument," taking an "I know it when I see (or hear) it" approach to the prohibition. The problem is exacerbated by the multiple tests (or, more accurately, rules of thumb) that are used to identify argument. The result is that the rule against argument varies widely from jurisdiction to jurisdiction, from courthouse to courthouse, and even from judge to judge.

Distinguishing argumentative statements from those that are not is difficult. There is a fine line between an appropriate description of the evidence in the opening statement and forbidden argument, and it is frequently unclear where the line is or when it has been crossed. Many decisions in this area require distinguishing between various shades of gray, not simple distinctions between black and white.

---

[12] Portions of this section previously appeared in Perrin, *From O.J. to McVeigh: The Use of Argument in the Opening Statement*, 48 EMORY L.J. 107 (1998). Used with permission.

1.   *The Tests for Argument*

The opinions of appellate courts, at best, give only general guidance about the proper content of the opening statement, noting that the purpose of the opening statement is to:

- "*State* what evidence will be presented"[13]

- "*Outline* the theory of the case"[14]

- "*Inform* the jury of the nature of what counsel expects the evidence to be"[15]

- "*Apprise* the trier of fact of what the state or defense expects to prove"[16]

- "*Explain* the case to the jury"[17]

Although these broad strokes do not provide much practical guidance for the practitioner, they do paint a picture of what might be called the "proof test" for argument, which broadly equates argument with the discussion of anything outside the party's evidence.

Experienced trial lawyers realize that the scope and content of the opening statement are matters that rest firmly in the discretion of the trial judge, who must decide in the context of the facts of the case whether counsel has crossed over the line into improper argument. With very few exceptions, the trial judge's ruling on argument is final and the judge's notion of what is and is not permissible will dictate the remarks of counsel before the jury. The relative unguided independence of trial judges leads to great uncertainty among trial lawyers about the application of the rule.

a.   The Witness and Inference Tests

There are two tests that most judges and lawyers use to apply the rule against argument. For ease of reference, they might be labeled as (1) the witness test and (2) the inference test.

The more popular of the two tests is undoubtedly the witness test, which—as the label suggests—simply asks whether the advocate has a witness (or an exhibit) who can competently attest to the disputed portion of the opening statement. If the answer is "no," then the lawyer's comments constitute improper argument. Thus, a lawyer could describe a witness' expected testimony that she saw the defendant commit the crime, but not that the defendant did so intentionally, because the defendant's mental

---

[13] *See, e.g., United States v. Dinitz*, 424 U.S. 600, 612 (1976) (Burger, C.J., concurring).

[14] *See, e.g., Browne v. State*, 933 P.2d 187, 190–91 (Nev. 1997).

[15] See, e.g., Fields v. Commonwealth, 343 S.E.2d 379, 382–83 (Vir. Ct. App. 1986).

[16] *See, e.g., Thompson v. State*, 381 A.2d 704, 706 (Md. Ct. Spec. App. 1978).

[17] *See, e.g., State v. Sanchez*, 923 P.2d 934, 945 (Haw. Ct. App. 1996).

state is not subject to observation. No witness could competently testify to the defendant's intent (with the possible exception of a mental health professional). It is an admittedly conservative test, and is rarely enforced strictly by judges.

The other frequently referenced rule of thumb—the "inference test"—draws the distinction between improper argument and proper description by focusing on the extent to which the advocate tells the jury how to view the facts. Under this approach, a lawyer is prohibited from drawing inferences or conclusions or otherwise interpreting the evidence for the jury. Thus, for example, a lawyer would be permitted to tell the jury "the defendant was going 50 m.p.h. in a 30 m.p.h. zone," but would be precluded from telling the jury that "the defendant was speeding."

b. The Tools of Argument

"Argument" describes not only the words uttered by the advocate, but also the manner in which those words are delivered. In fact, the advocate's tone may be the most significant factor in avoiding, or conversely, inviting objections based on argument. Common sense confirms that the same statement can carry very different meanings and have quite disparate effects on the listener by merely varying the style and tone of delivery. Moreover, it is often significantly easier to identify an argumentative tone than it is to identify an argumentative statement. The latter may require a careful analysis of the evidence, a time consuming task indeed. One's tone of voice, however, is subject to immediate characterization requiring no real thought or analysis. It is not surprising, then, that judges fall prey to the ease of being guided by their sensory perceptions, sustaining (or overruling) objections during the opening statement based on sound instead of content.

In addition to an argumentative tone, advocates infringe the rule against argument when they use certain rhetorical devices. For example, the use of rhetorical questions, analogies, anecdotes, appeals to common sense, repetition, or other techniques, by definition constitute argument and thus are not appropriate during the opening. If anything is foreclosed by the rule against argument it includes the specific tactics that one would characterize by their very nature as "argumentative."

In summary, advocates in the opening are limited by the rule against argument in at least four ways. They may explain or present their proof, but they must:

- be able to identify a competent witness or exhibit in support of each statement made

- not draw inferences or interpret the evidence for the jury

- avoid adopting an "argumentative" tone

- not use any rhetorical devices

Despite the prohibition on argument in the opening, advocates argue anyway. In fact, few, if any, rules of trial practice are violated as frequently as is the rule against argument. The reality is that some argument finds its way into most every opening statement and the rule against argument is rarely strictly enforced by trial judges.

2. *Strategies for Avoiding and Overcoming Argument Objections*

The amount of lawyer angst over the rule against argument would lead an observer to believe that a sustained argumentative objection is the worst imaginable horror for a trial lawyer. The reality, however, is that a sustained objection for argument is no worse than any other sustained objection. And, in fact, its bark is worse than its bite. The entire experience typically consists of nothing more than an objection from opposing counsel and the word "sustained" uttered by the judge. In the hurly-burly of the trial, the jurors may not even know what happened. That does not mean that lawyers should ignore the rule against argument or that they should blindly argue their case during the opening regardless of the consequences. It does mean, however, that lawyers should alleviate their anxiety about the rule against argument to a great degree and should have confidence as they deliver their openings. The techniques identified below constitute tried-and-true strategies for avoiding objections for argument altogether and for overcoming such objections once they are made.

a. Use Caution When Characterizing People, Events, or Evidence

Just as certain words are fighting words because they elicit strong reactions from listeners, certain words in the opening statement are inherently argumentative and almost certain to draw an objection for improper argument. Consider these two descriptions of the same event.

 Illustration Comparing Argumentative with Non-Argumentative Phrasing

Argumentative: The defendant committed this brutal and heinous murder because he was insanely jealous. If he couldn't have her, no one could.

Non-argumentative: We will prove that the defendant committed the murder of his wife and why he did so. Several of defendant's own friends will testify that he told them more than once, "If I can't have her, then no one can." That's right. The defendant took his wife's life, stabbing her repeatedly in the face and chest and back, because he couldn't let go of her.

The first choice makes judgments about the defendant's actions. The murder was "brutal" and "heinous" and the defendant was "insanely jealous."

The second choice, on the other hand, avoids the temptation to make those judgments for the jury instead relying on the facts to make the point clear. The use of partisan or prejudicial characterizations during the opening is one of the fastest ways to attract an objection. Limiting their use will reduce the likelihood of objections. That does not mean, however, that the lawyer should avoid characterizations altogether. The objective is to use action words and conclusions that find support in the testimony or are reasonable inferences therefrom. Facts are more powerful than empty conclusions. Precision and accuracy are more effective than inflammatory rhetoric.

b. Argue Through Themes and Theories

A case theme, by definition, is an argument. It is a rhetorical tool used for its persuasive force. And yet, advocates regularly use themes as one means of arguing their cases to jurors during the opening and judges typically tolerate the practice. There is almost an unwritten exception to the rule against argument that allows advocates to introduce their case themes and theories during the opening. This custom relates to another similar exception to the rule recognized by judges—one of timing. Advocates are allowed greater leeway to argue at the beginning and ending of their opening than during the middle. Thus, a strong statement by counsel of why their client is in the right, placed at the beginning and reinforced at the ending, can prove to be a safe means of avoiding the rule's limitations.

c. Support Conclusions with an Expert's Opinion Testimony

Expert witnesses testify in almost every modern trial and interpret the evidence for the jury. Their opinions are not limited to abstract propositions of science; rather, they testify in the form of opinions about what the facts mean. The liberal rules regarding expert witnesses allow experts to provide the jury with "mini summations" during the trial, and also radically expand the permissible scope of the opening statement. Under even the restrictive witness test, lawyers can tell the jury what they will hear from the expert even though the expert's expected testimony is conclusory and interpretive. Thus, rather than being limited to facts, the advocate can tell the jury what the facts mean, at least to the extent that an expert will support each conclusion. One might correctly conclude that the boundaries of the opening statement are often marked by the opinion testimony that will be offered during the trial and one way to avoid argument objections is to ensure that conclusions offered in the opening are supported by competent expert testimony.

d. Avoid an Argumentative Tone

The next means of avoiding argument objections has almost nothing to do with what advocates say and everything to do with how they say it. As the advocate's voice grows louder and more intense during the opening, the likelihood of an objection increases. Regardless of what the advocate is actually saying, it will sound argumentative. It reminds one of a base-ball umpire who claimed to be able to call balls and strikes by how they sounded. The rule against argument is a limit on *what* lawyers can say during the opening, not on *how* they say it. And yet, judges do rule according to sound, and thus lawyers must avoid "sounding argumentative." That does not mean that the lawyer should employ a monotone or should avoid the use of inflection or changes in volume and intensity. The rule against argument does not require that the advocate be boring or uninteresting. Instead the advocate should simply avoid the kind of intensity—outrage, righteous indignation, a plea for justice—that belongs only at the end of the trial, when the jury shares the advocate's emotional intensity.

e. Preface Argumentative Comments with a Predictive Phrase

The final strategy is the "oldest trick in the book," at least for lawyers trying to avoid objections during the opening. For generations, lawyers have prefaced their most argumentative statements in the opening with "the evidence will show" or "you will learn" or "I will prove." The insertion of the predictive phrase has seemingly magical qualities. In one fell swoop it calms both opposing counsel and judge, allaying fears that the statement that followed the predictive phrase was improper. The use of such phrases will often head off an argumentative objection or cause the judge to deny one that has been lodged.

The reality, of course, is that the predictive phrase changes nothing. If the statement is argumentative without the phrase it is argumentative with it. The statement "the defendant, acting out of revenge and hate, killed the victim in cold blood" is argumentative just as the statement "I will prove to you that the defendant, acting out of revenge and hate, killed the defendant in cold blood" is argumentative. But the latter statement softens the blow a bit, reminding the jurors (and the judge) that the statement is not evidence but only a prediction of what the evidence will be.

This advice does not mean that advocates should preface every statement with "the evidence will show." Far from it. Predictive phrases weaken the opening, continuously reminding the jurors that the lawyer's words are not evidence, but merely the lawyer's view of the evidence. Instead, use "the evidence will show" or "you will hear" sparingly, such as to introduce particularly strong conclusions or to otherwise avoid or overcome objections.

 ## Illustration of Objection for Improper Argument

Counsel 1:	We will prove to you that the defendant tobacco companies conspired to conceal the true risks of smoking and that they intentionally misled and deceived smokers in doing so.
Counsel 2:	Objection, improper argument.

Judge:	Response counsel?
Counsel 1:	Your Honor, we have a good faith belief that one of defendant's former employees, Bryan Bixby, will testify about what the defendants knew and the efforts they undertook to conceal the truth.
Judge:	Overruled.

B. Reference to Inadmissible or Excluded Evidence

A second and related requirement of the opening statement is that advocates limit their remarks to evidence that they have a good faith belief will be admissible during the trial. Counsel must not mention or make reference to any evidence that has been ruled inadmissible pursuant to a motion *in limine* or that the advocate knows or reasonably believes will not be admitted. The rule extends even to evidence of doubtful admissibility and, of course, to evidence that simply does not exist. To the extent advocates are unsure about the propriety of discussing a particular piece of evidence, they have two options: (1) file a motion *in limine* in advance of trial, or (2) simply avoid reference to the evidence during the opening. If the judge takes a motion *in limine* under consideration, without ruling on it, counsel should use caution in discussing the disputed evidence during the opening. Many judges expect counsel to avoid discussion of matters the admissibility of which the judge is actively considering. If unsure, counsel should seek clarification from the court.

 Illustration of Objection for Reference to Inadmissible Evidence

Lawyer:	Ladies and gentlemen, during the course of the trial you will hear that this is not the first time the defendant has been in trouble with the law. In fact, he was previously convicted for—
Opposing Lawyer:	Objection, that's not proper evidence in this case.
Judge:	Sustained.

Sanctions for violations of this rule can range from severe to merely annoying. On the severe end of the spectrum, in the event that the evidence mentioned is extremely prejudicial, discussion of the inadmissible evidence can result in a mistrial. The more likely result, however, is that the sanction will fall in the annoyance category, such as a curative instruction by the judge advising jurors that the evidence discussed by counsel is not properly considered by them in the case. Somewhere between the two is the unusual sanction levied by Judge Ito in the O.J. Simpson criminal prosecution, wherein he allowed the prosecution to deliver a supplemental opening statement because of the defense's discussion of inadmissible and previously undisclosed evidence.

C. Discussion of the Law

The third limitation on the opening restricts counsel from engaging in lengthy discussions of the legal principles that control the case or from otherwise arguing the law. The closing argument, which comes after the lawyers have met with the judge to decide upon the jury instructions, is the time for counsel to discuss, explain, and analyze the governing legal principles. In the opening, before the jury charge is known or the contested issues developed, extended discussion of the law or legal principles is premature.

However, that does not mean that counsel is precluded completely from some references to the law or introduction of the jury to important legal principles. Unfortunately, lawyers and commentators sometimes refer to this principle for shorthand purposes as precluding any discussion of the law. That is not correct. The advocate can always provide the jury context for the evidence they will be hearing and explain to them legal standards that will govern the jury's decision-making. The critical requirement, of course, is that the advocate must be accurate and fair in his explanations. For example, in a criminal prosecution involving a claim of self-defense the defendant would be hard pressed to make an opening statement without some mention and discussion of his defense. He might even desire to give the jury the legal definition of self-defense so that the jury has some context for the evidence they will hear. For example:

 Illustration of Proper Discussion of Law

Defense Lawyer: We don't deny that Gabe Manning was there when Mr. Waxler died or that he was the one who pulled the trigger that tragic night. Mr. Manning will take the stand and he will tell you himself of those fateful events. However, you will not hear evidence that Mr. Manning is guilty of murder or that he intended to kill anyone. Instead, we will prove to you that Mr. Manning acted in self-defense; that he pulled the trigger not as an act of aggression, but as an act of desperation; that he feared for his life and he shot Waxler because he was left with no other choice. At the end of this trial Judge Marshall will tell you what it means to act in self-defense. She will tell you that if Manning believed he was in imminent danger of death or severe bodily harm at the time he acted, then he acted in self-defense and he committed no crime. That is exactly what happened here, as you will hear through the sworn testimony.

The same principle applies in a civil case involving, for example, a claim of defamation. Assume that a defendant is accused of defaming the plaintiff, a co-worker, by accusing her of embezzlement. The defendant can raise two defenses: truth and qualified privilege. The defense of truth should require little explanation to the jury in the opening statement, but the defense of qualified privilege is a different matter entirely. To start with, it is an unfamiliar concept to the jurors and it has very specific legal requirements. If the advocate waits until closing argument to explain to the jury what it means, it may be too late. The jury will likely have already taken sides and done so without the benefit of a full and accurate understanding of one of defendant's defenses. Thus, the advocate should—the advocate must—introduce the jurors to the concept during the opening and give them some idea how it applies to the facts in the case before them.

In summary, the limitation on discussion of the law during the opening should be taken seriously, but it should not be made into something it is not. The rule is not an absolute prohibition. Rather, it is a caution or limitation on how far counsel should go—a helpful tool to prevent counsel from getting the cart too far ahead of the horse.

Illustration of Objection for Improper Discussion of Law

Lawyer: One of the issues in this case is whether Mr. Johnson intentionally killed Fred Winston. And the judge will instruct you on the difference between an intentional act and an unintentional one. And it's important that you listen closely to the judge when he tells you about that distinction, because in this case the defendant's acts were accidental, and thus unintentional. It's the difference between meaning to do something, planning for it, and specifically intending to do it, and having something happen accidentally that you did not plan for.

Opposing Lawyer: I'm sorry, Your Honor, but I have to object to that as an improper discussion of the law.

Judge: Sustained.

D. The Advocate's Personal Beliefs or Opinions

Advocates must avoid the expression of their personal beliefs or opinions about the merits of the case or the credibility of witnesses. The lawyer will not testify as a witness, nor will he undergo cross-examination. Thus, the particular opinions of the advocate about the case are simply not pertinent to the jury's task of considering the evidence. Moreover, advocates presumably gain an unfair advantage when they use their role as advocate to personally vouch for the evidence and its sufficiency or reliability.

Vouching is a greater temptation during the closing argument than the opening statement, but the rule is the same in each instance. Examples of statements that constitute improper vouching in the opening statement might include the following:

 Illustration of Improper Vouching

- I have tried many cases before juries and I have never seen this much proof of a crime. Take my word for it: the defendant is guilty.

- One of our witnesses will be Julie Winters, an onlooker at the time of the accident. I have met Ms. Winters and I have looked into her eyes when she previously testified in a deposition, and I can tell you in no uncertain terms, Ms Winters is a liar. I know when a person is lying to me and I can tell you that she will get on the stand today and lie to you.

- The plaintiff will try to convince you that you should not believe Dr. Wayne's testimony because he is being compensated as an expert and because he has testified for Acme Industries before. I'm here to tell you, I know Dr. Wayne. I've worked with him before and he is a friend of mine. He is a good man. He cannot be bought. I trust him and you should too.

In each instance, counsel goes far beyond mere advocacy of a position and into expression of personal opinion. It is one thing for counsel to argue that Dr. Wayne should be believed because of the evidence in the case and another entirely to base the argument on counsel's personal relationship with the expert.

However, the rule does not preclude every use of first person by trial counsel. To the contrary, it is perfectly appropriate for counsel to tell the jury in the opening, "I will prove to you today ..." or "I'm confident that you will find in favor of the defendant" or other first person expressions, provided that they are tied to what the evidence will show and not the personal beliefs or opinions of counsel.

E.   The Ethical Considerations for Opening Statement

The opening statement presents the advocate with a number of serious ethical obligations and responsibilities. Some are obvious and redundant of the legal obligations discussed above. Do not misrepresent the evidence to the jury. Do not make use of fictional evidence. And do not discuss evidence that will not be introduced during the trial. For example, the criminal defense attorney may not use the opening statement as an opportunity to discuss the defendant's expected testimony if she knows that the defendant will never take the stand. Efforts to manipulate the jury by exposing them to inadmissible, nonexistent, or fictional evidence constitute a clear violation of counsel's obligation of candor to the court and the jury. The ABA Model Rules of Professional Conduct specifically address this issue, providing that counsel must not "allude to any matter that the lawyer does not reasonably believe is relevant or that will not be supported by admissible evidence." (*See* ABA Model R. Prof. Conduct 3.4(e).)

Moreover, counsel must not refer to evidence excluded by the court's ruling on a motion *in limine*. Counsel must not express personal opinions about the case or witnesses in the case. Counsel must not ask the jury to put themselves in the position of one of the parties (the so-called "golden rule" argument). Counsel must not ask the jurors to return a verdict based on any improper purpose or appeal to their passions or prejudices.

The ethical limits of the opening statement are marked by the familiar twin pillars of good faith and reasonableness. Advocates should discuss in the opening statement only the evidence that they reasonably and in good faith believe will be admitted during the trial. Advocates must limit themselves to the evidence that the jury will hear and must seek a verdict based on that evidence and nothing else.

F. Objections, Curative Instructions, and Mistrials

1. *Good Manners and Lawyer Etiquette*

Despite the well-established and rather strict rules discussed above, lawyers rarely object during opening statements. Historically, lawyers have followed an unwritten rule of lawyering etiquette—that advocates should politely allow their opponents to deliver their opening statements without interruption, unless they argue in the extreme. This notion of good manners leads some judges to actively discourage objections during the opening and to basically ignore objections that are raised. The rule makes some sense. Inasmuch as each side gets an opportunity to present an opening statement, there is no real reason to vigorously enforce the rule against argument. Unless the opponent is playing unfairly in the opening remarks, such as by referring to inadmissible evidence or suggesting inferences not supported by the evidence, the advocate may be well suited to resist the temptation to object.

Beyond mere professional courtesy, there are other reasons not to object. Every objection carries a cost—it may raise concerns about the advocate's incivility or create questions about his desire to keep certain information from the jurors. Moreover, objections to the opening statement carry very little consequence. Typically, the only thing counsel gets for his trouble is a terse "sustained." It hardly seems worth the trouble. Accordingly, objections during the opening should be reserved for only those arguments and maneuvers that truly hurt the party or unfairly mislead the jury.

When lawyers make an objection they must do so in a timely and specific manner. The timeliness requirement means that the objection must be made within a reasonable time after the error is apparent. Obviously, the lawyer must object when the improper comment is made and not minutes, hours, or days later. The specificity requirement means that advocates must state the specific grounds for the objection. In the opening statement that will typically mean stating the grounds, "improper argument." In addition the lawyer should stand when addressing the court to interpose the objection. The lawyer who objects during the opening statement is in a somewhat different position than one objecting to a direct examination or the like. The lawyer is interrupting the remarks of the opponent and breeching lawyer etiquette. Because of those concerns, the lawyer who stands to object during the opening may want to display some deference and humility. Instead of, "Objection, argument!," the advocate might try a kinder, gentler approach. Perhaps, something like: "I'm sorry your Honor, I hate to interrupt Ms. Williams, but her argument is not proper during the opening statement." The difference will not be lost on the jurors.

2.   *Curative Instructions and Mistrials*

Depending on the severity of the damage done by opposing counsel's improper comments, steps beyond the bare objection may be necessary. The first remedy beyond a mere objection is a curative instruction from the judge. If opposing counsel improperly argues or refers to inadmissible evidence, counsel can seek an instruction from the judge for the purpose of curing the presumed harm. For example, in response to improper argument, the following exchange might take place.

 Illustration of Curative Instruction

Lawyer:	Objection, improper argument, Your Honor.
Judge:	Sustained counsel, limit yourself to the facts.
Lawyer:	Your Honor, I request that the jury be instructed to disregard the improper comments from counsel.
Judge:	Ladies and gentlemen, this is the opening statement; it is not evidence. Nothing the lawyers say constitutes evidence in this case. The opening statement is simply to give you an overview of the case and a preview of each side's evidence. You may continue counsel.

One risk with seeking a curative instruction is that it may serve to reinforce the opponent's words rather than to truly defuse them. It is a strategy best reserved for extreme abuses of the opening and, even then, only if the objecting party has already spoken and will not have a chance to respond until closing argument.

The final remedy for opening statement errors is mistrial. Not surprisingly, the mistrial is reserved for only truly outrageous abuses by counsel, such as a prosecutor's comments in a criminal case that violate a defendant's constitutional rights. "The declaration of a mistrial is a drastic remedy and should be granted only in those circumstances when the incident is so grievous that the prejudicial effect can be removed no other way."[18] A wide variety of factors must be taken into account before deciding to request a mistrial, including the extent to which the party is confident about the likelihood of success on the merits, the party's desire to have the case tried quickly, and the nature of the misconduct by the other side. Judges are extremely reluctant to grant mistrials based on comments in the opening statement, believing that curative instructions effectively eliminate any potential prejudice.

VI. THE LEGAL REQUIREMENTS OF THE OPENING STATEMENT

Despite the fact that counsel's words during the opening statement do not constitute "evidence," they do matter for reasons that go beyond their persuasive force with the jury. They also may have a legal effect. For example, if counsel concedes his client's liability on a claim in the opening statement, affirmatively shows that his client has no right to recover on one or more claims, or admits that the state cannot prove all of the elements of a crime with which the defendant is charged, the opponent may obtain a directed verdict based on nothing more than counsel's admissions in the opening. The rule only applies, however, if counsel has had a full opportunity to correct any ambiguity, error, or omission, and only if the party has made a clear, affirmative, and intentional admission.[19]

When such an admission is made during the opening, the opposing advocate can seek judgment on the conceded claim before proceeding with the evidence. In the face of such a request, the adversely affected counsel has several options. If the party does not intend to pursue the claim or defense or simply cannot prove the claim or defense, then the party should agree to the entry of judgment. Alternatively, if the admission was inadvertent or unintentional, and the party intends to pursue the claim or defense, the party can ask the court for an opportunity to clarify the opening statements. The supplemental remarks should be directed to the disputed point and counsel should show exactly how she intends to prove the claim or defense, and make clear that she does not concede or admit the matter.

---

[18] *State v. Thurlo*, 830 S.W.2d 891 (Mo. Ct. App. 1992).

[19] *See Best v. District of Columbia*, 291 U.S. 411, 415 (1934); *Hanley v. United States*, 416 F.2d 1160, 1164 (5th Cir. 1969); *Morgan v. Koch*, 419 F.2d 993, 999 (7th Cir. 1969); *Webb v. United States*, 191 F.2d 512, 515 (10th Cir. 1951).

Chapter Six

DIRECT EXAMINATION[1]

---

[1] The genesis of this chapter was an article written by Caldwell, Perrin, Richard Gabriel, and Sharon Gross, *Primacy, Recency, Ethos & Pathos: Integrating Principles of Communication into the Direct Examination* 76 NOTRE DAME LAW REVIEW 423 (2001).

I. OBJECTIVES AND OBSTACLES

A. Objectives

Direct examination is the heart and soul of an advocate's case. Nearly all of the information a party needs to communicate to the jury comes from direct examination. With rare exceptions, trials are won on the strength of a party's case, not on the weakness of the opponent's case.

An effective direct examination is a sophisticated and complex undertaking. The successful examiner must recognize and overcome the obstacles to an effective examination, carefully and thoroughly prepare each witness, and integrate into each direct examination certain basic principles of effective communication and persuasion. Those principles, discussed in Section III below, provide the essential tools for powerful and compelling direct examinations. They include: blocking and headlining, personalization and rapport building, use of pathos, effective staging, logical and dramatic development of the action sequence, use of exhibits and demonstrative evidence, disclosure of weaknesses, emphasis and repetition of important testimony, and adoption of a winning attitude and demeanor.

There are three goals to be accomplished through direct examination:

1.   Present evidence that is sufficient to prove the party's claim or defense

2.   Convince the fact finder of the integrity of the party's evidence, and the credibility of the party's witnesses

3.   Nullify the opponent's claims or defenses

Conventional wisdom advises that direct examination is the one point in the trial when advocates should shift the spotlight away from themselves and onto their witnesses. The lawyer should relinquish control and allow the jury to hear the testimony of the witness with as little interference as possible. We agree. The witness' testimony should hold center stage during the direct examination. All too often, however, lawyers have misunderstood that advice as meaning that they do not have an active role in the direct examination, and instead that their role is largely passive. This is not so: it is the lawyer/examiner who must construct the direct examination in such a way that the jury's attention is drawn to the witness; it is the lawyer who must prepare the witness to tell her or his story despite the intimidating glare of the spotlight; and it is the lawyer who must ensure that all of the testimony needed from each witness is elicited in a clear and memorable way.

The success of the direct examination ultimately depends upon whether the jury believes and likes the messengers. In the context of the direct examination, the messengers are not only the witnesses who testify from the witness stand, but also the examiners who call the witnesses and elicit the testimony, for they implicitly (during direct examination) and explicitly (during closing argument) vouch for the credibility of their witnesses.

B.   Obstacles

As a tool of communication, the direct examination presents a number of imposing obstacles to the examiner. Unlike the opening statement or closing argument, advocates cannot communicate directly with the jury, but rather only indirectly through the testimony of their witnesses. Unlike cross-examination, the examiner on direct examination may not ask witnesses leading questions or otherwise argue the case to the jury through those questions. Moreover, the examiner on direct examination is subject to objections by opposing counsel, either to the questions asked or the answers given.

These unique challenges might be depicted graphically as a triangle, with the examiner (A) at one corner, the witness (B) at the top, and the jury (C) at the third corner. During *voir dire*, opening statement, and closing argument, the advocate is able to speak directly to the jury: that is, to go from A to C without having to transmit the message through B (the witness) (see Figures 6.1 and 6.2). Consequently, the lawyer speaks to the jury without filter or restraint. *Voir dire* allows the even greater

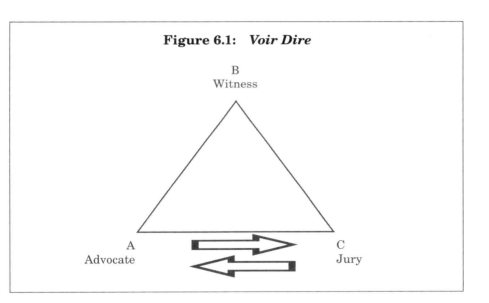

Figure 6.1: *Voir Dire*

B
Witness

A
Advocate

C
Jury

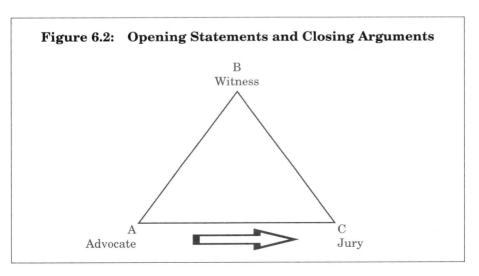

Figure 6.2:   Opening Statements and Closing Arguments

B
Witness

A
Advocate

C
Jury

luxury of enabling the lawyer to speak directly with the jurors and to hear their responses to questions.

On the other hand, the direct examination necessitates traveling two legs of the triangle, from the examiner (A) to the witness (B) and from the witness (B) to the jury (C), substantially complicating the communication process (see Figure 6.3). Although the cross-examination also requires a trip through the witness, the ability to ask leading questions enables the lawyer to communicate his message to the jury much more directly than during the direct examination, even making it possible for the lawyer, without regard

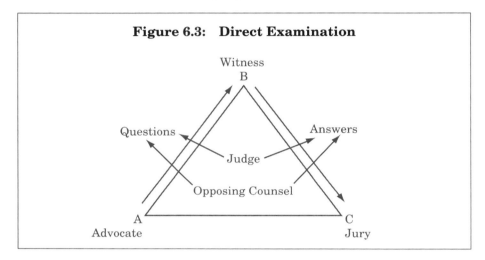

Figure 6.3:   Direct Examination

to the cooperation of the witness, to communicate a point to the jury by the questions asked, and thus in effect to travel directly from A to C.

The direct examination is not only complicated because of the need to communicate through the witness, but also because of the other players in the courtroom drama–opposing counsel and the judge. They both reside in the middle of the triangle (D and E) poised to interrupt the direct examination. The opposing lawyer can disrupt the direct examination between A and B by interposing an objection to the question asked or disrupt the direct examination between B and C by interposing an objection to the answer given.

In either event, the judge can sustain the objection and prevent the information from reaching the jury or can lodge an objection *sua sponte*. In addition, the judge can order a side bar or call a recess. Each disruption robs the examination of the natural rhythm desired by the advocate. Put in perspective, these challenges combine to make the direct examination a complicated and challenging means of transmitting the witness' story to the jury.

II.   PREPARING FOR DIRECT EXAMINATION

The many barriers to communicating through direct examination demonstrate the central importance of careful and thorough preparation of witnesses before they testify. Good direct examinations do not just happen; they are the result of thorough preparation and careful planning. There are no shortcuts or excuses. The hard work of preparation is essential to successful direct examinations.

Preparation takes several forms, including,

- anticipation of evidentiary objections

- analysis of the testimony needed to prove the party's claim or defense

- consideration of the foundational requirements for any exhibits or demonstrative aids to be used

- equipping witnesses with the tools they need to testify fully, accurately, and convincingly about what they know

A.   Preparing the Witness

1.   *Fact-Gathering*

Witness preparation is a two-step process. The first step is the fact-gathering phase, during which the lawyer's goal is simply to obtain all of the information in the witness' possession and to put that information into some form that will preserve it for future use. Much of this work takes place at the beginning of the case when the lawyer is trying to determine what happened. Witness interviews that are simply for fact-gathering purposes should consist largely of open-ended questions designed to get the witness talking and appropriate follow-up questions to fill in the gaps left after the witness' answers. The attitude of the lawyer should be open and non-judgmental toward the witness. Generally, the lawyer should have witnesses commit their information to writing or take other steps to preserve the witness' knowledge. Witness statements can be used later if needed to help refresh a forgetful witness' memory or to impeach witnesses who change their testimony.

2.   *Preparing Witnesses for Deposition or Trial*

The second step in witness preparation is preparing the witness to testify at trial, deposition, or hearing. This process is very different from fact-gathering and naturally involves different concerns. First, preparing a witness to give testimony must include not only a review and discussion of information known by the witness and the likely areas of inquiry during the direct examination, but also how the witness should deliver the testimony. Second, the advocate must recognize the discomfort and anxiety that many witnesses experience when confronted with testifying before a judge and jury. Explaining the process and removing the mystery are significant steps in alleviating witness anxiety. Third, preparation for trial or deposition must provide the witness with the skills and ammunition the witness will need to survive hostile questioning on cross-examination. Fourth, witness preparation must be conducted while mindful of the rights of adverse parties to obtain the information used or documents reviewed during witness preparation. Finally, the preparation must be done consistent with the ethical obligations imposed on the lawyer under the codes of professional conduct. Each of these aspects of preparation is discussed below.

a. Preparation by Themes or Topics

The first and most important task of witness preparation is to help witnesses testify fully and clearly about what they know and to give their testimony in a way that conveys to the trier of fact the witness' trustworthiness. Too often lawyers treat the preparation of witnesses as a rehearsal for a theatrical production in which the lawyer and the witness have lines that must be learned and then delivered on cue. That approach to witness preparation leads lawyers to script the direct examination and then to simply lead the witness through the script when preparing them to testify. Trial testimony is much too dynamic for any kind of scripted preparation. In the hurly-burly of trial, the witness will almost certainly fail to remember all of her "lines" and will deliver the ones she remembers out of order. Moreover, objections will disrupt the questioning and throw off "the script." And even if everything goes perfectly, the testimony will *sound* scripted, giving the jury the impression that the witness' testimony is simply the product of the lawyer's machinations. Finally, preparation by scripting fails to give witnesses any sense of where their testimony fits into the case as a whole and leaves the witness vulnerable to the opponent's cross-examination. The witness will know only the "correct" answers to a finite set of questions and will have little understanding of how her testimony fits into the larger whole.

Instead of preparing witnesses by rehearsing the actual questions and answers, witnesses should be prepared according to the themes of the case and the topics about which the witness will testify. If witnesses understand the big picture and how their testimony fits into the larger story of the case, they will be better prepared to handle cross-examination and better able to answer questions in the context of the disputed issues in the case. This mode of preparation necessitates that the lawyer spend some time with each witness explaining the disputed issues and the contentions of the lawyer's client with regard to those issues, and the role of the witness in the case. Next, the lawyer should identify for the witness the particular topics that will be covered with the client during the direct examination, discussing with the witness his knowledge of each topic, rather than just his specific answer to a particular question.

Thematic preparation prepares witnesses to give their testimony in "blocks" (topical subparts of the direct examination), and to think about their testimony not as a series of questions and answers, but as a part of a larger direct examination and a still larger case. It also provides the lawyer with a good sense of how the witness will respond to the direct examination questions and whether the lawyer will need to exert more or less control over the witness at the trial or hearing. During the actual preparation session(s), the lawyer will need to periodically stop and discuss specific responses given by the witness—suggesting better word choices, clarifying the witness' understanding of the pertinent events, or reminding the witness of past statements the witness has made about the same material. Yet, the lawyer should avoid suggesting that there is a particular right answer to any particular question or that the questions will be asked in a certain way.

This manner of preparation should lead to direct examinations that come across as genuine conversations between the lawyer and witness and not as preconstructed Qs and As that have been carefully scripted in advance. It also ensures smoother execution of the direct examination, because the lawyer does not risk the panic that strikes when the witness gets "off script." Instead, the absence of a script forces the lawyer to ask natural follow-up questions of the witness to elicit any material needed to complete a "block" or fill in a gap.

b. Removing the Mystery about Testifying

In addition to careful preparation of what the witness will say, the lawyer must also consider *how* the witness will deliver his testimony. Many, if not most, of the individuals called to testify at trial or deposition will be first time witnesses, meaning that the process will be foreign to them and more than a little bit intimidating. The lawyer must work through the preparation process to put the witness at ease and to give the witness the skills needed to be a good witness. Of course, the best way to make a witness comfortable is through thorough preparation. Knowledge inspires confidence. At the same time, it is helpful to remove as much of the mystery from the process as possible. A witness testifying at trial for the first time might benefit from a visit to the courtroom beforehand. He might even sit in the witness chair to get a clear sense of how the courtroom looks and feels. Advocates might accomplish much the same thing by showing the witness a video that depicts witness testimony at a deposition or trial and identifies some of the traps and pitfalls of being a witness.

c. Testimonial Tips and Traps

Perhaps the more difficult task in the preparation process is ensuring that prospective witnesses understand how to testify in a manner that is persuasive and credible. Many lawyers begin with a checklist of points that they go over with witnesses orally, or in writing, or both. The first and most important of these testimonial tips, of course, is for the witness to tell the truth. In no event should the lawyer do anything either explicitly or implicitly that would lead the witness to shade the truth or to tell an outright lie.

Perhaps the second most important piece of advice to the witness is the same for both direct examination and cross-examination: the witness must listen carefully to each question. Unfortunately, this is also the hardest instruction for witnesses to follow. They tend to answer the question that they expected the examiner to ask or the question that they think the lawyer meant to ask. Most witnesses need practice and encouragement to become good listeners.

Witnesses also must understand the role of all of the individuals in the courtroom (or in the deposition). The judge's authority over the proceeding, the motivations of the opposing side's lawyer, and even the role of the court clerk and bailiff may need some explanation. For example, the advocate needs to tell witnesses that in the event of an objection to an answer, she should stop speaking and wait for the court's ruling. Similarly, the witness needs to know how to handle exhibits, if any, and perhaps even what to do during recesses.

On a more substantive level, it may be helpful to conduct mock cross-examinations of certain witnesses and even to videotape the examination so that the witness can actually see how he appears when testifying. Often witnesses' nervous habits are unknown to them until they can see them on video. The witness' tendency to say "you know" several times in each sentence may become obvious only when the witness observes firsthand just how distracting it is. Practicing cross-examination also serves to diffuse the disorientation of the actual cross. The witness is given the opportunity to anticipate some of the likely questions, to see some of the traps that await and, perhaps more importantly, to simply experience questioning at the hands of a hostile examiner.

d. Preparing for Cross-Examination

An important part of witness preparation is ensuring that the witness is prepared to withstand the rigors of cross-examination. Part of that preparation is content-based. That is, you should apprise the witness of likely lines of inquiry on cross-examination and ensure that the witness is prepared to respond fully and accurately to those questions. This process must include, at a minimum, reviewing with the witness any past statements the witness has made about the subject matter of his testimony. This review helps the witness avoid unintentional conflicts between his current testimony and past statements, reducing the likelihood that the witness will be impeached. Preparation should also include an overview of the opposing party's claims or defenses and the party's theory about what happened. Nothing provides better protection against cross-examination than a clear perspective on the questioner's motives and objectives.

In addition, the preparation process must include guidance to the witness about the basic principles of giving cross-examination testimony. The instructions should advise the witness not to volunteer information to the cross-examiner, but rather to answer only the question asked. The witness should be told to pause before answering (so the witness can briefly reflect on the question and to give the advocate the opportunity to object if appropriate) and then to answer the question directly, if possible. If the question calls for a "yes" or "no" answer, the witness should answer "yes" or "no." If the question cannot be answered "yes" or "no," the witness should say so. The witness should never guess or estimate. If she does not know the answer, she should say "I don't know."

The instructions should also describe certain kinds of questions that may trap an unwary witness. For instance, witnesses should be careful answering compound questions because the answer may or may not apply to all parts of the question. Witnesses should be warned about questions that make false assumptions about the evidence, such as the "when did you stop beating your wife" question. Witnesses should resist invitations to make sweeping generalizations or to testify about matters beyond their knowledge or expertise. They should not fall prey to the "pregnant pause," when the questioner pauses before asking another question after the witness' answer in hopes that the witness will feel the need to keep talking simply to fill in the dead air. Rarely will the witness' additional comments be helpful.

e.   The "Have you talked to your lawyer?" Question

When preparing a witness to testify at deposition, hearing, or trial the lawyer must always be mindful of the potential implications of how the preparation is conducted. One concern is that the lawyer's preparation of the witness might cause the jury to believe, if they learned of the preparation efforts, that the lawyer improperly coached the witness, and thus call into question the credibility of both the witness and the advocate. This concern can never be totally eliminated, but its potential for harm can be limited by telling the witness that he may be asked about meeting with you and ensuring that the witness knows that there is nothing improper or inappropriate about your preparation meetings. Simply preparing the witness for the question, "Isn't it true that you met with your lawyer [or plaintiff's lawyer] before you came here today?," will substantially limit the potential impeachment. The witness, if prepared for the question, can answer with a confident "Absolutely, I certainly did," instead of stammering and stuttering as witnesses often do when they are surprised by the question, assuming that there must have been something wrong with the meeting.

f.   Rule 612 and Production of Preparation Materials

Preparation of witnesses, if not carefully structured and executed, may also put the lawyer at risk of having to produce to the other side any materials used to prepare a witness to testify despite the lawyer's belief that the materials were privileged or otherwise protected from production. Rule 612 of the Federal Rules of Evidence provides that the adverse party is entitled to review any writings used to refresh a witness' memory before the witness testifies "if the court in its discretion determines it is necessary in the interests of justice." (Fed. R. Evid. 612.) Some jurisdictions hold that a party waives the protected status of a document, regardless of whether the protection is based on work product or attorney client privilege grounds, by showing a document to a witness to refresh the witness' memory before the witness testifies. Thus, a lawyer who selects one hundred documents out of the more than one thousand documents involved in the case and shows only those one hundred documents to a witness in preparation for the witness to testify at deposition could be forced under Rule 612 to produce to the opposing party the selected documents despite the fact that the attorney's selection of the documents clearly falls within attorney work product under Rule 26(b)(3) of the Federal Rules of Civil

Procedure. Other jurisdictions interpret Rule 612 more narrowly, refusing to require production of documents used with witnesses before testifying unless the examining party can show that particular documents actually refreshed the witness' testimony and helped the witness to testify.

However, the very existence of Rule 612 counsels in favor of a cautious approach to witness preparation. When a witness is shown privileged documents during the preparation process, the advocate runs the risk that she will have to disclose the documents to opposing counsel. The risk is equally great for deposition testimony. One of the first questions lawyers love to ask at the beginning of depositions is, "What documents have you looked at in preparation for your deposition today." Not only must witnesses be prepared for that question, but advocates must be prepared for it as well and know how they will respond when their opponent demands production of the documents reviewed by the witness.

g.   The Rules of Ethics and Common Sense in Witness Preparation

Finally, the lawyer must conform to professional rules of conduct and basic principles of ethics and common sense when preparing witnesses to testify. Obviously, the advocate must not do anything that causes or encourages witnesses to change their truthful testimony. (A.B.A. Model R. of Prof. Conduct 3.4(b).) An advocate's duty of candor to the court and her position as an officer of the court demand that she insist that witnesses tell the truth whether it helps or hurts the advocate's side, and that the advocate refuses to offer evidence that she knows or "reasonably believes" to be false. (Rule 3.3(a)(4).) Moreover, advocates should take appropriate steps to discourage witnesses from lying and should quickly move to reveal and correct any false testimony that they discover has been given by a witness. (Model Rule 3.3(a)(2), (4).)

B.   Preparing the Examination

1.   *Proof of the Claim or Defense*

The best-prepared witness and the most stylistically pleasing presentation are worthless if the examination fails to elicit the testimony necessary to prove the party's claims or defenses. The lawyer's most fundamental obligation is to ensure that the legal proof requirements are satisfied through the party's case-in-chief. Thus, planning direct examinations requires attention both as to which persons must be called as witnesses to prove the case and what evidence must be elicited from each witness.

A matter as important as this must not be left to chance. Advocates must develop a means of systematically identifying the evidence that must be produced to prove the party's claims or defenses and then ensure that there is witness testimony, an exhibit, or both, that will prove each point. Advocates must further ensure that each witness is competent to testify and that the exhibit will be admissible at trial. Once the trial begins, advocates should use a written chart or checklist to track the actual testimony and exhibits as they come into evidence and confirm that each claim or defense was established in the manner expected.

2. *Order of Witnesses*

In addition to ensuring that all necessary testimony and exhibits are introduced at trial, advocates must consider the best order in which to call the witnesses. Of course, the best order may vary from case to case and will depend on many variables. For instance, the expert witness might be unavailable to appear when the proponent would have hoped because of scheduling conflicts, or the case might have moved more quickly than the proponent expected, forcing a party to call witnesses out of order to fill out the trial day.

However, when possible, some general principles should be followed. As discussed earlier, first impressions are important throughout the trial, and the principle of primacy certainly applies to witness ordering and presentation. Thus, present a strong, credible witness, or one who is emotionally appealing, at the beginning of the case. That witness may be followed with a "weaker" witness, that is, a witness who is timid or less significant, or a "chain" witness who serves merely as a link. For example, call as the first witness someone who can testify that the defendant used the gun and who can identify the gun. Next, call the "chain" witness who can identify the exhibit gun as the one received from the case investigator and logged into evidence. The next witness might be the case investigator who retrieved the gun from the defendant.

Juries love to hear stories and, when possible, witnesses should be called in an order that allows the jury to appreciate the "narrative" of the case. Thus, order the witnesses chronologically when it makes sense to do so. Chronological order in a medical malpractice case would begin with the initial diagnosis and continue to the resolution of the defendant's culpability. For example, the patient notices symptoms, which she reports to her physician, who orders lab tests. The lab tests indicate abnormalities, which suggest a particular illness, but the physician who receives the results misdiagnoses the condition and the patient suffers an injury. The chronological order of witnesses would be patient (plaintiff), lab technician, and then expert witness. This not only presents the witnesses chronologically, but also follows a strong, weak, strong order of presentation. If the circumstances dictate calling the defendant doctor as an adverse witness, begin with the plaintiff and then call the lab technician, the defendant doctor, and the expert witness. Presenting the defendant's testimony immediately before the expert witness would create a stark contrast, and still retain the desired chronology.

In a criminal case the chronology could flow from the commission of the crime to the end of the crime. For example: the victim is walking down the street; the defendant grabs and assaults him; his screams attract a passerby who rescues him; the passerby holds the suspect for the police who take the suspect into custody and take a statement. The chronological order of witnesses would be the victim, the passerby, and the officer.

If the order cannot be chronological, it should be logical. For example, a defendant is charged with five counts of residential burglary that occurred in multiple areas over a one-month period of time. The police connect the defendant to the crime by fingerprints. The same agency evidence technician processed each burglary scene. The logical presentation of the evidence would be to have the five homeowners testify in the order of first in time to last in time, or in the order of counts one through five of the information. After the homeowners, the technician and expert should testify. Not only does the jury understand the evidence as to each count, but they get the impact of the defendant's busy month of activities.

Similarly, logic dictates that "foundational" witnesses should be called before the expert witness testifies. For example, if an accident reconstructionist will testify that the automobile skid marks show that the plaintiff was traveling 45 miles per hour, it would be wise to call the witnesses who can testify about the actual length of the skid marks and can link the skid marks to the particular accident before the expert testifies.

Moreover, first present witnesses who can lay a credible foundation for a vulnerable witness, before calling the vulnerable witness himself. In a narcotics case, for example, it is logical to call the undercover officer before the informant. An informant is frequently vulnerable because of a criminal history, a motive to help the officer, or a history of drug abuse. The jury will more readily believe that the defendant sold drugs to the officer and the informant if they hear it from the officer first.

3.   *Selection of Witnesses*

The selection of which witnesses an advocate will actually put on the witness stand will play an important role in deciding the ultimate order of those witnesses. Advocates should be wary of calling too many witnesses to prove the same fact because it is time consuming, and may insult the intelligence and patience of the trier of fact. Multiple witnesses may also cause credibility problems if they all sound alike, leading the jury to decide that they were "scripted." If each purports to have seen the same thing and then describes it differently, a new unnecessary issue is raised that must be resolved. At the same time, however, if you have two credible witnesses who saw the same event then you may want to call both of them despite the additional time required. In fact, multiple witnesses can be helpful in repeating the essential facts of the case and reinforcing by corroboration the credibility of each of the witnesses.

When it is necessary to choose between multiple witnesses on the same issue, choose the witness who can serve some other strategic purpose. For example, if most of the jurors are older women, choose the "older woman witness" to testify on the point. Or, if one of the witnesses can improve or build on the testimony of another, choose that witness.

Be cautious when deciding not to call an obvious witness. Although the jury is instructed not to speculate on the missing witness, individual jurors may wonder why a proponent failed to call that witness. For example, if it is clear that there were two, but only two, non-party eyewitnesses to an accident, the jurors may wonder why the plaintiff called only one and may conclude that the missing witness would not have been favorable to the plaintiff. This type of speculation may jeopardize an otherwise strong case, so that the best course of action may be to call the second witness even though she does not add to what the first witness can establish.

In sum, when possible choose those witnesses who have testimony that helps to prove the case, who have some jury appeal, who meet jury expectations, and who corroborate each other and move the case toward a successful resolution.

C.   Structuring the Testimony

Each direct examination should begin with an introduction of the witness to the jury, including basic information such as name, marital status, family size, occupation, residence, and status or position in the community. Lawyers often mindlessly begin direct examinations by asking witnesses to state their name "for the record." That thoughtless approach, which suggests that neither the lawyer, nor anyone else in the courtroom, really cares about the name of the witness, but rather that the person's name is simply a necessary formality, immediately sends the wrong message to the jury. If the judge does not elicit the witness' name before the advocate begins the examination, he should ask: "Ms. Jones, please introduce yourself to the jury." Even on a point as seemingly trivial as eliciting the name of the witness, the difference in the two approaches is significant. At every turn, advocates must demonstrate by what they do and say that their witnesses are credible and worthy of respect, and that principle holds particular importance at the very beginning of the direct examination.

If the witness is an expert, you must, of course, develop his or her educational and professional background. Call professional witnesses by their title, for example, Doctor, Detective, Reverend, or Officer. Showing proper respect in this way builds the credibility of the witness and reduces the witness' nervousness. This "getting to know the witness" phase should consist of "easy" questions that allow the witness to adjust to the physical environment of the courtroom and to the many staring faces.

Next, address the purpose of the witness' presence in court and set the stage for the witness' testimony. Is this the victim, a friend of the defendant, or an expert witness? If identification is the purpose, begin with the facts that support the credibility of that identification and thoroughly outline the time, place, and manner of the witness' observation. Tell the jury about previous identifications: for example, at the show-up, line-up, or the preliminary hearing. Highlight unique characteristics of the defendant that the witness found remarkable. Then move quickly and dramatically to an in-court identification.

After the stage is set you should move to the "action sequence," the critical testimony this witness has to offer, always letting the witness tell the story in her words. Leading questions discredit the testimony and are objectionable. At the same time, of course, do not lose control of the witness.

Strive to keep the direct examination streamlined. Ask crisp and well-placed questions and then listen to the answers. Whenever possible, try to finish the direct examination at the same time the court takes a break. The principle of recency teaches that this tactic will cause the testimony to settle in the minds of the jurors more firmly than it otherwise might.

III. PRINCIPLES FOR EFFECTIVE DIRECT EXAMINATIONS

PRINCIPLES FOR DIRECT EXAMINATIONS

❖ Ask Clear and Understandable Questions

❖ Use Blocking and Headlining

❖ Personalize Witnesses

❖ Incorporate Pathos

❖ Set the Stage

❖ Fully Develop the Action Sequence

❖ Emphasize Important Testimony

❖ Use Exhibits and Demonstrative Aids

❖ Disclose Material Weaknesses

❖ Adopt a Winning Attitude and Demeanor

An effective direct examination should do more than simply establish the legal elements of a claim or defense, though it must surely do that. The direct examination must also resonate with the jury. It must be clear, memorable, and compelling. The direct examination should be carefully organized so that it tells an easily understood and memorable story. It should cast the spotlight on the witness and allow him to testify in his own words. Successful direct examinations require mastery of certain basic techniques of communication. The ten techniques that follow provide a sure and steady path to better and more persuasive direct examinations.

❖ Principle Number One: Ask Clear and Understandable Questions

Direct examination is a process of questions and answers. Each question must be framed to elicit a direct, simple, and known response. The answer must be responsive to the question and must be based on the witness' personal knowledge. The first step toward eliciting a helpful answer is to ask a concise and clear question.

1. *Ask Open-Ended Questions*

The jury wants to hear the witness testify, not the examiner, thus direct examination questions should be mostly non-leading. Leading questions are generally not permitted on direct examination except when necessary to develop the witness' testimony or on preliminary matters. (Fed. R. Evid. 611(c).)

The classic definition of a leading question is a question that suggests the answer. Thus, the question "You wouldn't know a leading question if it bit you on the nose, would you?" is obviously leading. However, the question "Did you ask the witness a leading question?" would likely not fall within the definition in that it does not suggest any particular answer. In other words, the mere fact that a question calls for a "yes" or "no" answer does not mean that it is leading. The suggestiveness of the question controls its characterization as leading or not. One means of avoiding objections for leading is by giving the witness a choice in the question. For example, you might ask "Did you ask a leading question or was it open-ended?"

Of course, the best method to avoid such objections is to ask open-ended questions that encourage the witness to tell their story fully and completely. Who, what, when, where, or how should be the first word of most direct examination questions. The perfect question on direct examination is "What happened next?" or better yet, "How so?" or best of all, "Why?"

Despite the general prohibition on leading, there are situations when leading is not only appropriate on direct examination, but absolutely necessary. For example, when laying foundations for exhibits or other evidence, or eliciting testimony about undisputed matters you may lead the witness. Similarly, if the witness is forgetful, very young, or hostile, you may ask leading questions. (Fed. R. Evid. 611.) Leading is also permissible if for the purpose of developing the witness' testimony, such as through the use of headlines or other transitional aids.

Advocates should not let the leading question prohibition cause them to ask unintelligible or awkwardly phrased questions. For example, a favorite question on direct examination for many lawyers is: "What, *if any-thing*, happened next?" The "if anything" is inserted, presumably, to avoid an objection that the examiner has not yet established that anything happened next—"assumes facts not in evidence" or "leading." But the fear of objection from omission of "if anything" is irrational. In the first place, "real people" do not use phrases like "if anything," and the question makes the examiner sound like a lawyer. In the second place, the potential objection is easily overcome because something must have happened next or the witness would not be testifying on the witness stand!

2. *Ask Easily Understood Questions*

Avoid the temptation to show off your impressive vocabulary during the direct examination. The language of the direct examination should be simple and easily understood. Resist the urge to sound like a lawyer. Instead of asking, *"Officer, what happened after you exited your vehicle?"* ask, *"Officer, what happened after you got out of your car?"* Moreover, advocates should use word choices that personalize their clients and cases. For example, ask the burglary victim to describe the condition of his home, not his house; call the deceased victim by her first name. This makes the case more personalized and evokes greater empathy from the jury.

At the same time, advocates should avoid asking questions in the negative or questions that leave the record unclear when answered. Questions that begin, "Is it not true that then you left ..." will puzzle even the sharpest witness and attentive juror. Ask questions such that a "yes" or "no" answer to the question has a readily understandable meaning to the jury and will be clear in the transcript.

Finally, advocates should adopt the terms required by law to make the witness' testimony legally sufficient. Ask a robbery victim specifically about "fear" and ask a rape victim specifically about "penetration." Those particular words are used in the instructions to the jury and the advocate must elicit testimony to prove those facts.

3.   Use the "Double Direct" to Gain Repetition

Repetition of important testimony is one means of ensuring that the jury remembers the testimony and the "double direct" is one technique to obtain such repetition. The double direct examination involves the advocate's repetition of the key words from the witness' answer at the beginning of the advocate's next question. For example:

Illustration of Double Direct Examination

Lawyer: What did the man with the gun say to you?

Witness: He said, "Hand me your wallet or I'll blow your head off."

Lawyer: After he said, "Hand me your wallet or I'll blow your head off," what did you do?

However, the double direct examination should be reserved for important testimony that the examiner desires to emphasize. Otherwise, the tactic will lose its effectiveness and may draw a sustained cumulative objection.

❖   Principle Number Two: Use Blocking and Headlining

1.   The Jury's View of the Direct Examination

An important step toward constructing a clear and coherent direct examination is to fully appreciate the jury's condition as it listens to witness testimony. First, the jurors have no opportunity to interact with the witness. Instead, they are passive recipients of the testimony. Second, the witness' story does not come to the jurors as a narrative whole, but rather is revealed to them in pieces, constantly interrupted by another question, an objection, or a recess. Third, much testimony is communicated in legal language and unfamiliar case terminology. These barriers to any kind of fluid or clear revelation make the direct examination quite difficult for the jurors to comprehend, and require the advocate's constant attention to the jury's perspective during the direct examination. Viewed from the jury's perspective, effective direct examinations must continually give the jury updates about what the witness has said, what the current topic of discussion is, and why that topic is important.

2. *The Theory Behind Blocking and Headlining*

Every witness' testimony consists of discrete parts and subparts. Witnesses will reveal some information about their personal or professional background and will discuss various aspects of the events in question. Each part or block of the direct examination should begin with a headline or signpost alerting the jury to the subject matter of the upcoming part. The headline should be followed by a series of short, prodding questions that allow the witness to relate the pertinent information. Each block should conclude with a wrap-up of the information imparted during that block and then a transition to the next block.

This contrasts starkly to the traditional approach, which is to chronologically work through the information and to do so with an unbroken chain of questions and answers. While at first blush this approach may make sense, it frequently degenerates into a mind-numbing continuum incapable of being retained. Blocking, on the other hand, recognizes the jury's need for help in making sense of direct testimony and recognizes that *every* direct examination is made up of component parts.

Parallels to the use of blocks and headlines in other forms of communication abound. Just as well-formed paragraphs have topic sentences and good essays have a clear and easy-to-follow organization, so must an effective direct examination have clear and identifiable blocks introduced by headlines. For instance, in examining a percipient witness to an automobile collision, it is first necessary to understand the perspective, or vantage point, of the witness who viewed the collision. That vantage point should be elicited separate and apart from the actual action sequence, the part of the testimony wherein the witness relates what occurred. Under the continuum approach, a good examiner would elicit information relating to the witness' perspective prior to moving to the accident. However, the examiner will not break or sever those two discrete topics in any noticeable way. Instead, the first simply bleeds into the second. In contrast, if the advocate addresses these two topics individually, the jurors would have an opportunity to focus on first one and then the other and to know the purpose and content of each block in advance. Blocking allows jurors the opportunity to take the testimony in smaller doses that are more easily retained. Blocking breaks direct examination into "digestible" subparts, so that learning and retention are optimized.

Headlining and blocking recognizes the decreasing attention spans of most Americans and increases the likelihood that the target audience will retain the testimony. Because the attention span of the typical juror has been reduced to the time between television commercials, blocks should be limited accordingly. Accommodations must be made to keep abreast of changing audience information demands and blocking is just such an accommodation.

3. *Headlining and the Prohibition on Leading Questions*

Each block should begin with a headline or signpost. This headline is a simple statement announcing the next topic to be discussed followed by a question. It is designed to clearly set forth the subject matter of the forthcoming block. The headline alerts the jurors to the subject matter of that particular block and signals that the examiner is now shifting topics and is setting the stage for that new topic. Given the general prohibition against asking leading questions during direct examination, lawyers are often reticent to utilize headlines. Even many lawyers aware of the need for headlines allow the leading question prohibition to severely restrict their use of headlines. Thus, they often say to a witness, "directing your attention to the night of May 1 ..." rather than separating the headline from the question. Instead, the examiner should clearly separate the headline from the next question, as follows: "Now that we are familiar with your education, let's talk about the professional positions you've had. What was your first job out of college?"

That paralyzing fear of suffering a leading question objection is misplaced in any event. The Federal Rules of Evidence and state evidence codes exempt transitional statements from the leading question prohibition. For example, Rule 611(c) of the Federal Rules of Evidence specifically states that leading questions may be used on direct examination "as may be necessary to develop the witness' testimony." The headline, followed by a non-leading question, is nothing more than an effort to develop the witness' testimony.

4. *Transitioning From One Block to the Next*

Transitions during the direct examination provide an opportunity for the examining lawyer to boldly set the stage for the jurors and the witness. Once the headline is in place, the examining lawyer must figuratively step back and re-focus the jurors' attention solely on the witness. This is perhaps the only part of the trial where the lawyer should relinquish the white-hot spotlight. The short, prodding "What happened next?" type questions are ideally suited for this purpose. Instead of constantly shifting from the examiner to the witness, these questions allow the jurors to devote their exclusive attention to the witness.

Each headline, in addition to setting the stage for the new block of testimony, should also contain a transition that segues from the just completed block. This transition serves not only to shift topics, but also as an opportunity to recap the just completed block. The examiner can briefly highlight for his audience the essence of what they should have retained from the just completed block.

The number of blocks will vary depending on the complexity of the witness' testimony. A witness to a car accident may involve as few as four blocks, whereas the direct examination of an expert witness in a product liability case may involve a dozen blocks. When in doubt, go to another block. As a general guide, potential blocks might include: a background or personalization block; an expertise, experience, or education block; a staging or context block; an action sequence or observation block; an opinion or characterization block; and a summary block.

5. *Advantages of Blocking and Headlining*

One significant advantage of blocking is that each new block provides the examiner, the witness, and most importantly, the jury with the opportunity to start over. Each block is a fresh start. Because each block is self-contained, with a beginning (headline), middle (short prodding questions), and end (wrap-up and transition to next block), if a particular block becomes confused, or the witness loses focus, the problem is minimized as soon as that block is completed. In the subsequent block, the examiner, the witness and particularly the jury will start anew, refocused on the new subject. In contrast with the continuum method, once the rhythm or concentration is lost and confusion ensues, it is very difficult to set things right. Blocking, with its frequent breaks, allows all parties to regroup and refocus.

In a jury research project involving contract issues and a default between a bank and land developers, one mock juror spoke about his confusion: "I got very lost when he [the witness] was discussing all the letters back and forth. Once I got lost, it was hard for me to get back into it. It would have been very helpful if he had refuted the plaintiff's position point by point. He also should have elaborated more on the chronology of events leading up to the lawsuit."[2] This illustrates how jurors can get lost in testimony and how blocking assists them in segmenting information so that they can more easily remain focused and retain that information.

The following illustrates headlining and blocking during direct examination. In this case, liability turns on whether the decedent, Mrs. Putman, was in the crosswalk or fifteen feet beyond the intersection, when she was struck by defendant's car. In the preceding block, the plaintiff's attorney elicited the witness' background information, including the fact that she is employed as a crossing walk guard. The examination now picks up with a headline.

 Illustration of Blocking and Headlining[3]

BLOCK #1:   *So now that we know you were a crossing guard on duty at the time of the accident, let's turn to your vantage point just before the accident. Where were you?*

---

[2] Caldwell, et al., *Primacy, Recency, Ethos, and Pathos: Integrating Principles of Communication into the Direct Examination,* 76 NOTRE DAME L. REV. 423, 460 (2001). Used with permission.

[3] This illustration is based on the hypothetical case *Potter v. Shrackle,* Kenneth S. Broun and James H. Seckinger (4th ed. 1990, National Institute of Trial Advocacy).

Witness:	I was standing on the southwest corner of Boulder and Cameron.
Lawyer:	What were you doing?
Witness:	I had just stopped a little boy who had run across the crosswalk. I was bent down and talking to him.
Lawyer:	How were you positioned in relation to the intersection?
Witness:	I was facing the intersection.
Lawyer:	Was there anything blocking your view of the intersection?
Witness:	No.
Lawyer:	It was late afternoon, was the sun a factor?
Witness:	No.
Lawyer:	Why was that?
Witness:	The sun was at my back.
BLOCK #2:	***Now that we know your position at the Southwest corner of Boulder and Cameron while you were facing the intersection, let's turn our attention to what happened. Please tell the jury when you first saw Mrs. Putman.***
Witness:	I first saw her while I was talking to the little boy.
Lawyer:	And where was she?
Witness:	She was crossing Boulder Avenue in the crosswalk.
Lawyer:	What drew your attention to her?
Witness:	The fact that she began crossing the street—it's my job to pay attention when anyone is in the crosswalk.
Lawyer:	Describe how she was walking, was she running?
Witness:	No, she was not running, she was walking in an average stride.
Lawyer:	How far was she from you when you first noticed her?
Witness:	Well, she was just approaching the median area so I would have to say that she was about forty, forty-five feet from me.
Lawyer:	What did you notice next?
Witness:	I noticed defendant's car.
BLOCK #3:	***Let's stop right there. As you were standing at the intersection and had an unobstructed view of Mrs. Putnam and defendant's car, what drew your attention to defendant's car?***
Witness:	Well, I remember being concerned when I saw Mrs. Putman crossing because she didn't wait for my assistance. It's a busy intersection

and that's why the city has hired a crossing guard during peak traffic times. So, when I saw Mrs. Putman crossing, I looked to see if any cars were coming.

Lawyer: How far was defendant's car from you when you first noticed it?

Witness: It was about fifty or fifty-five feet from me.

Lawyer: Were there any obstructions blocking your view of defendant's car?

Witness: No.

Lawyer: When you saw defendant's car, was it moving or stopped?

Witness: It had slowed down to turn but it kept moving.

Lawyer: How fast would you say defendant's car was going?

Witness: I would estimate between 10–15 mph.

Lawyer: What happened next?

Witness: Well, Mrs. Putman continued to cross the street. Like I said, she was about halfway through the intersection. I looked away for a second or two to watch the little boy walk down the street when I suddenly heard a loud thud followed by screeching brakes. Immediately I looked back and saw Mrs. Putman on the hood of the car. It was horrible. I have never seen anything like that before.

Lawyer: Where was the defendant's car in relation to the intersection when you saw Mrs. Putman on its hood?

Witness: Just a couple of feet past the intersection.

Lawyer: How many feet is a couple?

Witness: Three or four.

Lawyer: How long had you looked away before you saw Mrs. Putman on the hood of the defendant's car?

Witness: Half a second or two. It was very brief.

Lawyer: And where was Mrs. Putman just before you looked away?

Witness: She was in the crosswalk.

This example provides three blocks: a staging block about where the witness was and what she was doing, a second staging block reiterating her vantage point and describing her observations just prior to the accident, and then an action sequence block where the witness describes the actual accident. In the headline for the first staging block, the examiner wrapped up the preceding section so that the jury had a second opportunity to hear the information already provided and then previewed the current block. By tying the previous information to the next point of focus, the examiner gave the jury a framework on which it could build, thus augmenting the jury's ability to retain the testimony. From the first staging block the jury learned that this witness was responsible for knowing who was in the intersection and that the witness was looking directly at the crosswalk for almost the entire action sequence. The second staging block precisely described her observations just before the accident. When there are several eyewitnesses to an accident, all with differing vantage points and testimony, the examiner must establish the credibility of his witness as opposed to the others who merely happened on the scene or were preoccupied with other activities when the accident occurred. With the completion of the staging blocks, the examiner has set the stage for a compelling action sequence. The more understandable and compelling the testimony, the more the jury will attend to and retain that testimony.

❖ Principle Number Three: Personalize Witnesses to Build Rapport Between Witnesses and Jurors

1. *Overview of Personalization and Rapport Building*

Just as it is true that every direct examination consists of parts and subparts, it is equally true that each witness who testifies on direct examination is a flesh-and-blood human being with a story to tell. From the jury's perspective, it is just as important to know *who* is testifying as it is to know *what* they know. Thus, *every* direct examination should begin by personalizing the witness, to reveal some of the witness' background. This getting-to-know-the-witness block should begin with a headline explaining the purpose of the block and should then go on to develop a personal overview, including areas such as marital status, children, significant nonprofessional activities and even the part of the country the witness is from. These personal facts give jurors a way of identifying with the witness. Personalization creates a rapport between the witness and the jury, which leads to credibility and trust.

2. *The Relevance of Background Material*

There is a reticence, even an outright refusal on the part of many trial lawyers, to personalize each witness called for direct examination. This reluctance is confounding, given that jurors often make critical decisions based on intangibles such as personal relationships and subjective impressions. This resistance to personalization is primarily due to the fact that the witness' personal history is perceived as not essential or even material to the particular events of the case. Whether a witness is married with two children and coaches his daughter's soccer team is legally irrelevant to the witness' expert testimony about the care rendered by the defendant. A closer look, however, reveals that each witness' (including expert's) human side is central to every case. Disclosure of the witness' personal background builds common bonds with the jurors, gives the testimony more practical meaning, and ultimately gives it more weight and credibility. The legal objection can often be overcome by responding that this is simply background information so that the jury will be able to better evaluate the witness' credibility and thus more fully appreciate his testimony. Judges typically allow some background questioning with all witnesses, and substantial background questioning with parties.

3. *Advantages of Personalization*

One reason that personalization enhances the weight of the testimony is that it makes the witness more accessible to the jurors. Accessibility provides a sense of connection between jurors and the witness, and more readily allows the jurors to view the testimony from the witness' perspective. This maxim is so obvious that it is often overlooked. This rapport process takes place in two stages: (1) prior to the informational segment of the examination, and (2) while the witness is relaying the "relevant" facts. In the rush to get to the heart of the case, to get to the facts, trial lawyers overlook the fact that jurors make critical decisions based on intangibles such as likeability and trust. If the jurors like and trust a witness, they are more likely to side with that witness' view of events.

In the demonstration of personalization below, the examiner begins direct examination by "getting to know the witness." The witness in this example is the plaintiff in a wrongful termination action. The examiner, wholly apart from the facts of the employment situation, takes the time to bring this witness' personal life before the jury.

 ## Illustration of Personalization and Rapport Building

Block #1:   *Mr. Stevens, before we get to the events surrounding your employment and later discharge, I want to ask you some questions about your personal background to help the jurors learn about you and better understand your testimony. First, tell us a little about yourself.*

Witness: Well, I'm married and have two children.

Lawyer: What is your wife's name?

Witness: Anna.

Lawyer: How long have you and Anna been married?

Witness: Eight years.

Lawyer: How would you describe your marriage?

Witness:	Anna and I have a good life together. We are perfect partners: we have so many things in common. We like the outdoors and camping and cycling and together with our children we do those kinds of things most every weekend. She has a great sense of humor. She kids me all the time.
Lawyer:	Tell us about your two children.
Witness:	Okay. Kristen is six. She is a radiant little girl. Extremely precocious and willful. She can be a handful sometimes.
Lawyer:	And your second child?
Witness:	Little Kyle just turned two and he is a wild baby. He was walking at nine months and it seems like he is in perpetual motion. He is just like "Curious George." He gets into everything.
Lawyer:	Describe your relationship with your two kids.
Witness:	Well, the highlight of my day is coming home and being greeted by Kristen and Kyle. I am learning to play the piano with Kristen. And the four of us are trying to learn Spanish together. I find I don't even want the kids to go to bed, sometimes.
Lawyer:	Where do you and your family live?
Witness:	We live here in Yorktown, at 25001 South Victoria.
Lawyer:	How long have you lived there?
Witness:	About six and a half years.
Lawyer:	How did you end up in Yorktown?
Witness:	Oh, I've always lived here except for college. I grew up in Yorktown, went all the way through high school here, and I'm enjoying raising my kids here.
Block #2:	**Thank you Mr. Stevens. Now that we know a little about you and your family I'd like to move to . . . .**

A witness who takes the stand and is immediately directed to the facts in dispute is not going to warrant the same weight as a witness whom the jurors feel they personally know and respect. In the same vein, personalizing also allows the witness an opportunity to identify values the jurors may find important in assessing the ultimate credibility of the witness. Even though the facts of this witness' personal life do not directly bear on whether or not he was wrongfully discharged, and thus may not be legally relevant in a technical sense, they are nonetheless vitally important to the people who ultimately must decide this case, the jury. The jurors do not sit and react in a vacuum. Instead, they tend to view the evidence as a story, full of real flesh-and-blood characters. Witness testimony is only as meaningful as the witness is credible. A meaningful gauge of credibility is how a person lives his life, who that person loves, who loves him, and how that person reacts to life's blessings and curses. These are the keys to building bonds with the jury.

Personalization is idiosyncratic. If jurors perceive that personal information is contrived or "corny," witness credibility can plummet. Thus, the advocate must provide substantive reasons for witnesses to describe aspects of their personal life. Counsel should also consider including an innocuous negative about the person to avoid the perception that they are portraying a false "rosy" picture of the witness. In the previous illustration, note that the headline suggested to the jury the importance of personalization in understanding the testimony. Be sensitive that personalization doesn't appear to be merely a ploy designed to tug at the heart-strings of the jurors.

❖ Principle Number Four: Incorporate Pathos

Every trial lawyer has experienced the situation where a direct examination that should have been dynamic and fraught with emotion failed to engage the jurors. There can be any number of reasons for this: the witness was a poor communicator, the testimony sounded rehearsed, or more likely than not, the examiner did not put the witness in a position to effectively communicate his story.

Personalization, as discussed, can lead not only to trust and likeability but also to empathy or pathos. Witness personalization allows jurors to connect with the witness on an emotional level, not just a factual one, and to appreciate the larger implications of the case. Apart from personalizing, this "getting to know the witness" block may be the opportunity for the witness to "open up" to the jurors and disclose personal information or feelings that will further humanize their testimony. Likewise, a well-placed "feelings" question can be an extremely powerful tool. For instance in an unlawful termination case, the examiner may ask the plaintiff "How did you feel when you were told you were fired?" The plaintiff's response is likely to be emotional and to convey to the jurors the deep sense of loss suffered. Such a question allows the witness to share his feelings with the jury and to create a bond built on that empathy. This questioning should be built on the framework of the witness' background. As such, a personal or "feelings" question will not seem gratuitous or designed to play on the juror's sentiments. If personalization questions are carefully designed, they will seem like a neutral extension of the examination and will elicit a positive response from jurors.

The following illustration involves a lawsuit for unlawful discharge. And while the nuts and bolts of the employment contract and the other important circumstances surrounding that contract must be set forth during an earlier block of the direct examination, it is the actual point of termination that screams for a "feelings" question to allow the plaintiff to open up to the jurors and tell of his pain.

Illustration of "The Feelings Question"

Lawyer:	Mr. Stevens, now that we know about the three year employment contract you entered into with the defendant, I would like to turn to the afternoon of October 5 two years ago. What were you doing that afternoon?
Witness:	I was working at the store.
Lawyer:	Did the defendant come in?
Witness:	Yes he did.
Lawyer:	Tell us what happened.
Witness:	It was late in the afternoon, the night manager has just arrived and I was getting ready to go home.
Lawyer:	Go on.
Witness:	Mr. Talford asked if we could go to the back office and talk.
Lawyer:	What happened next?
Witness:	He told me he was very disappointed with how the store was doing. I tried to explain that I thought things were starting to turn around but he cut me off and told me I was being let go.
Lawyer:	By let go, what did you take that to mean?
Witness:	He fired me.
Lawyer:	Mr. Stevens, I want to stop you right there. Right then, right at the point you were told you were fired, **how did that make you feel?**
Witness:	First I was just stunned but then as it sunk in I felt this overwhelming sense that I had let down my family. I wondered how I could face my wife and my kids. It wasn't just my life but all four of our lives. I didn't know how we were going to make it. I had never felt so helpless in my life.

This description of how the plaintiff felt and what thoughts ran through his mind provides the jury with information that will help them identify with the plaintiff's predicament. The case is no longer about a fired store employee. It is now about a family man, a man upon whom his loved ones were depending, suddenly unable to provide for the basic needs of his wife and children. While the jurors may not be able to empathize with the sudden loss of employment—because, if nothing else, it is outside their life experience—each juror can understand and empathize with the feeling of helplessness that the witness described.

❖ Principle Number Five: Set the Stage

The goal of any direct examination is for the jury to believe the witness' account of the events in question. With that in mind, some might suggest the examination should begin and end with just the facts directly bearing on the events in question. After all, lawsuits are about getting to the bottom of things, getting to the facts. However, to hold to this naive point of view is to turn a blind eye to the reality of human learning and common sense. Jurors, like all of us, want and demand to know the context in which the events took place. Part of the context is a sense of the environment or world of the parties involved in the case. Jurors, again like most of us, frequently bring a set of assumptions (perhaps even erroneous assumptions) about some of the circumstances involved in the trial. For example, some of the jurors may have assumptions about the process of claim handling in bad faith insurance cases or about how doctors utilize patient histories. Those assumptions may or may not be accurate. Consequently, direct examination often must start generally before moving to the specific. For instance, have the insurance expert testify as to the typical way a claim is processed well before turning to the specifics in the case at trial.

This process of eliciting those circumstances is *staging*. The staging block precedes the action sequence and should contain sufficient detail and background information for the jury to fully appreciate the forthcoming description of the critical events in the case. With the foundation of the necessary material in place, the action sequence will be more clearly and powerfully communicated and more easily understood.

In addition to providing a general context before moving on to specifics, staging may also involve a thorough understanding of a physical layout or design. For example, the layout of a warehouse in a personal injury forklift accident case may need some detailed description, including photographs and diagrams before the actual events that caused the injury are described. With that information in place the jurors understand that the witness could have seen what she claims to have seen. Staging may also involve an understanding of the relationship between various actors or parties. For instance, it would be important to know that the victim and an eyewitness once had a dating relationship. Staging demands that the essential background details be clear as the witness moves to the events in question. Staging is important because it provides the jurors with the necessary context for understanding the testimony about the critical events.

Proper staging also protects against jury distractions. Distractions are anything that impedes the ability of the jurors to focus on the essential facts. The most compelling way to avoid distractions is by clearly and coherently recounting the incident in question, without unnecessary detail or clutter. A direct examination that has progressed to the action sequence without proper staging must temporarily divert from the action testimony to fill in necessary details. This diversion detracts from what should be compelling testimony by breaking up the witness' account. The action sequence delivered in stops and starts will not have the same vitality or impact as a story told without interruption or distraction. For instance, assume that a percipient witness is about to describe how one car slammed into the side of another, when her testimony is suddenly interrupted because the examiner, now aware that he has failed to properly set the stage, is forced to back up and ask about traffic conditions and whether there was a left turn lane. Without staging such necessary details, the action sequence is at best unclear and at worst confusing. Consequently, what should have been the crescendo of that witness' testimony has been disrupted and has lost much of its narrative drive.

The illustration of staging that follows is based on the direct examination of a rape victim. Assume that in the block preceding this one, the witness was personalized. In this block, which will come before the action sequence, the stage is being set. All the background questions are being asked and answered so that there will be no distractions once the examiner moves to the action. The overarching issue in this case is the victim's identification of her rapist. She will testify she was startled awake from her mid-morning sleep by an attacker standing in the doorway to her apartment. At that point she saw his face. As the attacker then moved from the doorway to her bed, he pulled up a bandana covering his face below his eyes. The goal of this staging block is to reinforce the certainty of her eyewitness identification of the assailant.

 ## Illustration of Staging[4]

Block #1:   *Ms. Taylor, now that we've had an opportunity to learn about your personal life and about your university experience, and before we turn to the morning you were attacked, it is important that the jurors understand the layout of your apartment. At the time of the attack did you live alone?*

Witness: Yes.

Lawyer: Tell us about where you lived.

Witness: It was a studio apartment on Baltic Avenue. It was about three blocks from the university.

Lawyer: Is your unit a large apartment complex?

Witness: Yes, there are probably forty units. It is pretty big.

Lawyer: Is your unit upstairs or downstairs?

Witness: Downstairs.

Lawyer: Describe your apartment for us.

---

[4] This illustration is based on the hypothetical case *State v. Stone,* James H. Seckinger (4th ed. 1990, National Institute of Trial Advocacy).

Witness:	It's an end unit. It is pretty small, but up until then, I liked it just fine.
Lawyer:	I understand. Well, tell me about the design.
Witness:	It's a studio apartment, which means it doesn't have a bedroom. When I wasn't in bed, the bed folded back up into a closet.
Lawyer:	How about a kitchen?
Witness:	It has a cute little kitchenette. There is a small stove, an oven, a sink and some cupboards. I had bought a small table with two chairs to eat at.
Lawyer:	Ms. Taylor, I want the jurors to get a sense of how big your apartment is. How long would you say it is?
Witness:	I'm not very good with distances. Maybe from me to where you are standing.
Lawyer:	Your Honor, may the record reflect I am about thirty feet from Ms. Taylor?
Court:	That seems about right.
Lawyer:	And about how wide?
Witness:	Maybe about two-thirds of that.
Lawyer:	I take it there is just one door.
Witness:	That's right.
Lawyer:	Does that door open into a hallway or directly to the outside?
Witness:	It opens into a hallway.
Lawyer:	Ms. Taylor, where is the bed in relation to the door?
Witness:	The bed is across the room from the door, not quite from me to you.
Lawyer:	Well, because I am about thirty feet from you, would you estimate between twenty and twenty-five feet?
Witness:	That seems about right.
Lawyer:	Let's turn to the windows in your apartment. How many are there?
Witness:	Just the one by the door on the joining wall.
Lawyer:	Describe that window.
Witness:	It's a pretty good sized window, maybe three feet by five feet.
Lawyer:	Is there any covering for the window?

Witness:	Yes, it has a set of curtains.
Lawyer:	Would you say that these are heavy or light curtains?
Witness:	They are thick curtains, but they are unlined. There is a lot of light that comes in around the top and sides. I don't mind, though. I don't need to have it pitch black when I sleep.
Lawyer:	Were the curtains open or closed at the time you were attacked?
Witness:	They were closed.
Lawyer:	Were there any lights on in your apartment at the time of the attack?
Witness:	I had been reading when I fell back asleep and my bedside lamp was still on.
Lawyer:	Was that light shining in your eyes in any way when you woke up?
Witness:	No, it has a shade on that softens the light. I don't like bright light when I am reading.
Block #2:	*Thank you, Ms. Taylor, I think we have a pretty good idea of how things are in your apartment in mid-morning. We now need to turn to that mid-morning back on November 22 when you were raped.*

This staging block was designed primarily to address the witness' ability to identify the defendant. First, there is the distance from the bed, from where the victim first saw the defendant, to the doorway, where the defendant was standing. Next, there is the issue of the back-lighting of the defendant as he stood in the doorway. Because the door opened into a hall and not directly to the outside, backlighting should not be an issue. And finally, the lamp at the victim's bedside would have provided some light to view the defendant's partially concealed face. With this staging block in place the examination would then move to a block in which the witness identifies the rapist and describes the rape itself.

❖ Principle Number Six: Fully Develop the Action Sequence

The culmination of direct examination is the action sequence block. It is here when the witness testifies as to what happened. The information relayed in this block is the reason this witness was called to testify. The quality of this block is largely dependent on what came before. If the examiner has properly personalized the witness, so that the jurors appreciate the perspective of the witness, and has properly staged the examination such that the essential details are clear, the witness will be able to testify in a clear and compelling manner about the action sequence.

The action sequence is much like the last act of a play. In the preceding acts we learned who the characters are, what motivates them, their relevant histories and only then do we lift the curtain on the final act. As that curtain opens, the advocate proceeds with the assurance that the audience has all the necessary information essential to fully understanding the action sequence.

1. *Telling the Story*

It is important during the action sequence to allow the witness to relate her testimony in the most clear and compelling manner possible. Generally, that means that the examiner should develop the testimony chronologically and avoid distractions. Material relayed in chronological order will likely be more easily understood, and thus better retained by the jury. Likewise, the witness' "story" should not have unnecessary digressions to go back in time and fill in information that could have been elicited in staging block. Such interruptions may well "break" the drama or the compelling force of the witness' story. Cross your t's and dot your i's before you get to the action sequence.

With that said, it is not sufficient for the examiner to simply begin the examination with a generic "What happened?" question and then let the witness testify to the entire action sequence. There are a number of techniques that can be used within the action sequence block to enhance its clarity and impact. Not all of the techniques suggested will work during every examination. Rather the facts, the nature of the case, and even the witness' personality will be driving factors in determining which techniques should be employed during any one examination.

2. *"Freezing" the Action for Important Points*

One such technique involves stopping the witness at a critical moment during her examination to call special attention to what the witness is about to say. At first, it might appear that stopping the witness could violate the rule against interruptions during the action sequence. However, the technique, far from being a potential distraction, actually helps the witness heighten the jurors' attention in the testimony at a critical moment in the telling of the story. The following is an illustration of this freeze-frame technique in which the witness has just heard the voice of a would-be rescuer. The witness, in this case the defendant, was lying at the base of a cliff in the dark and admittedly failed to warn the would-be rescuer that there was a cliff between the rescuer and the defendant. Subsequently, the would-be rescuer fell over the cliff to his death. It is essential that the witness explain his failure to warn in a memorable way. The following illustration picks up the testimony in the middle of the action sequence.

Illustration of "Freezing" the Action for Important Points[5]

Lawyer:	Mr. Green, how long did you lie at the base of the cliff?
Witness:	It had to have been several hours. When I fell it was still light out and when the paramedics arrived it was pitch black.
Lawyer:	How did you first become aware that the paramedics were in the vicinity looking for you?
Witness:	I heard some voices.
Lawyer:	Could you tell where they were coming from?
Witness:	Yes, it seemed to me that they were somewhere above my location approaching the cliff.
Lawyer:	Mr. Green, **I want to stop you right there.** When you first heard those voices and realized the men were approaching the cliff why didn't you warn them of the cliff?
Witness:	I can't tell you how many times I've played that scene over in my mind. I had been lying there a long time all alone, and I knew I had a badly broken leg that wouldn't allow me to move. It was getting very cold and I had been shaking on and off for awhile. I just wasn't in my right mind when I first heard the paramedics. All I could think to say was, "Please hurry, I'm hurt."
Lawyer:	What happened next?
Witness:	One of the paramedics fell over the cliff and landed right next to me.

In stopping the witness mid-action sequence, when the juror's attention is on full alert, Mr. Green's explanation for his failure to warn receives maximum attention. Its placement draws the jurors to the witness' reason for his action or, in this case, his failure to act.

A second use of the freeze-frame is to allow the witness to relate her feelings at a critical juncture of the action. Again recognizing that, generally, interruption during the action sequence arrests the development of the action, there are exceptions. The well placed "feelings" question, as described earlier in the pathos section of this chapter, allows the witness to convey the full extent of his feelings as they are relevant to the action.

---

[5]   This illustration is based on the hypothetical case *Wrigley v. McGuire* (2002, Association of Trial Lawyers of America).

3. *Filling in the Gaps in the Story*

A second technique to consider concerns the situation where a witness relates several significant facts in response to a single question. Most often this is the result of the witness' nervousness. Nonetheless, significant facts, instead of coming forth point-by-point, are lumped together and their individual importance may be lost in the overall answer. When this occurs the examiner should permit the witness to complete his answer and then re-cover the individual points raised. There is often a reluctance to do this out of a fear of an asked and answered objection, or even a cumulative objection. The first concern is unwarranted in that the bulk of the answer was not in response to the question. The cumulative objection is more of a concern; however, most courts will allow the examiner to clarify an answer that went beyond the call of the question.

In the following illustration, that same witness who was lying at the base of the cliff is being asked how it was he came to be there. Again we pick up the block as it is underway.

Illustration of Filling in the Gaps in the Story[6]

Lawyer: Mr. Green what happened next?

Witness: I lost my grip and started to slide down, next thing I knew I was at the bottom of the cliff with a broken leg and a throbbing head. I must have been hysterical at that point because everything seemed confusing to me.

Lawyer: **Lets back up a little. I want to first talk about how it was you fell. Can you explain that?**

Witness: Yes I can. I was about halfway up the cliff when I lost my grip. Perhaps it was perspiration but my hand just slipped.

Lawyer: As you lost your grip what happened then?

Witness: At first I slid down several feet and then I lost contact with the cliff and fell.

Lawyer: Describe where you landed.

Witness: Like I said, I was at the bottom of the cliff. It was a rocky shelf.

Lawyer: Describe how you landed.

Witness: My body fell awkwardly right on my leg. I could hear the bone in my calf actually break.

Lawyer: You mentioned that your head throbbed. Did you strike your head?

---

[6]   This illustration is based on the hypothetical case *Wrigley v. McGuire* (2002, Association of Trial Lawyers of America).

Witness:	When I landed on my leg my head struck a rock protruding out from the base of he cliff.
Lawyer:	Where on your head did you strike the rock?
Witness:	On the left side, the temple area. I've got to tell you, I was seeing stars.
Lawyer:	You mentioned that you felt confused, please explain that.
Witness:	I don't know if it was the pain in my leg or the throbbing in my head but I felt dazed, kind of disoriented as I lay there.

The examiner has taken that first answer and through adroit questioning developed each of the four parts of the original answer. In so doing each of the points can be assessed individually. In addition, the advocate successfully re-covered and thus emphasized important testimony for the jurors.

4.   *Using Demonstrative Aids to Tell the Story Again*

After the witness has testified to the action sequence consider using demonstrative aids to cover the same testimony again. The benefits are substantial. First, the jurors are given yet another perspective from which to evaluate the events described by the witness. Second, the use of a picture or diagram allows the jurors to see rather than simply to listen, leading to greater retention of the testimony. And third, the central events are repeated, thus emphasizing their importance. It goes without saying that visual material is more readily retained by jurors.

> **Tech Tip**
> *Forms of Equipment*
>
> ✓ Timelines
> ✓ Text document, emphasis with box, circle, or line
> ✓ Organizational charts
> ✓ Statistical charts
> ✓ Storyboards

An obvious concern is that such testimony is cumulative. However, it will most often be permitted because a different medium is being used—a picture instead of words. For instance, after the witness has just testified about how she struck her head on an angle iron while climbing on the defendant's playground structure, the examiner should have her step down from the witness stand and describe how the injury occurred using a picture of the playground structure.

❖   **Principle Number Seven: Emphasize Important Testimony**

One danger of asking only open-ended questions on the direct examination, one after another, is that after all is said and done, the most important portions of the witness' testimony may appear to the jury to be no different and no more important than the trivial and unimportant portions. To the average juror, every answer may appear to have the same value to the case as the one before it and the one after it. Every piece of information revealed by the witness receives the same time and attention from the jury as every other piece of information. Counsel may well spend the same amount of time on the color of the defendant's car and the weather conditions, as on the actual collision between the plaintiff's and defendant's cars. The result: no answer is obviously more important than any other.

And yet, some testimony given on direct examination is critically important and other testimony is not. Some testimony decides whether a party wins or loses and by how much. Some testimony has emotional resonance with the jury—the plaintiff's injuries or damages in a personal injury case or the impact of a crime on victims in criminal cases—and thus, must be milked by the advocate for greater impact on the jury.

We have already discussed one method of achieving some emphasis of important testimony during the direct examination, namely the so-called "double direct." When using the double direct examination, the advocate incorporates part or all of the witness' answer into the next question, as follows.

 ## Illustration of Double Direct Examination[7]

Witness: And then the defendant told me that he wanted to "nail the bitch," referring to Ms. Foster!

Lawyer: **After the defendant told you that he wanted to "nail the bitch,"** what did he do next?

The double direct examination does allow the advocate to draw attention to important testimony, but its effectiveness is limited because it allows the advocate to repeat the statement only once. The technique can be used only sparingly (so as to avoid objection) and it must always be used in connection with an open-ended question, thus limiting its versatility.

A more effective, powerful, and versatile means of emphasizing important testimony is to dwell on the pertinent event or topic for an extended period of time by asking the witness close-ended, narrowly framed questions about the specific details of the critical event or happening. The most dramatic or traumatic elements of a party's claim or defense must not be lost in lengthy, narrative answers by witnesses. Instead, the advocate must keep the moment before the jury for as long as possible by slowing down the witness' description of the event or sequence of events so that the events unfold one frame at a time. To accomplish all of that, the advocate must:

---

[7] This illustration is based on the hypothetical case *Mitchell v. Mitchell,* Judge Jerry Parker (Texas Young Lawyers Association).

- ask close-ended questions

- keep questions limited in time and scope

- focus questions on the specific details of the event

This technique is sometimes called "parking"—an appropriate term to describe the practice. In other words, turn off the motor and stay for a while. Keep the testimony in one place and eliminate all other distractions. This technique requires patience from advocates. They must not be in too big a hurry to get through the critical sequence of events during the direct examination. It also calls for careful questioning, with each question framed so that the question calls for non-cumulative testimony and provides relevant details about the event.

For the prosecution, the critical testimony might be the victim's description of her rape; for the criminal defense lawyer, it might be the defendant's description of his decision to pull the trigger of his pistol to save his own life; for the plaintiff's lawyer, it might be the helpless moments just before the 18 wheeler hit plaintiff's car and the immediate aftermath of the collision; for the civil defendant, it might be the hectic moments after an accident on the defendant's premises as heroic efforts were made to save the plaintiff. Regardless of the specific testimony that needs emphasis, advocates can increase the testimony's immediate impact on the jury, and enhance the jury's ability to remember the testimony later by using this technique.

In the illustration below, plaintiff is a young girl who suffered severe burns and scarring when as a nine month old she was scalded by extremely hot water coming from the faucet in her apartment bathroom. Plaintiff alleges that the owner of the apartment complex negligently maintained the premises. The witness in the illustration is the young girl's mother who attempted to rescue her from the hot water. Notice the details elicited by the examiner, some of which may not be significant in and of themselves, but serve to give additional texture and detail to the events and, equally important, help to keep the jury's attention focused on the young girl's tragic injury for an extended period of time.

 Illustration of "Parking" on Important Testimony[8]

Lawyer:	What happened next?
Witness:	I heard the water come on in the bathroom and then I heard little Jessica screaming, so I ran into the bathroom and there was Jessica on all fours under a stream of hot water.
Lawyer:	How could you tell that the water was hot?

---

[8] This illustration based on the hypothetical case *Riley v. Garfield House Apartments* (Association of Trial Lawyers of America).

Witness:	There was steam rising from it and you could feel the heat coming off of the water. And only the hot water handle was turned.
Lawyer:	What do you mean when you say that Jessica was "on all fours"?
Witness:	She was on her hands and knees right under the faucet.
Lawyer:	So the water was hitting her on her back?
Witness:	Yes, right across the back.
Lawyer:	Was Jessica crying when you first got into the bathroom?
Witness:	She was screaming and crying really hard and loud.
Lawyer:	Was she moving, trying to get away from the water?
Witness:	It was the strangest thing because she wasn't moving. She seemed stuck underneath the faucet.
Lawyer:	What did the skin on her back look like?
Witness:	It was bright pink, almost red. It looked like she had a really bad sunburn.
Lawyer:	What did you do?
Witness:	As quickly as I could I turned off the water and then I tried to pick her up, to get her out of the tub.
Lawyer:	How did you go about trying to pick her up?
Witness:	I put one hand under each of her arms. I was just going to lift her out.
Lawyer:	What happened when you went to lift her out of the tub?
Witness:	Well, as I was reaching down to lift her up, I touched her back, and her skin just came right off on my hand.
Lawyer:	Came off?
Witness:	Yes, it just came off in my hand.
Lawyer:	Which hand had you touched her with, your right or your left?
Witness:	I believe it was my right hand.
Lawyer:	How did seeing her skin come off in your hand effect you?
Witness:	I panicked. I was scared. I couldn't believe this was happening to my little girl.
Lawyer:	Were you able to get her out of the tub?
Witness:	Well, it all happened really quickly, but every time I would touch her, more skin would come off.
Lawyer:	Can you remember the specific places you touched her?

Witness:	I know I touched her on her back and under her arms and on her neck.
Lawyer:	What did the Jessica's back look like after the skin peeled off?
Witness:	It looked like someone had ripped the skin off of her. It was horrible.
Lawyer:	After you turned off the water, did Jessica stop crying?
Witness:	Not really. The loud screaming stopped, but not the crying. It was more like prolonged moaning. She sounded like she was really hurting.
Lawyer:	Were you able to get her out of the tub?
Witness:	Yes, finally, I thought to grab a towel and I wrapped it around her and pulled her out of the tub.
Lawyer:	How did you hold her?
Witness:	I had the towel wrapped around her and was holding her like a baby across my chest, like this.
Lawyer:	Let the record show that Ms. Steinhorn has indicated that she was holding Jessica across her chest, with Jessica's head in the crook of Ms. Steinhorn's right arm and her body supported by Ms Steinhorn's hands. Was this your first chance to see Jessica's face since you heard the water come on?
Witness:	Yes, it was.
Lawyer:	What did her face look like?
Witness:	She looked sad, distressed. Her eyes were barely open, her brow was wrinkled and furrowed, and she was intermittently crying and moaning. I could tell she had been crying hard.
Lawyer:	What did you do next?
Witness:	I just held her for a minute, put my face to hers and kissed her gently. Then I laid her down on my bed and called 9-1-1.

❖ Principle Number Eight: Use Exhibits and Demonstrative Aids

Demonstrative evidence and other visual aids are necessary components of many direct examinations. In fact, the benefits of visual aids are so pronounced that advocates need to carefully consider their use with every witness. Visual aids and demonstrative evidence:

- demonstrate and reinforce witness testimony

- increase jury retention of witness testimony

- make complex testimony more understandable

- organize witness testimony

The ultimate goal in the selection and use of demonstrative evidence during direct examination is to increase the persuasive impact of witness testimony.

1. *Demonstrative Aids Explain, Illustrate, and Reinforce Witness Testimony*

Counsel must determine which media is best suited to explain, illustrate, and reinforce the points being made by the testifying witness. After the witness has orally testified to the events of the car collision, having her use a simple poster board depicting the intersection and the movement of the cars explains, illustrates, and reinforces her oral testimony. A video of a crime scene taken under similar conditions as the evening of the crime will demonstrate that the witness had sufficient light to see her attacker and thus reinforce her oral testimony. Expert witnesses in product liability and construction defect cases may use animations or models to further explain and thus reinforce their testimony. Further, an expert using a white sheet of paper, flip chart, or PowerPoint might best show the calculation of damages.

2. *Demonstrative Aids Increase Juror Retention*

As noted in earlier chapters, information that jurors only hear, is easily forgotten; but, information they hear and see will likely be remembered. Visual reinforcement of testimony is critical to juror retention and should be used in conjunction with all critical evidence. Oral testimony enhanced by a visual aid becomes significant and memorable to jurors, and as such they will most likely be retained.

Moreover, an enormous, but often overlooked, benefit of using visual aids during direct examination is that they provide something other than the oral give-and-take of question and answer. Sometimes just doing something different will help the jurors remain alert and focused on the testimony. The most vital aspect of retaining information is first learning of it.

3. *Demonstrative Aids Make the Complex Understandable*

Beyond simply combating juror boredom, visual aids can make the complex understandable. A heart surgeon will be better able to explain the by-pass surgical procedure more effectively if he uses a model of the heart. Likewise, the

Tech Tip
✓ Simple works best!
✓ Stimulate the juror's senses
✓ The visual reinforces the audio

computations as to the future-earnings of the decedent can best be shown using paper and marker. And an automobile accident reconstructionist can better communicate his opinion as to the cause of the rollover using a computer-generated simulation of the rollover.

4. *Demonstrative Aids Organize Witness Testimony*

Testimony involving intricate events, such as the numerous offers and counter-offers of protracted contract negotiations, can become a jumble of dates and events. The chance of jurors getting lost during such testimony is great. A time line depicting the various points during the lengthy negotiations would certainly give the jury a clearer picture of those dealings than oral testimony alone. Likewise, having an expert witness write out the four reasons for his opinion allows him to organize and thus simplify what most likely is complex testimony.

❖ Principle Number Nine: Disclose Material Weaknesses

Perhaps the truest measure of trial advocates is their ability to confront facts adverse to their theory of the case and either mitigate the damage created by those facts or, better yet, integrate those adverse facts into their theory of the case. It requires no great advocacy to prevail when all the facts uniformly support the advocate's theory of the case. But, with rare exception, those cases never see the polished interiors of a courtroom. *Every* advocate at *every* trial confronts a fact, or more likely facts, that are inconsistent with, or even contrary to, his view of events. The particular weaknesses will vary from case-to-case—a past that is less than spotless, a loss of memory, a prior inconsistent statement, a bias or prejudice that might affect credibility, a claim that simply does not seem to add up, or even actions that are contrary to common experience. Whatever the weakness, direct examination is the primary opportunity to confront such adverse facts.

With that said, it is equally true that confronting adverse facts is not a task relegated solely to direct examination. Rather, it is necessary to confront and begin the integration/mitigation process from the outset of the trial. "Bad facts" should be leaked to prospective jurors even as early as *voir dire*, as well as at opening statement, and even through closing argument. Sound advocacy requires exposing those facts. However, confronting, mitigating, and integrating adverse facts and circumstances is a task that primarily remains for direct examination. For it is during direct examination that the witness with the "problem" must own up to it and explain it.

1. *Disclosure Enhances Credibility*

The first, and paramount, reason for early and thorough disclosure of materially adverse facts is credibility. As discussed earlier, the credibility of the advocate and his witnesses is the well-spring from which persuasion follows. Damage to the credibility of either is tantamount to erecting a skyscraper on marshy ground. Failure to address contrary facts at the first available opportunity leaves the jurors with the impression that the advocate and the witness have misrepresented their case and are not to be trusted. The advocate's first opportunities to confront are during jury selection and opening statement. And a failure to disclose may be a death knell to his credibility. The first opportunity for the witness is during his direct examination. He must get it out and deal with it first before cross-examination. Jurors hearing these "bad facts" from the witness himself likely will hold to the belief that because he told us about these facts which hurt his position, he must be credible and is to be believed in all he says. Furthermore, the advocate's credibility is enhanced as he is the conduit of the witness' disclosure. Also, assuming opposing counsel is aware of the problematic facts, it is naive to think he will not showcase them to the best advantage of his case and to the disadvantage of his opponent. If that contrary fact or weakness is known to both sides, disclosure on terms most favorable to the advocate is the only viable option.

Additionally, a significant advantage gained by self-disclosure of material weaknesses is that the advocate gains tremendous tactical advantage by having the first opportunity to shape how these facts will be perceived by the jurors. She who goes first has the opportunity to stamp her view on problematic facts. And if done well, that first view is difficult to change.

2.   *Disclose Only Material Weaknesses*

Not all facts that do not line up with the theory of the case represent problem areas that must be disclosed and either integrated or mitigated. Rather, only those facts that are material, that matter to the outcome, should be disclosed. A fact is material if it could reasonably bear on the jury's decision making. If the fact does not matter, by raising it, the advocate gives it undue prominence and significance. Instead, the advocate should ignore the *de minimus* weakness. If opposing counsel elects to raise it—it is likely that the jurors will think less of him for making an unwarranted attack.

For instance, assume in a wrongful death case in which the defendant was alleged to have caused the death of plaintiff's spouse by driving recklessly, it developed that the defendant, in an entirely unrelated matter, had pled guilty to petty theft eight years ago. Is this the type of contrary evidence defense counsel should disclose? Or is he better off ignoring the prior event? Even if admissible, what will the juror's think of that fact? Will it matter to them as they absorb the evidence in this wrongful death case? If defense counsel simply ignores the prior event will it enhance the plaintiff's case if the defendant is "impeached" with the petty theft while being cross-examined? It would seem that the prior is a non-event for purposes of this trial. The jurors might think that because he did raise the fact he must be concerned with it, and therefore the jury should be concerned as well. On the other hand, if the fact first surfaces while plaintiff's counsel is cross-examining the defendant, it may appear to be an unwarranted, even a mean-spirited, attack. If so, plaintiff's counsel suffers at the hands of the jury.

3.   *Integrating Problematic Facts*

When the contrary fact is material, and thus must be disclosed, there are two approaches that should be considered. The first approach is to examine the problematic fact or weakness with an eye to integrating or absorbing the fact into the overall theme of the case. Contrary facts should first be analyzed for their positive potential and only if entirely unusable should the weakness be mitigated. For example, consider the following. While offering essentially the same testimony about a shooting, the testimony of the two eye-witnesses differed in several respects. The first witness testified that the gunman already had his gun drawn when he entered the convenience store. The second witness testified the defendant pulled the gun from his pocket just before he shot the clerk. The first witness testified that the defendant had a goatee, the second said he was clean shaven. Both witnesses, however, identified the defendant as the shooter at a line-up and again at trial. The defendant presented an alibi defense, thus reducing the trial to the reliability of the eyewitnesses' identifications.

How should the prosecutor treat the two discrepancies? These are indeed contrary facts. Do they matter? Are they material? If not, the prosecutor can simply ignore them. But given that the reliability of the identifications is at issue, any discrepancies between the witnesses do matter. These are facts the jurors will indeed weigh. Consequently, the prosecutor must deal with these inconsistencies one way or the other. Her approach may be that the inconsistencies in fact strengthen each witness' reliability, in that each must have arrived at his identification independently. If the testimony of the witnesses mirrored one another, it would suggest, perhaps, that they had discussed the case between themselves or even that a third party (the prosecutor or her investigator) had suggested aspects of their testimony. To rebut that concern, the prosecutor might argue that two individuals witnessing the same event may well offer accounts that differ in some aspects; but what is consistent is that each *independently* identified the defendant as the shooter, one may have just seen him from a different angle at which he only saw a clean shaven cheek. In fact the discrepancies, the "problem facts," might actually enhance each witnesses' reliability.

4. *Mitigating Damaging Evidence*

In the event contrary facts cannot be integrated or absorbed into the theory of the case, those facts must be mitigated. Mitigation may be something as simple as putting a particular event in context. Facts that appear so stark at first blush take on gradations, when explained, that soften the impact. For instance, a prior petty theft conviction standing alone is a damning indictment of a person's honesty and integrity. However, when put in the context of an overworked, tired, young mother of two, who failed to pay for the bottle of shampoo she had put in her purse and forgotten because she was carrying one baby and tugging another, the impact of that unadorned prior is certainly lessened. Sometimes the explanations behind the material weaknesses are sufficient to mitigate their severe impact.

It is highly likely that some material weaknesses cannot be completely neutralized. That is a function of the circumstances and there are limits to even effective advocacy. However, even the most burdensome facts must be raised and dealt with despite their adverse impact. Disclosure, even under those circumstances, still has the substantial corresponding benefits of enhancing the advocate's credibility, shaping the juror's initial impression of that fact and preventing the harsh exposure from the opponent.

5. *How to Make the Disclosure During the Direct Examination*

Perhaps the two greatest risks when making the disclosure is appearing overly defensive or causing the weakness to take on greater significance than it warrants. In short, take care that the disclosure does not look like a disclosure. Sometimes it is impossible to avoid that appearance, such as when disclosing a witness' prior felony conviction. Other times, however, the lawyer can weave the disclosure into the direct examination so that it is not apparent that something is being revealed. This can be done by explaining the context of the problem, so that the jury understands how the mistake was made.

The content of the disclosure will obviously turn on the nature of the weakness being revealed. In the conventional situation, in which the desired disclosure relates to a potential impeachment point, the lawyer making the disclosure must walk a fine line between making full and complete disclosure and overemphasizing the harmful information. On the one hand, the disclosure should be sufficiently detailed to defuse the impact of the cross-examination questioning on the matter. At the same time, however, resist the temptation to devote too much time and attention to the problem area so that it diverts the jury's attention from the witness' testimony and becomes the primary focus of the examination. One of the ways to dilute the impact of the disclosure is to follow up with questions that emphasize the positive steps taken to remedy the situation or problem. As in most of life, balance is the key to effective disclosure: provide the jury with enough information about the weakness, but not too much. Striking the right balance comes with experience.

a. The Conventional Disclosure

In the typical situation, the technique for disclosing a weakness is not nearly as important as making the disclosure in the first place and making it in a timely manner. The disclosure itself is simply a matter of eliciting the critical facts and giving the witness a chance to explain. The example that follows comes from a most difficult set of circumstances. The excerpt is from the direct examination of the defendant in a prosecution for the murder of his ex-wife. The defendant had a previous conviction for disorderly conduct where he physically abused his now deceased wife. He pleaded *nolo contendere* and completed counseling and community service. Obviously, one might legitimately decide not to call the defendant with such a significant boil to prick. Assume for purposes of this exercise, however, that the defendant was called to testify. After spending some time developing the defendants' personal background, his early years, and his professional career, the examiner turned to the defendant's relationship with the victim. First, the defendant tells the story of their meeting and falling in love. The weakness is placed at its logical point in the direct examination—the point in time when the defendant turned violent toward the victim.

Illustration of Conventional Disclosure

Lawyer:	***Now that we have a sense of who you are, where you came from and what you do to make a living, I want to turn to your relationship with Nicole. Let's start at the beginning, how did the two of you meet?***
Witness:	We had a mutual friend who thought we might hit it off, so he invited both of us for a barbeque at his house.
Lawyer:	When was that?
Witness:	Let's see. That was in 2006.
Lawyer:	And did the two of you hit it off?
Witness:	Oh yes. And we started seeing each other right away. It quickly became a serious relationship.
Lawyer:	How did the relationship develop from there?
Witness:	Nicole moved in with me a couple of months later and in December 2007 we got married.
Lawyer:	Tell us about the relationship you and Nicole had developed.
Witness:	It was great. Before I met Nicole I didn't think I would ever get married. But what I felt toward her and she toward me was such an overwhelming love that I needed to make the strongest commitment to her that I could.
Lawyer:	What kinds of things did the two of you do together?
Witness:	It seemed like we did everything together. Everything worked for us. We were in a position where we could take long vacations, we golfed at lot, we had a wide array of friends. Life was wonderful. We were as in love and as happy as a couple can hope to be.
Lawyer:	***Now I want to move ahead to November 2009. I understand there was a problem. Tell us about that.***
Witness:	This is one of the most shameful things in my life. I lost my temper and slapped Nicole.
Lawyer:	Please tell us the circumstances.
Witness:	Nicole was a beautiful woman and because of that she frequently would have men express interest in her, looking at her. You know,

checking her out. That wasn't always so easy for me, but I handled it pretty good except for that one time.

Lawyer: What happened?

Witness: We had been golfing and at the clubhouse I noticed a man really looking Nicole over. I was more or less used to that, so I didn't think it was a big deal. But then a little later I noticed Nicole look back at him and it just got to me. I can't explain it rationally. It just got to me.

Lawyer: What happened then?

Witness: When we got home I asked her about the guy at the clubhouse. And I remember she looked at me and said, "Don't be a jerk. It's a free country." Her remark surprised me and then angered me and without thinking I slapped her in the face with my hand. As soon as I did it, I couldn't believe that had been me. I was so ashamed.

Lawyer: What happened then?

Witness: I tried to apologize to her, to hug her. But she wouldn't have any of it. She called the police and I was arrested.

Lawyer: Go on.

Witness: I was charged with domestic violence and I knew I was guilty. So at the first court appearance I wanted to plead guilty but my lawyer told me to plead *nolo contendere*. And that's what I did.

Lawyer: So you admitted that you slapped her?

Witness: Yes.

Lawyer: What was your sentence?

Witness: I paid a fine, performed 150 hours of community service, and received counseling.

Lawyer: Tell me about the counseling.

Witness: Sure. At first I really resented it. After all it was once a week for a year. But once I got into it I found it very helpful and it allowed me to come to terms with the jealous feelings I often had. By the end of the year I truly believe I was a better person and certainly a better husband than I had been before.

Lawyer: How did this whole episode affect your relationship with Nicole?

Witness: She forgave me. She told me that she didn't believe I was violent and that this had just been a mistake. We were able to pick up and like I said our marriage actually got stronger as a result.

The examiner in the example carefully developed the relationship between the defendant and the deceased, his one time wife, before revealing the prior criminal offense. Yet, the advocate did not elicit the weakness and then abandon it as if it was some infected object. Instead, the lawyer gave the witness the opportunity to explain the relationship's development since the abuse and to articulate the lessons learned since that time. Thus, the disclosure is made toward the middle of the examination and even toward the middle of the relationship block itself. Moreover, the disclosure is full and complete. It does not try to minimize the nature of the wrong or to otherwise withhold critical facts. In that way, it strips the cross-examiner of her ability to dramatically unveil the prior conviction. Moreover, the disclosure enables the witness to explain the conviction and to personalize its effects on the defendant's relationship with his wife.

b. The Challenge Question

A different, but equally important, kind of disclosure arises with witnesses who testify to a claim or an event that defies common sense or severely stretches one's imagination. In that situation, the lawyer does not direct the witness to a "disclosure" as much as the lawyer challenges the witness to fully explain to the jury why the testimony, despite its apparently incredible nature, actually does make sense and should be believed. The disclosure should come in response to a challenge question: a question that challenges the witness' version of the underlying events. This technique is particularly essential when witnesses have explanations for critical events that seem farfetched. The advocate, instead of simply eliciting the questionable explanation without comment, must take on the role of the skeptical juror and ask the question that one might imagine the juror asking: "You mean to tell me that you were not intoxicated even though you were swerving all over the road and failed three field sobriety tests?" The challenge question allows the lawyer to associate with the jury's skepticism, and at the same time, helps direct that skeptical juror to the answer.

The excerpt below is from the direct examination of the plaintiff in a hypothetical defamation case. The plaintiff, a high school football coach, sued the defendant for libel and slander after the defendant told others that the plaintiff had illegally recruited students to play football at his school. The defendant defended the suit by claiming his statements were true, based on two letters the plaintiff allegedly sent to an 8th grade football player enticing him with scholarships and a job for his parent. The plaintiff claimed that he did not send the letters, but instead believed that his overactive booster club was likely responsible for the misdeeds. After developing the plaintiff's childhood, schooling, and coaching career, the examiner should move into his work as coach at the current school and the claims that he tried to recruit the 8th grader.

Illustration of the Challenge Question[9]

Lawyer:	**Coach, I want to ask you some questions about Kermit Bell, the 8th grader the defendant claims you tried to recruit. When did you first come to know about Kermit Bell?**
Witness:	I knew about him from the time he was in 4th grade—9 years old—when he was playing youth football.
Lawyer:	What position did he play?
Witness:	Quarterback, always quarterback.
Lawyer:	Did you keep track of his career?
Witness:	Oh yes. He was fun to watch—a natural athlete. I watched some of his games and read about his exploits in the local newspaper.
Lawyer:	Why did you keep up with him?
Witness:	First of all, I'm a football fan. I love the game and it's always fun to watch someone who has that innate ability to play the game. Second, I keep up with the players coming up through the ranks to give me a better sense of what the future holds for my program.
Lawyer:	Let's move to the year that Kermit was in 8th grade—2008.
Witness:	Okay.
Lawyer:	How good was he as an 8th grader?
Witness:	He was good, very good. I compared him to Steve Young, the great San Francisco 49er's quarterback. I used to watch him when he was a kid too. This kid had all the skills.
Lawyer:	Did you ever tell anyone else about Kermit's promise in football.
Witness:	You bet. I'm sure I told lots of people about him, including his mother, Mrs. Bell.
Lawyer:	How about your athletic booster club at school, did you ever tell them about Kermit?
Witness:	Absolutely. You know how boosters are. At the spring meeting they all want to know about next year, about who the new players will be and who might be joining our program. I know that on more than one occasion I mentioned Kermit as a local player who would be a tremendous football player in the future and someone I would dearly love to have on my team.

---

[9] This illustration is based on the hypothetical case *Cooper v. Cooper,* Judge Jerry R. Parker (National Institute of Trial Advocacy).

Lawyer:	Why did you do that?
Witness:	As I recall, I was simply trying ·to answer a booster's question about outstanding area players.
Lawyer:	Did you ever attempt to influence Kermit Bell to play football at your school?
Witness:	No way.
Lawyer:	Did you ever send Kermit or his mother a letter enticing them to attend your school?
Witness:	I did not.
Lawyer:	Why not?
Witness:	That would have been recruiting. That's against the rules and I personally don't believe in doing that.
Lawyer:	Your Honor, I have what's been marked as defendant's exhibit 1 for purposes of identification only. May I approach the witness?
Judge:	You may.
Lawyer:	Do you recognize Defendant's exhibit 1?
Witness:	No, I don't.
Lawyer:	Whom is the letter addressed to?
Witness:	It is addressed to Kermit Bell's mother, Mary.
Lawyer:	And who signed the letter?
Witness:	Well it has my name signed on it, but I know for a fact that I didn't sign or send this letter.
Lawyer:	How can you be so certain?
Witness:	I do not send letters to potential players or their parents, promising them jobs and the like, trying to get kids to play football for me. That would be recruiting and I don't do it.
Lawyer:	***Why not? The benefit is worth the risk, isn't it?***
Witness:	It's not a matter of weighing the benefit versus the cost. I take my role as an example for my players very seriously and I value my reputation as a high school football coach. Recruiting is against the rules—it's cheating—and I don't do it. We only take on students that are enrolled in school.
Lawyer:	So is it your belief that someone forged your signature on that letter?
Witness:	Somebody must have. I know I didn't sign it.

Lawyer:	Coach, I need to stop you right there. I want to focus your attention on this letter for just one more moment. **How in the world do you explain that this letter, defendant's exhibit 1, on your personal stationary, made it from your office to Kermit Bell's house?**
Witness:	I only know one thing for certain. I didn't send it. You have to understand that I have a very active booster club. It has over 1000 members and it meets every week. It lives and breathes football. Also you have to understand that my office, which is where my personal stationary is kept, is a gathering place for boosters during the week. We have newspaper clippings and current statistics for the team and consequently the boosters tend to congregate in that area. We send out a newsletter to the boosters every month and I write a little column and at the end it has my signature. Finally, I had talked to the booster club about Kermit before these letters were sent. We've changed how we do things now—we're not as open as we used to be. But at the time of these letters an overactive booster club member could have quite easily gotten some of my stationary and traced my signature on the letters. If they did so, they did it without my knowledge or permission. We don't need to cheat to win. We are doing just fine playing by the rules.

The defendant faces a tactical choice when confronted with the highly incriminating letter. He can deny that he sent it and then bury his head in the sand, disclaiming any knowledge of how it got to Kermit Bell's house. Alternatively, he can take the approach demonstrated above—deny that he sent it and then provide the jury with a plausible explanation for the letter. The tendency for advocates is to avoid directly confronting the really difficult questions in a case. The challenge question takes the opposite approach, directly confronting the hard questions and telling the jury why they should decide the question in favor of the examiner. The transcript includes two challenge questions, both of which give voice to the jury's skepticism and provide the witness a chance to overcome that skepticism. The questions build the credibility of the lawyer and witness. The jury will presumably respect and ultimately trust the party that refuses to dodge the tough questions, and instead gives answers to those questions, providing a comprehensive narrative of defendant's case.

6. *When to Make the Disclosure on Direct Examination*

The final consideration when making a disclosure is in determining its placement in the direct examination sequence. The principles of primacy and recency dictate that the harmful information should not be placed close to the beginning or ending of the direct examination. If the direct examination begins with a damaging admission, then the jury's impression of the witness is permanently tainted. If you end with the disclosure, it takes on disproportionate importance as the fact the jury hears last and remembers best about the witness. Ideally then, the information should be elicited in the middle of the examination. The exception to this rule is when the disclosure is so central to the case that counsel must address it first before the jury is willing to listen to anything else. The disclosure must also be made at a logical point during the direct examination. If the disclosure is made abruptly or awkwardly it also draws the jury's attention to it. For instance, if the direct examiner transitions from asking about where the witness was at the time of the car accident to questions about a prior felony conviction ("By the way, have you ever had any trouble with the law?"), the lawyer will likely do more harm than good. When planning witness testimony, decide what you want the jury's final impression to be.

❖ Principle Number Ten: Adopt a Winning Attitude and Demeanor

The final technique for effective direct examinations shifts the focus away from the structure and content of the direct examination and onto the examiner and his attitude and demeanor. Even the best-prepared direct examination of a witness with a compelling story to tell can fail to move a jury if the advocate ineptly executes the examination. The style and demeanor of the advocate can enhance or detract from the message; they can make it easier or harder for the jury to listen to the evidence; they can convey powerful, but unspoken, messages to the jury about a party's case. The demeanor of the advocate is on display before the jury from the moment she begins each examination. Her actions often speak as loudly as her words. Thus, matters as divergent as how the advocate treats witnesses during the direct examination, to what the examiner does while a question is being answered, to where the lawyer is positioned during the direct examination, may be of critical importance.

1. *Do Not Rely on Notes*

The temptation of most inexperienced trial lawyers is to prepare a script for each direct examination, setting forth each question and answer and then rely on the script during the direct examination. Understandably, the novice views the script as a combination of the Holy Grail and Linus' security blanket. The script holds the answers to the mysteries of life or at least the next question to be asked on direct examination and provides the advocate great comfort in the midst of the stressful and unpredictable examination. As noted earlier, however, scripts simply do not work at trial for at least three reasons. First, the examiner and witness never successfully follow the script. The witness invariably gives an answer that eats up the next three questions, or conversely, an answer that omits a critical piece of information on which the following series of questions depends. Or the lawyer will add an unscripted question during the direct examination and the witness will not know what the "correct" answer is. Second, scripted direct examinations will sound scripted, and to a juror's discerning ear, nothing could be more fatal to the witness' credibility. If the jurors decide that the witness is simply parroting answers contained in a script, they will disregard the testimony and question the advocate's credibility. Third, a script acts as both a magnet and a straightjacket. The advocate's attention will inexorably be drawn to the script. Yet, the script will simultaneously constrain the examiner's freedom to make adjustments to the direct examination as trial developments inevitably will merit.

Instead of using a script, examiners should conduct direct examination with no notes at all, thus minimizing distractions and maximizing flexibility. The "no notes" approach forces the lawyer to actually listen to the answers and then ask natural follow-up questions. The result is a much more natural, conversational exchange between the lawyer and the witness, and the jury will perceive the testimony as spontaneous and genuine instead of artificial and scripted. Most lawyers tremble at the very thought of conducting a direct examination without notes, fearing that undoubtedly they will fail to elicit important information or they will present the information in a disorganized and confusing order. While understandable, both fears are unfounded. Use of the blocking technique (described in section III, Principle Number Two, above) remedies the lawyer's fear of omission. By eliciting the testimony topically or in "blocks" the examiner is freed from having to remember specific questions and answers and instead must only remember the five or six topics to be covered. Furthermore, the examiner can avoid omitting important information by simply taking the time on direct examination to ask the questions necessary to fill in the gaps inside each block and, if necessary, by consulting his notes to ensure that no blocks were missed. At most the examiner should prepare an outline of the direct examination, including each of the blocks that he plans to cover and the key pieces of information that should be elicited in each block. In no event, however, should the outline contain the specific questions to be asked or the particular answers to be given. And in no event should the lawyer rely on any such notes to the point that the advocate appears to be reading questions directly from the notes.

2. *Listen to the Answers*

The excessive use of notes also complicates the advocate's ability to listen to the answers given by a witness. This problem arises from the fear shared by many lawyers of not knowing the next question. That is, after the witness answers the pending question, the lawyer faces the disturbing prospect of having to come up with another question. A second, but closely related fear, is the lawyer's concern about prolonged silence during his direct questioning. Most lawyers are uncomfortable enduring any period of silence after the witness completes the answer while the lawyer thinks of another question. Those two fears tempt the lawyer to look down as the witness answers the question, find the next question from the lawyer's notes, and immediately fire it at the witness when the prior answer is completed.

When the lawyer looks down to his notes before the answer is completed, he sends a powerful message about his attitude toward the witness and the case. Either he does not care about the answer (and thus the jury should not care either) or he already knows the answer (and thus the entire proceeding is just a well orchestrated charade). The "look down" also distracts the lawyer, making it difficult, if not impossible, to listen to the answer. If the lawyer is not listening to the answer, how can she ask the natural follow-up or clarify a mis-impression left by the witness? Effective direct examinations depend on active listening by the lawyer, and anything that interferes with that must be avoided. Moreover, the lawyer's focus on the witness during the direct examination bolsters the witness' credibility by sending a message to the jury that the testimony is important.

The tendency of lawyers to check their notes while the witness answers results not only from fear, but also from a fundamental misunderstanding of the rhythm of the direct examination. Most seem to believe that the correct rhythm is question, answer, question, answer, question, answer and so on. In reality, the better rhythm is question, answer, pause, question, answer, pause, and so on. The pause allows the jury time to digest the answer and prepare for the next question. It also allows the lawyer time to identify the next question, if she needs to do so after the question is complete.

3. *Do Not Echo the Answer*

Fear of silence in the courtroom not only motivates examiners to look down during the answer, but it also causes them to audibly comment on the answer after it is given. It is common for lawyers to nervously insert an "Okay" after every answer, or an "I see" or even to repeat the last part of the answer. These comments disrupt the rhythm of the direct examination, distracting the jury from focusing on the answer from the witness, and revealing the lawyer's nervousness or uncertainty.

4. *Stand Close to the Jury Box*

The position of the lawyer during the direct examination varies from jurisdiction to jurisdiction according to local custom and judicial prefer-ence. For example, federal judges often exercise greater control over the movement of lawyers in the courtroom than state court judges. Lawyers conducting direct examinations in federal court may be required to stand at the podium at all times. On the other hand, in some state courts lawyers have traditionally questioned witnesses while seated at counsel table. Both of those options are far from optimal. Instead, when permitted, the lawyer should conduct the direct examination from the corner of the jury box. The primary benefit of that position is that the witness, when answering ques-tions, is forced to look at the jury when he or she directs the answer to the lawyer. Secondary benefits include the proximity of the lawyer to the jury (thus allowing for the development of rapport between them) and the law-yer's accessibility and appearance of control by not hiding behind a podium or slumping behind a desk.

IV. REDIRECT EXAMINATION

Following the opponent's cross-examination, the direct examiner may conduct a redirect examination of the witness. The redirect examination is limited in scope to those matters inquired into during the cross-examination and attempts to rehabilitate the witness. The first question for counsel is whether it is even necessary to conduct a redirect examination of the witness. There is no small measure of satisfaction in rising at the completion of the opponent's cross and boldly stating, "No redirect of this witness, Your Honor. May the witness be excused?" Translated, counsel has declared that the opponent inflicted no serious wounds during the cross; that there was nothing severe enough to demand repair. A small victory? Perhaps. But victory nonetheless.

Redirect examination is appropriate if:

- the witness' testimony has been impeached during the cross and there is some available and helpful rehabilitation,

- the witness' testimony on an important point has become confused as a result of the cross, or

- there is important testimony that bears repeating by the witness.

Take the last point first. The mere fact that a witness has already testified to a point during direct examination does not preclude additional questioning about the very same matter on redirect examination provided that the cross-examiner asked about the matter during his cross-examination. Thus, the defendant's testimony on direct examination that he could not have committed the offense because he was out of town on a business trip could be repeated again during redirect examination if the prosecution attacked the defendant's alibi during the cross-examination. Redirect examination can be an effective tool for repetition of key testimony from the witness, a kind of last word from the witness (though the opponent can always conduct recross, of course).

Redirect examination also provides an immediate opportunity to rehabilitate an impeached witness. Many times the rehabilitation will be nothing more than a denial of the attempted impeachment—the expert's denial that money had any effect on his opinion, the eyewitness' response to defendant's claim that she couldn't have seen what she claims to have seen, the witness' explanation of why he made seemingly inconsistent statements about the sequence of events. Other times the rehabilitation may include bringing forth additional evidence to support the impeached witness' testimony. For example, the party might offer prior consistent statements of the witness to prove that she has not forgotten what happened or to rebut a claim that she has recently fabricated her testimony as the result of some improper influence or motive.

In the latter situation, prior consistent statements are admissible to prove the truth of the matter asserted, provided that the prior statements were made before the alleged improper motive arose. (*See, e.g.,* Fed. R. Evid. 801(d)(1)(C).) Other prior consistent statements may be used for the non-hearsay purpose of rehabilitating the witness' credibility (such as statements that rebut an attack on the witness' memory).

The use of prior consistent statements simply requires proof that the witness made the prior statement and proof of when he did so. If the objective is to rebut an attack on memory, counsel would want to point out that the prior statements were made closer in time to the events, when memory was fresher, and that they do not differ materially from the witness' trial testimony. If the purpose is to rebut a claim of fabrication, counsel should have the witness establish that the statements predate the witness' alleged improper influence or motive. In the example below, plaintiff's counsel has just completed the cross-examination of a witness, Jack Sullivan, who was a passenger in plaintiff's car at the time of the car accident. Plaintiff's counsel has attempted to impeach Sullivan during the cross, based on Sullivan's monetary settlement with the defendant before trial. Defense counsel's redirect examination demonstrates an effort to rehabilitate Sullivan.

Illustration of Rehabilitation on Redirect Examination

Lawyer:	When did your settlement with Mr. Morris take place?
Witness:	Just two weeks ago or so. I believe we signed the papers on August 15th.
Lawyer:	Had you discussed the accident with anyone before that settlement agreement?
Witness:	Of course I had, many people at various times.
Lawyer:	Did you ever discuss it with a claims adjuster, a Ms. Buford?
Witness:	Yes, I did, sometime shortly after the accident.
Lawyer:	Did anything come of your conversation with Ms. Buford?
Witness:	I remember that she had it all typed up, everything I had told her, and then she gave it to me to sign as my statement.
Lawyer:	Did you sign it?
Witness:	I sure did.
Lawyer:	When was that?
Witness:	I don't know exactly, but it was more than a year ago, just a matter of weeks after the accident.
Lawyer:	Was it before or after you settled with the defendant?
Witness:	Long before our settlement.
Lawyer:	And what did you tell Ms. Buford?
Witness:	I told her the same things I said here today, that Billy (plaintiff) wasn't paying attention at the time of the accident, that he was on his cell phone and messing with his iPad.

| Lawyer: | So that's been your testimony from the beginning? |
| Witness: | Absolutely. |

The final point to remember on redirect examination is that the same rules of procedure and questioning that apply to the direct examination apply to the redirect examination. For example, counsel may not ask leading questions on redirect examination, and yet, it is not unusual to find counsel doing just that because of the rhythm established from the just-finished cross-examination. The better practice is to consciously lapse back into the rhythms and good practices of the direct examination–to use headlining and blocking, ask short, prodding questions, and keep the redirect examination as short as reasonably possible while still accomplishing counsel's objectives.

V. SPECIAL WITNESSES

The basic techniques and principles discussed above apply to almost all direct examinations and *almost all* witnesses. They do not cover every witness or every situation. Some witnesses present special challenges and require different treatment. We discuss three of those "special witnesses" in this section, including: (1) the forgetful witness, (2) the adverse witness, and (3) the child witness.

A. The Forgetful Witness

Every trial attorney will have the experience of having a witness forget some important information. It is critical, therefore, to know how to revive the witness' ability to recall or, if that is not possible, to know what evidence is available to substitute for the witness' testimony concerning the forgotten information. There is a three-layered approach that should be followed: lead the witness, refresh recollection, and offer past recollection recorded.

1. *Jogging the Memory with Leading Questions*

As noted previously, leading questions are generally not permitted on direct examination. They are permitted, however, as may be necessary to develop the witness' testimony. (Fed. R. Evid. 611(c).) In other words, it is permissible to use a leading question to help jog the memory of the witness. For example, in a wrongful termination case the advocate's client terminated the manager in one of her restaurants for several reasons: a steep decline in profits, customer complaints about the cleanliness of the restaurant, two negative citations by the County Health Department, and a complaint by a server at the restaurant that the manager had made unwanted sexual advances toward her. In response to questions concerning the reasons for terminating the manager, the client mentioned the first three reasons but omitted the complaint from the server. In such a case, a carefully phrased leading question might refresh or jog the witnesses' memory.

Illustration of Use of Leading Questions to Jog Memory

Lawyer:	Alright, Mr. Jones, you have testified that your decision to terminate Mr. Adams was due to declining profits, as well as your concerns over whether cleanliness standards were being met at the restaurant. Was there anything else that contributed to your decision to terminate Mr. Adams?
Witness:	Well, uh, it was a combination of several things.
Lawyer:	Mr. Smith, had you received any complaints about Mr. Adams from any other employees at the restaurant he managed?

The last question is leading, in that it suggests that a complaint or complaints from co-workers was a factor leading up to the manager's termination. Yet, it is fairly broadly phrased and does not come as close to testifying for the witness as it would if it were differently phrased. Consider the following: "Mr. Smith, had a waitress in the restaurant complained to you that Mr. Adams was sexually harassing her?" While the latter question may be somewhat more likely to refresh the witness' memory than the former, it also will leave the jury with the impression that the lawyer is creating the witness' testimony. The first question should be sufficient to jog the witness' recall without giving the impression that the witness is merely saying what his lawyer wants him to say. If, however, the leading question does not jog the memory, it is time to proceed to the next layer and attempt to refresh the recollection of the witness.

2.   *Refreshing Recollection*

Where a witness is unable to recall facts important to the case, it is permissible to attempt to refresh the witness' recollection. Although virtually anything that will revive the witness' memory can be used to refresh recollection, the most successful memory aid is usually the very words of the witness herself. This may be in the form of a deposition transcript of the witness' prior testimony, a report or communication actually drafted by the witness, or it may be the report of someone else (*e.g.*, an investigating police officer) which recorded the witness' own words.

It is important to lay the appropriate foundation for refreshing the witness' recollection. First, it must be established that the witness lacks recall. Then it must be shown that some document or other item exists which, if exposed to the witness, may have the effect of reviving the memory of the witness.

Illustration of Refreshing Recollection

Lawyer: Mr. Smith, were there any other factors that led to your decision to terminate Mr. Adams' employment.

Witness: You know, I'm sure there were. But it has been three years, and some details aren't as clear in my mind as they once were.

Lawyer: If I showed you a copy of a memorandum you sent to your partners concerning your decision to terminate Mr. Adams, might that refresh your recollection?

Witness: I am almost certain it would.

At that point, the document or other item being used to refresh recollection can be shown to the witness. If it succeeds in refreshing the witness' recollection, the witness will then be permitted to testify based upon his revived memory. The document or thing used to refresh should be retrieved from the witness before the witness continues her testimony. The opposing counsel must be informed of what counsel is using to refresh and opposing counsel is entitled to use the document or thing on cross-examination of the witness and to offer it into evidence. (*See, e.g.,* Fed. R. Evid. 612.) If, however, the witness still cannot recall the detail that the attorney seeks to elicit, it will be necessary to replace witness testimony with some other means of presenting the evidence. If available, a memorandum or record prepared by the witness may be offered. In addition, a record prepared by someone else may be offered if it can be shown it was adopted by the witness at a time when the matter was fresh in the witness' memory.

3.   *When Memory Fails, Past Recollection Recorded*

Although hearsay rules generally prohibit introduction of a witness' own out-of-court statements, an exception to this general proscription exists for recorded recollection. (Fed. R. Evid. 803(5).) While there may be some variation in the rules concerning the admissibility of this type of hearsay evidence, its use is generally permissible if a proper foundation is laid. First, it must be shown that the writing or record concerns something of which the witness once had knowledge but has now forgotten or insufficiently recalls. The writing or record must be shown to have been made or adopted by the witness while the matter recorded was fresh in the witness' memory, and it must be shown to have accurately recorded the witness' knowledge.

If these foundational requirements are met, the writing or record may be read into (or played into) evidence. It is received in evidence in its written or recorded form only if the adverse party wishes.

 Illustration of Past Recollection Recorded

Lawyer: Mr. Smith, did you write a memorandum to your business partners concerning your reasons for terminating Mr. Adams' employment?

Witness: Yes I did.

Lawyer: Your Honor, may I approach the witness?

Court: You may.

Lawyer: I am handing you what has been marked for identification as Defendant's Exhibit 16. Do you recognize it?

Witness: I do.

Lawyer: How do you recognize it?

Witness: I wrote it and signed it. It is the memorandum I sent to my partners explaining why I had let Mr. Adams go.

Lawyer: When did you write that memorandum?

Witness: The same day that I terminated Mr. Adams.

Lawyer: Were the events leading up to your decision fresh in your mind when you wrote the memorandum?

Witness: Oh, yes.

Lawyer: And did your memorandum accurately report the events that led you to decide to terminate Mr. Adams' employment?

Witness: Of course.

Lawyer: Your Honor, at this time I would move Defendant's Exhibit 16 into evidence and would ask that the witness be permitted to read it into evidence.

Court: Defense Exhibit 16 is received in evidence. The witness may read it aloud to the jury.

Note that the document is read into evidence rather than given to the jurors. That is the method of introduction mandated by the Federal Rules of Evidence and followed in most state courts. It avoids the risk that jurors will place greater weight on a witness' written words than they place on testimonial evidence.

B.   The Adverse Witness

The second witness for whom special consideration must be given is the adverse witness, that is, a witness who is hostile to the party calling the witness to testify. One can imagine any number of situations in which an advocate might encounter an adverse witness. In a criminal case, the prosecutor might call the alleged victim of domestic abuse to testify even though she has recanted her allegations of abuse. Or, the prosecutor might call one of defendant's friends or even a family member to rebut the defendant's alibi. In a civil case, the plaintiff might call the defendant or an employee of the defendant during the plaintiff's case-in-chief to testify about the defendant's actions (and omissions).

There are four critical differences between the typical direct examination and the direct examination of an adverse witness:

- personal preparation of the witness is generally unavailable

- surprise is a potent weapon

- leading questions to the witness are allowed (and essential to success)

- the examiner, not the witness, is on center stage

As these points so clearly demonstrate, conducting a direct examination of an adverse witness is more akin to cross-examination than to direct examination. And the techniques and principles for preparing and executing the direct examination are more like those that apply to cross-examinations, and not direct examinations. (See Chapter Eight.) Typically, the advocate has no opportunity to meet with or to prepare the adverse witness beforehand. And by the very nature of the witness' hostility toward the advocate's client, matters of witness control loom large for the examiner, unlike the ordinary direct examination. The rules of evidence recognize these significant challenges for the examiner, most notably by allowing leading questions with such witnesses. (*See, e.g.*, Fed. R. Evid. 611(c).) Leading questions are a necessity when "directing" adverse witnesses, because the last thing adverse witnesses are interested in doing is following the direction of the lawyer for the party that is suing them or is somehow aligned against their interests. Moreover, the examiner may need to impeach the witness or otherwise discredit the witness' testimony.

Sometimes the hostility of the witness will be obvious to everyone in the courtroom, including the judge, and will require no foundation or motion by the party. For example, when the plaintiff calls the defendant as her first witness, no one will question that the defendant is an adverse witness and that plaintiff's lawyer can use the tools of cross-examination while questioning the witness. However, in other situations it may not be so clear-cut and the examiner may be required to establish the witness' hostility. For example, when the prosecution calls the defendant's close friend to testify about the defendant's whereabouts the night of the murder, it is not immediately apparent that the witness is adverse to the prosecution. In fact, if the witness testifies to the facts anticipated by the prosecution, the witness should in fact be helpful, not hostile. However, if the witness, once on the stand, demonstrates such hostility, either by suddenly changing his testimony or manifesting a general lack of candor in his testimony, the advocate can move to have the witness declared hostile, thus invoking the loosened rules of examination that apply to adverse witnesses. The judge, of course, has wide discretion to decide whether a particular witness is hostile.

In the example that follows, assume that the prosecutor is examining the alleged victim of an assault and battery. According to the prosecution, the defendant, Dirk Corbin, severely injured the victim after a disagreement over the distribution of the victim's earnings from her work as a prostitute. Immediately after the attack, the victim identified the defendant as the attacker and signed a statement to that effect. On the stand, however, she changes her story and points the finger at someone else.

 Illustration of Examination of Adverse Witness

Lawyer: Ms. Walters, at some point that night did you and Mr. Corbin get into an argument?

Witness: No, not that I recall.

Lawyer: Well, didn't Mr. Corbin strike you across the face at some point that night?

Witness: Oh no. He would never do anything like that. I know I said that before but I was upset at him because he was not treating me right. I accused him of beating me up just to get even with him.

Lawyer: So, it's your testimony today that the defendant never touched you?

Witness: That's right, never laid so much as a hand on me.

Lawyer: Would you say that you and the defendant are good friends?

Witness: I don't know what you mean by "good." We know each other, we're friends.

Lawyer: Well you have maintained your friendship with him since you were injured, haven't you?

Witness: Sure.

Lawyer: And the defendant has continued to manage your business activities?

Witness: Yes, he does.

Lawyer: And now you have changed your story from the one you gave police at the time you were injured.

Witness: Yes, I have. I never should have falsely accused Dirk like that.

Lawyer: Your Honor, the people request permission to treat the witness as hostile.

Judge: [*Looking to defense counsel*] Any objection?

Opposing Counsel: Yes, Your Honor, counsel's made no showing of hostility. Just because they don't like her answers doesn't mean they should get to treat her as an adverse witness.

Judge: Overruled. The witness may be treated as hostile by the prosecution.

At this point, the examiner may use leading questions. The examiner will also benefit by having the court declare the witness as "hostile," which alerts jurors to the fact that the witness has a motive to be less than candid in response to the advocate's question.

C.   The Child Witness

A third category of special witnesses is the child witness. Children present special concerns about their competency to testify as witnesses, including their ability to communicate what they know, to distinguish between truth and falsehood, and to withstand the rigors of giving testimony in adversary system. They require particularly careful preparation and special consideration and accommodation while on the witness stand.

1. *Competency of Child Witnesses*

Unlike the common law principles of competency, the federal rules of evidence presume that children are competent to testify (Fed. R. Evid. 601). There is no minimum age requirement before children are considered competent to testify in federal court, though some states still impose such limitations. The federal approach simply means that the chronological age of a child will not be dispositive of the child's competency to testify in court. Instead, the court will independently examine the child's maturity, her ability to understand the oath, and her ability to communicate to the jury. Judges typically conduct a *voir dire* of young children before allowing them to testify, during which the judge attempts to explore the child's understanding of reality and ability to recognize what is the truth and what is a lie. For example, the judge might ask the child, "Do you understand what a lie is?" Or perhaps, "What happens when you tell a lie?" "If I said that the tie I'm wearing has green stripes would that be true or would that be a lie?" If the child appears to appreciate the distinction and to be capable of responding to questions, the court will likely find the child competent to testify.

2. *Accommodations for Child Witnesses*

Assuming that the judge determines that the child is competent to testify, the next question is under what conditions will the child give her testimony. In many jurisdictions, child victims of physical or sexual abuse may be allowed to testify outside the presence of the defendant in criminal cases, by way of closed circuit television or by other means. The specific showing required depends upon the terms of the jurisdiction's statute, of course, but generally speaking the proponent of the witness (typically the prosecution) must show that the procedure is necessary to further an important interest. This interest is usually demonstrated by showing that forcing the child to testify in the courtroom would be so traumatic that it would either render the child unable to testify, thus depriving the prosecutor of reliable evidence, or that it would severely traumatize the young victim. The showing will often require testimony from mental health experts who can testify about the potential injury to the child in an individualized way.

Even in cases in which the child is required to testify in the presence of the defendant, courts will typically allow the examiner some extra leeway in questioning the child. The formal environment of the courtroom and the unfamiliar nature of the proceeding make testifying particularly difficult for children. They often experience extreme nervousness and anxiety about the whole ordeal. And so, depending on the maturity and capabilities of the child, the examiner may be allowed to ask leading questions of the witness and to be more involved in helping the witness to express and explain her testimony. However, the examiner should also look for means of making the child comfortable and lessening the trauma experienced by the child. That might mean ensuring that the witness has some comfort toy with them on the stand (a teddy bear or blanket, for instance), or having the lawyer who the child knows best conduct the examination, or spending extra preparation time with the child showing her exactly what to expect (including a "dress rehearsal" of the child's testimony under simulated conditions, with someone playing the judge and opposing counsel, etc.).

Perhaps the most important thing advocates can do, however, is to maintain an informality and accessibility in their interaction with child witnesses, beginning well before the child is required to testify. The advocate should spend some time with the child in a setting comfortable to the child. At trial, the advocate should call the child by her first name, use a conversational tone of voice, spend some time in the initial questioning of the witness discussing areas of interest for the child to put the child at ease, and use simple and understandable words in questions and responses. The more comfortable the child is on the witness stand, the better and more comprehensive her testimony will be.

In the example that follows, the witness is Jimmy, a six year old child who saw his younger brother get hurt while climbing on the outside of a play structure at a privately maintained community park. The child's mother has brought a lawsuit, claiming that the toy structure was defectively and dangerously designed.

Illustration of Direct Examination of a Child Witness

Lawyer: Good morning, Jimmy. How are you doing this morning?

Witness: I'm okay I guess.

Lawyer: Jimmy, can you tell us your whole name, first and last?

Witness: Jimmy Dale Norton.

Lawyer: Thank you, Jimmy. Does your mom sometimes call you by your whole name when you are in trouble?

Witness: Yeah, sometimes she does.

Lawyer: How old are you Jimmy?

Witness: I'm six and-a-half.

Lawyer: Wow! When will you turn seven?

Witness: October 15th.

Lawyer: Jimmy can you tell me about your family? Do you have any brothers or sisters?

Witness: Yes, I have a brother, Jesse.

Lawyer: How old is Jesse?

Witness: He's only four. He's my younger brother.

Lawyer: Who else is in your family?

Witness: I have a dog. His name is Tramp.

Lawyer: Oh really? Do you take care of Tramp?

Witness: Not really. My mom does mostly.

Lawyer: Are your mom and brother here today?

Witness: My mom is, she's right over there [*pointing*].

Lawyer: Let the record show that Jimmy has pointed to Ms. Norton, sitting at plaintiff's counsel. Now that we know about your family, can you tell us what you like to do just for fun?

Witness: I don't know.

Lawyer: Do you like to play baseball?

Witness: Yes, I'm on the Cardinals.

Lawyer:	So you play on a team?
Witness:	Yeah.
Lawyer:	What position do you play?
Witness:	I like first base, but usually I play in the outfield.
Lawyer:	What's the thing you like most about baseball?
Witness:	I don't know ... I like hitting, I guess that's it.
Lawyer:	What else do you like to do for fun?
Witness:	I'm not sure.
Lawyer:	Do you like to play with your brother?
Witness:	Sometimes, but he's not very good at baseball.
Lawyer:	What do you enjoy playing with your brother?
Witness:	I don't know. I guess Nintendo. Sometimes we play Super Mario Brothers.
Lawyer:	Who's better, you or your brother?
Witness:	I am. I always win.
Lawyer:	Do you ever go to the park with your brother, play at the park with him?
Witness:	Yeah, sometimes.
Lawyer:	I want to talk to you about one time when you went with your brother to the park and he got hurt. Do you remember that?
Witness:	Yeah.
Lawyer:	You do?
Witness:	Yeah, I remember. We were at the new park by my friend's house.
	[*Counsel proceeds with questioning about events at the park.*]

Chapter Seven

TRIAL EXHIBITS AND DEMONSTRATIVE EVIDENCE

I. Overview and Purpose of Exhibits

The diagram of an intersection, a broken seatbelt, a photograph of a wrecked truck, a DNA sample, or a chart depicting a downturn in earnings are commonly offered as trial exhibits. They stand apart from the testimony that comprises most of the evidence presented in trials, but serve equally important purposes. Exhibits may be an essential part of proving the case,

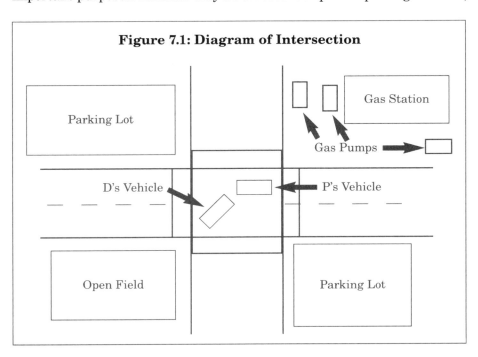

Figure 7.1: Diagram of Intersection

Parking Lot

Gas Station

Gas Pumps

D's Vehicle

P's Vehicle

Open Field

Parking Lot

such as the contract in a breach of contract case, or they may serve to circumstantially prove the party's case, such as the murder weapon in a criminal case. Exhibits also explain, clarify, and reinforce trial testimony. Further, they assist in maintaining juror interest and focus throughout the trial.

Exhibits bring an extra dimension to all parts of a trial. They are tangible, and appeal to other sensory functions besides hearing. It has been well established that things which can be seen, felt, or smelled resonate more powerfully and more memorably than those things which can only be heard. Thus, preparation for a successful trial *must* include an assessment of which exhibits and demonstrative aids will further the case. The question is not *whether* exhibits will be used, but rather *which* exhibits will be used.

In the not so distant past, demonstrative aids were limited to butcher paper and markers, blowups, and overhead transparencies. In many cases, those time-honored aids still suffice. However, the options for advocates have significantly increased in number and technological sophistication. For instance, the overhead projector and butcher paper have given way to a document camera, presentation software, and trial presentation systems in helping to organize and present information to the trier of fact. But the age-old truth that "seeing is believing" is truer than ever. Whether it is television, computers, video games, movies, or DVDs, today's juror is accustomed to electronic stimulation.

Exhibits and demonstrative aids help to:

- explain or clarify testimony

- reinforce the evidence and enhance juror retention

- maintain and heighten juror interest

- satisfy juror expectations

A.   Exhibits Explain and Clarify Testimony

The intuitive notion that complex matters are made more comprehensible by the use of charts, photographs, diagrams, models, computer-generated re-creations and simulations is supported by both practice and theory. For instance, in assisting the plaintiff's testimony describing how the defendant's vehicle ran the light before striking his car, a diagram of the intersection detailing the plaintiff's version of events is vital in understanding that testimony. In prosecuting a driving under the influence case, the arresting officer's testimony of the erratic driving pattern of the defendant will be more clear and will have more impact if he is asked to detail that driving pattern on a diagram. Exhibits or demonstrative aids must be used in all types of litigation: in medical malpractice cases, to explain the internal operations of the body; in a multi-party conspiracy, to depict the names and roles of each actor; in complex tort cases, to show graphic depictions of vehicular accidents; and in other trials to provide helpful and understandable explanations of obscure scientific principles, complicated fact scenarios, damage calculations, and even the sequence of events.

Exhibits can also play an important role in helping jurors understand expert witness testimony. With the astounding proliferation of expert witnesses in most trials, expert testimony must be made understandable to the layperson, particularly in technical or complex scientific fields. One approach is to have the expert witness create or use a visual aid to augment and explain her testimony. The visual aid may be as simple as a chart, a diagram, or a list. For instance, during the direct examination of plaintiff's expert, after the expert has just offered her opinion that the defendant's playground equipment was defectively designed, the advocate could ask the expert to write on a flip board a bullet-point list of the reasons for her opinion. This allows the jurors to both hear and see the reasons for the expert's opinion and come to a better understanding of that testimony. At the other end of the spectrum, the visual aids can be complex and more costly, such as a computer-generated simulation that illustrates the expert's testimony.

B.   Exhibits Reinforce Testimony and Enhance Juror Retention

In addition to providing jurors with a clarity of understanding that words alone cannot accomplish, exhibits also enhance the ability of jurors to remember the essential evidence in an advocate's case. During closing argument, advocates can emphasize particular evidence so that it will be more readily recalled by jurors during deliberations. But it is also essential that "critical" evidence be memorable as it comes into evidence so that the closing argument reinforces, rather than creates, a memory. Creating the memories as the testimony comes in is best accomplished with visual images. Exhibits are more memorable than oral testimony and consequently will be recalled more readily because they create associations for the jurors that they can recall more easily during deliberations.

Consider, for example, the effectiveness of lists. A well-constructed list is an important tool both at closing argument and during the testimony of an expert witness. When displayed before the jury, a list synthesizes and organizes the testimony for the jurors. This simplest of visual aids reinforces what is being said and significantly increases the impact of the message on the jury.

Visual images also create associations for jurors that can be valuable during the closing argument. Consider an example from Abraham Lincoln's most famous trial, the so-called "Almanac Trial." The prosecution charged Lincoln's client with a nighttime murder based on the testimony of one eyewitness. During Lincoln's cross-examination, the witness conceded that he had been able to see what happened by moonlight only because the moon had been high in the nighttime sky at the time of the murder. Lincoln then used an almanac for the pertinent year to prove that, at the time of the murder, the moon was just rising and thus would have been low in the sky.[1] The jury now associated the almanac with an outright lie by the

---

[1] *See* JOHN J. DUFF, A. LINCOLN: PRAIRIE LAWYER 350, 357 (1961).

prosecution's main witness. By simply holding up the almanac during the closing, Lincoln could avail himself of that association, reminding the jury of the untrustworthy witness and his lies.

C.   Exhibits Heighten and Maintain Juror Interest

There is nothing like a good demonstrative aid to heighten juror interest in what is being said. No words could equal the impact on the jurors of watching O.J. Simpson try on the bloody glove allegedly worn by his ex-wife's murderer and seeing that the glove did not fit. You had to see it. Once the jurors had seen it, Simpson's lawyers needed only to pick up the glove and show it to the jurors to reinforce the point. In a drug possession case, a baggie of heroin placed on the jury rail during closing argument is certain to capture juror interest. Likewise, in a drunk driver case, the prosecutor during closing argument might communicate the quantity of beer consumed by the defendant by placing beer cans, one after another, on the jury rail. The beer cans, on display in front of the jury, speak far more loudly and more powerfully than the prosecutor's words. And the demonstration itself is so out of the norm that it is sure to be memorable.

Of course, technological innovations have greatly expanded the range of options for advocates. Perhaps the technological tool most easily available to advocates is presentation software. It allows advocates to create lists, time lines, charts, and diagrams, as well as label photographs and project documents in color with motion and sound. In short, it can do much more than any transparency or flip board, and thus, it can serve as a valuable means of keeping the jurors tuned in to the trial.

Additionally, there are even more sophisticated options, such as computer-generated, full motion animations, re-creations, and simulations. A computer-generated animation depicting the vehicle roll-over and how the occupants of the vehicle were injured will certainly maintain juror interest and enhance their comprehension. It can also be terribly persuasive with jurors. Yet, there are some problems associated with using computer simulations. We are so accustomed to receiving information from "television-like" monitors that the re-creation may well be viewed by some jurors as fact, even though it represents only one party's view of the events. Such a re-creation may be excluded by the court because of its potential for unfair prejudice. Another concern of such high-tech exhibits is cost. Not many litigants will have access to the resources necessary for such exhibits. Yet, when it is feasible to use these exhibits, they can be very effective in heightening juror interest and keeping the jurors focused.

D.   Exhibits Satisfy Juror Expectations

A final benefit of the use of exhibits is that they satisfy the expectations of modern jurors. That does not mean that advocates must utilize the latest technology in every case. And it does not mean that advocates should put away their magic markers and flip charts once and for all. It does mean, however, that jurors are sophisticated consumers when it comes to the tools of communication. Advocates must make their presentations interesting and accessible to jurors and should use available technology when it makes sense to do so. Exhibits and demonstrative aids are essential to satisfy a juror's need for visual stimulation.

II.   TYPES OF EXHIBITS AND DEMONSTRATIVE AIDS

Trial evidence consists of the sworn testimony of witnesses, the exhibits admitted during the trial, and any stipulations made by the parties (plus matters judicially noticed by the court). Testimonial evidence comes from the witnesses. Exhibits and demonstrative aids are the documents and other tangible objects used to prove the claim or defense or to enhance, explain, confirm, or demonstrate the testimony of witnesses.

Most tangible objects a party might use at trial can be placed into one of three categories:

- real evidence

- documentary evidence

- demonstrative evidence

These categories provide a helpful starting point because the requirements for admission turn in large part on the kind of object counsel is attempting to introduce. Accordingly, we briefly describe the three categories of exhibits before we address their foundational requirements.

A.   Real Evidence

Real evidence is sometimes referred to as original or physical evidence. It is a tangible item that is directly involved in the dispute. The handgun used in the murder, the torn seatbelt from the plaintiff's automobile, the cocaine found on the defendant, the plaintiff's injured hand, or the contract entered into by plaintiff and defendant are all examples of real evidence, as they can all independently establish the existence or nonexistence of a relevant fact.

While real evidence is usually thought of as an actual object involved in the events, it is not so limited. Real evidence would also include a bullet shot from the defendant's gun used for comparison with a bullet taken from the victim's body. Even though the comparison bullet was not involved in the crime charged, it is real evidence because it establishes a material fact in the case.

B.   Documentary Evidence

Documentary evidence refers to writings or recordings that are offered to prove their content. Documentary evidence is a type of real evidence in that it has independent probative value. Like real evidence, it is often an item or object that is, or is alleged to have been, involved in the dispute. However, unlike real evidence, testimony cannot be substituted for this type of evidence. Documents must be introduced into evidence to prove their contents under the best evidence doctrine. (Fed. R. Evid. 1002.) Documentary evidence would include the handwritten pages the plaintiff claims was decedent's will, a contract allegedly signed by defendant, the defendant's handwritten confession, and even a bank statement.

C. Demonstrative Evidence

Demonstrative evidence generally refers to tangible evidence that illustrates or explains a fact the advocate must prove. Demonstrative evidence is distinguished from real or documentary evidence in that it has no independent probative value (in that it played no role in the actual events in dispute); rather, it is used in conjunction with witness testimony to clarify cumbersome, complicated, or confusing testimony, to highlight particular aspects of a witness' testimony, or to emphasize and reinforce evidence crucial to the advocate's case. Demonstrative evidence includes such items as drawings, maps, models, diagrams, photographs, charts, lists, courtroom demonstrations, and computer simulations. The scope of demonstrative evidence is limited only by the advocate's creativity.

III. ADMISSION OF EXHIBITS AND DEMONSTRATIVE AIDS

A. Foundational Requirements

Each piece of evidence offered during the trial must have a proper foundation laid by the attorney and approved by the judge before it can be introduced to the jury. For example, testimonial evidence—the actual words spoken by witnesses from the stand—must come from witnesses who have personal knowledge, have taken and understand the oath, and have the cognitive capacity to communicate what they know. And, of course, the testimony must be relevant, reliable, and not subject to any rule of exclusion.

In the same way, the advocate must lay the foundation for introducing exhibits before they can be shown to the jury. In other words, exhibits must be relevant and reliable, and they must be "authentic." For all exhibits other than those that are self-authenticating, authentication requires foundational testimony from a witness. In the language of the Federal Rules of Evidence, the party offering the exhibit must show that the exhibit "is what its proponent claims." (Fed. R. Evid. 901(a)). That means that the party must present sufficient proof that a reasonable juror could find the exhibit is what the party claims it is. For example, testimony based on a witness' personal knowledge that he recognizes the knife as the one used in the attack would ordinarily be sufficient to authenticate the knife.

Perhaps not surprisingly, the most frequent method of authentication is the testimony of a witness with personal knowledge of the events. When the tangible evidence is unique and identifiable on the basis of its distinctive appearance, evidence that the object is what the proponent purports it to be can usually be offered through the testimony of a witness who has personal knowledge. For instance, the testimony of the arresting police officer would be sufficient to authenticate a particular pair of gloves as ones that the defendant was wearing at the time of the arrest. With other evidence that is not distinctive, such as twenty-five grams of cocaine, additional foundation about the chain of custody may be necessary for the item.

B. Special Considerations for Electronic Evidence

We live in an age where electronic data is overwhelming. Data is passed through the Internet at lightening speed every millisecond. Between cell-phones, blogs, web pages, instant messaging, e-mail, Myspace, Facebook, Twitter, and many other electronic modes of communication, information is being shared among people more often and faster than ever. It is not surprising, then, that some of this information becomes critical evidence in trials.

Since most electronic data can be easily manipulated, it poses a special challenge to advocates trying to lay a proper evidentiary foundation. Regardless of its increased likelihood of falsification, the authentication standard for electronic evidence is the same as that for any other type of evidence: the advocate only needs sufficient proof that a reasonable juror could find the exhibit is what the party claims it is. Thus, the advocate need not worry about ruling out all other possibilities inconsistent with authenticity, nor proving authenticity beyond a reasonable doubt. She must simply show that there is a reasonable likelihood that the evidence is what it purports to be.

Like other evidence, the number one way to authenticate electronic data is through testimony of a witness with knowledge. Other ways to authenticate electronic evidence include:

- distinctive characteristics

- voice identification

- the reply doctrine (not only does this apply to telephone calls, but also e-mail addresses, screen names, and threads on blogs)

- association with a screen name/e-mail address

- parties sending photos of themselves from their screen names

- a plan/action communicated online and carried out in real life

- communication of information that could only be known by the party

- phone number or IP address registered to the party

- files found on party's computer to which he had sole access

There is, however, one sticky issue over which courts are torn when it comes to electronic evidence: the best evidence rule. Some courts rule that any "copy-pasting" of chat logs or computer printouts of internet communications violate the best evidence rule. This is due to the higher risk of manipulation when a conversation or photo is copied and pasted into a separate document where editing could take place without the knowledge of the court. Some courts, however, allow copied-and-pasted transcripts in most situations. The trend seems to lean more toward the best evidence rule being satisfied, as long as someone can testify that the conversation as copied or printed, accurately represents the actual conversation.

C. Laying Foundations and Introducing Exhibits

In some courtrooms, the argument over the admission of exhibits takes place well before the trial begins. Certain judges may require that exhibits be pre-marked and even be admitted or excluded by the court before the trial even begins. Pre-marking exhibits has distinct advantages. The advocates know with certainty before trial which exhibits will be admitted, thus eliminating the uncertainty that an exhibit may be excluded during trial. Additionally, pre-marking exhibits is efficient, eliminating the rather elaborate and time-consuming process that must be undertaken when moving in exhibits during witness testimony. Nonetheless, pre-marking exhibits may not be an option in all trials and is not preferred by all judges. And certainly pre-admission of exhibits will not always take place. Consequently, advocates must be intimately familiar with the process for introducing exhibits into evidence during witness testimony.

1. *Describe the Exhibit*

The first step in admitting exhibits is to describe the exhibit with some particularity. This is especially significant if the exhibit is not easily distinguishable from other similar items, such as a can of Pepsi or a baggie of heroin. The description should be objective and neutral, designed solely to ensure that the record is clear about what the advocate is doing.

 Illustration of Describing Exhibit

Lawyer: Your Honor, may the record reflect I am holding a knife that is approximately 12 inches long? It has a fixed blade and wooden handle.

---

2. *Mark the Exhibit for Identification Purposes*

The second step is for the advocate to ask leave of court to approach the clerk and have the exhibit marked for identification. Obviously, this step is unnecessary if the parties have pre-marked the exhibits. Whether exhibits are designated with numbers or letters depends upon the preferences and protocol of the court. Some jurisdictions use numbers to mark plaintiff and prosecution exhibits, whereas defense exhibits are designated by letters. Others use numbers (or letters) for both sides' exhibits. Simply having the exhibit marked for identification has no evidentiary value; it is simply a convenient manner of tracking the exhibit. If opposing counsel has an objection to the exhibit, it would be premature to offer the objection at this point since the proponent has not yet offered the exhibit into evidence.

 Illustration of Marking Exhibit

Lawyer: Your Honor, may I approach the clerk and have the knife marked for identification as People's next in order?

Court: You may. The exhibit will be People's Exhibit Number Five for identification purposes.

3.   *Show Exhibit to Opposing Counsel*

The third step is to show the exhibit to opposing counsel. By taking and showing the marked exhibit to opposing counsel, the proponent of the exhibit signals to the jury that she is being fair and open, giving her opponent a full opportunity to examine the exhibit prior to moving it into evidence. This step ensures that opposing counsel does not complain that the proponent is somehow acting unfairly by depriving counsel of the chance to view the exhibit before it is offered into evidence.

 Illustration of Showing Exhibit to Opponent

Lawyer: Your Honor, may the record reflect I am showing People's Exhibit Five for identification to opposing counsel?

Court: The record will so reflect.

4.   *Give Exhibit to Witness, Lay Foundation*

The fourth step for counsel, after retrieving the exhibit from opposing counsel, is to seek permission to approach the witness and to ask the necessary questions of the witness to lay a foundation authenticating the exhibit. Some judges will require that counsel always ask permission before approaching the witness, while others maintain a more informal courtroom. The specific foundation required will depend on the nature and intended use of the exhibit. As noted earlier, the most common means of authentication is by personal knowledge of the authenticating witness, requiring simply that the witness identify the object as being what the proponent claims it is. In fact, the foundation can sometimes be laid with no more than two questions, the first establishing that the witness knows what the exhibit is and the second establishing the basis of the witness' knowledge. With demonstrative evidence, counsel must also establish that the exhibit fairly and accurately conveys the thing that is being depicted (*e.g.*, intersection, car, weapon, etc.).

 Illustration of Laying Foundation

Lawyer:	Your Honor, may I approach Mr. Loury with People's Exhibit Five for identification?
Judge:	You may.
Lawyer:	Mr. Loury, referring to People's Exhibit Five for identification, have you ever seen that item before?
Witness:	Yes, I have.
Lawyer:	Tell us the circumstances.
Witness:	When I entered my parents' home and found my father's body, that knife was laying across his chest.
Lawyer:	How can you be certain it was the same knife as the knife marked as People's Number Five?
Witness:	I recognize it as one of the knives from the set my parents keep in their kitchen. It was the only knife missing from the set.

---

5. *Move Exhibit into Evidence*

Once an adequate foundation has been laid and the exhibit has been authenticated, all that remains is for the proponent of the exhibit to move it into evidence. An important consideration is when exhibits should be moved into evidence—at the time the foundation is laid, at the conclusion of the witness' direct examination, or at the conclusion of the party's case. Depending on the circumstances, there may be good reasons for choosing any of these possibilities. The strategy regarding timing is discussed later. For present purposes, assume the party chooses to introduce the exhibit immediately.

 Illustration of Moving Exhibit into Evidence

Lawyer:	Your Honor, at this time I move People's Five for identification into evidence.
Judge:	*[looking to opposing counsel]* Any objection?
Opposing Counsel:	No, Your Honor.
Judge:	People's Exhibit Five is admitted.

If opposing counsel believes that an adequate foundation has not been laid, he must object before the exhibit is admitted into evidence. If the judge sustains the objection, the proponent of the exhibit may, with leave of court, resume questioning and once again attempt to lay an adequate foundation, and then again attempt to move the exhibit into evidence.

The opponent of the offered exhibit, in addition to making a foundation objection, also has the option of taking the witness on *voir dire*, challenging the adequacy of the foundation for the exhibit. The *voir dire* examination is limited, of course, to the question of the exhibit's foundation. Any question that ventures beyond that limited area is subject to a scope objection. Once the opponent of the exhibit has completed her *voir dire* examination, she can then renew her objection.

Illustration of *Voir Dire* Questioning about Foundation

Lawyer:	Your Honor, I object. There is no foundation that People's Exhibit Five is the same knife that the witness saw on the body. May I take the witness on *voir dire*?
Judge:	You may.
Lawyer:	The knife you found did not have any distinctive markings, did it?
Witness:	No.
Lawyer:	And you certainly did not mark that knife, did you?
Witness:	What do you mean?
Lawyer:	You did not put your initials on that knife?
Witness:	No.
Lawyer:	Nor did you put it in a baggy and mark the baggy?
Witness:	No.
Lawyer:	Other than the fact that it looked like one of the knives your parents keep in their kitchen, it was not distinctive to you, was it?
Witness:	No.
Lawyer:	Your Honor, I renew my foundational objection. This witness is simply not competent to testify that People's Five is the same knife he saw lying across his father's chest.

6. *Publish Exhibit to the Jury*

The final step, after an exhibit has been admitted, is to publish the exhibit to the jury; that is, give the jury the opportunity to see, read, touch, hold, and examine the exhibit. The particular method of publication can take many forms and will depend on the nature of the exhibit and the purpose for its introduction in the case. Of course, the timing and manner of publication must first be cleared with the judge.

Consider the possibilities. With documentary exhibits, the advocate might provide a copy of the exhibit for each juror (the judge and opposing counsel) or collect all of the documentary exhibits in a notebook for each juror (in cases involving numerous documentary exhibits), or enlarge the document and show it to the entire jury at the same time. With real evidence, such as the baggy of cocaine or the defendant's glove found at the murder scene, the advocate may hand the object to the jurors and allow them to pass it around the jury box or display it on courtroom monitors with the aid of a document camera. Whatever form the publication takes, low-tech or high-tech, a foam board enlargement, an old fashioned "pass the exhibit around the jury box," or a digitalized enlargement of the exhibit on a plasma screen, the act of publication is critical. It is the pay-off for the advocate's work in laying the foundation.

Three rules should govern the advocate's approach to publication of exhibits:

1. *There is no substitute for sensory stimulation when it comes to jurors.* Whenever appropriate, advocates should give jurors the chance to *experience* the exhibit by touching and holding it.

2. *The act of publication should not disrupt or distract attention from the examination.* Publication should be timed to maximize impact and minimize disruption. The exhibit should be shown to the jury roughly simultaneously to the witness' discussion of the exhibit before the jury. However, distribution of copies of documentary exhibits to the jurors should be carefully timed so that the jurors are not distracted from the direct examination of the witness by reading the document while the witness is testifying about other matters.

3. *The exhibit, when published, must be plainly visible and accessible to every juror.* Publication is ineffective if one or more of the jurors are unable to fully participate in the viewing or handling of an exhibit.

✎ Illustration of Publication of Real Evidence

Lawyer:	Your Honor, at this time, we ask that the jurors be allowed to examine People's Exhibit A, the glove found at the crime scene.
Judge:	Any objection?
Opposing Lawyer:	No, Your Honor.
Judge:	You may publish it to the jury.

Illustration of Publication of Enlarged Documentary Exhibit

Lawyer: Your Honor, we request permission to show to the jury a verbatim enlargement of Plaintiff's Exhibit C, which we have already shown to opposing counsel.

Judge: You may.

D.   Foundations for Specific Types of Exhibits

The process for admitting exhibits into evidence is only part of the story. Trial lawyers must also know the specific foundational requirements for each exhibit they need to introduce into evidence. This section provides numerous examples of those foundational requirements, divided into the three categories described above: (1) real evidence; (2) documentary evidence; and (3) demonstrative evidence.

1.   *Real Evidence*

As noted above, real evidence consists of the tangible pieces of evidence involved in the circumstances giving rise to the claims or defenses at issue in the trial. For instance, in the illustration involving the knife, discussed above, the knife is real evidence. The prosecutor has laid the necessary foundation for admission of the knife by offering testimony that it was the very same knife the witness saw on his father's body the night his father was killed. As in that example, the foundation for such evidence can often be established through the personal knowledge of a single witness.

On occasion, authentication of real evidence may require testimony from multiple witnesses to establish the chain of custody for the exhibit. In particular, chain of custody evidence is required for those exhibits that are not easily distinguishable from other similar objects. All cocaine looks basically the same, just as counterfeit currency bears very close similarity to authentic currency. And in cases involving such fungible exhibits, the proponent must show that the witness or party has some means of distinguishing the item from other similar items. Thus, the prosecution must show that the white granular material in the baggy is the same material that was tested by the state's chemist and found to be cocaine and that it is the same material that was found on the defendant when he was arrested. Law enforcement agencies attempt to anticipate these authentication issues by their practice of carefully labeling evidence when it is seized, recording its receipt into an evidence storage locker, and tracking its movement through the police lab and elsewhere. Nevertheless, the prosecutor must establish the cocaine's chain of custody to connect it back to the defendant.

How rigorously do courts enforce the chain of custody requirement? It depends. In criminal cases, courts tend to enforce the requirement more stringently than in civil cases. Yet, even in a criminal prosecution, not every person who constitutes a link in the chain must be called as a witness, though each of the important links will likely be needed to testify about their handling of the exhibit. The foundation need not conclusively establish the authenticity of the exhibit; rather, the advocate must merely establish that a reasonable juror could find that the exhibit is what the proponent claims it is. (Fed. R. Evid. 901(a)). The omission of insignificant or minor parts of the chain of custody should not preclude authentication of the evidence.

 Illustration of Establishing the Chain of Custody

Link 1—The narcotics detective:

Lawyer:	[*After satisfying the initial steps of authentication, including marking and identifying the exhibit and showing the exhibit to opposing counsel, counsel proceeds as follows.*] Detective Green, I hand you what has been marked as People's Exhibit Number One for identification. What is it?
Witness:	It is a plastic baggy that contains a vial with a white granular substance inside, which I found in the defendant's duffel bag when I searched it on May 5.
Lawyer:	What did you do with the vial and its contents when you found it in the defendant's duffel bag?
Witness:	I placed the vial in a clear baggy, as you see here [holding up People's Number One] and I labeled the outside of the baggy with the date and my signature and tagged it with an evidence label.
Lawyer:	Then what did you do?
Witness:	I then placed the evidence baggy into a large paper sack, along with other evidence seized from the scene and placed the sack into my car.
Lawyer:	What did you do with the vial seized from the defendant's duffel after you completed your investigation?
Witness:	Well, I drove it back to the police station and placed it in my evidence locker.
Lawyer:	Describe for the jury what you mean by "evidence locker."
Witness:	My evidence locker is the place where I store evidence that I've collected pending its use in a hearing or trial or testing.
Lawyer:	Who has access to your evidence locker?

Witness:	No one other than the lead narcotics detective and me.
Lawyer:	Did you ever remove the baggy, People's Number One, from your evidence locker?
Witness:	I did. The next day, May 6, I took the baggy to the police lab for testing.
Lawyer:	Describe that process.
Witness:	In the police lab there is an intake desk where you sign in evidence for testing. I signed the baggy in, and it was given a tracking number for processing purposes.
Lawyer:	What was the tracking number given for People's One?
Witness:	It was EI 4954.
Lawyer:	Did you ever retrieve the baggy, People's One, from the lab?
Witness:	Yes, about a week later, on May 14, I got a call from the lab and went down there and checked the baggy out from the lab and returned it to my evidence locker.
Lawyer:	Has People's One remained in your locker until today?
Witness:	Yes. This morning, before I testified, I got the baggy from my evidence locker and brought it to court.
Lawyer:	Is it in the same condition today as when you first seized it?
Witness:	Yes, it appears to be.

Link 2—The chemist:

Lawyer:	[*After qualifying the expert and identifying the exhibit*] Dr. Brown, I hand you what's been marked as People's Number One for identification. Do you recognize it?
Witness:	Yes, I tested the white granular substance inside the baggy to determine what it was.
Lawyer:	How did you first gain possession of the baggy, People's One?
Witness:	Well, I got the baggy from the evidence intake desk in the lab. They receive evidence that needs testing from investigating officers and detectives, assign tracking numbers to them, and log them in on the log sheet.
Lawyer:	Do you know what tracking number People's Number One was assigned?
Witness:	Yes, it was assigned EI 4954.
Lawyer:	How do you know that?

Witness:	I know it because I noted the tracking number for the baggy on my testing report, and because the log sheet for that day reflects the same information.
Lawyer:	What did you do with the contents of the baggy, People's One?
Witness:	I tested the contents of the vial to determine what it was.
Lawyer:	Before we discuss the results of your testing, what did you do after you completed your testing of the contents of the baggy?
Witness:	I returned the vial and its contents to the baggy, returned the baggy to the lab's intake desk, and phoned Detective Green to tell him the results of the tests and tell him that he could come get the baggy with the vial.
Lawyer:	And does People's One contain the same vial and contents that you tested?
Witness:	I certainly believe so. It has the same tracking number and its physical appearance is consistent with the vial I saw and the material I tested.
Lawyer:	At this time, Your Honor, I move for the admission of People's Number One into evidence.

2. *Documentary Evidence*

Documentary evidence, which consists of relevant writings that a party seeks to have admitted during the trial, can be authenticated by a number of means, depending on the circumstances and the nature of the document. For example:

- Personal observation of the document being prepared or signed (Fed. R. Evid. 901(b)(1))

- Lay witness opinion on handwriting (Fed. R. Evid. 901(b)(2))

- Expert witness opinion on handwriting (Fed. R. Evid. 901(b)(3))

- Jury comparison of handwriting (Fed. R. Evid. 901(b)(3))

- Distinctive contents of the writing (Fed. R. Evid. 901(b)(4))

- The reply doctrine (letter received in reply to previous letter dealing with same subject matter) (Fed. R. Evid. 901(b)(4))

- Public record (Fed. R. Evid. 901(b)(7))

- Ancient document (more than twenty years old) (Fed. R. Evid. 901(b)(8))

In addition to these means of authentication under the Federal Rules, some documents are self-authenticating (Fed. R. Evid. 902), including business records if accompanied by an affidavit or declaration from the custodian establishing the authenticity of the records. The larger point is that there are many ways to authenticate writings, and the advocate's task is to find the most efficient and most persuasive approach available.

In addition to authentication issues, documents also raise hearsay issues and best evidence issues for which advocates must prepare. With regard to hearsay, every document offered at trial, by its very nature, constitutes an out of court statement and must either be offered for some purpose other than the truth, or fall within some exemption or exception to the hearsay rule. The best evidence rule, on the other hand, is generally satisfied by introduction of a copy of the document whose contents are being proven. However, in the event that the opposing party raises a genuine question regarding the authenticity of the original, the proponent must introduce the original and not a duplicate. (Fed. R. Evid. 1003).

Below we discuss the authentication requirements for five different kinds of documents, including business records authenticated by a custodian of records, an e-mail authenticated by a combination of different methods, a letter authenticated by the reply doctrine, a will authenticated by lay witness opinion, and a summary used with an expert witness.

a. Authentication of Business Records

Perhaps the most common type of document offered in civil trials is the business record. This category includes diverse records, including medical records, accident reports, business memoranda, financial data, employee evaluations, and interoffice correspondence, to name a few. The foundation necessary to admit business records requires consideration of both authentication and hearsay requirements. The proponent must establish that the records are both authentic and fall within the hearsay exception for business records (or some other provision). Under recent amendments to the federal rules and in accordance with the rules of many state jurisdictions, business records can be admitted through an affidavit or declaration by the custodian of records establishing that the records are those of the company and fit within the business records hearsay exception. (*See, e.g.*, Fed. R. Evid. 902(11)). Alternatively, they may be authenticated by a witness who is familiar with how the records were created and can competently testify about that process.

Under the federal business records exception (Fed. R. Evid. 803(6)), the proponent must establish that:

- The document was made at or near the time of the events it describes

- It was made by someone with personal knowledge or based upon information from someone with personal knowledge who had a business duty as an employee to report or record the information

- The document was kept in the regular course of regularly conducted business activity

- It was the regular practice of that business activity to make the record

Each of these requirements must be met and counsel must, to the extent possible, track the precise language of the rule in laying the foundation.

The example below assumes that a hospital's custodian of records is on the witness stand and is being asked about the plaintiff's medical records.

 ## Illustration of Business Record Authenticated by Custodian of Records

Lawyer: *[After establishing the witness' position and responsibilities as custodian of the hospital's records and the witness' familiarity with the hospital's record keeping practices]* Ms. Miller, I hand you a folder of documents containing forty-six pages, which has been marked as Plaintiff's Exhibit C. The pages in the folder have been numbered sequentially 1–46. Can you identify the contents of that folder?

Witness: Yes, this contains the medical file for Ms. Layton's hospital stay from November 5, 2001 to November 9 of the same year.

Lawyer: How do you know that?

Witness: Sometime ago I was asked to retrieve Ms. Layton's records at the hospital since the beginning of 1999, and these are the documents that I found in our archived files.

Lawyer: Have you had the chance to review the specific contents of this folder?

Witness: Yes, I have.

Lawyer: Without describing the contents of any documents, can you give us a sense of the types of documents contained in the folder?

Witness: Sure, there are daily nurses' notes and doctors' instructions, pre- and post-operative notes and reports, lab results, and the like.

Lawyer: Are those documents made in the regular course of the hospital's regularly conducted business activity?

Witness: Yes, they are.

Lawyer: Was it the regular practice of the hospital to make the records contained in the folder?

Witness: It certainly was.

Lawyer:	Were the records made at or near the time of the activities, events or conditions described by the records?
Witness:	Yes they were.
Lawyer:	And were the records made by a person with knowledge or from information provided by a person with knowledge?
Witness:	Yes, they were.

Notice that many of the questions asked by the examiner are leading questions, which is made necessary by the very precise requirements of the business records hearsay exception. Leading questions are appropriate on direct examination when the examiner is asking questions that relate to foundational matters. (*See* Fed. R. Evid. 611(c)).

b. Authentication of E-mail Messages[2]

Undoubtedly, e-mail messages are an increasingly common piece of evidence in modern litigation, as e-mail has rapidly become the primary means of communication within organizations and businesses. Although e-mail messages are often just another business record, their authentication is not as simple as a business record or a letter, because the recipient of the message may have no means of readily identifying the sender (such as by the sender's signature) and the sender of the message may have no means to readily determine whether the intended recipient received the message. The somewhat complicated electronic processes involved in sending and receiving e-mails makes authentication a potentially difficult matter. E-mail is not simply the Pony Express at hyper speed. Instead, it involves a relatively complex system of communication among various networks and servers situated in different locations. At the same time, however, advocates may be able to use a variety of established methods to authenticate e-mails. For example:

- A person's own e-mail messages might be authenticated by the preparer's personal knowledge.

- E-mails received by a person could be authenticated by the reply doctrine if the e-mail was received in reply to a prior message

- Distinctive content of the e-mail, if it contains information that only the sender would know.

- Consistency with the e-mail address on another e-mail sent by the Defendant

- The e-mails inclusion of similar requests or details brought up by the Defendant in other contexts

---

[2] *See generally* EDWARD J. IMWINKELRIED, EVIDENTIARY FOUNDATIONS 59–69 (4th ed. 1998).

Otherwise, the proponent of the message may have to use a chain of custody approach to authenticating the e-mail, demonstrating the path of the message from the sender's computer to the recipient's computer.[3]

c.   Authentication by Lay Witness Opinion

Lay witness opinion provides another means of authenticating a writing. (Fed. R. Evid. 901(b)(2); 701). The examiner must establish that the authenticating witness has personal knowledge of the handwriting or signature of the person who wrote or signed the document sufficient that she can recognize the handwriting or signature when she sees it. Moreover, the witness must not have acquired her knowledge of the person's handwriting in anticipation of the litigation. In the following example, the authenticating witness has substantial familiarity with the decedent's signature and acquired that knowledge long before the instant litigation begins, thus enabling her to offer her opinion testimony.

Illustration of Authentication of a Will with Lay Witness Opinion Testimony

Lawyer:	Mrs. Green, what was the nature of your relationship with Mr. Wills?
Witness:	I was Mr. Wills' secretary for ten years.
Lawyer:	In your capacity as secretary, did you have opportunities to view his handwriting?
Witness:	Every day.
Lawyer:	How many times would you say you've seen Mr. Wills' signature?
Witness:	It's too many to count. Thousands of times, to be sure.
Lawyer:	Would you be able to recognize his handwriting—that is, to distinguish it from the handwriting of others?
Witness:	Mr. Wills had a very distinctive hand. I would know it in a heartbeat.
Lawyer:	Your Honor, I am holding a single handwritten page that is entitled "Last Will and Testament of Hugh Wills." May I approach the clerk and have it marked as Plaintiff's One for identification?
Court:	You may.
Lawyer:	May the record reflect I am showing Plaintiff's One for identification to defense counsel?

---

[3] For a detailed description of such a foundation, *see* IMWINKELRIED, EVIDENTIARY FOUNDATIONS 59–69 (4th ed. 1998).

Court:	So reflected.
Lawyer:	Leave to approach the witness with Plaintiff's One?
Court:	You may.
Lawyer:	Mrs. Green, I'm handing you this document which has been marked as Plaintiff's One for identification. Have you seen it before?
Witness:	The first time I saw it was in your office about three months ago.
Lawyer:	Mrs. Green, do you recognize the handwriting on Plaintiff's One?
Witness:	Yes, I do.
Lawyer:	Whose handwriting is it?
Witness:	Without question, Mr. Wills wrote that document.
Lawyer:	How can you be certain?
Witness:	As I've stated, I've seen Mr. Wills' handwriting thousands of times. I would recognize it anywhere.

d.   Authentication by the Reply Doctrine

An additional means of authenticating a writing, when personal knowledge is not available to a party, is by any distinctive characteristics of the writing, either in its appearance, contents, or internal patterns. (Fed. R. Evid. 901(b)(4)). One recognized application of this provision is the reply doctrine, which allows authentication of a letter "by content and circumstances indicating that it was in reply to a duly authenticated one." (Fed. R. Evid. 901(b)(4), advisory committee's note). Thus, if the proponent can establish that the witness sent a letter to another and subsequently received a reply to that letter addressing the same subject matter as the original letter, the proponent can authenticate the subsequently received letter even in the absence of any testimony that the responding party actually wrote the response. The circumstances alone suffice for purposes of authentication.

Illustration of Letter Authenticated by the Reply Doctrine

Lawyer:	Mrs. Lowry, I'm showing you what has been marked for identification as Plaintiff's Exhibit 7. What is that document?
Witness:	That is a letter I wrote to the defendant after his dog attacked me in my front yard.
Lawyer:	How do you know that?

Witness:	I wrote it and signed it. I remember very clearly the day that all happened.
Lawyer:	What was the date that you mailed that letter, Exhibit 7?
Witness:	I sent it out the same day that I wrote it, August 31, 2010.
Lawyer:	Did you ever get a response to that letter?
Witness:	I did, about a week later I got a handwritten note from the defendant.
Lawyer:	Your Honor, I have what appears to be a handwritten note dated September 8, 2010, on a piece of 8 ½ by 11 inch notebook paper. It's been marked as Plaintiff's Exhibit 8 . . . . [*after showing document to opposing counsel and witness, the examination continues*] What is Plaintiff's Exhibit 8?
Witness:	It is the handwritten note I received from the defendant.
Lawyer:	Do you recognize the handwriting in the note?
Witness:	No, I've never seen the defendant's handwriting before.
Lawyer:	Then how do you know it is from the defendant?
Witness:	Well, the timing for one thing. I found it stuck in my door about a week after I mailed my letter. And its content, for another thing. The letter addresses the concerns that I raised in my previous letter to him.
Lawyer:	Your Honor, I move for the admission of Plaintiff's Exhibits 7 and 8.
Judge:	[*Looking at opposing counsel*] Any objection?
Opposing Counsel:	Your Honor, we have no objection to Exhibit 7, but Exhibit 8 should be excluded. No foundation's been laid. The witness admits she has no idea if that's the defendant's handwriting.
Judge:	[*Looking to the direct examiner*] Counsel?
Lawyer:	Your Honor, Exhibit 8 has been authenticated under the reply doctrine, Rule 901(b)(4) of the Federal Rules. Counsel's concerns go to the weight, not admission of the exhibit.
Judge:	Objection overruled. Exhibits 7 and 8 are admitted.

e.   Summaries

The final example of documentary evidence is not a "document" at all, but a substitute for documents in the form of a summary. Summaries are useful aids for advocates and witnesses in cases involving a large number of documents that would be difficult, unwieldy, or just plain boring if they were all shown to the jurors. The foundational requirement for use of a summary is that the underlying documents on which the summary is based were made available to the opposing party at a reasonable time and place before trial, that the underlying documents would be admissible into evidence if offered, and that the summary fairly summarizes the underlying documents.

Examples of helpful summaries might include:

- Summary of the results of various DNA tests performed by the witness on DNA extracted from the blood found at the crime scene, compared to test results from DNA taken from defendant's blood samples

- Summary of plaintiff corporation's earnings history (both before and after defendant's alleged predatory pricing) based on extensive financial data maintained by the corporation

- Summary of unpaid charges accrued by plaintiff subcontractor based on underlying daily work orders and tally sheets completed by subcontractor's employees

Summaries can play a particularly valuable role in enhancing the direct examination of an expert, helping jurors to understand the documents relied upon by the expert or explaining the outcomes of the expert's analysis of the evidence in the case.

Illustration of Expert Witness Testimony Utilizing a Summary

[*After satisfying the court that opposing counsel was provided with copies of the defendant's bank statement*]

Lawyer:	You are an accountant, aren't you, Mr. Green?
Witness:	Yes I am.
Lawyer:	Have you had an opportunity to review the defendant's bank statements for the three years beginning February 2006 through February 2009?
Witness:	Yes, I have.
Lawyer:	Were you able to identify in those statements the deposits made to the defendant's bank accounts during that period of time?
Witness:	Yes I was.
Lawyer:	Did you prepare a chart that summarizes the deposits shown on those statements by date and amount of the deposit?
Witness:	Yes I did.

Lawyer:	May I approach the witness?
Court:	You may.
Lawyer:	Mr. Green, I am handing you a chart pre-marked for identification as State's Exhibit 9. Do you recognize it?
Witness:	I do. It is the chart I prepared reflecting the defendant's bank deposits based upon his bank statements from 2006 to February of 2009.
Lawyer:	Your Honor, may State's Exhibit 9 be received in evidence?
Court:	[*To defense lawyer*] Any objection?
Defense lawyer:	None, Your Honor.
Court:	State's Exhibit 9 is received in evidence.

3. *Demonstrative Evidence and Visual Aids*

The third category of evidence that requires authentication before introduction is demonstrative evidence and visual aids. Because demonstrative evidence only illustrates the actual thing that has significance in the case—a diagram of the intersection or a model of the human brain, for example—the required foundation requires more than a showing of personal knowledge. The proponent must also establish that the demonstrative evidence "fairly and accurately depicts the thing as it was (or is)." Those words are as familiar to trial lawyers and judges as any spoken in the courtroom, and accordingly, lawyers and judges expect to hear them when a photograph or map is being authenticated. At the same time, however, it is not necessary to have the creator of the drawing or the photographer testify to the accuracy of the drawing or the picture. Anyone who is familiar with the thing depicted can so testify, provided they use those "magic" words.

a.   Charts, Drawings, Diagrams, and Maps

The events leading to a car crash in an intersection might be depicted through a simple diagram of the intersection; the eyewitness' identification of the defendant might be demonstrated through the police sketch based on her description; the defendant's efforts to elude the police might be shown through a map pinpointing his travels; or the plaintiff's steep decline in earnings might be shown through a chart depicting those earnings. Each of these items is demonstrative evidence and each visually demonstrates to the jury an important point in the case, and does so simply and efficiently. Does the diagram have to be to scale? Do drawings have to be precise in every detail? No and no. The key is whether the drawing is fair and accurate. If it will mislead the jury on a material point, it should be excluded. If it falsely portrays spatial relationships in some critical respect, it may need to be redone. But the mere fact that the drawing is hand-drawn during the course of trial and fails to get the size and distance exactly right is ordinarily a matter that goes to the weight of the evidence and not its admissibility.

Illustration of Laying a Foundation for a Diagram

Lawyer: Officer Marks, are you familiar with the intersection of Main Street and First Avenue?

Witness: Yes.

Lawyer: How is it that you are familiar with that intersection?

Witness: I am a patrol officer and that intersection is within my patrol area. I've traveled that intersection hundreds of times.

Lawyer: Your Honor, leave to approach the witness with Defendant's Exhibit Two for identification?

Judge: You may approach.

Lawyer: I am now showing you Defendant's Two. Do you recognize it?

Witness: Yes, I do.

Lawyer: What is it?

Witness: It is a diagram of the intersection of Main Street and First Avenue.

Lawyer: Does Defendant's Two *fairly and accurately* depict the intersection as it existed on January 14 of last year?

Witness: Yes, it does.

Lawyer: To your knowledge, is Defendant's Two drawn to scale?

Witness: No, it isn't.

Lawyer: Would Defendant's Two assist you in explaining your testimony concerning the accident that occurred on January 14 of last year?

Witness: Yes.

In the event the advocate anticipates the witness marking on the exhibit, he should not move the exhibit into evidence until after the witness has completed using the exhibit. Once the exhibit is accepted into evidence, it becomes the sole domain of the court and as such is not to be altered or modified.

When the witness marks on an exhibit, the advocate must orally describe those actions to create a complete record. For instance, the witness may point to a particular place on a diagram and testify, "I was right about here." The advocate must immediately follow up: "May the record reflect that the witness indicated Point A on People's Three for identification." It is easy to forget that the record is blind and can only hear what is spoken in the courtroom. Consequently, it is the advocate's responsibility to always keep the record in mind. For instance, the witness, in response to a question asking how far apart the defendant and victim were just before the defendant struck the victim, might simply hold his hands apart indicating the distance. The advocate must follow-up the response by stating, "May the record reflect that the witness has just held his hands approximately two feet apart, indicating the distance between the two individuals."

b. Photographs

Photographs are treated for authentication purposes as simply another form of demonstrative evidence, no different from a diagram or drawing. The proponent must establish that the picture "fairly and accurately" depicts the things shown in the picture, but anyone familiar with the thing depicted can testify to establish that. The photographer need not be called to testify unless there is some question about techniques used by the photographer that may have materially distorted the picture. Moreover, for purposes of the best evidence rule, any print is treated as an original. Assume that in the transcript below, a homeowner has sued his insurer for claims related to earthquake damage to the homeowner's residence. The homeowner is authenticating after-the-fact photographs of the inside of the home.

 Illustration of Authentication of Photographs

Lawyer:	I'm showing you Plaintiff's Exhibits 8-15 for identification, what are they?
Witness:	They are pictures of various parts of the inside of my home after the initial earthquake struck.
Lawyer:	How do you know that?
Witness:	Well, I saw it for one thing, I saw the damage caused by the earthquake; it's not something you can easily forget.
Lawyer:	Do the pictures fairly and accurately depict the inside of your house as it appeared immediately after the earthquake?
Witness:	Yes they do.
Lawyer:	Your Honor, at this time I move for the admission of Plaintiff's Exhibits 8-15.

At that point, the photographs should be admitted into evidence, though that in no way means that counsel's questioning about the photographs is completed. Counsel should post enlarged copies of each picture in front of the jury and discuss what portion of the house is being shown, the specific damage each picture depicts, and so forth. Counsel may want to elicit testimony concerning who took the pictures and approximately when they were taken. All of those details are helpful in fleshing out the full meaning and significance of the pictures, but none of them are necessary to gain admission of the pictures into evidence.

c. Videotapes

Authentication of the third category of demonstrative evidence—videotapes or motion pictures—does not vary substantially from that required for photographs. Most courts will accept as sufficient, authentication testimony from someone who has personal knowledge of the events recorded on the tape and that the tape accurately depicts those events. For instance, the infamous tapes of the beating of Rodney King might be authenticated by anyone present who could affirm that the tapes fairly and accurately show the events as they actually happened.

Historically, however, courts have required much more before accepting videotapes into evidence, imposing on proponents the following requirements: (1) the operator of the camera was qualified; (2) the equipment was suited for the task and was working properly; (3) the operator operated the camera properly in filming the event; (4) someone accounts for the custody of the film—no material edits or alterations were made; (5) the movie was developed properly; and (6) the movie fairly and accurately depicts the event. Even in the absence of strict enforcement of such requirements, it may make sense to have the person who shot the video testify to its authenticity when possible. The operator of the camera can detail the technical aspects of the tape in a way that enhances the credibility of the tape.

Below the prosecution seeks to introduce a videotape of a murder scene by calling the videographer to testify.

 Illustration of Videotape Authentication

Lawyer:	Mr. Carrol, in what capacity are you employed with the sheriff's department?
Witness:	My job is to photograph or videotape crime scenes as directed by the investigating detectives.
Lawyer:	Did you respond to apartment 115 located at 5050 Lombard Street on October 15 of last year?
Witness:	Yes, I did.
Lawyer:	Did you videotape the interior of that apartment on that date?

Witness:	Yes I did.
Lawyer:	Your Honor, I am holding a standard videotape cassette marked "Cassell Apartment." May I approach the clerk and have the cassette marked as People's Number Sixteen for identification?
Judge:	You may.
Lawyer:	May the record reflect I am handing People's Sixteen for identification to opposing counsel?
Judge:	So reflected.
Lawyer:	Leave to approach the witness with People's Sixteen?
Judge:	You may.
Lawyer:	Sir, I am handing you People's Sixteen. Do you recognize it?
Witness:	It's the tape I made of the Cassell apartment.
Lawyer:	How is it that you know that this is the tape you made of the Cassell apartment?
Witness:	I printed "Cassell Apartment" on the cassette.
Lawyer:	Have you had an opportunity to view the videotape in preparation for your testimony here today?
Witness:	I watched it yesterday.
Lawyer:	Do the images on that videotape accurately reflect the interior of the apartment as they appeared on October 15th of last year?
Witness:	They do.
Lawyer:	Your Honor, at this time I move People's Sixteen into evidence.
Judge:	Hearing no objection, People's Sixteen is in evidence.

d.   Tape Recordings

Tape recordings can be critical pieces of evidence at trial whether it is the defendant agreeing to purchase illegal drugs or an employer conspiring to retaliate against a whistleblower or a key witness expressing his racial biases. The foundation for tape recordings roughly parallels the requirements for videotape. The traditional requirements have included:

- the operator of the equipment was qualified to operate it

- the equipment was in good working condition

- the content is accurate and there have been no material edits or alterations

- the speakers on the tape are properly identified

However, courts recognize that a participant to the conversation recorded on the tape can authenticate the recordings without testifying to each of the elements of the foundation. That is, if a person who was present and heard the recorded conversation testifies that the recording accurately reflects the contents of the actual conversation and can identify the speakers on the tape, that testimony will suffice to authenticate the recording. In the absence of testimony from a participant, however, the proponent will have to elicit testimony from the operator of the machine and those who have had custody of the tape to demonstrate its authenticity, and will have to call a witness who can identify the voices on the tape.

The requirement of voice identification simply means that the proponent must have a witness who has previously heard the voices of the people on the tape and can identify their voices from listening to the tape. The testimony is proper lay witness opinion under Rule 701 of the Federal Rules of Evidence. Moreover, unlike lay witness opinion about handwriting, it is permissible for the witness' knowledge about the voice of another to be acquired in anticipation of trial.

One practical concern that arises frequently with the use of tape recordings is the quality of the recording itself. Will the jury be able to hear the tape if it is played in open court? Many tapes sound like prolonged gargling when played at a high volume, creating more frustration than anything else. The solution is to prepare a transcript of the tape so that the jurors can use the transcript to help follow the tape as it is being played. The transcript is not evidence and should be used solely to aid the jurors in understanding the tape. However, if the tape recording includes a conversation in a foreign language, an English transcript must be prepared, and authenticated, by an expert translator. In that case, the transcript is evidence.

There may be additional concerns relating to the origin of the tape itself. Was it obtained illegally, without the knowledge of one or more of the participants to the recorded conversations? Counsel should be aware of the tape's origins and cautious that her use of the tape does not abridge state or federal law.

In the example below, the prosecution seeks to introduce a tape recording of the defendant agreeing to purchase a large quantity of cocaine from an undercover officer. The undercover officer is the witness on the stand.

 ## Illustration of Authentication of Audiotape Recording

Lawyer:	Officer Hiller, did you tape record the conversation that took place at defendant's apartment?

Witness:	Yes, we did. On an earlier visit I had planted a small recording device in defendant's apartment and it recorded our conversation.
Lawyer:	Who operated the recording equipment?
Witness:	Another narcotics detective, Detective Narcon, was in a van on the street outside operating the recording equipment.
Lawyer:	Have you listened to the tape recording of the conversation from that day?
Witness:	Yes, I have.
Lawyer:	Is the tape an accurate recording of the conversation you had that day?
Witness:	Yes it is.
Lawyer:	Have there been any edits or other alterations of the tape?
Witness:	No there have not.
Lawyer:	Can you identify the individuals who speak during the recorded conversation?
Witness:	Yes. The first speaker on the tape is the defendant, he is referred to as "Big Dog" or "Biggy" throughout the tape. I'm the second speaker on the tape, called "Leonard" or "L." And the third speaker is Monroe Lewis, a friend of the defendant's. He is called "Monkey"and "ML" on the tape.
Lawyer:	I'm showing you the tape, which has been marked as People's Exhibit 5. Is that the tape of the conversation you had with defendant at his apartment that day?
Witness:	Yes it is.
Lawyer:	How do you know?
Witness:	It's labeled Big Dog—8/11/10, which is the day of this conversation and I listened to the tape again before coming here today. It is the tape.
Lawyer:	Your Honor, the People move for the admission of the tape, Exhibit 5, into evidence and for permission to play the tape for the jury.

---

e. Computer Animation

With the proliferation of cell-phone cameras, it sometimes seems as if every time anything significant or unusual happens, someone is standing by with a camera to record it. "Film at 11." But in reality, most events that end up the subject of trials are not taped by anyone, and there is no visual record of what happened. In those cases, computer animation provides a means of filling the void by re-creating for the jury how the critical events unfolded. Through computer simulation, a party can create computer-generated images that both appeal to the juror's need for visual stimulation and demonstrate the party's theory about the case. Animations are popular and effective because of their incredible flexibility, allowing the jurors to view events from any angle or point of view and to see the events unfold in slow motion or even one frame at a time. Typically, computer animation is used during the direct examination of an expert witness to illustrate the expert's opinion about how the accident happened or during the direct of an eyewitness to illustrate what the witness saw.

When used illustratively, the foundation is no more complicated than with a diagram or photograph. If the witness can testify that the animation correctly illustrates the witness' testimony or accurately portrays the events the witness observed, the animation should be admitted. Even when used for the limited purpose of illustration, the party will likely need to call the person responsible for creating the animation to explain the equipment and software used and the process of creation.

When the animation is used more ambitiously, not as demonstrative evidence but as substantive proof of how the accident happened, the foundational requirements are more stringent. The proponent must establish that the animation is based on reliable principles of math and science, that the software used is capable of producing simulations, that it was properly programmed to apply the math and science principles properly, that the software could reliably convert those principles into images, that the factual data provided was trustworthy and was entered reliably, and that the computer recorded the images onto video tape or a DVD, which the witness recognizes as the output from the program used.[4] The authenticating witnesses will likely include the person who created the animation, someone who can testify to the reliability of the math and science principles used to create the animation, and the expert witness who is testifying about the matters contained in the animation. Courts tend to view animations with some degree of suspicion, particularly when they are offered as substantive evidence, and they tend to strictly enforce the foundational requirements.

The primary limitation on the use of computer animations is an imminently practical one: money. They tend to be quite expensive, and thus are typically reserved for cases with relatively high stakes or parties with sufficient resources to foot the bill. The illustration below involves the use of computer animation to illustrate the plaintiff's expert opinion about the cause of a rollover of an SUV. Assume that the developer of the computer animation has previously testified about the technical aspects of its creation.

 ## Illustration of Authentication of Computer Animation

Lawyer: Dr. Robbins, I'm showing you what has been marked as Plaintiff's Exhibit 17, can you tell me what that is, sir?

Witness: Yes, that is a videotape of a computer-generated animation that has been prepared to show how the rollover happened.

---

4   *See* IMWINKELREID, EVIDENTIARY FOUNDATIONS 109–10 (4th ed. 1998).

Lawyer:	Did you prepare the computer animation?
Witness:	I participated in each step of its preparation, but the actual technical aspects of the animation were coordinated by Trial Consultants, Inc., a firm that specializes in that kind of thing.
Lawyer:	Why was the computer animation prepared, if you know?
Witness:	It was prepared at my request. I thought it would help to show the precise nature of my conclusions in this case with regard to how the accident happened.
Lawyer:	What was your role in the preparation of the animation?
Witness:	The first thing I did was conduct my typical investigation, review the facts, visit the scene of the accident and reach an initial conclusion about what happened. Next, I did three things to assist in the creation of the computer animation: first, I reviewed all of the available case materials—depositions, police reports, results from my personal visits to the scene of the accident and so forth—and developed the basic known facts of the accident to put into the computer simulation program; second, I worked with the folks at Trial Consultants, Joe Greene among others, to identify and verify the principles of physics that we would need to apply to accurately simulate plaintiff's accident; and third, I reviewed the animation produced by the computer to determine whether it was consistent with my conclusions about the accident.
Lawyer:	So you have viewed the animation contained on the videotape marked as Plaintiff's Exhibit 17 for identification?
Witness:	Yes, I have.
Lawyer:	Does the animation fairly and accurately depict the way the accident happened based on your experience and your expert analysis of the facts?
Witness:	It does.
Lawyer:	Would it assist in illustrating and explaining your testimony to show the jurors Exhibit 17, the videotape?
Witness:	Absolutely. The tape illustrates my conclusions about the accident much better than my words ever could.
Lawyer:	Your Honor, at this time, plaintiff moves for the admission of Exhibit 17 for demonstrative purposes only.

f. Models and Other Demonstrative Objects

An expert witness can use a hammer, for example, to illustrate her opinion about how the victim was struck and killed, without establishing that it was the actual hammer used. The hammer is only used to illustrate the witness' testimony, not to establish that it was in fact the actual hammer used in the homicide.

Demonstrative evidence can also be used to illustrate such tangible items as the murder weapon, the damage to the defendant's spinal column, or the flawed design of a huge concert hall. In a case in which the police are unable to find the murder weapon, the prosecution might have the eyewitness show the jury a hammer that is consistent in size and shape with the hammer the witness saw the defendant wielding when he attacked the victim. In a personal injury case involving paraplegia on the part of the plaintiff, counsel might have his expert use a model of a spinal column to show the jury how the accident led to the severe injury. In a suit against an architect for malpractice, counsel might have a model of the defendant's design built to demonstrate through an expert exactly how and why it was flawed. In each instance, the foundational requirement is basically the same: the witness would have to establish that she is familiar with the thing depicted, and that the demonstrative evidence fairly and accurately depicts the object or thing. In the case of the hammer the party would need to show that it was substantially similar to the actual hammer. In the instance of the models, the witness may also have to show that the models are necessary to explain the witness' testimony. In the example that follows the prosecution is attempting to present a hammer similar to the one observed by an eyewitness.

Illustration of Authentication of Demonstrative Evidence of Murder Weapon

Lawyer: Ms. Dixler, when you saw the defendant attacking June Alvarez, were you able to determine whether he had anything in his hands?

Witness: Yes, I could see what looked like a hammer in his right hand.

Lawyer: How close were you to the defendant when you saw the hammer?

Witness: Not more than 25 feet or so.

Lawyer: How was the lighting?

Witness: There was a street lamp close by. I could see the defendant clearly.

Lawyer: Could you tell how long the hammer was?

Witness: It looked to be about 12 inches I'd say. It was a good bit longer than his hand.

Lawyer: Did it have any distinctive features?

Witness: No, just a regular, run-of-the-mill hammer.

Lawyer: Your Honor, I have what's been marked as People's Exhibit 13 ... [*after going through preliminary steps, counsel proceeds as follows*]. Do you recognize this hammer?

Witness:	It's not the hammer that I saw in defendant's hands that night, but it looks to be the same size and shape as the hammer defendant was carrying that night.
Lawyer:	Would you say that this hammer, Exhibit 13, is substantially similar to the hammer defendant had?
Witness:	Absolutely, yes.

The hammer is admitted for the sole purpose of demonstrating the dimensions and appearance of the hammer that was seen in the defendant's hands. It is not the murder weapon, and the defendant is entitled to a limiting instruction to reinforce that fact.

g.   Demonstrations

Not all demonstrative evidence involves the admission of something into evidence. In fact, one of the most basic forms of demonstrative evidence is a simple demonstration of what happened by a percipient witness. The demonstration might be conducted in court in the presence of the jury or filmed beforehand and shown to the jury. For an in-court demonstration, the witness should first testify about the relevant events and then should be asked to re-enact the event in front of the jury. For example, in a driving under the influence case, the officer-witness may be examined about how the defendant performed on a particular field sobriety test and then may be asked to step from the witness box and actually demonstrate the defendant's efforts. The oral testimony establishes that the witness had first-hand knowledge of the events, thus providing the foundation for offering the in-court demonstration. During this or any in-court demonstration the specific conduct of the witness must be described for the record.

While such a demonstration is visually powerful, it is certainly not without risk. Live demonstrations can go awry in the courtroom, perhaps even inadvertently giving credence to the opponent's contentions. Obviously, much planning and preparation should precede any such demonstration and then such a demonstration should never be done in such a way that the advocate loses control of the demonstration. Further, opposing counsel can re-create the demonstration, change the parameters, and possibly change the outcome.

 Illustration of In-Court Demonstration

| Lawyer: | Officer, can you describe for the jury which field sobriety tests you performed on the defendant? |
| Witness: | Yes, I performed two tests, the heel to toe test where I asked the defendant to walk in a straight line placing his heel right in front and touching the toes of his other foot for a short distance and |

the touch the nose test where I asked the defendant to stand up, extend his arms to his side, close his eyes and touch his nose with the index finger of each hand one at a time.

Lawyer: How did the defendant perform on the tests?

Witness: On the heel to toe, he performed very poorly. He was unable to complete even one step without falling off to one side. On the finger to nose, he was able to touch his nose about one in three attempts.

Lawyer: Officer would you be able to demonstrate for the jury exactly how the defendant performed on these tests?

Witness: Yes, I could.

Lawyer: Your Honor, may the witness have leave to step down for the purpose of demonstrating the witness' performance on the field sobriety tests?

Judge: Yes, you may step down, Officer.

Lawyer: Beginning with the heel to toe test can you demonstrate the defendant's conduct?

Witness: Sure. He did something like this . . . . [*demonstrating*]

Lawyer: Your Honor, may the record show that the Officer placed his right foot in front of his left foot, lost his balance, and fell off to the right side?

Judge: The record will so reflect.

Lawyer: How many times did the defendant attempt to perform the heel to toe test?

Witness: Three or four times. And every time, same result.

Lawyer: Now can you demonstrate the finger to nose test?

Witness: Certainly . . . . [*demonstrating*]

Lawyer: Your Honor, let the record show that the Officer held both hands straight out from his side, closed his eyes and then with his right hand poked himself in his own right eye, with his left hand touched his chin and then with his right hand touched his nose.

Judge: The record will so reflect.

An alternative that provides counsel with more control over the demonstration while reducing the risk that something will go wrong is to videotape the demonstration, and then to play the tape for the jury. The more complicated the demonstration, the greater the need for videotaping beforehand. In laying the foundation, the proponent need not elicit testimony from the videographer about when the tape was made. Instead, the proponent must establish merely that the demonstration will assist the jury in deciding a disputed fact issue and that the tape bears substantial similarity to the conditions at or near the time of the original incident.

h. Visual Aids

The final category of demonstrative evidence trial lawyers use at trial is visual aids such as charts or lists. Though visual aids are not evidence and are not properly admitted into evidence, they can nevertheless be critically important tools of advocacy during the opening statement and closing argument. During the opening statement, counsel might write a list of key points on a flip board or create a time line of important events. During closing argument, counsel might create a chart of plaintiff's damages or a list of what you must believe to find in favor of the defendant. None of these items would be properly introduced into evidence or used by the jury during their deliberations. But they are proper visual aids for explaining and arguing the advocate's case.

The standard for which visual aids counsel can use, and which ones he cannot use, turn largely on the rules that govern that particular portion of the trial. A list or timeline used in the opening statement must not be argumentative and it must not refer to inadmissible evidence. A chart or PowerPoint slide used in the closing must not appeal to passion or prejudice or refer to evidence that was not introduced during the trial. Otherwise, trial lawyers are limited only by their own creative instincts in deciding how to reinforce the key points in the case through some kind of visual depiction.

E. The Timing of Offering and Publishing Exhibits

The final question when handling exhibits during trial is when counsel should actually offer them into evidence and, once admitted, when counsel should publish them to the jury.

1. *When to Offer Exhibits*

Advocates have at least three options concerning when they can offer exhibits into evidence. Exhibits might be offered:

- immediately after the foundation is laid,

- at the end of the attesting witness' testimony, or

- at the end of the party's case.

There are potential advantages and disadvantages to each approach. Offering an exhibit at the time of the witness' testimony about the exhibit ensures that (1) counsel does not forget to admit the exhibit; (2) the witness is still available in the event that the initial foundation laid by counsel is insufficient; and (3) the witness can use the exhibit and explain it to the jury as the witness is testifying. At the same time, however, offering the exhibit gives opposing counsel the opportunity to raise an objection to the admission of the exhibit, perhaps foreclosing use of the exhibit (in the event of a sustained objection) and, at the very least, interrupting counsel's examination.

Offering exhibits at the close of the direct examination of the witness minimizes the risk of disruption from an objection while still ensuring that the witness is available in the event of a foundational problem. The witness can use the exhibit during her testimony provided that the party has laid an adequate foundation for its admission. Moreover, the simple fact that counsel is offering multiple exhibits into evidence at the same time, as opposed to offering them one at a time, may limit the number of objections raised by the opponent. The major disadvantage is that counsel ends the direct examination with the relatively unexciting and uninteresting admission of exhibits into evidence. And he risks ending the direct on a sustained objection, if the judge refuses to allow admission of an exhibit. Accordingly, counsel should end the examination and then, just before sitting down, ask the court to admit the exhibits introduced during the witness' testimony. For example:

 ## Illustration of Offering Exhibits into Evidence

Lawyer: Your Honor, before I sit down, I move for the admission of Plaintiff's Exhibits 1-7 into evidence.

Judge: [Looking at opposing lawyer] Any objection?

Opposing Lawyer: Your Honor, could we have a moment?

Judge: Of course.

Opposing Lawyer: We do have an objection, Your Honor, to exhibit 4, the letter. It's hearsay.

Judge: Any response, counsel? [Looking to Lawyer 1]

Lawyer: It's a business record, Your Honor. The witness established that in her testimony.

Judge: Objection overruled.

The third possibility, offering the exhibits only at the end of the party's case, presents some serious challenges and has one obvious advantage. Under this approach, the advocate waits until the very end all of the opponent's objections to the admission of the party's exhibits and then dumps all of the exhibits into evidence at once. In cases involving more than a few exhibits, the likelihood is that the opponent will not object to most of the exhibits and the judge will not be interested in entertaining extended discussion about the admission of each exhibit. However, by offering exhibits at the end of the case the party takes some substantial risks, most notably that any witnesses needed to lay additional foundation for exhibits will not be available or will have to be recalled. That risk is not worth the modest advantage gained by this approach, and thus, it is the least desirable alternative. Most, if not all, exhibits should be offered into evidence when the attesting witness is still on the witness stand.

Some exhibits, however, require multiple authenticating witnesses, such as chain of custody exhibits. When should counsel seek the admission of those exhibits? One option available to advocates is to offer the exhibit into evidence through the first witness who testifies about the exhibit, but to offer it subject to completing the foundation through other witnesses who will be called later. Counsel will, of course, have to make a proffer to the judge of what evidence she expects to elicit from the subsequent witnesses, so that the court can determine whether the proffered evidence will be sufficient to authenticate the exhibit. Presuming an adequate proffer, the exhibit can then be admitted subject to later connection. If the party fails to present the expected proof, the court must strike the exhibit from the record and instruct the jury to disregard it if requested to do so.

2.   *When to Publish Exhibits*

In addition to deciding when to offer exhibits, counsel must also consider when to publish them once they are admitted. With some exhibits, publication is of no concern at all. For example, when using blow-ups of documents or diagrams, publication occurs whenever counsel places the enlargement in front of the jury. However, with other exhibits, such as regular sized documents or objects not easily visible to the jurors (bullets or ball bearings, for example), the act of publication will be critical to the jury's ability to learn the contents or features of the exhibit. In those instances, counsel must remember to publish the exhibit to the jury, but must do so in a way that does not distract the jurors from listening to the evidence or paying attention to the trial proceedings. For example, counsel should never publish a document or group of documents by distributing them to the jurors while a witness is testifying on the stand. The jurors will quite naturally read the documents they have been given while ignoring the witness' testimony. The better alternative is to highlight the critical portion of the document, perhaps through an overhead transparency, pre-prepared enlargement, or document camera, so that the jury can follow along with the witness' testimony, and then to publish the actual document to the jury only at the close of the witness' testimony. In that way, counsel avoids the risk of jury distraction, and leaves the problem to the opposing counsel.

If counsel needs for the jury to personally examine a piece of evidence to understand certain testimony, he has at least two means of avoiding the old-style jury pass around. First, counsel can use a document camera to display the object to all of the jurors at once or, second, he can give the object to the jurors but wait until the object has made its way through the jury box before continuing with his examination. The latter option, however, may test the patience of judges who subscribe to the view that there should be no dead air during a trial. The preferable approach is to use available technology to show the object to all of the jurors at once, and then to allow the jurors to handle the object only after the examination is completed.

IV. PRINCIPLES FOR MAXIMIZING THE USEFULNESS AND PERSUASIVE IMPACT OF EXHIBITS

❖ Principle Number One: Keep Demonstrative Exhibits Simple, Clear, and Easily Understandable

Demonstrative exhibits serve to illustrate, clarify, and emphasize the evidence or issues. They should not contain too much information or present the information in a way that is difficult to understand. Otherwise, instead of clarifying, the exhibit will likely overwhelm and, perhaps, even confuse the jury.

For instance, assume that plaintiff has presented an expert witness to testify about the future earnings of the plaintiff. In such a case it may be appropriate to have a graphic display prepared detailing how the expert arrived at her computations. However, if the chart contains too much detail or is simply too difficult to understand, it only exacerbates already complicated testimony and is not helpful in clarifying or simplifying the testimony. Exhibits

> **PRINCIPLES FOR MAXIMIZING THE USEFULNESS AND PERSUASIVE IMPACT OF EXHIBITS**
>
> ❖ Keep Demonstrative Exhibits Simple, Clear, and Easily Understandable
>
> ❖ Disclose One Piece of Information at a Time
>
> ❖ Keep Exhibits Proportionate to the Case and Opponent
>
> ❖ Do Not Rely on Exhibits to the Exclusion of Advocacy
>
> ❖ Be Careful of Overselling
>
> ❖ Anticipate Evidentiary Hurdles
>
> ❖ Practice, Practice, Practice
>
> ❖ Ensure that Exhibits Can Be Seen by Jurors

should be kept as simple as possible. While the advocate and his witness will have the chance to explain an exhibit, it is far better that each exhibit can be understood on its own. If even the least sophisticated juror has difficulty understanding the exhibit—the exhibit is a failure. Exhibits must necessarily play to the lowest denominator.

❖ Principle Number Two: Disclose One Piece of Information at a Time

A chart or list that contains several pieces of information should be set up so that only one piece of information is revealed at a time. Each point should be written and then discussed before writing or revealing the next point, or all but one point should be covered and then the next uncovered in time. Otherwise, the jurors will continue reading the entire exhibit instead of listening to the witness or advocate. Exhibits should complement what the witness or attorney is saying, rather than competing against them.

❖ **Principle Number Three: Keep Exhibits Proportionate to the Case and Opponent**

The exhibits must fit the trial. Exhibits that are disproportionate to the "size" of the case convey the wrong message to the jury. In a multi-million dollar insurance "bad faith" case, it may be appropriate for both sides to utilize sophisticated technology in presenting their respective cases. Both sides have the resources and as such the jurors may well expect a certain kind of presentation. Conversely, a slip and fall case with relatively minor injuries is presumably not the kind of case in which a computer-enhanced re-enactment would be called for. Such an expense is so vastly disproportionate to the case that many in the jury box will question the common-sense of the advocate.

Another consideration is the nature and sophistication of the exhibits your opponent is using. If the opponent is using expensive, professionally prepared exhibits it may be appropriate to counter with the same kind of exhibits. On the other hand, you may choose to go low-tech for the very purpose of drawing a stark contrast—we are the underdog, the oppressed, the "little guy" fighting the establishment. By the same token, using expensive exhibits when your opponent is drawing on butcher paper may create the impression that your client is wealthy and powerful.

❖ **Principle Number Four: Do Not Rely on Exhibits to the Exclusion of Advocacy**

With the advent of animations and other new technologies, there may be a temptation to rely on exhibits to the exclusion of effective advocacy. A brilliant computer-created animation depicting the cause of the car rollover is undoubtedly a powerful and persuasive tool. Given that potent persuasiveness, the trial lawyer may forget about or ignore other critical aspects of the trial. If the re-creation or animation says it all, why do I need to say more? However, your opponent will most likely not sit idly by and allow your exhibit to carry the day. Your exhibit may be met with a like exhibit, perhaps even reducing the trial to "dueling" animations.

Exhibits, especially animations and re-creations have very real limits. They are, of course, subject to manipulation and as a consequence many jurors may remain skeptical as to their accuracy. It is for the lawyer to advocate both the reliability of his exhibits, and the unreliability of his opponent's. And in the larger sense, it is for the advocate to recognize that trials are not won or lost on the strength of exhibits, but rather on the merits of the case coupled with the advocacy skills of the lawyers.

❖ **Principle Number Five: Be Careful of Overselling**

Advocates must exercise some degree of caution when using demonstrative aids. Indeed, an exhibit may belie the advocate's claims. For example, the car's damage, when finally shown to the jury, may seem disappointing to the jury after the exaggerated build-up by plaintiff's counsel. Obviously, the visual images that advocates display before their juries should serve to confirm, not contradict what the advocate has said and should serve to impress, not disappoint the jury with the advocate's claims.

❖ Principle Number Six: Anticipate Evidentiary Hurdles

It is axiomatic that exhibits will be met with evidentiary challenges. An advocate should anticipate that *every* exhibit will draw an objection. Given that admonition, it is the height of incompetence to encounter an objection unprepared. While there may be instances during trial when unanticipated objections might be raised, that should never be the case with exhibits.

❖ Principle Number Seven: Practice, Practice, Practice

It is critical for trial lawyers to practice using the exhibits they intend to show to the jury. If the demonstrative aid involves the use of a television, DVD player, or computer, a whole host of additional concerns arise relating to the dependability of the equipment. The significant advantages of visual imagery can be quickly lost if the use of the image is awkwardly presented or inadequately controlled. The excruciatingly painful and embarrassing experience of having a judge and jury stand by while the advocate (or the advocate's legal assistant or technology guru) tries to figure out how to work the document camera must be avoided if at all possible. Experience teaches that everything that can go wrong, will go wrong. Careful planning and preparation, however, can help to limit the number of variables involved in the presentation. Perhaps most importantly, however, the advocate should always have a back-up plan, just in case disaster strikes and the equipment malfunctions.

❖ Principle Number Eight: Ensure that Exhibits can be Seen by Jurors

Visual and demonstrative aids are worthless if the jurors are unable to see them. The same is true for real and documentary evidence. Thus, advocates must consider the jurors and their perspective each and every time they position or use an exhibit. Can every juror easily see the screen or easel? The advocate should sit in each seat in the jury box before the trial to determine the optimum place for visual aids or enlargements of documentary evidence. In addition, any writing or other images on the screen or board must be large enough for each juror to easily read or see. Is counsel blocking a juror from being able to see the board or exhibit? The advocate must always be aware of his position in relation to the visual aid. He should stand to the side or back to avoid blocking juror views. The real success of exhibits is often found in such details.

Chapter Eight

CROSS-EXAMINATION

I.   OVERVIEW & OBJECTIVES

Cross-examination can be a remarkable tool for ferreting out the truth. Professor Wigmore's classic statement, that cross-examination "is beyond any doubt the greatest legal engine ever invented for the discovery of truth,"[1] makes the point well. Cross-examination is the cornerstone of the adversary system—the opportunity to confront one's accuser and to

---

[1]   5 J. WIGMORE, EVIDENCE § 1367 (Chadbourn rev. 1974).

test the truthfulness of the opposing witness's testimony. It is a raid behind enemy lines; an incursion into occupied territory. The advocate's mission is to search and destroy. Or at least that is the image of cross-examination that predominates among trial lawyers. Most lawyers hold firm to the notion that cross-examination is a battle between opposing forces—a battle of wills and a battle of wits. For proponents of this view, it is in cross-examination that cases are won or lost and it is in cross-examination that trial lawyers demonstrate their mastery by forcing the opposing witness to confess to the crime or admit responsibility for the injury.

Perhaps the venerable television prosecutor, Perry Mason, personifies this view of the cross most clearly. However, as devoted viewers know, Perry Mason would go one step beyond merely getting a confession from the witness he was subjecting to his penetrating cross-examination. That was kid stuff for the master lawyer Perry Mason. His questioning on cross-examination was so forceful and logical, so pointed and powerful, that someone from the gallery—not a party, not a witness, but a spectator—would feel compelled to stand up and make a full confession to the crime. That scenario is as farfetched as it is harmful to the psyches of cross-examiners. The message of the fictional Perry Mason, and those who have followed in his stead, is that if the lawyer is good enough and asks the right questions in the right way, advocates really can win the case through cross-examination. Coerce the confession. Reveal the smoking gun. Win the case.

Reality, however, is altogether different. While, indeed, cross-examination can be a remarkable tool for ferreting out the truth—it is still just a tool, not *the* tool. Cross-examination is one of the essential components of trial, but not *the* essential component of trial. Cases are rarely won on cross. Instead, most of the time they are won because of the facts.

Nevertheless, the unrealistic expectations of cross-examination lead lawyers to ask questions that they should not ask and to adopt strategies that they should not adopt, resulting in a cross-examination that actually does more harm than good. Thus, instead of cross-examining witnesses with the objective of single-handedly winning the case through that particular cross, trial lawyers should approach each cross-examination as having more limited utility. The more modest objective of cross-examination should be *not to lose the case*. The cross-examiner must avoid allowing the witness to repeat her testimony during the cross or to explain why the examiner's case theory is wrong.

Once advocates adjust their grandiose visions of experiencing magical "Perry Mason moments" during their cross-examinations, they will recognize that real success is measured by whether they are able to:

- elicit favorable testimony from the witness

- discredit the witness' testimony and/or

- limit the witness' testimony

The primary challenge in achieving these goals is gaining and maintaining control over the witness. The witness on cross-examination is, in most instances, hostile to the advocate and his client, and motivated to frustrate the examiner's efforts. The extent to which advocates maintain control of such witnesses will, in large part, dictate their ultimate success or failure on cross-examination.

II.   PREPARATION

Preparation for cross-examination requires a thorough understanding of the case and an intimate familiarity with the opponent's witness. It is only through understanding the case that the examiner will be able to understand the role of the witness and appreciate the value of potential lines of questions for that witness. Such thorough familiarity will ensure that the examiner will identify each potential area of impeachment or attack.

Preparation follows a four-step process. First, develop a master list of all the potential points that can be established through the examination of the witness, whether areas of agreement, impeaching points, or direct attacks. Second, hone the master list down to only the most powerful points, those that will best assist the advocate in proving his case or will exact the most damage to the opponent's case. Third, organize the points in a logical order, but not in chronological order or in the same order as the direct examination testimony was delivered. And finally, make the decision whether, in light of the available cross-examination materials, it is necessary or helpful to rise and question the witness at all. It may be that the risk of harm will outweigh the potential benefit. It is never a foregone conclusion that every witness should be cross-examined.

A.   Brainstorming: Identifying Potential Areas of Inquiry

The cross-examiner's first step is to collect all of the information available about the witness: the witness' past statements, testimony given in depositions, grand juries, or preliminary hearings, and any statements made or testimony given by others about that witness. Once counsel knows what the witness has said before, he can begin to identify potential lines of cross-examination. Does the witness agree with the cross-examiner's witnesses on any points that are material to the issues in dispute? Is the witness' account of the events subject to rebuttal or attack? Can the witness be impeached because of a bias, a defect in perception, or a prior inconsistent statement? A good starting point is the list of potential impeaching points that are discussed later in this chapter. Viewing each witness through the universe of impeaching points will invariably prove fruitful.

In addition to these possibilities, counsel may find other sources helpful as well. For example, counsel's own witnesses may provide potential lines of attack on cross-examination, based on their knowledge of the facts in the case or the witness' background. Counsel should also not overlook the possibility of simply reinforcing the party's theme or critical facts through the witness. An effective cross-examination may consist of little more than reiteration of the main points of the cross-examiner's case through an opposing witness.

For party witnesses, counsel should examine the party's conduct at the time of the incident under review to determine if another course of action was available to the party. For example, in a criminal case, instead of reentering the bar where he had been arguing with the decedent, perhaps defendant should have left the area or called the police. In a civil case involving a claim of trademark infringement, the plaintiff's lawyer might do much the same thing by questioning the defendant's manager about options other than unlawfully infringing on a competitors trademark. The examination of a party's options may well reveal a more reasonable or safer alternative than the one chosen.

Each point identified by counsel should be noted for potential inclusion. This is not the time to assess the relative strengths and weaknesses of the points. That will come later. At this stage the objective is to explore the witness' knowledge and relationships such that every possible attack on the witness' testimony is identified.

B.   Honing: Making the Final Cut

The second step is to take the list of potential cross-examination points and identify the strongest and safest ones. In this process counsel should be guided by three principles:

(1)   each point must be consistent with and advance the party's theme and theory of the case;

(2)   difficult, subtle, unclear, or objectionable points should be avoided, if possible; and

(3)   the number of points should be limited—cross-examination should be kept as brief as possible, while still eliciting the necessary information or concessions from the witness.

The process of honing the cross-examination cannot begin until counsel has developed a theme for the case and a theory about what happened and why. Theme and theory development provide the framework within which to evaluate the potential cross-examination questions. As to each cross-examination point, counsel must constantly consider whether the point advances the party's theme and is consistent with the party's theory. For example, it may be foolish for a prosecutor to mercilessly impeach a witness who concedes that the defendant had a motive to commit the crime or contradicts the defendant's claim that the witness was with the defendant at the time of the offense. Just because impeachment is available does not mean that it is wise or helpful.

The second step in honing the list is to consider the ease or difficulty with which counsel will be able to execute the questions required to make the point. Will the jurors be able to understand the reason or reasons for the questions? Will counsel be able to make the desired point without prolonged argument or quarreling with the witness? Is counsel protected by prior statements of the witness in the event that the witness changes her story on the stand? Some points are simply too subtle or too difficult for the narrow constraints of cross-examination. The jury should have some sense when the cross-examiner sits down, of why he asked the questions he did. It is true that the cross-examination points can be explained and clarified during the closing argument, but they should have some resonance, some meaning at the time they are asked.

The next step in the honing process is to evaluate the potential cross-examination points and consider which points are likely to make the strongest impact on the jury. Which points will advance the party's case without losing control over the witness or creating an unnecessary risk that the witness will be able to do harm to the examiner's case? A few strong points on cross are much better than a few strong points mixed with moderate or even weak points. The longer the cross-examination lasts, the greater the chance that something may go wrong, that the witness will rehash the direct examination testimony. A cross-examination that quickly deflates the witness' direct testimony with only a few pointed questions can make a more powerful impression on jurors than an exhaustive, marathon-length cross that explores every nook and cranny of the witness' life. As the great Irving Younger commanded: "Three points are good; two points are better; one point is best." The honing process should eliminate points that are unnecessary or unhelpful so that every question advances the cross-examiner's case.

The final step in developing a list of cross-examination points is consideration of the permissible scope of the cross-examination. In federal courts (and many other jurisdictions), the scope of cross-examination is constrained by the scope of direct rule, which limits questioning on cross-examination to those matters covered on direct examination and any matters that bear upon the credibility of the witness. (Fed. R. Evid. 611(b)). Other jurisdictions do not limit cross-examination, permitting any and all questions provided they are relevant and not otherwise objectionable. (See, e.g., Tex. R. Evid. 611(6) ("A witness may be cross-examined on any matter relevant to any issue in the case, including credibility."). Undoubtedly, the scope of direct rule limits the ability of counsel to introduce new topics with witnesses during cross-examination. The greatest impact of the rule is likely felt during the cross-examination of witnesses who have a limited purpose for testifying, such as a witness who testifies about a single fact or event. Preparation for the cross-examination of any witness must include analysis of whether each potential line of questioning fits within the proper scope of cross-examination.

C. Organizing: Ordering the Cross-Examination Points

The third step in the preparation process is to organize the points in a logical sequence, but not one that the witness will find comfortable or natural. Four central premises should generally govern organization:

- Avoid using chronological order

- Do not put the points in the same order as the testimony that was covered during direct examination

- Place facts helpful to the cross-examiner's case at the beginning of the cross

- End with a strong, but safe (meaning not objectionable) point

The two organizational structures that every witness knows and with which every witness is comfortable are chronological order and the order of the direct examination. Counsel should disrupt that natural order on cross-examination whenever possible; avoid putting the witness at ease or making it easy for the witness to anticipate the direction of the examination. Begin the cross at the end of the sequence of events, where the direct examination ended. Arrange the points so that they move from one topic to another and do not seem to follow any particular order (at least no order apparent to the witness).

That does not mean that the points should be jumbled such that the jury cannot make sense of them. The goal is to keep the witness uncomfortable, not to keep the jurors guessing. Each series of questions, designed to make a single point to the jury, should be clear and follow logically one question after another. But once a point is completed, counsel should move to a different time period or otherwise unrelated events or conduct.

With that said, some areas of cross-examination should occur at logical points during the cross. For instance, common sense dictates that counsel should elicit helpful information from the witness before impeaching the witness. Witnesses become hostile when attacked and may be less inclined to be agreeable about anything. However, if there are no helpful facts to be elicited from the witness, then consider beginning the examination with an impeachment or correction of the witness if such opportunities are present. A successful impeachment at the very beginning of a cross-examination is akin to a hard jab to the nose at the outset of a boxing match. It sends a message to the witness that the cross-examiner is prepared and in control and will not tolerate any attempts by the witness to stray from her prior testimony. A witness whose nose is bloodied at the outset tends to be much more compliant and cooperative thereafter.

The cross-examination, consistent with the psychological principle of recency, should end on a strong point, but also a safe one. A safe point is one that is immune from a successful objection. Some lawyers want to end their cross-examinations with a bang, so they save a big finish for the end. The question goes something like this: "Isn't it true that you went over to your ex-wife's home that night, angry, jealous, out of control, and you waited for her to get home, and then you slashed her throat and the throat of her friend in cold blood and left them on the pavement to die?" After the judge sustains an objection because the question is argumentative, compound, and subject to several other objections, the cross-examiner says,

"Withdrawn," and sits down. That is no way to end a cross-examination. For one thing, an advocate never wants to sit down on a sustained objection. It is a sign of weakness, a humiliating admission of defeat, to end an examination to the tune of the judge's "sustained!" For another thing, it is unprofessional to ask questions known to be objectionable, intending to withdraw it in the face of an objection. Instead finish on a point that will inflict some damage on the witness and/or advance the party's case on the merits, but stands little or no chance of being struck down by an objection.

D.   Deciding: Choosing Whether to Cross-Examine the Witness

The last step in the preparation process is to decide whether it is even necessary or advisable, in light of the potential impact of the cross-examination on the jury, to conduct a cross-examination of the witness. While counsel may feel pushed to cross-examine all witnesses called by the opponent, not every witness requires cross-examination. This final step in the preparation process must, of course, follow the first three steps. Until counsel knows the universe of potential examining points with a witness, the sequence of the points, and their potential impact, she is in no position to assess the fundamental question of whether to cross-examine.

Consider three factors in making this final determination:

(1) the potential impact of the cross-examination in advancing the cross-examiner's case or damaging the opponent's case;

(2) the risk that the cross-examination will alienate the jurors or damage the cross- examiner's standing before the jury; and

(3) the reaction/disappointment of jurors from counsel's failure to cross-examine the witness

The last factor recognizes the fact that jurors tend to expect the advocate to cross-examine every witness, and a decision not to cross-examine a witness implies acceptance of the witness' testimony on direct. However, that must be balanced against the second concern, which recognizes that cross-examining certain witnesses will only damage the advocate's credibility and engender sympathy for the opponent's witness. For example, in personal injury cases the advocate may wisely choose not to cross-examine the family member of the injured/deceased person who testifies only about the loss created by the person's injury or death. These witnesses, sometimes referred to as "grunt and groaners" by defense lawyers, are highly sympathetic witnesses. Counsel's attempts to suggest that the loss really wasn't that bad or that the injuries were not as severe as the witness claims, all while the witness silently weeps on the witness stand, tend to backfire, leaving the advocate looking insensitive and callous. The better approach with such a witness may be for the advocate to stand up and announce that he will not be conducting a cross-examination of the witness.

III. PRINCIPLES FOR EFFECTIVE CROSS-EXAMINATION

The first and most important skill for successful cross-examinations is for advocates to maintain control of the witness. It is also the most difficult skill to master. The ideal cross-examination consists of the examiner making a series of pronouncements or assertions, each of which elicits a simple affirmation from the witness with no explanation. The principles discussed below are designed to achieve maximum witness control and to guide lawyers through the perilous waters of cross-examination.

> **PRINCIPLES FOR EFFECTIVE CROSS-EXAMINATION**
> - ❖ Wear the White Hat
> - ❖ Ask Only Leading Questions
> - ❖ One Fact, One Question
> - ❖ Maintain Control by Repeating the Question
> - ❖ Maintain Control by Listening to the Answers
> - ❖ Do Not Ask Questions that Lose Control
> - ❖ Be Protected on Every Question
> - ❖ Argue Using Cross-Examination Questions

❖ Principle Number One: Wear the White Hat

The popular view of the cross-examination is that it is the time to get mean and nasty. The gloves come off; all rules of etiquette and decorum are suspended; and the lawyers can do as they please. The lawyer can yell and scream, intimidate and interrupt, harass and harangue. Such a notion is *nonsense*. An antagonistic or aggressive approach will not play well with the jury. In the minds of many, lawyers are suspect simply by virtue of their profession. And a lawyer who fulfills that negative stereotype by attacking a witness will most likely pay a terrible price with the jury. Trial lawyers must earn the respect and trust of the jury, and mistreating witnesses is not the way to engender either.

Trial advocates should maintain the same attitude and disposition on cross-examination they had with their own witnesses during direct examination. They should treat the witnesses on cross with courtesy and respect. They should avoid *ad hominem* attacks, resist the urge to yell or scream, and reject the tactics of intimidation or bullying. Advocates should not immediately go into battle mode every time they rise to cross-examine. They should wait until the witness has shown that he does not deserve the advocate's or the juror's trust and respect and has caused the jurors to want the witness to be upbraided.

❖ Principle Number Two: Ask Only Leading Questions

Cross-examination requires that the examiner be in control. The best and most effective mechanism for controlling witnesses during cross-examination is the use of leading questions. Ask *only* leading questions. Every time, without fail. Every question should be tailored to elicit a simple, monosyllabic "yes" or "no." But that is not enough. The question must leave no doubt what answer the advocate desires. Consider the contrast between the questions set forth below:

Lawyer 1:   Did you purchase a gun from Fred's Gun Emporium?

Lawyer 2:   Isn't it true, you purchased a gun from Fred's Gun Emporium?

— or —

Lawyer 3:   You purchased a gun from Fred's Gun Emporium, correct?

The questions asked by Lawyers 2 and 3 are both leading in that they leave no doubt about the desired answer, whereas Lawyer 1's question, while seeking a yes or no answer, does not signal the correct answer. The precise form of the leading question is not as important as the fact that it is leading. Nevertheless, an easy method for ensuring that every question is appropriately leading is for the examiner to make a series of assertions, each preceded or followed, if necessary, by a word or phrase to make a question. Questions by Lawyers 2 and 3 above, are examples of this form. In any event, advocates should vary the form of questions. Beginning *each* question "Isn't it true that ..." is monotonous to hear and may become annoying to the jurors.

The question is more important than the answer on cross-examination. Leading questions allow the examiner to speak past the witness and directly to the jury. The examiner makes his point directly to the jurors. Not only by the structure of the question, but by voice and gesture. Counsel relinquishes control by asking questions that are not leading, allowing hostile witnesses to reiterate their harmful testimony, and potentially compromising the examiner's case.

Master trial advocates may find it useful, on occasion, to ask non-leading questions of witnesses on cross-examination, when they are fully protected or when the witness has nowhere to hide. Those who are yet to reach the level of mastery, however, will exercise greater witness control and find greater success on cross-examination by asking only leading questions.

❖ Principle Number Three: One Fact, One Question

In addition to asking leading questions, advocates must ask short questions that seek only one fact each. The longer the question, the more facts contained in the question, the greater the likelihood that the witness will find something to disagree with and will feel the need to explain exactly where the examiner went wrong. Cross-examiners must eliminate opportunities for the witness to give expansive or evasive answers and the best means of doing that is by asking short and simple questions—one fact, one question. In propounding a question that contains more than one variable, the examiner unwittingly gives the witness the freedom to go beyond a "yes" or "no" response.

Illustration of Multiple Fact Question

Lawyer: When you and your companions went to the mall, you drove in your 1964 Pontiac, didn't you?

Witness: No, that's not right. I only went with Reggie, not some companions. And besides that, I wasn't driving. Reggie drove his mom's minivan.

This simple, but multi-fact question caused the witness to provide more than a simple "yes" or "no" response. The question contained numerous variables—the number of persons involved, their destination, the identity of the driver, and the make and year of the car. Here is how questioning might be improved by the one fact, one question approach:

Illustration of One Fact, One Question

Lawyer: You went to the mall, didn't you?

Witness: Yes.

Lawyer: You went with Reggie?

Witness: That's right.

Lawyer: Reggie drove?

Witness: Yes.

Lawyer: The car was a 2009 Camry, wasn't it?

Witness: Yes.

One fact, one question. Limiting each question to one fact eliminates opportunities for the witness to venture beyond the question and allows the examiner to stay in control. It also allows the examiner to draw out, and thus emphasize, certain facts. The examiner is able to elicit critical testimony, slowly and incrementally, so that the witness slowly bleeds before the jury. Instead of asking, "You chased Carrie Mae down the hall with a board then hit her on the head with it, didn't you?" The examiner should emphasize each aspect of the defendant's conduct by asking about each aspect of it separately.

Illustration of Emphasizing Damaging Testimony[2]

Lawyer:	Carrie Mae ran from the room, correct?
Witness:	That's right.
Lawyer:	And you went after her, didn't you?
Witness:	Yes.
Lawyer:	In fact, you were chasing her?
Witness:	Yeah, I guess I was.
Lawyer:	You had a board in your hands, didn't you?
Witness:	Yes.
Lawyer:	In fact, you held that board while you chased her?
Witness:	Yeah, but it wasn't like that. I wasn't trying to hurt her.
Lawyer:	Mr. Burns, you were chasing Carrie Mae, correct?
Witness:	Yeah.
Lawyer:	And at the time you were chasing her you were holding a board, weren't you?
Witness:	Yeah, I guess so.
Lawyer:	Is that a yes?
Witness:	Yes, it is.
Lawyer:	You caught up to Carrie Mae, didn't you?
Witness:	Yes.
Lawyer:	You hit her with the board, didn't you?
Witness:	Yes.

A final advantage to narrow questioning is that it helps the lawyer identify the exact point of disagreement with the witness. In the illustration above, if the witness disagreed at any point it could be quickly remedied, whereas when several facts are loaded into one question, and the witness takes issue with even one fact, confusion ensues and control is compromised.

---

[2] This illustration is based on the hypothetical case *State v. Horace Johnson*, Jean Montoya (National Institute of Trial Advocacy).

❖ Principle Number Four: Maintain Control by Repeating the Question

The moment of truth on cross-examination comes when the witness refuses to answer the examiner's "yes or no" questions with simple "yes" or "no" answers. For example:

Lawyer:	Isn't it true that you were at George's apartment at 2 a.m. on June 12, 2001?

Witness 1:	Yes, I was there, but only for a few minutes and then I left and went straight home. I wasn't there when the fight broke out.

— or —

Witness 2:	The fight didn't even happen at George's place, man. It happened out in the parking lot. Some biker dudes from across town started it. We were only defending ourselves.

In the first example (Witness 1), the witness answered the question, but kept going, answering much more than the question asked. In the second example (Witness 2), the witness failed to even answer the question, but instead answered an entirely different question.

1. *The Wrong Approaches*

Almost every cross-examination will have similar moments when the witness refuses to be limited by the lawyer's questions. What should the lawyer do to control these "blurt outs"—the unnecessary explanations and attempted evasions? There are at least three ill-advised strategies that trial lawyers sometimes choose to address the problem of witness control on cross-examination:

A. the admonition;

B. the interruption; and

C. the objection.

a. The Admonition

Some advocates anticipate the witness' desire to give expansive answers on cross-examination and they admonish witnesses about their answers even before the first cross-examination question. For example:

Lawyer:	Good afternoon, Mr Greenleaf. How are you today?
Witness:	Fine.
Lawyer:	I have a few questions I'd like to ask you today and they will all call for a "yes or no" answer. And before I get started, I'd like to get your agreement that you will keep all of your answers to "yes" or "no." Can you do that for me?
Witness:	I'll try, I guess. It will depend on what you ask me.

This preemptive strike may well be objectionable. It just might be that not all questions can be answered with a simple "yes" or "no," that a question is confusing and cannot be answered at all, or that a question requires explanation. If opposing counsel fails to object to the cross-examiner's admonition, the judge might. Additionally, this kind of preemptive strike sends the jury the wrong message entirely. In the first place, the witness has not yet done anything to deserve this condescending admonition. In the second place, counsel signals to the jury that he is concerned about what the witness might say. Neither message improves the advocate's position with the jury or advances the advocate's case.

Alternatively, instead of using the preemptive strike, counsel may delay admonishing the witness until the witness first strays from the straight and narrow path of "yes" or "no" responses. Counsel might tell the witness:

Lawyer: I'm sorry, Mr. North, but that question only called for a "yes" or "no" answer, and I'd appreciate it if you would limit your answers to "yes" or "no" from now on.

However, this tactic is only slightly better than the preemptive strike, because it suggests that counsel is fearful of what the witness might say and the jury might well conclude that counsel is afraid of the truth.

b.   The Interruption

Another misguided attempt to control witnesses' explanations and evasions is to interrupt the witness when the witness tries to explain an answer. Instead of allowing the witness to finish her answer, the lawyer abruptly cuts her off and demands that she limit her answers to "yes" or "no."

Witness: No, that's not right. I didn't go there to start a fight, I . . .

Lawyer: Excuse me for interrupting, Mr. Diemer, but I didn't ask you *why* you went to the club that night, only that you went to the club for the purpose of fighting. Yes or No. Please only answer the question I'm asking.

The interruption signals to the jury that counsel has something to fear from the answer and that he is willing to overpower the witness, to intimidate her, to shout her down if necessary, to prevent the jury from hearing what she has to say. The second reason that the interruption is a flawed strategy is simple: it is rude and impolite. When advocates interrupt witnesses, they temporarily sacrifice their likeability. Alert opposing counsel will point out the cross-examiner's brutishness by requesting that the witness be allowed to finish her answer and that counsel be admonished to allow the witness to answer the questions being asked.

c. The Objection

The final mechanism sometimes used to control unruly witnesses is an objection for lack of responsiveness. When a witness gives an answer that is not responsive, counsel can object by saying "non-responsive," and request that the answer be stricken from the record. The exchange might look something like the following:

Witness:	Yes, I suppose so, but it's not what you're suggesting. We never meant to hurt anyone. From the beginning we intended and worked to ensure that everyone got the return they had been promised.
Lawyer:	Objection, non-responsive as to everything after "yes."
Judge:	Sustained.
Lawyer:	Request that the answer be stricken and the jury admonished to disregard the answer.
Judge:	So ordered.

There is nothing improper about such an objection. Indeed, the rules specifically permit it. However, when advocates make objections based on the witness' non-responsiveness they admit that they cannot fight their own battles, that they must rely on the all-powerful judge to control their witnesses for them. Such an objection puts the advocate in an unmistakable position of weakness before the jury. The jurors are left to wonder what was so wrong with the witness' answer that it should be stricken, and why won't the advocate let the witness explain her answers?

Admittedly, there are times when a non-responsive objection is necessary to preserve error or to punish a stubbornly uncooperative witness. For instance, if the witness blurts out an answer that discloses inadmissible matters or particularly prejudicial testimony, counsel may need to lodge an objection to avoid waiving the error or to prohibit its use by the other side. When used solely as a means of control, however, an objection should not be the advocate's strategy. Advocates are better off when they exercise control over their witnesses, without objections, admonitions, or interruptions.

2. *The Right Approach: Repeat the Question*

So, what is the advocate to do? When the witness blurts out a non-responsive answer or evades a question, how should the lawyer exercise control over the witness and still wear the white hat? *Simply repeat the question.* No cajoling or intimidating. No glares or grimaces. Just repeat the question. This approach has some distinct advantages. The examiner maintains a respectful demeanor toward the witness before the trier of fact; and, by repeating the question, the examiner shows the jury that it is the witness who is being evasive, rather than the lawyer. And if jurors perceive the witness' attempted manipulation of the process, they will discount the witness' testimony much more severely than if the advocate tried to convince them of it. This is a subtle form of impeachment, but an effective one.

When counsel first repeats the question, he should initially take responsibility for the witness' failure to answer the question properly. It must have been a bad question. But with each succeeding repetition, the advocate should be less forgiving as the witness shows that, in fact, he is the problem and is unwilling to answer the question being asked.

 Illustration of Repeating the Question

Lawyer:	You and the defendant knew each other before the contract was signed, didn't you?
Witness:	Well, I don't know if you can say we knew each other. I had seen him around.
Lawyer:	I'm sorry, Mr. Lonergan, perhaps my question wasn't clear. Let me try again. You and the defendant knew each other before the contract was signed, didn't you?
Witness:	I had met him before.
Lawyer:	Is that a yes?
Witness:	Yes, that's a yes.

Once it is clear to the witness that counsel is willing to doggedly stay the course and get the "right" answer, and to make the witness appear evasive in the process, the witness in all likelihood will be less willing to stray in his next answer.

❖ Principle Number Five: Maintain Control by Listening to the Answers

In addition to the simple tactic of repeating the question, advocates can control witnesses by carefully listening to their answers. Despite the seeming simplicity of the advice, it is not necessarily simple to put into practice. Cross-examiners have many distractions on cross-examination that keep them from hearing the witness' answers, primarily their pre-planned, carefully thought out attack on the witness. The questions are written down, word-for-word, and they are read by the examiner just as they are written. The problem with a stiff, rigid agenda on cross-examination is that the witness is a member of the other team, or at least, a friend of the other team, and he is not privy to, nor interested in, counsel's set agenda. Further, witnesses on cross will say the most amazing things. They will make extreme claims that defy common sense; they will open the door to evidence the judge previously ruled inadmissible; or they will make statements inconsistent with what they have said before. But if the advocate is not listening, he will miss it. And if the advocate misses it, there is not anything he can do about it, and consequently, he has lost a great opportunity.

There is nothing wrong with careful planning. Preparation is essential to success on cross-examination. And there is nothing wrong with having an agenda for the cross-examination and attempting to execute that agenda. That too is essential for success. What is wrong, however, is becoming so married to the plan that the examiner cannot make mid-course corrections or adjustments when the witness invites the examiner to do so. By necessity, the cross-examiner must be able to adjust and adapt to changing circumstances and changing testimony, because the agenda on cross-examination will be ever-changing.

Listening closely to every answer enables trial advocates to exercise greater control over the witness, because they can respond immediately and effectively to the witness' tactics. Two such tactics merit specific mention:

- efforts by witnesses to be evasive by not giving definitive answers or by giving unclear ones; and

- attempts by witnesses to include additional information in their answers that is harmful to the cross-examiner's case or beneficial to the party for whom the witness is testifying.

Witness weaseling is an age-old art and the examiner will miss the witness' equivocal responses or qualified answers unless he is listening. If the advocate catches the attempted evasion, he can pin the witness down.

In the same way, "witness dumping," wherein the witness attempts to dump as much of her case as possible into the opponent's cross-examination, is a time honored practice. One effective device to deal with such efforts, discussed above, is to simply repeat the question. Another technique, however, is to discipline the witness for going beyond the scope of the question, to teach the witness that such attempts to subvert the cross-examination will not be tolerated. One particularly effective tool for this task is impeachment by common sense. As often as not, the things witnesses blurt out to defend themselves do not withstand close examination and do not comport with common sense. And a few questions that force the witness to take her position to its logical extreme will reveal the sham for what it is.

Other tools of impeachment work as well, including impeachment by prior inconsistent statement or by omission. Moreover, sometimes witnesses, in their overzealous efforts to defend themselves and to disrupt the cross-examiner's efforts, will make statements that open the door to evidence that would otherwise not be admissible. Few events in a trial will more quickly chasten witnesses than the realization that they have opened the floodgates by their own foolish responses to the cross-examiner's questions.

These "unplanned" questioning forays should follow the same principles of cross-examination already discussed. The questions should be leading and should contain only one fact each. The examiner should only ask questions to which the advocate knows the answer or for which there is only one logical, common sense possibility. And counsel should return to the familiar and comfortable environment of the advocate's original agenda as soon as possible.

Illustration of Nailing Down an Equivocal Witness

Lawyer: As you approached the intersection, you were going 50 miles per hour, true?

Witness: I guess that's right.

Lawyer: I'm sorry, Mr. Weasley, I don't want you to guess. You were going 50 miles per hour, true?

Witness: I suppose so.

Lawyer: You were going 50?

Witness: Yes.

 ## Illustration of Impeachment by Common Sense

Lawyer: When you lifted the surfboard to carry it to the check-in area, you could tell that it was heavier than normal, couldn't you?

Witness: No, not really. It felt no different than normal, the same as it always felt.

Lawyer: You are a competition surfer, right?

Witness: Yes.

Lawyer: You carry your own surfboard when you surf?

Witness: Of course, yes.

Lawyer: So, you lift your surfboard a number of times every time you go surfing?

Witness: Yes.

Lawyer: And as a competition surfer, you surf a lot, don't you?

Witness: Yes.

Lawyer: So, it would be fair to say that you lift surfboards probably thousands of times each year?

Witness: Sure.

Lawyer: A surfboard is carefully balanced, isn't it?

Witness: Yes, good ones are.

Lawyer: As a competition surfer you use good boards, don't you?

Witness:	That's right.
Lawyer:	Would it be fair to say that that balance is affected by the weight distribution of the board?
Witness:	That's a factor.
Lawyer:	So, as a competition surfer, a person who makes his living from surfing, you would be sensitive to the weight distribution in a surfboard?
Witness:	That's true.
Lawyer:	But this particular board didn't seem any different to you?
Witness:	No, not at all.
Lawyer:	It's your testimony that the fifteen pounds of cocaine packed into the tip of the surfboard you were carrying didn't make it feel any different from any other board?
Witness:	That's right. No different.

❖ **Principle Number Six: Do Not Ask Questions that Lose Control**

As important as it is to ask short, leading questions on cross-examination, it is equally important to avoid certain kinds of questions that are guaranteed to lose control of the witness. Examples of particularly dangerous questions include, for example:

- open-ended questions

- questions that include characterizations of people or events

- questions that refer to the witness' past testimony

- questions that invite an explanation

- the one question too many

(i) *Open-ended questions:* The dangers of open-ended questions should be obvious. Such questions invite the witness to expound on a topic, which effectively relinquishes control of the examination to the witness.

(ii) *Characterizations:* When advocates ask witnesses on cross-examination to agree with the advocate's characterizations of events or people, the witness may feel compelled to explain why the characterization is wrong or inaccurate. The more provocative the characterization, the more likely the witness will not simply answer "yes" or "no." For example:

Illustration of Use of Characterization

Lawyer: You were talking on your cell phone when the accident happened weren't you?

Witness: Yes, I had just called my mom.

Lawyer: Wouldn't you agree that was a foolish thing to do—driving and talking on the phone?

Witness: No, I wouldn't agree with that. What was foolish was Mr. Smith stopping abruptly in the middle of the road to turn around. The cell phone had nothing to do with what happened.

Asking the defendant to admit that he acted maliciously, or asking a plaintiff to admit that his conduct was careless is sure to provoke a prolonged explanation, detailing exactly why the questioner is wrong. Instead of asking the witness to agree to counsel's characterization, counsel should begin with facts, commit the witness to the facts, and then walk the witness up the ladder of increasingly helpful characterizations of her conduct.

Illustration of Walking Witness Up the Ladder

Lawyer: The night of December 31st, the very night that you and your wife had the fight that brings us here today, you and your wife went to a New Year's Eve party, true?

Witness: Yes, that's true.

Lawyer: The party was at your friend's house, Dominic La Russo, correct?

Witness: Yes.

Lawyer: And at the party there was music and dancing?

Witness: That's right.

Lawyer: Champagne was served?

Witness: Yes.

Lawyer: And you danced with your wife?

Witness: Yes, I did.

Lawyer: Your wife also danced with others, didn't she?

Witness: Yes, I believe she did.

Lawyer: She danced with your friend Dominic, the host?

Witness:	Yes, several times.
Lawyer:	And that bothered you a little bit, didn't it?
Witness:	I guess so. It wasn't that she was dancing with Dominic though, it was that she was making a fool of herself.
Lawyer:	You thought your wife should behave herself, didn't you?
Witness:	Yes, I thought she should act her age.
Lawyer:	She was flirting with some of the men at the party?
Witness:	Yes.
Lawyer:	She was drinking?
Witness:	Yes.
Lawyer:	At some point you pulled her aside, didn't you?
Witness:	Yes, she needed to pull herself together.
Lawyer:	And you told her that?
Witness:	Yes, or at least words to that effect.
Lawyer:	You were perturbed by your wife's behavior at this point, weren't you?
Witness:	I don't know, maybe.
Lawyer:	You were frustrated?
Witness:	Yes, frustrated.
Lawyer:	And when you talked to her, she didn't respond very kindly, did she?
Witness:	Not at all.
Lawyer:	She told you to leave her alone, to let her have some fun?
Witness:	Something like that.
Lawyer:	And that made you mad, didn't it?
Witness:	Yes, I was upset.
Lawyer:	You were angry with your wife?
Witness:	Wouldn't you have been?
Lawyer:	I'm sorry, sir, but I need you to answer the question. You were angry with your wife when she spoke to you the way she did, weren't you?
Witness:	Yes, I was angry. I left the party without her.

(iii) Prior testimony: Another type of question to avoid is the question that harkens back to the witness' prior testimony on direct examination or in an earlier deposition or hearing. Witnesses almost never agree that counsel has properly characterized the testimony and the result is that the witness again feels the need to explain what he said before and why. The better approach is to simply ask about the underlying facts. Do not couch the facts in terms of the witness' prior testimony. For example, do not ask: "Mr. Weston, you testified earlier that you had never met the defendant face-to-face before this meeting on June 1st, correct?" Rather, ask: "You had never met the defendant face-to-face before the meeting on June 1st, had you?"

(iv) Questions that invite an explanation: A properly structured leading question should only elicit a "yes" or "no." Yet, despite the examiner's best efforts, some witnesses will attempt to explain or qualify their answers. And sometimes the explanation will surprise, perplex, or frustrate the examiner. Perhaps the answer varies from the witness' deposition testimony or relates new information not previously revealed by the witness. In that unguarded emotional state—surprised, perplexed, frustrated—the examiner asks, "Well, how can that be?" The result, of course, is to totally and completely cede control of the examination to the witness. Cross-examination is not the time for explanations or open-ended questions. Cross-examiners must find the discipline and composure to suppress the instinct to ask for an explanation.

(v) The one question too many: The final question that must be avoided during the cross-examination is the question that attempts to make the ultimate point of the questioning transparent for the jury. It is the one question too many because it is guaranteed to elicit an explanation from the witness and to defuse the impact of the point with the jurors. Not every point during cross-examination must be developed with absolute clarity and precision. By pushing too hard to make a point crystal clear, the examiner may unwittingly provide the witness with an opportunity to explain.

Illustration of Asking One Question Too Many

Lawyer:	It is your testimony here today that you did not speak to Ruben Avila just before the fire, is that right?
Witness:	That's right.
Lawyer:	Mr. Hastart, you were interviewed by a police officer at the scene of the fire, weren't you?
Witness:	Yes.
Lawyer:	You knew at that time that the officer was investigating the cause of the fire?
Witness:	Sure.

Lawyer:	You knew it was important to be clear and accurate in what you told him, isn't that right?
Witness:	I was doing the best I could.
Lawyer:	And you knew it was important to be clear and accurate in what you told him, correct?
Witness:	Yes.
Lawyer:	You told him the truth, didn't you?
Witness:	Yes, I did.
Lawyer:	Isn't it true, Mr. Hastart, that on the very night of the fire you told the officer that you and Reuben Avila had a conversation just before the fire?
Witness:	Yeah, I guess that's what I said then.
Lawyer:	Perhaps my question was not clear, on the very night of the fire you told the Officer that you and Reuben Avila had a conversation just before the fire, is that right?
Witness:	Yes.
Lawyer:	Well, Mr. Hastart, what's it to be, were you not being honest then or are you not being honest now?
Witness:	That's not fair. The night of the fire was terrible. People had just died. It was very traumatic and things were very confusing. It was very hard to sort things out. I was doing the best I could under very trying circumstances.

This examination should have ended one question earlier. The impeachment is there for all to see. Even if a juror somehow missed it, that can be remedied during closing argument. Meanwhile by asking the classic "Were you lying then or are you lying now" question, the witness is given an opportunity to either explain away or at least mitigate his "inconsistency."

❖ Principle Number Seven: Be Protected on Every Question

Control on cross-examination comes not only from making sure that the form of each question is leading or from avoiding questions that may cause the advocate to lose control, but also from exercising good judgment about which areas should be avoided altogether and recognizing the limits of cross-examination. The greatest risk on cross-examination is the unknown. And when advocates ask questions to which they do not know the answer, they venture into the great unknown where almost anything can happen, most of it bad. The witness' answer may be innocuous (if the advocate is lucky) or it may be a blockbuster answer that turns the case against the advocate. Given even a slight opportunity, the witness may, and most probably will, offer testimony that is harmful to the examiner's case. Thus, a good rule of practice on cross-examination is that advocates should avoid questions to which they do not know the answer. If the examiner does not know what the response will be, he should not ask the question. To the contrary, advocates should ask only those questions to which they are confident of the answer.

The liberal discovery available in civil cases and, to a lesser extent, in criminal cases, means that both sides should know the content of each witness' testimony before the witness testifies. An essential part of thorough preparation for cross-examination includes careful review and analysis of all such past statements or testimony by the witness. And cross-examination questions should largely flow out of what the examiner knows the witness has said before, such that if the witness varies from her past statements, the witness can be impeached. That requires, of course, that counsel have close at hand all previous statements of the witness during the cross-examination of the witness and quick access to the statements if needed. One practical means of organizing cross-examination is by indexing each question to its source, whether that is prior deposition testimony, an exhibit, or another witness. Thus, next to each question, counsel should reference the specific document, page, and line where the prior statement can be found. Should the witness testify in a manner that is inconsistent with her prior statements, the examiner can then use the prior statement to impeach her. By these simple tips, advocates can avoid fumbling through pages of discovery or other documents while the jurors and judge wait.

Sometimes it is simply not possible to be completely protected by some prior statement or exhibit on every question advocates need to ask on cross-examination. It may be that little or no discovery was available in the case or that a witness testified in a manner that was not anticipated by the cross-examiner. In those instances when counsel must venture unprotected into an area of cross-examination, he should rely on the probabilities and on his own common sense in deciding which questions to ask. What is the likelihood, based on everything the examiner knows about the witness, that the witness' answer will be X as opposed to Y? For obvious reasons, advocates should not linger any longer than necessary when questioning witnesses about such uncertain matters. The fewer questions asked by the advocate when unprotected, the less the risk that the witness will testify to something damaging to the examiner's case.

❖ Principle Number Eight: Argue Using Cross-Examination Questions

This is the first and last principle of cross-examination. The focus during cross-examination should be on the examiner, not the witness; the spotlight should be on the question, not the answer; the organization should be centered on the cross-examiner's own theme and theory of the case, not on the testimony of the witness. That is, advocates, when they prepare for cross-examination, should not become so lost in the details and minutiae of a witness' testimony that they lose sight of the larger themes and theories they must prove to prevail.

A fundamental difference between direct-examination and cross-examination is that advocates, through the effective use of leading questions on cross-examination, can effectively bypass the witness and argue their cases directly to the jury. The questions asked during the cross should harken back to the opening statement and foreshadow the closing argument. Each question should build on the one before, invoking the party's theme, emphasizing the key points in the case, and always arguing the party's claim or defense. Further, visual aids can be just as vital in cross-examination as any other part of the trial, especially since cross should not go in chronological order. As you make points that help your client, commit them to some sort of visual aid, such as writing them down as a key word on a board or a flip chart. Seeing the cues in writing solidifies their meaning with the jury, and makes a lasting impression.

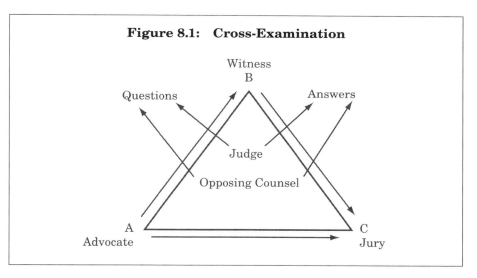

Figure 8.1: Cross-Examination

Take for example, a civil case wherein the plaintiff sued her ex-husband, a police officer, for malicious prosecution after he falsely accused her of possession of illegal drugs and signed an affidavit detailing the allegedly false charges. Plaintiff's theory is that defendant was motivated by hostility toward his ex-wife based on his belief that he had gotten a raw deal in the divorce and that she had been unfaithful and was subjecting their child to an unhealthy home environment. Plaintiff claimed that defendant had planted the drugs in plaintiff's home and used his insider position as an officer to bring about her arrest. Plaintiff's theme? Access, access, access, access. At every point the defendant had the means and opportunity to execute his master plan—access to the marijuana, access to the plaintiff's bathroom, access to the justice system. Observe how plaintiff's counsel develops the point of access slowly and incrementally, one fact at a time, and then argues plaintiff's theme directly to the jury through the questioning of the defendant:

Illustration of Arguing Using Cross-Examination Questions[3]

Lawyer: In your work as a patrol officer, you occasionally deal with people who are in possession of illegal narcotics, true?

Witness: That's right.

Lawyer: People with illegal drugs?

Witness: Yes.

Lawyer: Cocaine?

Witness: Occasionally.

Lawyer: Heroin?

Witness: Rarely.

Lawyer: Marijuana?

Witness: Yes, a lot of marijuana.

Lawyer: You've had many occasions when you stopped people with marijuana, right?

Witness: It happens pretty regularly.

Lawyer: And it happened pretty regularly before May 1, 2008, when Sally North [the plaintiff] was arrested for possession of marijuana, didn't it?

Witness: Yes, it's a regular pattern. When you work patrol, you come across a fair amount of marijuana possession.

Lawyer: When you find someone in possession of marijuana, you arrest them, correct?

Witness: Usually, but not always.

Lawyer: If you do arrest them, you take the marijuana from them, right?

Witness: Yes, I put it in an evidence envelope and mark it for identification.

Lawyer: Then you take it back it to the evidence storage area at the police station, right?

Witness: I either take it to the storage unit or the lab.

Lawyer: You mentioned that you don't always arrest people that you find in possession of marijuana, is that true?

---

[3] This illustration is based on the hypothetical case *Mitchell v. Mitchell*, Judge Jerry R. Parker (Texas Young Lawyers Association).

Witness:	That's true. Sometimes it just doesn't make sense to arrest a teen-ager for smoking a joint or to arrest a cancer patient for having a small stash.
Lawyer:	In those situations you seize the marijuana, but you don't turn it in to the police lab, true?
Witness:	Well, I'll just destroy it on the spot. Throw it down the sewer or flush it down the toilet. Just get rid of it.
Lawyer:	And these amounts that you take it on yourself to destroy, those would be rather small amounts, right?
Witness:	Yes, very small amounts. Just a roach or a few grams at the most.
Lawyer:	And these small amounts that you occasionally would seize, but not turn in, they would easily fit inside one of your pockets?
Witness:	I suppose so.
Lawyer:	So it would be fair to say that you, on occasion, have **access to small amounts of marijuana,** true?
Witness:	I guess so.
Lawyer:	I'm sorry. You do on occasion have **access to small amounts of marijuana,** don't you?
Witness:	Yes, but only small amounts.
Lawyer:	On May 1, 2008, you were inside your ex-wife's apartment, true?
Witness:	Yes I was, to check on my daughter. She was sick.
Lawyer:	And while you were inside Sally's apartment you went into the bathroom?
Witness:	Yes, I did.
Lawyer:	You were in the bathroom alone, true?
Witness:	No one else was in there, that's right.
Lawyer:	And while you were in the bathroom, you had **access to the medicine cabinet,** right?
Witness:	Access? I don't know what you mean.
Lawyer:	**Access, meaning that you could reach the medicine cabinet?**
Witness:	I suppose I could have.
Lawyer:	You had **access in that you could have opened the medicine cabinet,** correct?
Witness:	I didn't, but I guess I could have.
Lawyer:	I'm sorry sir, but my question was whether you could have opened the medicine cabinet if you had a reason to do so?

Witness:	Yes, I could have.
Lawyer:	And later that day, marijuana was found in that bathroom, wasn't it?
Witness:	Yes.
Lawyer:	It was found inside the medicine cabinet, right?
Witness:	Yes, but I sure didn't put it there.
Lawyer:	But it was found inside that medicine cabinet, right?
Witness:	Yes.
Lawyer:	And the amount found was a small amount, true?
Witness:	It was 19 grams, I understand.
Lawyer:	Well it was an amount that could easily fit in one's hand, correct?
Witness:	Sure.
Lawyer:	Nineteen grams could easily fit inside a person's pocket, couldn't it?
Witness:	I suppose so.
Lawyer:	Is that a "yes" it could fit within a person's pocket?
Witness:	Yes.

Through this meticulous cross-examination, plaintiff's counsel was able to reinforce its theme of access, access, access.

IV. IMPEACHMENT

Impeachment is a hostile act, designed to discredit the witness' testimony before the trier of fact. While a successful impeachment can greatly enhance a cross-examination, an illadvised or poorly executed impeachment can damage the cross-examiner's credibility and set back the examiner's case. There are several basic means of impeachment available to the cross-examiner, including:

- interest, bias, or prejudice
- inadequate observation or inability to perceive
- inability to recall
- conduct inconsistent with events
- prior convictions
- nonconviction misconduct probative of truthfulness

- impeachment by omission

- impeachment by prior inconsistent statement

- impeachment by common sense or contradiction

In addition, advocates should be mindful of another powerful means of impeaching witness credibility: the use of a separate witness who can testify concerning the witness' character for veracity. This, however, is not a technique for cross-examination.

A.   Bias, Prejudice, Interest, or Motive

Perhaps the most common type of impeachment is bias, proof that the witness is not simply a disinterested observer, but has an interest in the outcome of the case or some other motive to testify untruthfully. Bias, prejudice, interest, and motive evidence comes in all shapes and sizes.

- Is the witness a party or otherwise interested in the outcome?

- Is the witness related to a party in the action?

- Does the witness have an adverse relationship to either party?

- Does the witness have an employment or business relationship with one of the parties?

- Has the government granted the witness immunity or promised him leniency in exchange for testimony?

- Is the witness being paid to testify as an expert?

- Has the witness settled a claim with one of the parties?

- Has the witness been coached or influenced by the direct examiner in her testimony?

If during examination the witness denies any of these sources of bias, extrinsic evidence supporting the bias may be introduced.

The means of eliciting the witness' bias, prejudice, interest, or motive depends on the nature of the bias and the role of the witness in the case. For example, if the advocate is cross-examining the defendant's mother who is the defendant's sole alibi witness, she may need to do no more than simply elicit the existence of that relationship.

 Illustration of Impeachment by Bias

Lawyer: Mrs. Smith, you are related to the defendant, aren't you?

Witness: Yes, I'm his mother.

Lawyer: No further questions of this witness, Your Honor.

Even though the answer does not likely add new information beyond what was elicited on direct examination, the fact that it is being asked on cross-examination conveys to the jurors that they should consider the bias of the mother in evaluating whether to credit her testimony.

On the other hand, if the bias is not as disqualifying as the maternal relationship, the advocate may need to give more thought to maximizing the impact of the bias on cross-examination. One way to maximize the impact of bias evidence is to link it to the particular testimony the advocate wants to discredit. A witness' employment relationship to a party might be linked to his favorable testimony for that party. Or, an expert witness' relationship to the party who called the expert to testify (financial and otherwise) might be linked to the expert's hurtful opinion or testimony. For example, instead of merely asking the expert a few perfunctory questions about her payment from the plaintiff (*e.g.*, "You are being paid by the plaintiff for your testimony here today, isn't that right?"), advocates should link the fact of payment to the testimony they believe the jury should discount or ignore altogether.

 Illustration of Impeachment of Expert for Bias[4]

Lawyer: It's your opinion that defendant's playground structure complied with the government guidelines, correct?

Witness: Yes.

Lawyer: And that it was Ms. Jones' [the plaintiff] misuse of the playground structure that caused her injuries?

Witness: That's right.

Lawyer: And you are being paid by the defendant to testify here today, aren't you?

Witness: I am being paid my normal rate for providing my consulting services, yes.

Lawyer: In point of fact, you are "on the clock" for the defendant right now as you answer the questions I am asking you, true?

Witness: I suppose you could say that. I am being paid my normal rate for testifying at trials.

Lawyer: And likewise, you were working for the defendant when you testified on direct examination that the playground built by the defendant was perfectly safe, isn't that correct?

Witness: Yes, but that certainly had no effect on my opinions.

---

[4]   This illustration is based on the hypothetical case *Dawson v. Anderson* (Association of Trial Lawyers of America).

Lawyer:	When all is said and done, the defendant has agreed to pay you more than $20,000 for your work in this case, correct?
Witness:	I don't know the exact amount, but my services do not come cheaply.
Lawyer:	Excuse me, sir, perhaps my question was not clear. Isn't it true the defendant has agreed to pay you more than $20,000 for your work in this case?
Witness:	Yes.

Of course, jurors are not surprised to learn that expert witnesses are paid for their expert testimony but this kind of more detailed inquiry reveals the true extent of the financial interest of the expert witness. Indeed, the cross-examiner may be able to go further if, for example, the expert derives a substantial amount of his annual income testifying for the defense in similar cases.

B.   Inadequate Observation or Lack of Perception

The second means of impeachment involves the witness' ability to perceive or understand what the witness claims to have perceived or understood. In preparing to impeach the witness for some sensory or mental incapacity, the inquiry should be:

- Was the witness in a position to adequately observe what she is now testifying to?

- *e.g.*, Was the "eyewitness" to the traffic collision paying close attention to the intersection?

- Did events happen too quickly for the witness to clearly comprehend what took place?

- Was the witness hindered in any way in accurately observing the events?

- Does the witness suffer from poor vision or poor hearing?

- Does the witness have the requisite knowledge or experience to accurately testify about what she saw?

- *e.g.*, Would the witness be able to recognize marijuana if he saw it?

- Does the witness have any mental impairment that might limit his ability to testify accurately?

- *e.g.*, Was the witness using drugs or alcohol at the time of the events?

- Does the witness suffer from any kind of mental illness or impairment?

If the witness denies the inability to perceive or the lack of observation, extrinsic evidence can be introduced to prove the point.

 Illustration of Impeachment Based on Lack of Perception[5]

Lawyer:	Mr. Richards, you own and operate the gas station near the intersection of First and Main, don't you?
Witness:	Yes.
Lawyer:	You have a number of responsibilities and duties as the owner/manager?
Witness:	It keeps me hopping.
Lawyer:	At about 3:00 P.M. the day of the accident, you were in one of the service bays in your station?
Witness:	That's right.
Lawyer:	And you were having a discussion?
Witness:	True.
Lawyer:	You were discussing a bill with a customer?
Witness:	That's right.
Lawyer:	And it was during that discussion inside the service bay when you heard the collision?
Witness:	I'll never forget it.
Lawyer:	You turned in the direction of the sound?
Witness:	That's right.
Lawyer:	But because you were in one of the service bays in your garage, you didn't see the collision, did you?
Witness:	Well as soon as I heard that terrible sound I ran to the doorway and looked.
Lawyer:	That's right, first you heard the collision?
Witness:	Right.
Lawyer:	Then you ran to the doorway?
Witness:	Right.

---

[5]   This illustration is based on the hypothetical case *Potter v. Shrackle*, Kenneth S. Broun and James H. Seckinger (National Institute of Trial Advocacy).

Lawyer:	And at that time the plaintiff was lying in the street?
Witness:	The accident had just happened, I was at that door in a heart beat.
Lawyer:	I understand that, Mr. Richards. Let me ask my question again. At the time you reached the doorway, the plaintiff was already lying in the street, wasn't she?
Witness:	Yeah that's right.
Lawyer:	So your first view of the scene was after the accident had occurred, isn't that correct?
Witness:	Okay.

C. Faulty Memory

The third impeachment possibility is a failure of the witness' memory. By showing that the witness has forgotten important facts, the lawyer calls into question other parts of the testimony that the witness claims to be able to remember and raises doubts about the certainty of the witness' testimony. With each witness, the examiner should ask:

- Has there been a significant passage of time since the event?

- Has the witness admitted to a lack of memory regarding the events?

- Is the witness' memory loss selective or total, genuine or feigned?

- Is the witness' memory sufficiently clear to distinguish the event from other similar events?

For instance, assume that the arresting highway patrol officer in a driving under the influence case is testifying about his observations that took place six months ago. Specifically, he testifies that the defendant stumbled on one of the field sobriety tests. There are two potential impeaching points in this scenario. First, the events happened six months ago, and second, the officer has most likely made a number of other traffic stops and arrests in the interim and may not be able to distinguish the specific details of this arrest from other arrests.

 Illustration of Impeachment Based on Lack of Memory

Lawyer:	Officer, over the past six months would you estimate that you have made over one hundred twenty vehicle stops?
Witness:	At least that.
Lawyer:	And would it be fair to say that at least forty of those stops have been for suspected driving under the influence?

Witness:	Again, I would say at least that.
Lawyer:	During each of those forty plus stops you administered field sobriety tests, didn't you?
Witness:	Yes, I did.
Lawyer:	In fact, on a driving under the influence stop, you administer at least three and as many as four or five field sobriety tests, don't you?
Witness:	I almost always administer five tests.
Lawyer:	So, that would work out to approximately two hundred individual field sobriety tests in just the past six months, correct?
Witness:	That's right.

Note that the cross-examination either terminates at this point or moves on to another area. The examiner has the essential evidence to make the argument at closing that this officer is hard pressed to truly distinguish this one test from the two hundred others. However, to go any further and drill home the point may well be the one question too many and allow the witness to explain himself.

D.   Conduct Inconsistent with Events

The fourth means of impeaching a witness, is to identify conduct by the witness that is inconsistent with the testimony of the witness relating to how the events took place. The examiner might consider: Did the witness do something at the time of the event that was inconsistent with his testimony concerning the event? For instance, if on direct examination the witness testified that he was the first person to come upon a serious automobile accident and he saw two people in great pain, yet other evidence shows that he did not stop his car to render aid or take any action to call for assistance, his actions were clearly inconsistent with his testimony.

Tech Tip

Visual Aids for Impeachment

Visual aids can be helpful in proving conduct or prior statements were inconsistent with events. Try using:

✓ Timelines

✓ Marked transcripts

✓ Deposition video excerpts

 ## Illustration of Impeachment by Conduct

Lawyer:	You testified that you actually saw the accident occur, correct?
Witness:	Yes.
Lawyer:	And that it was such a horrifying event that you cannot forget how it happened?

Witness:	That's right.
Lawyer:	But you didn't stop and help the individuals in the accident, did you?
Witness:	Well I called 9-1-1 on my cell phone.
Lawyer:	You did not wait for the police officers to arrive at the scene, did you?
Witness:	No, I didn't.
Lawyer:	And you didn't speak to those officers about what happened, true?
Witness:	I didn't stay, so I wasn't able to speak to anyone at the scene.
Lawyer:	You didn't speak to any emergency medical technicians at the scene?
Witness:	No.
Lawyer:	That's right. You left the scene before the police or medical personnel even arrived, didn't you?
Witness:	Yes, I had a hair appointment.
Lawyer:	You left, what you have described as a horrifying event, to get to a hair appointment, right?
Witness:	Yes, unfortunately, that's right.

E.   Criminal Record

Prior criminal convictions of a witness provide the fifth type of impeachment. In federal court, Rule 609 of the Federal Rules of Evidence governs the admission of prior convictions. It rests on two fundamental premises:

(1) all felony convictions are probative of the truthfulness of witnesses, and

(2) convictions more than ten years old are typically too remote to assist the jury in evaluating issues of credibility.

The Rule essentially divides the world into two kinds of witnesses: "the accused" and everyone else. The term "the accused" refers only to criminal defendants. The Rule similarly addresses two kinds of criminal convictions: crimes involving dishonesty or false statement and felony convictions.

Under Rule 609(a)(1), to impeach the criminal defendant with a prior conviction (other than convictions for crimes involving dishonesty or false statement), the prosecution must show that the conviction is a felony offense, is less than ten years old (measured from the date of the conviction or the date of release from confinement, whichever is later), and is more probative than prejudicial. (Fed R. Evid. 609(a)(1)). The burden is on the prosecution to make the required showing of the probative value of the conviction for impeachment purposes. Prior felony convictions (other than convictions for crimes involving dishonesty) of all other witnesses, including defendants in civil cases, are admissible for purposes of impeachment if they are less than ten years old and the probative value of the conviction is not substantially outweighed by the danger of unfair prejudice, the Rule 403 balancing test.

Under Rule 609(a)(2), convictions that involve crimes of dishonesty or false statement, such as perjury, forgery, embezzlement, or fraud, are per se admissible, regardless of the nature of the crime (whether a felony or misdemeanor) or the identity of the witness (the criminal defendant or otherwise). (Fed. R. Evid. 609(a)(2)). The ten year time limit still applies to these convictions. However, convictions more than ten years old may be admitted only if the judge finds that the probative value of the conviction substantially outweighs the danger of unfair prejudice and the proponent of the evidence has provided written notice of the party's intent to offer this evidence. (Fed. R. Evid. 609(b)).

Most judges strictly limit the specific information that the cross-examiner may elicit from the witness about the conviction. For instance, the factual details of the crime that led to the conviction are not admissible. Instead, the examiner may ask about the name of the crime for which the person was convicted, the date of the conviction, and, in some jurisdictions, the sentence imposed for the conviction. Despite these limits, advocates should attempt to exploit the conviction by breaking down the information about the prior conviction into as many questions as possible. If the witness denies the prior conviction, extrinsic evidence (typically a certified copy of the judgment of conviction itself) may be introduced. The federal rules, and many state evidence provisions, limit the use of certain types of convictions, such as juvenile convictions and convictions for which a pardon has been granted.

Illustration of Impeachment by Prior Conviction

Lawyer:	You've been convicted of a felony before, haven't you?
Witness:	Yes, about two years ago.
Lawyer:	In fact, that was an embezzlement charge, wasn't it?
Witness:	Yes, it was.
Lawyer:	A jury convicted you of that offense in this very courthouse on September 29, 2008, isn't that correct?
Witness:	Yes.
Lawyer:	And you were sentenced to two years in a federal prison, right?
Witness:	Yes, though I only spent about one year in prison.

F. Nonconviction Misconduct

The use of prior convictions to impeach is merely one of three ways an examiner can use character evidence to impeach a witness on cross-examination. The second tool is commonly known as nonconviction misconduct and its use in federal court is governed by Rule 608(b) of the Federal Rules of Evidence. Under Rule 608(b), an examiner may ask a witness during cross-examination about instances of misconduct that are probative of the witness' trustworthiness. Some fruitful areas of inquiry include:

- Are there past instances when this witness has lied or engaged in untruthful conduct?

- Did the witness lie on his resume?

- Did the witness lie on her employment application?

- Did the party lie about his status to the social security disability board?

- Has the defendant misled his probation officer?

Of course, the examiner is precluded from simply making up past misdeeds of the witness. The examiner's questions must have a good faith basis. It is somewhat unusual to be aware of past specific instances of untruthfulness by the witness, and thus, Rule 608(b) is not available with every witness. However, when the occasion arises it can make for very powerful questioning.

One caveat about Rule 608(b): unlike most other impeaching techniques, the rule does not allow the past misconduct to be proven by extrinsic evidence. (Fed. R. Evid. 608(b)). Accordingly, if the witness denies the past misconduct when asked about it on cross-examination, the examiner must accept the answer and cannot inquire further with the current witness or produce evidence from another witness or a document to prove the alleged misconduct.

Illustration of Impeachment by Nonconviction Misconduct

Lawyer: You live in South Park, isn't that correct?

Witness: Yes.

Lawyer: And you've lived there for more than two years, haven't you?

Witness: Yes—it's actually been about five years now.

Lawyer: Isn't it a fact that two years ago you registered your youngest son to attend a school located in North Park?

Witness: Yes, my child attends that school.

Lawyer:	When you were registering your youngest child for that school you indicated on the registration materials that you actually lived in North Park, didn't you?
Witness:	No, I didn't.
Lawyer:	And you lied about your residency to try to get your child into the North Park School District?
Witness:	Absolutely not.

At this point, even if the questioner has a copy of the form that shows the misrepresentation, it is not admissible because it would be improper extrinsic evidence. The only avenue available is as follows:

Lawyer:	Mr. Smith, may I remind you that you have taken an oath to tell the truth, and any deviation from the truth may be punishable as perjury?
Witness:	Fine. I lied about the residency. The North Park School is much nicer. I didn't think the lie would be a big deal. It wasn't hurting anyone.

At this point, had the witness refused to tell the truth and stuck to his claim of truthfulness, there would be nothing more the advocate could do to prove otherwise, except hope that the jury could see through his lies by observing his demeanor. The advocate takes a risk in this situation, however, because reminding the witness he is under oath, and then having the witness blatantly lie anyway, may cause the jury to believe he is telling the truth when he is not.

G. Impeachment by Omission

It is an all too common and potentially devastating occurrence: a witness for the opposing party suddenly, for the first time, testifies at trial to an event or a statement that the witness failed to include in any of his prior statements, reports, or deposition testimony. It is a problem that presents a challenging impeachment opportunity. The examiner must first consider whether the omission merits impeachment. This requires a common sense determination of whether the new fact is material to the case. Next, and most critically, the examiner must consider whether the omission of the fact from prior statements or testimony defies expectation; in other words, would the witness be expected to have included the event or statement in the earlier statement or testimony if indeed it is true. The witness will not be impeachable if she can credibly answer that no one asked the right question or that it simply did not occur to her to mention the fact earlier.

Impeachment by omission requires that the advocate carefully validate the witness' prior statement in which one would have expected the witness to include the newly revealed information. That document may be a deposition, an expert report, an internal memorandum, or a police report. Setting the trap that the witness knew the importance of the information at the time he made the statement is critically important so that later the witness cannot easily escape the impeachment. If the prior statement is a deposition, the advocate should establish that the witness took an oath to tell the whole truth, that she in fact told the whole truth, that she knew the parties and advocates would rely on her testimony, that she never amended or corrected her testimony despite having the opportunity to do so, and that her memory was fresher at the time of the deposition than at the time of trial. Once the validation is complete, the advocate can spring the trap by confronting the witness with the fact that her current testimony does not appear in her prior statement or testimony in the case.

 ## Illustration of Impeachment by Omission

Lawyer:	You've been a sworn police officer for thirteen years, isn't that right?
Witness:	Yes.
Lawyer:	Over the course of that time you have written many police reports, haven't you?
Witness:	Of course.
Lawyer:	You are aware, of course, that your reports are examined by the District Attorney's office to determine if criminal charges are to be filed?
Witness:	I am aware of that.
Lawyer:	In fact, you know from experience that in many cases your report will be the sole basis for making a filing decision, isn't that right?
Witness:	I suppose so.
Lawyer:	So, don't you appreciate the significance of the reports you write as a sworn peace officer?
Witness:	Yes I do.
Lawyer:	It is important to be truthful and accurate in including the events as you perceived them?
Witness:	That's right.
Lawyer:	And you seek to include all pertinent information in your reports, true?
Witness:	I certainly do.

Lawyer:	You testified on direct examination that Mr. Miller stumbled and fell during one of the field sobriety tests, correct?
Witness:	Yes, he did.
Lawyer:	That fact was not in your report, was it?
Witness:	No, I don't include every detail in my reports. That simply is not necessary.
Lawyer:	Officer let me ask again. That fact was not in your report, was it?
Witness:	No.
Lawyer:	In fact, Officer Johnson, this is the first time in the history of this case that you have testified in court to that fact, isn't it?
Witness:	I guess it is.
Lawyer:	Is that a yes?
Witness:	Yes.

Note how carefully the examiner established the witness' knowledge of the importance of her report. With that foundation, the witness' explanation for non-inclusion rings hollow and the impeachment is successful.

H.   Prior Inconsistent Statements

The favorite form of impeachment for lawyers, and perhaps the most damning, is prior inconsistent statements. The opportunity to use the witness' own words to contradict his trial testimony can deliver a crippling blow to the witness' credibility.

Yet, there are a number of ways this impeachment opportunity can be derailed. First, lawyers sometimes fail to recognize an impeachment opportunity when it arises. If the impeaching point is merely a slight misstatement by the witness, or involves matters collateral to the disputed issues in the case, the examiner should generally resist the temptation to impeach. To impeach in these circumstances detracts from meaningful impeachment and risks damaging the advocate's credibility by creating the impression that the advocate is just trying to pick a fight or is making a mountain out of a molehill. Use the common sense test: Does it matter? Will the jurors care? If the impeachment is on a point that does not matter or about which the jurors will not care, the examiner will look petty or perhaps even mean-spirited or dishonest.

Second, the examiner may fail to firmly commit the witness to the witness' current testimony, thus allowing the witness to equivocate once the impeachment is under way. The commitment should be obtained without alerting the witness that an impeachment is forthcoming. If the witness senses danger she may attempt to qualify her statement thus reducing, if not eliminating, the opportunity to impeach.

Third, the examiner may not lay an adequate foundation for the prior statement, validating its existence and its importance. If the prior statement was made in a deposition, the advocate should elicit from the witness the circumstances of the deposition, including that the witness was under oath at the time and, if applicable, that the witness verified the accuracy of her testimony as recorded in the transcript.

Fourth, the examiner may be tempted to cede control to the witness by allowing the witness to read her prior inconsistent statement aloud to the jury. Don't do it! Instead, the advocate should simply read the statement from counsel table or, alternatively, should approach the witness and show him the statement. Under the latter approach, the advocate must maintain control by reading the statement himself while the witness simply follows along. Either approach allows the lawyer to remain in control. Both approaches are consistent with the federal rules, which do not require that the witness be given the chance to see the deposition before the impeachment. (Fed R. Evid. 613(a)).

The natural tendency after the impeachment is to ask another question, just to rub the point in. The classic example is: "So, are you lying now or were you lying then?" That's a bad question, not only because it is objectionably argumentative, but also because it gives the witness the chance to explain the prior inconsistent statement. End the impeachment with the reading of the inconsistent answer and save the rest for closing argument. The jury will understand the significance of the witness being caught in a lie.

Illustration of Impeachment by Prior Inconsistent Statement

Lawyer: Before we really get started, Mr. Anderson, I want to clear up my notes from your examination. I just want to make sure I've got things right. You said during direct examination that you didn't enter the house before the shooting, is that right?

Witness: That's right.

Lawyer: Mr. Anderson, you gave a deposition concerning the events in this case, didn't you?

Witness: Yes.

Lawyer: Your attorney was with you at your deposition, wasn't he?

Witness: Yes, he was.

Lawyer: At the conclusion of the deposition you were given an opportunity to review the answers you gave, weren't you?

Witness:	Yes, I was.
Lawyer:	And you were told you could correct any errors or misstatements?
Witness:	I believe so.
Lawyer:	Mr. Anderson, you took an oath and swore to tell the truth at that deposition, didn't you?
Witness:	Yes.
Lawyer:	In fact, that's the same oath to tell the truth that you took today, wasn't it?
Witness:	I guess it was.
Lawyer:	Counsel, I am referring to page sixteen, lines six through thirteen of the transcript of that deposition. Isn't it true, Mr. Anderson, that during your deposition you were asked, and I quote, "Did you enter the house at any time before the shooting"?
Witness:	Yes, I was asked that.
Lawyer:	And, Mr. Anderson, isn't it true you said, and again I quote, "I went in the house about ten minutes before the shooting."
Witness:	Well, that's not exactly what happened.
Lawyer:	Mr. Anderson, perhaps you did not understand my question. Let me repeat it. Isn't it true you said, "I went in the house about ten minutes before the shooting"?
Witness:	That's what I said.
Lawyer:	Thank you.

Note that the examiner firmed up the witness' statement from the just completed direct examination. This is essential in preventing the witness from attempting to qualify his answer once he recognizes that an impeachment is forthcoming. Also note that once the impeachment was completed the examiner stopped and resisted the temptation to ask the one question too many.

When seeking to cross-examine a witness with a prior inconsistent statement, it is not unusual for a witness to claim a loss of memory about the underlying events or circumstances. The witness may take this approach for either of two reasons: (1) The witness has genuinely forgotten what happened; or (2) The witness recognizes that she is about to be impeached and the witness hopes that a claim of memory loss will defuse or frustrate the impeachment.

How should the examiner handle an allegedly forgetful witness in the midst of an attempted impeachment? The first issue is whether memory loss by the witness at trial is inconsistent with the witness's prior statement about the matter. Every jurisdiction agrees that feigned loss of memory by the witness is indeed inconsistent with prior statements by the witness. Thus, if the witness claims while testifying at trial that she is unable to recall events that she previously addressed, and the cross-examiner is able to demonstrate to the judge that the claimed memory loss is feigned, impeachment by prior inconsistent statement is permitted.

There is less uniformity about whether genuine memory loss is sufficient to open the door to impeachment by prior inconsistent statement. In California, for example, courts require a cross-examiner to establish feigned memory loss as a condition of such impeachment. *See People v. Simmons*, 177 Cal. Rptr. 17, 19–20 (Cal. App. 1981). This more restrictive approach follows from California's more generous treatment of prior inconsistent statements. Under the California Evidence Code, section 1235, all prior inconsistent statements are admissible for the truth of the matter asserted and not merely for impeachment purposes. This liberal standard of admission is paired with a more restricted definition of what is "inconsistent."

In other jurisdictions, including federal courts, the treatment of memory loss is less uniform. The issue of whether the memory loss must be feigned is rarely squarely addressed by courts and when it is the answers are not consistent. In practice, lawyers regularly treat loss of memory— whether genuine or feigned—as being inconsistent with a witness's prior statements about the matter and at least some courts do allow the use of this kind of impeachment. *See, e.g., United States v. Ragghianti*, 560 F.2d 1376, 1380 (9th Cir. 1977).

Picking up the same illustration as above, at its mid-point, look closely at how to refresh recollection within an impeachment.

 ## Illustration of Refreshing Recollection/Impeachment by Prior Inconsistent Statement

Lawyer: Isn't it true, Mr. Anderson, that during your deposition you were asked, and I quote, "Did you enter the house at any time before the shooting?"

Witness: You know I'm a little nervous right now, and I don't remember being asked that question.

Lawyer: I understand, Mr. Anderson. If you have an opportunity to review your deposition do you believe it would refresh your recollection?

Witness:	That would probably help.
Lawyer:	Your Honor, may I approach with the deposition?
Court:	You may.
Lawyer:	Mr. Anderson, please read page sixteen to yourself.
Witness:	Okay.
Lawyer:	Have you finished?
Witness:	Yes, I have.
Lawyer:	And do you now recall your testimony during your deposition?
Witness:	I do.
Lawyer:	Isn't it true, Mr. Anderson, that during your deposition you were asked and I quote, "Did you enter the house at any time before the shooting"?
Witness:	Yes, I was.
Lawyer:	And isn't it true you said, and again I quote, "I went in the house about ten minutes before the shooting."
Witness:	Yes.

I. Impeachment by Common Sense or Contradiction

There may not always be an omission or prior inconsistent statement on which to build the advocate's impeachment. Sometimes the only basis for impeachment is common sense. Impeachment by common sense is best used when the witness testifies to a version of events that simply defies ordinary expectations. Rather than wait until closing argument to point out how outrageous the other party's claims are, the advocate should make the point during cross-examination while the witness' testimony is fresh in the jurors' minds.

To impeach by common sense the advocate should show the jury how extreme and extraordinary the witness' testimony is. For example, assume that plaintiff, a high school football coach, sued a fellow coach for defamation when the defendant claimed that the plaintiff illegally recruited players. The defendant pleaded truth as an affirmative defense, pointing to a letter to an eighth grader's mother appearing to offer certain inducements if the child attended the plaintiff's school. The letter contained the plaintiff's signature, but plaintiff claimed that he did not sign it. Remarkably, he claimed that his signature was forged. Here is the relevant portion of the cross-examination of the plaintiff:

Illustration of Impeachment by Common Sense or Contradiction[6]

Lawyer:	Coach Cooper, I'm handing you defendant's exhibit one, a letter dated May 15th. That letter contains what looks to be your signature, doesn't it?
Witness:	Yes, but it's not my signature.
Lawyer:	That's right, you claim that someone forged your signature on that letter, right?
Witness:	That's right.
Lawyer:	You know it was forged because you would never send a letter like defendant's exhibit one, would you?
Witness:	No, I most certainly would not.
Lawyer:	Because this letter is a recruiting letter, isn't it?
Witness:	That's right, it's not the kind of thing I ever send to prospective students.
Lawyer:	I understand, and that's because recruitment would be a violation of league rules, wouldn't it?
Witness:	That's right.
Lawyer:	And it would be a violation of your own school's rules?
Witness:	That's right.
Lawyer:	If you didn't sign the letter, then someone must have forged your signature on the letter, isn't that right?
Witness:	I suppose so.
Lawyer:	Well is there any other way for your signature to have gotten on this letter if you didn't do it yourself?
Witness:	No, not that I can think of.
Lawyer:	So you would agree that your signature is forged?
Witness:	That's right.
Lawyer:	Let me see if I can understand how this must have happened. Someone must have broken into your office and gotten a piece of your official stationary, right?

---

[6] This illustration is based on the hypothetical case *Cooper v. Cooper*, Judge Jerry R. Parker (National Institute of Trial Advocacy).

Witness:	I don't know how it happened. I have no idea.
Lawyer:	But the letter is on your official stationary, true?
Witness:	Yes, it is.
Lawyer:	And you keep your official stationary in your office, isn't that right?
Witness:	Yes, that's true.
Lawyer:	And after they got some of your official stationary, they had to forge your signature, right?
Witness:	Sure, but that wouldn't be difficult, I sign a column in our booster club newsletter every week during football season. Someone could copy my signature from that.
Lawyer:	Yes, I understand that, but the person who sent this letter would have to take one of those old newsletters or some other document with your signature on it and trace it, isn't that right?
Witness:	Well, that's one way it might have happened, but not the only way.
Lawyer:	You agree, don't you, that the signature on defendant's exhibit one matches your signature almost perfectly?
Witness:	Yeah, it really does.
Lawyer:	So, isn't it fair to assume that whoever did this had to spend some time to get it just right?
Witness:	Probably so, I've got some rabid boosters at my school.
Lawyer:	That's right. You believe that members of your booster club probably sent out the letter without you knowing about it, don't you?
Witness:	Well, that makes the most sense I think. Obviously, I don't know for sure. Maybe it was one of the other coaches in the district.
Lawyer:	After the person got your official stationary and forged your signature, the person would have to get the address for this eighth grader and send the letter, right?
Witness:	Yes, that's right I suppose.

With each step the examiner has made the story more implausible: from obtaining the correct stationary, to copying a near perfect signature, and on to obtaining and sending the letter to a highly sought-after player. Such a chain of circumstances is so unlikely, that it defies common sense.

Chapter Nine

OBJECTIONS

I. OVERVIEW & OBJECTIVES

The very act of making an objection at trial is full of drama and suspense. All of the gears of the adversary system grind into action. The objecting advocate rises and interrupts the proceeding to interpose an objection to the evidence offered by the opponent. The responding advocate must then quickly identify the proper grounds for admission of the evidence. The judge must assess, in a heartbeat, the arguments for and against admission, and render a ruling. And the jurors come to attention, watching and wondering.

The term itself—"Objection!"—forces one to take notice. It is a powerful word in the courtroom. It stops the proceeding in its tracks, at least for a moment, and demands the attention of every trial participant. It is also a dangerous word, one that should be used with care. Wielded as a weapon of destruction, objections may cause serious self-inflicted wounds. Used as a shield, however, objections provide an important tool for trial advocates, essential to fend off evidence that may unfairly prejudice their client or improperly distract or corrupt the jurors.

Making and responding to objections are integral parts of any trial; and yet, objections are often little more than afterthoughts for trial lawyers. Advocates reason that propounding and responding to objections is reactive, and perhaps even spontaneous, and thus, not something that merits a great deal of forethought. Alternatively, advocates believe that to the extent evidentiary problems can be anticipated, they are generally dealt with during pre-trial motions. However, not all evidentiary concerns can be anticipated before trial. And furthermore, direct and cross-examinations are fraught with objectionable questions and sometimes unexpected and objectionable answers. An overall trial strategy that fails to include consideration of objections, and even an objection strategy, is inadequate and incomplete.

Trial lawyers make objections for many reasons, some proper and others not. They object to exclude inadmissible evidence, of course, but also to disrupt the opponent's examination, to interrupt a witness' damaging answer, to test the judge, or to argue a point to the jury. However, there are only two proper reasons to object:

- to exclude inadmissible evidence

- to preserve a point of error for appeal

Any other reason for an objection, such as to gain a supposed strategic advantage, is not appropriate and should be resisted. And, even when an objection is available to a party, advocates should not reflexively make the objection. Under certain circumstances, the advocate may gain an advantage from not objecting, despite having the right to do so.

II.   PROCEDURAL REQUIREMENTS FOR OBJECTIONS AND OFFERS OF PROOF

Objections serve three fundamental purposes in an adversary system. First, they alert the trial judge to the potential error and allow the judge to make rulings based on the arguments of the parties. Second, they give notice to the examining counsel of the alleged defect in the advocate's evidence and an opportunity to correct any deficiencies. Third, the ability to object is a tool of efficiency, cutting off the rights of parties who fail to preserve their rights by objecting when appropriate.

A.   Requirements for Objections

Objections must be timely and specific. (*See, e.g.*, Fed. R. Evid. 103(a)). The timeliness requirement means that objections should be made as soon as the error becomes apparent to the advocate. In the context of witness examination, that typically means that the advocate should raise objections to questions before the answer is given and objections to answers before the next question is asked. Sometimes that is impossible and the standard is simple reasonableness. Did the lawyer make the objection within a reasonable time after the erroneous evidence was offered?

The specificity requirement means that advocates must make the legal basis of their objection clear to the court, unless it is clear from the context of the objection. Thus, it is insufficient to make a generic objection to evidence. Advocates must offer the specific grounds at the time they object—such as hearsay, speculation, or leading.

With very few exceptions (such as plain error or constitutional error), an objection is necessary to preserve a point of error for appeal. That means that if a party fails to object to the admission of inadmissible evidence during the trial, the party cannot complain about the judge's admission of the evidence on appeal. The point is waived.

B.   Requirements for Offers of Proof

When the court refuses to admit evidence offered by a party, an objection is not sufficient to preserve the error. Instead, the party must make an offer of proof. The offer of proof creates a record of the nature and content of the excluded evidence, so that a reviewing court will have some basis on which to evaluate the correctness of the trial court's ruling.

Following the court's ruling of exclusion, the adversely affected party should request the opportunity to make an offer of proof. The offer should be made outside of the jury's presence. The advocate may choose from several options in making the offer. She might actually call to the witness stand the witness whose testimony was excluded and elicit the excluded testimony in a conventional question and answer format. Some courts, however, may prefer a more efficient alternative, such as having the advocate summarize the expected content of the excluded evidence for the court (and on the record) without having the witness testify. Offers of proof may be made at any time before the case is submitted to the jury.

III. PRINCIPLES OF OBJECTION STRATEGY AND PROTOCOL

❖ Principle Number One: Keep Objectionable and Harmful Evidence from the Jury

Some advocates wield objections like clubs and attempt to beat their adversaries into submission. Objections are not weapons that should be used to wreak havoc, but rather are tools to ensure the admission of fair and probative evidence. The goal of objections is not to preclude introduction of proper (albeit harmful) evidence, but rather to preclude evidence that is objectionable *and* harmful. Thus, advocates, before objecting, should assess whether the opponent's attempts to introduce inadmissible evidence, or to examine witnesses using improper questions, is harmful to the advocate's case. The question is: "Does it hurt?" If the evidence is objectionable, but not harmful, the advocate should wisely choose not to object. Indeed, objections should be made only when necessary to preclude evidence that inflicts real damage to the party's case.

> **PRINCIPLES OF OBJECTION STRATEGY AND PROTOCOL**
>
> ❖ Keep Objectionable and Harmful Evidence from the Jury
> ❖ Anticipate Objections
> ❖ View Oral Argument as the Last, Best Chance for Admission or Exclusion of the Evidence
> ❖ Prepare Witnesses for Objections
> ❖ Avoid Unnecessary Sidebar Conferences
> ❖ Do Not Address Opposing Counsel
> ❖ Avoid Speaking or Standing Objections
> ❖ Concede Appropriate Objections
> ❖ Avoid Being Overly Aggressive
> ❖ Limiting Instructions Cure Nothing

Most of the testimony elicited by your opponent, however, will likely be proper and admissible, and thus, not objectionable. And advocates should resist objecting to admissible evidence or properly phrased questions for a whole host of reasons, including:

- Proper and admissible evidence should be heard by the trier of fact.

- Futile objections draw additional attention to the answer.

- The integrity of the objecting advocate's case will be compromised, as the jurors are left to wonder why that party is attempting to conceal evidence they have a right to hear.

- The credibility of the advocate himself will be called into question as he may be viewed as an obstructionist and a zealous partisan who cannot be trusted.

Each of these concerns is examined in turn below.

First, every party to a lawsuit has the right to be heard and to present admissible evidence in support of the party's position. Equal access to the courts carries with it the right to present one's evidence to the trier of fact for a fair and impartial determination. And any contrivance or connivance that impinges on that right is a disservice to the rule of law.

Second, an objection that is made and overruled tends to draw additional attention to both the question and the answer. An objection interrupts the cadence of the question and answer give and take, and simply, by virtue of the interruption, the jurors will pay particular heed to the evidence that drew the objection. Testimony that might have simply slipped by unnoticed is now drawn out for emphasis, and jurors may conclude that the evidence must be significant and detrimental to the objector to have drawn an objection in the first place.

The third reason is that such objections compromise the integrity of the objecting advocate's case. The jurors may decide that the advocate's objection was made out of desperation, perhaps because his evidence is insufficient to prove his claim or defense or to rebut the opponent's evidence. Even worse, the objecting advocate may be viewed as conceding that his case cannot prevail if all the facts are disclosed.

The final, and perhaps most compelling reason vitiating against such objections is that the integrity of the advocate himself is compromised. Lawyers have an ethical responsibility to object only when there is a good faith basis to do so. An advocate who becomes a zealous partisan with a win-at-all-costs mind-set not only violates his duty as a lawyer, but also will not be considered a credible source of information by jurors. The integrity of the advocate is the wellspring of success at trial. If at any point that integrity is called into question, the advocate's ability to effectively present his client's case is severely compromised.

❖ Principle Number Two: Anticipate Objections

Not all evidentiary matters can be covered in pre-trial motions. Many evidentiary matters are only capable of resolution as they develop during witness testimony. However, that task is not solely relegated to the whims of chance or sudden bursts of insight, but rather is another aspect of trial that advocates must anticipate and for which advocates must carefully plan. Whether making or responding to objections, advocates should not be taken by surprise. An essential task in preparing for the examination of any witness is to anticipate the objections from opposing counsel and to know in advance appropriate responses. An advocate who draws a hearsay objection during a direct examination and has no response is akin to a deer in the headlights. And needlessly so. The objection should have been foreseen and an appropriate response prepared.

The task differs only slightly in making objections. With the liberal discovery system that earmarks contemporary trials, it is difficult to imagine a witness testifying to matters that surprise the opposing advocate. Because the advocate knows what is coming, he should be armed in advance with his objections.

That said, however, not all objections can be anticipated. Sometimes witnesses become confused or anxious and their testimony varies from their previous statements. Sometimes the way an advocate asks her question can elicit unanticipated testimony. The best preparation for such contingencies is to be thoroughly familiar with the facts of the case and to recognize any variance with previous or anticipated answers.

Anticipating objections is not limited to foreseeing the problematic areas of the case, but can also apply to the timing of objections. When a question calls for improper opinion testimony, the objection should be made before the witness begins the answer. Not merely to preserve the error, but also because a tardy objection that allows even a partial answer may put harmful and objectionable testimony before the jury. Even though the answer may be stricken from the record and the jury admonished to disregard it, the bell has been rung, and the damage done. In reality, asking that an answer be stricken from the record and the jury admonished to disregard the answer is a fool's mission. The jurors have heard it and cannot now somehow purge it from their thoughts. If anything, the tardy objection and the request that the answer be stricken most likely will only serve to draw attention to the hurtful testimony.

❖ Principle Number Three: View Oral Argument as the Last, Best Chance for Admission or Exclusion of Evidence

An advocate's argument before the court regarding the admission or exclusion of evidence may well be the advocate's best, and effectively her last, chance to get the relief she seeks. Appellate courts review most evidentiary rulings at trial under an abuse of discretion standard, meaning that many trial rulings are effectively insulated from reversal on appeal. And the harmless error rule further reduces the likelihood that an evidentiary error will form the basis for reversal on appeal. Thus, the judge's ruling on any point of evidence may constitute, for all intents and purposes, the last word on the matter.

Accordingly, advocacy by the lawyer is critically important. Advocates must not only be prepared to anticipate potential objections before trial, as suggested in the previous principle, but they must also be prepared to effectively and doggedly advocate for the admission or exclusion of the evidence. They must be armed with appropriate authority from the rules of evidence or case law and persuasive arguments supporting the party's position. Further, they must be diligent in their attempts to obtain admission of the evidence, arguing alternative theories of admission or renewing the objection as the landscape of the trial evolves. Trying cases for appeal is foolhardy. The best hope of success is at trial, and advocates should make every effort to get a good result without having to pursue an appeal.

❖ **Principle Number Four: Prepare Witnesses for Objections**

Do not assume that witnesses understand how the question and answer of examination works. Do not assume they understand that cross-examination follows direct examination or that the direct examiner can engage in re-direct questioning. Do not assume that they understand the impact or meaning of objections. In fact, witnesses can become confused by objections. They may not even appreciate what "sustained" or "overruled" means. Advocates should explain to their witnesses that they should stop answering a question when an objection is made. And, they should encourage their witnesses to pause briefly before answering the opponent's question, both to momentarily reflect on how best to answer, and to give the advocate an opportunity to object.

❖ **Principle Number Five: Avoid Unnecessary Sidebar Conferences**

When an unanticipated evidentiary matter surfaces, it may be necessary to confer with the judge outside the jury's presence—a so-called "sidebar conference." Sidebar conferences should be requested sparingly. As discussed earlier, most complex evidentiary matters should be anticipated and dealt with pretrial or at a time when the jury is not present. Moreover, jurors tend to feel excluded during the sidebar and may even become suspicious of the motives of an advocate in requesting a sidebar conference. For the examiner, sidebar conferences constitute an unwelcome disruption of the examination and should be avoided if possible.

❖ **Principle Number Six: Do Not Address Opposing Counsel**

All communication in the courtroom should be directed to the judge, the witnesses, or the jurors. There is *no* occasion to address, or be addressed by, opposing counsel; all questions concerning the conduct of the trial are to be ultimately decided by the court, not the lawyers.

Occasionally, during the heat of trial—specifically in making and responding to objections—counsel may find himself in a heated exchange with his opponent. However, that exchange must be directed through the judge and not to opposing counsel. Do not turn and argue directly to opposing counsel.

❖ Principle Number Seven: Avoid Speaking or Standing Objections

Advocates should generally avoid argument on their objections unless invited by the court to do so. When objecting, the advocate should stand and simply state, "Objection, calls for hearsay." An extended argument about the evidence is a speaking or standing objection, and may well incur the wrath of the court because the argument is within the jury's hearing. If additional argument is necessary on the issue, the court will call for a recess or a sidebar.

 ### Illustration of a Standing Objection

Lawyer: What did Mr. Corkle say to you?

Opposing Lawyer: Objection, Your Honor, that question calls for the witness to offer hearsay testimony. The answer is offered for no reason other than its own truth. It does not fit within any recognized exception. It's the worst kind of hearsay—and I have no way to cross-examine the truthfulness of the statement.

Court: I'll sustain the objection, but admonish counsel to refrain from making any further standing objections.

Speaking objections arise out of the concern that the court will not understand the basis of the objection. If, indeed, there is a concern that the objection will not be immediately recognized by the court as proper, the objecting advocate is free to ask leave of the court to explain his objection, as follows:

Lawyer: Objection, hearsay.

[*No immediate ruling or response from the court.*]

Lawyer: Your Honor, may I be heard further?

Court: Proceed.

Lawyer: This question is seeking to . . . .

The lawyer is, in essence, inviting the court to ask him to explain or clarify the basis for the objection.

❖ Principle Number Eight: Concede Appropriate Objections

There are occasions when an examiner agrees with the opponent's objection. For example, the advocate may agree that the witness' lengthy answer has become a narrative, she may realize that she needs to lay a better foundation, or she may recognize that the question she asked was inadvertently leading. When the objection has merit, advocates should concede and offer to withdraw or rephrase the question.

If the objection is likely to be sustained anyway, advocates should attempt to gracefully extricate themselves from the situation and even turn the opportunity to their advantage. Such a reasonable response will be appreciated by the court and, more importantly, will be taken by jurors as demonstrating the advocate's desire to try the case within the rules and to be fair. On the other hand, fighting a losing battle may well demonstrate that counsel is a mere partisan who will oppose anything, and therefore, is less deserving of the jury's trust.

❖ Principle Number Nine: Avoid Being Overly Aggressive

Every aspect of an advocate's behavior during a jury trial is constantly evaluated and re-evaluated by jurors. Jurors may not appreciate interruptions caused by objections and especially disdain advocates whose objections are repeatedly overruled by the judge. Jurors will even tend to distrust advocates who *win* objections, unless the objectionable nature of the question or the evidence it seeks to elicit is clear to them. Advocates must be aware of how they are being perceived by the jury. If the jurors perceive an advocate as being overly "aggressive" in objecting, so that she appears to be attempting to obstruct the opposing side from presenting his case and thus preventing the jurors from hearing evidence, their perception of that advocate's credibility, as well as the integrity of the advocate's case, will be severely damaged.

Thus, advocates should be polite, even when objecting. Tone and style communicate to the jury an advocate's civility, and his respect for his opponent and the dignity of the proceedings. For example, let the opponent finish his question before making an objection, unless the question itself suggests hurtful and improper testimony and even then, the advocate should apologize for the interruption.

❖ Principle Number Ten: Limiting Instructions Cure Nothing

When evidence is admissible for one purpose, but not for another, a party may request that the court give the jury a limiting instruction. (*See, e.g.*, Fed. R. Evid. 105). For example, inadmissible hearsay evidence reasonably relied upon by an expert may be admissible to assist the jury in evaluating the expert's opinion, but it is not admissible to prove the truth of the hearsay statements. The party opposing the expert could request that the judge instruct the jury to consider the expert's inadmissible basis for his opinion for the nonhearsay purpose of explaining the expert's opinion.

Limiting instructions purport to cure the potential unfair prejudice that would result from the jurors' consideration of the evidence for the forbidden purpose. But as one Supreme Court justice so aptly put it, "The naive assumption that prejudicial effects can be overcome by instructions to the jury ... all practicing lawyers know to be unmitigated fiction."[1] And so, limiting instructions are, for the most part, unhelpful. They cure nothing. The jurors have heard the testimony and, despite a carefully worded admonition from the court that they may only consider testimony in a limited way, the jurors will use that evidence in any way that makes sense to them. In fact, the limiting instruction may actually work against the advocate who requests it by emphasizing the evidence again. An advocate who is successful in getting crucial evidence before the jury, albeit only for a "limited purpose," has won that battle.

IV.   OBJECTIONS

This list is not intended as comprehensive of all possible objections during witness testimony, but it does include the most frequently invoked objections. We have chosen to divide the objections into two categories: objections to inadmissible evidence and objections to the form of the question.

A.   Objections to Inadmissible Evidence

The substantive rules of evidence for a jurisdiction will determine the admissibility of testimonial evidence that the examiner's questions seek to elicit. It is beyond the scope of this book to consider the rules of evidence in depth, but the appropriate federal rules of evidence will be referenced. In addition to the objections listed below, the advocate must be mindful of pretrial rulings by the court, which limit the use of particular evidence in the instant case. Obviously, any questions that seek evidence that the court has ruled inadmissible should be objected to on those grounds.

1.   *Irrelevant; Unfairly Prejudicial*

An answer that does not logically, naturally, or by reasonable inference relate to an issue of fact or law in dispute tends to distract or misdirect the jury. (Fed. R. Evid. 401, 402). Relevancy objections frequently arise when the examiner is offering circumstantial evidence to prove or disprove a fact from which an inference can be drawn about a fact in dispute. Often the connection either between the circumstantial evidence and the inference to be drawn, or between the inference and the fact in dispute, is unclear. In objecting to such evidence, be wary of the examiner's promise that he will "link it up." That claim is a mere assertion that may not come to pass; and if the evidence is admitted, the jury has heard it whether it is later linked up or not. If there is a doubt that the evidence will be linked up, the proponent should be pressed for an offer of proof. The offer of proof should be given at sidebar, or otherwise outside the presence of the jury.

Additionally, even relevant evidence can be excluded if its probative value is substantially outweighed by the danger of unfair prejudice (Fed. R. Evid. 403), or if there are other policy considerations that have

---

[1]   *Krulewitch v. United States*, 336 U.S. 440, 453 (1949) (Jackson, J., concurring).

made particular types of evidence inadmissible. Included in that latter category is evidence of subsequent remedial measures (Fed. R. Evid. 407), settlement offers (Fed. R. Evid. 408), payment of medical or other expenses (Fed. R. Evid. 410), evidence of liability insurance (Fed. R. Evid. 411), and evidence of a rape victim's past sexual conduct (Fed. R. Evid. 412).

Illustration of Irrelevant Line of Questioning

[In the cross examination of the alleged victim in a rape case.]

Lawyer:	You drove to the nightclub that night, right?
Witness:	Yes.
Lawyer:	You went alone, didn't you?
Witness:	Yes.
Lawyer:	You didn't have a date?
Witness:	I went alone.
Lawyer:	You did anticipate dancing at the club, didn't you?
Witness:	Yes.
Lawyer:	So it was your intention to meet people at the club and dance with them?
Opposing Lawyer:	Objection. Irrelevant.
Court:	Sustained. Counsel, I am hard pressed to see how this bears on the issue of consent.

2. *Hearsay*

Hearsay is an out-of-court statement, made by someone other than the witness while testifying, that is offered to prove the truth of the matter asserted. (Fed. R. Evid. 801). Hearsay is excluded primarily because it cannot be tested by cross-examination, thus providing no opportunity to measure the declarant's sincerity, bias, perception, memory, or intent. (Fed. R. Evid. 802).

Of course, in responding to a hearsay objection, there are a vast range of exclusions and exceptions that must be considered. (Fed. R. Evid. 803-807). Generally, once a hearsay objection is made, it is incumbent on the proponent of the statement to establish either that the statement is not hearsay or that it comes within one of the exclusions or exceptions.

Illustration of Testimony Eliciting Hearsay

Lawyer: Officer Franklin, what did the victim tell you when you arrived at the scene of the rape?

Opposing Lawyer: Objection, hearsay.

Lawyer: Excited utterance, Your Honor.

Court: Lay a foundation, counsel.

Lawyer: Officer Franklin, how did the victim appear when you arrived?

Witness: She was crying and quite hysterical.

Lawyer: What did she tell you when you first arrived?

3. *Lacks Foundation*

Witnesses generally may not testify to matters about which they lack personal knowledge. (Fed. R. Evid. 602). A witness who is asked which car ran the red light should not be permitted to answer unless there is evidence (which can include that witness' own testimony) that she witnessed the event. Foundational deficiencies arise in a number of ways. For example, exhibits are not admissible unless a foundation has been laid establishing the authenticity of the evidence—that it is relevant to the case and is what it purports to be. In a breach of contract action, a copy of a contract cannot be admitted until a witness establishes that it is *the* contract between the parties. Although authenticity is required by the relevancy rules, many jurisdictions have specific evidentiary provisions concerning how the proper foundation establishing authenticity should be laid. (Fed. R. Evid. 901, 902).

Illustration of Foundational Concern

Lawyer: Who was the first person to arrive at the meeting?

Opposing Lawyer: Objection. Lacks foundation.

Court: Sustained.

Lawyer: Were you present when the first person arrived for the meeting?

Witness: Yes I was.

Lawyer: Did you see who was the first person to arrive at the meeting?

Witness:	Yes, I did.
Lawyer:	Who was it?

4.   *Calls for Speculation*

A question that invites a witness to speculate or guess is objectionable. Witnesses are to testify to facts and the jurors must decide whether to credit those facts. Witness testimony is limited to those matters about which the witness has personal knowledge. (Fed. R. Evid. 602). While even lay witnesses are permitted to testify to their opinions (Fed. R. Evid. 701), those opinions must be founded upon personal knowledge. It is improper to ask a witness to speculate or guess about matters concerning which the witness lacks personal knowledge.

Illustration of a Question that Calls for a Witness to Speculate[2]

Lawyer:	What would have caused Mr. McKyton to send an email accusing Lucas of adultery?
Opposing Lawyer:	Objection. Calls for speculation.
Court:	Sustained.

5.   *Impermissible Opinion Testimony*

Conclusions and opinions are the end result of reasoning that flows from a fact or series of facts. It is generally the role of lay witnesses to relate the facts and jurors are left to draw their own conclusions and opinions based on those facts. Thus, questions that invite lay witnesses to offer conclusions or opinions may be generally objectionable. (Fed. R. Evid. 701, . . .701). With that said, there are significant exceptions to this rule. A lay witness is permitted to testify and give his opinion about inferences and deductions drawn from facts when it will assist the jury in interpreting the facts and the opinion is rationally based on the perception of the witness. For instance, it would be proper to ask a lay witness, "Did he seem disoriented?" It is within the common experience to draw such a conclusion and it would be helpful to the jury. (Fed. R. Evid. 701, 702).

---

[2] This illustration is based on the hypothetical case *Reiter v. McKyton*, Judge Jerry, R. Parker (Texas Young Lawyers Association).

Illustration of Impermissible Lay Opinion Testimony

Lawyer: Did the defendant appear to be in his right mind?

Opposing Lawyer: Objection. Calls for opinion.

Court: Sustained.

Lawyer: Did the defendant appear disoriented?

Witness: Yes, he did.

Lawyer: How?

The other primary exception permitting opinion testimony concerns expert witnesses. As described in Chapter Ten, there has been a vast expansion of the use of expert witnesses under the Federal Rules of Evidence. The extensive use of experts is due in large part because they can give opinions and conclusions about the events at issue based on their expertise in a specific area of endeavor and their specific knowledge of the facts of the case. It is incumbent on opposing counsel to be vigilant as to the specific opinions and conclusions offered by an expert. It is not uncommon for an expert to venture beyond the limited confines of her expertise.

Illustration of Impermissible Expert Witness Testimony

[*The witness' specific area of expertise is limited to automobile rollovers.*]

Lawyer: Mr. Jarvis, now that we've heard the reasons for your conclusion as to the design defect that led to the car's rollover, let's turn to the adequacy of the seatbelts in that model car to avoid further injury. Do you have an opinion concerning the seatbelts in the model car in which the plaintiff was injured?

Opposing Lawyer: Beyond the scope of this witness' expertise.

Court: You may be heard further.

Opposing Lawyer: Judge, this man's a design engineer specializing in vehicle stability. For him to be able to venture into the adequacy of seatbelts is well outside his expertise.

Court: Sustained.

6. *Best Evidence*

The "best evidence" of any writing is the original document. By producing the original document there is assurance that the contents have not been altered. This objection applies to writings, recordings, or photographs and only when a party seeks to prove the contents of the writing, recording, or photograph itself. (Fed. R. Evid. 1001-1007). Duplicates of the original are admissible to the same extent as the original except under limited circumstances pursuant to Rule 1003 of the Federal Rules.

To discourage the destruction of original evidence by a party who wishes to avoid its admission, the opposing side may produce other evidence of the writing if the original is unavailable through no fault of her own. (Fed. R. Evid. 1004).

An advocate who is facing a best evidence objection may argue that the original is unavailable through no fault of his client, or that the terms of the writing are not in dispute or are only collateral to the issues in the case. Moreover, it could be argued that the offered evidence comes within one of the exceptions to the rule, such as a summary of voluminous writings or a duplicate. (Fed. R. Evid. 1003, 1006).

 Illustration of Best Evidence Concern

Lawyer: What did the contract specify as the date of completion?

Opposing Lawyer: Objection. Not the best evidence.

Court: Sustained.

7. *Privileged*

A communication made in confidence between people in certain relationships may be privileged. These relationships include: attorney-client, doctor-patient, psychotherapist-patient, husband-wife, and priest-penitent. Confidential communications between the parties in these relationships are protected in order to encourage frank and open communication. The privilege is lost if the objection is not made. The existence and scope of these privileges vary from jurisdiction to jurisdiction. Whether the matter discussed is subject to a privilege, whether a waiver has occurred, and who may assert the privilege are issues of substantive law that must be thoroughly researched.

 Illustration of a Question Invoking Privilege

[*Cross examination of a priest called as a defense witness in a criminal case.*]

Lawyer: You talked to the defendant that very night he was arrested, isn't that right?

Witness: That's right.

Lawyer: In fact, you and the defendant talked about the murder of Nicole, correct?

Opposing Lawyer: Objection, Your Honor. Any statement, if made, is privileged within the priest-penitent privilege.

8.   *Cumulative*

Rule 403 of the Federal Rules of Evidence excludes not only evidence that is unfairly prejudicial to a party, but also evidence that is cumulative of other evidence already before the jury or evidence that would constitute a waste of time. (Fed. R. Evid. 403). Though parties may present multiple witnesses who all testify to the same point, the judge may limit the extent of duplication, and the same witness may not testify to the same fact multiple times. Thus, anytime a witness says, "As I said before …" the answer that follows is almost certainly cumulative. And when the opponent presents five witnesses to testify to the defendant's good character, the prosecutor might well appeal to the judge's concern for unnecessary duplication.

Illustration of Objection for Cumulative Evidence

Lawyer: Now that we understand the reasons for your opinions in the case, I'd like for you to step down to the board and list them out for the jury. Your Honor, may the witness step down?

Opposing Lawyer: Objection, Your Honor. This is cumulative.

Court: Sustained.

9.   *Impermissible Character Evidence*

With limited exceptions, character evidence is not admissible to prove that a person acted in conformity with a particular trait of character. (Fed. R. Evid. 404). Thus, questions that seek information concerning the type of person a party is, or particular patterns of conduct a party has engaged in, should alert the advocate to the possibility that she should object based on the ground that the question seeks impermissible character evidence.

Illustration of a Question Eliciting Impermissible Character Evidence

Lawyer: Ms. Blue, isn't it a fact that the defendant is known in the community to be a violent person?

Opposing Lawyer: Objection. Impermissible character evidence.

Court: Sustained.

However, the character evidence rules do permit the use of specific instances of prior conduct, including crimes or other wrongful acts, for a purpose other than to show a person's character and that he acted in conformity with that character. These proper purposes can include proof of motive, opportunity, intent, preparation, plan, knowledge, identity, or absence of mistake or accident. (Fed. R. Evid. 404(b)).

 Illustration of a Question Eliciting Evidence of a Prior Act to Show Motive

[In a criminal case in which the defendant is accused of embezzling funds from her employer]

Lawyer: You enjoy visiting Las Vegas on a regular basis, don't you, Ms. Horn?

Witness: I do enjoy it, yes.

Lawyer: In fact, you gamble quite a bit while you are there, don't you?

Witness: I gamble some.

Lawyer: In June of 2001, you had accumulated gambling debts totaling over $20,000, hadn't you?

Opposing Lawyer: Objection. Irrelevant and impermissible character evidence.

Lawyer: Goes to motive, Your Honor.

Judge: Overruled.

The advocate must be mindful of the requirement in the federal rules, and in many state jurisdictions, that the prosecutor is required in criminal cases to provide a "reasonable notice" in advance of trial of its intent to use non-propensity evidence under Rule 404(b) at trial and of the general nature of the type of evidence that will be offered. This provides the defense attorney with an opportunity to move *in limine* to exclude the evidence and to reconsider whether to have the defendant testify if the evidence will be admitted.

10. *Beyond the Scope*

Cross-examination is generally limited in federal court to the subject matters covered during direct examination and any matters affecting credibility. (Fed. R. Evid. 611). The reason for this restriction is to maintain the focus on the case-in-chief of the party calling the witness. To permit the cross-examiner to examine the witness beyond the subject matter of direct would permit the cross-examiner to interrupt his opponent's case with evidence that is presumably more favorable to the cross-examiner's case. In the event the cross-examiner desires to question about subject matter beyond what was covered during direct, he will have to call the witness himself to make such inquiry. (The exception being the defendant in a criminal case.) The re-direct examination cannot go beyond the scope of the cross-examination, re-cross cannot go beyond the scope of the re-direct, and so on. The only exception to this restriction is that matters pertaining to witness credibility are not subject to scope objections. Credibility is always at issue.

Illustration of a Question that Asks the Witness to Go Beyond the Scope of the Previous Examination

[In a case where the direct examination was limited to the color of the traffic light at the time of the accident.]

Lawyer: Isn't it true that the plaintiff's car had bald tires?

Opposing Lawyer: Objection. Beyond the scope of direct.

Court: Sustained.

11. *Improper Impeachment*

Impeachment of a witness can take many forms. It can be undertaken by showing a witness' bias or prejudice, that he made a prior inconsistent statement, that he lacked the ability to observe or recall, that he suffered a prior conviction, or even that he has a poor character for honesty or veracity.

However, there are a number of limitations concerning impeachment. For instance, the court has discretion to exclude collateral evidence if its probative value is substantially outweighed by the danger of unfair prejudice. (Fed. R. Evid. 403). Likewise, if a prior conviction does not fit within the confines of the pertinent evidentiary rule it cannot be used. (Fed. R. Evid. 609).

In attempting to impeach a witness with a prior inconsistent statement, the impeaching statement (the prior statement) must differ from the witness' testimony. Any material variance between the testimony and the prior statement is sufficient to constitute grounds for impeachment.

While the rules are generally permissive in allowing evidence to be used to impeach the credibility of witnesses, some types of evidence cannot properly be used to impeach. In particular, rules of evidence restrict the use of prior criminal convictions (Fed. R. Evid. 609), specific past instances of conduct (Fed. R. Evid. 608), and evidence of religious beliefs or lack thereof (Fed. R. Evid. 610) for the purpose of impeaching a witness.

Illustration of a Question that Seeks to Improperly Impeach

Lawyer: Isn't it a fact that twenty years ago you sustained a juvenile conviction for shoplifting?

Opposing Lawyer: Objection. Impermissible impeachment evidence.

Court: Sustained.

B. Objections to the Form of the Question

The second group of objections we discuss are objections to the way the question is framed rather than objections to the evidence that the question seeks to elicit. To a lesser degree, the rules of evidence limit the form of the question. Most of these objections, however, are grounded in common sense.

1. *Leading*

During direct examination witnesses must be allowed to "speak" directly to the jury. The advocate is not the source of the information, but rather, the facilitator. A lawyer who interferes with this direct communication—witness to juror—is interrupting the most significant aspect of trial. The witness must be allowed to tell what he knows about the events that are relevant to the dispute. It is the witness who is testifying, not the lawyer. And an advocate who suggests to the witness the answer he wants, or expects to hear, is leading the witness.

A common misconception is that a question that calls for a yes or no answer is leading. That is not necessarily so. To ask, "Did you go out to dinner the night of the accident?" calls for a yes or no answer, but suggests neither answer is more appropriate than the other. It is not a leading question. However to ask, "You went out to dinner the night of the accident, didn't you?" is considered leading because the phrasing of the question suggests the answer.

 Illustration of a Leading Question

Lawyer: At the time of the accident you were driving at no more than 35 miles per hour, correct?

Opposing Lawyer: Objection. Leading.

Court: Sustained.

Another common misconception is that leading questions are always prohibited during direct examination. They are not. For example, Rule 611(c) the Federal Rules of Evidence expressly permits leading questions on direct examination in certain circumstances when necessary to assist the witness in developing her testimony. In particular, the very young and the very old, the very timid and the very forgetful, all may have difficulty testifying, but their testimony still must be heard. Further, when laying foundations or making transitions during direct examination advocates are allowed to lead.

Illustration of Leading a Witness While Laying a Foundation

Lawyer:	You are the custodian of the business records of Acme Equipment Supply, aren't you?
Witness:	Yes, I am.
Lawyer:	And you have been in that position for the past ten years?
Witness:	Yes.
Lawyer:	Referring to what's been marked as Plaintiff's Two for identification, these records are kept in the regular course of business, aren't they?
Witness:	Yes.
Lawyer:	They are not just kept for purposes of litigation?
Witness:	No, they are not.
Lawyer:	At this time, Your Honor, I move Plaintiff's Two into evidence.

2. *Argumentative*

An argumentative question—one which badgers the witness—states a proposition in the form of a question, and tries to convince the witness to change his mind and agree with the proposition. In fact, the lawyer is really arguing his point to the jury rather than seeking information from the witness. The objection is most often made in response to questions propounded on cross-examination.

Illustration of an Argumentative Question

Lawyer:	Your explanation of why you pursued Mr. Jacobi rather than assisting Ms. Hanson really doesn't make sense, does it?
Opposing Lawyer:	Objection. Argumentative.
Court:	Sustained.

3. *Calls for a Narrative*

It is often difficult to ascertain that a particular question calls for the witness to narrate. However, it is fairly easy to recognize when an answer has become narrative. Consequently, an objection that "the answer calls for a narrative" is less apt to be successful than an objection that the witness is giving a narrative answer.

Narrative testimony occurs when a witness relays testimony beyond what was specifically sought in the question. The "answer" has essentially eschewed the question-and-answer format in favor of just telling what happened. A narrative answer may contain inadmissible testimony that can slip in before an objection can be made. In constraining the witness to stay within the confines of the question-and-answer format, objectionable testimony is more easily recognized and a timely objection is more feasible.

Illustration of a Question that Calls for a Narrative Response

Lawyer: Please describe the events that happened at your place of employment from the time you arrived on June 23.

Opposing Lawyer: Objection. Calls for a narrative.

Court: Sustained.

4. *Nonresponsive Answer*

A response that goes beyond the call of the question is objectionable. The purpose of this objection is to stop a witness from "taking off" on a question, and perhaps blurting out inadmissible testimony. There are typically two scenarios when this may occur. First is with the eager witness who is attempting to be helpful. The question may call for a short response; however the witness, attempting to be helpful, goes beyond the called-for response and, in fact, becomes nonresponsive. Opposing counsel should limit such responses because the extended response may contain objectionable testimony and, as discussed under narrative answers, such a response often times is more compelling than the give and take of questions and answers.

The second scenario in which an examiner is likely to be confronted with nonresponsive answers is on cross-examination. Even though the question is leading and clearly calls for a simple "yes" or "no," the hostile witness may launch into a nonresponsive, qualifying answer. Here the examiner, rather than opposing counsel, may object to the excess portion of the answer and move to have it stricken. However, as suggested in Chapter Eight, Cross-Examination, the wiser course may be to ask the question again, emphasizing that the question calls for a "yes" or "no." This latter approach may be preferable, in that it puts the damaging question before the jury again. Moreover, in not responding appropriately to the question, the jurors may well begin to question the sincerity—if not the integrity—of the witness.

Illustration of a Nonresponsive Answer

Lawyer: So, you did not actually see my client, Mike Jones, hit Sam Smith, did you?

Witness: Well, Mike told me he was going to beat the stuffing out of Sam.

Opposing Lawyer: Objection. Nonresponsive. Move to strike.

Court: Sustained.

5. *Compound*

Asking two or more questions within the framework of a single question may confuse the witness and also the jury. For instance, an examiner may ask, "Does Smith Industries, or did Smith Industries, at the time of the injury, produce widgets that your company was likely to purchase?" By answering "no" is the witness responding to all questions or only one? The witness may feel compelled to answer, and that answer, even though unclear, is now in evidence and can be considered by the jury. This question is fraught with problems. The verb tense shift at the outset confirms that at least two questions are being asked. However, it is easy to see how the examiner made the error. He began in the present tense and then attempted to correct himself by shifting to the past tense. Unfortunately, he did not simply begin the question anew after his initial error.

Illustration of a Compound Question

Lawyer: Did you report the incident to your employer, or was there some reason why you might have felt it was not wise to do so?

Opposing Lawyer: Objection. Compound.

Court: Sustained.

6. *Misstates the Evidence*

A question that misstates facts already in evidence is confusing to jurors, and to the witness, and can lead to mistaken conclusions. Any question misstating evidence that has already been presented must draw an objection, and the record must be clarified to cure any misimpressions.

Illustration of a Question that Misstates the Evidence

[Where the witness has testified that the blue car entered the intersection first.]

Lawyer: After the light changed and the green car entered the intersection, which car was second to enter the intersection?

Opposing Lawyer: Objection. Misstates the evidence.

Court: How so, counsel?

Opposing Lawyer: It has not been established by any testimony that the green car entered the intersection after the light changed.

Court: I'll sustain the objection.

7. *Assumes Facts Not in Evidence*

A question that includes a material fact that is in dispute is objectionable because the jury may incorrectly believe the disputed fact is true, and the jury may believe the witness implicitly agrees that the fact in dispute is true. Questions that begin "Would it surprise you if I told you," or "Did you know," generally assume facts not in evidence. This objectionable question frequently arises when a hypothetical question is asked. Generally, hypothetical questions—other than those addressed to expert witnesses—can include all material facts in evidence, but not facts that are not in evidence.

If the opponent attempts to introduce facts not in evidence in his examination, it is important to object forcefully, and make certain the jury understands that the fact(s) in the questions are not conceded as true.

Questions that assume facts are only permissible when they are used to impeach a witness' credibility or when used to question an expert witness.

Illustration of a Question that Assumes Facts Not in Evidence

[Where there has been no testimony as to the speed of the cars involved in an accident.]

Lawyer: From where you stood you were clearly able to see the defendant's car speed into the intersection, weren't you?

Opposing Lawyer: Objection. Assumes facts not in evidence.

8. *Asked and Answered*

As discussed in Chapter One, the principle of frequency stands for the proposition that jurors are more likely to remember that which is repeated. During witness examinations, advocates occasionally may seek essentially the same information a second or even a third time to help define and reinforce that testimony. While such a tactic may constitute effective advocacy, it is objectionable not only because it places undue emphasis on that particular question and answer, but also because repeating the question and answer consumes undue court time.

While judges have considerable discretion over how much examination to permit on a given subject, most judges will sustain objections made on the ground that counsel is merely re-hashing testimony previously given. Judges have the power to limit repetitive questioning to avoid needless consumption of time and witness harassment. (Fed. R. Evid. 403 & 611).

Illustration of an Asked and Answered Question

Lawyer: All right, Mrs. Brown, just to clarify, would you please recount again for the jury what you saw when you got out of your car?

Opposing Lawyer: Objection. Asked and answered.

Court: Sustained.

9. *Unintelligible, Vague, or Confusing*

At times, even an experienced trial attorney will ask a question that is so poorly phrased it cannot be understood or is likely to be misunderstood. It would be unfair to require the witness to answer such a question and any attempt to do so is likely to create confusion among the jurors. Those questions must be objected to, and the judge is likely to direct the propounding attorney to rephrase the question.

Illustration of an Unintelligible Question

Lawyer: Did you ever see the assailant, either before or after the attack, so that your identification of him might have been confusing him with another event that had nothing to do with the attack but might just have been something you recalled from some other opportunity to view him?

Opposing Lawyer: Objection. Unintelligible.

Court: Sustained.

Chapter Ten

EXPERT WITNESSES

I. OVERVIEW: THE UNIQUE ROLE OF EXPERTS

Expert witnesses play an increasingly prominent role in modern litigation. Most cases tried today include testimony from multiple expert witnesses. In fact, a study of civil trials has demonstrated that the "battle of the experts"—experts retained by opposing parties on the same issue—is commonplace, occurring in more than half of all cases tried in the state studied.[1] The ability to conduct an effective examination of an expert witness is a basic skill that every trial lawyer must master.

The popularity of expert witnesses results in part from the many testimonial advantages that they enjoy. Unlike fact witnesses, who are generally limited to testifying to what they saw or heard, experts can offer their opinions about what happened and who was responsible, even though the expert usually has no personal knowledge of the events. In that way, experts create evidence in the form of their opinions about the disputed issues, and parties use that newly created evidence when establishing their claims and defenses. Experts are not only unburdened by the rules requiring a witness' personal knowledge (Fed. R. Evid. 602) and the rule limiting the admissibility of opinion evidence (Fed. R. Evid. 701), but they are also allowed to rely on inadmissible evidence, including hearsay, in forming their opinions (Fed. R. Evid. 703). They are also allowed to offer opinions that encompass the ultimate issue in the case. (Fed. R. Evid. 704(a)). These testimonial perks enjoyed by experts help explain, at least in part, why they are such desirable witnesses.

Experts are employed by lawyers not merely for an advantage, but out of necessity, in light of the substantive legal requirements of some claims. For example, in professional negligence cases—such as medical or legal malpractice or a products liability case—expert testimony may be required to establish liability. In most medical malpractice lawsuits, for example, courts require that a properly qualified medical doctor testify to establish the standard of care that governed the defendant's conduct and to determine whether the defendant satisfied that standard. In other cases, expert testimony may not be required by the substantive law, but may be perceived as helpful to a party's claim or defense, such as testimony by an accident reconstruction expert in a personal injury suit arising out of a car accident.

But testimonial advantages and legal necessity are not the only reasons experts are so frequently employed. The sad reality is many lawyers retain experts because of the control lawyers are sometimes able to exercise over experts and what they say on the witness stand or write in an expert report. Experts differ from lay witnesses not only in that they testify in the form of opinions, but also in that they are paid for their services. The prospect of payment can serve as a corrupting influence, causing the lawyer to expect the expert to become a member of the trial team and deliver testimony necessary to prove the client's claim.

This corrupting influence of money is perhaps greatest when experts are professional expert witnesses and receive all—or substantially all—of their income from testifying in depositions and at trials. Such experts are motivated to meet the expectations of their clients and their lawyer-employers because of their need for repeat business. They become "insiders," capable of manipulating the system because of their integral understanding

---

[1] *See* Samuel R. Gross and Kent D. Syverud, *Don't Try: Civil Jury Verdicts in a System Geared to Settlement*, 44 UCLA L. REV. 1, 33 (1996).

of how the system works. All of this serves to make the lawyer's task, when retaining or dealing with experts, quite complicated. Lawyers must take care to resist the temptation to misuse expert witnesses or exert undue control over their opinions.

Rather than treating experts and their opinions as commodities available for purchase, lawyers should view experts as helpful, and sometimes even critical, repositories of information, who can serve an important role in the adversary system. At their best, experts bring clarity to difficult and confusing topics and assist jurors in bridging the gap between what the facts are in a case and what those facts mean.

II.   A PRIMER ON THE EVIDENTIARY REQUIREMENTS FOR EXPERT WITNESS TESTIMONY

The very notion of "expert testimony" suggests something specialized and beyond the understanding of lay witnesses. And yet, everyone is an expert, or at least it seems that way. "Experts" are everywhere, from the ubiquitous day-time talk show to the nightly news, and they opine on everything, from bioterrorism risks to gardening techniques to fashion pitfalls. The courtroom is not all that different. Experts are commonplace today and their testimony runs the gamut of topics. The Federal Rules of Evidence, Rules 702-706, regulate the admission of testimony by experts at trial. The Rules provide the answers to the following questions:

- Who is an expert?

- What can an expert say?

- What can an expert rely on in forming opinions?

- When can experts give their opinions?

A.   Who is an Expert?

The Federal Rules give a generous definition to the term "expert," including anyone who through "knowledge, skill, experience, training, or education" has acquired "scientific, technical, or other specialized knowledge." (Fed. R. Evid. 702). Any of the listed means of acquiring expertise, whether "skill" or "education" or "knowledge," is sufficient under the Rule. Thus, an auto mechanic could qualify as an expert on the parts and operation of automobile transmissions solely based on his special "skill," while an individual with a Ph.D. in engineering would qualify as an expert based on nothing more than her "education." The advisory committee's note to Rule 702 specifically provides that "skilled witnesses," such as bankers and landowners, qualify as experts under the rule. Rule 702's generous definition of "expert" has caused one commentator to suggest, "Almost everyone qualifies as an expert in one field or another."[2]

---

[2] Michael H. Graham, *Expert Witness Testimony and the Federal Rules of Evidence: Insuring Adequate Assurance of Trustworthiness*, 1986 U. ILL. L. REV. 43, 73.

That is not to say that there are no limits, of course. Experts are limited in their testimony to their particular areas of expertise and must not venture into other areas in which they have no skill, training, education, or experience. For example, doctors must limit their testimony to medical matters, not economics, and economists must limit themselves to opinions relating to economics, not medicine.

B.   What Can an Expert Say?

Once qualified, experts are free to testify to their opinions, provided that those opinions are:

(1) helpful to the jury,

(2) based on reliable theories or techniques,

(3) supported by sufficient underlying facts or data, and

(4) relevant to the issues in dispute.

In December of 2000, Rule 702 of the Federal Rules of Evidence was amended to specifically require that expert witness testimony must be not only relevant, but also reliable. The addition of an explicit reliability requirement in Rule 702 followed on the heels of two decisions by the United States Supreme Court, *Daubert v. Merrill Dow Pharmaceuticals, Inc.,*[3] and *Kumho Tire Company v. Carmichael,*[4] both of which interpreted the original Rule 702 as including such a requirement. One must understand the contours of these two opinions to fully appreciate the meaning of the amended Rule 702 and to apply the new rule to actual expert testimony.

1.   Daubert, Kumho Tire, *and Evidentiary Reliability*

When *Daubert* was decided by the Supreme Court in 1993, lower federal courts were split over the standard for admitting expert testimony based on scientific principles or theories. Most federal courts applied the so-called *Frye* "general acceptance test" to such testimony, while a minority of courts applied a more liberal relevance test. The *Frye* test was taken from a 1923 decision by the District of Columbia Court of Appeals, in which the court held that an expert's testimony about a crude precursor to the polygraph machine was not admissible because the expert's underlying theory had not yet gained general acceptance in the pertinent scientific field or discipline.[5]

Other courts used a "relevance test" that asked about the reliability and relevance of the theories relied upon by the expert. Under this test,

---

[3]   509 U.S. 579 (1993).

[4]   526 U.S. 137 (1999).

[5]   *See Frye v. United States*, 293 F. 1013, 1014 (D.C. Cir. 1923).

the fact that a theory had not yet gained "general acceptance" was not fatal to its admission, provided it was otherwise shown to be relevant and reliable.[6]

In *Daubert* the Court concluded that the language of Rule 702 did not point to the drafters' adoption of the *Frye* general acceptance test. Instead, the Court found that Rule 702 required that experts have "good grounds" for their opinions. In other words, the theories and techniques experts use to reach their opinions must be "scientifically valid." The Court identified five factors (the "*Daubert* factors") as a guide for courts in determining reliability:

1. whether the theory or technique has been or can be tested;

2. whether the theory or technique has been subjected to peer review and/or publication;

3. the error rate, if any, for the theory or technique;

4. whether there are standards maintained for the application of the theory or technique; and

5. whether the theory or technique has been generally accepted by experts in the pertinent field.

The Court also held that expert opinions under Rule 702 must be relevant, meaning that the opinions must "fit" the issues in dispute.

Subsequently, the Supreme Court decided *Kumho Tire Company v. Carmichael*[7] in an attempt to resolve lingering controversy about the scope of *Daubert*. *Kumho Tire*, which involved expert testimony by a tire failure analyst—an admittedly nonscientific area of expertise—addressed the question of whether the *Daubert* factors and the requirement of reliability applied to all experts or only those using scientific theories or techniques. The Court concluded that Rule 702 did not distinguish between "scientific" expert testimony and other types of expert testimony, and that the reliability requirement applied to all experts. The Court recognized that the factors laid out in *Daubert* would have only limited application for some nonscientific experts and stressed that the court's analysis under Rule 702 must be flexible, taking into account the nature of the expert testimony involved and the issues to which the opinion relates. Not all jurisdictions have followed the Supreme Court's lead, and instead have continued to follow the general acceptance test under *Frye*.

2. *Reliability Under Rule 702*

The amendment to Federal Rule 702 requires that every expert who testifies at trial, from the plumber to the doctor to the vocational

---

[6] *See, e.g., United States v. Downing*, 753 F.2d 1224, 1233 (3d Cir. 1992).

[7] 526 U.S. 137 (1999).

rehabilitation expert, must give testimony that "is the product of reliable principles and methods." That means that experts must do more than simply tell the jury, in essence, "trust me." Experts must demonstrate that their opinions are based on some identifiable methodology, that the methodology used is sufficient to ensure a valid outcome, and that the methodology was reliably applied in the instant case. The standard applies to scientific and nonscientific testimony alike, to testimony based largely on the expert's experience in the field, and to testimony based on precise and verifiable scientific tests.

In addition to demonstrating the reliability of the principles and methods used to form their opinions, experts must also show that they have "applied the principles and methods reliably to the facts of the case." (Fed. R. Evid. 702). This requirement recognizes that the expert's "conclusions and methodology are not entirely distinct from one another" and that experts must carefully and appropriately use and apply the principles and methods at their disposal. Thus, an expert who uses generally accepted methods, but reaches an opinion that others in the field would not reach, is subject to strict review from the trial court. (Fed. R. Evid. 702, advisory committee's note to 2000 amendment to Rule 702). The burden on trial lawyers in this strange new world is to educate experts about the reliability requirement, to help experts think through the approach they use to reach conclusions in such cases, and to help ensure that the expert applies its methodology in a consistent and reliable way to the case facts.

3.   *Opinions on the Ultimate Issue*

The rules also address the very practical question of how far experts can go in stating their opinions. Can an expert express an opinion in terms of the ultimate issue in the case? For example, in a product liability case, the plaintiff's design engineer might opine, "In my opinion, Joe Smith's car was defectively designed by defendant Acme Corporation." Is that acceptable? The common law rule was that expert opinions could not embrace the ultimate issue in the case because such opinions invaded the jury's province. The drafters of the Federal Rules of Evidence, however, recognized that such opinions were still subject to rejection by the jury, and thus, do not in fact invade the jury's province. Accordingly, Rule 704 abandoned the common law approach, with one exception. That exception, set forth in Rule 704(b), applies to experts testifying to the mental state or condition of criminal defendants. All experts are precluded from testifying that a defendant in a criminal case did or did not have the mental state constituting an element of a crime. Thus an expert could not testify that a defendant premeditated before committing a crime or that the defendant was insane at the time of the commission of a crime.

The liberalization of the rule simply means that there is no longer an objection for "goes to the ultimate issue, Your Honor." However, opinions that embrace the ultimate issue may be objectionable for other reasons. For instance, an opinion that the defendant was "negligent" may constitute an improper legal opinion or be inadmissible under Rule 403 as unduly prejudicial. Some jurisdictions permit experts to offer opinions using legal terms or causes of action provided that the expert is relying on a correct legal definition. Other jurisdictions require that opinions be offered in non-legal terms (*i.e.*, "unreasonable" in place of "negligent").

As a practical matter, Rule 704 means that you may be entitled to offer expert opinions using legal jargon, but you should probably avoid doing so. Juries are less likely to understand the meaning of the term negligence than the term unreasonable, less likely to fully appreciate defective than unsafe or dangerous. The opinions come at a dramatic point in the direct of every expert. To take full advantage of the opportunity, the expert should express the opinion in plain English and without unnecessary verbiage.

C.   What Can an Expert Rely on in Forming Opinions?

Opinion testimony from experts, by its very nature, is based on assumptions and supporting premises. Some commentators have analogized expert testimony to syllogistic reasoning in which there are one or more major premises, one or more minor premises, and a conclusion. Opinions must be based on something, and in the case of experts, that something must be sufficient to support the expert's opinion. For example, an expert's opinion about the cause of an accident based upon astrology would be rejected. Astrology is an inadequate basis for accident reconstruction. On the other hand, if the opinion was based upon careful measurements taken at the scene, inspection of the damage to the cars, review of pertinent reports and depositions, calculation of the relevant speeds of the cars and angles of the impact, and so forth—all done by a person experienced or trained in the field—it would undoubtedly be a sufficient basis for the opinion. The adequacy of the basis is significant, because under the amendment to Rule 702, it is a requirement for admission of the opinion itself. If the expert has an insufficient basis, then the expert's opinion should be excluded.

At the same time, however, Rule 703 authorizes experts, in forming their opinions, to rely on information they know or information they are told, including inadmissible evidence. The rule provides: "If of a type reasonably relied upon by experts in the field in forming opinions or inferences upon the subject, the facts or data need not be admissible in evidence . . . ." (Fed. R. Evid. 703). Thus, experts can rely on hearsay or other inadmissible evidence provided that it is reasonable in the expert's field to do so. Notice that the standard is not that reliance is "customary." It is not enough that everyone in the expert's field relies on the data in forming such opinions, but instead it must be shown that reliance under the circumstances is reasonable. At the very least, the standard requires the expert to testify that his reliance on inadmissible hearsay is reasonable under the circumstances.

If experts can rely on inadmissible evidence, can they disclose that evidence to the jury? The answer is "it depends." In an attempt to correct perceived abuses under the former rule, the 2000 amendment to Rule 703 severely restricts the admission of inadmissible facts or data relied on by experts. In fact, such facts or data may be disclosed only if "the court determines that their probative value in assisting the jury to evaluate the expert's opinion substantially outweighs their prejudicial effect." Thus, the rule creates a presumption of exclusion. Moreover, if the facts or data *are* deemed admissible, they are subject to a limiting instruction that they "must not be used for substantive purposes." (Fed. R. Evid. 703, advisory committee's note).

Neither the Rule nor the advisory committee's note provides much guidance on how courts should decide whether the expert may disclose such facts or data. The advisory committee does suggest that the court should consider the likely effectiveness of a limiting instruction under the circumstances. To the extent a limiting instruction would be ineffective, there is a greater likelihood of prejudice from the admission of the facts or data. The court may also consider whether the expert is being used as a mere conduit for hearsay or whether the expert legitimately needed to rely on the inadmissible evidence to form an opinion. The nature of the underlying facts relied upon by the expert may be important as well. If the facts or data go to a hotly contested issue or are inherently prejudicial, the court may refuse admission. Finally, if the party appears to be using Rule 703 as a means to avoid cross-examination of the evidence and in fact could call a witness who has personal knowledge of the underlying information, the court may well consider the prejudice to the opposing party too great to allow admission.

D.   When Can Experts Give Their Opinions?

The last aspect of expert witness testimony is the question of timing. When can an expert offer his expert opinion? Rule 705 provides that counsel may elicit the expert's opinion without "first testifying to the underlying facts or data." (Fed. R. Evid. 705). That means that once an expert is qualified as such, counsel is free to begin asking the expert about his opinions. No explanation of how the expert arrived at the opinion or what the expert did to reach the opinion is required. It does not mean, however, that the court might not require the disclosure of such information (outside the jury's presence) to determine the admissibility of the expert's opinion or for other reasons. It also does not mean that the opponent cannot question the expert about his underlying basis during cross-examination. He can; but the advocate has the right to choose the order of presentation.

Some commentators advise lawyers to take advantage of Rule 705 by eliciting the expert opinions as early as possible in the direct, and only after the opinions are disclosed to spend some time explaining the basis of and reasons for the opinions. The advantage to this approach is that the jury hears the opinions closer to the beginning of the testimony (when they are more attentive) and then receives the explanations (which tend to be less interesting). Despite the invitation of Rule 705 (and the advice of commentators who espouse this approach), we do not believe that early disclosure of the opinions is the best course for the direct examination of experts. To the contrary, we believe that the jury needs to know of the expert's preparation—the tests he performed, the documents he reviewed, the calculations he made—before it hears the opinions. The basis material builds the expert's credibility and prepares the jury for the opinion, so that when it comes it is expected and, more importantly, it is credible.

E.   Prepare Your Expert Well Before Trial Begins

An area that should not be overlooked when using experts is witness preparation. Just like any other witness, it is vital that advocates work with their expert witnesses before trial. The advocate should explain the trial process to the expert, and the expert should explain her conclusions to the advocate. The last thing an advocate wants is an optional witness harming his client's case when it could have been avoided by a little preparation.

Firstly, the advocate must make sure the expert understands the legal elements that must be proven at trial in order to win the case; then, the advocate should explain how the expert's testimony will support that effort. That is not to say that the advocate should in any way try to influence the expert's findings. He simply must take the expert's findings as they are, and show the expert how he will use those findings to support his client's position.

Secondly, advocates should inform their experts of any legal language that may be required by the Rules of Evidence or used as key terms in jury instructions, and ask the experts to use it. For example, it is more effective for an expert to testify that, "Mr. Yakishito clearly fell below the required standard of care when performing Mr. Ying's heart transplant;" rather than "Mr. Yakishito didn't do his job correctly, in my opinion."

Lastly, advocates should make sure they explain the standard of proof necessary to win the case at hand. Experts can often be reluctant to confirm statements like "always," "no doubt," and "permanently;" they can get caught up in the idea that nothing is certain. Remind them, they are not proving that X happened beyond "any" doubt, simply that X happened beyond a "reasonable" doubt.

III.   The Structure and Content of the Direct Examination of Experts

A.   The Challenges and Opportunities of Experts

Expert witnesses present special challenges for advocates on direct examination, both because of their specialized knowledge and their status as paid witnesses. The "expertise" of experts requires substantial preparation by the advocate. The advocate must become sufficiently acquainted with the expert's field, at least as it applies to the specific testimony the expert will present in the case, so that the advocate can identify the logical and necessary areas of inquiry and can simplify the material so that it is understood by the lay jury. At the same time, the advocate must work to preserve the independence of the experts and avoid reinforcing the stereotype that every expert is a mere paid partisan in the presentation of the expert's testimony. Experts provide unique opportunities for advocates because of the powerful testimonial tools available to them. As already noted, experts may create new evidence for a party in the form of opinions, which may encompass the ultimate issues in the case. Further, the expert's opinions may be based on inadmissible facts or data—provided the opinions are relevant, based on reliable theories and methodologies, and based on sufficient underlying facts and data. No other type of witness offers a similar array of testimonial tools.

B.   The Content of the Direct Examination

The successful direct examination of any witness, whether lay or expert, depends in large part upon adherence to the basic principles and techniques discussed in Chapter Six, Direct Examination. The techniques of asking clear and understandable questions, blocking and headlining, and disclosing weaknesses or problems, for example, apply with the same force to the direct of experts as they do to the direct of lay witnesses. The balance of this section supplements those basic techniques, addressing the specific concerns that arise during the direct examination of expert witnesses, and discussing the particular techniques needed to ensure success when examining experts.

1.   *Personalization*

The direct examination of an expert witness should begin in the same manner as the direct of any other witness, with the personalization of the expert. The need for personalization is perhaps greatest with experts because of the distance created by their often intimidating credentials and sometimes incomprehensible testimony. Personalization allows the expert to begin building rapport with the jury by demonstrating that the expert is more than a collection of degrees, or a body of expert knowledge, but is a personable and likable individual who holds much in common with the members of the jury. The expert's place of residence, marital and family status, and other pieces of personal information can help the jury bridge the gulf between the expert and the jury.

Our advice—that advocates should personalize experts—is undoubtedly in the minority among trial advocacy commentators. Most opine that personal information about experts is not legally relevant, and beyond that, is not interesting to jurors. They simply do not care about the personal biographical information of experts. The first objection—the legal relevance of the information—is a legitimate concern. Whether an expert is married or unmarried, a father or a mother, does not seem to make a fact of consequence in the case more or less likely; and thus, may initially appear to fail the relevance test of Rule 401 of the Federal Rules. The same could be said of background information about most percipient witnesses, and yet, judges routinely allow such testimony for the purpose of identifying the witness and acquainting the jury with his or her background. The same argument should apply to experts. Nevertheless, some judges refuse to entertain such testimony from experts, considering it a waste of the jury's (and the judge's) time. Other judges will indulge the expert at least as to some basic biographical information. We believe advocates should risk the relevance objection because of the importance of building the expert's credibility and rapport with the jury. The worst that can happen is a sustained objection, forcing a transition to the expert's educational background.

The other reason voiced to avoid an expert's personal background—apathy on the part of the jurors—overlooks the critical role that likability plays in the jury's assessment of the expert's credibility. The more the jury perceives it shares similar experiences and backgrounds with the expert, the greater the jury's inclination to trust the expert's testimony. With experts, that similarity is most likely to be revealed in the expert's appearance, body language, and background. If the expert lives and works in the same town as the trial or has two school-aged children or has been married for twenty-seven years to the same person, the jury will likely draw certain favorable conclusions, such as that the expert is one of us (a home-grown product) or a regular guy or a stable, reliable person. Those favorable impressions are invaluable and worth the risk of an objection.

Illustration of Personalization of Expert

Lawyer: Good morning, Dr. Strangelove, will you please introduce yourself to the jury?

Witness: Yes. My name is Dr. Herbert Strangelove, and I live right here in New Town.

Lawyer: Doctor, before we get into your qualifications and opinions, I want to ask you questions about your life here in New Town so the jury can get to know you better. How long have lived here, doctor?

Witness: I was actually born and raised here. I went away to college and then medical school, but I came back to set up my practice.

Lawyer: Are you married, doctor?

Witness: I am. I've been married for twenty-two years to Amy, my high school sweetheart, and we have been blessed with three beautiful children.

Lawyer: What are the names and ages of your kids?

Witness: Tyler is my oldest, he's eighteen; then Nick, he's fifteen; and finally Elise, she's eleven.

Lawyer: Thank you, doctor. Now that we know a little about you, I want to . . . .

2.   *The Preview Question*

The role played by expert witnesses at trial may not be readily apparent to jurors. Jurors must not only translate the expert's complex testimony, but also they must understand what the expert is doing and why he is doing it. Experts do not testify to the facts. They are not eyewitnesses. They are not parties. Expert testimony does not follow the structure of other witnesses and does not have the same character or feel as other testimony. Accordingly, jurors need some help early in the expert's direct examination to understand why the expert is testifying and what he is going to say.

One way to enhance juror understanding is by posing a question after the personalization of the expert to "preview" the role of the expert in the proceeding. The preview question gives the expert the opportunity to explain his or her role in the trial and to foreshadow the ultimate objective of the expert's direct examination. It also provides segue from the personal block to the professional block.

 Illustration of Preview Question

Lawyer:	Dr. Strangelove, why are you here today?
Witness:	I am here to testify to the conclusions I've reached about the cause and severity of plaintiff's lung cancer based upon my experience and knowledge as a cancer specialist and my examination of plaintiff.
Lawyer:	Doctor, before we discuss your conclusions, I would like to ask you some questions about what qualifies you to testify to those conclusions . . . .

---

3. *Professional Qualifications*

The preview question provides a perfect transition into the expert's qualifications and gives the jury some context about why the lawyer is exploring the academic credentials or workplace experience of the witness in the first place. The expert's qualifications are critically important because they:

1. satisfy the basic legal requirements of Rule 702;

2. preempt an objection from the opponent; and

3. build the expert's credibility as a person fully qualified to testify about one or more of the issues in the case.

During the qualifications block advocates should:

- show genuine interest in the expert's background through body language, voice inflection, eye contact, and appropriate follow-up questions;

- comprehensively cover the expert's qualifications;

- link specific aspects of the expert's education, experience, or training to the issues in the case; and

- prick the boil of the expert's payment or other biases

a. Show Genuine Interest in the Expert's Qualifications

Unfortunately, lawyers tend to view questioning about the expert's qualifications as unimportant, tedious, boring, and uninteresting. As a consequence, they tend to mindlessly ask the qualification questions, showing little or no real interest in the answers. They use checklists to make sure every point is covered, rarely stopping to follow-up on an interesting answer or to clarify the significance of a credential or accomplishment. The use of a checklist itself is not the problem. Checklists can help ensure comprehensive coverage of the pertinent matters. However, when the checklist replaces the advocate's own effort in working through and thinking about the particular matters to be covered and becomes a kind of crutch leading to *pro forma* questioning of the expert, then the checklist approach can cause more harm than good.

Advocates must use the qualifications block as an opportunity to do more than merely demonstrate that the expert has the requisite credentials to testify. Credentials alone do not win lawsuits. The advocate must demonstrate that the expert has something of value to say about the issues in the lawsuit and is someone to whom the jury should listen. A significant measure of success can be achieved simply through the advocate's attitude in asking the qualifications questions. Act interested. Pay attention.

A few telltale signs of disinterest include:

1. looking away or shuffling papers while the expert is answering a question;

2. reading the questions from notes or checking them off after they are asked or answered;

3. maintaining a flat, monotone voice while asking the questions;

4. asking the questions quickly without any follow-up questions and without any apparent regard for the answers; and

5. failing to show any physical response to witness answers, such as a nod or shake of the head or a raised eyebrow or other natural reactions.

Advocates must maintain a high level of energy during this part of the questioning because the jury will take their cue about its relative importance (or unimportance) from the advocate. Advocates should stand up straight and maintain eye contact with the expert throughout the expert's answers. They should nod their head at appropriate times to reflect understanding and laugh when appropriate to show appreciation of the expert's humor. They should use voice inflection, varying the pitch, volume, and pace of their speech to show interest in what the expert is saying. They should ask natural follow-up questions to show that they are listening and that the expert's credentials are, in fact, both interesting and important. They should ask the questions naturally, without reliance on any script or checklist. Questions like "Where did you go to school?" and "What do you do for a living?" are hardly the kind of matters that need to be written down. After all, if you are truly interested in what the person does, the right questions will come naturally as you try to let the jury know everything it needs to know about the expert.

b.   Cover the Qualifications Comprehensively

As important as the advocate's attitude is to success, matters of substance are equally significant. As a starting point, the advocate must elicit all of the expert's pertinent qualifications, including every credential that makes the expert appear authoritative to the jurors. Advocates must build strong and unshakable foundations for each expert's testimony for at least two reasons. In the first place, the rules of evidence require a foundation before experts can offer their opinions. And although the rules are generous in their definition of who is an expert, every expert— without fail—must satisfy the rule's requirements. The second reason that argues in favor of comprehensiveness is a practical one. The better and stronger the expert's credentials, the more convincing he will be to the jury.

The specific information that should be elicited from the expert about his qualifications depends on the expert's specialty and the issues in the case. However, one can identify several general categories for inquiry, including educational background, employment history, publications, professional awards or honors received, and memberships in professional associations or organizations. For example, with blue-collar experts such as plumbers or auto mechanics, the qualifications should focus on the person's training and certifications, if any, and the person's work experience. For a Ph.D., more time is likely to be spent on the person's educational accomplishments, particularly the person's post-graduate education. It is not enough, however, for the advocate to merely elicit the expert's credentials. Those credentials must be linked to the specific facts and issues in the case.

c.   Link the Expert's Qualifications to the Issues in the Case

The mere fact that a person is a medical doctor does not mean a jury will readily accept every conceivable opinion on a medical topic offered by that doctor. The mere fact that an expert is an engineer by training and education does not mean that the person knows about the inner workings of automobile restraint systems. The technique of linkage remedies these concerns, helping to move the expert's qualifications from the general to the specific, and from the theoretical to the practical. The advocate, in essence, invites the witness to link his past education, experience, or writing to the specific matters about which the expert will testify later. This technique helps the qualifications come to life and allows the jury to obtain a preview of the expert's conclusions.

Thus, in a case involving a claim that the plaintiff's exposure to asbestos caused the plaintiff to develop cancer, the plaintiff must do much more with her expert than simply elicit that the doctor has a Ph.D. in epidemiology and teaches at a university. In addition, plaintiff must link the expert's qualifications to the issues in the case, the causal link between asbestos and cancer. This, of course, will require some introduction to epidemiology and some specifics about the expert's interest in the field and her work on the effects of exposure to asbestos. In the same way, an engineer's education and experience may be quite impressive and leave no doubt that the expert is intelligent and accomplished. But if those qualifications do nothing to help the jury comprehend how he understands the inner workings of automobile restraint systems—how they work and why they fail—then the jury will be less prepared than they should be to listen to and trust the expert's opinions on that topic. That is, in the absence of explicitly making connections between the expert's qualifications and his opinions for the jury, it will not necessarily be apparent to the jury how the expert's expertise relates to the issues in the case.

Illustration of Linkage of Expert Qualifications to Testimony

Lawyer: Mr. Hughes, when you were a graduate student in engineering did you receive any hands-on training?

Witness: Actually, a great deal. Engineering is all about hands on. All engineers want to know how things work and how to make them work better.

Lawyer: What kinds of hands-on experience did you receive as a graduate student?

Witness: As part of my course requirements, I was assigned to work at the Nissan car assembly plant in Auburn Hills.

Lawyer: So, were you an employee of Nissan?

Witness: No, I was a student studying under the Nissan engineers.

Lawyer: What specific aspects of automobile assembly were you involved in?

Witness: Several aspects, including the one involved in this trial. In fact, most of my six months at Nissan was spent with the engineers who oversaw the installation of restraint systems.

Lawyer: Not to get too far ahead of ourselves, Mr. Hughes, but was that hands-on experience valuable to you in working on this case, even though this case involves a Ford vehicle?

Witness: Absolutely. The basics of automobile restraint systems are pretty much the same regardless of the make of the car.

Lawyer: Mr. Hughes, what else did your graduate studies involve?

d.   "Prick the Boil" of the Expert's Payment or Other Biases

The final task of the examiner during the qualifications block is to disclose any bias the expert may have because of any payment the expert is receiving from the party calling the expert or because of any relationship the expert has with the party. It is, of course, routine for experts to be paid for their services, and it is highly likely that both sides will have paid experts testifying for them. Nevertheless, counsel should bring out the fact of payment during the direct simply to preempt the opponent's attack. The key points of disclosure are that the compensation is for the expert's time—his services, not his testimony—and that the payment did not purchase a result but only a full and comprehensive review of the issues in the case. By placing the disclosure near the end of the qualifications block, counsel gets the benefit that comes with disclosure—enhanced credibility and control over the release of the information—and also the benefit of placing the fact of payment in the middle of the examination where it is unlikely to be particularly memorable.

Another tactic to defuse the fact of payment is to use the expert's experience in the courtroom as a sign of his qualification to testify as an expert. Lawyers frequently use the fact that their expert has previously been qualified as an expert in the pertinent field as another reason to support the expert's standing in the present case. For example, "Dr. Jones, have you previously been qualified as an expert in the field of commercial banking by the courts of this state?" The expert's answer that he has been qualified on numerous occasions helps turn a liability into a potential asset, as the expert is made to look like a highly qualified and sought after expert.

The following illustration involves the qualification of the prosecution's expert, a medical examiner, to offer his opinion in a manslaughter trial about whether the decedent died from alcohol poisoning or from a blow to the head.

 Illustration of Qualifications Block for a Medical Examiner [8]

Lawyer: Before we discuss your opinions, Dr. Kildare, I want to ask you about what qualifies you to testify about your autopsy of Ms. Bradshaw

---

[8]   This illustration is based on the hypothetical case *State v. Horace Johnson*, Jean Montoya (National Institute of Trial Advocacy).

	and the cause of her death, beginning with your educational background. Where did you go to college?
Witness:	I went to the University of Texas and majored in biology.
Lawyer:	Why biology?
Witness:	I've always been fascinated by the human body and I wanted to go on to medical school. Biology seemed like a good foundation for that.
Lawyer:	After college were you able to go to medical school?
Witness:	Yes, I was. I went to Johns Hopkins and got an M.D. in 1996.
Lawyer:	In medical school did you develop any areas of particular interest?
Witness:	I did. I was particularly fascinated with the field of pathology and decided to pursue a residency in that area.
Lawyer:	What is pathology?
Witness:	Pathology is the study of diseases, and more particularly, the changes to the body's structure and function caused by diseases.
Lawyer:	You mentioned a residency; were you able pursue a residency in pathology?
Witness:	Yes, fortunately enough I obtained a residency in pathology at Duke Medical Center and worked there from 1996–2000.
Lawyer:	What did you do after your residency?
Witness:	I applied for and obtained a fellowship in forensic pathology at the USC Medical Center in Los Angeles, California.
Lawyer:	How is forensic pathology different from pathology as you described it earlier?
Witness:	Forensic pathology is simply one specific application of pathology. It involves the use of pathology as an investigative tool for criminal litigation, most typically as a medical examiner performing autopsies.
Lawyer:	And did you in fact have the opportunity to perform autopsies during the course of your fellowship?
Witness:	I did, and I found that forensic pathology was an interesting and challenging line of work. I decided to pursue a job in the field.
Lawyer:	Now that we know about your educational background, I want to ask about your work experience in the field of pathology. Where was your first job in the field?
Witness:	I got a job as a deputy medical examiner in LA in 2001 after my fellowship ended and I've been there ever since.

Lawyer: What do you do in that position?

Witness: I perform autopsies, prepare reports of my findings, and, when necessary, testify in court about my findings.

Lawyer: How many autopsies have you performed?

Witness: Oh gosh, too many to count. The last time I tried to add it up I counted more than 2,500 autopsies.

Lawyer: Can you give us an idea, just generally, of some of the more common causes of death you've seen in your years as a medical examiner?

Witness: It runs the gamut, from the kinds of things you might expect such as fatal gunshot wounds and knife wounds, blunt force traumas to the victim's head, to drug overdoses and deaths resulting from purely natural causes.

Lawyer: You mentioned drug overdoses. Have you had cases where excessive alcohol usage played a role in a person's death?

Witness: You bet. It's unusual in my experience for alcohol to cause a person's death—for someone to drink himself to death—though it does happen on a rare occasion. But it is not as unusual for alcohol use to cause impairment of one's senses and lead to conduct that causes the person's or someone else's death.

Lawyer: You also mentioned blunt force trauma injuries as a common cause of death. In those cases, in your experience, does death always follow closely on the heels of the fatal blow?

Witness: It depends. Depending on the severity and location of the trauma, death might come immediately or it might come only after hours or even days have elapsed. Blows to the head in particular can result in unseen damage to the brain, which, over time, will cause a person to die. I have performed a number of autopsies over the years, similar to this one, where the death of the victim occurred some time after the fatal blow was struck.

Lawyer: Dr. Kildare, in addition to your work as a medical examiner, are you a member of any professional associations?

Witness: Yes, I was fortunate to be named a diplomat of the College of Forensic Pathologists, an invitation-only organization for accomplished forensic pathologists. I'm also a member of the national organization of forensic pathologists and have served on the organization's executive board for the last two years.

Lawyer: Have you previously been qualified as a forensic pathologist in the courts of this state?

Witness: Absolutely. I regularly am asked to testify about my autopsy findings and in every instance, over one hundred cases now, I've been qualified by the court as an expert.

Lawyer: And who is paying for your time here today?

| Witness: | I'm an employee of the county and they're paying me just as they would if I was back at the office doing an autopsy. |

[The lawyer then moves from general to specific, asking the expert how his background is pertinent to this case.]

A number of things were accomplished during these qualification blocks. Note the linking questions demonstrating an early professional interest in pathology that ultimately led to a fellowship into a particular type of pathology and then into actually performing autopsies during the fellowship. The examiner then transitioned from the doctor's educational background to his professional work experience. In the professional experience block, the examiner has once again linked issues in the witness' background to contested issues in this case, specifically relating to alcohol-related and blunt force trauma deaths. And finally, note the placement of compensation at the end of the block when it is least likely to draw much notice.

4.   *The Basis*

The third block of an expert's direct examination concerns the facts and data that support the expert's opinion: the basis. Before experts actually reveal their opinions to the jury, they should carefully and thoroughly explain the process by which they have reached those opinions. The explanation should cover both the general and specific. That is, the block should begin by explaining the methodology or technique generally used by experts in the field to reach conclusions about the issues involved as well as the specific steps taken by the expert in this case to reach their opinions, including the specific documents reviewed or analyzed, the particular tests conducted, and calculations made. The larger point is that the more the jury understands when the opinion is finally given, the more likely it is that the jury will embrace the opinion when it is disclosed.

In the basis block, counsel should:

- adequately prepare the way for the expert's opinion so that the jury understands the opinion and appreciates where it came from when it is revealed;

- begin with a general description of the expert's methodology and then move to a specific description of how the expert applied and used the methodology in the present case; and

- disclose pertinent portions of the content of the material relied on by the expert, not simply a list of the kinds of material the expert used.

The Supreme Court's decisions in *Daubert* and *Kumho Tire*, and the amended Rule 702, discussed above, require that experts use some valid, reliable methodology in reaching their opinions. The task of advocates during this block is to help their experts explain the process or methodology they used to form their opinions and to ensure that the jurors understand that process. The reasons for revealing the basis for the opinions before the opinions themselves are many, but include two particularly salient ones: (1) the expert gains credibility by showing that he followed a recognized methodology in reaching his conclusions, and (2) the expert effectively prepares the jurors for the opinion by educating them about the basic principles in the expert's field so the jurors are not surprised or perplexed by the opinion when it is finally revealed.

a.   Prepare the Way for the Expert's Opinion

The ultimate objective of the basis block is to prepare the jury for the opinions it will hear from the expert. By the time the basis block is concluded, the jurors should have the sense that they know essentially everything the expert knew when he formed his opinion and they know every step the expert went through to form that opinion. A jury in that position will not be surprised or perplexed by the expert's opinion, but rather will view it as the natural and logical outcome of the expert's careful and thorough analysis. And accordingly, the jury will be more likely to claim the opinion as its own and to view the expert as a credible and reliable witness.

b.   From General to Specific

In most, if not all, instances the basis block should begin with a general description of the expert's approach to the issues raised by the facts and then move to the specific work done by the expert to prepare his opinion in the present case. Thus, the medical doctor might begin this portion of the direct examination with a description of how she typically diagnoses a patient, while a safety engineer might first describe the steps one takes to identify the cause or origin of an accident, before proceeding to explain the specifics of their work in the present case. Beginning with the general allows experts to serve as a teacher for the jurors, their guide in uncharted waters. As the teacher, the expert becomes the authority figure in the courtroom, someone the jurors can respect and to whom they can look for answers. In addition, the general to specific approach enhances the jury's understanding of the expert's basis, giving jurors the opportunity to hear an uninterrupted explanation of the expert's methodology. Finally, this approach builds the credibility of the expert by demonstrating that the expert reached his conclusions based on the same methodology that he and others in the field typically use for that purpose.

Take the economist in a personal injury case as an example. Before eliciting the specific information about the decedent's wage earning history and his expected future income, the advocate should have the economist explain how he ordinarily calculates lost income. By the end of this section, the jury should have the entire formula before them and should have at least a basic understanding of what a discount rate is and how personal consumption figures in the calculation. Once the jury has the basics, they are ready for the economist to plug in the specific information regarding the decedent and to explain the origin of each piece of information. This kind of careful development of the underlying basis will prepare the jury to accept, and equip them to understand, the expert's opinions.

c. Disclose the Content of the Underlying Facts or Data

The basis block should do more than merely reveal the various types of information upon which the expert relied. It should also include the content of the information and the importance of that content to the expert's opinion. The difference is significant. Under the former approach, the expert simply lists, by category, the documents he has reviewed. For example, the expert tells the jury, "I reviewed the plaintiff's and defendant's depositions, the police report, photographs of the scene and the cars, and I personally inspected and analyzed the scene" and then the lawyer moves on to the expert's opinions. Under the "full disclosure" approach, experts go beyond mere categorization and they tell the jury what information, if any, they learned from each document or action, and how that information was helpful in the formation of their opinions.

Perhaps the greatest challenge with this approach is striking the right balance between giving the jury enough information to be fully prepared for the expert's opinion, but not so much information that the jury is confused and overwhelmed or the opinions become anticlimactic. The advocate should elicit mostly descriptive information in this block—what did the expert do, why did he do it, what did he learn—as opposed to evaluative information. For the most part, the expert's evaluation and analysis should be reserved for the opinion block. If the expert read the depositions of the parties in preparing to testify, he should be asked to explain why he did so and what he learned that was helpful to his evaluation. If the expert visited the scene of the accident, he should be asked to explain what he did there and what helpful information he obtained. If the expert relied on the police report, again he should be asked to explain why and discuss the specific information that he learned from the report.

This advice comes with a very important caveat: anticipate hearsay objections from the opponent during this part of the direct. To the extent the information the expert is disclosing is inadmissible hearsay, such as the deposition testimony described above, the advocate must lay a proper foundation for the expert's reliance and disclosure. As discussed above, Rule 703 allows experts to rely on inadmissible facts and data only if the reliance is reasonable, and allows disclosure of the hearsay to the jury only if the probative value of disclosure substantially outweighs the danger of unfair prejudice. That means that advocates must lay the requisite foundation before eliciting inadmissible facts or data, both as to the reasonableness of the expert's reliance on the material and the importance of the material to the expert's opinion.

Illustration of Basis Block for an Economist in a Personal Injury Case

Lawyer: Now that we know about your education and experience in economics, I want to discuss with you in general terms how you go about the task of assessing a person's loss of wage earning capacity. Can you describe for the jury the first step you take when trying to make that assessment?

Witness: The first step is to collect all of the data you can about the person's wage earning history. The best indication of what a person will earn in the future is what they have made in the past. So, I collect their past income tax returns, pay check stubs or bank records for the ten years or so prior to the person's death. With that information, I can determine the average increases in income experienced by the person and I can begin to project what their income would have been in the future.

Lawyer: What is the next step?

Witness: In addition to their earning past, I try to determine how long the person would have worked had they not died. To do that, I consider the person's occupation—there is a vast difference in the longevity of professional athletes compared to business executives—and the available statistical data put out by the government and others about average work life expectancies in the pertinent field.

Lawyer: Why do you do that?

Witness: I need to determine how long the person would have likely worked so I can know how many years of lost income the person likely suffered.

Lawyer: What comes next?

Witness: Then I determine the appropriate discount rate.

Lawyer: What's that?

Witness: Well, when you project lost earnings ten or twenty years into the future, you have to discount those earnings to present value to determine how much income a person would need today to compensate the person for their future losses. For example, if a person would have had an income of $50,000 five years from now, it would take something less than that amount today to compensate him for that loss because the person can invest the money today and gain some kind of return. You have to consider two factors: the projected rate of inflation which will eat away at the value of that money and the potential return the person can get for that money by investing it. To the extent the investment return is likely to be greater than the inflation rate then the amount of loss should be reduced by the difference between the two.

Lawyer:	So, the discount rate would decrease the amount of the person's lost income?
Witness:	That's right.
Lawyer:	Doctor, would it be helpful to the jury to show them visually how this calculation looks?
Witness:	Yes, I think it would.
Lawyer:	Your Honor, may the witness step down to the board for the purpose of demonstrating this calculation to the jury?
Judge:	Certainly. You may step down, Sir.

[Continue through the general until it is completed, then move to the specific.]

Lawyer:	Now that we understand how you generally go about assessing lost income, I'd like to turn to the specific work you did in this case to determine the income lost by the Jones family from their father's death. How did you go about your task?
Witness:	Well, I followed the same four steps I have just described. First, I collected data on Mr. Jones past earnings history, including fringe benefits. Second, I determined how long he likely would have worked but for his death. I then determined the appropriate discount rate, and discounted the loss to present value. Finally, I ascertained the amount of consumption that would have been attributable to Mr. Jones and reduced the loss by that amount.
Lawyer:	Doctor, let's begin with the first step you described. What data were you able to collect about Mr. Jones' past earning history?
Witness:	I collected his income tax returns for the last ten years, as well as, his W-2 forms.
Lawyer:	What did you learn from that information?
Witness:	I learned that Mr. Jones had enjoyed steady increases in his income over the last ten years at an average of 6.7 percent. His income began at $38,500.00 in 1999 and by the time of his death was $73,638.00.
Lawyer:	How was that earnings information helpful to you in determining Mr. Jones' lost earnings?
Witness:	It provided me with a baseline, a beginning point for my assessment of his likely future earnings and his likely wage increases in the future.
Lawyer:	Let's discuss the second thing you did—determining Mr. Jones work life expectancy. How did you go about that?

[The advocate continues through each step until completed.]

5. *Opinions*

The direct examination reaches its climax with the disclosure of the expert's opinions. With most experts, the opinions are the primary— perhaps *the only*—reason for calling the expert to testify in the first place, and thus, their disclosure should be the most dramatic and most highlighted portion of the direct. The advocate must send a signal to the jury that it is time to sit up and pay particular attention to what is happening. At this point, advocates should change their voices, lean in to the witness, use their hands, and choose words that will unequivocally signal that an important answer is forthcoming. The advocate's headline introducing the opinion block can help signal that important testimony is coming. Words such as "focus," "freeze," or "zero in" help communicate the importance of the testimony without explicitly and improperly telling the jury, "this is important."

The specific questions used to elicit the opinions of experts traditionally have involved a two-step sequence. The first question asks whether the expert has formed an opinion: "Do you have an opinion about … ?;" the second question asks for the opinion itself: "What is that opinion?" This form is familiar to judges and provides opposing counsel with an opportunity to object, while building anticipation with the jury.

The exact wording of the opinion question demands careful attention from the advocates and the expert. The first question should be preceded with a review of the expert's basis for the opinion. For example, the questioner might say: "Based upon your education, including your Ph.D. in epidemiology, your twenty years of experience as a researcher for the Center for Disease Control, your review of the depositions taken in this case, your analysis of the prior studies regarding the causal link between the ingestion of Bendectin during pregnancy and limb reduction defects in babies, and your consideration of the reports prepared by the plaintiff's experts in this matter, do you have an opinion about … ?" In this way the questioner directly connects for the jury the expert's qualifications and the basis with the expert's opinion.

Moreover, the words used by the questioner to describe the expert's opinion should communicate the subject matter of the expert's conclusions clearly, should satisfy the substantive legal requirements, and should fall within the scope of the expert's qualifications. For example, in a medical malpractice case alleging negligence by the defendant doctor, the examiner might ask: "Based upon [insert basis for opinion], do you have an opinion about whether defendant's medical treatment of Mr. Smith [the plaintiff] was reasonable [or "was appropriate" or "fell within the standard of care for orthopedic surgeons"]?" The questions should be specific regarding the nature of the opinion that is being sought—not just the generic, "Do you have an opinion?".

In the same way, as part of the preparation process, advocates should work with experts to hone their answers to the opinion question so that they couch their answers in terms that are legally sufficient, powerful, and clear. For example, plaintiff's expert might opine in a product liability case that the product's design was unsafe, unreasonable (another term for negligence), dangerous, or unfit for its intended use. In a negligence case, the plaintiff's expert might testify that the defendant acted unreasonably or that his conduct fell below the standard of care in the defendant's field.

Traditionally, courts have required that expert opinions be more than mere speculation and that they be based on a reasonable degree of certainty or probability in the expert's field. Thus, an engineer would testify that his opinion was "to a reasonable degree of engineering certainty" and a doctor would say that his opinion was "to a reasonable degree of medical probability." The federal rules no longer require such formalistic expressions from the expert, but some state jurisdictions do, and more importantly, some judges and lawyers have this approach so ingrained in their psyche that they continue to expect to hear these "magic" words. Advocates must know the presiding judge's preferences and use the expression if the jurisdiction or judge requires it.

An additional consideration is whether or not the expert should use the term "opinion" in expressing his determinations about the issues he has analyzed. There is some suggestion that the term "opinion" reduces the weight of the expert's testimony and leaves open the very real possibility of other contrary opinions. Everybody has an opinion and in our post-modern, post-positivist world, populated as it is with talk shows that often consist of nothing more than guests espousing wildly contradictory opinions about the issue *du jour*, it may make sense to avoid any language that suggests that the expert is just another eccentric academic with an opinion. Perhaps the terms "conclusion" or "determination" carry more heft and invite less doubt from the jury.

 ## Illustration of Medical Examiner Opinion Block[9]

Lawyer: Based upon your medical school education, your residency at Duke, your fellowship at USC, your eleven years as a deputy medical examiner with the L.A. Medical Examiner's office, the more than 2,500 autopsies you have performed in that time, the autopsy you performed on Ms. Veritas, and your assessment of the findings from that autopsy, including the toxicological tests performed on her blood, have you reached a conclusion about Ms. Veritas' cause of death?

Witness: Yes, I have.

Lawyer: And what is your conclusion about the cause of her death?

Witness: I have concluded that she died from edema of the brain, or uh, a swelling of her brain, which resulted from a severe blow to her head several hours earlier.

Lawyer: What do you mean by edema or swelling of the brain?

Witness: When the brain is hit with any kind of blunt force, as happened in this case, it begins to bleed and to swell. But, of course, the skull limits the extent to which it can swell. The result is a build up of pressure that over time can lead to death.

---

9   This illustration is based on the hypothetical case *State v. Horace Johnson*, Jean Montoya (National Institute of Trial Advocacy).

6. *Reasons*

Immediately following the revelation of the expert's opinion, the advocate should elicit the expert's reasons for the opinion. This is the chance for the expert to provide the jury with a summary of the party's case, a kind of mini-closing argument. The expert should synthesize for the jury why it is that one party is at fault or why the product is safe or unsafe. It is a unique opportunity, one available only to experts, and accordingly, it should be used by advocates to the fullest possible advantage.

If at all possible, the expression of the expert's reasons shall be introduced in the form of a list. Enumeration of the points makes them easier for the jury to remember and highlights their importance. The use of a list also simplifies organization of the material for the advocate, witness, and jury, allowing the advocate to question the witness about each point on the list sequentially.

The list of reasons that support the expert's opinion is, in essence, a list of the reasons why the advocate's client should prevail. Accordingly, the points on the list should be developed with great care and attention. Three or four reasons work best because they can be best remembered by the jury. More points may overwhelm the jury, but too few points and there is not a true list. The reasons should be just that—reasons. They should help the jury appreciate the logic and force of the expert's opinion. They should not merely rehash the basis portion of the direct. Consider the reasons block of the medical examiner who gave his opinions in the previous excerpt.

 Illustration of Reasons Block[10]

Lawyer: Why have you concluded Ms. Veritas died from a swelling of her brain?

Witness: Four reasons. First, the two centimeter gash above her left eyebrow; second, the .4 centimeter bruise of the left occipital lobe of the victim's brain; third, the time lapse between the infliction of the trauma and the victim's death; and fourth, engorgement or swelling of the blood vessels of the surface of the brain and the hemorrhaging detected in various places in and around the brain.

Lawyer: Let's talk about the first reason you gave, the two centimeter gash above the left eyebrow of Ms. Veritas. How did that lead you to your conclusion about her cause of death?

Witness: Well, the gash was two centimeters deep, penetrating the covering of the left roof of the brain. It was a sufficiently deep blow that it actually bruised the victim's brain, thus leading to the internal bleeding and swelling.

---

[10] This illustration is based on the hypothetical case *State v. Horace Johnson*, Jean Montoya (National Institute of Trial Advocacy).

Lawyer:	When you say two centimeters, can you translate that into inches for those of us who are metric impaired?
Witness:	Sure. That's the same as about 1/4 of an inch.
Lawyer:	That leads us to the second point you gave, a .4 centimeter bruise of the left occipital lobe of the brain. First of all, what does that mean?
Witness:	That simply refers to the portion of the brain on the person's left hand side, toward the top upper half of the head.
Lawyer:	How did that help you determine the cause of death for Ms. Veritas?
Witness:	The bruise lined up with the quarter inch gash and was caused by it. That showed me exactly where the bruising and bleeding of the brain came from—it came from the blow that caused that gash.
Lawyer:	The third reason you gave, the time lapse, how did that lead you to your conclusion?

[*The advocate continues through each reason until they are each fully explained and illustrated for the jury.*]

---

7. *Multiple Opinions/Rebutting the Opposing Expert's Opinions*

Experts regularly testify to more than one opinion. For instance, in the case of the medical examiner described in several excerpts above, the witness may opine not only that the victim died from edema of the brain resulting from the gash on her forehead, but also that the gash was likely caused by a wooden board of certain characteristics as opposed to being caused by a fall. Each opinion given by experts must be within the scope of their expertise, have a reasonable basis, be based upon a reliable methodology, and be relevant to the issues in the case. Thus, each opinion should be treated in the same way demonstrated above. It may be necessary with an expert's second opinion to go back and discuss additional qualifications of the person or to identify the additional bases of the second opinion to the extent they differ or go beyond the basis for the initial opinion. The key is to maintain the same logical order of presentation and the same attitude toward the disclosure of each opinion.

There is one additional area that can be quite fruitful during the expert's direct examination: rebuttal of the opponent's expert testimony. Whether the expert is testifying for the plaintiff or defendant, counsel should consider the possibility of specifically and directly rebutting the opposing expert's opinions. Depending on the facts and the expert, this rebuttal may take different forms. For example, the prosecutor may want the medical examiner described above to respond to the opinion of defendant's expert that the victim died from alcohol poisoning related to her extremely high blood alcohol content. Of course, the coroner rebuts that opinion by his testimony that edema of the brain was the cause of death. But, the point can also be made more directly by giving the expert a chance to specifically tell the jury why the opposing expert reached the wrong conclusion or exactly where the expert went wrong. That block may most naturally fit at the end of the direct or immediately after the expert has given his opinions about the disputed issue.

IV. PRINCIPLES FOR EFFECTIVE DIRECT EXAMINATIONS OF EXPERTS

There is more to an effective direct examination of an expert than a logical and organized structure, though that is an excellent start. What follows is an assortment of techniques to help ensure that the direct is understandable, credible, interesting, and memorable.

❖ Principle Number One: Use Plain Language

Much like lawyers, experts often find it hard to communicate to jurors in plain English. The more degrees the witness has, the more difficult it is for that witness to speak the jury's language. Instead, experts use technical jargon and terms of art that require an unabridged dictionary to decipher. The expert's impressive vocabulary will almost certainly dazzle the jury. They will have no doubt that the witness really does have four graduate degrees. At the same time, however, the technical terms and multi-syllabic words will distance the expert from the jury and will create a barrier to the jury's understanding of the testimony.

> **PRINCIPLES FOR EFFECTIVE DIRECT EXAMINATION OF EXPERTS**
>
> ❖ Use Plain Language
>
> ❖ Disclose Payment and Other Bases for Bias
>
> ❖ Use Visual and Demonstrative Aids
>
> ❖ Use Lists
>
> ❖ Know the Preference of the Trial Judge About Whether to Tender Experts (And Don't Tender Unless You Have To)
>
> ❖ Keep it Simple; Use Metaphors and Analogies to Explain and Clarify Testimony
>
> ❖ Refuse to Treat Experts as Commodities

The advocate's task is twofold: (1) use the preparation process to allow the expert to practice communicating complex concepts in plain English, encouraging him to substitute common terms for technical ones whenever possible and (2) help experts during their testimony to translate any terms of art used into understandable definitions and descriptions. The bottom line is that advocates must resist the temptation to adopt the expert's terminology, and must insist that the expert adopt the advocate's plain English.

Some believe that the big words and complicated sounding ideas actually enhance expert credibility, demonstrating their superior knowledge and education. After all, the argument goes, you should get your money's worth for the expert. The expert's credibility, however, is not found in technical jargon or the like. The expert's credibility is found in the expert's helpfulness. The jury wants to know: Does the expert give a clear explanation of the issues in the case? Does the expert provide logical and supported conclusions about those issues?

Nevertheless, despite the best efforts of advocates, some terms and expressions seem to defy simplification. A doctor's diagnosis, for example, most likely mandates the use of particular terms of art. Severe anxiety neurosis does not go by any other name. It is what it is. In those instances, advocates should have the witness explain the meaning of the term or give a definition. In the case of severe anxiety neurosis, that would mean having the witness explain the symptoms associated with the illness and the illness' typical origin. Thereafter, when the expert refers to the diagnosis, the jury will at least have some understanding of the term.

❖ Principle Number Two: Disclose Payment and Other Bases for Bias

As discussed earlier in this chapter, the elephant in the room when an expert testifies is that the expert, unlike all of the lay witnesses in the courtroom, is being paid to testify for the party who called him. The likelihood, of course, is that both sides are paying their experts, which, in a sense, levels the playing field (depending on a variety of other factors). However, that does not change the party's need to voluntarily disclose the fact of payment during the direct examination. If the jury first hears about the payment during cross-examination it will damage the expert's credibility by raising suspicion about why the expert and his lawyer failed to come clean when they had the chance to do so.

The disclosure of payment should be made near the middle of the direct, as opposed to close to the beginning or end of the direct. And the disclosure should be at a logical point of the exam, made within the flow of the direct itself. For example, at the end of the qualifications block, when the expert has just testified that he has a consulting firm that periodically consults with parties involved in litigation, the advocate might raise the payment issue, as follows:

 Illustration of Disclosure of Payment

Lawyer: What does your consulting firm do?

Witness: My consulting firm periodically consults with individuals or corporations involved in litigation.

Lawyer: When you engage in that kind of consulting, how are you paid for your services?

Witness: The individual or corporation who hired us pays our hourly fee.

Lawyer: And, is that what is happening in this case?

Witness:	Yes. I am being paid for the services I've rendered in this case by Acme Corporation.
Lawyer:	How much are you being paid for your work in this case?
Witness:	We charge $150.00 per hour for our preparation before trial. For in court testimony, like today, we charge a per day fee of $1,200.00.
Lawyer:	How much do you expect to charge Acme for your services in this case?
Witness:	The total bill will probably be about $7,500.00.
Lawyer:	Dr. Jones, does Acme's payment of you depend in any way on the outcome of this case?
Witness:	Absolutely not. I'm paid for my consulting services, not for a particular opinion or outcome.

As demonstrated by the lawyer in the example, advocates should not shy away from the disclosure questions. It is more preferable for them to come out during the direct, when counsel can exercise some control, than during the cross when the opponent controls the agenda. Therefore the disclosure should include not just the fact of payment, but also the details of billing rates and the total amount. Importantly, it must be clear that the payment is not for the witness' testimony or for a certain opinion. The payment is only for the expert's professional services rendered before, during, and after the trial.

Other biases need to be disclosed as well. If the expert is an employee of the party, the employment relationship must be disclosed and explained. If the expert has testified previously for the same lawyer or party, disclosure of the relationship should be made. If the expert has a particular relationship to the issue about which the expert is testifying, such as an expert testifying about the defendant's future dangerousness in the penalty phase of a capital murder case when the expert is a member of an organization of psychiatrists who take the position that psychiatrists are competent to state such opinions (contrary to conventional wisdom in the field), the positional bias should be disclosed up front. In short, any bias that might cause the expert's impartiality in the case to be questioned should be disclosed and explained during the direct.

❖ Principle Number Three: Use Visual and Demonstrative Aids

Perhaps more than any other type of testimony, expert witness testimony requires the use of visual and demonstrative aids. With experts, demonstrative aids are not merely helpful, they are indispensable. They enhance expert testimony by:

- explaining and clarifying complex or confusing expert testimony

- placing the expert in the role of a teacher

- summarizing the expert's analysis and conclusions.

The possibilities are unlimited: Pictures, diagrams, charts, graphs, models, computer animations, summaries, lists, demonstrations. Perhaps the best argument for the liberal use of visual aids during the expert's direct is what happens when they are not used: few things are more painful or mind-numbing than the talking head expert, who sits in the witness chair for hours on end in a perfectly stationary position (or worse yet, speaks through the television screen via a video deposition).

Demonstrative aids can enable jurors to get past an expert's theoretical explanations of his field and actually see and experience the practical dimensions of what the expert does or how the expert goes about reaching a conclusion. Take, for example, several different types of forensic expert testimony. A witness who is an expert in forensic DNA testing can show the jury the actual radiographs that resulted from the DNA tests and demonstrate the "matches" between the defendant's DNA and the DNA found in the blood in the victim's home. A fingerprint expert can project the disputed fingerprints onto a large screen and show the correlations between the defendant's prints and those found on the murder weapon. A forensic document examiner can conduct for the jury a side-by-side comparison of defendant's handwriting and the handwriting located on the forged document. Each juror's ability to make the comparison themselves, and in doing so to reach the "obvious" conclusion reached by the expert, and actually see the analysis play out before their eyes, ensures that those jurors will remember the testimony in vivid terms. This, in turn, makes it more likely they will hold firm to their conclusions during deliberations (assuming that the jurors believe and trust in the science on which the expert's conclusion is based).

Other visual aids may allow the jury to better understand the basic principles of the expert's field, the underlying premises of the expert's opinion. For example, a heart surgeon might use a model of the heart to illustrate its various parts, as well as the nature of the surgical procedure undertaken by the defendant doctor. A tire failure analyst might use a tire similar to the one that blew out to demonstrate what causes tires to blow out and how an expert can look at a tire and determine the likely cause of the problem. A firearms expert might use a firearm identical to the one that accidentally discharged and injured the plaintiff to demonstrate the gun's pertinent design features and the basics of the gun's safe operation. The list of possible examples is as long as the list of different types of expertise. And the complexity of the possible demonstratives one might use is as wide as the technology gap between pen and paper and computer animation. The key to it all is to view the expert's testimony from the eyes of the uninitiated lay jurors. What points will they need clarified? Where in the expert's testimony will they need additional explanation? Identify the points that will benefit most from visual depiction and consider the optimum demonstrative aid in light of the case budget and the point being made.

The second benefit derived from the use of visual aids with experts is that visual aids place the expert in the role of a teacher or guide, helping the jury through the intricacies of the expert's opinions. Teachers stand before their students and teach, and exhibits or visual aids provide experts with the opportunity to do the same. The demonstrative aid gives counsel a reason to get the expert out of the witness chair and over to the visual aid (which should be positioned directly in front of the jury box). Once there, the expert can explain the demonstrative aid, pointing out to the jurors the pertinent aspects of the model, diagram, or chart. Regardless of what the expert actually says while out of the witness chair, the jurors' interest in the expert will be renewed and enhanced by the simple fact of his movement. And of even greater importance, the expert will be in a position of authority with the jurors. The jurors will likely pay closer attention to the expert's words and better remember what he says.

The third potential benefit from demonstrative aids is repetition and reinforcement of the expert's key points. Demonstrative aids provide an opportunity to go back through the expert's testimony for the purpose of showing the jury what the expert was talking about when he explained the point with words only. In this way demonstrative aids are a legitimate means of achieving repetition without running afoul of the rules of evidence.

❖ Principle Number Four: Use Lists[11]

The use of a list can greatly enhance an expert witness' testimony. It provides structure to the direct in much the same way as headlining and blocking, by helping to categorize and organize the material for the jury in a memorable and understandable way. At the same time, a good list is much like a visual aid in that it gives the jury another way to store the information and it translates easily into visual depiction. Lists aid juror retention of the expert's testimony by allowing jurors to actually take down in note form the list of salient points.

Undoubtedly, the jury will receive almost any list during the expert direct with open arms. The list is like a life jacket tossed to the jury as they are drowning in a sea of technical and complex testimony. In the midst of their life-and-death struggle, the list gives the jurors something to hold on to. They tend to listen to the testimony more closely, remember it more clearly, and view the expert—and party—more kindly.

One of the great advantages of lists is they force experts to communicate to the jury in understandable terms. In developing lists, experts must distill their opinions into pithy sound bites. Experts must turn the sophisticated

---

[11] Caldwell, Perrin, and Frost, *Primacy, Recency, Ethos, and Pathos: Integrating Principles of Communication into the Direct Examination*, 76 NOTRE DAME L. REV. 510-12 (2001). Used with permission.

analysis in their reports into short and understandable bullet points. They help experts remember that their audience is the lay jurors and that they must target their remarks to them and not to their professional peers. It also helps to ensure that experts have engaged in the critical, but difficult, task of analyzing the reasons that support their opinions and ensuring that they persuasively demonstrate the validity of their opinions.

Perhaps more significantly, each item in a list reinitiates the principle of primacy, recapturing the jury's attention anew. After the expert has identified his three reasons for reaching his opinion, the lawyer can then ask about each point separately, confident that the jury will be tuned into the testimony. In fact, an effective and well-timed list gives jurors confidence that they have a grasp of the expert's testimony and have something tangible to take with them into deliberation. The expert, in enumerating the list, sends a message to the jury that, at the end of the day, the three points in the list are what the jury needs to remember about the expert's testimony.

As suggested above, the list can be used to advantage in developing the expert's reasons for his opinion. The expert's three or four reasons that support his opinion are critical to ultimate success. They should be highlighted in any way possible and emphasized to the jury as significant. A listing of the reasons does just that, followed by short, prodding questions to explore each of the reasons, and, if permitted by the court, summarized on a flip board.

 ## Illustration of Expert's Use of a List

Lawyer: Dr. Mayflower, now I want you to focus on the conclusions you have reached about the safety of the defendant's seatbelt design. Based on your twenty five years of engineering experience, your many years spent designing automobile seatbelt systems, your personal inspection of the seatbelt in Ms. Jones' [the plaintiff's] car, your careful evaluation of the accident scene and the other physical evidence, and your review of the depositions taken in this case, have you reached a conclusion about whether the seatbelt in Ms. Jones car was properly designed by the defendant for its intended purposes?

Witness: Yes, I have reached a conclusion.

Lawyer: What is your conclusion?

Witness: My conclusion is that the seatbelt in Ms. Jones' car was unsafe for use as a restraint system because it was not properly designed for that purpose by the defendant manufacturer.

Lawyer: Why?

Witness: **Three reasons. First,** the very fact that the seatbelt split into two pieces; **second,** the poor retractor design for the seatbelt system; and **third,** the severity of the plaintiff's injuries.

Lawyer:	**Let's start with your first reason.** How does the fact that the seatbelt split into two pieces support your opinion that it was not properly designed by defendant?
Witness:	Seatbelts are designed to prevent injury, not to cause them. A seatbelt that comes apart during an accident involving only moderate speeds, such as the one here, must be defective in some way. That is especially true when the seatbelt is in a relatively late model car such as plaintiff's. A properly designed and manufactured seatbelt does not break apart on impact.
Lawyer:	**How about the second reason for your opinion**—that the retractor design was not a good design—how does that support your opinion that the defendant's seatbelt system was unsafe?
Witness:	As I mentioned earlier, the car's restraint system caused the ultimate failure of the seatbelt. In defendant's car, the webbing of the seatbelt is routed through a loop that is attached to the interior of the car above the driver's left ear. This loop was designed to rotate to maximize the comfort of the driver. However, that design caused the webbing of the seatbelt to bunch up against the closed end of the loop, significantly reducing the webbing's strength and leading to the tearing of the belt. The bunching of the seatbelt is demonstrated by the marks on the guide loop on only one end, the closed end. If there had been no bunching, then the marks would be uniform across the guide loop. But they are not.
Lawyer:	**How does your third reason—the injuries suffered by Ms. Jones**—support your opinion that the defendant's seatbelt design was unsafe?
Witness:	Ms. Jones' accident was not at a terribly high speed. Yet, the injuries she suffered were much greater than those suffered by the crash dummies in the thirty miles per hour crash tests performed by defendant in the safety testing of their cars. That demonstrates that plaintiff was effectively unrestrained in the car, and that the seatbelt broke at the very beginning of the accident sequence, thus causing the plaintiff's body to slam into the dashboard and steering wheel with great force.

❖ Principle Number Five: Know the Preference of the Trial Judge About Whether to Tender Experts (And Do Not Tender Unless You Have To)

American judges and jurisdictions are split on whether advocates must tender expert witnesses to the court and have the experts accepted as qualified to testify before they can reveal their opinions or conclusions. A few judges and jurisdictions require it, though most do not. To tender an expert simply means to submit a witness to the judge as an expert in a particular field or discipline. The proper time to tender an expert witness is following the establishment of the expert's qualifications as an expert.

The advocate states: "Your Honor, at this time Chris Isaac (the plaintiff) tenders Dr. Wishbone to the court as an expert in the field of biomedical engineering." The court then provides the opponent an opportunity to raise an objection to the expert's qualifications, if one exists, and to make appropriate argument or take the expert on *voir dire*. If the court finds the expert to be properly qualified, it announces to the jury, "The court accepts Dr. Wishbone as an expert in the field of biomedical engineering." If the court rejects the expert, it then precludes any expert opinions from the expert unless the party is able to correct the foundational deficiency.

Tendering is not mandated by the Federal Rules of Evidence. Nevertheless, some federal judges require it in their courtrooms, as do a number of state court judges.

The primary advantage to tendering experts is a boost to the expert's credibility that results from the imprimatur of the judge. The judge announces to the jury that the expert is recognized by the court as an expert in the pertinent field, a powerful endorsement indeed. The primary disadvantage is that the act of tendering invites the opponent to object to the expert's qualifications and it creates the possibility that the judge will limit the expert's testimony or exclude it altogether. When a party makes a tender, the judge typically invites the opposing party to raise any concerns they have about the expert's qualifications before the judge rules. That invitation will likely result in more objections than one would otherwise encounter, simply because lawyers are more likely to interpose an objection when asked to do so than when not similarly invited. The heightened risk of objection, and the attendant disruption of the direct examination from arguing about the qualifications of the expert or the pertinent field of expertise, substantially diminishes the benefits of tendering. Accordingly, we generally advise lawyers to avoid tendering experts unless they have no choice. In the event that the judge requires experts to be tendered, the lawyers have no choice and they should make the tender at the proper time and try to gain maximum advantage from it.

❖ Principle Number Six: Keep It Simple; Use Metaphors and Analogies to Explain and Clarify the Testimony

The temptation with expert witnesses is to give jurors a crash course in the expert's discipline so that they can become mini-experts in the field. And without a doubt, jurors must know enough about the underlying principles of an expert's testimony to intelligently assess the expert's conclusions. However, too much detail, too many terms of art, or too much of highly-technical information will lead to the jurors' eyes glazing over and their ears tuning the expert out. Unfortunately, then when the expert's important findings are revealed, the jurors may miss them altogether. Therefore, an important principle of the direct examination of experts is to keep it simple.

One way to achieve simplicity without sacrificing understanding and completeness is through the expert's use of analogies and metaphors. Even the most well-intentioned examiner and the most plain-spoken expert may still fail to make the expert's testimony clear and understandable to the jury. Some terms of art do not have easy to understand synonyms and just seem to defy the best efforts at simplification. Well-constructed analogies and metaphors taken from every day life bridge the jurors' gap between what they hear from experts and what they understand.

Take an expert in a criminal case who is testifying about forensic DNA testing, for example. Few topics can match DNA analysis for complexity, the terms are foreign, (genes, alleles, polymers, to name just a few), the tests are like alphabet soup, (RFLP, PCR, and D1S80) and the testing process is a total mystery (RFLP testing includes, for example, electrophoresis, Southern blotting, and the use of radiographs). And that does not even begin to include the complexities of statistical probabilities and the work of population geneticists. Attempts to explain the precise scientific principles of DNA testing to a lay jury are for the most part unnecessary and are almost certainly doomed to failure. Instead the expert should identify some common images that will give the jury a working knowledge of how scientists and police use DNA as an investigative tool. The distinctiveness and usefulness of DNA might be compared favorably to a person's fingerprints. It is quite distinctive (though not exclusive) and it tells us where a person may have been, though not necessarily when. In describing the organization of genetic information in DNA, one scientist has analogized it to an encyclopedia:

> The genetic information contained in the DNA is organized and packaged into chromosomes, much as printed information is organized into volumes. Just as a specific passage in the encyclopedia can be identified by specifying a volume, page, and line number, a specific genetic passage or location, known as a locus, can be identified . . . . For example, if we see the designation D4S139 in a report, then we know exactly what gene has been analyzed.[12]

Everyone has read an encyclopedia, and thinking about DNA in those terms will improve the jurors' understanding.

Developing effective metaphors or analogies is an essential part of the process of preparing an expert for testimony at trial and it is a job for both lawyer and expert. The expert may be a good source for such explanatory devices inasmuch as experts have the expertise and experience in the field. At the same time, however, the advocate knows the facts of the case better than anyone and may be able to see applications of the expert's theory that are not readily apparent to the expert.

❖ Principle Number Seven: Refuse to Treat Experts as Commodities

Expert witnesses have become indispensible to trial lawyers. That is both good news and bad news, because experts can be expensive *or*

---

[12] HOWARD COLEMAN & ERIC SWENSON, DNA IN THE COURTROOM: A TRIAL WATCHER'S GUIDE 31 (1994).

invaluable; helpful *or* a liability; impartial *or* partisan. When it comes to experts, it is fair to say about trial lawyers, "can't live with 'em, can't live without 'em." Yet, trial lawyers can and do decide how they will select, prepare, and actually use experts in their cases. Advocates can refuse to treat expert witness testimony as a commodity to be purchased, and they can refuse to treat experts as partisans available for the right price. That is, advocates in their zeal to win must resist the ever-present temptation to join those who view experts in simple utilitarian terms, as nothing more than instruments needed to ensure victory at trial.

The most difficult issues that arise in the examination of experts mostly relate to money. The fact that experts are paid makes them more susceptible to corruption and makes lawyers more prone to exploit that vulnerability by exerting undue influence and pressure on the expert to do and say whatever is necessary to prevail. The basic governing principles for dealing with the experts should be obvious. First and foremost, experts may not have any direct financial interest in the lawsuit, such as by means of a contingent fee agreement with a party. The expert's payment must be for the services provided, and not for a particular outcome in the case. Experts should not become a part of the trial team—just another advocate for the party who is footing the bill. Instead, experts should be allowed, and even required, to maintain a professional detachment from the parties.

Second, lawyers should select experts based on their expertise and skill in a pertinent field and not because of their partisanship. Experts who will say anything for anybody should be carefully avoided, as should experts who maintain blind allegiance to a particular position regardless of the specific facts or circumstances of a case.

Third, lawyers should prepare experts in a way that does not dictate the particular result the party wants or needs. The lawyer should provide the expert with all of the necessary information and allow the expert the ability to form his or her opinions without exerting any overreaching partisan influences.

Fourth, and finally, lawyers should present expert testimony in a way that is consistent with the standards in the expert's own professional discipline. Lawyers should not pressure experts to express their opinions more definitively than is appropriate in light of what is known and what the expert's discipline would allow. Moreover, lawyers should not expect experts to express opinions in a way that encompasses the ultimate issues in the case, but instead in terms and with qualifying words appropriate for their discipline.

The high stakes of litigation and the corrupting influence of money make a combustible combination when it comes to expert witness testimony. Trial lawyers, as officers of the court, and with an obligation of candor to the judge and jury, bear the brunt of the obligation to ensure that their use of experts furthers the search for truth instead of frustrating it. It is a high calling and a difficult one in today's environment, but a worthy one for those entrusted with ensuring that justice is done.

V. THE CROSS-EXAMINATION OF EXPERTS

The general principles of cross-examination discussed in Chapter Nine are equally applicable to the cross-examination of expert witnesses. Advocates conducting a cross-examination of an expert should ask leading questions, maintain effective control of the witness, and take advantage of the principles of primacy and recency when organizing the cross. The balance of this chapter addresses specific concerns that arise during the cross-examination of expert witnesses and suggests particular techniques to help ensure a successful examination.

A. Special Challenges in the Cross-Examination of Experts

The cross-examination of expert witnesses presents trial lawyers with particularly difficult challenges and concerns. In the first place, experts are just that, experts. Presumably, they have specialized knowledge in the area about which they are talking, which gives them a head start and no small amount of self-assurance. They know the field better than the advocate ever will. In the second place, they are often veterans of the courtroom. In fact, the expert is likely to have had more experience in the courtroom than the advocate. Experienced experts are comfortable in the courtroom, and can be difficult to nail down or control. In the third place, the expert is likely to be an articulate and effective speaker. Not surprisingly, professional experts have charm, sincerity, and polish that can make them seem immune to attack. These conditions—the knowledge, experience, and personality of experts—combine to make cross-examination of experts a difficult task.

However, the task need not be feared. Experts can be cross-examined successfully. The road to such success is charted below, but it begins where all trial success begins—with careful and thorough preparation. Preparation begins with learning everything possible about the area of expertise involved in the case. It includes some tutoring at the hands of a consulting expert or perhaps even the party's own testifying expert. Furthermore, it includes careful and detailed review of each expert's report, deposition testimony, articles, publications, and other writings, or statements that may indicate potential areas of attack. Once the background preparation work has been completed, the advocate is ready to prepare the cross-examination questions themselves.

B. Potential Areas of Inquiry

1. *Constructive Facts and Areas of Agreement*

Cross-examining experts involves more than attempting to show that the opponent's expert witnesses are mercenaries who will say anything for a dollar. In fact, the cross of experts provides an excellent opportunity to advance the cross-examiner's own case by establishing or confirming key facts or propositions. Sometimes the best place to begin the cross-examination of an expert is not with an impeachment or attack, but with inquiry about areas of agreement between the parties, if any exist. Typically, such "constructive facts" can be found with every expert. For example, the opposing expert may recognize the examiner's expert as a leader in the field. He may admit that the assumptions made by the examiner's expert or the facts relied on by him were fair and reasonable. He may concede that the methodology used by the examiner's expert was proper and correct (while disagreeing with the opinion reached). In each instance the point of agreement is worth emphasizing to the jury. The opposing expert's confirmation simultaneously bolsters your expert's credibility and establishes the point as undisputed.

This tactic is analogous to hitchhiking; the advocate hitches a ride with the opponent's expert, eliciting testimony from the expert that moves the advocate closer to proving the claims or defenses that he must prove to prevail. The time to hitchhike is at the beginning of the cross, before the cross-examiner attempts to discredit or attack the opposing expert's opinions. The reason is a simple matter of human nature. Once the attacks begin, the expert will be much less likely to be helpful and much less willing to agree to anything the advocate asks.

Beyond constructive facts, there are, of course, many potential lines of attack and impeachment during the cross-examination of experts. In fact, one can identify and analyze potential attacks by evaluating each aspect of the expert's direct testimony and asking whether the expert is susceptible to criticism or impeachment on that point. Thus, one might ask, by way of example: Is the expert properly qualified? Does the expert have an adequate basis for her opinion? Did the opposing expert fail to undertake any of the steps the examiner's expert took? Do the expert's opinions make sense? Are they supported by some articulated methodology? And finally, is the expert subject to impeachment by prior inconsistent statement or by omission or otherwise? Each line of attack is discussed in the order it would normally appear during the direct, beginning with the expert's qualifications.

2. *Attacking Qualifications*

The opponent's qualifications may be a rich source of cross-examination material. There are two quite different approaches when attacking an opposing expert's qualifications. The first is to seek to preclude the expert from testifying in the case (either entirely or as to a particular opinion), and the second is to attack the weight the jury should give to the expert's testimony. Naturally, preclusion is substantially more difficult to obtain than a successful attack on the weight of the expert's opinion. As noted above, the Federal Rules of Evidence adopt a generous standard for experts, allowing them to acquire their specialized knowledge from any of five methods, including education, training, or experience. Moreover, judges have traditionally been reluctant to exclude expert testimony because of the impact of such a ruling. Nevertheless, the recent Supreme Court rulings in *Daubert* and *Kumho Tire* and the amendment of Rule 702 may have toughened the resolve of some judges and made them more sympathetic to these challenges.

a. Precluding the Testimony: *Voir Dire* of Experts

The typical procedural means for seeking exclusion of expert testimony is through the filing of a motion *in limine* before the trial begins. This approach does not directly implicate cross-examination, but is simply a matter of making the necessary legal arguments to the court about the shortcomings of the expert's qualifications to testify. An alternative means of seeking preclusion is to object at the time the expert is tendered to the court or immediately prior to the expert's opinion testimony. In this scenario, the advocate's proof of the expert's lack of qualifications may involve taking the expert on *voir dire,* meaning that the cross-examiner would question the expert specifically about any alleged deficiencies before the expert would be allowed to offer his opinions.

Voir dire is not a term or process reserved solely for questioning jurors as part of the juror selection process. It is also used with witnesses to resolve questions about their qualifications to testify. Used properly, it is a powerful tool. In essence, *voir dire* allows an advocate to conduct a portion of his cross-examination of the expert right in the middle of the opponent's direct examination. It allows the advocate to raise questions about the expert's credentials before the jury even hears the expert's opinions. And it enables the advocate to disrupt the direct examination of the rhythm and flow that all direct examiners need and want.

Voir dire is appropriate when a party raises a legitimate question about the qualifications of a person to testify as an expert on a particular issue. The right to *voir dire* rests firmly in the discretion of the trial judge. A party who desires to conduct a *voir dire* of the opposing expert must raise an objection when the expert attempts to testify to any opinion that exceeds the expert's expertise or for which the expert is unqualified to give. The proper objection is "lack of foundation." The objection signifies that the direct examiner has literally failed to lay an adequate foundation under Rule 702 for this witness to testify as an expert as to the particular opinion sought. Typically, the judge will then entertain argument from counsel for and against the objection.

In the course of argument, the objecting counsel may request the opportunity to *voir dire* the expert as a means of supporting the party's motion. Or, in the alternative, the judge may invite counsel to take the expert on *voir dire*. In either event, the *voir dire* is limited to the challenged lack of qualifications and may not range into other unrelated matters. The proponent of the expert must vigilantly protect against a wide-ranging *voir dire* in which the opponent essentially conducts his entire cross-examination under the guise of conducting a *voir dire*.

 Illustration of *Voir Dire* Examination

Plaintiff's lawyer: Dr. Smith, what is your opinion about whether the design of the defendant's front loader was safe for its intended use?

Defense lawyer:	Objection, lack of foundation.
Judge:	[*To Plaintiff's counsel*] Any response counsel?
Plaintiff's lawyer:	Yes, Your Honor. We have established that Dr. Smith has a Ph.D. in mechanical engineering and teaches courses at Westside Community College in this field. He is clearly qualified under Rule 702 of the Federal Rules.
Judge:	Counsel?
Defense lawyer:	Your Honor, if I could take Dr. Smith on *voir dire*, I believe I could demonstrate to the court that he is not qualified to offer an opinion about the safety of the design of Acme's front loader.
Judge:	You may.

Voir Dire Examination by Defendant's Counsel:

Lawyer:	Dr. Smith, you have never designed a front loader, have you?
Witness:	No, I haven't.
Lawyer:	In fact, you have never even participated in the design of a front loader, true?
Witness:	That's true.
Lawyer:	And you've never worked for a heavy machinery manufacturer, right?
Witness:	That's right.
Lawyer:	You have never consulted with a heavy machinery manufacturer on the design of a front loader, have you?
Witness:	I have not.
Lawyer:	All of your professional life you have been in academia, isn't that right?
Witness:	Well, not entirely. I consult with a number of commercial entities on a wide range of engineering issues.
Lawyer:	I understand, but you have always either been a student or a professor, true?
Witness:	That's correct.
Lawyer:	You've never worked full time in the private, for-profit sector?
Witness:	That's true.
Lawyer:	Your Honor, at this time I renew my objection to Dr. Smith's testimony. He has no practical, real world basis on which to evaluate the design of the front loader that is in issue. His testimony should be excluded.

b. Attacking Weight

In the likely event that the effort to preclude the expert from testifying fails, the cross examiner's task is to attack the weight the jury should give to the expert's testimony. In these instances, the deficiency in the expert's qualifications is not so great as to prevent the expert from testifying altogether, but rather suggests that the expert—though marginally qualified to testify—should be greeted by the jury with skepticism or outright disdain. Consider just a sampling of the possible attacks on expert qualifications:

- Contrasting the superior credentials of the cross-examiner's expert to the credentials of the opposing expert

- Identifying the remarkable variety and range of matters about which the opposing expert has testified, suggesting that he is a partisan expert who testifies about anything and everything

- Demonstrating that the expert is testifying beyond the scope of her expertise

- Showing that the expert, while marginally qualified as an expert under the rules, is not adequately qualified or experienced to give a credible opinion in the particular field or discipline at issue.

i. Contrasting Credentials

When both sides call an expert to testify on a particular issue, creating a real battle of the experts, the question arises as to which expert to believe. Which of the two experts is best suited to offer an opinion? Which expert is more credible and better qualified? One attack on the opponent's expert opinion testimony exploits any advantages held by the cross-examiner's own expert in terms of superior credentials or experience in the pertinent field. Perhaps the most obvious application of this attack is in cases in which one expert has an advanced degree and the opposing expert does not. However, it also might apply when one expert has extensive hands-on experience in the field, while the other has only academic exposure to the issue. In other words, advocates must identify those advantages they enjoy in comparing the competing credentials of the competing experts and must attempt to exploit any advantage.

 Illustration of Cross-Examination of Experts (Contrasting Expert Credentials)

Lawyer:	Mr. Copeland, the extent of your education in the field of electrical engineering was a bachelors degree obtained from Western State in 1963, is that right?
Witness:	Yes, that's correct.
Lawyer:	And you never went back and obtained a doctoral degree in electrical engineering, did you?

Witness:	No, I immediately got a job in the field and went to work.
Lawyer:	You never got a masters degree in electrical engineering either, true?
Witness:	Yes, that's right.
Lawyer:	In fact, since you obtained your bachelor's degree almost forty years ago, you've not taken any courses toward an advanced degree, isn't that right?
Witness:	That's true, but misleading. I've taken continuing education courses every year since I started to work to keep my engineering license current.
Lawyer:	Well, all engineers have to take those continuing education courses, don't they?
Witness:	Yes, they do.
Lawyer:	And isn't it true that Dr. Livingston, the electrical engineering expert for Mary Worth in this case, has a doctorate in electrical engineering?
Witness:	That's my understanding.
Lawyer:	And his degree is from New York Technical University, right?
Witness:	Again, that's what I understand.
Lawyer:	New York Technical University has one of the premier engineering programs in the world doesn't it?
Witness:	Yes, it's highly respected.
Lawyer:	And a doctorate in electrical engineering requires four or five years of schooling after college, does it not?
Witness:	I believe that's right.
Lawyer:	Well, you would agree that Dr. Livingston went to school a good bit longer than you did?
Witness:	Absolutely.
Lawyer:	And he has an advanced degree in the field of electrical engineering that you simply do not have, true?
Witness:	That is true.

ii.   The All-Purpose Expert

The dramatic growth in the use of experts over the last thirty years has created a cottage industry of so-called "professional experts" who derive all or most of their income from serving as expert witnesses in litigated matters. They are expert witnesses first, and engineers, economists, or physicians second. That development opens the expert to impeachment in two ways—perhaps the expert has developed a particular position or approach to an issue, such that he offers the same opinion in every case regardless of the facts or he is available for hire on any issue for any party. That is, the advocate might confront the all-purpose professional expert at one extreme or the single-issue expert at the other. The single-issue expert suggests a kind of bias, sometimes called "positional bias," which will be discussed a bit later. The all-purpose expert suggests someone who is both biased ("he will do anything for a buck!") and unqualified. After all, no one can be an expert on everything, and the more areas the expert has testified in, the greater the likelihood that the jury will find him exceeding his actual area of expertise. The familiar axiom "jack of all trades, master of none" comes to mind. The cross-examination should simply lay out the remarkable array of areas of alleged expertise in past cases. The result can and should be devastating.

 ## Illustration of Cross-Examination of the All-Purpose Expert

Lawyer:	Mr. Flanagan, you have testified as an expert before today, haven't you?
Witness:	Yes, I've done this a number of times.
Lawyer:	In fact, you've given expert testimony in six other cases just this year, true?
Witness:	I don't know the exact number, but I have had a number of cases I was working on go to trial. Maybe four, five, six times, I can't be certain about it.
Lawyer:	Well, in the case of *West v. Frigid Air, Inc.,* in January of this year, you testified about a defect in the design of the West's air conditioning system, didn't you?
Witness:	Yes, I did.
Lawyer:	That testimony required mechanical engineering expertise on your part, true?
Witness:	Yes, that's fair.
Lawyer:	And you were paid by the plaintiffs for your services in that case, weren't you?
Witness:	Yes, of course, in the same way as all experts.
Lawyer:	That's right. And in February, in the case of *Davidson v. Westmont Industries*, you testified about the unsafe conditions that existed on Westmont's premises, correct?
Witness:	That's correct.

Lawyer:	And that testimony required expertise in the field of industrial hygiene and safety, right?
Witness:	That's true, based on my many years as a plant foreman.
Lawyer:	I understand Mr. Flanagan. And you were paid by Davidson, the plaintiff in that case, true?
Witness:	Yes, once again, per the normal practice in this field.
Lawyer:	Later in February, you testified again, didn't you?
Witness:	I couldn't say, Counsel; that was a while ago.
Lawyer:	The case of *Hiller v. Dixon*, you remember that case?
Witness:	Of course, yes.
Lawyer:	And in *Hiller* you testified about the cause of the automobile accident between Hiller and Dixon, correct?
Witness:	Yes, I did—nothing more than elementary physics.
Lawyer:	I'm sorry Mr. Flanagan. My question was whether you testified about the cause of the accident?
Witness:	Yes, yes.
Lawyer:	And that testimony required expertise in accident reconstruction?
Witness:	That's true.
Lawyer:	The plaintiff paid for your services in that case as well, true?
Witness:	I believe that it was the lawyer who actually paid me, but I was paid, yes.
Lawyer:	You were paid for your services as an accident reconstructionist by someone associated with the plaintiff?
Witness:	Yes, I was.
Lawyer:	And then in March of this year, the next month, you testified in the case of *Norse v. BCH Enterprises and the West Valley Fire Department*, right?
Witness:	Yes.
Lawyer:	And in that case you testified about the cause and origin of a fire that injured Mr. Norse, true?
Witness:	Yes, I did. It started from a defective space heater in his home.
Lawyer:	And you testified about the substandard conduct of the firefighters at the scene, true?
Witness:	Yes, in support of plaintiff's claims against the Fire Department.

Lawyer:	And your testimony in Hiller required expertise in the standard of care for firefighters, true?
Witness:	Yes.
Lawyer:	As well as expertise in fire investigation?
Witness:	Yes.

The process can continue on through the many wildly divergent areas of expertise, all the while reinforcing the point that for this expert, education or experience are not barriers to testifying for whatever the party paying him needs him to say. Notice the logical rhythm of the questioning. It follows the same pattern for each case: first, the date and name of the case; second, the nature of the expert testimony; then, the particular expertise required to give the testimony; and finally, the fact of payment for the testimony. The questions do not give the expert an opportunity to explain. They are simple and straightforward, allowing little weasel room.

There are other means of pressing the case that the expert should not be trusted because of the expert's insufficient expertise. Careful attention must be paid to the specific area of expertise claimed by the expert and efforts to exceed that area must be pointed out to the jury. In the midst of battle it is not unusual for lawyers and experts to stretch expertise beyond its proper boundaries. It is a sure sign of the expert's bias in the case and must be highlighted for the jury. Similarly, some experts satisfy the generous standard in Rule 702, but simply do not measure up for the case at hand. Point out the deficiencies; illuminate the absent training, education, knowledge, skill, or experience.

3. *Attacking Motivation—Bias or Prejudice: Fees, Relationships, Preconceptions*

A third, fertile area in the cross-examination of experts is the expert's bias or prejudice. Payment of witnesses is ordinarily strictly forbidden—although expert witnesses are almost always paid for their services—and a party's payment of an expert raises obvious issues regarding the effect of the money on the expert's impartiality. While the payment of experts is likely the most obvious form of expert bias, it is far from the only one. Other forms of bias might include:

- The expert currently has, or at one time had, an employment relationship with the party.

- The expert has previously given expert testimony for the party *or* advocate.

- The expert always testifies for the same side in litigated cases (*e.g.*, expert always testifies for defendant manufacturer in crashworthiness cases).

- The expert always testifies to the same conclusion in every case.

- The expert has some other interest in the case or issues involved, whether economic, professional, or personal.

The bias created by an expert's payment is about as straightforward an impeachment opportunity as one could hope to have. It does not require any sophistication to recognize that an expert who was paid a substantial sum of money by one party may well have some degree of bias in favor of that party, particularly when the expert's conclusions inexorably favor the paying litigant. Nevertheless, despite the obvious logical force of the evidence, the expert's payment, standing alone, does not necessarily carry much persuasive force with juries for at least two reasons: (1) both side's experts in the case are likely being paid for their services, and they have reached conflicting opinions (thus forcing the jury to look to other factors in deciding who to believe); and (2) both experts will sincerely and vigorously deny any connection between their payment and their opinions. Therefore, the impeachment question on cross, "Isn't it true that you are being paid by plaintiff for your testimony here today?" does little, by itself, to materially advance the defendant's case.

The limited utility of that question does not mean, however, that counsel should simply avoid inquiry into the expert's payment altogether. Rather, it means that advocates must find creative ways to make the point more meaningful, to show juries the corrosive influence that money can have in the work of experts. Perhaps the best means of making that showing is by linking the fact of payment to the aspect of the expert's direct testimony that best supports the claim that the expert is biased. For example, an expert's opinion on behalf of a cigarette producer that nicotine is not addictive would, in and of itself, suggest that the expert may have a bias in favor of the cigarette company that is paying him. However, juxtaposition of the expert's seemingly extreme opinion and the fact that he was paid by a cigarette company to offer it makes the point more powerful and memorable. Here is an illustration of how that technique might be used specifically to demonstrate bias.

 Illustration of Linkage of Expert's Payment

Lawyer:	Dr. Drake, in forming your opinion today, you have considered all of the scientific evidence about whether nicotine is addictive, haven't you?
Witness:	There is a wealth of literature out there, some helpful, some not. So, it probably overstates it a bit to say I've considered everything. I have considered the significant studies and data that shed light on the question, yes.
Lawyer:	And included in the material you reviewed was the Nyquist Study, correct?

Witness:	Well, I didn't specifically rely on the Nyquist Study because I don't agree with its methodology, but I certainly am aware of it.
Lawyer:	That's right, you are aware of it, true?
Witness:	Yes, I am aware of it.
Lawyer:	The Nyquist study concluded that nicotine is addictive, correct?
Witness:	Yes, it did.
Lawyer:	When you were preparing for your testimony today, you were also aware of the California Public Health Study on the effects of nicotine on behavior, were you not?
Witness:	Yes.
Lawyer:	You were aware of that study?
Witness:	Yes, I was.
Lawyer:	That study is the largest such study ever conducted on this issue, true?
Witness:	Yes, I believe it studied the most smokers over the longest period of time.
Lawyer:	And that study also concluded that nicotine has addictive qualities, isn't that right?
Witness:	That's fair.
Lawyer:	It found nicotine to be addictive, true?
Witness:	Yes.
Lawyer:	But your testimony here today is that nicotine is not addictive.
Witness:	That's right. Not in the classic sense of that concept. People stop smoking every day in this country.
Lawyer:	So, your testimony here today is that, despite these studies that have found to the contrary, you believe that nicotine is not addictive?
Witness:	That's right.
Lawyer:	**[Linkage question number 1]** And you offer that opinion on behalf of a producer of cigarettes, true?
Witness:	Yes.
Lawyer:	**[Linkage question number 2]** And, in fact, you offer that opinion while you are being paid by that defendant cigarette producer, correct?
Witness:	Yes, but the opinion has nothing to do with being paid.

Lawyer:	Well, isn't it true that you are being paid $1,000.00 for your time spent testifying today?
Witness:	Yes, that's my standard rate for one day of trial testimony.
Lawyer:	And you've already been paid more than $10,000.00 for your work in this case, true?
Witness:	Yes, that sounds about right.

4. *Attacking the Expert's Basis*

The expert's basis provides another potentially rich source of cross-examination material. An expert's opinion is only as good as the facts or data on which it is based. Thus, the axiom "garbage in, garbage out" applies with obvious force to expert witness testimony. Once advocates demonstrate that experts have inadequate or unreliable bases for their opinions, the jurors are almost certain to discount the opinions as well. Potential attacks on the basis include unsupported assumptions, inadequate or faulty preparation or investigation, lack of personal knowledge, and errors made by the expert in preparing his opinions. Each attack is discussed and illustrated below.

a. Unsupported Assumptions

All experts make assumptions when they form opinions; it is impossible to form an opinion without assuming something. Economists testifying about future lost wages have to predict the future with regard to the deceased or injured plaintiff, and in doing so, they must make assumptions about how long the person would have worked but for the injury, how much they would have made, what raises they would have received, and how the general economy would perform, etc. An accident reconstruction expert makes assumptions about who is telling the truth about what happened, how fast cars were moving at the point of impact, and so on. Real estate appraisers make assumptions about the rate of depreciation for the property they are appraising and the market value of the improvements to the property. Some assumptions are based on future events, others on past behavior, others on national statistics, and still others on industry practice. But they are assumptions nonetheless—unproven facts—and they are critical to the validity of the opinions of most experts.

In preparing to cross-examine an expert, the advocate should:

1. identify the assumptions the expert has relied on in forming her opinion;

2. question the expert about her assumptions during her deposition;

3. retain a consultant with similar expertise who can help identify the assumptions relied upon by the opposing expert; and

4. test the assumptions against the facts in the case.

Do the assumptions make sense in light of what is known about the person? Are they consistent with standards in the expert's own field? Do they make unsupported leaps of logic? During the cross, the examiner can:

1. reveal to the jury the expert's assumptions, demonstrating the tenuous nature of the expert's conclusions;

2. challenge the expert's assumptions as unsupported by the facts, logic, or accepted practices in the expert's discipline; and/or

3. change any incorrect assumptions to proper ones and force the expert to reassess his or her opinion in light of the changes.

Illustration of Attacking Expert Economist's Assumptions[13]

Lawyer: Dr. Chen, in forming the opinions you've offered here today, you made a number of assumptions about Mr. McFarland's future didn't you?

Witness: Yes, I did.

Lawyer: In fact, you could not have reached an opinion about McFarland's lost income in the future without making those assumptions, true?

Witness: That's the nature of what I do.

Lawyer: That's right, you rely on assumptions about what will happen in the future, correct?

Witness: Yes.

Lawyer: And if the assumptions you have made do not happen, that will change the loss you claim was suffered by Mr. McFarland, right?

Witness: Yes, changes could increase or decrease his future lost income.

Lawyer: One of the assumptions you made is that Mr. McFarland will live for twenty-three more years, true?

Witness: Yes, that's true, based on life expectancy tables.

Lawyer: Those tables are averages for all Americans, right?

Witness: That's right.

Lawyer: They don't take into account a person's family history of heart disease, do they?

---

[13] This illustration is based on the hypothetical case *Farrell et al. v. Strong Line, Inc. et al.*, Thomas F. Geraghty (National Institute of Trial Advocacy).

Witness:	Not specifically, they represent national averages.
Lawyer:	And in this case, Mr. McFarland had a notable family history of heart disease, didn't he?
Witness:	Yes, he has some history of heart disease in his family.
Lawyer:	If Mr. McFarland lived for only eighteen more years, instead of the twenty-three years that you assumed, that would change your opinion about the extent of his lost income, would it not?
Witness:	Yes.
Lawyer:	In the summary chart you prepared, plaintiff's exhibit C, you would stop calculating the plaintiff's loss after year eighteen, correct?
Witness:	Yes, that's right.
Lawyer:	And that changed assumption would reduce the amount of loss you claim by almost $357,000.00, true?
Witness:	I would have to do the calculation to figure that out.
Lawyer:	Please go ahead and do so.

[*Expert recalculates lost income.*]

Witness:	Okay, I'm done.
Lawyer:	Go ahead.
Witness:	The change would be a reduction of $356,768.46 in the amount of future lost income for Mr. McFarland.

[*The cross-examiner continues working through the expert's assumptions, one at a time*].

b. Lack of Personal Knowledge

Broadly speaking, there are two types of experts: those who participated in some way in the events that give rise to the lawsuit or its aftermath and those who participate only after the fact and must rely on a cold record and imperfect memories in determining what happened and why. In the former category is the design engineer who participates in the design of a vehicle that is subsequently alleged to be defectively designed or a doctor who treated the injured plaintiff immediately after an accident or the coroner who performs an autopsy of the body. These experts are hybrid fact/ expert witnesses in that they have both personal knowledge of pertinent facts in the case and expertise on disputed issues. Most experts, however, are retained long after the facts of the case and have no personal knowledge of the facts. Instead, they have to rely on what others say happened and they often have to form their opinions without the benefit of knowing everything that they would like to know.

This limitation faced by many experts creates opportunities for the cross-examiner. One surefire means of limiting the import of the opponent's expert is by making the point that the expert was not present at the time, that he or she does not know to an absolute certainty what happened, and that the expert is relying on the memories and perspectives of many others and the assessment of circumstantial evidence in reaching an opinion. The attack on the expert's lack of personal knowledge makes explicit a point that is *always* implicit with experts—that their work involves the evaluation and assessment of facts and data after the fact, not the direct or personal observation of the disputed events.

 Illustration of Attacking Expert's Lack of Personal Knowledge

Lawyer:	Dr. Jones, it's your opinion that the accident was the result of defendant's failure to stop at the red light, true?
Witness:	Yes, that's right.
Lawyer:	But you weren't there when the accident happened, were you?
Witness:	No, I wasn't there, but I've seen the accounts of those who were there and they are consistent with what I've concluded.
Lawyer:	Well, the defendant says that the light was still yellow when she went through the intersection, doesn't she?
Witness:	Yes, that's true she does claim that.
Lawyer:	But you have disregarded what she says happened haven't you?
Witness:	No, I haven't disregarded it, I've concluded that it is not consistent with the other available evidence.
Lawyer:	And you didn't see the defendant's car run that red light, did you?
Witness:	No, of course not.
Lawyer:	For that matter, you didn't see whether or not the plaintiff's car went into the intersection before the light turned green did you?
Witness:	No, I was not there.

c.   Inadequate Preparation

Another potential area of cross-examination is the adequacy of the expert's preparation. Did the expert actually visit the scene of the accident or personally inspect the allegedly defective part? Did the expert collect the information necessary to reach an opinion on the pertinent issue in the case? Did the expert take each step required by the standards or protocols in the expert's discipline before arriving at an opinion? Did the expert account for other possible explanations or causes of the disputed events before drawing a conclusion? There are almost always questions the expert did not ask, places she did not go, measurements she did not take, tests she did not run, alternatives she did not consider. Each misstep is an opportunity to demonstrate that the expert's work was incomplete, haphazard, or even shoddy, and that the expert's preparation is inadequate to support the opinion.

Illustration of Cross-Examination on Expert's Inadequate Preparation

Lawyer:	Dr. Jones, you were retained as an expert by defense counsel over three years ago, isn't that right?
Witness:	Yes, I believe that is correct.
Lawyer:	In fact, as I do the mental calculation, it has actually been forty-two months since you were hired by the defense, correct?
Witness:	That sounds about right.
Lawyer:	From that time forty-two months ago until this very day, as you sit in that witness chair testifying for the defense, you have not once gone to the scene of the collision involved in this case, have you?
Witness:	It wasn't necessary.
Lawyer:	Actually, that wasn't my question, Dr. Jones. Isn't it true that in the forty-two months since you have been retained by the defense, you have not once gone to the scene of the accident?
Witness:	No, I have not.
Lawyer:	Dr. Jones, you were present when Mr. Miller testified, weren't you?
Witness:	Yes.
Lawyer:	His expert opinion is that the defendant made an improper left turn that caused the accident, true?
Witness:	That's what he testified to.
Lawyer:	Mr. Miller went to that intersection of Baton and Main Street, didn't he?
Witness:	That's what he said.

Lawyer:	That's right. In fact, he told us he went to the intersection two times, isn't that right?
Witness:	That's what he said.
Lawyer:	You have no reason to disbelieve him, do you?
Witness:	Of course not.
Lawyer:	Mr. Miller's first site inspection was during the mid-day, to visually inspect the intersection, and his second visit was at 3:30 p.m., which was the time of day the collision in this case took place, isn't that what he told us?
Witness:	That's right.
Lawyer:	Dr. Jones, since you did not go to the collision site, you were never able to visually inspect and assess the intersection, were you?
Witness:	Counsel, I have reviewed the police files, including their accident reconstruction reports. Those reports contain all the necessary measurements and other pertinent data. It was not necessary for me to personally visit the site.
Lawyer:	Just to be clear. You at no time made a visual inspection of that intersection?
Witness:	That's right.
Lawyer:	And it is your testimony that inspecting the site at the same time of day as the accident would have in no way been beneficial in reaching your expert conclusion?
Witness:	That's right.
Lawyer:	Dr. Jones, did the accident investigation report indicate the amount of traffic that typically passes through that intersection on weekday afternoon at approximately 3:30 p.m.?
Witness:	No.
Lawyer:	Did the accident investigation report indicate whether this intersection was in a heavily commercial area?
Witness:	No.
Lawyer:	Did the accident investigation report indicate whether there were any schools in the area, from which students might be walking home?
Witness:	No.
Lawyer:	Did the accident investigation report indicate the angle of the sun for a motorist traveling westbound at 3:30 in the afternoon?
Witness:	No.

d. Mistakes or Errors of Computation, Reporting, Recording, or Analyzing

A final method of attacking the expert's basis is to identify a mistake the expert made in the expert's report or direct examination testimony and then confront the expert with the mistake during the cross. The impact of such a tactic on both the jury and the witness cannot be over-estimated. The mistake shows the jury that the expert is fallible—and perhaps also biased, depending on the nature of the mistake—and also signals to the expert that the questioner is well prepared and will catch slip-ups by the witness. The latter point is a critical lesson for experts. They often have quite a bit of experience in the courtroom, a healthy dose of confidence as a witness, and familiarity with the process, which can make them difficult to control during cross-examination. A quick jab to the nose in the form of a correction will go a long way to reduce the likeli-hood of future battles. The behavioral impact of an early correction argues in favor of making the point early in the cross-examination, if there is no "hitchhiking" to be done, so that the advocate can maximize the benefit gained from the attack

The correction might be any kind of mistake, as long as it is mate-rial to the case and important to the expert's opinions: a mathematical error, an incorrect measurement, a wrong fact. In the O.J. Simpson crimi-nal prosecution, the defense, during the cross-examination of Dr. Bruce Weir, a statistician and population geneticist, identified a mistake he made in his calculation of the probability that certain DNA found in blood had come from someone other than Simpson. The exchange between the defense attorney, Peter Neufeld, and Dr. Weir is reproduced below.[14]

Illustration of Attacking Miscalculation in Forming an Opinion

Lawyer:	Let me ask you this, Dr. Weir, just to change gears for a second: During your career, Sir, have you ever made any mistakes as a professional?
Witness:	Oh, I'm sure I have.
Lawyer:	Have you ever made errors in either calculations or computations?
Witness:	I'm sure I have.
Lawyer:	Have you ever in your career asserted facts that turn out not to be correct?

---

[14] The excerpt of Neufeld's cross-examination is taken from Westlaw's database of notable trials. *People v. Simpson*, Cause No. BA097211 (June 23, 1995), 1991 WL 394321, *12–21 (Cal. Super. Ct.).

Witness:	Well, you will probably refresh me with some. I hope not.
Lawyer:	Okay. Would it be fair to say that you may have made mistakes during your career in certain facts that were asserted?
Witness:	I may have made a mistake in my career, yes.
Lawyer:	Okay. And would you also agree, Doctor, that perhaps you have even propounded theories that, at some time in the future, ultimately were refuted?
Witness:	I don't believe so. I don't—I can't think of any published refutations of any of my papers.

[*After a discussion of other matters, Neufeld returns to Weir's calculations.*]

Lawyer:	. . . . [O]ne of the things you did do, at least initially, is you would sum the frequencies of the different pairs of genotypes; isn't that right?
Witness:	That's correct, yes, we have all the possible ways of getting those four alleles.
Lawyer:	And it was your intent when you did this, Dr. Weir, was it not, to sum up all the possible pairs? You don't want to leave any out?
Witness:	It was my intent and I certainly hope I didn't leave any out.
Lawyer:	And would you agree, Sir, that the more pairs that you include, the more common the ultimate frequency is?
Witness:	That's right, yes.
Lawyer:	So it is essential, to be fair to the defendant in any case or to Mr. Simpson in this particular case, that you include all possible pairs; isn't that right?
Witness:	That's correct, yes.
Lawyer:	And if you left out some pairs, then your number could be biased against Mr. Simpson; isn't that correct?
Witness:	It sounds as though you are finding that I left one out. I hope I haven't.

[*After an exchange about the ability of genetic marker 1.2 to mask itself (that is, to not appear on the test strip) under certain circumstances, Neufeld turned to Dr. Weir's mistake.*]

Lawyer:	If I may, I call your attention to—I would like to put up as a next exhibit, Dr. Weir's table 25-A and 25-B.
Judge:	All right. That will be People's 1199—excuse me, Defense 1199.

[*The tables are displayed for the jury.*]

Lawyer:	Do you see that, Dr. Weir?
Witness:	Yes, I do.
Lawyer:	Dr. Weir, on this table, ... 25-A and -B ....
Witness:	Yes.
Lawyer:	You see the little asterisk you have there underneath the line?
Witness:	I see it, yes.
Lawyer:	And you see where it says "Allele 1.2 if present would not be detected"?
Witness:	Yes.
Lawyer:	Now, in this particular table, Dr. Weir, given the statement results from the DOJ laboratory—
Witness:	Yes.
Lawyer:	As you have for table 24-B, the table I just showed you, in this instance you chose to accept the possibility that the allele, namely 1.2, which is the possible allele, could be masked and therefore not be there?
Witness:	Yes.
Lawyer:	Isn't that correct, sir?
Witness:	Well, I don't know what you mean. The statement holds of course all high calculations include the possibility of it being there.
Lawyer:	And your calculations also include, in this particular table, the possibility of it not being there; isn't that right?
Witness:	That's correct. I have—I have a whole range of possibilities either with it being present or not present.
Lawyer:	So for table 25-A, which were certain mixed stains on the glove, G1 and G4, you chose to include both the frequencies, given the assumption that allele 1.2 is there and the assumption that allele 1.2 is not there; isn't that correct, sir?
Witness:	That looks like right, yes.
Lawyer:	Whereas in the table—by the way, as a result of taking that approach, Sir, in table 25-A, how many different pairs did you have to sum up for the DQ-Alpha type?
Witness:	It looks like 18.
Lawyer:	.... And so you have 18 different frequencies that you sum up on this particular table for those particular items; isn't that correct?

Witness:	That's correct.
Lawyer:	And you did that in a situation where there is a possible 1.2 allele which may or may not actually be there because of the masking phenomena; isn't that correct?
Witness:	That's correct.
Lawyer:	Now, going back, Sir, to—to table 24-A—
Judge:	1198.
Lawyer:	Exhibit 1198, again the same, it being a mixture; is that correct, sir?
Witness:	That is what—that is a mixture, yes.
Lawyer:	And consequently, the 1.2 allele in that particular mixture may actually be there or may actually not be. there; isn't that correct?
Witness:	That's correct.
Lawyer:	But this time, Sir, unlike the other items on the glove, you chose not to include the frequencies of those pairs assuming the 1.2 allele wasn't there; isn't that correct?
Witness:	I think you found my mistake, Mr. Neufeld.
Lawyer:	Well, let's talk about what that mistake means, Sir. In this particular instance, Dr. Weir, your calculations are based only on summing frequencies for six pairs; is that right?
Witness:	That's right.
Lawyer:	And would you agree, Sir, that if you sum the frequencies for an additional dozen pairs, which would be three times as many as you started off with, you would arrive at a probability for that mixture which would be much more helpful to Mr. Simpson; isn't that correct?
Witness:	I might question the word "Match." It depends on the frequency of the 1.2 alleles.
Lawyer:	Well—
Witness:	It is kind of interesting that the frequencies in both these tables are comparable in magnitude.
Lawyer:	Sir, would you agree and didn't you say a little while ago on cross-examination, that if you add additional pairs of frequencies you will arrive at a frequency that is more common than if you add fewer pairs of frequencies?
Witness:	That's correct.

5. *Attacking Opinions*

The final potential area of cross-examination is the actual opinion proffered by the opposing expert. The opinion is ripe for attack because, by definition, it constitutes a foray into the unknown—and sometimes, the unknowable. That fact alone raises a number of questions about the expert's opinion, including:

- bias—Did the expert reach his opinion because of the side that is paying him?

- competence—Is the expert qualified to offer his opinion?

- basis—Does the expert have adequate underlying facts and data for his opinion?

- consistency—Is the expert's testimony consistent with common sense principles and professional norms?

- methodology—Did the expert use a valid and reliable methodology in forming his opinion?

We have discussed the first three areas of attack in the three previous sections. The point of each of those attacks is to demonstrate to the jury that the expert's opinion should be questioned or even disregarded entirely, because of a problem with the expert's trustworthiness, credentials, or preparation.

A fourth possibility is that the jury should ignore the expert's testimony because he's simply wrong. That is, even assuming that the expert is objective and qualified and thoroughly prepared, his opinion should still be rejected because it defies common sense or violates professional norms. Experts do take leaps of logic, ignore unhelpful facts, and give into the temptation to be more definitive in their testimony than the underlying data supports and cross-examiners must be prepared to confront the witness with such errors.

The final area of attack is on the expert's methodology in reaching his or her opinion. The theory or technique used by experts in forming an opinion is the very cornerstone of their testimony at trial. Obviously, if experts use a flawed methodology, an unproven theory, or an unreliable technique in forming their opinions, the resulting opinions themselves are highly questionable. Identification of such flawed methodologies begins in the discovery process. Through mandatory disclosures, interrogatories, and depositions, parties should be able to learn the basic theory or methodology relied upon by the opposing expert. In addition, the advocate's own experts, both consulting and testifying experts, can assist in identifying opinions that are derived from theories that are either unproven, debunked, or entirely outside the mainstream of the discipline.

The advocate's first step with such unreliable opinions should be to file a motion *in limine* seeking exclusion of the testimony. Opinions based on unreliable or invalid theories do not satisfy Rule 702 of the Federal

Rules of Evidence. However, if the trial court refuses to exclude the testimony, the attack must shift to the cross-examination of the expert and the presentation of contrary evidence. The attack may zero-in on the flaws in the expert's methodology, contrasting the opposing expert's approach to the generally accepted approach to the issue; or the examiner might use excerpts from a learned treatise (discussed below in section C.1) to point out the unreliability of the expert's approach; or the advocate might simply impeach the expert's approach with common sense.

Experts will say the most amazing things. Consider these three examples of expert testimony actually offered during real trials:

- Testimony from an astronomer claiming that he could date a photograph by making certain calculations from the "directional angle of the shadow cast by [an] object," despite the lack of any testing or verification of his theory.[15]

- Testimony from experts reasoning that "because [the children] sustained birth defects ... and their parents used Shaklee's alfalfa tablets, and because some alfalfa tablets had contained an EtO residue, the parents must have ingested the EtO residue tablets!"[16]

- Testimony from experts that traumatic events, such as car accidents and the like, cause the occurrence of cancer.[17]

Each expert used patently flawed approaches in arriving at their conclusions. The astronomer stretched the field of astronomy far beyond its useful limits; the EtO expert made a leap of logic unsupported by the known facts; and the medical expert found a causal connection that had no valid scientific basis or support. In each instance, cross-examination can effectively reveal the fatal errors committed by the experts.

A related attack on the methodologies used by experts focuses on their application of the methodology to the facts in the case. Rule 702 requires that the principles and methods used by an expert be applied reliably to the facts in the case. Even established methodologies, applied improperly by experts, can result in unreliable opinions. For example, forensic DNA testing, which has been widely accepted by courts, could still be applied to the facts of a case improperly, such as by mishandling of the defendant's blood, or by misinterpretation of the radiograph or by misstatement of the statistical probability that an unknown random person was the source of the tested DNA. Attacking a flawed application of reliable principles or accepted methodologies provides an excellent opportunity to emphasize the expert's bias. Why would someone misapply well-accepted principles or methodologies unless they were only interested in a particular outcome? Linkage of the expert's error in application to his payment makes

---

[15] *See United States v. Tranowski*, 659 F. 2d 750, 752–54 (7th Cir. 1981)

[16] *Sorenson v. Shaklee Corp.*, 31 F.3d 638, 649 (8th Cir. 1994).

[17] *See Daly v. Bergstedt*, 126 N.W.2d 242 (Minn. 1964).

indelible for the jurors the connection between the expert's opinion and his payment.

In testing expert witness opinions and in developing lines of cross-examination that attack flawed opinions, trial lawyers should use as their guides a strong dose of common sense and a healthy skepticism about "knowledge." "Does the expert's opinion make sense, both logically and factually?" "Does the expert's opinion go beyond what his discipline can determine or beyond what can legitimately be known?" If the expert's opinion defies common sense or espouses a position that is simply unknowable, an attack may be in order. If the opinion does not make sense to you, it probably does not make sense to the jurors either, and the cross-examiner can take advantage of the jury's confusion by pointing out the counterintuitive nature of the expert's testimony.

The facts in the Supreme Court's decision in *Kumho Tire Company v. Carmichael*, discussed above, provide an excellent example of an expert using a flawed methodology and applying it to the facts of the case in an illogical, nonsensical, and flawed manner. The plaintiff's expert in that case, a mechanical engineer and "tire failure analyst," testified in his deposition that plaintiff's tire had failed because it was designed or manufactured defectively by defendant. The Supreme Court ultimately determined that the expert's testimony was properly excluded by the trial court, because it was unreliable under Rule 702.[18] Nevertheless, it provides an instructive example of how one might go about the cross-examination of the expert if he testified at trial. A hypothetical cross-examination of that "expert" follows:

 Illustration of Attack on Expert's Flawed Methodology

Lawyer:	Mr. Carlson, it's your opinion that the right rear tire of Mr. Carmichael's car blew out because of a defect in its design or manufacture, is that true?
Witness:	Yes, it is. That's my opinion.
Lawyer:	And in initially reaching that opinion you viewed photographs of the tire, didn't you?
Witness:	Yes, I did, though I later personally inspected the tire as well.
Lawyer:	That's right, but your initial opinion about the tire was based on photographs, true?
Witness:	That's right, a number of photographs.
Lawyer:	And later you personally inspected the tire, right?

---

[18] *See* 526 U.S. 137 at 158.

Witness:	Yes, I did.
Lawyer:	It was important for you to personally inspect the tire, wasn't it?
Witness:	Sure, yes.
Lawyer:	Your personal inspection gave you the chance to touch and feel the tire, right?
Witness:	That's right.
Lawyer:	To see how much tread was left?
Witness:	Yes, I was able to measure the remaining tread.
Lawyer:	To assess the physical condition of the tire?
Witness:	Certainly.
Lawyer:	One of the reasons for you to physically inspect the tire is so you can determine whether the tire's failure was caused by a problem with its design or manufacture or by "overdeflection," true?
Witness:	Yes, the inspection is helpful in making that determination.
Lawyer:	"Overdeflection" means that the tire is under inflated or is carrying too much weight, correct?
Witness:	That's right.
Lawyer:	Either of those problems can lead to separation of the tire from its inner steel belted carcass, true?
Witness:	True.
Lawyer:	And that separation causes the blow out?
Witness:	Yes, that's right.
Lawyer:	And your theory is that if the blow-out was not caused by overdeflection, then it must have been caused by a design or manufacturing defect, is that right?
Witness:	Yes, that's my basic theory based on years of experience doing this.
Lawyer:	Your theory, have you ever published it in any professional journals?
Witness:	No, not that I can think of.
Lawyer:	And you've never submitted your theory to review by other engineers or tire failure analysts, have you?
Witness:	Well, not in the sense of a peer-reviewed journal, but I've certainly discussed it with colleagues and discussed it in cases before.

Lawyer:	You've never conducted a study on the accuracy of your theory have you?
Witness:	No, but my many years of experience dealing with tires and their failures gives me a lifetime's worth of knowledge in support of my theory.
Lawyer:	But you've never tested it in any scientific way, have you?
Witness:	No.
Lawyer:	Mr. Carlson, you believe that a tire that has been subject to over-deflection should show certain physical signs of that, don't you?
Witness:	Yes, it should.
Lawyer:	And those signs include tread wear on the tire's shoulder that is greater than the tread wear along the tire's center, true?
Witness:	Yes, that would be one symptom of overdeflection.
Lawyer:	In fact, the plaintiff's tire showed greater wear on the shoulder than in the center didn't it?
Witness:	Well, yes and no. There was to a limited degree greater tread wear on one shoulder, but if there was overdeflection you would expect to see it on both shoulders of the tire, and here you didn't have that.
Lawyer:	But it is true, isn't it, that there were parts of the tire that had no tread left at all, right?
Witness:	Yes.
Lawyer:	And there was greater wear on one shoulder of the tire than in the middle of the tire, correct?
Witness:	Yes, that is true.
Lawyer:	And you believe that a second sign of overdeflection is deterioration of the sidewalls of the tire?
Witness:	Yes.
Lawyer:	That deterioration might include discoloration of the sidewall?
Witness:	Yes, that's one sign of deterioration.
Lawyer:	And here, you found some discoloration on the sidewalls of plaintiff's tire, didn't you?
Witness:	Yes, I did, but only a very small amount of discoloration. Not enough to suggest overdeflection.
Lawyer:	But you agree that there was some discoloration on the sidewalls, right?
Witness:	Yes, there was a limited amount.

Lawyer:	A third sign you look for in determining whether the blowout resulted from overdeflection is marks on the tires rim flange?
Witness:	Yes, that's right.
Lawyer:	In addition to worn tread on the shoulder, discoloration of the sidewalls, marks on the tire's rim flange, and the presence of bead groove, the tire had also previously been punctured, isn't that right?
Witness:	Yes, it did have two punctures that had been repaired.
Lawyer:	That's right. There were two punctures of the tire?
Witness:	Yes.
Lawyer:	And someone had attempted to repair those punctures?
Witness:	That's true.
Lawyer:	But, in fact, the repairs were inadequate?
Witness:	Yes they were.
Lawyer:	And in addition to everything else, the tire had been in use for five years before it blew out, true?
Witness:	Well, I don't know how old the tire was, but I assumed for purposes of my assessment that the tire was about five years old, that's correct.
Lawyer:	You also don't know how many miles the tire had been driven before it blew out, do you?
Witness:	No, I don't know the precise number of miles.
Lawyer:	It could have been 20,000 or 50,000 or more?
Witness:	I suppose so. You cannot determine that from an inspection of the tire.
Lawyer:	Nevertheless, you believe that the tire had been driven thousands and thousands of miles during its life, right?
Witness:	Yes, that's fair.
Lawyer:	And according to Mr. Carmichael, he had driven his car more than 7,000 miles in just the two months before the tire blew out, true?
Witness:	That's my understanding, yes.

The cross-examiner may be tempted at that point to go for the kill and to force the witness to admit that his theory is flawed and his testimony biased. The question, "despite all the signs and symptoms of overdeflection, you still claim the failure was due to a design or manufacturing defect" is the one question too many. It invites a response from the witness and ensures that the examiner will lose control of the examination. The point has been made, the jury understands the point, and the ultimate argument about the expert's flawed methodology should be reserved for the direct of defendant's tire failure expert and closing argument.

C. Tools for Cross-Examination of Experts

When advocates rise to conduct a cross-examination of an expert they have at their disposal some tools that are simply not otherwise available— such as learned treatises and hypothetical questions—and other tools that are generally available, but have specific (and somewhat unique) applications when used with experts—such as prior inconsistent statements and impeachment by omission.

1. *Learned Treatises*

The term "learned treatise," as used in Rule 803(18) of the Federal Rules of Evidence, is broader than it sounds. It is not limited to "treatises" in the sense that the work must be long, comprehensive, and thoroughly boring. Rather, the term embraces any piece, regardless of its length, that is written primarily for professionals and is subject to scrutiny and exposure for inaccuracy (Fed. R. Evid. 803, advisory committee's note). It includes papers, pamphlets, periodicals, books, regulations, and professional or association standards on any pertinent subject including "history, medicine or other science or art." (Fed. R. Evid. 803(18)).

During cross-examination, a learned treatise can be used to impeach the expert's testimony by demonstrating that the methodology or opinion of the expert conflicts with the accepted practice or established authority. To use a learned treatise on cross, the examiner must establish that the treatise is a "reliable authority." That showing can be made in one of three ways:

1. the admission of the witness;

2. the testimony of another expert; or

3. judicial notice.

Thus, counsel can use treatises during cross-examination even though the expert rejects the treatise as an authority in his field. The rule simply requires that some qualified witness vouch for the authoritative nature of the document, even if that person is a witness for the party using the treatise.

Once advocates establish a treatise as authoritative and gain its admission into evidence, they should show the pertinent portions of the treatise to the jury and read them aloud. Counsel should never cede control of the treatise to the witness and allow him to read it to the jury. The witness will make every effort to blunt the force of the treatise. Once introduced before the jury, the treatise becomes an impeachment tool and can be used by counsel to demonstrate the conflict between the expert's testimony and the information contained in the treatise. Counsel should enlarge the portions of the treatise that he wants to use or project them onto a screen so that the jury can follow along as the treatise is read aloud.

As noted above, the requisite foundation to use the treatise depends on whether the opposing expert recognizes the treatise as an authoritative or reliable source in the expert's field. If the opposing expert concedes the reliability of the treatise, then the cross-examiner can establish both the authority of the treatise and the impeachment during the cross-examination itself. Otherwise, counsel must establish through another qualified expert, presumably counsel's own expert, that the treatise is authoritative.

Assume that in a criminal prosecution, the government's expert testified on direct that fingerprinting has an error rate of zero; that it is always correct when done correctly by a qualified examiner. On cross-examination, defense counsel wants to impeach the expert with a fingerprinting treatise, entitled the *Art and Science of Fingerprint Analysis,* which recognizes that the interpretation of fingerprints is inexact, leading to occasional errors of analysis and an error rate that may be as high as twenty-five percent. The expert, when asked, denies that the proffered treatise is authoritative, stating, "I've been doing this for a long time and I've never seen or heard of that book before." At that point, the examiner must either delay the impeachment until the defense case, when the examiner can show that the treatise is authoritative through his expert, or seek permission to use the treatise with plaintiff's expert subject to laying the foundation during the defense case. The latter approach will require a proffer from defense counsel, demonstrating that he has a witness who can establish the authoritativeness of the treatise. Judges are typically willing to admit evidence that is supported by such a proffer subject to a motion to strike if the foundation is never laid.

The exchange between defense counsel and the judge might look something like this:

Lawyer:	Your Honor, I would request leave to use the treatise with this witness subject to the testimony of Dr. Prosser during the defense case.
Judge:	What is your proffer?
Lawyer:	Dr. Prosser will testify that *The Art and Science of Fingerprint Analysis* is a leading text in the field, and is used in teaching fingerprint analysis and is relied on as an authoritative source by those in the field.
Judge:	I'll allow its use subject to a motion to strike.

The only caveat with learned treatises is that under the Federal Rules (Fed. R. Evid. 803(18)) and most state rules of evidence (*see, e.g.,* Cal.

Evid. Code § 1341), the treatise itself is not admissible into evidence as an exhibit. That is, counsel (or the witness) can read the treatise excerpts into evidence, but cannot have the jury take possession of the treatise or use the treatise itself during deliberations.

Illustration of Use of Learned Treatise on Cross-Examination

Lawyer:	Dr. Reddel, it's your opinion that defendant's handheld grinder, which contained no automatic kill switch, was a completely safe design, true?
Witness:	The defendant's grinder was properly designed for its intended use and for its intended users; it had a safe design, yes.
Lawyer:	Dr., you are familiar with the American National Safety Institute, aren't you?
Witness:	Yes, I am.
Lawyer:	It's known as ANSI, true?
Witness:	Yes.
Lawyer:	That is an organization that establishes standards for the design and manufacture of many different products, true?
Witness:	Yes.
Lawyer:	And its membership consists of manufacturers and businesses involved in the sale and distribution of these products, right?
Witness:	Right.
Lawyer:	There are ANSI standards for the design of handheld grinders, true?
Witness:	Absolutely.
Lawyer:	These standards are recognized as a reliable authority by the member manufacturers and businesses, aren't they?
Witness:	Well, the ANSI standards are not binding in any way, but they are one source to consult regarding safety in design.
Lawyer:	You consider the ANSI standards reliable, don't you?
Witness:	Sometimes they are helpful, sometimes not.
Lawyer:	But that is an authoritative source regarding the design of, for instance, handheld grinders?
Witness:	That's fair.

Lawyer:	In fact, all members have the chance to give input on standards before they are adopted, true?
Witness:	Yes, they do.
Lawyer:	And the standards must be approved by the executive committee, which consists of industry representatives, right?
Witness:	That's right.
Lawyer:	Your Honor, I have ANSI standard 1.21 regarding handheld grinders, which has been marked as Plaintiff's Exhibit 51, and I'm showing it to opposing counsel. Permission to approach?
Judge:	You may.
Lawyer:	Dr. Reddel, do you recognize Exhibit 51 as standard 1.21 of the ANSI standards regarding handheld grinders?
Witness:	Yes, I do.
Lawyer:	This is the provision that specifically addresses the advisability of an automatic kill switch for a handheld grinder, true?
Witness:	Yes.
Lawyer:	Your Honor, may I display for the jury on the screen an enlarged version of standard 1.21?
Judge:	Yes.
Lawyer:	Dr. Reddel, can you see the screen okay?
Witness:	Yes.
Lawyer:	Read along as I read 1.21 out loud to make sure I get it right. 1.21 says: "Handheld grinders should be equipped with automatic kill switches to minimize the risk of injury during normal usage." Did I read that correctly?
Witness:	Yes, you did.

2. *Hypothetical Questions*

Another cross-examination tool unique to experts is the hypothetical question. Hypothetical questions are questions that ask experts to assume certain facts or principles in determining the answer. And they can be properly used with experts as a technique to force the opposing expert to analyze the case using the cross-examiner's view of the facts. The primary limit on the hypothetical is that the facts and inferences in the question find support in the evidence, either the evidence already admitted, evidence that will be admitted, or facts or data reasonably reviewed or relied upon by the expert in forming the expert's opinions. Thus, as noted earlier, the examiner can ask the expert to change her assumptions, or to incorporate into her analysis facts that she ignored initially.

In the following illustration, the chief defense expert is a retired fire chief who testified during direct examination that the decedent firefighter—the spouse of the plaintiff—acted unreasonably in his rescue attempt, and that his own negligence was the cause of his death.

 Illustration of Use of Hypothetical Question on Cross-Examination[19]

Lawyer:	Chief Buckholtz, just to be clear, it is your conclusion that it was Firefighter Brennan's own unreasonable actions that resulted in his death, is that correct?
Witness:	That's right.
Lawyer:	Chief, I would like to explore some of the factors you relied on in coming to that opinion. One of those is that Mr. Brennan was running over the terrain and as a result did not see the cliff, correct?
Witness:	That's correct.
Lawyer:	And it is your belief that conduct was unreasonable under the circumstances?
Witness:	Right.
Lawyer:	And that contributed to his death?
Witness:	That's correct.
Lawyer:	Another factor that you believe contributed to firefighter Brennan's death was his failure to heed the warning given by Mr. Brown [the fallen climber]?
Witness:	That's right. Mr. Brown, from the bottom of the cliff, called out and warned Mr. Brennan about the cliff.
Lawyer:	And that fact was significant in arriving at your opinion that Mr. Brennan acted unreasonably, wasn't it?
Witness:	That was an important factor.
Lawyer:	And you believe that fact contributed to his death?
Witness:	Right.
Lawyer:	Chief Buckholtz, I am going to ask you for your opinion, based on two assumptions. First, assume that Mr. Brennan, just before

---

[19] This illustration based on the hypothetical case *Wrigley v. McGuire* (Association of Trial Lawyers of America).

> falling, had stopped and turned and yelled to his partner to be careful, not to run, because the terrain was uneven; and second, assume that the Defendant did not ever say to Brennan, "Be careful I'm at the bottom of a cliff," but simply said, "Hurry, I'm hurt. Over here." Under those conditions, would it still be your opinion that Firefighter Brennan's actions were unreasonable?

Regardless of the expert's "answer," the common sense answer, given the two changed circumstances, should be self-evident. Consequently, the jury will see that the "correct" view of the two facts in dispute—the decedent's "running" and the defendant's "warning"—will directly lead one to conclude that the plaintiff was not at fault.

3. *Past Writings or Testimony— Inconsistencies*

Unlike lay witnesses, expert witnesses often have a lengthy paper trail following them into the courtroom. Consider a typical scenario. The plaintiff retains an engineering expert in a product liability case. The expert is a university professor who regularly consults with manufacturers in products liability cases and occasionally works on the plaintiff's side as well. He has given numerous depositions, prepared many expert reports, and testified a few times at trial. In his capacity as a professor, he has written a large number of articles in academic journals. In the instant case, the expert has prepared a report and given deposition testimony. Moreover, if the case is being tried in federal court, the plaintiff is required under Rule 26(a)(2)(b) of the Federal Rules of Civil Procedure to disclose "any ... cases in which the witness has testified as an expert at trial or by deposition within the preceding four years." Thus, without any independent investigation, counsel should have information about the expert's testifying experience and the ability to track down the expert's past testimony.

The larger point is that there is often a substantial amount of material— prior statements, expert reports, deposition and trial testimony, and articles and books—available to the cross-examiner to test the expert's testimony. With the technological tools enjoyed by trial advocates today, it is easier than ever to access testimony given or opinions reached by experts in former cases. Some organizations maintain searchable databases, which collect testimony given by experts who regularly appear for the side opposing the organization's membership. Particularly for experts who are repeat players, these tools open up excellent impeachment opportunities. The basic tool of impeachment with a prior inconsistent statement can become a powerful weapon against an expert who is advocating a position at odds with the expert's position in a previous case, or is using an approach the expert previously criticized. The impeachment itself is no different than with a lay witness (See Chapter Nine, *supra*). However, the richness of the potential impeaching material distinguishes this form of impeachment from lay witnesses.

When accessible, counsel should obtain the past testimony and writings of opposing experts and carefully review it for inconsistencies or, conversely, for a positional bias held by the expert. Either discovery will reinforce the expert's bias. If the expert has changed his position or approach because of the needs of the party who is paying him, the expert's bias is clear. If the expert always reaches the same opinion regardless of the facts, the expert's bias is equally clear.

4.   *Impeachment by Omission*

Another impeachment tool that has particularly powerful possibilities during the cross-examination of expert witnesses is impeachment by omission. Experts in state and federal courts are typically expected to prepare expert reports setting forth the expert's opinions and the reasons therefore. Moreover, most experts are deposed and questioned about their opinions and the supporting basis for them. The unpredictability of trials, however, makes it difficult for parties or experts to know definitively in advance what evidence the opponent will use in its case. Consequently, experts, on occasion, develop new opinions at trial, or modify existing ones, or they identify new facts or reasons to support their testimony. Advocates have several options in responding to these last minute adaptations, including moving to exclude the testimony as violative of discovery and disclosure obligations, or seeking a continuance. A third option is to impeach the expert for not making disclosure earlier, and to create the impression that the "new" material should be ignored by the jury.

The expert's failure to include the new fact or opinion in his report or deposition testimony should suggest that the opinion and/or fact is suspect. There are three key points to hit when using this type of impeachment:

1.   establish the care and thought that went into the expert's report and/or deposition testimony

2.   develop the expert's knowledge about the important role of the report or deposition in the case for the lawyers and parties

3.   reveal that the expert failed to mention or include the new opinions or facts in the expert's original report or testimony

The expert's omission of the now critical information may suggest any number of inferences depending on the circumstances:

1.   the expert did a sloppy job in her initial evaluation of the case and is now trying to correct those initial problems;

2.   the party and/or expert has realized that additional evidence is needed to establish the parties claims or defenses and have created the necessary evidence through the expert; or

3.   recently discovered facts or evidence have materially changed or impacted the expert's original evaluation.

Whichever circumstance caused the change, the expert is now subject to criticism. One way or the other, it reflects poorly on the expert's preparation, motives, or knowledge. Ultimately, the impeachment should cause the jury to view the expert's opinions with greater suspicion and concern.

Chapter Eleven

CLOSING ARGUMENT[1]

---

[1] The genesis of this chapter was an article written by Caldwell, Perrin, and Frost, 76 TULANE LAW REVIEW 961 (2002). Used with permission.

I. OVERVIEW AND PURPOSE OF THE CLOSING ARGUMENT

"An advocate can be confronted with few more formidable tasks than to select his closing arguments . . . ."

—Robert Jackson, Chief Counsel for the United States
before the Nuremberg War Crimes Tribunal, 1946[2]

Closing argument is the final act, the last five minutes of a hard-fought title game, the ninth inning. It is the high drama of the trial. It is when the trial lawyer steps up and, through the majesty of his oratory, wins the case. Or, at least that is the common perception. Yet, while closing argument is the time for the lawyer to pull the evidence and law together into a compelling and persuasive whole, many, if not most, jurors will have reached tentative conclusions at some point earlier in the trial.[3] Nonetheless, there is much that must be accomplished at close. At the very least, it is the final opportunity to convince the trier of fact to accept the advocate's view of the disputed issues and to render a verdict accordingly.

The trial lawyer's success during the closing argument requires the mastery of a range of skills, including:

- explaining the relevant law

- integrating trial testimony into the law

- incorporating selected testimony into the party's theme

- confronting, integrating, and deflecting contrary evidence

- striking the proper emotional tone

---

[2] LIEF, CALDWELL, AND BYCEL, LADIES AND GENTLEMEN OF THE JURY: GREATEST CLOSING ARGUMENTS IN MODERN LAW, 29 (Scribner 1998).

[3] *See* MARGARET C. ROBERTS, TRIAL PSYCHOLOGY 41 (1987); Michael F. Colley, *The Opening Statement: Structure, Issues, Techniques,* TRIAL, Nov. 1982, at 54 (citing H. KALVEN AND H. ZEISEL, THE AMERICAN JURY (1966)).

These many and varied tasks require that the advocate serve as friend, teacher, salesman, entertainer, storyteller, motivator, strategist, and even psychologist during closing argument. And advocates must do all of this with the ultimate goal of persuading the trier of fact to view the case from their perspective.

For those jurors already committed to the advocate's side, the closing argument marks an opportunity for the advocate to resolve any lingering questions and to solidify their allegiance. In addition, those jurors sympathetic to the lawyer's view need the tools to persuade others in the deliberation room so that they can further advocate for their chosen side. For the uncommitted or unsympathetic jurors, the closing argument provides the advocate one last, critical chance to make the case—to reason through the evidence and to persuade them to come to the correct outcome.

Closing argument is the time to integrate the component pieces of the trial into a finished product; to give perspective, meaning, and context to the evidence introduced throughout the trial; to weave the sometimes disparate and conflicting pieces of evidence into a clear statement that explains what transpired and who is responsible. It is for the close—the only time where persuasive discourse is explicitly permitted and expected at trial—to chart the lessons learned and the deeds misdone.

Against this backdrop of responsibilities and opportunities, we face the grim reality that too many closing arguments fail to persuade, and that the "argument" too often devolves into a numbing regurgitation of testimony without any effort to connect that testimony to a theme or the relevant law. These efforts at closing wander and drift without mooring, leaving the jurors puzzled, bored, and even dismayed that they are not receiving help from the advocate in making sense of the testimony and the law. Such efforts are a gross abdication of the responsibility advocates owe their clients and the jury.

II.   THE STRUCTURE OF THE CLOSING ARGUMENT

The path to an effective closing argument begins with a structure that will give the jurors a clear agenda and a memorable framework for decision-making. Some seasoned trial lawyers might be offended at the notion that there should be a set structure or organization to closing arguments. Indeed, some may argue that for the closing to be effective it must be delivered from the heart, and is not something that can be completely planned or calculated. Nothing could be further from the truth. Such a notion contemplates that a thought-out structure must be necessarily devoid of energy, emotion, and passion. Structure does not render the closing passionless. Organization does not constrict the life from the close. Rather, a logically organized closing argument channels the trial lawyer's energy, logic, and emotion for maximum effectiveness.

Structure and organization are particularly important for an effective closing argument because of the number of tasks the advocate must accomplish. The advocate must explain the law, integrate the facts into the law, confront, integrate, and deflect contrary evidence, recognize and harness the emotional currents of the trial, and clearly and precisely tell the jury what they are to do. To leave these tasks to the spontaneity of inspired oratory is to ensure that not everything that should be addressed will be addressed, and that the jury will be left without adequate guidance for its deliberations. With that said, it must be noted that there is no set formula for the order of the closing argument. Indeed, with the obvious exception of delivering a compelling introduction, the balance of the close should be structured in a logical manner according to the particular facts and issues involved. We address the structural components of an effective closing argument below.

A.   Deliver a Powerful Introduction

Closing arguments, like any other speech, must begin by immediately engaging the audience. First impressions harden like cement. The rule of primacy compels the speaker to immediately capture his audience's attention. Every closing has a critical first moment when the jurors, whether consciously or subconsciously, are making the pivotal decision whether to continue to actively listen or to drift off. Thus, those first words must be memorable.

The introduction or "grab" should:

- re-introduce the theme

- personalize the party's view of the facts

- capture the emotional high ground

The masters of trial advocacy recognize the value of the grab. Justice Robert Jackson, while on leave from the United States Supreme Court, was charged with the responsibility of prosecuting those involved in the horrific crimes committed during the reign of the Third Reich in World War II. He began his legendary closing argument against the Nazi hierarchy at Nüremberg with the following:

 1st Illustration of the Grab

Jackson: An advocate can be confronted with few more formidable tasks than to select his closing arguments where there is a great disparity between his appropriate time and his available material. In eight months—a short time as state trials go—we have introduced evidence which embraces as vast and varied a panorama of events as ever has been compressed within the framework of a litigation.

It is impossible in summation to do more than outline with bold strokes the vitals of this trial's mad and melancholy record, which

> will live as the historical text of the twentieth century's shame and depravity.[4]

In but three sentences, Jackson executed the quintessential grab. He re-introduced his theme, "the trial's mad and melancholy record. . . ." He underscored his party's (the United States) view of the facts, "which will live as the twentieth century's shame and depravity." And in so doing, he captured the emotional high ground.

As a second example, the introduction of the defense's closing argument for the wrongful death of a firefighter who died trying to rescue the defendant might proceed along these lines:

2nd Illustration of the Grab[5]

> It is courage and heroism that sends them out, but it is teamwork and discipline that brings them home . . . . It is raw courage and unabated heroism that drives emergency service providers to leave the safety of the fire station to help those in need, but it's teamwork, common sense, and most importantly, discipline, that allows them to do their dangerous jobs *properly* and then return to the fire station *safely* . . . . Even heroes have to do their jobs properly . . . even heroes have to do it right.

This introduction accomplishes two essential tasks. First, while acknowledging that the firefighter who died was a hero—a hero who died trying to help another—this introduction establishes that firefighters' jobs are dangerous and that the threat of injury or death is a constant. And, second, this introduction clearly sets forth the defense theme that a firefighter must act reasonably throughout the rescue attempt.

There is a tendency for trial lawyers to expend those first precious moments of the close by thanking the jurors for their service or acknowledging how long and difficult the trial has been. Those comments have a time and place in the closing argument, but not at the expense of a powerful grab that immediately begins advancing the argument. There is but one beginning, and advocates must maximize its potential.

B.   Present the Law

The most powerful facts and compelling stories are meaningless unless the law recognizes that those facts can give rise to a crime, tort,

---

[4]   Lief, Caldwell, and Bycel, Ladies and Gentlemen of the Jury: Greatest Closing Arguments in Modern Law 29 (Scribner 1998).

[5]   This illustration is based on the hypothetical case *Wrigley v. McGuire* (2002, Association of Trial Lawyers of America).

or some other recognized cause of action or defense. Accordingly, advocacy at trial does not take place in a vacuum. Instead, every decision by the trial advocate—ranging from the witnesses called to the theory or theories pursued—is informed and shaped by the law. The elements of a claim or defense dictate what evidence is relevant in a civil case, just as the elements of the crime or defense determine the boundaries of the permissible proof in a criminal case. But more than that, the jury's decision in a case is ultimately a determination about whether the available evidence proves— or fails to prove—a cause of action or violation of law. The law provides the grids and supports of every case, no matter the complexity or simplicity of the facts. Yet, the lawyer is rarely allowed to discuss the law with the jury. During *voir dire* the lawyer can do little more than seek commitments from the members of the venire that they will follow the law in the case. In the opening statement the lawyer is severely restricted in attempting to discuss the law, limited to generalities or a brief overview. And during witness examination no discussion of the law is ever appropriate.

The one time of the trial specifically set aside for full disclosure of the law to the jury is when the judge reads the jury instructions. Yet typically this charge to the jury fails to explain to jurors how those rules, applied to the facts, will guide them to their verdict. In fact, few events are as painfully boring or less memorable than when the judge reads the final instructions to the jury. Depending on the case, the reading of the instructions can last for hours. The instructions are rarely worded in plain English, instead using legal terms of art and less-than-helpful definitions. Moreover, the instructions are given all at once leaving the jury with a serious case of information overload. It is, in short, a sleep-inducing experience, and one poorly designed to give the jury meaningful assistance in deciding the case. And yet, as all trial lawyers know, the instructions on the law are critically important, for they give the jury the tools it will need to decide the case.

That is where good advocacy comes in. The closing argument is the lawyer's one opportunity to explain the law to the jury and to discuss its application to the issues in the case. Unlike *voir dire* or the opening statement, the advocate is free during the close to argue, explain, and illustrate the law. It is an opportunity that must be seized and used for everything it is worth. No closing argument is complete or even legally sufficient without an explanation from the advocates of the critical legal principles involved. However, prior to discussing and illustrating the task of explaining the law, and incorporating the law into the evidence, it is necessary to first ascertain what law is to be given.

1. *Jury Instructions*

Jury instructions are based on the law governing the charges, claims, or defenses involved in the case. In the earliest phases of trial preparation the advocate must identify the law that will be used to instruct the jury and to use the proposed jury instructions as a guide throughout trial preparation and the trial itself.

Jury instructions fall into two categories. "General" jury instructions include procedural matters, such as selecting a foreperson and how the jurors are to approach the task of deliberation. They also include standard instructions of law that apply without regard to the specific subject matter of the case, such as those concerning the burden of proof, evaluating witness credibility, and the distinctions between direct and circumstantial evidence, to name a few.

The second broad category of jury instructions is usually referred to as "special" jury instructions. These are the instructions specific to the facts and issues presented during that trial. Even these "special" instructions will typically be based on form or pattern instructions that will be used from case to case. For instance, a pattern instruction setting forth the elements necessary to convict for robbery will most likely be used in every robbery trial. Likewise, in an automobile collision case alleging negligence, the pattern instruction on negligence will be given to the jurors.

Although the jury is instructed at the end of the trial, usually after closing arguments have been presented, the process of considering, compiling, and submitting jury instructions actually begins well before the start of the trial. Practice varies from court to court, but it is not uncommon for a judge to require the advocates to lodge their proposed jury instructions with the court before the trial begins.

As with jury selection, there is a wide variation in practice among court systems, and even among judges within a court system, concerning the process of deciding what instructions will be given to the jury. It is essential that the advocate familiarize herself with the particular practices of the judge presiding over the trial.

While most courts require that a set of requested jury instructions be lodged with the court before the trial begins, inevitably situations arise during trial that require the submission of new instructions or modification to the instructions already submitted. Thus, the proposed jury instructions may be supplemented during trial. In addition, occasionally the court will find it necessary to instruct the jury on a particular point during trial. An example of this occurs if evidence is admitted for one purpose but is inadmissible for another purpose. It is customary for the judge to instruct the jury immediately after the evidence is offered to limit its use of the evidence.

2.   *Sources of Jury Instructions*

Jury instructions are based upon the law that governs the particular case or evidentiary issue. Thus the sources of the jury instructions are the sources of law generally: statutes, case law, and constitutions. Fortunately, pattern or form jury instructions cover most circumstances, thereby eliminating the need to reinvent the wheel for each trial. These pattern or form jury instructions are compiled in books that are readily available in law libraries. In some jurisdictions there may be more than one compilation. For example, federal courts in the Ninth Circuit hearing a criminal case may use the Ninth Circuit Manual of Model Jury Instructions–Criminal, published by West; or the Modern Federal Jury Instructions–Criminal, published by Matthew Bender. If more than one compilation exists in a particular jurisdiction, the advocate must ascertain which the trial judge prefers.

The compilations contain general and special jury instructions that cover common issues and elements for numerous claims, charges and defenses. In addition to these claim-specific instructions, there are also form instructions to cover myriad specific evidentiary issues that could arise. Pattern or form jury instructions exist for the vast majority of the issues that will arise at trial. If there is no pattern or form jury instruction to govern a particular issue, or if the existing instruction requires modification, the advocate can rely upon case law, statutes, or the constitution to craft a jury instruction. The instruction, of course, must accurately reflect the law.

3.   *Making the Law Understandable*

Just as jurors rely on their collective common sense and common experiences in evaluating the claims and contentions of the parties, they also rely on the judge's instructions on the law to understand the legal significance of the evidence. The advocate's task in closing argument is to give meaning to the jury instructions by showing the jurors how to apply the law to the facts established by the evidence. Discussing the law also provides the advocate with a chance to associate with the judge. Each and every time the advocate mentions an instruction, she should mention the judge. For example, "As Judge Jones will tell you in a few minutes, this case involves a claim of negligence." The benefits are two-

> **Tech Tip**
>
> ✓   Consider creating PowerPoint slides listing elements that must be proved or disproved
>
> ✓   Build the list one point at a time so jurors do not get ahead of you

fold: first, the lawyer is aligned with the judge, the one person in the courtroom the jurors most respect and admire; and second, in those jurisdictions that read the instructions after the closing arguments, the lawyer's accurate description of the judge's instructions may enhance the jurors' perception of the advocate's credibility.

In most cases the jury instructions can be divided into three discrete categories:

- the burden of proof

- the elements or requirements of the pertinent crime, claim, or defense

- evidentiary issues specific to the case

The importance of the burden of proof depends on the nature of the case and the position of the advocate. The traditional burden in civil cases, the preponderance of the evidence standard, does not usually require extended explanation. In fact, the plaintiff's most important task may be distinguishing this burden from the much more demanding burden of proof in criminal cases. Defendants may want to reinforce that the burden is on the plaintiff and not on the defendant.

Whenever possible, parties should be assertive when discussing the burden of proof. That is, the defendant should show the jury that he was not negligent, rather than merely arguing that the plaintiff failed to prove by a preponderance of the evidence that he was negligent. And the plaintiff should not be satisfied with merely meeting the preponderance standard, but should demonstrate to the jury how the plaintiff established the defendant's negligence beyond dispute. Granted, this is more than the legal requirement of meeting the burden of proof, but to do otherwise would leave open the possibility, for example, that the jurors may conclude the defendant is negligent, but the plaintiff's attorney just failed to prove it. This could cause the jurors to wish to "correct" the failure of proof.

The burden of proof in criminal cases is often difficult for juries to comprehend, and requires more attention from advocates. What does it mean for a juror to have a "reasonable doubt"? What constitutes an "abiding conviction"? One means of explaining "reasonable doubt" to a jury is through a story or anecdote—an example of what it means to have a reasonable doubt, or to be certain beyond a "reasonable doubt." Stories can help the jury understand the application of the abstract legal standard to real events, and can help the jury see that the standard was—or was not—satisfied in the case.

Other instructions can help explain the meaning of the burden of proof. For example, one standard jury instruction concerning the sufficiency of circumstantial evidence in criminal cases states in part:

> [I]f the circumstantial evidence permits two reasonable interpretations, one of which points to the defendant's guilt and the other to [his] [her] innocence, you must adopt the interpretation that points to the defendant's innocence, and reject that interpretation that points to [his] [her] guilt.[6]

Where applicable, the defense lawyer's argument should apply this rule of law to the circumstantial evidence in the case and guide the jurors to draw the inference that the law requires that the evidence points to the defendant's innocence.

The second category of instructions—those addressing the elements of crimes, claims, or defenses—should play a central role in every closing argument. Once again the elements of the crime, cause of action, or defense may be explained to the jury in the form of a story or analogy or simply by paraphrasing the instruction. The plaintiff might paraphrase negligence as meaning that the defendant "wasn't paying attention" or "didn't stop to think." In the *Silkwood* trial, Spence went much further, providing the jury a masterful explanation of strict liability:[7]

---

[6]   1 California Jury Instructions, Criminal § 2.01 (1996).

[7]   Lief, Caldwell, and Bycel, Ladies and Gentlemen of the Jury: Greatest Closing Arguments in Modern Law 159 (Scribner 1998).

Illustration Explaining Strict Liability Instruction

Spence:

Well, we talked about "strict liability" at the outset, and you'll hear the court tell you about "strict liability," and it simply means: "If the lion got away, Kerr-McGee [the defendant] has to pay." It's that simple —that's the law. You remember what I told you in the opening statement about strict liability? It came out of the Old English common law. Some guy brought an old lion on his ground, and he put it in a cage—and lions are dangerous—and through no negligence of his own—through no fault of his own, the lion got away. Nobody knew how—like in this case, "nobody knew how." And, the lion went out and he ate up some people—and they sued the man. And they said, you know: "Pay. It was your lion, and he got away." And, the man says: "But I did everything in my power—I had a good cage— had a good lock on the door—I did everything that I could—I had security—I had trained people watching the lion—and it isn't my fault that he got away." Why should you punish him? They said: "We have to punish him—we have to punish you—you have to pay. You have to pay because it was your lion—unless the person who was hurt let the lion out himself. That's the only defense in this case: unless in this case Karen Silkwood was the one who intentionally took the plutonium out, and "let the lion out," that is the only defense. . .

Strict liability: "If the lion gets away, Kerr-McGee has to pay," unless Karen Silkwood let the lion loose. What do we have to prove? Strict liability. Now, you can see what that is? The lion gets away. We have to do that. It's already admitted. It's admitted in the evidence. They admit it was their plutonium. They admit it's in Karen Silkwood's apartment. It got away. And, we have to prove that Karen Silkwood was damaged. That's all we have to prove. Our case has been proved long ago, and I'm not going to belabor you with the facts that prove that. It's almost an admitted fact, that it got away, and that she was damaged.

Spence's connection of Kerr-McGee's loss of plutonium to the escape of the lion gave the jury an easy way to understand a difficult concept and provided his memorable refrain: "If the lion got away, Kerr-McGee has to pay." It also fit perfectly with his theory of the case, that if plutonium got out of the plant and contaminated Silkwood, then Kerr-McGee was liable, regardless of anything else, unless Ms. Silkwood took the plutonium herself.

In every case there are jury instructions that the lawyer must apply to the evidence. For example, most jurors have never thought in a systematic way about how to decide whether a person is telling the truth. They simply use their intuition. A typical jury instruction on credibility gives the jury some objective means of deciding credibility and the lawyer can assist the jurors to see how they can use the guidance of the instruction in evaluating witness credibility. Consider the following common instruction:

A witness who is willfully false in one material part of his or her testimony is to be distrusted in others. You may reject the whole testimony of a witness who willfully has testified falsely as to a material point, unless, from all the evidence, you believe the probability of truth favors his or her testimony in other particulars.[8]

In the O.J. Simpson criminal case, Detective Mark Fuhrman denied ever having used a racial epithet, but was later heard doing so in a tape-recorded conversation. Imagine how the defense might use the credibility instruction to attack Fuhrman.

 Illustration Explaining Witness Credibility Instruction

Lawyer:

I'm sure you remember the testimony of Mr. Fuhrman. Detective Mark Fuhrman. Sworn to uphold the law. Sworn to tell the truth. If you are like me, you'll probably never forget the moment he testified. It was chilling. To think that he would lie to you so coldly and calculatingly, to assume that you would never find out the truth. But we did find out the truth, we discovered the real Mark Fuhrman, the racist Mark Fuhrman, the lying Mark Fuhrman. And you might be asking, sincerely and fairly, so what? Does it matter *in this case* that he lied about having used those despicable epithets in the past? Well, remember that the prosecution's case depends on Mark Fuhrman's credibility. He supposedly found that second glove on Mr. Simpson's property and if you are going to conclude he found the glove there, you have to believe and trust Fuhrman. You have no other choice. Can you believe Fuhrman about the glove when you know that he looked you in the eye and lied to you about what he had said in the past?

In a moment, when the judge tells you about the law and gives you his instructions before you deliberate, he will tell you that "a witness who is willfully false in one material part of his testimony is to be distrusted in others" and that "you may reject the whole testimony" of a witness who has lied to you. And that's exactly what you should do here. Fuhrman lied. He lied about using the racial epithet and he lied about the glove and you should throw it all out because it's all garbage.

Another common example of an instruction that may deserve some attention is the instruction on circumstantial evidence. Jurors often operate under the mistaken belief that circumstantial evidence is less persuasive than direct evidence and that circumstantial evidence is insufficient without some corroborating direct evidence. Of course, that notion is directly contrary to the jury instructions. To overcome such misperceptions the advocate may need to explain to the jury what circumstantial evidence is and how persuasive it can be. Lawyers love to use the footprints in the sand from *Robinson Crusoe* to demonstrate the power of circumstantial evidence, though other more current and even more personal examples

---

[8]   1 California Jury Instructions, Criminal § 2.21.2 (1996).

may work better. Regardless of the device the advocate uses, however, the point is quite important: we make important decisions every day based on nothing more than circumstantial evidence and we do so because such evidence can be both compelling and convincing.

The advocate's presentation of the law during the closing argument will not likely come all at once, and the best place to discuss particular aspects of the law will depend on the issues in the case. Yet, as a general rule, it often provides a helpful structure to the closing argument to discuss the burden of proof and the essential elements of the charge, claim or defense near the beginning, directly after the advocate has delivered his grab. The burden of proof provides context for what follows. The discussion of the elements of the charge, claim, or defense provide the body of most closing arguments, and thus, will likely be discussed in the middle of the typical closing. The placement of the other instructions is difficult to generalize, in that it will greatly depend upon which instructions are being discussed and which issues they relate to.

C.   Integrate the Law Into the Facts

In addition to giving the law context, advocates must integrate that law and the facts, explaining how the facts of a case do (or do not) satisfy the legal burdens and standards. We use the word "integrate" precisely. To "integrate" is defined as "to make into a whole by bringing all parts together."[9] It implies to meld together, to make as one. It is the attorney's job to do the integrating, to weave the facts of the case into the legal elements, tying up the loose ends, and otherwise critical evidence as it relates to the law.

Failure to integrate the facts and the law will leave the jury unprepared to reach a verdict. The law, on its own, without establishing its significance to the facts, leaves the jury unguided in deciding how the law applies to the evidence. The jurors may or may not make the necessary connections to reach the desired verdict. A trial lawyer who fails to integrate facts and law vests vast discretion in the jurors, which they are not necessarily equipped to properly exercise. Worse yet, it leaves to opposing counsel the opportunity to "connect" the facts and law in a way advantageous to his case.

Vincent Bugliosi in his closing argument in the *Charles Manson* prosecution explicitly demonstrated to the jury how the facts in the case satisfied the legal requirements of conspiracy. He set forth the elements of conspiracy and then integrated the evidence produced at trial to establish Manson's responsibility for the acts of his followers.

 Illustration Integrating the Facts into the Law

Bugliosi: Once a conspiracy is formed, each member of the conspiracy
                        is criminally responsible for it and equally guilty of the crimes

---

[9]   AMERICAN HERITAGE DICTIONARY 937 (3d ed. 1992).

committed by his conspirators which were in furtherance of the object of the conspiracy. For example, A and B conspired to murder X. Pursuant to the agreement, B actually murders X. A, although he is not the party that actually murdered X, is equally guilty of that murder even if he was not present at the scene. He could have been playing badminton somewhere. It wouldn't make any difference. If he was a member of that conspiracy, he is guilty of that murder.

Although the evidence at trial shows that Charles Manson was the leader of the conspiracy to commit these murders, there is no evidence that he actually personally killed any of the seven victims in this case. However, the joint responsibility rule of conspiracy makes him guilty of all seven murders.[10]

This straightforward passage effectively explained the law of joint responsibility and applied it to the facts established at trial. Bugliosi made the necessary connections for his jury.

As this passage from Bugliosi's closing demonstrates, integrating the facts and the law need not be complicated or prolonged. In fact, the goal should be to show the jury how simple and obvious it is that the facts of one's case clearly satisfy—or fail to satisfy—the applicable legal standards. And while the advocate should focus on the key pieces of evidence that prove or disprove a particular element, trying to incorporate every piece of evidence that holds a tenuous connection to a particular element elevates quantity over quality, and will likely draw more juror skepticism than praise. The jury will be inundated with information, and the importance of a key piece of evidence will be lost in the haystack of evidence the jury is asked to remember.

While the integration need not be complex, it should be specific. Advocates should harken the jury back to specific pieces of evidence. They should recall with the jury the specific testimony of particular witnesses, emphasizing the point with such phrases as "Mrs. Jones sat on that witness stand right there, and under oath, she testified that. . . ." This presentation is best accentuated by reading from the actual transcript. The advocate may also be specific by actually showing the jury pieces of physical evidence. This is particularly effective when the evidence is the subject of dispute at trial, such as whether something is a "deadly weapon" for purposes of a charge of assault with a deadly weapon. If the jury is not impressed by the deadly nature of the object with which the victim was assaulted—which need not be something so menacing as a knife or gun—the defendant may walk away with a lesser included assault conviction, or be freed based on the jury's contempt for an overzealous prosecutor.

Additionally, the integration of facts and law should be thorough. When preparing a closing argument, every advocate must determine what evidence the jury must consider when deciding whether a particular legal element has been proved. The advocate should ensure that every critical

---

[10] VINCENT BUGLIOSI & CURT GENTRY, HELTER SKELTER 407–412 (W.W. Norton & Co. 1994) (original publication date 1974).

piece of evidence is impressed upon the jury during closing argument. Evidence should not be left out simply for the sake of brevity, lest the case be unnecessarily minimized.

But then there is the rub. If the advocate must integrate the law and the facts, how can he make sure that all key pieces of evidence are argued, and do so in a manner that the jury will be able to recall them? This is where a list can be tremendously helpful.

D. Use a List to Emphasize the Key Points

One challenge for advocates in the closing argument is to cover all of the essential evidence in a persuasive manner that will maximize the jury's ability to focus on and recall those points necessary for success. The use of a list can prove an immensely helpful tool both to persuade jurors and to enhance their retention. The list should comprise the key points in support of the advocate's view of the case. During even less complicated trials, jurors are presented with a vast amount of information. And even the most astute jurors are often hard pressed to accurately sort through the data and arrive at crucial conclusions.

A list can sort, prioritize, and provide structure. It can also give meaning to what many jurors perceive as a vast morass of evidence. A thoughtful and fair list can be very helpful for them, and consequently, can be very persuasive. It should encapsulate the core of the trial, so that the jurors will refer to it during deliberation. In fact, it should set the jurors' agenda for their deliberations.

Lists not only persuade, they enhance juror retention. People are visual learners, and individuals who see information, rather than simply hear it, are much more likely to remember it. We all use lists to help us remember information. We take grocery lists to the store, and keep "to do" lists on our desks. The list in the closing argument works in much the same way. It allows the advocate to stress the information he considers important, and expects the jury to remember. Finally, the list can enable the advocate to confidently break free from notes. While providing the jurors with a visual aid to help recall important points in the case, the same list can remind the advocate of each point she will need to cover during closing argument, thus making it easier for the advocate to dispense with the use of notes.

The list, however, must be used properly. First and foremost, it should be simple, both in form and substance. The list must not incorporate every detail of the case; rather, it should be aimed at hitting the key points. It contains the reasons the advocate's view of the case is correct.

Tech Tip

✓ Consider a PowerPoint slide setting forth the list points

✓ It is better to build the list one point at a time such that the jurors are focused to the particular point being discussed

✓ There is noting wrong with going "old school" and using a white board or even butcher paper and marker – this may actually endear you to your jurors

Some cases may lend themselves to a short, three point list, while others require more points. But lists should rarely require more than six or seven points. And each point should be in bullet form, never full sentences. Each item is intended as a talking point. A list should not cover areas not in dispute. Although the attorney will certainly want to tell the jury how those elements have been met, they do not deserve the special attention that a list provides. For instance, in a malicious prosecution case, the plaintiff (the ex-wife of defendant police officer) has accused the defendant of planting marijuana in her residence, reporting the marijuana to a narcotics detective, and then urging a prosecutor to file criminal charges. It developed during the testimony that the defendant, on occasion, had failed to turn over marijuana he had confiscated in making drug arrests. It also came out during trial that the defendant was in the plaintiff's apartment previous to the marijuana being found in the plaintiff's apartment.[11]

During closing argument the plaintiff's list would be:

 ## Illustration of the Use of a List

    1.   defendant had access to marijuana

    2.   defendant had access to apartment

    3.   defendant had access to detective

    4.   defendant had access to prosecutor

This list now provides four significant talking points that paint a damning picture of the defendant and his dubious conduct.

While a list should be as simple as possible, it should also be comprehensive. The advocate should include only the key points, but *all* of the key points that he wants the jury to focus on. Yet, it still serves the client to strive for simplicity at the expense of completeness. What possible reason could there be to only include three pieces of evidence if six could help prove a particular, disputed element of a cause of action? If the advocate does not do so, the jury may be left remembering only half of the story.

It is best to display the list to the jury one point at a time. Otherwise, jurors will read ahead, instead of focusing on what is being said. An attorney can avoid this juror temptation in one of two ways: first, the attorney can pre-prepare, and partially mask the list. Or second, the attorney can write each point on a board and then talk through that point before writing up the next point. Sometimes the most helpful tools are butcher paper and markers.

---

[11] This illustration is based on the hypothetical case *Mitchell v. Mitchell*, Judge Jerry R. Parker (2002, Texas Young Lawyers' Association).

E. Exploit Opposing Party's Weaknesses

Why didn't the defense call the very expert they hired?

Why didn't the plaintiff tell anyone about the accident until the next day?

Why did the defendant refuse to take any of the blood alcohol tests?

The points undergirding each of the rhetorical questions at the outset of this section are "negatives" drawn from some failure or perceived failure of the opposition. It could be a failure to call a witness who would seem to be logical given the circumstances that developed during trial. It may be a failure of the opposing party to act in a manner that is consistent with his theory of the case. Whatever the failure, exposing it in all its glory for the trier of fact can make for persuasive argument.

One means to effectively emphasize "negatives" is through the use of rhetorical questions. Each of the three questions at the beginning of this section illustrates the potent impact of rhetorical questions in stressing the "negatives" in the opposition's case. Coupling those questions with even more rhetorical questions helps showcase the point to be made. For instance, in fully exploiting the point to be made from the first question, the argument might follow this sequence:

1st Illustration Using a Rhetorical Question to Exploit a Weakness

> Why didn't the defense call the very expert they hired? They hired him to examine the defendant. Yet they failed to call this expert to testify on the overarching issue in this trial. What are we to gather from this? How should we view their failure to call him? What is it they are afraid of? Do you think, for one second, that if their expert could have contradicted what we heard from the plaintiff's expert who did testify, they wouldn't have had him testify?

Such a sequence can be very persuasive in exposing the full extent of the opponent's failures. As a further point of illustration, take another of the questions posed at the outset of this section and frame the argument.

2nd Illustration Using a Rhetorical Question to Exploit a Weakness

> Why did the defendant refuse to take any of the blood alcohol tests? If his story is true, then any of the tests offered would have proved his case. If he had only had two beers, why not take the perfect opportunity to prove that he is telling us the truth? What does an innocent man have to fear from taking a blood alcohol test?

The advocate should always look for ways to exploit the opponent's weaknesses in the closing argument. Make the other side pay for its failures.

Finding the negatives in the opponent's case is not necessarily routine business. Some negatives, such as a prior felony conviction, are straightforward and require little work or preparation. But others are not so readily recognized. It is a good practice to "step back" from the case and view not only your side, but your opponent's side from a non-lawyer's perspective. What would a layperson see that you did not? But with that said, for the most part, the "negatives" are identified only through a thorough understanding of the case from both the advocate's and the opposition's perspective. The payoff is worth the effort, because the weaknesses in the opposing party's case can prove to be extremely persuasive evidence.

F.   Confront, Integrate, and Mitigate Contrary Evidence

As suggested throughout, *every* case in every trial has adverse facts and circumstances. It is a true measure of effective trial advocacy to successfully confront those adverse facts and either mitigate their impact or, better yet, integrate them into the advocate's theory of the case. Confronting problem areas, however, is not a task relegated solely to closing argument. Rather, it is vital to confront and begin the integration/mitigation process from the very outset of trial. "Bad facts" should be discussed with prospective jurors at *voir dire*. This is an opportunity to actually put the matter before the jurors and have a dialogue in which their particular feelings concerning the matter can be gauged. (*See* Chapter 4, Section IV). Opening statement is the second opportunity to confront problematic circumstances. At opening the advocate can place the adverse facts in the context of the larger events that gave rise to the trial, and in so doing, mitigate or even begin the integration of those facts into the advocate's view of the case. Confronting, integrating and mitigating adverse facts, however, is primarily accomplished during the direct examination of the witness burdened with the problem. As discussed in Chapter Five, that is the time to deal with the difficult areas and get answers and explanations right from the horse's mouth.

It then remains for closing argument to reap the full benefits of the successful efforts throughout trial to "prick the boils." For instance, in the defense closing of a criminal case the advocate should acknowledge, rather than ignore, the prior conviction of his client. That portion of the argument might proceed along these lines.

Illustration of Confronting and Mitigating Harmful Evidence

It was appropriate during this trial that Mr. Matthews himself told you about his conviction for theft. It was important for you to hear that because one of your essential tasks is to determine the credibility of everyone who has testified. That determination

> should include as much information about all the witnesses as is permissible within the rules of trial. And certainly an incident such as this is important to know about. Just as it is important for you to learn that that incident happened over eight years ago; since that time Mike Matthews has held the same job for seven years, he met and married a loving and supportive wife and he has become a stable and hardworking member of our community. He can't run or hide from his past, but he can acknowledge it honestly, overcome it and become a better person.

Not only has the "boil been pricked," but also by alluding to the defendant's life following his conviction, we learn that he has overcome his mistake and become better for it. Moreover, the credibility of the advocate shines through, since he was the instigator of the honest disclosure.

G.   Conclude: Clearly and Precisely Tell the Jury What You Want Them to Do

The last piece of the closing should be the simplest—a clear and precise statement to the jurors about what they are to do. The bulk of the closing argument is explaining to the jurors why they need to take particular action. The conclusion tells them precisely what that action should be.

Informative speaking serves the primary goal of simply informing or educating the audience. Persuasive speaking, however, requires much more. In its most basic sense, persuasive speaking seeks to convince the listeners that they should adopt a particular position, and, often times, act on that position in a particular way. By definition, then, an otherwise persuasive speaker has failed in the most fundamental and phenomenal way if the jury is left wondering what it is being asked to believe, or to do. Unfortunately, it is here where many attorneys fail. They fail not because they are ill-prepared, or because they themselves do not know what they want the jury to do, but because they miss the forest for the trees. They become engrossed in the nuances and complexities of a trial and may overlook the fact that the jury has a purpose to serve by voting on the issues in the case. For example, in a robbery prosecution in which the jury must decide guilt or innocence, attorneys may spend so much time arguing over why a particular piece of evidence is or is not credible, that they focus the jury's attention on that small concern at the expense of the larger picture.

> **Tech Tip**
>
> *Effective Closing: Show and Tell!*
>
> ✓ Enlarge a visual aid of the jury instructions by using a projector or ELMO.
>
> ✓ Explain to the jury how to integrate the facts and the law to answer the key questions of trial.

Moreover, in cases that involve multiple claims, counterclaims, or special verdict forms, counsel may fail through inadvertence or otherwise to specifically inform the jury of the desired answer to each question or claim. Obviously, a defendant with counterclaims against a plaintiff, or claims against third parties or other defendants, seeks more than just a verdict that he is not liable. He also wants affirmative relief. Counsel must make sure that the jury understands the multiple tasks it must complete and how each should be completed.

Special verdict forms present a similar issue inasmuch as they require the jury to determine particular factual issues in response to specific questions. Most often these factual questions will form the necessary basis for determinations of liability. Inconsistent jury responses to the questions contained in a special verdict form may result in a mistrial, new trial, and/or reversal on appeal. As such, the attorney should explain clearly and precisely the manner in which he expects *every single question* to be answered. To ensure that there is no doubt in the minds of the jurors, the advocate should walk the jury through the verdict form itself.

There should be a time in the closing argument when the advocate states to the jury some variation of, "Ladies and gentlemen, the evidence shows, and justice demands, that you find the defendant not guilty." This should happen with every question the advocate expects the jury to answer. Messages like this need to be repeated for reinforcement. By stating clearly and plainly what the juror should do, and in a manner that the jury will be sure to unmistakably understand, the advocate increases her chances of success exponentially.

III.   PRINCIPLES OF EFFECTIVE CLOSING ARGUMENTS

It is one thing to advise an advocate to be persuasive at closing argument. It is quite another thing to take that generalized advice and transform it into a blueprint for a successful argument. While the specific blueprints for a closing argument are necessarily case and attorney specific, certain overarching and fundamental principles remain constant from one case to another and from one lawyer to another. This chapter will seek to illuminate those fundamental principles, to provide concrete instruction on how to develop a compelling closing argument, and to identify the limitations placed on closing arguments.

> **PRINCIPLES OF EFFECTIVE CLOSING ARGUMENTS**
>
> ❖ Build and Maintain Credibility
>
> ❖ Integrate the Case Theme
>
> ❖ Engage in a Horizontal Dialogue with the Jury
>
> ❖ Employ the Tools of Argument
>
> ❖ Use Demonstrative Aids and Exhibits
>
> ❖ Recognize the Limits of Your Audience
>
> ❖ Adopt a Persuasive Style
>
> ❖ Display Passion and Conviction; Invoke Both Logic *and* Emotion
>
> ❖ Take the Rebuttal Seriously

❖ Principle Number One: Build and Maintain Credibility

First and foremost to making an effective closing argument is the credibility of the advocate before the jury. If the jury does not trust the advocate or the advocate's evidence, then the argument is in vain. The importance of building and maintaining credibility, and the steps the advocate can take to do so, were discussed at length in Chapter One. That material will not be repeated here. Instead this chapter will consider those steps an advocate can take specifically during closing argument that will further enhance and promote his credibility in the eyes of the jurors.

Credibility springs forth from truthfulness. Conversely, misrepresentations and false statements destroy credibility. Any misrepresentation by an advocate will plant seeds of doubt in the jurors' minds, causing them to question both the truth of the advocate's statements, as well as whether some weakness in the case has caused him to feel the need to exaggerate or deceive. Worse yet, the jury may punish the advocate's client for the advocate's attempts to deceive them or seek an unfair advantage. While most advocates would never purposefully seek to mislead the jury or misrepresent the record, these types of mistakes can occur inadvertently. However, the consequences to the advocate's credibility from even inadvertent misrepresentation may be no less severe than if the misstatement was intentional.

A sure means of avoiding inadvertent misrepresentations during the closing argument is to actually read from pertinent parts of the transcript (if available) instead of paraphrasing witness testimony based on the lawyer's notes or memory. The impact of the lawyer holding up the actual transcript and reading selected portions of testimony verbatim can be powerful, particularly if the other side has failed to rely on the actual transcripts or has failed to accurately relate the testimony of a witness. Advocates avoid any risk of misstatement and reinforce to the jurors that they can trust the advocate to provide completely accurate information. If a transcript is not available, careful reliance on notes is preferable to reliance on mere memory. Tell the jury: "I thought that Ms. Jones' testimony was so important that I wrote it down word-for-word. You remember her testimony, don't you? She said, and I quote, 'Mr. Garcia was absent from the termination meeting because of a family emergency. . . .'"

Advocates also build and maintain their credibility when they are genuine, sincere, straightforward, and authentic. One manner of establishing sincerity and authenticity during closing argument is to show some vulnerability before the jury, to pull back the facade of unflappable confidence and to reveal one's own fears and foibles. Gerry Spence, perhaps more than any other, successfully invokes his own fear as a means of building credibility with the jury. In the highly publicized defense of Randy Weaver, Spence began his closing argument by telling the jurors,

> I wish I weren't so afraid. I wish after all these years in the courtroom I didn't feel this way. You'd think I would get over it. I'm afraid I won't be able to make the kind of argument to you that Randy Weaver deserves . . . . I'm afraid I won't measure up. I wish I were a better lawyer.[12]

---

[12] GERRY SPENCE, HOW TO ARGUE AND WIN EVERY TIME 57 (1995).

As demonstrated by Weaver's acquittal, Spence's disarming candor was effective. Honest personal disclosures are powerful tools and they can be directed to any of the countless fears or concerns one might have about a case. Honestly revealing those fears to the jury breaks down the barriers between the jury and advocate, and serves to enhance the jury's trust of the advocate. Although it may seem counter-intuitive that revealing one's fears actually enhances credibility, it simply goes to show that credibility is often enhanced when advocates act least like advocates.

Another counter-intuitive step toward building credibility is to disclose the weaknesses in one's own case. Disclosing weaknesses during closing argument directly rebuts the notion that the lawyer is merely out to win. In the same way, an advocate's concession on points that the opposing party has established through the evidence, and which are not fatal to the advocate's case, can demonstrate his fairness and objectivity.

Similarly, advocates should resist the urge to argue every point no matter how trivial or unsupported by the evidence. Instead, they should be selective, arguing only the strongest points, only those supported by competent, credible evidence. An argument—whether inside a courtroom or not—is only as strong as its weakest link and an advocate's credibility is only as strong as the plausibility of his weakest argument.

Yet another means of building credibility—this one so simple that it risks being missed—is to display kindness and respect to everyone. Strive to be the one lawyer in the courtroom who gets along with everyone: the one who makes it impossible for the jury not to like him or her. The jurors will notice the way the advocate treats others in the courtroom, and will grow suspicious if the advocate is kind and considerate to them, but cold and brash with the bailiff or court clerk, or is disrespectful in referring to witnesses who have testified during the trial.

An advocate who is respectful and courteous is also less likely to be perceived as arrogant. While advocates should maintain strong confidence in their cases, such confidence should never be confused with arrogance. A jury that perceives an attorney to be arrogant is likely to be more critical of him and less forgiving of his position. An arrogant, but eminently competent attorney will receive no sympathy from a jury, while a sincere, but bumbling attorney will likely receive every consideration. Advocates should strive to have juries perceive them as committed, diligent, and even tough, but not as intimidating bullies. As much as the attorney should believe in her case, she must always remember that the jury has the final say, and therefore, the *power*. It is the advocate's task to guide jurors down the *right* path to show them the *truth*, not to harangue, coerce, or otherwise offend in some manner that will send the jury rushing headlong into the hands of the opposition.

Credibility is the bedrock of a successful close, the foundation on which all effective closings are built. Without it, an attorney can do everything else right, and still never gain the trust—or more importantly, the vote—of the jury. Conversely, once an attorney has managed to establish and maintain that credibility with the jury, she can begin to consider other principles that will help to build an effective closing argument.

❖ Principle Number Two: Integrate the Case Theme

The case theme is the matrix upon which the entire trial has been built. Indeed, no meaningful trial preparation can be undertaken until the theme has been identified. And from that point forward, every aspect of the trial is built on the foundation of that theme. The theme is introduced during jury selection, developed during opening statement, and nurtured throughout witness examinations, but it comes to full realization during closing argument. It is for the advocate during closing argument to unleash the full impact of the case theme: to weave together the law and evidence into a cohesive and compelling whole. The closing is the final opportunity to give the perspective, meaning, and context of all that has come before.

Good closing arguments are built on themes that account for what happened and why it happened. A good theme does not require the advocate to bend some facts and ignore others. Rather, it makes sense of the events that led to trial. It resonates with the jurors and becomes *their* story of the case.

Closing arguments without a core theme will be soon forgotten. Without the glue of a theme the jury will have a general notion of what transpired, they will recall some particulars, but they will lack a means to put the testimony together in a way that makes sense. A good theme, however, gives those same jurors a mechanism to remember the significant facts because it now fits into their story. Facts that otherwise would have been lost are now remembered.

❖ Principle Number Three: Engage in a Horizontal Dialogue with the Jury

While credibility is a fundamental prerequisite to persuasion, "horizontal dialogue" is an indispensable tool of persuasion. It contemplates an exchange between equals, not a lawyer talking down to jurors condescendingly or an advocate talking pompously over the heads of jurors. The ability to communicate with the audience, like two friends discussing serious matters over coffee, builds rapport between the advocate and the jury and forms the dividing line between brilliant advocates and merely competent trial lawyers.

One can best explain horizontal dialogue by breaking it into its component parts. The "horizontal" aspect means the jurors must feel that the advocate is speaking at their level—not speaking to them from a position of authority or superiority. The jurors should feel connected to the attorney, as if he is speaking with them in an ordinary, every day conversation. Nothing magical happens when one enters a courtroom that places the lawyer on a higher plane of discourse. The attitude of advocates when they appear before the jury should be that of a friend or neighbor. Undoubtedly, effective trial strategy and case preparation require real intellectual prowess. However, that intellect must be tempered by an ability to relate to "the common man." Speaking in too technical or complicated a manner is likely to leave jurors confused, disheartened, or worse, asleep. At that point, bringing the jurors back into the fold can be a painstaking, if not impossible, task.

Perhaps a sin far more deadly than speaking in too sophisticated a manner, however, is being condescending. Speaking more eloquently or technically than jurors can understand is likely to frustrate the jurors, and make their job more difficult. But sounding condescending is insulting, and can spark anger or resentment in the jury box, alienating the very people who hold the fate of the advocate's client in their hands.

Indeed, the essence of horizontal dialogue is finding that delicate balance wherein one is able to speak at an appropriate level of sophistication, yet with simplicity, and do so with six, nine, or twelve people at the same time. One aid in finding this balance is to recognize that horizontal dialogue is participatory. Horizontal dialogue is obviously not a dialogue in the ordinary sense; it is not possible during closing argument to have an actual two-way conversation with the jurors. Instead, it is a dialogue because the advocate invites the jurors into the argument and includes them in it. Jurors feel as if they are active participants in the discussion.

Despite the jury's compelled silence during the course of the proceedings, the jurors communicate with counsel in many ways throughout the close. The most obvious way, of course, is through each juror's body language. A juror may smile or frown, or nod his head approvingly or shake his head in disagreement. A juror will express surprise with a raised eyebrow or show apathy by looking away. In these circumstances, the juror is actively conveying a message to the advocate. And that message assists in understanding what arguments are working and what arguments are not. By paying attention to what each juror is communicating, an advocate is better able to continue an effective "dialogue." If "all the world is a stage and we are merely players," then the advocate must not ignore prompts from his or her supporting cast of jurors.

This horizontal dialogue model is in stark contrast to the "hard sell" approach employed by many trial lawyers. In the "hard sell" approach, advocates aggressively argue that their conclusions are correct, but do so without supporting those conclusions; or advocates argue that a particular point is black and white—that the evidence supports only one conclusion—when it appears to jurors to be an issue that is susceptible to more than one reasonable interpretation.

When jurors perceive that the advocate is threatening their freedom by limiting their choices, and is doing so without justification, the jurors are highly motivated to restore that freedom. The greater the illegitimacy of the restriction, the greater the resistance of the jurors. Consequently, advocates must resist the temptation to deliver one conclusion after another or to oversimplify difficult issues by suggesting one unequivocal correct answer. If advocates push too far or too hard into the province of the jurors, cognitive resistance builds within the jurors, and the effectiveness of the advocate is eroded. Establishing a horizontal dialogue requires not only a participatory attitude but also the tools of closing argument. Those tools are set forth in the next section.

❖ Principle Number Four: Employ the Tools of Argument

The main objective of the closing argument, as the name suggests, is to argue the case. And yet, many advocates spend the closing argument either summarizing the evidence or trying to force their desired conclusions down the jury's throat. Neither approach works. Instead, the closing argument is a time for reasoned and thoughtful consideration of the evidence. Rather than the "hard sell," it is better to reason with jurors to the desired conclusion. Instead of an emphatic series of declarative statements and personal opinions, it is better to help the jurors discover the truth for themselves. Sharing the supporting facts prior to offering the conclusion allows the jurors to "share" in the reasoning process that led to the conclusion and, because of their "involvement," the conclusion will be more readily accepted by the jurors. Jurors who maintain a sense of "ownership" over the decision process will adhere to that conclusion with greater conviction.

There are a number of tools of argument at the advocate's disposal. One tool is to selectively recall particular pieces of evidence to make specific points rather than to tell the jury what they have already heard. Another persuasive technique often employed during the closing argument is the rhetorical question. This verbal tool can direct and focus the jury on the critical issues in the case. Likewise, analogies, anecdotes, and stories have long been used to communicate messages in a simple, yet powerful way. Finally, an often-overlooked aspect of persuasion, the advocate's appeal to common sense, can help the jury see the simple truth of the case. Each of these four techniques is discussed in turn.

1. *Recall, Do Not Rehash*

While the opening statement should be treated as a story—an opportunity to inform jurors of the evidence they will hear, giving them both context and a "non-argumentative" roadmap—the closing argument stands in marked contrast. By the time closing arguments are presented, the jury has already heard the story, and does not need or want to hear it again. Jurors are likely to perceive any "rehashing" of facts as both condescending ("Does he think we didn't hear him the first time?") or boring ("Not this again!"). Rather, the attorney should use the closing argument as an opportunity to discuss the law, and then selectively use pieces of evidence to show how the required legal elements have or have not been met.

As the number of witnesses and amount of evidence mounts, it becomes more difficult for the jury to remember, contextualize, and understand all of the information. Yet, juror retention during closing argument is critical in order for the strengths of the advocate's case to be set forth and to be discussed meaningfully during deliberations. The advocate's selective recall of the evidence, used in place of a review of all the trial evidence, allows the advocate to remove the onus from the jurors by highlighting the strengths of his case in a manner that assists jurors to retain that information. But selectively recalling evidence is just that—selective. Some facts are just not important enough to mention in the closing. In any closing argument, one must choose what evidence must be selectively pulled out and put before the jury. For instance, in the following illustration the plaintiff's lawyer is arguing that the defendant was negligent in attempting a rock climb from which he fell and which, in turn, led to the death of the rescuer firefighter (plaintiff's spouse).

 ## Illustration of Selective Recall[13]

It seems that the crucial question before us today is whether the defendant acted negligently in trying to climb that cliff. Now Judge Frye will give us a tool to help gauge the defendant's conduct. He will tell us that negligence is a question of reasonableness. And that a person is negligent if they didn't act reasonably and as a result someone got hurt.

Now, what have we heard during this trial that helps shed some light on the defendant's actions? What testimony have we heard that must be looked at and examined to help us figure out if he acted reasonably. Well, as you can imagine, I've been thinking about this and it seems there are three things we heard that might be helpful in answering that question.

First, what about defendant's experience?

[Counsel writes "#1—Def's Experience" on dry erase board.]

Think back with me to the testimony from the defendant himself. You will recall I had a chance to ask him about that. What did we learn? No classes. No guide. In fact, he told us that he had never been climbing before.

[Counsel writes on board and completes first point—which now reads "#1—Def's Experience—None."]

Let's turn to the second point . . . .

Jurors simply cannot remember everything. Selective recall is useful in preserving the advocate's account of what happened in the minds of the jurors. It can effectively frame the trial for the jury, reigning in the boundaries of what is being argued and what the jury should focus upon as decision-makers.

---

[13] This illustration is based on the hypothetical case *Wrigley v. McGuire* (Association of Trial Lawyers of America).

2. *Use Rhetorical Questions*

A true question is offered to elicit an answer. The questioner is seeking a response. Not so with rhetorical questions. Rhetorical questions are offered to elicit a predictable, but unspoken answer. Rhetorical questions allow advocates to focus their listeners on the point being made.

Even though rhetorical questions are statements rather than questions, they are persuasive in that they require the audience to both follow the argument that culminates in the assertion and then to supply the exclamation point to the assertion. Such "questions" are only effective to the extent that the audience understands the train of thought that builds to the "question" and then answers the question itself. Consequently the audience participates in the process. When rhetorical questions are used effectively, the advocate controls the conclusion that the jury will draw, yet allows the jury to feel empowered, as if they reached that predetermined conclusion on their own. Even though the advocate never answers the question, knowing the answer is clear, the jurors feel they have participated in deciphering a complicated issue or resolving a key factual dispute.

The rhetorical question is a powerful tool, and must be wielded with care and forethought. The advocate must ensure that the topic about which he is offering the rhetorical question does in fact lend itself to only one logical conclusion. When a rhetorical question is properly framed there is little risk that the jury will reach an unanticipated conclusion. For instance, it is entirely appropriate to state: "Is it truly reasonable to believe the defendant was asleep the entire night when she had bragged to her friends the next day that she was at the victim's house for several hours?" Such a statement/question can only lead to one answer and therefore is a proper subject for rhetorical. Whereas an advocate should be much more careful in stating "Given these overwhelming inconsistencies in the prosecution's case can we say that there is reasonable doubt?" The response the jury may have to this question may not be what the advocate had hoped. In this instance, the advocate is forcing the jury to make up their minds and come to a seminal conclusion, yet he has not adequately laid the foundation needed to ensure that the jury will answer the rhetorical in the prescribed manner. When this happens, the advocate has failed to actually ask a rhetorical question, he has instead asked an open-ended question to which he has no way of ensuring that the jury will come to the conclusion he desired.

3. *Use Analogies, Anecdotes, and Stories*

Long before the development of the jury trial, communicators employed anecdotes, analogies, and stories to express their message in simple, yet powerful, ways. People from all ethnic and racial backgrounds and from every generation have been taught life's lessons through stories. Ancient Chinese, Greek, and Roman myths were passed on from generation to generation to explain the mysteries of nature and life. The stories contained in great religious texts such as the Bible and the Koran have inspired generations of believers. Shakespeare, Dickens, and their progeny have shared tales of love, betrayal, heroism, and social injustice and, in doing so, have delivered insights into the soul of the human experience. A well-crafted story can encapsulate an idea, a theme, or even a call to action. Stories, analogies, and anecdotes can be critical parts of any closing argument.

During the closing argument there are two contexts in particular that lend themselves to the story. The first is to provide an explanation of legal concepts and terms. The second is to explain conduct, or to distinguish right from wrong, so that the jurors can better appreciate and understand the actions of the parties in the trial.

The art in explaining a complex notion is to educate the jurors without boring or alienating them. The dangers of causing the jurors to lose interest are obvious, but the concerns of alienation are perhaps not so manifest. Gaining and keeping the attention of jurors is foundational. Trial lawyers must recognize the short attention span of most jurors and continually gauge the jurors' level of interest to keep them focused. When the lawyer must, out of necessity, delve into the explanation of a particular legal principle or factual theory, the battle for the jurors' attention is at its fiercest.

The use of a story, anecdote, or analogy has at least three distinct advantages:

- The story will prove more interesting than the advocate's explanation, thus better maintaining the jurors' attention.

- A well-chosen story or anecdote will communicate the concept more clearly and persuasively than the non-story approach.

- Stories reduce the risk of juror alienation.

As to the first benefit, the more interested the jurors, the more likely it is that they will stay focused on the topic. Given the choice between hearing an extended discussion of the inferential value of circumstantial evidence or a story about a child whose foray into the cookie jar was discovered because of the cookie crumbs on her face, jurors would prefer to hear the latter. It relates to their common experience and explains the concept of circumstantial evidence in a way that is easily grasped, as well as being entertaining. Appeals to the jurors' experiences and the activation of the jurors' imaginations add "flair and panache" to the closing argument, keep the jurors attentive, and make the closing more memorable.

The second benefit is that the right story or analogy will more clearly and effectively communicate the point. Stories and analogies allow the jury to transcend the particular facts and events involved in the legal dispute before them and to find a more familiar context for understanding and resolving the issues presented. At their best, they bring about an "Aha!" moment when jurors make the connection between the story or analogy and the issues in the case, leading the jurors to understand the right outcome. Stories and analogies reveal basic truths about the case, but do so in a way that makes the jurors participants in the argument and with a light touch that disarms defensive jurors.

That raises the third benefit from stories and analogies: reducing the risk of juror alienation. Conventional explanations by advocates of the issues or legal principles in a case run the risk that the advocate, unwittingly or not, will alienate the jurors by speaking to them in a condescending manner, or conversely, an unintelligible manner. On the one hand, the advocate knows what the jury does not know and he may be perceived as talking down to the jurors, much like a parent or teacher explaining difficult material to a child or pupil. On the other hand, the advocate may be perceived as speaking over the head of the jurors, momentarily forgetting his audience and proceeding to discuss foreign legal concepts and convoluted technical issues in legalspeak. Obviously, such perceptions by jurors hamper, if not destroy, any rapport between the advocate and the jury. In contrast, stories and anecdotes actually build rapport with the jurors and help maintain the horizontal relationship.

The story at closing argument, of course, is only effective if it fits the facts and theory of the case. A summation for a murder or a rape trial necessarily deals with a serious and sensitive subject matter, which should be taken into consideration when a decision is made about the use of a particular anecdote or analogy. A light, airy, or even humorous story obviously would be inappropriate, such as to call into question the lawyer's sensibilities. Other cases, however, may benefit from a lighter touch and may allow a sense of humor or sharp wit to shine through to the jury.

The universe of stories to illustrate and explain is numerous. A century and a half ago, Lincoln in defense of a man accused of excessive force was confronted with opposing counsel's argument that the defendant should have protected himself without inflicting such severe injuries on his attacker. Lincoln rebutted the argument.

Illustration of an Anecdote as a Tool of Argument

Lincoln: That reminds me of the man who was attacked by a farmer's dog, which he killed with a pitchfork. "What made you kill my dog?" demanded the farmer. "What made him try to bite me?" retorted the defender. "But why didn't you go at him with the other end of your pitchfork?" persisted the farmer. "Well, why didn't he come at me with his other end?" was the offender's retort.[14]

Lincoln's short, pithy analogy effectively answered the claim of excessive force as it perfectly captured his theory of the case. Just as importantly, Lincoln accomplished his goal of explaining the law without speaking to his audience in a way that interfered with his horizontal dialogue.

Just as a story can be used to explain and illustrate the law and other nebulous concepts, it can also be a tool to explain conduct, and even

---

[14] *See* FREDERICK TREVOR HILL, LINCOLN THE LAWYER 216–17.

to distinguish right from wrong. Examples abound. For instance, take William Kunstler's brilliant close in defending the Chicago Seven, which was built around the story of the American Patriots battling the British in 1770 Boston.[15]

 Illustration of an Analogy as a Tool of Argument

Kunstler: You don't have to look for rebels in other countries. You can just look at the history of this country.

You will recall that there was a great demonstration that took place around the Custom House in Boston in 1770. It was a demonstration of the people of Boston against the people who were enforcing the Sugar Act, the Stamp Act, the Quartering of Troops Act. And they picketed at the one place where it was important to be, at the Custom House, where the customs were collected.

You remember the testimony in this case. Superintendent Rochford said, "Go up to Lincoln Park, go to the Bandshell, go anywhere you want, but don't go to the amphitheater."

That was like telling the Boston patriots, "Go anywhere you want, but don't go to the Custom House," because it was at the Custom House and it was at the amphitheater that the protesters wanted to show that something was terribly and totally wrong. They wanted to show it at the place it was important, and so the seeming compliance of the city in saying, "Go anywhere you want throughout the city. Go to Jackson Park. Go to Lincoln Park," has no meaning. That is an excuse for preventing a demonstration at the single place that had meaning, which was the amphitheater. The Custom House in Boston was the scene of evil and so the patriots demonstrated. They ran into Boston. You know what happened. The British soldiers shot them down and killed five of them . . . . They were shot down in the street by the British for demonstrating at the Custom House.

You will remember that after the Boston Massacre, which was the name the colonies gave to it, all sorts of things happened in the colonies. There were all sorts of demonstrations. . . .

Kunstler's simple and straightforward analogy of his clients to the patriots of the American revolution not only explained their conduct, but also put them on near hallowed ground. Kunstler painted compelling visual images of great events and established that his clients were part of a greater cause; his story successfully moved the jurors to view the Chicago Seven in a far more positive light than the prosecution desired.

---

[15] *See* Lief, Caldwell, and Bycel, Ladies and Gentlemen of the Jury, 112-113.

The story, the anecdote, and the analogy have always been time-honored methods for effective communicators and likewise have always been indispensable tools in the arsenal of the trial lawyer.

4. *Appeal to Common Sense*

Some truths are so obvious that they speak for themselves. Sometimes a series of occurrences fit together too neatly to be a coincidence. Some claims are so outlandish that they do not pass "the smell test." And when an advocate confronts such an obvious argument, she should appeal to the jurors' common sense, their intuitive sense of how the world works.

Common sense serves as a powerful tool of persuasion during closing argument because it invites the jury to participate in the argument and provides a means by which the jury can test the evidence in the case against each juror's understanding of how things work. The appeal to common sense empowers jurors and enhances the advocate's horizontal dialogue with the jury. It tells the jury that no matter how alien the proceedings seem and no matter how out of place they feel in the courtroom, the decision-making process relies upon their acquired wisdom; it is the product of their past experiences. They may and, in fact, *must* examine the facts and contentions in the case in light of their own experiences and perceptions.

The use of common sense as a means of argument is also beneficial because it enables the advocate to see weaknesses in the opposition's case that the jury instructions or witness testimony might not reveal. The prism of common sense may also help identify a creative means of arguing the weaknesses of the other side's case that would otherwise go unnoticed.

Appeals to common sense may arise in any number of circumstances, including credibility disputes and circumstantial evidence disputes. To illustrate the former, imagine the following scenario taken from the hypothetical "Bonnie Lynch" case.[16] The simulated criminal trial was showcased at the convention of the American Bar Association in 1979, with John Burgess of San Francisco representing the defendant, Bonnie Lynch. She had been charged with "knowingly harboring and concealing a fugitive from a federal warrant and then helping him cross a state line, knowing it was his purpose to commit a felony." Over a weekend Bonnie Lynch had hosted in her home a man named Frank Adams and then had driven him to the bus station. There were only two problems: (1) Frank Adams was a fugitive; and (2) Bonnie Lynch drove him across the state line–to Texarkana–when she dropped him at the bus station. The central issue in the case was whether Bonnie Lynch knew that Frank Adams was a fugitive and that he intended to commit a felony when she took him across the state line.

The main state's witness was Bonnie's old acquaintance, Jesse Nolan. He was the one who had talked Bonnie Lynch into putting up Frank Adams

---

[16] JAMES W. MCELHANEY, MCELHANEY'S TRIAL NOTEBOOK 499–501 (2d ed. 1987). Copyright 1987 American Bar Association and James W. McElhoney. Reprinted with permission.

for the weekend, but he had received a grant of immunity in return for his testimony. His trial testimony consisted of his clear and unequivocal statement that he told Bonnie Lynch "all about" Frank Adams.

Burgess argued the case twice during the convention, each time before a different jury composed of legal secretaries from Dallas law firms. The lawyer who played the role of the United States Attorney tried the case the exact same way both days, and Burgess did the same, except for one change he made to his closing argument on the second day. The first jury voted to convict Lynch by a vote of seven to five.

Burgess, of course, vigorously attacked Nolan's immunity deal both days, but the second time Burgess added a twist. He recreated for the jury the telephone conversation between Nolan and Lynch, graphically showing the jury the unlikelihood that Nolan was telling the truth about his alleged full disclosure to Lynch. Here is his argument.

 ## Illustration of the Use of Common Sense as a Tool of Argument

Burgess: Ladies and gentlemen, there is only one way that Bonnie Lynch can be guilty: This "immunity witness," Jesse Nolan, must be telling the truth.

You remember his testimony. He told you that he called Bonnie Lynch on the telephone to see if she would be willing to put up Frank Adams for the weekend. He admitted that she was reluctant to do so at first because she lives alone with her little girl, Gretchen. But Nolan says that he talked Bonnie into it, and insists that he told Bonnie Lynch all about Frank Adams in that conversation.

Now, his honor, Judge Higginbotham, is going to instruct you at the end of the case. He will tell you the law you must follow. One thing he is not going to do is tell you to leave your common sense at the door when you go in that deliberation room.

If Jesse Nolan is telling you the truth, how must that telephone conversation have gone?

"Hello?"

"Hello, Bonnie?"

"Yes. Who is this, please?"

"This is Jesse—Jesse Nolan."

"Oh, hi, Jess. How are you?"

"I'm fine. Say, Bonnie, I wonder if you might do me a favor."

"I will if I can. What is it, Jesse?"

> "I have this friend from out of town, and I have to find a place for him to stay. I wonder if you might put him up for the weekend?"
>
> "Gee, Jesse, I don't know. There is just me and Gretchen living here—I am not sure."
>
> "Oh, he wouldn't be any trouble. He's a real nice guy."
>
> "I'm really not sure, Jesse. Who is this person, anyway?"
>
> "His name is Frank Adams, and he is an old friend of mine."
>
> "Oh, Jesse, I don't think so. . . ."
>
> "Bonnie, don't worry. He is a real good guy. He is a bag man for the mob in Nashville. There is a federal fugitive warrant out for his arrest, and he is on his way to Dallas to bribe a local official."
>
> "Well, if that's the case, send him right over."

At that point, the jury's response was predictable. Upon appreciating, perhaps for the first time, the lunacy of the prosecution's argument, the jury broke into laughter and quickly returned a unanimous verdict of not guilty. Burgess' argument was an explicit appeal to common sense. By helping the jury to see that the testimony of the state's star witness could not be trusted, Burgess changed the dynamic of the case and obtained a favorable verdict, though only a simulated one.

The same principle works in other contexts as well. Instead of telling the jury that a particular witness is a liar, show them that his testimony simply does not add up. Instead of telling the jury that a particular inference the other side wants to draw is not supported by the evidence, show the jury how the inference is unsupported. Help the jury look at the evidence through the lens of common sense.

❖ Principle Number Five: Use Demonstrative Aids and Exhibits

The intuitive notion that complex matters are made more comprehensible by the use of charts, diagrams, models, or even computer simulation is supported by both practice and theory. Demonstrative evidence provides jurors with a quality of information and a clarity of understanding that words alone cannot accomplish and as such are a necessary staple of the closing. People are essentially "visual learners." Information jurors are told they may remember; information they are told *and* shown they will remember. It is that simple. The ability to store and recall visual images is remarkable. Thus, advocates must avail themselves of exhibits, demonstrative evidence, and other visual aids during the closing argument.

Lawyers have almost unlimited latitude in how they present their arguments, including the use of demonstrative evidence, and the range of possible demonstrative aids is vast. The relatively wide-open parameters of closing make it an ideal medium for reinforcing the words with pictures, models, diagrams, and other visual and tangible aids. Effective advocates design their closing arguments acutely aware of the jury's need for visual cues and use their creativity to identify the demonstrative aids that will best communicate the case to the jurors while heightening their interest in the case.

Tech Tip
A non-exhaustive list of the most popular visual aids
✓ Bullet point lists
✓ Labeled photos
✓ Relationship charts
✓ Timelines
✓ Copies of documents
✓ Flip-charts
✓ Illustrations
✓ Videos

Less dramatic visual aids can be equally effective. With nothing more than butcher paper and markers, a flip chart, or even a dry erase board, the advocate can create a memorable and effective presentation for the jury. The most basic demonstrative device, such as a diagram, photographs of the scene of an accident, or a timeline of the key events in the case can enhance juror interest by satisfying the juror's need for visual stimulation. The jurors are more likely to stay focused simply because the lawyer is doing something other than just talking.

The jury instructions provide an excellent opportunity for the creation and use of visual aids. Pertinent portions of the charge can be enlarged and displayed before the jury on foam board, transferred onto overhead transparencies, or entered into some type of presentation software. Whether you go high-tech or low-tech, however, the important point is to do something that will allow the jury to both hear and see the critical instructions so that they will make a lasting impression.

In addition to creating heightened interest in the jurors, demonstrative aids also enhance juror retention of the closing argument. The visual image is more memorable for jurors and will be more readily recalled during deliberations. As discussed earlier, a well-constructed list serves as an important part of a closing argument. When displayed before the jury, a list synthesizes and organizes the evidence for the jurors, demonstrating that when boiled down to its essence, the case is comprised of four or five points. As the advocate talks through each point, she writes a bullet point on the board. This simplest of visual aids serves as a significant reinforcement of what the advocate is saying, but by seeing it as well as hearing it the impact of that point on the jury is significantly increased.

❖   Principle Number Six: Recognize the Limits of Your Audience

1.   *Be Brief*

Mark Twain once apologized for writing a long letter explaining that he did not have time to write a short one. Brevity in Twain's context did not contemplate lack of effort or forethought, although such sloth knows no time constraint. In Twain's view, brevity was the by-product of a thoughtful and thorough effort, not to be confused with simply having little to say.

Likewise, the need for brevity in a closing argument in no way implies lack of effort or omission of critical points. Rather, advocates must be sensitive to the limits of the jury and address each and every critical point efficiently and thoughtfully, without excessive verbosity or needless re-hashing.

The case for brevity at closing argument is compelling, and quite simple. As any accomplished public speaker will attest, keeping the audience interested and focused is always job one, and it is a rare individual who can maintain audience attention for any great span of time. While it may be true that attention spans have shrunk to the time between television commercials, that fact alone does not account for juror loss of interest. One culprit may be the unduly lengthy closing. Attorneys not only face jurors who would be unable and unwilling to follow and maintain interest in such a lengthy argument, they also face judges who are unwilling to tolerate such long-windedness.

Further, jurors are alienated by the sheer length of some arguments. They lose their focus because of the advocate's unnecessary repetition, incessant rehashing, and excessive verbiage. Such rehashing and base repetition implies that the lawyer does not trust the jurors. The message is that jurors are incapable of understanding or remembering what transpired during the taking of testimony, and it is the job of the all-knowing lawyer to tell them what they heard and to explain its significance. The notion of a horizontal dialogue, discussed earlier, contemplates the lawyer communicating with the jurors as equals, not talking beneath them in a way that is condescending. The jurors heard the same testimony as the lawyers, and the master advocates understand that simple fact and argue their cases accordingly.

2. *Keep it Simple*

An important part of the art of trial advocacy is to understand when enough is enough. Sometimes less is more. Sometimes simpler is better. More words, more witnesses, more exhibits, and more questions are not always necessary, or even helpful. In fact, too much information or needlessly complex arguments will only serve to dampen the jurors' interest and exacerbate their confusion. There are a number of areas in particular in which advocates must be sensitive to the need for simplicity. From word choices to the selection of themes, advocates must place the needs of the jurors above all else.

A good start is for advocates to simplify their vocabulary. They should use short action words and minimize three and four syllable words that are not in most jurors' common parlance. Proper word selection helps facilitate horizontal dialogue. So too does recognizing that most jurors do not think technically. Thus, for example, compass directions should rarely be used. If an advocate states that "Mr. Peters was driving east on Broadway preparing to turn south on Main," many jurors will become confused and will spend the next moments trying to figure out what Mr. Peters was doing. If you must use directionals, use a diagram for clarity. The jurors are more likely to stay with your arguments if you are speaking their language. Use of jargon is also a concern. An advocate should strive to speak the language of the jury, not that of police officers, expert witnesses, or gangbangers. Proper word usage reduces the risk of creating an intellectual gap between the advocate and jurors.

Similarly, the advocate should use simple universal themes. The theory of the case, as discussed earlier, should reflect a universal, easily understood and accepted basic truth. It need not be sophisticated and certainly should not be complicated. Rather, it should resonate with everyone in the jury box. Although it may seem to defy logic, simplicity is particularly important in complicated cases.

The principle of keeping the case simple, however, does not and should not serve as an excuse for not thoroughly and meticulously preparing the case. Indeed, advocates cannot know how to simplify their cases or how to focus on what is important if in preparation they have not turned every stone. It is only then that the advocate can separate the wheat from the chaff, to cull out the heart of the case and present it to the jury in simple terms.

❖ Principle Number Seven: Adopt a Persuasive Style

What of persuasion? What is it that Clarence Darrow did or Gerry Spence does, so that they can move an audience, a jury, or a judge to their point of view. In the execution of the six principles discussed above there is a style, an attitude, that can further enhance the persuasive impact of the closing argument. This style or attitude requires that advocates understand and make effective use of nonverbal communication and that they eliminate barriers between them and the jurors.

1. *Understand and Utilize Non-Verbal Communication*

Lawyers communicate not only with their words, but with their gestures, expressions, and movements. Nonverbal communication plays a critical role in an advocate's effort to build credibility with jurors, to develop a horizontal dialogue with them, and to persuade them of the justness of the advocate's cause. Thus, while we have already discussed how a jury may communicate with the attorney through nonverbal behavior, attorneys, of course, communicate to jurors in the same way, whether they realize it or not. Jurors will notice and ascribe meaning to each and every gesture or expression by the lawyers in the case, both those that are intentional and those that are unintentional. Thus, advocates must be aware of their kinesics—or bodily behavior—to ensure that they are communicating to the jury what they intend to communicate.

Maintaining eye contact with jurors is perhaps the most obvious and most important aspect of nonverbal communication. It helps focus the jurors' attention on the advocate and it demonstrates the advocate's confidence and trustworthiness. An advocate should also maintain an open body posture, and face the jury as squarely as possible; a profile can inhibit jury exposure to the advocate's facial expressions. Standing squarely before the jury indicates that the advocate has nothing to hide and shows his openness and confidence in the case. The same is true of showing the jury the palms of one's hands when gesturing. Gestures should be smooth, deliberate, and natural. Finally, the advocate should move about the courtroom during the closing, but any such movement should be intentional and purposeful, not random or distracting. Movements should be for the purpose of emphasizing a point or at appropriate points of transition. Pacing will distract the jury from hearing the advocate's words, but standing motionless will bore the jury and cause them to lose interest. The advocate should strike a balance.

2. *Eliminate Barriers to Your Message*

Effective communication requires maximum attention by all parties. Any form of distraction to either party, by definition, obstructs communication. Physical barriers are the most obvious impediments to effective communication, and can be the most distracting. The courtroom is a place where tales are told and dramas unfold. The judge sits elevated above the attorneys and jurors, who are placed at "starkly symmetrical counsel tables" and within a secluded jury "box." With this in mind, it is important for the advocate to examine the court itself and the props present within it, just as an actor examines and choreographs his stage. Advocates must be comfortable and familiar within the walls of the courtroom and must see that their communication with the jury is uninhibited.

Perhaps the single most common physical barrier between the advocate and the jury is one that is placed there by the advocate himself—the podium. Delivering a closing argument from behind a podium may be appropriate in establishing a formal tone, but the advocate risks being viewed as merely a "talking head." Additionally, once behind the podium, advocates are likely to use the podium as a crutch, hiding their face while they read their notes, or leaning on it for physical or psychological support. Even in federal court, where the judge may require the advocate to use the podium, the attorney should move to the side of the podium, allowing the jury to see his full frame and sending the message that he will not allow anything to disrupt the conversation.

In the same vein, when allowed to do so, the attorney should not be afraid to approach the jury box during opening statement and closing argument. While it is impossible to know how close to the jury is too close for advocates, it is beyond dispute that rapport building is much easier for the advocate face-to-face and person-to-person in front of the jury box rather than behind the podium. Leaning on the jury rail may be too close, causing the jury to feel overwhelmed, as if the attorney is invading their personal space. Standing too far away, on the other hand, may leave the jury feeling disconnected. Nobody goes to a concert intending to sit in the back row; the jury should not be made to feel as though they have been banished to that same back row.

Exactly how close the attorney should stand to the jury depends on the height, size, and gender of the attorney, as well as the part of the country in which the trial is being held. A large man is going to seem more imposing standing close to a jury than a petite female. The male advocate may have to fight stereotypes of aggressiveness and dominance, while the petite female may need to overcome preconceived notions of weakness and passivity. Modifying the distance between the advocate and jury can help an advocate overcome some of those stereotypes. Geography may play a part in one's notion of personal space. Some suggest that people on the two coasts tend to have much larger zones of personal space than those in the middle and southern United States.

The attorney who must resort to legal pads, the taking and reading of notes, or the shuffling of questions creates the same dilemma. He is forsaking the opportunity to establish eye contact with jurors and to absorb the jurors' nonverbal cues. The risk of using notes is that they act as a magnet for the eyes, virtually compelling the advocate to rely on them. Nevertheless, if notes must be used, they should be used minimally so as to avoid any appearance that the argument is scripted. If jurors see that advocates are concentrating on their notes rather than on the jurors, the argument may well fall on deaf ears. The antidote to the use of notes is comprehensive preparation and practice.

The advantages to lessening one's reliance on notes are obvious. First, the extemporaneous speaker enjoys the freedom and flexibility that comes with not having a script. Naturally, a trial will likely take many twists and turns, and the absence of a script allows advocates the room they need to make appropriate adjustments. Second, over-reliance on notes erodes the advocate's credibility by suggesting the advocate does not know the case well enough to argue it without notes or that the attorney is simply a mouthpiece for the client. Third, the notes or memorized lines become a crutch, a security blanket for the advocate, preventing the advocate from maintaining eye contact with the jury and causing the advocate to become disconnected from the jury. In short, notes can easily become an intellectual barrier between the jury and the advocate.

But notes are not the only intellectual barriers that can come between an advocate and his audience. Advocates must also be aware of particular word choices or speech patterns. Overly formal speech can serve to distract jurors. The advocate risks "outsmarting" the jury, and he risks sounding scripted, unnatural, and contrived. Other dangers also lurk, including mumbling, profanity, jargon or slang, a monotone presentation style, and nervous reliance on "fillers," such as "okay," and "um" or "uh."

Perhaps the most significant barrier to effectively communicate during the closing, however, is the jurors' preconceived notion of their role as passive. Jurors may believe that their participation only becomes active once deliberation begins. An attorney must convince jurors that they are an active part of the trial itself. Throughout the trial, advocates must engage and involve the jurors. Jurors must feel that they are participants in the process. They must have the sense that they have personally worked through the evidence and arrived at their own conclusions. Techniques such as recalling testimony rather than rehashing it and using rhetorical questions are but two examples. A third technique is the use of inclusive language. The advocate's selection of words can serve to emphasize that the trial is a collaborative process, a joint search for the truth involving the attorney and the jurors working together. For example, as the attorney guides the jury to a desired conclusion, words such as "I" or "you" should be replaced by "we" and "us." Thus, in discussing an important piece of evidence, the advocate might say: "Remember back to Mr. Madison's testimony, when he told us that 'no one had entered the house.' What did we conclude from that, why was that important to what we are discussing now?" The language of inclusion puts the advocate in the jury box as the thirteenth juror, a co-laborer in the trial.

❖ Principle Number Eight: Display Passion and Conviction; Invoke Both Logic *and* Emotion

Successful attorneys must do more than simply enunciate the legal strengths of their cases. Rather, the advocate must gather the morsels of a case, those points or issues that suggest a larger truth than the facts themselves, and show the jury why the case matters, why the jury should care. It may be an overriding legal principle such as due process or equal protection, or merely the abundance of evidence that supports a particular factual position. Whatever the particular truth may be, attorneys must convey to the jury passion and conviction in every case. Without conviction, any closing argument, no matter the legal strengths of the case, risks being lost on a bored or unsympathetic jury, and most likely doomed to failure.

The overarching goal at closing argument, of course, is to convince each juror that the advocate's position is correct and worthy of the juror's vote. A juror who perceives that the advocate does not believe what she is saying, that the advocate has a lack of conviction, will follow the advocate's clear message by also not believing the argument and not voting for the advocate's client.

Demonstrating conviction requires a delicate balance of emotion and logic. Emotion is necessary because it adds life to a case—gives the jury the sense that the advocate truly believes in his case, his duty, and his client, and that the jury should too. Logic is necessary because it prevents an emotional plea from becoming empty sensationalism.

Clarence Darrow brought conviction, emotion, and logic into his argument to spare Leopold and Loeb from the death penalty.[17]

Illustration of Logic Tempered with Conviction and Emotion

Darrow: I could say something about the death penalty that, for some mysterious reason, the state wants in this case. Why do they want it? To vindicate the law? Oh, no. The law can be vindicated without killing anyone else. It might shock the fine sensibilities of the

---

[17] *See* LIEF, CALDWELL, AND BYCEL, LADIES AND GENTLEMEN OF THE JURY, 177–78.

state's counsel that this boy was put into a culvert and left after he was dead, but, Your Honor, I can think of a scene that makes this pale into insignificance. I can think, and only think, Your Honor, of taking two boys, one eighteen and the other nineteen, irresponsible, weak, diseased, penning them in a cell, checking off the days and the hours and the minutes, until they will be taken out and hanged. Wouldn't it be a glorious day for Chicago? Wouldn't it be a glorious triumph for the State's Attorney? Wouldn't it be a glorious triumph for justice in this land? Wouldn't it be a glorious illustration of Christianity and kindness and charity? I can picture them, wakened in the gray light of morning, furnished [with] a suit of clothes by the state, led to the scaffold, their feet tied, black caps drawn over their heads, stood on a trapdoor, the hangman pressing a spring, so that it gives way under them; I can see them fall through space—and stopped—by the rope around their necks.

In going about the task of getting the jury to care and feel about the case, an attorney should not, and cannot, inject his or her personal opinions into the trial. These opinions are irrelevant and potentially prejudicial (*see* Part IV of this Chapter). That does not mean, however, that an attorney should not be passionate about his case, interjecting emotion into appropriate aspects of the closing argument. Particularly in a period of time when there have been notorious instances of juror nullification, reliance on the legal strengths of a case and ignoring the emotional side will leave a case half-prepared and half-presented.

Attorneys can demonstrate emotion in a number of ways including voice modulation, facial expression, and hand and body movement. Attorneys can also display emotion by doing nothing at all. A single pause, when the advocate seems to freeze in time, and focuses his eyes on one particular juror, can add a dramatic punctuation mark to an important point. At the same time, the cessation of activity will allow jurors a moment to process the message, and by selectively choosing which jurors deserve that moment of silent eye contact, allow the attorney to draw wandering jurors back into the fold.

Of course, the attorney must vary his emotion at appropriate times, lest the jury become desensitized, overwhelmed, or even exhausted. An advocate may move from righteous indignation, to humorous interpretation, to stoic recollection. Variation gives the audience a momentary reprieve and prevents key points from becoming lost in an endless sea of static emotion. This is particularly true in closing arguments, which often center around complex, technical, or sensitive matters.

In the end, the attorney must convince the jurors that they are making an important decision that will fundamentally affect a person or people in dramatic ways. One simple but effective step toward accomplishing that objective is to make the jurors care about the advocate's client by personalizing him or her. The client is not just that, but is a person, or group of persons. The attorney should never refer to the client as "my client," but by name. Although it seems like flyspecking, this alone could make the difference between the jurors viewing the attorney as a hired gun, or an advocate sworn to protect the interests of another human being.

This can be particularly difficult when the client is not a person, but a corporation or governmental entity. Under those circumstances, the corporation is not a multi-million dollar deep pocket, but an association of humans, each seeking to do good and earn an honest living. A prosecutor does not represent the state, but the good people living in that state.

Contrast this with the way the attorney should refer to the opposing party. Names are not appropriate. Rather, the opposite principles apply. The State's attorney is just that. The corporation is a faceless, emotionless, unfeeling conglomerate. And even the individual opponent is not "John Smith," father of two, but the "plaintiff" or "defendant."

To demonstrate meaningful conviction, however, an advocate must temper emotion with logic. Logic, which is derived from the Greek word "logos," appeals not to a jury's emotional side, but to the jury's sense of order and reason. Raw emotion, absent logic, may appear as nothing more than superfluous remonstration. A logical analysis provides the justification for the emotion, appealing to the thoughtful rather than the visceral.

One effective technique for utilizing logic is to appeal to the notion that sometimes things are what they seem. The more creative the defense, the better this argument. In simplistic terms, this argument suggests that despite the desperate stories the opposing parties have created, the proof is in the logical, the obvious, the apparent. Just as two plus two equals four, the defendant's fingerprints were on the murder weapon because he is the one who used it.

On the flipside, one logical appeal that is overused and ineffective is to argue to the jury that "My client could not possibly have been so thoughtless as to. . . . " And one can fill-in-the-blank with whatever crime or misdeed the client is accused of committing. The danger with this appeal is self-evident. A jury could very easily disagree. It is wholly within the realm of possibility that a jury will believe that a person would do such a thing, and in fact did commit the crime. In other words, the advocate may be suggesting to the jury that, not only is the accused guilty, but also is not too bright. Contrast this with the argument that the facts are exactly what they appear to be, which is easier for the jurors to appreciate because it appeals to their common experiences. No great leaps of faith and logic are required. Believing to the contrary would require the jury to go through some mental gymnastics and to view the case as falling outside the normal course of events.

In the end, advocates must build their closing arguments and rest their convictions on a foundation of both emotion and logic; they must appeal to both the heart and the mind. Without arguments and appeals based on both pathos and logos, juries will be left with little more than a paralyzing recitation of testimony and legal principles.

❖ Principle Number Nine: Take the Rebuttal Seriously

The familiar psychological principle of recency stands firmly ensconced as one of the bedrocks of good trial advocacy. The refrain that trial lawyers should "end strong" finds its way into almost every piece of literature about trial advocacy. The reason for this ubiquitous advice is that mountains of empirical data prove the point: people really do remember best the last thing they hear about a person or event and that which goes last does have a disproportionate impact on the listener. The one part of trial that demands an appreciation of the principle of recency more than any other is the rebuttal closing argument, when the party with the ultimate burden of persuasion in the case gets to talk to the jury without any opportunity for the other side to reply. It is literally the opportunity to have the last word. And accordingly, it is a unique advantage that must be taken seriously and exploited for its full effect.

The sad truth is that most advocates fail to specifically prepare or plan for the rebuttal at all. Instead, the typical advocate views the rebuttal as an opportunity to "rebut" what the other side said during the closing. So the advocate, with yellow legal pad in hand, simply goes down her notes of the opponent's close and checks off each point as it is rebutted. That approach concedes control of the agenda to the other side and ensures that the rebuttal will be eminently forgettable.

Perhaps the problem is the name, "rebuttal." Instead of "rebuttal," advocates should think of it as a second opportunity to speak to the jury, a "final closing argument," or better yet, "The Last Word." At the very least, that more accurately captures the advocate's opportunity when he or she stands before the jury. The opportunity to have the jury's undivided attention and to convey to the jury the essence of the case without any reply or counterpoint from the opponent is priceless and should be treated as such.

The rebuttal should be prepared ahead of time, just as the plaintiff's or prosecution's initial closing argument must be prepared in advance. The reasons are not overly complicated. In the first place, the opponent's arguments should be familiar to you by the time of the closing arguments so that the advocate can anticipate what arguments will be made. In the second place, advocates must not allow their opponents to seize control of the agenda. A point-by-point rebuttal does just that, responding to the arguments the other side made and in the order in which the other side made them. Some of those arguments may not be worth rebutting and others may be better rebutted in the context of the party's already developed theme or theory of the case. In the third place, the precious minutes available for rebuttal are too valuable to be exhausted responding to the other side's every claim. Such an approach trivializes the important issues in the case, distracts the jury's attention away from those key issues, and disrupts the organization of the rebuttal. A good rule of thumb is that 75–80 percent of the rebuttal should be prepared beforehand, leaving only 20–25 percent for responding to unforeseen arguments or analogies or metaphors used by opposing counsel.

But even with the "new stuff," the rebuttal material should be placed in the structure and context prepared beforehand by the advocate.

Thus, instead of a debate-style, extemporaneous "rebuttal," advocates should treat the rebuttal argument as a continuation of their argument, but with the benefit of having heard the other side's argument. A successful rebuttal will not come as a result of clever, seat-of-the-pants retorts, but because of careful preparation and a large dose of creativity. Great thoughts rarely appear fully formed at just the right time.

The advocate should pursue four objectives in the rebuttal argument:

- convey to the jurors the importance of their task and the significance of the case (beyond the facts themselves)

- reinforce the key points in the case, including the party's theme

- rebut the arguments made by the opponent, but only within the advocate's timetable and structure

- leave the jury with a memorable, lasting image to take into the jury room

One trap the advocate should take pains to avoid on rebuttal is the trap of the "The Challenge Question." The advocate representing the defendant regularly will pose certain questions to the jury during his or her closing argument, and challenge the other side to answer them. It is kind of an adult "double dog dare," but one that is couched in important sounding words, as if the fate of the free world depended on the answer to the question. The hope, of course, is that the advocate will spend his time answering the question or questions and will then be unable to make the critical points to the jury. Do not do it! If the questions are important to the case, answer them in the context of your prepared rebuttal. If they are not important, do not waste your time with them. Whatever you do, however, do not begin the rebuttal by answering the questions because by doing so you have ceded control of your argument to the other side.

Finally, keep the rebuttal brief. The advocate's instincts may well tell him to keep talking until he has rebutted every thing the other side said in its close. That is unwise for the reasons stated above and because by this time in the trial the jury is ready to get on with their deliberations. The advocate must make every word count during the rebuttal, and must know when to stop. The jury will appreciate the advocate's efficient use of the rebuttal time and his recognition that the jury has heard enough.

IV.   LIMITATIONS ON CLOSING ARGUMENT

One of the joys of closing argument is the relative lack of restraint placed upon the advocate. Whereas the advocate is constrained to avoid argument in opening, in closing the tools of argument can be fully employed in a final effort to persuade the jury. That does not mean, however, that there are no limitations on what an advocate can say or do in the close. There are. And transgressing the limitations will subject the advocate to objections—which break the flow of the argument—and to loss of credibility if the objections are sustained.

A.   Prohibitions on Closing

We have compiled a list of the things the advocate should avoid in closing argument. These boundaries are set by the law of closing, and there may be some variation of that law from jurisdiction to jurisdiction. If in doubt as to how far is too far, advocates are well advised to research the law. On closing, it is wise to be conservative. The advocate is generally better off forgoing tactics that risk objection, rather than suffering those objections which, even if overruled, break the flow of the argument.

1.   *Avoid Misstating the Evidence*

Jurors are limited in their deliberations to considering the evidence presented and the inferences they may draw therefrom. Advocates must carefully confine their argument to the evidence presented, and must not misstate that evidence. As mentioned previously, if a transcript of witness testimony is available, its use can eliminate the chance that an advocate will misstate the substance of the witness' testimony. Additionally, the advocate must be wary of referring to facts that were never admitted in evidence. The exception is that most courts permit attorneys to refer to well known historical facts—such as the World Trade Center attack—to illustrate points made during argument. Likewise, as suggested throughout this chapter, stories and analogies may properly be used. Perhaps the easiest way to distinguish between proper and improper use of matters outside the record is to ask whether the jurors' consideration of the matters would be material to their decision. Proper objections to this improper argument include "misstates the evidence," "assumes facts not in evidence," "arguing excluded matter," and "states (or assumes) facts outside the record."

2.   *Avoid Personal Opinion*

It is improper for the advocate to interject her personal opinions or beliefs about the evidence, the guilt/innocence, or liability of the parties into the argument. It is for the jurors, not the advocates, to express their opinions by means of rendering a verdict. A variation on the "no personal opinion" rule is the prohibition against vouching for a witness. Just as an advocate may not express her opinion that an opponent's witness is a liar, neither should she express a personal opinion that bolsters the credibility of her witnesses.

Proper objections to this type of argument include "improper opinion by counsel" and "improper vouching for a witness."

3.   *Avoid "Golden Rule" Arguments*

"Golden Rule" arguments ask the jurors to put themselves into the shoes of one of the parties. When arguing damages it is improper to ask the jury to step into the shoes of a party. The concern is that jurors who are asked to imagine what it must have felt like (as opposed to considering what the plaintiff actually told them it felt like) are relying on matters outside the record—and on an emotional appeal—to decide an issue. This can lead to damages awards not supported by the record, either because they are too high or, when the defendant makes such an appeal, too low.

Prosecutors can also run afoul of the "Golden Rule" prohibition when they urge the jurors to place themselves in the shoes of the crime victim. Such arguments distract jurors from their proper function, which is to decide guilt. If the crime was particularly heinous, that is a matter for the judge to consider during sentencing.

A proper objection to this type of argument is that "counsel is encouraging the jurors to decide the case based on personal interest or inflamed emotions rather than on the evidence."

There is at least one exception to the "Golden Rule" prohibition that applies in criminal cases. That exception exists when there is a self-defense issue. Since the jurors will have to consider whether the defendant reasonably defended himself, they will have to view the facts of the case from the defendant's perspective.

4. *Avoid Any Reference to Excluded Evidence*

Evidence that was excluded during pretrial motions or during the trial itself is, of course, not a proper subject for closing argument. Occasionally testimony will be introduced and later stricken. Such testimony is not evidence and is not to be discussed during closing argument. The objection is "counsel is referring to inadmissible evidence."

5. *Avoid Disparaging Opposing Counsel or the Opposing Party*

The courtroom is no place for a display of incivility, and name-calling certainly has its limits. For instance, in the prosecution's closing argument against a defendant accused of being a serial rapist it most likely would be error to state that "a snake crawls on its own belly, but this human vulture crawls on the bellies of our helpless and defenseless women."[18] Traditionally, such remarks are improper unless they are supported by the evidence. If they are not supported the remarks may constitute misconduct in that they have compromised the defendant's ability to receive a fair trial.[19] On the other hand, it is permissible to demonstrate to the jurors that a witness or party lied under oath.

---

[18] *Hill v. State* (1941) 144 Tex. Crim. 415, 423 (This comment was surprisingly not found improper as the reviewing court held it was a reasonable deduction from the facts: "It is commonly known that a snake crawls on its belly and it is also commonly known that men who, by force, overcome the resistance of helpless women and commit rape, crawl on the bellies of such women.).

[19] Caldwell, *Name Calling at Trial: Placing Parameters on the Prosecutor*, 8 AM. J. TRIAL ADVOC. 385 (1986).

6. *Avoid Racial, Religious, Ethnic, or Economic Bias*

Advocates should never urge that a case be decided based upon biases or prejudices that may be held by jurors. Nor should damage awards be based upon arguments that the defendants can afford to pay or plaintiffs need or do not need the money.

Proper objections to these arguments include "irrelevant," "unfairly prejudicial," "appeals to passion and prejudice," and "tends to inflame the jury."

7. *Avoid Grandiose Assertions*

It is tempting, and often good advocacy, to make the case seem bigger than the facts justify. Advocates need jurors to care about the case. However, the jurors must not be misled into deciding that case in a way not supported by the evidence. The tired "send a message" appeals have occasionally been found improper in criminal cases, whereas they may be appropriate in civil cases when seeking punitive damages. Likewise, care must be used in urging that the jurors are acting as the conscience of the community or that their verdict is an important battle in the war on terrorism, drugs, crime, violence, or any other popular target. An example of the proper use of the "send a message" argument was employed by Gerry Spence in the *Silkwood* case.[20]

 Illustration of the Successful "Send a Message" Theme

Spence: I couldn't get over it—I couldn't sleep—I couldn't believe what I had heard. I don't know how it affected you. Maybe you get so numb after a while—I guess people just stand and say, "Exposure, exposure, exposure, exposure, exposure—cancer, cancer, cancer, cancer, cancer, cancer, cancer, cancer, cancer, cancer, cancer, cancer, cancer, cancer, cancer, cancer, cancer," until you don't hear it anymore. Maybe that is what happens to us. I tell you, if it is throbbing in your breast—if cancer is eating at your guts, or it's eating at your lungs, or it's gnawing away at your gonads, and you're losing your life, and your manhood, and your womanhood, and your child, or your children, it then has meaning—they are not just words. You multiply it by hundreds of workers, and thousands of workers, that is why this case is the most important case, maybe, in the history of man. That is why I'm so proud to be here with you. That's why I'm so glad you're on this jury, and that we are a part of this thing together.

---

[20] *See* LIEF, CALDWELL, AND BYCEL, LADIES AND GENTLEMEN OF THE JURY 126 (Scribner 1998).

8. *Avoid Comment on a Criminal Defendant's Failure to Testify or to Produce Evidence*

Criminal defendant's have an unqualified constitutional right to not testify. The Fifth Amendment expressly prohibits compelled self-incrimination. Anything said by the prosecutor that may be construed as a comment on the defendant's failure to testify is a monumental error and will almost certainly result in an immediate mistrial.

Illustration of Prosecutor's Comment on Defendant's Failure to Testify

> The defense produced one witness, the defendant's girlfriend, who said that she was with him at the time of the shooting. That's it. That's their defense. One witness. One witness with a definite axe to grind. Wouldn't it have been helpful to hear more? Wouldn't we have all liked a better explanation? You know what I'm talking about.

Objections to this type of argument include "improper comment on defendant's decision not to testify."

9. *Avoid Urging Jury Nullification*

Jurors are required to follow the law, even if they do not agree with it. It is improper for an attorney to argue to the jurors that they should disregard the law. It is also unwise, as it can be taken as an admission that one's evidence is insufficient under the law—otherwise why urge the jury to disregard the law? For example, in the case of a battered wife now on trial for killing her abusive husband, the law requires a showing of an immediate threat before the wife can claim either self-defense or voluntary manslaughter. In the absence of that immediacy, defense counsel may be tempted to argue that the jury should ignore that aspect of the law and "do the right thing." Such an argument is, of course, improper. Defense counsel under such circumstances must argue within the law and perhaps suggest that under the circumstances confronting his client her actions were in fact immediate.

An objection to this type of argument can be stated "improper argument urging jury nullification."

B.   Objection Strategy on Closing

At no other time during the trial can the mere interposition of an objection do as much damage as it can during the closing argument. This is the time when counsel most needs to hold the jurors' attention and keep them focused upon the logic of the argument. Any interruption detracts from the ability to do this. Recognizing this, many judges discourage objecting during closing argument, and counsel should be careful not to make frivolous objections calculated merely to interrupt the argument. This will not only anger the judge—not to mention the opponent—but it will likely be seen through by the jurors, who will be certain to find it irritating.

With that said, in the event that counsel transcends the bounds of proper argument, the advocate must object in order to correct the error or, if overruled, to preserve the issue for appeal. While some objections, such as disparaging counsel, are essential, most are not. It would be foolish to permit a misstatement of the evidence to be taken into the deliberation room or to permit jurors to consider the case based upon improper bases. Thus, while the advocate should be wary of interposing frivolous objections during closing argument, at this time—as in all other stages of the trial—a well-taken objection is an essential tool of effective trial advocacy. Objections may become particularly important during the rebuttal, when defense counsel is left with no other effective means of correcting the record.

APPENDIX

FEDERAL RULES OF EVIDENCE

Effective July 1, 1975

Complete through December 1, 2010

RULES OF EVIDENCE FOR UNITED STATES COURTS
AND MAGISTRATES

ARTICLE I
GENERAL PROVISIONS

RULE 101. Scope

These rules govern proceedings in the courts of the United States and before the United States bankruptcy judges and United States magistrate judges, to the extent and with the exceptions stated in rule 1101.

(Amended, eff 10-1-87; 11-1-88; 12-1-93)

RULE 102. Purpose and Construction

These rules shall be construed to secure fairness in administration, elimination of unjustifiable expense and delay, and promotion of growth and development of the law of evidence to the end that the truth may be ascertained and proceedings justly determined.

RULE 103. Rulings on Evidence

(a) Effect of erroneous ruling.—Error may not be predicated upon a ruling which admits or excludes evidence unless a substantial right of the party is affected, and

(1) *Objection.*—In case the ruling is one admitting evidence, a timely objection or motion to strike appears of record, stating the specific ground of objection, if the specific ground was not apparent from the context; or

(2) *Offer of proof.*—In case the ruling is one excluding evidence, the substance of the evidence was made known to the court by offer or was apparent from the context within which questions were asked.

Once the court makes a definitive ruling on the record admitting or excluding evidence, either at or before trial, a party need not renew an objection or offer of proof to preserve a claim of error for appeal.

(b) Record of offer and ruling.—The court may add any other or further statement which shows the character of the evidence, the form in which it was offered, the objection made, and the ruling thereon. It may direct the making of an offer in question and answer form.

(c) Hearing of jury.—In jury cases, proceedings shall be conducted, to the extent practicable, so as to prevent inadmissible evidence from being suggested to the jury by any means, such as making statements or offers of proof or asking questions in the hearing of the jury.

(d) Plain error.—Nothing in this rule precludes taking notice of plain errors affecting substantial rights although they were not brought to the attention of the court.

(Amended, eff 12-1-00)

RULE 104. Preliminary Questions

(a) Questions of admissibility generally. Preliminary questions concerning the qualification of a person to be a witness, the existence of a privilege, or the admissibility of evidence shall be determined by the court, subject to the provisions of subdivision (b). In making its determination it is not bound by the rules of evidence except those with respect to privileges.

(b) Relevancy conditioned on fact. When the relevancy of evidence depends upon the fulfillment of a condition of fact, the court shall admit it upon, or subject to, the introduction of evidence sufficient to support a finding of the fulfillment of the condition.

(c) Hearing of jury. Hearings on the admissibility of confessions shall in all cases be conducted out of the hearing of the jury. Hearings on other preliminary matters shall be so conducted when the interests of justice require, or when an accused is a witness and so requests.

(d) Testimony by accused. The accused does not, by testifying upon a preliminary matter, become subject to cross-examination as to other issues in the case.

(e) Weight and credibility. This rule does not limit the right of a party to introduce before the jury evidence relevant to weight or credibility.

(Amended, eff 10-1-87)

RULE 105. Limited Admissibility

When evidence which is admissible as to one party or for one purpose but not admissible as to another party or for another purpose is admitted, the court, upon request, shall restrict the evidence to its proper scope and instruct the jury accordingly.

RULE 106. Remainder of or Related Writings or Recorded Statements

When a writing or recorded statement or part thereof is introduced by a party, an adverse party may require the introduction at that time of any other part or any other writing or recorded statement which ought in fairness to be considered contemporaneously with it.

(Amended, eff 10-1-87)

**ARTICLE II
JUDICIAL NOTICE**

RULE 201. Judicial Notice of Adjudicative Facts

(a) Scope of rule. This rule governs only judicial notice of adjudicative facts.

(b) Kinds of facts. A judicially noticed fact must be one not subject to reasonable dispute in that it is either (1) generally known within the territorial jurisdiction of the trial court or (2) capable of accurate and ready determination by resort to sources whose accuracy cannot reasonably be questioned.

(c) When discretionary. A court may take judicial notice, whether requested or not.

(d) When mandatory. A court shall take judicial notice if requested by a party and supplied with the necessary information.

(e) Opportunity to be heard. A party is entitled upon timely request to an opportunity to be heard as to the propriety of taking judicial notice and the tenor of the matter noticed. In the absence of prior notification, the request may be made after judicial notice has been taken.

(f) Time of taking notice. Judicial notice may be taken at any stage of the proceeding.

(g) Instructing jury. In a civil action or proceeding, the court shall instruct the jury to accept as conclusive any fact judicially noticed. In a criminal case, the court shall instruct the jury that it may, but is not required to, accept as conclusive any fact judicially noticed.

**ARTICLE III
PRESUMPTIONS IN CIVIL
ACTIONS AND PROCEEDINGS**

RULE 301. Presumptions in General in Civil Actions and Proceedings

In all civil actions and proceedings not otherwise provided for by Act of Congress or by these rules, a presumption imposes on the party against whom it is directed the burden of going forward with evidence to rebut or meet the presumption, but does not shift to such party the burden of proof in the sense of the risk of nonpersuasion, which remains throughout the trial upon the party on whom it was originally cast.

RULE 302. Applicability of State Law in Civil Actions and Proceedings

In civil actions and proceedings, the effect of a presumption respecting a fact which is an element of a claim or defense as to which State law supplies the rule of decision is determined in accordance with State law.

ARTICLE IV
RELEVANCY AND ITS LIMITS

RULE 401. Definition of "Relevant Evidence"

"Relevant evidence" means evidence having any tendency to make the existence of any fact that is of consequence to the determination of the action more probable or less probable than it would be without the evidence.

RULE 402. Relevant Evidence Generally Admissible; Irrelevant Evidence Inadmissible

All relevant evidence is admissible, except as otherwise provided by the Constitution of the United States, by Act of Congress, by these rules, or by other rules prescribed by the Supreme Court pursuant to statutory authority. Evidence which is not relevant is not admissible.

RULE 403. Exclusion of Relevant Evidence on Grounds of Prejudice, Confusion, or Waste of Time

Although relevant, evidence may be excluded if its probative value is substantially outweighed by the danger of unfair prejudice, confusion of the issues, or misleading the jury, or by considerations of undue delay, waste of time, or needless presentation of cumulative evidence.

RULE 404. Character Evidence Not Admissible to Prove Conduct; Exceptions; Other Crimes

(a) **Character evidence generally.**— In a criminal case, evidence of a person's character or a trait of character is not admissible for the purpose of proving action in conformity therewith on a particular occasion, except:

(1) *Character of accused.*— In a criminal case, evidence of a pertinent trait of character offered by an accused, or by the prosecution to rebut the same, or if evidence of a trait of character of the alleged victim of the crime is offered by an accused and admitted under Rule 404(a)(2), evidence of the same trait of character of the accused offered by the prosecution;

(2) *Character of alleged victim.*—In a criminal case, and subject to the limitations imposed by Rule 412, evidence of a pertinent trait of character of the alleged victim of the crime offered by an accused, or by the prosecution to rebut the same, or evidence of a character trait of peacefulness of the alleged victim offered by the prosecution in a homicide case to rebut evidence that the alleged victim was the first aggressor;

(3) *Character of witness.*—Evidence of the character of a witness, as provided in rules 607, 608 and 609.

(b) **Other crimes, wrongs, or acts.**—Evidence of other crimes, wrongs, or acts is not admissible to prove the character of a person in order to show action in conformity therewith. It may, however, be admissible for other purposes, such as proof of motive, opportunity, intent, preparation, plan, knowledge, identity, or absence of mistake or accident, provided that upon request by the accused, the prosecution in a criminal case shall provide reasonable notice in advance of trial, or during trial if the court excuses pretrial notice on good cause shown, of the general nature of any such evidence it intends to introduce at trial.

(Amended, eff 10-1-87; 12-1-91; 12-1-00)

RULE 405. Methods of Proving Character

(a) **Reputation or opinion.** In all cases in which evidence of character or trait of character of a person is admissible, proof may be made by testimony as to reputation or by testimony in the form of an opinion. On cross-examination, inquiry is allowable into relevant specific instances of conduct.

(b) **Specific instances of conduct.** In cases in which character or a trait of character of a person is an essential element of a charge, claim, or defense, proof may also be made of specific instances of that person's conduct.

(Amended, eff 10-1-87)

RULE 406. Habit; Routine Practice

Evidence of the habit of a person or of the routine practice of an organization, whether corroborated or not and regardless of the presence of eyewitnesses, is relevant to prove that the conduct of the person or organization on a particular occasion was in conformity with the habit or routine practice.

RULE 407. Subsequent Remedial Measures

When, after an injury or harm allegedly caused by an event, measures are taken that, if taken previously, would have made the injury or harm less likely to occur, evidence of the subsequent measures is not admissible to prove negligence, culpable conduct, a defect in a product, a defect in a product's design, or a need for a warning or instruction. This rule does not require the exclusion of evidence of subsequent measures when offered for another purpose, such as proving ownership, control, or feasibility of precautionary measures, if controverted, or impeachment.

(Amended, eff 12-1-97)

RULE 408. Compromise and Offers to Compromise

(a) **Prohibited uses.**—Evidence of the following is not admissible on behalf of any party, when offered to prove liability for, invalidity of, or amount of a claim that was disputed as to validity or amount, or to impeach through a prior inconsistent statement or contradiction:

(1) furnishing or offering or promising to furnish or accepting or offering or promising to accept, a valuable consideration in compromising or attempting to compromise the claim ; and,

(2) conduct or statements made in compromise negotiations regarding the claim, except when offered in a criminal case and the negotiations related to a claim by a public office or agency in the exercise of regulatory, investigative, or enforcement authority.

Permitted Uses. This rule does not require exclusion if the evidence is offered for purposes not prohibited by subdivision (a). Examples of permissible purposes include proving a witness's bias or prejudice negating a contention of undue delay; and proving an effort to obstruct a criminal investigation or prosecution.

RULE 409. Payment of Medical and Similar Expenses

Evidence of furnishing or offering or promising to pay medical, hospital, or similar expenses occasioned by an injury is not admissible to prove liability for the injury.

RULE 410. Inadmissibility of Pleas, Plea Discussions, and Related Statements

Except as otherwise provided in this rule, evidence of the following is not, in any civil or criminal proceeding, admissible against the defendant who made the plea or was a participant in the plea discussions:

(1) a plea of guilty which was later withdrawn;

(2) a plea of nolo contendere;

(3) any statement made in the course of any proceedings under Rule 11 of the Federal Rules of Criminal Procedure or comparable state procedure regarding either of the foregoing pleas; or

(4) any statement made in the course of plea discussions with an attorney for the prosecuting authority which do not result in a plea of guilty or which result in a plea of guilty later withdrawn.

However, such a statement is admissible (i) in any proceeding wherein another statement made in the course of the same plea or plea discussions has been introduced and the statement ought in fairness be considered contemporaneously with it, or (ii) in a criminal proceeding for perjury or false statement if the statement was made by the defendant under oath, on the record and in the presence of counsel.

(Amended, 12-12-75; 4-30-79, eff 12-1-80)

RULE 411. Liability Insurance

Evidence that a person was or was not insured against liability is not admissible upon the issue whether the person acted negligently or otherwise wrongfully. This rule does not require the exclusion of evidence of insurance against liability when offered for another purpose, such as proof of agency, ownership, or control, or bias or prejudice of a witness.

(Amended, eff 10-1-87)

RULE 412. Sex Offense Cases; Relevance of Alleged Victim's Past Sexual Behavior or Alleged Sexual Predisposition

(a) **Evidence generally inadmissible.** The following evidence is not admissible in any civil or criminal proceeding involving alleged sexual misconduct except as provided in subdivisions (b) and (c):

(1) Evidence offered to prove that any alleged victim engaged in other sexual behavior.

(2) Evidence offered to prove any alleged victim's sexual predisposition.

(b) **Exceptions.**

(1) In a criminal case, the following evidence is admissible, if otherwise admissible under these rules:

(A) evidence of specific instances of sexual behavior by the alleged victim offered to prove that a person other than the accused was the source of semen, injury or other physical evidence;

(B) evidence of specific instances of sexual behavior by the alleged victim

with respect to the person accused of the sexual misconduct offered by the accused to prove consent or by the prosecution; and

(C) evidence the exclusion of which would violate the constitutional rights of the defendant.

(2) In a civil case, evidence offered to prove the sexual behavior or sexual predisposition of any alleged victim is admissible if it is otherwise admissible under these rules and its probative value substantially outweighs the danger of harm to any victim and of unfair prejudice to any party. Evidence of an alleged victim's reputation is admissible only if it has been placed in controversy by the alleged victim.

(c) Procedure to determine admissibility.

(1) A party intending to offer evidence under subdivision (b) must:

(A) file a written motion at least 14 days before trial specifically describing the evidence and stating the purpose for which it is offered unless the court, for good cause requires a different time for filing or permits filing during trial; and

(B) serve the motion on all parties and notify the alleged victim or, when appropriate, the alleged victim's guardian or representative.

(2) Before admitting evidence under this rule the court must conduct a hearing in camera and afford the victim and parties a right to attend and be heard. The motion, related papers, and the record of the hearing must be sealed and remain under seal unless the court orders otherwise.

(Effective 10-28-78; amended, eff 11-18-88; 12-1-94)

RULE 413. Evidence of Similar Crimes in Sexual Assault Cases

(a) In a criminal case in which the defendant is accused of an offense of sexual assault, evidence of the defendant's commission of another offense or offenses of sexual assault is admissible, and may be considered for its bearing on any matter to which it is relevant.

(b) In a case in which the Government intends to offer evidence under this rule, the attorney for the Government shall disclose the evidence to the defendant, including statements of witnesses or a summary of the substance of any testimony that is expected to be offered, at least fifteen days before the scheduled date of trial or at such later time as the court may allow for good cause.

(c) This rule shall not be construed to limit the admission or consideration of evidence under any other rule.

(d) For purposes of this rule and Rule 415, "offense of sexual assault" means a crime under Federal law or the law of a State (as defined in section 513 of title 18, United States Code) that involved—

(1) any conduct proscribed by chapter 109A of title 18, United States Code;

(2) contact, without consent, between any part of the defendant's body or an object and the genitals or anus of another person;

(3) contact, without consent, between the genitals or anus of the defendant and any part of another person's body;

(4) deriving sexual pleasure or gratification from the infliction of death, bodily injury, or physical pain on another person; or

(5) an attempt or conspiracy to engage in conduct described in paragraphs (1)-(4).

(Effective 7-9-95)

RULE 414. Evidence of Similar Crimes in Child Molestation Cases

(a) In a criminal case in which the defendant is accused of an offense of child molestation, evidence of the defendant's commission of another offense or offenses of child molestation is admissible, and may be considered for its bearing on any matter to which it is relevant.

(b) In a case in which the Government intends to offer evidence under this rule, the attorney for the Government shall disclose the evidence to the defendant, including statements of witnesses or a summary of the substance of any testi-

mony that is expected to be offered, at least fifteen days before the scheduled date of trial or at such later time as the court may allow for good cause.

(c) This rule shall not be construed to limit the admission or consideration of evidence under any other rule.

(d) For purposes of this rule and Rule 415, "child" means a person below the age of fourteen, and "offense of child molestation" means a crime under Federal law or the law of a State (as defined in section 513 of title 18, United States Code) that involved—

(1) any conduct proscribed by chapter 109A of title 18, United States Code, that was committed in relation to a child;

(2) any conduct proscribed by chapter 110 of title 18, United States Code;

(3) contact between any part of the defendant's body or an object and the genitals or anus of a child;

(4) contact between the genitals or anus of the defendant and any part of the body of a child;

(5) deriving sexual pleasure or gratification from the infliction of death, bodily injury, or physical pain on a child; or

(6) an attempt or conspiracy to engage in conduct described in paragraphs (1)-(5).

(Effective 7-9-95)

RULE 415. Evidence of Similar Acts in Civil Cases Concerning Sexual Assault or Child Molestation

(a) In a civil case in which a claim for damages or other relief is predicated on a party's alleged commission of conduct constituting an offense of sexual assault or child molestation, evidence of that party's commission of another offense or offenses of sexual assault or child molestation is admissible and may be considered as provided in Rule 413 and Rule 414 of these rules.

(b) A party who intends to offer evidence under this Rule shall disclose the evidence to the party against whom it will be offered, including statements of witnesses or a summary of the substance of any testimony that is expected to be offered, at least fifteen days before the scheduled date of trial or at such later time as the court may allow for good cause.

(c) This rule shall not be construed to limit the admission or consideration of evidence under any other rule.

(Effective 7-9-95)

ARTICLE V
PRIVILEGES

RULE 501. General Rule

Except as otherwise required by the Constitution of the United States or provided by Act of Congress or in rules prescribed by the Supreme Court pursuant to statutory authority, the privilege of a witness, person, government, State, or political subdivision thereof shall be governed by the principles of the common law as they may be interpreted by the courts of the United States in the light of reason and experience. However, in civil actions and proceedings, with respect to an element of a claim or defense as to which State law supplies the rule of decision, the privilege of a witness, person, government, State, or political subdivision thereof shall be determined in accordance with State law.

Rule 502. Attorney-Client Privilege and Work Product; Limitations on Waiver

The following provisions apply, in the circumstances set out, to disclosure of a communication or information covered by the attorney-client privilege or work-product protection.

(a) Scope of waiver. When the disclosure is made in a Federal proceeding or to a Federal office or agency and waives the attorney-client privilege or work-product protection, the waiver extends to an undisclosed communication or information in a Federal or State proceeding only if:

(1) the waiver is intentional;

(2) the disclosed and undisclosed communications or information concern the same subject matter; and

(3) they ought in fairness to be considered together.

(b) Inadvertent disclosure. When made in a Federal proceeding or to a Federal office or agency, the disclosure does not operate as a waiver in a Federal or State proceeding if:

(1) the disclosure is inadvertent;

(2) the holder of the privilege or protection took reasonable steps to prevent disclosure; and

(3) the holder promptly took reasonable steps to rectify the error, including (if applicable) following Federal Rule of Civil Procedure 26(b)(5)(B).

(c) Disclosure Made in a State Proceeding.—When the disclosure is made in a State proceeding and is not the subject of a State-court order concerning waiver, the disclosure does not operate as a waiver in a Federal proceeding if the disclosure:

(1) would not be a waiver under this rule if it had been made in a Federal proceeding; or

(2) is not a waiver under the law of the State where the disclosure occurred.

(d) Controlling Effect of a Court Order.—A Federal court may order that the privilege or protection is not waived by disclosure connected with the litigation pending before the court—in which event the disclosure is also not a waiver in any other Federal or State proceeding.

(e) Controlling effect of a party agreement.—An agreement on the effect of disclosure in a Federal proceeding is binding only on the parties to the agreement, unless it is incorporated into a court order.

(f) Controlling Effect of This Rule.—Notwithstanding Rules 101 and 1101, this rule applies to State proceedings and to Federal court-annexed and Federal court-mandated arbitration proceedings, in the circumstances set out in the rule. And notwithstanding Rule 501, this rule applies even if State law provides the rule of decision.

(g) Definitions.— In this rule:

(1) "attorney-client privilege" means the protection that applicable law provides for

confidential attorney-client communications; and

(2) "work-product protection" means the protection that applicable law provides for tangible material (or its intangible equivalent) prepared in anticipation of litigation or for trial.

(Amended 9-19-08)

ARTICLE VI
WITNESSES

RULE 601. General Rule of Competency

Every person is competent to be a witness except as otherwise provided in these rules. However, in civil actions and proceedings, with respect to an element of a claim or defense as to which State law supplies the rule of decision, the competency of a witness shall be determined in accordance with State law.

RULE 602. Lack of Personal Knowledge

A witness may not testify to a matter unless evidence is introduced sufficient to support a finding that the witness has personal knowledge of the matter. Evidence to prove personal knowledge may, but need not, consist of the witness' own testimony. This rule is subject to the provisions of Rule 703, relating to opinion testimony by expert witnesses.

(Amended, eff 10-1-87; 11-1-88)

RULE 603. Oath or Affirmation

Before testifying, every witness shall be required to declare that the witness will testify truthfully, by oath or affirmation administered in a form calculated to awaken the witness' conscience and impress the witness' mind with the duty to do so.

(Amended, eff 10-1-87)

RULE 604. Interpreters

An interpreter is subject to the provisions of these rules relating to qualification as an expert and the administration of an oath or affirmation to make a true translation.

(Amended, eff 10-1-87)

RULE 605. Competency of Judge as Witness

The judge presiding at the trial may not testify in that trial as a witness. No objection need be made in order to preserve the point.

RULE 606. Competency of Juror as Witness

(a) At the trial. A member of the jury may not testify as a witness before that jury in the trial of the case in which the juror is sitting. If the juror is called so to testify, the opposing party shall be afforded an opportunity to object out of the presence of the jury.

(b) Inquiry into validity of verdict or indictment. Upon an inquiry into the validity of a verdict or indictment, a juror may not testify as to any matter or statement occurring during the course of the jury's deliberations or the effect of anything upon that or any other juror's mind or emotions as influencing the juror to assent to or dissent from the verdict or indictment or concerning the juror's mental processes in connection therewith. But a juror may testify about (1) whether extraneous prejudicial information was improperly brought to the jury's attention, (2) whether any outside influence was improperly brought to bear upon any juror, or (3) whether there was a mistake in entering the verdict onto the verdict form. A juror's affidavit or evidence of any statement by the juror may not be received on a matter about which the juror would be precluded from testifying.

(Amended, eff 12-12-75; 10-1-87; 12-1-06)

RULE 607. Who May Impeach

The credibility of a witness may be attacked by any party, including the party calling the witness.

(Amended, eff 10-1-87)

RULE 608. Evidence of Character and Conduct of Witness

(a) Opinion and reputation evidence of character. The credibility of a witness may be attacked or supported by evidence in the form of opinion or reputation, but subject to these limitations: (1) the evidence may refer only to character for truthfulness or untruthfulness, and (2) evidence of truthful character is admissible only after the character of the witness for truthfulness has been attacked by opinion or reputation evidence or otherwise.

(b) Specific instances of conduct. Specific instances of the conduct of a witness, for the purpose of attacking or supporting the witness' character for truthfulness, other than conviction of crime as provided in rule 609, may not be proved by extrinsic evidence. They may, however, in the discretion of the court, if probative of truthfulness or untruthfulness, be inquired into on cross-examination of the witness (1) concerning the witness' character for truthfulness or untruthfulness, or (2) concerning the character for truthfulness or untruthfulness of another witness as to which character the witness being cross-examined has testified.

The giving of testimony, whether by an accused or by any other witness, does not operate as a waiver of the accused's or the witness' privilege against self-incrimination when examined with respect to matters that relate only to character for truthfulness.

(Amended, effective 10-1-87; 11-1-88; 12-1-2003)

RULE 609. Impeachment by Evidence of Conviction of Crime

(a) General rule. For the purpose of attacking the character for truthfulness of a witness.

(1) evidence that a witness other than an accused has been convicted of a crime shall be admitted, subject to Rule 403, if the crime was punishable by death or imprisonment in excess of one year under the law under which the witness was convicted, and evidence that an accused has been convicted of such a crime shall be admitted if the court determines that the probative value of admitting this evidence outweighs its prejudicial effect to the accused; and

(2) evidence that any witness has been convicted of a crime that readily can be determined to have been a crime of dishonesty or false statement shall be admitted regardless of the punishment.

(b) Time limit. Evidence of a conviction under this rule is not admissible if a period of more than ten years has elapsed since the date of the conviction or of the release of the witness from the confinement imposed for that conviction, whichever is the later date, unless the court determines, in the interests of justice, that the probative value of the conviction supported by specific facts and circumstances substantially outweighs its prejudicial effect. However, evidence of a conviction more than 10 years old as calculated herein, is not admissible unless the proponent gives to the adverse party sufficient advance written notice of intent to use such evidence to provide the adverse party with a fair opportunity to contest the use of such evidence.

(c) Effect of pardon, annulment, or certificate of rehabilitation. Evidence of a conviction is not admissible under this rule if (1) the conviction has been the subject of a pardon, annulment, certificate of rehabilitation, or other equivalent procedure based on a finding of the rehabilitation of the person convicted, and that person has not been convicted of a subsequent crime which was punishable by death or imprisonment in excess of one year, or (2) the conviction has been the subject of a pardon, annulment, or other equivalent procedure based on a finding of innocence.

(d) Juvenile adjudications. Evidence of juvenile adjudications is generally not admissible under this rule. The court may, however, in a criminal case allow evidence of a juvenile adjudication of a witness other than the accused if conviction of the offense would be admissible to attack the credibility of an adult and the court is satisfied that admission in evidence is necessary for a fair determination of the issue of guilt or innocence.

(e) Pendency of appeal. The pendency of an appeal therefrom does not render evidence of a conviction inadmissible. Evidence of the pendency of an appeal is admissible.

(Amended, eff 10-1-87; 12-1-90; 12-1-06)

RULE 610. Religious Beliefs or Opinions

Evidence of the beliefs or opinions of a witness on matters of religion is not admissible for the purpose of showing that by reason of their nature the witness' credibility is impaired or enhanced.

(Amended, eff 10-1-87)

RULE 611. Mode and Order of Interrogation and Presentation

(a) Control by court. The Court shall exercise reasonable control over the mode and order of interrogating witnesses and presenting evidence so as to (1) make the interrogation and presentation effective for the ascertainment of the truth, (2) avoid needless consumption of time, and (3) protect witnesses from harassment or undue embarrassment.

(b) Scope of cross-examination. Cross-examination should be limited to the subject matter of the direct examination and matters affecting the credibility of the witness. The court may, in the exercise of discretion, permit inquiry into additional matters as if on direct examination.

(c) Leading questions. Leading questions should not be used on the direct examination of a witness except as may be necessary to develop the witness' testimony. Ordinarily leading questions should be permitted on cross-examination. When a party calls a hostile witness, an adverse party, or a witness identified with an adverse party, interrogation may be by leading questions.

(Amended, eff 10-1-87)

RULE 612. Writing Used To Refresh Memory

Except as otherwise provided in criminal proceedings by section 3500 of title 18, United States Code, if a witness uses a writing to refresh memory for the purpose of testifying, either—

(1) while testifying, or

(2) before testifying, if the court in its discretion determines it is necessary in the interests of justice,

an adverse party is entitled to have the writing produced at the hearing, to inspect it, to cross-examine the witness thereon, and to introduce in evidence those portions which relate to the testimony of the witness. If it is claimed that the writing contains matters not related to the subject matter of the testimony the court shall examine the writing in camera, excise any portions not so related, and order delivery of the remainder to the party entitled thereto. Any portion withheld over objections shall be preserved and made available to the appellate court in the event of an appeal. If a writing is not produced or delivered pursuant to order under this rule, the court shall make any order justice requires, except that in criminal cases when the prosecution elects not to comply, the order shall be one striking the testimony or, if the court in its discretion determines that the interests of justice so require, declaring a mistrial.

(Amended, eff 10-1-87)

RULE 613. Prior Statements of Witnesses

(a) Examining witness concerning prior statement. In examining a witness concerning a prior statement made by the witness, whether written or not, the statement need not be shown nor its contents disclosed to the witness at that time, but on request the same shall be shown or disclosed to opposing counsel.

(b) Extrinsic evidence of prior inconsistent statement of witness. Extrinsic evidence of a prior inconsistent statement by a witness is not admissible unless the witness is afforded an opportunity to explain or deny the same and the opposite party is afforded an opportunity to interrogate the witness thereon, or the interests of justice otherwise require. This provision does not apply to admissions of a party-opponent as defined in Rule 801(d)(2).

(Amended, eff 10-1-87; 11-1-88)

RULE 614. Calling and Interrogation of Witnesses by Court

(a) Calling by court. The court may, on its own motion or at the suggestion of a party, call witnesses, and all parties are entitled to cross-examine witnesses thus called.

(b) Interrogation by court. The court may interrogate witnesses, whether called by itself or by a party.

(c) Objections. Objections to the calling of witnesses by the court or to interrogation by it may be made at the time or at the next available opportunity when the jury is not present.

RULE 615. Exclusion of Witnesses

At the request of a party the court shall order witnesses excluded so that they cannot hear the testimony of other witnesses, and it may make the order of its own motion. This rule does not authorize exclusion of (1) a party who is a natural person, or (2) an officer or employee of a party which is not a natural person designated as its representative by its attorney, or (3) a person whose presence is shown by a party to be essential to the presentation of the party's cause, or (4) a person authorized by statute to be present.

(Amended, eff 10-1-87; 11-1-88; 11-18-88; 12-1-98)

ARTICLE VII OPINIONS AND EXPERT TESTIMONY

RULE 701. Opinion Testimony by Lay Witnesses

If the witness is not testifying as an expert, the witness' testimony in the form of opinions or inferences is limited to those opinions or inferences which are (a) rationally based on the perception of the witness, and (b) helpful to a clear understanding of the witness' testimony or the determination of a fact in issue, and (c) not based on scientific, technical or other specialized knowledge within the scope of Rule 702.

(Amended, eff 10-1-87; 12-1-00)

RULE 702. Testimony by Experts

If scientific, technical, or other specialized knowledge will assist the trier of fact to understand the evidence or to determine a fact in issue, a witness qualified as an expert by knowledge, skill, experience, training, or education, may testify thereto in the form of an opinion or otherwise, if (1) the testimony is based upon sufficient facts or data, (2) the testimony is the product of reliable principles and methods, and (3) the witness has applied the principles and methods reliably to the facts of the case.

(Amended, eff 12-1-00)

RULE 703. Bases of Opinion Testimony by Experts

The facts or data in the particular case upon which an expert bases an opinion or inference may be those perceived by or made known to the expert at or before the hearing. If of a type reasonably relied upon by experts in the particular field in forming opinions or inferences upon the subject, the facts or data need not be admissible in evidence in order for the opinion or inference to be admitted. Facts or data that are otherwise inadmissible shall not be disclosed to the jury by the proponent of the opinion or inference unless the court determines that their probative value in assisting the jury to evaluate the expert's opinion substantially outweighs their prejudicial effect.

(Amended, eff 10-1-87; 12-1-00)

RULE 704. Opinion on Ultimate Issue

(a) Except as provided in subdivision (b), testimony in the form of an opinion or inference otherwise admissible is not objectionable because it embraces an ultimate issue to be decided by the trier of fact.

(b) No expert witness testifying with respect to the mental state or condition of a defendant in a criminal case may state an opinion or inference as to whether the defendant did or did not have the mental state or condition constituting an element of the crime charged or of a defense thereto. Such ultimate issues are matters for the trier of fact alone.

(Amended, eff 10-12-84)

RULE 705. Disclosure of Facts or Data Underlying Expert Opinion

The expert may testify in terms of opinion or inference and give reasons therefor without first testifying to the underlying facts or data, unless the court requires otherwise. The expert may in any event be required to disclose the underlying facts or data on cross-examination.

(Amended, eff 10-1-87; 12-1-93)

RULE 706. Court Appointed Experts

(a) **Appointment.** The court may on its own motion or on the motion of any party enter an order to show cause why expert witnesses should not be appointed, and may request the parties to submit nominations. The court may appoint any expert witnesses agreed upon by the parties, and may appoint expert witnesses of its own selection. An expert witness shall not be appointed by

the court unless the witness consents to act. A witness so appointed shall be informed of the witness' duties by the court in writing, a copy of which shall be filed with the clerk, or at a conference in which the parties shall have opportunity to participate. A witness so appointed shall advise the parties of the witness' findings, if any; the witness' deposition may be taken by any party; and the witness may be called to testify by the court or any party. The witness shall be subject to cross-examination by each party, including a party calling the witness.

(b) **Compensation.** Expert witnesses so appointed are entitled to reasonable compensation in whatever sum the court may allow. The compensation thus fixed is payable from funds which may be provided by law in criminal cases and civil actions and proceedings involving just compensation under the fifth amendment. In other civil actions and proceedings the compensation shall be paid by the parties in such proportion and at such time as the court directs, and thereafter charged in like manner as other costs.

(c) Disclosure of appointment. In the exercise of its discretion, the court may authorize disclosure to the jury of the fact that the court appointed the expert witness.

(d) Parties' experts of own selection. Nothing in this rule limits the parties in calling expert witnesses of their own selection.

(Amended, eff 10-1-87)

ARTICLE VIII
HEARSAY

RULE 801. Definitions

The following definitions apply under this article:

(a) **Statement.** A "statement" is (1) an oral or written assertion or (2) non-verbal conduct of a person, if it is intended by the person as an assertion.

(b) **Declarant.** A "declarant" is a person who makes a statement.

(c) Hearsay. "Hearsay" is a statement, other than one made by the declarant while testifying at the trial or hearing, offered in evidence to prove the truth of the matter asserted.

(d) Statements which are not hearsay. A statement is not hearsay if—

(1) *Prior statement by witness.* The declarant testifies at the trial or hearing and is subject to cross-examination concerning the statement, and the statement is (A) inconsistent with the declarant's testimony, and was given under oath subject to the penalty of perjury at a trial, hearing, or other proceeding, or in a deposition, or (B) consistent with the declarant's testimony and is offered to rebut an express or implied charge against the declarant of recent fabrication or improper influence or motive, or (C) one of identification of a person made after perceiving the person; or

(2) *Admission by party-opponent.* The statement is offered against a party and is (A) the party's own statement, in either an individual or a representative capacity or (B) a statement of which the party has manifested an adoption or belief in its truth, or (C) a statement by a person authorized by the party to make a statement concerning the subject, or (D) a statement by the party's agent or servant concerning a matter within the scope of the agency or employment, made during the existence of the relationship, or (E) a statement by a coconspirator of a party during the course and in furtherance of the conspiracy. The contents of the statement shall be considered but are not alone sufficient to establish the declarant's authority under subdivision (C), the agency or employment relationship and scope thereof under subdivision (D), or the existence of the conspiracy and the participation therein of the declarant and the party against whom the statement is offered under subdivision (E).

(Amended, eff 10-31-75; 10-1-87; 12-1-97)

RULE 802. Hearsay Rule

Hearsay is not admissible except as provided by these rules or by other rules prescribed by the Supreme Court pursuant to statutory authority or by Act of Congress.

RULE 803. Hearsay Exceptions; Availability of Declarant Immaterial

The following are not excluded by the hearsay rule, even though the declarant is available as a witness:

(1) *Present sense impression.* A statement describing or explaining an event or condition made while the declarant was perceiving the event or condition, or immediately thereafter.

(2) *Excited utterance.* A statement relating to a startling event or condition made while the declarant was under the stress of excitement caused by the event or condition.

(3) *Then existing mental, emotional, or physical condition.* Statement of the declarant's then existing state of mind, emotion, sensation, or physical condition (such as intent, plan, motive, design, mental feeling, pain, and bodily health), but not including a statement of memory or belief to prove the fact remembered or believed unless it relates to the execution, revocation, identification, or terms of declarant's will.

(4) *Statements for purposes of medical diagnosis or treatment.* Statements made for purposes of medical diagnosis or treatment and describing medical history, or past or present symptoms, pain, or sensations, or the inception or general character of the cause or external source thereof insofar as reasonably pertinent to diagnosis or treatment.

(5) *Recorded recollection.* A memorandum or record concerning a matter about which a witness once had knowledge but now has insufficient recollection to enable the witness to testify fully and accurately, shown to have been made or adopted by the witness when the matter was fresh in the witness' memory and to reflect

that knowledge correctly. If admitted, the memorandum or record may be read into evidence but may not itself be received as an exhibit unless offered by an adverse party.

(6) *Records of regularly conducted activity.*—A memorandum, report, record, or data compilation, in any form, of acts, events, conditions, opinions, or diagnoses, made at or near the time by, or from information transmitted by, a person with knowledge, if kept in the course of a regularly conducted business activity, and if it was the regular practice of that business activity to make the memorandum, report, record or data compilation, all as shown by the testimony of the custodian or other qualified witness, or by certification that complies with Rule 902(11), Rule 902(12), or a statute permitting certification, unless the source of information or the method or circumstances of preparation indicate lack of trustworthiness. The term "business" as used in this paragraph includes business, institution, association, profession, occupation, and calling of every kind, whether or not conducted for profit.

(7) *Absence of entry in records kept in accordance with the provisions of paragraph (6).* Evidence that a matter is not included in the memoranda reports, records, or data compilations, in any form, kept in accordance with the provisions of paragraph (6), to prove nonoccurrence or nonexistence of the matter, if the matter was of a kind of which a memorandum, report, record, or data compilation was regularly made and preserved, unless the sources of information or other circumstances indicate lack of trustworthiness.

(8) *Public records and reports.* Records, reports, statements, or data compilations, in any form, of public offices or agencies, setting forth (A) the activities of the office or agency, or (B) matters observed pursuant to duty imposed by law as to which matters there was a duty to report, excluding, however, in criminal cases matters observed by police officers and other law enforcement personnel, or (C) in civil actions and proceedings and against the government in criminal cases, factual findings resulting from an investigation made pursuant to authority granted by law, unless the sources of information or other circumstances indicate lack of trustworthiness.

(9) *Records of vital statistics.* Records or data compilations, in any form, of births, fetal deaths, deaths, or marriages, if the report thereof was made to a public office pursuant to requirements of law.

(10) *Absence of public record or entry.* To prove the absence of a record, report, statement, or data compilation, in any form, or the nonoccurrence or nonexistence of a matter of which a record, report, statement, or data compilation, in any form, was regularly made and preserved by a public office or agency, evidence in the form of a certification in accordance with Rule 902, or testimony, that diligent search failed to disclose the record, report, statement, or data compilation, or entry.

(11) *Records of religious organizations.* Statements of births, marriages, divorces, deaths, legitimacy, ancestry, relationship by blood or marriage, or other similar facts of personal or family history, contained in a regularly kept record of a religious organization.

(12) *Marriage, baptismal, and similar certificates.* Statements of fact contained in a certificate that the maker performed a marriage or other ceremony or administered a sacrament, made by a clergyman, public official, or other person authorized by the rules or practices of a religious organization or by law to perform the act certified, and purporting to have been issued at the time of the act or within a reasonable time thereafter.

(13) *Family records.* Statements of fact concerning personal or family history contained in family Bibles, genealogies, charts, engravings on rings, inscriptions on family portraits, engravings on urns, crypts, or tombstones, or the like.

(14) *Records of documents affecting an interest in property.* The record of a document purporting to establish or affect an interest in property, as proof of the content of the original recorded document and its execution and delivery by each person by whom it purports to have been executed, if the record is a record of a public office and an applicable statute authorizes the recording of documents of that kind in that office.

(15) *Statements in documents affecting an interest in property.* A statement contained in a document purporting to establish or affect an interest in property if the matter stated was relevant to the purpose of the document, unless dealings with the property since the document was made have been inconsistent with the truth of the statement or the purport of the document.

(16) *Statements in ancient documents.* Statements in a document in existence twenty years or more the authenticity of which is established.

(17) *Market reports, commercial publications.* Market quotations, tabulations, lists, directories, or other published compilations, generally used and relied upon by the public or by persons in particular occupations.

(18) *Learned Treatises.* To the extent called to the attention of an expert witness upon cross-examination or relied upon by the expert witness in direct examination, statements contained in published treatises, periodicals, or pamphlets on a subject of history, medicine, or other science or art, established as a reliable authority by the testimony or admission of the witness or by other expert testimony or by judicial notice. If admitted, the statements may be read into evidence but may not be received as exhibits.

(19) *Reputation concerning personal or family history.* Reputation among members of a person's family by blood, adoption, or marriage or among a person's associates, or in the community, concerning a person's birth, adoption, marriage, divorce, death, legitimacy, relationship by blood, adoption, or mar-riage, ancestry, or other similar fact of personal or family history.

(20) *Reputation concerning boundaries or general history.* Reputation in a community, arising before the controversy, as to boundaries of or customs affecting lands in the community, and reputation as to events of general history important to the community or State or nation in which located.

(21) *Reputation as to character.* Reputation of a person's character among associates or in the community.

(22) *Judgment of previous conviction.* Evidence of a final judgment, entered after a trial or upon a plea of guilty (but not upon a plea of nolo contendere), adjudging a person guilty of a crime punishable by death or imprisonment in excess of one year, to prove any fact essential to sustain the judgment, but not including, when offered by the Government in a criminal prosecution for purposes other than impeachment, judgments against persons other than the accused. The pendency of an appeal may be shown but does not affect admissibility.

(23) *Judgment as to personal, family, or general history, or boundaries.* Judgments as proof of matters of personal, family, or general history, or boundaries, essential to the judgment, if the same would be provable by evidence of reputation.

(24) [Transferred to Rule 807]

(Amended, eff 12-12-75; 10-1-87; 12-1-97; 12-1-00)

RULE 804. Hearsay Exceptions: Declarant Unavailable

(a) Definition of unavailability. "Unavailability as a witness" includes situations in which the declarant—

(1) is exempted by ruling of the court on the ground of privilege from testifying concerning the subject matter of the declarant's statement; or

(2) persists in refusing to testify concerning the subject matter of the declarant's statement despite an order of the court to do so; or

(3) testifies to a lack of memory of the subject matter of the declarant's statement; or

(4) is unable to be present or to testify at the hearing because of death or then existing physical or mental illness or infirmity; or

(5) is absent from the hearing and the proponent of a statement has been unable to procure the declarant's attendance (or in the case of a hearsay exception under subdivision (b)(2), (3), or (4), the declarant's attendance or testimony) by process or other reasonable means.

A declarant is not unavailable as a witness if his exemption, refusal, claim of lack of memory, inability, or absence is due to the procurement or wrongdoing of the proponent of a statement for the purpose of preventing the witness from attending or testifying.

(b) Hearsay exceptions. The following are not excluded by the hearsay rule if the declarant is unavailable as a witness:

(1) *Former testimony*. Testimony given as a witness at another hearing of the same or a different proceeding, or in a deposition taken in compliance with law in the course of the same or another proceeding, if the party against whom the testimony is now offered, or, in a civil action or proceeding, a predecessor in interest, had an opportunity and similar motive to develop the testimony by direct, cross, or redirect examination.

(2) *Statement under belief of impending death*. In a prosecution for homicide or in a civil action or proceeding, a statement made by a declarant while believing that the declarant's death was imminent, concerning the cause or circumstances of what the declarant believed to be impending death.

(3) *Statement against interest*. A statement that: (A) a reasonable person in the declarant's position would have made only if the person believed it to be true because, when made, it was so contrary to the declarant's proprietary or pecuniary interest or had so great a tendency to invalidate the declarant's claim against someone else or to expose the declarant to civil or criminal liabil-

ity; and (B) is supported by corroborating circumstances that clearly indicate its trustworthiness, if it is offered in a criminal case as one that tends to expose the declarant to criminal liability.

(4) *Statement of personal or family history*. (A) A statement concerning the declarant's own birth, adoption, marriage, divorce, legitimacy, relationship by blood, adoption, or marriage, ancestry, or other similar fact of personal or family history, even though declarant had no means of acquiring personal knowledge of the matter stated; or (B) a statement concerning the foregoing matters, and death also, of another person, if the declarant was related to the other by blood, adoption, or marriage or was so intimately associated with the other's family as to be likely to have accurate information concerning the matter declared.

(5) [Transferred to Rule 807]

(6) *Forfeiture by wrongdoing*. A statement offered against a party that has engaged or acquiesced in wrongdoing that was intended to, and did, procure the unavailability of the declarant as a witness.

(Amended, eff 12-12-75; 10-1-87; 11-18-88; 12-1-97; 12-1-2010)

RULE 805. Hearsay Within Hearsay

Hearsay included within hearsay is not excluded under the hearsay rule if each part of the combined statements conforms with an exception to the hearsay rule provided in these rules.

RULE 806. Attacking and Supporting Credibility of Declarant

When a hearsay statement, or a statement defined in Rule 801(d)(2)(C), (D), or (E), has been admitted in evidence, the credibility of the declarant may be attacked, and if attacked may be supported, by any evidence which would be admissible for those purposes if declarant had testified as a witness. Evidence of a statement or conduct by the declarant at any time, inconsistent with the declarant's hearsay statement, is not subject to any requirement that the declarant may have been afforded an opportunity to deny or explain. If the party against whom a hearsay statement has been admitted calls the declarant as a witness, the party is entitled to examine the declarant on the statement as if under cross-examination.

(Amended, eff 10-1-87; 12-1-97)

RULE 807. Residual Exception

A statement not specifically covered by Rule 803 or 804 but having equivalent circumstantial guarantees of trustworthiness, is not excluded by the hearsay rule, if the court determines that (A) the statement is offered as evidence of a material fact; (B) the statement is more probative on the point for which it is offered than any other evidence which the proponent can procure through reasonable efforts; and (C) the general purposes of these rules and the interests of justice will best be served by admission of the statement into evidence. However, a statement may not be admitted under this exception unless the proponent of it makes known to the adverse party sufficiently in advance of the trial or hearing to provide the adverse party with a fair opportunity to prepare to meet it, the proponent's intention to offer the statement and the particulars of it, including the name and address of the declarant.

(Effective 12-1-97)

ARTICLE IX
AUTHENTICATION AND
IDENTIFICATION

RULE 901. Requirement of Authentication or Identification

(a) **General provision.** The requirement of authentication or identification as a condition precedent to admissibility is satisfied by evidence sufficient to support a finding that the matter in question is what its proponent claims.

(b) **Illustrations.** By way of illustration only, and not by way of limitation, the following are examples of authentication or identification conforming with the requirements of this rule:

(1) *Testimony of witness with knowledge.* Testimony that a matter is what it is claimed to be.

(2) *Nonexpert opinion on handwriting.* Nonexpert opinion as to the genuineness of handwriting, based upon familiarity not acquired for purposes of the litigation.

(3) *Comparison by trier or expert witness.* Comparison by the trier of fact or by expert witnesses with specimens which have been authenticated.

(4) *Distinctive characteristics and the like.* Appearance, contents, substance, internal patterns, or other distinctive characteristics, taken in conjunction with circumstances.

(5) *Voice Identification.* Identification of a voice, whether heard firsthand or through mechanical or electronic transmission or recording, by opinion based upon hearing the voice at any time under circumstances connecting it with the alleged speaker.

(6) *Telephone conversations.* Telephone conversations, by evidence that a call was made to the number assigned at the time by the telephone company to a particular person or business, if (A) in the case of a person, circumstances, including self-identification, show the person answering to be the one called, or (B) in the case of a business, the call was made to a place of business and the conversation related to business reasonably transacted over the telephone.

(7) *Public records or reports.* Evidence that a writing authorized by law to be recorded or filed and in fact recorded or filed in a public office, or a purported public record, report, statement, or data compilation, in any form, is from the public office where items of this nature are kept.

(8) *Ancient documents or data compilation.* Evidence that a document or data compilation, in any form, (A) is in such condition as to create no suspicion concerning its authenticity, (B) was in a place where it, if authentic, would likely be, and (C) has been in existence 20 years or more at the time it is offered.

(9) *Process or system.* Evidence describing a process or system used to produce a result and showing that the process or system produces an accurate result.

(10) *Methods provided by statute or rule.* Any method of authentication or identification provided by Act of Congress or by other rules prescribed by the Supreme Court pursuant to statutory authority.

RULE 902. Self-authentication

Extrinsic evidence of authenticity as a condition precedent to admissibility is not required with respect to the following:

(1) *Domestic public documents under seal.* A document bearing a seal purporting to be that of the United States, or of any State, district, Commonwealth, territory, or insular possession thereof, or the Panama Canal Zone, or the Trust Territory of the Pacific Islands, or of a political subdivision, department, officer or agency thereof, and a signature purporting to be an attestation or execution.

(2) *Domestic public documents not under seal.* A document purporting to bear the signature in the official capacity of an officer or employee of any entity included in paragraph (1) hereof, having no seal, if a public officer having a seal and having official duties in the district or political subdivision of the officer or employee certifies under seal that the signer has the official capacity and that the signature is genuine.

(3) *Foreign public documents.* A document purporting to be executed or attested in an official capacity by a person authorized by the laws of a foreign country to make the execution or attestation, and accompanied by a final certification as to the genuineness of the signature and official position (A) of the executing or attesting person, or (B) of any foreign official whose certificate of genuineness of signature and official position relates to the execution or attestation or is in a chain of certificates of genuineness of signature and official position relating to

the execution or attestation. A final certification may be made by a secretary of an embassy or legation, consul general, consul, vice consul, or consular agent of the United States, or a diplomatic or consular official of the foreign country assigned or accredited to the United States. If reasonable opportunity has been given to all parties to investigate the authenticity and accuracy of official documents, the court may, for good cause shown, order that they be treated as presumptively authentic without final certification or permit them to be evidenced by an attested summary with or without final certification.

(4) *Certified copies of public records.* A copy of an official record or report or entry therein, or of a document authorized by law to be recorded or filed and actually recorded or filed in a public office, including data compilations in any form, certified as correct by the custodian or other person authorized to make the certification, by certificate complying with paragraph (1), (2), or (3) of this rule or complying with any Act of Congress or rule prescribed by the Supreme Court pursuant to statutory authority.

(5) *Official publications.* Books, pamphlets, or other publications purporting to be issued by public authority.

(6) *Newspapers and periodicals.* Printed materials purporting to be newspapers or periodicals.

(7) *Trade inscriptions and the like.* Inscriptions, signs, tags, or labels purporting to have been affixed in the course of business and indicating ownership, control, or origin.

(8) *Acknowledged documents.* Documents accompanied by a certificate of acknowledgment executed in the manner provided by law by a notary public or other officer authorized by law to take acknowledgments.

(9) *Commercial paper and related documents.* Commercial paper, signatures thereon, and documents relating thereto to the extent provided by general commercial law.

(10) *Presumptions under Acts of Congress.* Any signature, document, or

other matter declared by Act of Congress to be presumptively or prima facie genuine or authentic.

(11) *Certified domestic records of regularly conducted activity.*—The original or a duplicate of a domestic record of regularly conducted activity that would be admissible under Rule 803(6) if accompanied by a written declaration of its custodian or other qualified person, in a manner complying with any Act of Congress or rule prescribed by the Supreme Court pursuant to statutory authority, certifying that the record—

(A) was made at or near the time of the occurrence of the matters set forth by, or from information transmitted by, a person with knowledge of those matters;

(B) was kept in the course of the regularly conducted activity; and

(C) was made by the regularly conducted activity as a regular practice. A party intending to offer a record into evidence under this paragraph must provide written notice of that intention to all adverse parties, and must make the record and declaration available for inspection sufficiently in advance of their offer into evidence to provide an adverse party with a fair opportunity to challenge them.

(12) *Certified foreign records of regularly conducted activity.*—In a civil case, the original or a duplicate of a foreign record of regularly conducted activity that would be admissible under Rule 803(6) if accompanied by a written declaration by its custodian or other qualified person certifying that the record—

(A) was made at or near the time of the occurrence of the matters set forth by, or from information transmitted by, a person with knowledge of those matters;

(B) was kept in the course of the regularly conducted activity; and

(C) was made by the regularly conducted activity as a regular practice.

The declaration must be signed in a manner that, if falsely made, would subject the maker to criminal penalty under the laws of the country where the declaration is signed. A party intending to offer a record into evidence under this paragraph must provide written notice of that intention to all adverse parties, and must make the record and declaration available for inspection sufficiently in advance of their offer into evidence to provide an adverse party with a fair opportunity to challenge them.

(Amended, eff 10-1-87; 11-1-88; 12-1-00)

RULE 903. Subscribing Witness' Testimony Unnecessary

The testimony of a subscribing witness is not necessary to authenticate a writing unless required by the laws of the jurisdiction whose laws govern the validity of the writing.

ARTICLE X
CONTENTS OF WRITINGS, RECORDINGS, AND PHOTOGRAPHS

RULE 1001. Definitions

For purposes of this article the following definitions are applicable:

(1) **Writings and recordings.** "Writings" and "recordings" consist of letters, words, or numbers, or their equivalent, set down by handwriting, typewriting, printing, photostating, photographing, magnetic impulse, mechanical or electronic recording, or other forms of data compilation.

(2) **Photographs.** "Photographs" include still photographs, X-ray films, video tapes, and motion pictures.

(3) **Original.** An "original" of a writing or recording is the writing or recording itself or any counterpart intended to have the same effect by a person executing or issuing it. An "original" of a photograph includes the negative or any print therefrom. If data are stored in a computer or similar device, any printout or other output readable by sight, shown to reflect the data accurately, is an "original."

(4) **Duplicate.** A "duplicate" is a counterpart produced by the same impression

as the original, or from the same matrix, or by means of photography, including enlargements and miniatures, or by mechanical or electronic re-recording, or by chemical reproduction, or by other equivalent techniques which accurately reproduces the original.

RULE 1002. Requirement of Original

To prove the content of a writing, recording or photograph, the original writing, recording, or photograph is required, except as otherwise provided in these rules or by Act of Congress.

RULE 1003. Admissibility of Duplicates

A duplicate is admissible to the same extent as an original unless (1) a genuine question is raised as to the authenticity of the original or (2) in the circumstances it would be unfair to admit the duplicate in lieu of the original.

RULE 1004. Admissibility of Other Evidence of Contents

The original is not required, and other evidence of the contents of a writing, recording, or photograph is admissible if—

(1) Originals lost or destroyed. All originals are lost or have been destroyed, unless the proponent lost or destroyed them in bad faith; or

(2) Original not obtainable. No original can be obtained by any available judicial process or procedure; or

(3) Original in possession of opponent. At a time when an original was under the control of the party against whom offered, that party was put on notice, by the pleadings or otherwise, that the contents would be a subject of proof at the hearing, and that party does not produce the original at the hearing; or

(4) Collateral matters. The writing, recording, or photograph is not closely related to a controlling issue.
(Amended, eff 10-1-87)

RULE 1005. Public Records

The contents of an official record, or of a document authorized to be recorded or filed and actually recorded or filed, including data compilations in any form, if otherwise admissible, may be proved by copy, certified as correct in accordance with Rule 902 or testified to be correct by a witness who has compared it with the original. If a copy which complies with the foregoing cannot be obtained by the exercise of reasonable diligence, then other evidence of the contents may be given.

RULE 1006. Summaries

The contents of voluminous writings, recordings, or photographs which cannot conveniently be examined in court may be presented in the form of a chart, summary, or calculation. The originals, or duplicates, shall be made available for examination or copying, or both, by other parties at reasonable time and place. The court may order that they be produced in court.

RULE 1007. Testimony or Written Admission of Party

Contents of writings, recordings, or photographs may be proved by the testimony or deposition of the party against whom offered or by that party's written admission, without accounting for the nonproduction of the original.
(Amended, eff 10-1-87)

RULE 1008. Functions of Court and Jury

When the admissibility of other evidence of contents of writings, recordings, or photographs under these rules depends upon the fulfillment of a condition of fact, the question whether the condition has been fulfilled is ordinarily for the court to determine in accordance with the provisions of Rule 104. However, when an issue is raised (a) whether the asserted writing ever existed, or (b) whether another writing, recording, or photograph produced at the trial is the original, or (c) whether other evidence of contents correctly reflects the contents, the issue is for the trier of fact to determine as in the case of other issues of fact.

ARTICLE XI
MISCELLANEOUS RULES

RULE 1101. Applicability of Rules

(a) **Courts and judges.** These rules apply to the United States district courts, the District Court of Guam, the District Court of the Virgin Islands, the District Court for the Northern Mariana Islands, the United States courts of appeals, the United States Claims Court, and to United States bankruptcy judges and United States magistrate judges, in the actions, cases, and proceedings and to the extent hereinafter set forth. The terms "judge" and "court" in these rules include United States bankruptcy judges and United States magistrate judges.

(b) **Proceedings generally.** These rules apply generally to civil actions and proceedings, including admiralty and maritime cases, to criminal cases and proceedings, to contempt proceedings except those in which the court may act summarily, and to proceedings and cases under title 11, United States Code.

(c) **Rule of privilege.** The rule with respect to privileges applies at all stages of all actions, cases, and proceedings.

(d) **Rules inapplicable.** The rules (other than with respect to privileges) do not apply in the following situations:

(1) *Preliminary question of fact.* The determination of questions of fact preliminary to admissibility of evidence when the issue is to be determined by the court under Rule 104.

(2) *Grand jury.* Proceedings before grand juries.

(3) *Miscellaneous proceedings.* Proceedings for extradition or rendition; preliminary examinations in criminal cases; sentencing, or granting or revoking probation; issuance of warrants for arrest, criminal summonses, and search warrants; and proceedings with respect to release on bail or otherwise.

(e) **Rules applicable in part.** In the following proceedings these rules apply to the extent that matters of evidence are not provided for in the statutes which govern procedure therein or in other rules prescribed by the Supreme Court pursuant to statutory authority: the trial of misdemeanors and other petty offenses before United States magistrate judges; review of agency actions when the facts are subject to trial de novo under section 706(2)(F) of title 5, United States Code; review of orders of the Secretary of Agriculture under section 2 of the Act entitled "An Act to authorize association of producers of agricultural products" approved February 18, 1922 (7 U.S.C. 292), and under sections 6 and 7(c) of the Perishable Agricultural Commodities Act, 1930 (7 U.S.C. 499f, 499g(c)); naturalization and revocation of naturalization under section 310–318 of the Immigration and Nationality Act (8 U.S.C. 1421–1429); prize proceedings in admiralty under sections 7651–7681 of title 10, United States Code; review of orders of the Secretary of the Interior under section 2 of the Act entitled "An Act authorizing associations of producers of aquatic products" approved June 25, 1934 (15 U.S.C. 522); review of orders of petroleum control boards under section 5 of the Act entitled "An Act to regulate interstate and foreign commerce in petroleum and its products by prohibiting the shipment in such commerce of petroleum and its products produced in violation of State law, and for other purposes", approved February 22, 1935 (15 U.S.C. 715d); actions for fines, penalties, or forfeitures under part V of title IV of the Tariff Act of 1930 (19 U.S.C. 1581–1624), or under the Anti-Smuggling Act (19 U.S.C. 1701–1711); criminal libel for condemnation, exclusion of imports, or other proceedings under the Federal Food, Drug, and Cosmetic Act (21 U.S.C. 301–392); disputes between seamen under sections 4079, 4080, and

4081 of the Revised Statutes (22 U.S.C. 256–258); habeas corpus under sections 2241–2254 of title 28, United States Code; motions to vacate, set aside or correct sentence under section 2255 of title 28, United States Code; actions for penalties for refusal to transport destitute seamen under section 4578 of the Revised Statutes (46 U.S.C. 679); actions against the United States under the Act entitled "An Act authorizing suits against the United States in admiralty for damage caused by and salvage service rendered to public vessels belonging to the United States, and for other purposes," approved March 3, 1925 (46 U.S.C. 781–790), as implemented by section 7730 of title 10, United States Code.

(Amended, eff 12-12-75; 10-1-79; 10-1-82; 10-1-87; 11-1-88; 11-18-88; 12-1-93)

RULE 1102. Amendments

Amendments to the Federal Rules of Evidence may be made as provided in section 2072 of title 28 of the United States Code.

(Amended, eff 12-1-91)

RULE 1103. Title

These rules may be known and cited as the Federal Rules of Evidence.